Between two thieves

Richard Dehan

Alpha Editions

This edition published in 2024

ISBN : 9789367245644

Design and Setting By
Alpha Editions
www.alphaedis.com
Email - info@alphaedis.com

As per information held with us this book is in Public Domain.
This book is a reproduction of an important historical work. Alpha Editions uses the best technology to reproduce historical work in the same manner it was first published to preserve its original nature. Any marks or number seen are left intentionally to preserve its true form.

Contents

I .... - 1 -

II .... - 9 -

III .... - 13 -

IV .... - 16 -

V .... - 20 -

VI .... - 22 -

VII .... - 28 -

VIII .... - 36 -

IX .... - 44 -

X .... - 55 -

XI .... - 62 -

XII .... - 67 -

XIII .... - 69 -

XIV .... - 72 -

XV .... - 84 -

XVI .... - 96 -

XVII	- 106 -
XVIII	- 113 -
XIX	- 121 -
XX	- 130 -
XXI	- 136 -
XXII	- 145 -
XXIII	- 152 -
XXIV	- 159 -
XXV	- 164 -
XXVI	- 171 -
XXVII	- 177 -
XXVIII	- 182 -
XXIX	- 191 -
XXX	- 195 -
XXXI	- 200 -
XXXII	- 202 -
XXXIII	- 204 -
XXXIV	- 210 -
XXXV	- 217 -

XXXVI	- 223 -
XXXVII	- 232 -
XXXVIII	- 236 -
XXXIX	- 239 -
XL	- 247 -
XLI	- 253 -
XLII	- 256 -
XLIII	- 262 -
XLIV	- 268 -
XLV	- 278 -
XLVI	- 280 -
XLVII	- 286 -
XLVIII	- 290 -
XLIX	- 294 -
L	- 298 -
LI	- 304 -
LII	- 307 -
LIII	- 315 -
LIV	- 322 -

LV	- 329 -
LVI	- 335 -
LVII	- 341 -
LVIII	- 353 -
LIX	- 360 -
LX	- 366 -
LXI	- 373 -
LXII	- 379 -
LXIII	- 383 -
LXIV	- 385 -
LXV	- 389 -
LXVI	- 393 -
LXVII	- 404 -
LXVIII	- 408 -
LXIX	- 412 -
LXX	- 418 -
LXXI	- 424 -
LXXII	- 428 -
LXXIII	- 433 -

LXXIV	- 437 -
LXXV	- 442 -
LXXVI	- 447 -
LXXVII	- 454 -
LXXVIII	- 465 -
LXXIX	- 472 -
LXXX	- 478 -
LXXXI	- 482 -
LXXXII	- 491 -
LXXXIII	- 498 -
LXXXIV	- 510 -
LXXXV	- 514 -
LXXXVI	- 520 -
LXXXVII	- 526 -
LXXXVIII	- 534 -
LXXXIX	- 540 -
XC	- 546 -
XCI	- 554 -
XCII	- 555 -

XCIII	- 560 -
XCIV	- 568 -
XCV	- 573 -
XCVI	- 581 -
XCVII	- 586 -
XCVIII	- 591 -
XCIX	- 598 -
C	- 600 -
CI	- 603 -
CII	- 608 -
CIII	- 611 -
CIV	- 617 -
CV	- 619 -
CVI	- 626 -
CVII	- 628 -
CVIII	- 631 -
CIX	- 634 -

I

An old paralytic man, whose snow-white hair fell in long silken waves from under the rim of the black velvet skull-cap he invariably wore, sat in a light invalid chair-carriage at the higher end of the wide, steep street that is the village of Zeiden, in the Canton of Alpenzell, looking at the sunset.

Slowly the rose-red flush was fading behind the glittering green, snow-capped pinnacle of distant Riedi. A segment of the sun's huge flaming disk remained in view above a shoulder of her colossal neighbor Donatus; molten gold and silver, boiling together as in a crucible, were spilled upon his vast, desolate, icy sides; his towering, snow-crested helmet trailed a *panache* of dazzling glory, snatched from the sinking forehead of the vanquished Lord of Day, and even the cap of the Kreinenberg, dwarf esquire in attendance on the giant, boasted a golden plume.

The old man blinked a little, oppressed by excess of splendor, and the attendant Sister of Charity, who sometimes relieved the white-capped, blue-cloaked, cotton-gowned German nurse customarily in charge of the patient, observing this, turned the invalid-chair so that its occupant looked down upon the Blau See, the shape of which suggests a sumptuous glove encrusted with turquoises, as, bordered with old-world, walled towns, it lies in the rich green lap of a fertile country, deep girdled with forests of larch and pine and chestnut, enshrining stately ruins of mediæval castles, and the picturesque garden-villas built by wealthy peasants, in their stately shadow; and sheltered by the towering granite ranges of the Paarlberg from raging easterly gales.

The brilliant black eyes that shone almost with the brilliancy of youth in the wasted ivory face of the old man in the wheeled chair, sparkled appreciatively now as they looked out over the Lake. For to the whirring of its working dynamos, and the droning song of its propeller, a monoplane of the Blériot type emerged from its wooden shelter, pitched upon a steep green incline near to the water's edge; and moving on its three widely-placed cycle-wheels with the gait of a leggy winged beetle or a flurried sheldrake, suddenly rose with its rider into the thin, clear atmosphere, losing all its awkwardness as the insect or the bird would have done, in the launch upon its natural element, and the instinctive act of flight. The old man watched the bird of steel and canvas, soaring and dipping, circling and turning, over the blue liquid plain with the sure ease and swift daring of the swallow, and slowly nodded his head. When the monoplane had completed a series of practice-evolutions, it steered away northwards, the steady tuff-tuff of its Gnome engine thinning away to a mere thread of sound as the machine diminished to the sight. Then said the watcher, breaking his long silence:

"That is a good thing!... A capital—a useful thing!... An invention, see you, my Sister, that will one day prove invaluable in War."

The Sister, with a shade of hesitation, responded that Monsieur was undoubtedly right. For carrying dispatches, and for the more dreadful purpose of dropping bombs upon an enemy, the aeroplane, guided by a skillful pilot, would no doubt——

"Ah, tschah!... Bah!... br'rr!..." The old man hunched his thin, broad shoulders impatiently, and wrinkled up his mobile ivory face into a hundred puckers of comical disgust as he exploded these verbal rockets, and his bright black eyes snapped and sparkled angrily. "For dropping shell upon the decks of armored cruisers, or into camps, or upon columns of marching men, this marvelous machine that the Twentieth Century has given us might be utilized beyond doubt. But for the preservation of life, rather than its destruction, its supreme use will be in War. For the swift and easy removal of wounded from the field of battle, a fleet of Army Hospital Service Aeroplanes will one day be built and equipped and organized by every civilized Government, under the Rules of the Crimson Cross. Beautiful, beautiful!" The old man was quite excited, nodding his black velvet-capped, white-locked head as though he would have nodded it off, and blinking his bright eyes. "*Sapristi!*—I see them!" he cried. "They will hover over the Field of Action like huge hawks, from time to time swooping upon the fallen and carrying them off in their talons. Superb! magnificent! colossal! If we had had air-men and air-machines at Balaklava in '54, or at Magenta, or Solferino, or Gravelotte, or in Paris during the Siege!... Have the kindness, my Sister, to give me a pinch of snuff!"

The Sister fumbled in the pocket of the white flannel jacket—winter and summer, year in and year out, the old man went clothed from head to foot in white—and fed the thin, handsome old eagle-beak with pungent cheap mixture, out of a box that bore the portrait, set in blazing brilliants, of the Imperial Crowned Head whose gift it had been; as was recorded by the elaborate inscription engraved in the Russian character within its golden lid. The old man was particular that no dust of his favorite brown powder should soil the snowy silken mustache, waxed to fine points, that jutted above his long, mobile upper-lip, or the little imperial that was called by a much less elegant name when the birch-broom-bearded Reds heckled the President of the Third Republic for wearing the distinctive chin-tuft. After the pinch of snuff the old man became more placid. He had his chair slewed round to afford him a fresh point of view, and sat absorbed in the contemplation of which he never seemed to weary.

The sweet Spring day was dying. Vast brooding pinions of somber purple cloud already made twilight on the north horizon, where glooming ramparts topped by pallid peaks, and jagged sierras spiring up into slender minarets and aguilles, shone ghostly against the gloom. The horn of the herdsman sounded from the lower Alps, and neck-bells tinkled as the long lines of placid cows moved from the upper pastures in obedience to the call, breathing perfume of scented vetch and honeyed crimson clover, leaving froth of milk from trickling udders on the leaves and grasses as they went.

The sunset-hour being supper-time, the single street of Zeiden seemed deserted. You saw it as a hilly thoroughfare, bordered with detached timber-built houses, solid and quaintly-shaped and gayly-painted, their feet planted in gardens full of lilac and syringa and laburnum, daffodils and narcissi, violets and anemones and tulips; their walls and balconies tapestried with the sweet May rose and the pink and white clematis; the high-pitched roofs of the most ancient structures, green to the ridge-poles with mosses and gilded by lichens, rosetted with houseleek, and tufted with sweet yellow wallflower and flaunting dandelion. And you had just begun to wonder at the silence and apparent emptiness of the place, when, presto! it suddenly sprang into life. Doors opened and shut; footsteps crackled on gravel; gates clicked, releasing avalanches of barking dogs and laughing, racing children; the adult natives and visitors of Zeiden (Swiss for the most part, leavened with Germans and sprinkled with English and French) appeared upon the Promenade.... And the band of the Kursaal, magnificent in their green, white-faced, silver-tagged uniform, marched down the street to the Catholic Church, and being admitted by the verger—a magnificent official carrying a wand, and attired in a scarlet frock-coat, gilt chain, and lace-trimmed cocked hat—presently appeared upon the platform of the tower, and—it being the Feast of The Ascension—played a chorale, and were tremendously applauded when it was over.

"They play well, finely, to-night!" said the old man, nodding and twinkling in his bright pleased way. "Kindly clap my hands for me, my Sister. M. Pédelaborde may take it amiss if I do not join in the applause." So the *chef d'orchestre* was gratified by the approval of the paralytic M. Dunoisse, which indeed he would have been sorely chagrined to miss.

"I think that white-haired old man in the black velvet cap has the most noble, spiritual face I ever saw," said a little English lady to her husband—a tall, lean, prematurely-bald and careworn man, arrayed in a leather cap with goggles, a knicker suit of baggily-cut, loud-patterned tweeds, a shirt of rheumatism-defying Jaeger material, golfing hose, and such prodigiouslyclouted nailed boots, with sockets for the insertion of climbing-irons, as London West End and City firms are apt to impose upon customers who do their Swiss mountain-climbing per the zigzag carriage-road, or the cogwheel railway.

"Ah, yes! quite so!" absently rejoined the husband, who was Liberal Member for a North London Borough, and an Under-Secretary of State; and was mentally engaged in debating whether the six o'clock supper recently partaken of, and consisting of grilled lake-trout with cucumber, followed by curd-fritters crowned with dabs of whortleberry preserve, did not constitute a flagrant breach of the rules of dietary drawn up by the London specialist under whose advice he was trying the Zeiden whey-cure for a dyspepsia induced by Suffragist Demonstrations and the Revised Budget Estimate. "Quite so, yes!"

"You are trying to be cynical," said the little lady, who was serious and high-minded, and Member of half-a-dozen Committees of Societies for the moral and physical improvement of a world that would infinitely prefer to remain as it is "Skeptics may sneer," she continued with energy, "and the irreverent scoff, but a holy life does stamp itself upon the countenance in lines there is no mistaking."

"I did not sneer," retorted her husband, whose internal system the unfortuitous combination of cucumber with curds was rapidly upsetting. "Nor am I aware that I scoffed. Your saintly-faced old gentleman is certainly a very interesting and remarkable personage. His name is M. Hector Dunoisse." He added, with an inflection the direct result of the cucumber-curd-whortleberry combination: "He was a natural son of the First Napoleon's favorite *aide-de-camp*, a certain Colonel—afterwards Field-Marshal Dunoisse (who did tremendous things at Aboukir and Austerlitz and Borodino)—by—ah!—by a Bavarian lady of exalted rank,—a professed nun, in fact,—who ran away with Dunoisse, or was run away with. M. Pédelaborde, the man who told me the story, doesn't profess to be quite certain."

"I dare say not! And who is M. Pédelaborde, if I may be allowed to know?"

Infinite contempt and unbounded incredulity were conveyed in the little English lady's utterance of the foregoing words.

"Pédelaborde," explained her husband, sucking a soda-mint lozenge, and avoiding the wifely eye, "is the fat, tremendously-mustached personage who conducts the Kursaal Band."

"Indeed!"

"He has known M. Hector Dunoisse all his life—Pédelaborde's life, I mean, of course. His father was a fellow-cadet of your old gentleman's at a Military Training Institute in Paris, where Dunoisse fought a duel with another boy and killed him, I am given to understand, by an unfair thrust. The French are fond of tricks in fencing, and some of 'em are the very dev——Ahem!"

"I decline to credit such a monstrous statement," said the little lady, holding her head very high. "Nothing shall convince me that that dear, sweet, placid old man—who is certainly not to blame for the accident of his birth—could ever have been guilty of a dishonorable action, much less a wicked murderous deed, such as you describe! Do you know him? I mean in the sense of having spoken to him, because everybody bows to M. Dunoisse on the Promenade. You have!.... Next time you happen to meet, you might say that if he would allow you to introduce him to your wife, I should be pleased—so very pleased to make his acquaintance——"

"Ah, yes! Quite so! We have had a little chat or two, certainly," the dyspeptic gentleman of affairs admitted. "And I don't doubt he would be highly gratified." The speaker finished his lozenge, and added, with mild malignity: "That you would find him interesting I feel perfectly sure. For he certainly has seen a good deal of life, according to Pédelaborde.... He held a commission in a crack regiment of Chasseurs d'Afrique, and ran through a great fortune, I am told, with the assistance of his commanding officer's wife—uncommonly attractive woman, too, Pédelaborde tells me. And he was on the Prince-President's Staff at the time of the *coup d'État*, and after the Restoration—Pédelaborde positively takes his oath that this is true!—was shut up in a French frontier fortress for an attempt on the life of the Emperor. But he escaped or was released, when the Allies were pounding away at Sevastopol, in 1854, and Ada Merling—dead now, I believe, like nearly everybody else one has ever heard named in connection with the War in the Crimea—was nursing the wounded English soldiers at Scutari." The dyspeptic politician added acidly:

"Here comes M. Dunoisse trundling down the Promenade, saintly smile and all the rest of it.... Shall I give him your message now?"

But the speaker's better-half, at last convinced, indignantly withdrew her previous tender of cordiality, and as the invalid chair, impelled by the white-capped, blue-cloaked nurse, who had now replaced the nun, rolled slowly down the wide garden-bordered, orchard-backed *Place* of ancient timber houses that is Zeiden, the white-haired wearer of the black velvet cap, nodding and beaming in acknowledgment of the elaborately respectful salutations of the male visitors and the smiling bows of the ladies, received from one little British matron a stare so freezing in its quality that his jaw dropped, and his bright black eyes became circular with astonishment and dismay.

That an old man at whom everybody smiled kindly—an old man who had little else to live upon or for but love should meet a look so cold.... His underlip drooped like a snubbed child's. Why was it? Did not the little English lady know—surely she must know!—how much, how very much old Hector Dunoisse had done, and given, sacrificed and endured and suffered, to earn the love and gratitude of women and of men? He did not wish to boast—but she might have remembered it!... A tear dropped on the wrinkled ivory hands that lay helplessly upon the rug that covered the sharp bony knees.

"You have been guilty of a piece of confoundedly bad taste, let me tell you!" said the irritated Englishman, addressing his still vibrating wife. "To cut an old man like that! It was brutal!" He added, "And idiotic into the bargain!"

"I simply couldn't help it," said his wife, her stiffened facial muscles relaxing into the flabbiness that heralds tears. "When I saw that horrible old creature coming, looking so dreadfully innocent and kind; and remembered how often I have seen the little French and German and Swiss children crowding round his chair listening to a story, or being lifted up to kiss him"—she gulped—"or toddling to his knee to slip their little bunches of violets into those helpless hands of his—I could *not* help it! I simply had to!"

"Then you simply had to commit a social blunder of a very grave kind," pronounced her lord, assuming that air of detachment from the person addressed which creates a painful sense of isolation. "For permit me to inform you that M. Hector Dunoisse is not a person, but a Personage—whom the President of the Swiss Confederation and about half the Crowned Heads of Europe congratulate upon his birthday. And who—if he had chosen to accept the crown they offered him half a lifetime back—would have been to-day the ruling Hereditary Prince of an important Bavarian State. As it is——"

"As it is, he would forgive me the hideous thing I have done," the little lady cried, flushing indignant scarlet to the roots of her hair, "could he know that it was my own husband who deceived me.... Who humbugged me," she gulped hysterically. "*Spoofed* me, as our boy Herbert would hideously say,—with a whole string of ridiculous, trumped-up stories——" She hurriedly sought for and applied her handkerchief, and the final syllable was lost in the dolorous blowing of an injured woman's nose. Her husband entreated pusillanimously:

"For Heaven's sake, don't cry!—at least, here on the Promenade, with scores of people staring. What I told you is the simple truth.... Don't Roman Catholics say that the regular rips make the most thorough-going, out-and-out saints when they *do* take to religion and good works and all the rest of it? Besides ... good Lord!—it's Ancient History—happened years and years before our parents saw each other—and the old chap is ninety—or nearly! And—even supposing Dunoisse did what people say he did, only think what Dunoisse has done!"

Curiosity prevailed over injured dignity. The wounded wife emerged from behind a damp wad of cambric to ask: "What *has* he done?"

"What has he ... why—he has received all sorts of Votes of Thanks from Public Societies, and he has been decorated with heaps of Orders ... the Order of St. John of Jerusalem, and the Orders of the Annunziata of Savoy, and the Black Eagle; and he is a Commander of the Legion of Honor and a Knight of the Papal Order of St. Gregory, and Hereditary Prince of Widinitz if he liked, but he doesn't like ... goodness me! Haven't I told you all that already?" The M.P. for the North London borough flapped his hands and lapsed into incoherency.

"But surely you can tell me why these honors were bestowed upon M. Dunoisse?" asked his wife. "I am waiting for the answer to my question—what has he done to deserve them?"

The clear, incisive English voice asking the question cut like a knife through the consonantal, sibilant French, and the guttural be-voweled German. And a stranger standing near—recognizable as a French priest of the Catholic Church less by the evidence of his well-worn cloth, and Roman collar, and wide-brimmed, round-crowned silk beaver, with the shabby silk band and black enameled buckle, than by a certain distinctive manner and expression—said upon a sudden impulse, courteously raising his hat:

"Madame will graciously pardon an old man for presuming to answer a question not addressed to him. She asks, if I comprehend aright, what M. Dunoisse has done to deserve the numberless marks of respect and esteem that have been showered on him?... I will have the honor of explaining to Madame if Monsieur kindly consents?"

"Pleasure, I'm sure!" babbled the dyspeptic victim of the Suffragists and the Budget, yawning as only the liverish can. The priest went on, addressing the little lady:

"Madame, the invalid gentleman whose paralyzed hands rest upon his knees as inertly and immovably as the hands of some granite statue of an Egyptian deity, has given with both those helpless hands—gives to this hour!—will give, when we have long been dust, and these pretty infants playing round us are old men and aged women—a colossal gift to suffering Humanity. He has expended wealth, health, all that men hold dear, in founding, endowing, and organizing a vast international, undenominational, neutral Society of Mercy, formed of brave and skilled and noble men and women,—ah!—may Heaven bless those women!—who, being of all nations, creeds, and politics, are bound by one vow; united in one purpose; bent to one end—that end the alleviation of the frightful sufferings of soldiers wounded in War. Madame must have heard of the Convention of Helvetia?... But see there, Madame!... Observe, by a strange coincidence—the Symbol in the sky!"

The hand of the speaker, with a graceful, supple gesture of indication, waved westwards, and the little lady's eyes, following it, were led to the upper end of the wide, irregular châlet-bordered Promenade of Zeiden, where the wheel-chair of the invalid had again come to a standstill; possibly in obedience to its occupant's desire to look once more upon the sunset, whose flaming splendors had all vanished now, save where against a gleaming background of milky-pale vapor glowed transverse bars of ardent hue, rich and glowing as pigeon's blood ruby, or an Emperor's ancient Burgundy, or that other crimson liquor that courses in the veins of Adam's sons, and was first spilled upon the shrinking earth by the guilty hand of Cain.

"It is the sign," the priest repeated earnestly; "the badge of the great international League of love and pity which owes its institution to M. Hector Dunoisse." He added: "The face of Madame tells me that no further explanation is needed. With other countries that have drunk of War, and its agonies and horrors, Protestant England renders homage to the Crimson Cross."

II

Old Hector Dunoisse could not sleep that night. Sharp pains racked his worn bones; his paralyzed muscles were as though transfixed by surgical needles of finely-tempered steel. He would not permit the nurse to sit up, despite the physician's orders, therefore the medical Head of the Institution suffered the patient to have his way. So he lay alone in the large, light, airy room, furnished with all the appliances that modern surgical skill can devise for the aid of helplessness, and the alleviation of suffering, and yet a place of pain....

He would not suffer the nurse to lower the green Venetian blinds of the high, clear windows that fronted to the south-east and south-west; the moonbeams could not do him any harm, he declared. On the contrary! The mild, bright planet shining above the lonely *kulms* and terrible crevasses, shedding her radiant light upon the peasant's Alpine hut and the shepherd's hillside cave, as upon the huge hotel-caravanserais, glittering with windows and crowded with wealthy tourists, and the stately mediæval castles, ruined and inhabited by owls and bats and foxes, or lovingly preserved and dwelt in by the descendants of the great robber knights who reared their Cyclopean towers—was she not his well-loved friend?

So, as one waits for a friend, old Hector lay waiting for the moonrise; the white-haired, handsome, vivacious old face, with the bright black eyes, propped high upon the pillow, the wasted, half-dead body of him barely raising the light warm bed-coverings, the helpless arms and stiff white hands stretched rigidly along its sides.

And not only the man waited; the heavens seemed also waiting. The ghostly white ice-peaks and snowy mountain-ranges, crowded on the horizon as though they waited too. Corvus burned bright, low down on the south horizon; Spica blazed at the maidenly-pure feet of Virgo. Bootes looked down from the zenith, a pale emerald radiance, dimmed by the fierce red fires of the Dog Star.... The purple-dark spaces beyond these splendors were full of the palely glimmering presences of other stars. But the old man wanted none of these. He had forgotten to look at the almanac. He began to fear there would be no moon that night.

Old, sick and helpless as he was, this was a great grief to him. Useless the presence of others when we lack the one we need. And a little crack in a dam-wall is enough to liberate the pent-up waters; the thin, bright trickle is soon followed by the roaring turbid flood. Then, look and see what fetid slime, what ugly writhing creatures bred of it, the shining placid surface masked and covered.... The purest women, the noblest men, no less than we who know ourselves inwardly corrupt and evil, have such depths, where things like these are hidden from the light of day....

The pain was intolerable to-night,—almost too bad to bear without shrieking. Dunoisse set his old face into an ivory mask of stern resistance, and his white mustache and arched and still jet-black eyebrows bristled fiercely, and the cold drops of anguish gathered upon the sunken purple-veined temples upon which the silky silver hair was growing sparse and thin. Ouf!... what unutterable relief it would have been to clench his fists, even!... But the poor hands, helpless as a wax doll's or a wooden puppet's, refused to obey his will.

He lay rigid and silent, but his brain worked with vivid, feverish activity, and his glance roved restlessly round the white-papered walls of the airy, cleanly room. Shabby frames containing spotted daguerreotypes and faded old *cartes-de-visite* of friends long dead; some water-color portraits and engravings of battle-scenes, hung there; with some illuminated addresses, a few more modern photographs, a glazed case of Orders and Crosses, a cheap carved rack of well-smoked pipes, and—drawn up against the painted wainscot—an imposing array of boots of all nationalities, kinds and descriptions, in various stages of wear. His small library of classics filled a hanging shelf, while a pair of plain deal bookcases were stuffed with publications in half-a-dozen European languages, chiefly well-known reference-works upon Anatomy and Physiology, Surgery and Medicine; whilst a row of paper-bound, officially-stamped Government publications—one or two of these from his own painstaking, laborious pen—dealt with the organization, equipment and sanitation of Military Field Hospitals, Hospital Ships and Hospital Trains, the clothing, diet and care of sick and wounded, and, in relation to these, the Laws and Customs of grim and ghastly War. And a traveling chest of drawers, a bath, and a portable secretary, battered and ink-stained by half a century of honorable use; with the scanty stock of antique garments hanging in the white-pine press; a meager store of fine, exquisitely darned and mended old-world linen; an assortment of neckties, wonderfully out of date; some old felt wideawakes, and three black velvet caps, with a camel's hair *bournous*, that had served for many years as a dressing-gown; and the bust of a woman, in marble supported on a slender ebony pedestal set between the windows, completed the inventory of the worldly possessions of old Hector Dunoisse.

All that he owned on earth, these few shabby chattels, these dimmed insignia, with their faded ribbons—this man who had once been greatly rich, and prodigally generous, subsisted now in his helpless age upon a small annuity, purchased when he had been awarded the Nobel Prize. What bitter tears had been wrung from the bright black eyes when he was compelled to accept this charity! But it had to be; the burden of his great humanitarian labors had exhausted his last energies and his remaining funds; and Want had risen up beside his bed of sickness, and laid upon him, who had cheered away her specter from so many pallets, her chill and meager hand.

Ah, how he loved the glaring daguerreotypes, the spotty photographs, the old cheap prints! Far, far more dearly than the Rembrandts and Raphaels, the Watteaus and the three superb portraits by Velasquez that he had sold to the Council of the Louvre, and the Austrian Government and the Trustees of the National Gallery. The cabinets of rare and antique medals, the collection of Oriental porcelain and Royal Sèvres that had been bequeathed to him with the immense private fortune of Luitpold, the long-deceased Prince-Regent of Widinitz, that had also been disposed of under the hammer to supply his needs for funds,—always more funds,—had never possessed one-tenth of the preciousness of these poor trifles. For everything was a memento or token of something done or borne, given or achieved towards the fulfillment of the one great end.

The *chibuk* with the bowl of gilded red clay, the cherry-stick stem and the fine amber mouthpiece, an officer of the English Guards had forced upon Dunoisse at Balaklava. The inkstand, a weighty sphere of metal mounted on three grape-shot, with a detached fourth for the lid—that was a nine-pound shell from the Sandbag Battery. And the helmet-plate with a silver-plated Austrian Eagle and the brass device like a bomb, with a tuft of green metal oak-leaves growing out of the top, that was a souvenir of the bloody field of Magenta. It had been pressed upon Dunoisse by a flaxen-haired, blue-eyed Ensign of Austrian Infantry, whom he had rescued from under a hecatomb of dead men and horses, still living, but blackened from asphyxia, the colors of his regiment yet clutched in his cramped and blackened hands.

Even the *bournous*, the voluminous long-sleeved, hooded garment of gray-white camel's hair, bordered with delicate embroideries of silver and orange-red floss silk—that had its touching history; that had been also the legacy of one who had nothing else to give.

"He was an Arab of pure blood, a pious Moslem, Sergeant-Major in the First Regiment of Spahis, a chief in his own right. He fell in the assault upon the Hill of Cypres. Towards the end of the day, when the sun had set upon Solferino's field of carnage, and the pale moon was reflected in the ponds of blood that had accumulated in every depression of the ravaged ground, we found him, riddled with bullets, pierced with wounds, leaning with his back against a little tree, his bleeding Arab stallion standing by him as he prayed in the words of the Prophet: '*Lord, grant me pardon, and join me to the companionship on high!...*' He died two nights later upon a heap of bloody straw in the Church of Santa Rosalia at Castiglione. This had been strapped in the roll behind his saddle—his young bride had embroidered the gold and silken ornaments; in the field it had served him as a covering, and until the dead-cart came to remove the corpse,—as a pall."

More relics yet. The broken lock of a Garibaldian musket from Calatifimi. The guard of a Papal soldier's saber from Castel Fidardo, brown with Sardinian blood.

More still.... The gilded ornament from the staff-top of a Prussian Eagle—a souvenir of Liebenau, or was it Hühnerwasser? A Uhlan lance-head from Hochhausen. An exploded cartridge gathered on the field of Alcolea, where the Spanish Royalists were beaten in 1868. And a French *chassepot* and a Prussian needle-gun, recalling the grim tragedy of 1870 and the unspeakable disaster of Sedan. While a fantastically chased cross of Abyssinian gold, and a Bersagliere's plume of cocks' feathers, their glossy dark green marred with dried blood, were eloquent of the massacre of the Italian troops at Dagoli, in '87.

What memories were this old man's!

III

Old Hector could have told you that such crowded, thronging memories aggravate the dull, throbbing ache of loneliness to torment. To re-read letters written in faded ink by beloved hands that lie moldering underground, or are very far removed from us; or to brood upon the soulless image of a soulful face that, dead or living, we may never see with our earthly eyes again, does but exquisitely intensify the agony of loss. We who are old and wise should know better than to seek to quench the heart's thirst at such bitter Desert wells. Nevertheless, our eyes turn to the faded portrait, our hands touch the spring of the tarnished locket half-a-hundred times a day.

Upon the pillow beside the worn white head there invariably lay a stained and shabby Russia-leather letter-case, white at the edges with wear. It was fastened by a little lock of dainty mechanism, and the fine thin chain of bright steel links that was attached to it went round the old man's neck. He turned his head that his cheek might rest against the letter-case, and a slow tear over-brimmed an underlid, and fell and sparkled on the dull brownish leather that had once been bright and red. A silver plate, very worn and thin, bore an engraved date and a brief direction:

BURY THIS WITH ME

It would be done by-and-by, he knew; for who would rob a dead old man of his dearest treasure? Moreover, the contents of the leather case were valueless in ordinary eyes.

Just a package of letters penned in a fine, delicate, pointed, old-fashioned gentlewoman's handwriting to the address of M. Hector Dunoisse in half-a-dozen European capitals, and several cities and posting-towns of Turkey and Asiatic Russia; their condition ranging from the yellowed antiquity of more than fifty years back to the comparative newness of the envelope that bore the London postmark of the previous 22nd of December, and the Zeiden stamp of three days later. For once a year, at Christmas-tide, was celebrated old Hector Dunoisse's joy-festival—when such a letter came to add its bulk to the number in the leather case.

He would be fastidiously particular about his toilet upon that day of days, he who was always so scrupulously neat. His silken white hair would be arranged after the most becoming fashion, his cheeks and chin would be shaved to polished marble smoothness, his venerable mustache waxed with elaborate care. He would be attired in his best white flannel suit, crowned with his newest velvet cap, and adorned with all his Orders; while pastilles would be set burning about the room, fresh flowers would be placed, not only on the tiny altar with its twinkling waxlights and colored plaster presentment of the Stable at Bethlehem, but before a photograph in a tortoise-shell-and-silver frame that always stood upon a little table, beside his chair or bed. About the ebony pedestal of the marble bust that stood in the shallow bay of the southeast window a garland would be twined of red-berried holly and black-berried ivy, and delicately-tinted, sweet-scented hyacinths, grown under glass.... And then the hands of a nursing Sister or of a mere hireling would open the letter, and hold the feebly-written sheet before Dunoisse's burning eyes, and they would weep as they read, until their bright black flame was quenched in scalding tears.

Do you laugh at the old lover with his heart of youthful fire, burning in the body that is all but dead? You will if you who read are young. Should you be at your full-orbed, splendid prime of womanhood or manhood, you will smile as you pity. But those who have passed the meridian of life will sigh; for they are beginning to understand; and those who are very old will smile and sigh together, and look wise—so wise! Because they have found out that Love is eternally young.

Oh, foolish Youth!—that deems the divine passion to be a matter of red lips meeting red lips, bright eyes beaming into bright eyes, young heart beating against young heart. Intolerant, splendid Prime, that leaps to the imperious call of passion and revels in the delirious pleasures of the senses. For you love is the plucking of the ripe, fragrant, juicy fruit; the rose-tinted foam upon the sparkling wine that brims the crystal goblet; the crown of rapture; the night of jeweled stars and burning kisses that crowns the fierce day of Desire.

And ah! wise Age, experienced and deep, where Youth is all untaught, and Prime but a little more scholar-wise, and Middle Age but a beginner at the book.... For you Love is the jewel in the matrix of the stone; the sacred lamp that burns unquenched within the sealed-up sepulcher; the flame that glows in the heart's core the more hotly that snows of years lie on the head, and the icy blood creeps sluggishly through the clogged arteries; the sustenance and provender and nourishment of Life no less than the hope that smiles dauntlessly in the face of Death. For to die is to follow whither she has gone,—to meet with him again. Can those who seek to disprove the Being of their Creator with the subtle brain He forged be in the truest sense of the word—lovers? I say No! For Love is an attribute of the Divine.

Those written sheets in the locked case of dulled crimson leather, attached to the fine steel chain, told no tale of love....

Ah! the womanly, gracious letters, breathing warm friendship and kindly interest in the long-unseen, how diligently the old man had tried to read between their fine clear lines the one thing that he never found for all his searching. How devoutly they had been kept and cherished, how delicately and reverently handled.... But for seven long years now they had lain undisturbed in their receptacle, only seeing light when it was opened with the little key that hung upon the steel chain, so that the newest letter of all might be added to the treasured store.

Of late years, how brief they had become! From the three crowded sheets of more than fifty years back, to the single sheet of ten years—the quarter-sheet of five years ago—a mere message of kind remembrance, ending with the beloved name. It had been tragedy to Dunoisse, this slow, gradual shortening of his allowance of what was to him the bread of life. He could not understand it. Had he offended her in some way? He dared to write to her and ask, by aid of the paid secretary who typed from his painstaking dictation in a language which she did not understand. And the reply came in the caligraphy of a stranger. He realized then what he had never before dreamed possible, that his worshiped lady had grown old.... A photograph accompanied the letter. He recognized, with a joyful leap of the heart, that the sweet, placid, aged face with the delicate folds of a fine lace shawl framing it, was beautiful and gracious still. Thenceforward, in a tortoiseshell-and-silver frame, it stood upon the little table beside the bed.

But in another year or two heavy news reached him. She had grown feeble, barely able to trace with the gently-guided pen the well-loved initials at the foot of the written page! The shock of this unlooked-for, appalling revelation made him very ill. He was not himself for months,—never quite again what he had been.... A day was coming when ... the letters might come no more. Her initials were so faintly traced upon the last one that—that——

No, no! God was too kind to let her die before him. He clenched his toothless gums as he would have liked to clench his paralyzed hands, and clung desperately to his belief in the Divine Love.

IV

To lie, helpless and lonely and old, and racked by pain, and to keep on believing in the Divine goodness, requires a caliber of mental strength proportionately equal to the weakness of the sufferer. But it was too late in the day for Dunoisse to doubt.

And here was his dear Moon swimming into view, rising from the translucent depths of a bottomless lagoon of sapphire ether, red Mars glowing at her pearly knee. A childlike content softened the lines that pain and bitterness had graven on the old ivory face. He nodded, well pleased.

"There you are! I see you! You have come as punctually as you always do, making my pain the easier to bear," he murmured brokenly to the planet. "You shine and look at me and understand; unlike men and women who talk, and talk, and comprehend nothing! And you are old, like my love; and changeless, like my love; while yet my love, unlike you, is eternal; it will endure when you have passed away with Time. Dear Moon! is she looking at you too? Does she ever think of me? But that is a great question you never answer. I can only lie and wait, and hope and long ... in vain? Ah, God! If I could but know for certain that it has not been in vain!..."

Then, with a rush of furious crimson to the drawn cheeks and the knitted forehead, the barrier of his great and dauntless patience broke down before his pent-up passion's flood. His features were transfigured; the venerable saint became an aged, rebellious Lucifer. Words crowded from his writhing lips, despair and fury blazed in his great black eyes.

"How long, O God, implacable in Thy judgments," he cried, "must I lie here, a living soul immured in a dead body, and wait, and yearn, and long? 'Give thanks,' say the priests, 'that you have your Purgatory in this world.' Can there be any torture in Purgatory to vie with this I am enduring? Has Hell worse pains than these? None! for Despair and Desolation sit on either side of me. I rebel against the appointments of the Divine Will. I doubt the Love of God."

Rigor seized him, his racked nerves vibrated like smitten harp-strings, sweat streamed upon his clammy skin, the beating of his heart shook him and shook the bed, a crushing weight oppressed his panting lungs.

"It is so long, so very long!—sixteen years that I have lain here," he moaned. "I was content at first, or could seem so. 'Let me but live while she lives and die when she dies!—' had always been my prayer. I pray so still—yes, yes! but the long waiting is so terrible. When I had health and strength to labor incessantly, unrestingly, then I could bear my banishment. Through the din and shock of charging squadrons, the rattle of musketry and the roar of artillery, the ceaseless roll of the ambulances and the shrieks of mangled men, one cannot hear the selfish crying of the heart that starves for love. Even in times of peace there was no pause, no slackening. To organize, administer, plan, devise, perfect,—what work, what work was always to be done! Now the work goes on. I lie here. They defer to me, appeal to me, consult me—oh, yes, they consult me! They are very considerate to the old man who is now upon the shelf."

He laughed and the strange sound woke an echo that appalled him. It sounded so like the crazy laugh of a delirious fever-patient, or of some poor peasant wretch driven beyond his scanty wits by the horror and the hideousness of War. He shook with nervous terror now, and closed his eyes tightly that he might shut out all the familiar things that had suddenly grown strange.

"Let me die, my God! I cannot bear Life longer!" he said more calmly. "Let her find me crouching upon the threshold of Paradise like a faithful hound, when she comes, borne by Thy rejoicing Angels to claim her glorious reward. I am not as courageous as I boasted myself; the silence and the emptiness appal me. Let me die!—but what then of my letter that comes once a year?" he added in alarm. "No, no! I beseech Thee, do not listen to me, a sinful, rebellious old grumbler. I am content—or I would be if the time were not so long."

Something like a cool, light finger seemed as if drawn across his burning eyelids. He opened them and smiled. For a long broad ray of pure silvery moonshine, falling through the high southeast window upon the white marble bust that stood upon the ebony pedestal against its background of mountain-peaks and sky, reached to the foot of his bed, and rising higher still, had flowed in impalpable waves of brightness over the helpless feet, and covered the stiff white hands, and now reached his face.

This was the moment for which he nightly waited in secret fear, and breathless expectation and desire. Would the miracle happen, this night of all the nights? Would it visit him to bless or leave him uncomforted? He trembled with the desperate eagerness that might defeat its end.

The moon was full and rode high in the translucent heavens. To the lonely watcher the celestial orb suggested the likeness of a crystal Lamp, burning with a light of inconceivable brilliance in a woman's white uplifted hand. He knew whose hand. His black eyes softened into lustrous, dreamy tenderness, a smile of welcome curved about his lips, as the moon-rays illuminated the marble features of the bust that stood in the bay.

The face of the bust was the same as the old, beautiful face of the photographic portrait that stood in its tortoise-shell-and-silver frame upon the little table by his bed. You saw it as the sculptured presentment of a woman still young, yet past youth. Slenderly framed, yet not fragile, the slight shoulders broad, the long rounded throat a fitting pedestal for the high-domed, exquisitely proportioned head. Upon her rich, thick waving hair was set a little cap: close-fitting, sober, with a double-plaited border enclosing the clear, fine, oval face, a little thin, a shade worn, as by anxiety and watching.

The face—her face!—was not turned towards the bed. It bent a little aside as though its owner pondered. And that the fruit of such reflection would be Action, swift, unflinching, prompt, direct—no one could doubt who observed the purpose in the wide arching brows; the salient, energetic jut of the rather prominent, slightly-aquiline nose, with its high-bred, finely-cut nostrils; the severity and sweetness that sat throned upon the lips; the rounded, decisive chin that completed the womanly-fair image. A little shawl or cape was pinned about her shoulders; to the base of the pure column of the throat she was virginally veiled and covered.

And if the chief impression she conveyed was Purity, the dominant note of her was Reflection. For the eyes beneath the thick white eyelids were observant; the brain behind the broad brows pondered, reviewed, decided, planned.... It seemed as though in another moment she must speak; and the utterance would solve a difficulty; reduce confusion into sanest order, throw light upon darkness; clear away some barrier; devise an expedient, formulate a rule....

There was not a line of voluptuous tenderness, not one amorous dimple wherein Cupid might play at hiding, in all the stern, sweet face. She thought, and dreamed, and planned. And yet,...

And yet the full-orbed eyes, gray-blue under their heavy, white, darkly-lashed eyelids as the waters of her own English Channel, could melt, could glad, for he had seen!... The sensitive, determined mouth could quiver into exquisite tenderness. The most cherished memory of this old man was that it had once kissed him.

Ah! if you are ignorant how the memory of one kiss can tinge and permeate life, as the single drop of priceless Ghazipur attar could impart its fragrance to the limpid waters in the huge crystal block skilled Eastern artificers hollowed out for Nur Mahal to bathe in,—you are fortunate; for such knowledge is the flower of sorrow, that has been reared in loneliness and watered with tears. This one red rose made summer amidst the snows of a nonagenarian's closing years. He felt it warm upon his mouth; he heard his own voice across the arid steppes of Time crying to her passionately:

"Oh, my beloved! when we meet again I shall have deserved so much of God, that when I ask Him for my wages He will give me even you!"

What had he not done since then, what had he not suffered, how much had he not sacrificed, to keep this great vow? Had he not earned his wages full forty years ago? Yet God made no sign, and she had gone her ways and forgotten.

It was only in pity,—only in recognition of his being, like herself, the survivor of a vanished generation, almost the only human link remaining to bind this restless Twentieth Century with the strenuous, splendid days of the early Victorian era, that she had written to him once a year.

Only in pity, only in kindness was it, after all?

This one thing is certain, that at rare, irregular intervals, he reaped the fruit of his long devotion—his unswerving, fanatical fidelity—in the renewal of that lost, vanished, unforgettable moment of exquisite joy.

As he sat in his wheeled-chair upon the Promenade of Zeiden, as he lay upon his bed, he would feel, drawing nearer, nearer, the almost bodily presence of a Thought that came from afar. A delicate thrilling ecstasy would penetrate and vivify the paralyzed nerves of his half-dead body, the blood would course in the frozen veins with the ardent vigor of his prime. He would see her, his beloved lady, in a halo of pale moonlight, bending to comfort—descending to bless. Once more he would kneel before her; yet again he would take the beloved hands in his, and draw them upwards to his heart. And their lips would meet, and their looks would mingle, and then.... Oh! then the waking to loneliness, and silence, and pain.

V

He was prone, when the visitations of her almost tangible Thought of him were interrupted by periods of unconsoled waiting, to doubt the actuality of his own experience. That was the worst agony of all, to which the sharpest physical torments were preferable, when in the long, dreary, miserable nights a mocking voice would whisper in his reluctant ear:

"You have been deceived. She never thinks of you. Driveling old dotard! she has long forgotten that night at Scutari. Why in the name of Folly do you cling to your absurd conviction that she loved you then, that she loves you still? You have been deceived, I say. Curse her, blaspheme God, and die!"

"Be silent, be silent!" Dunoisse would say to the invisible owner of the mocking, jeering voice. "If I had the use of this dead right hand to make the sign of the Cross, you would soon be disposed of. For I know who and what you are, very well!"

And he would clamp his lean jaws sternly together, and look up to the carved walnut Crucifix with the Emblems of the Passion, that hung upon the wall beside his bed. And the thin, nagging voice would die away in a titter, and another Voice would whisper in the innermost shrine of his deep heart:

"My son, had I the use of My Arms when I hung upon the cross of Calvary? Yet, nailed thereon beyond the possibility of human movement, did I not pluck the sting from Death, and rise victorious over the Grave, and tread down Satan under My wounded Feet? Answer, My little son?"

And Dunoisse would whisper, falteringly:

"Lord, it is true! But Thou wert the Son of God most High, and I am only a helpless, suffering, desolate old man, worn out and worthless and forgotten!"

The Voice would answer:

"Thou art greater than a thousand Kings. Thou art more glorious than an Archangel, of more value than all the stars that shine in the firmament— being a man for whom Christ died! Be of good courage. This trial will not last long. Believe, endure, pray!... Hast thou forgotten thy compact with Me?"

Dunoisse would cry out of the depths with a rending sob:

"No! but it is a sin of presumption to seek to make bargains with God. The compact was impious."

The Voice would say:

"Perhaps, yet thou didst make it: and thou hast kept it. Shall I be less faithful than thou?"

Dunoisse would falter:

"I should have loved Thee for Thyself above any creature Thou hast made. To serve Thee for the love of even a perfect woman, was not this wrong?"

"It may be so!" the Voice would answer, "and therefore I have visited thee with My rods and scourgings. Yet, if I choose woman for My Means of Grace, what is that to thee?"

Dunoisse would not be able to answer for weeping. The Voice would continue:

"Moreover, it may be that in loving this woman, My servant, thou hast loved Me. For she is pure, and I am the Fountain of Purity; she is charitable, and I am Charity itself. She is beautiful of soul, beloved and loving, and I am unspeakable Beauty, and boundless, measureless Love. Be courageous, little son of Mine! Believe, and hope, and pray!..."

Dunoisse would stammer with quivering lips:

"I believe!... I hope!... Lord, grant me strength to go on believing and hoping!"

Then he would fall peacefully asleep upon a pillow wet with tears. Or he would lie awake and let his memory range over the prairies of dead years that stretched away so far behind....

Will you hear some of the things that this old man remembered? Listen, then, if it be only for an hour. That is a little space of time, you say, and truly. Yet I gave my youth and most of the things that men and women cherish, to buy this hour, dear, unknown friend!—of you.

VI

At sixteen years of age Hector-Marie-Aymont-von Widinitz Dunoisse fought his first duel, with a fellow-student of the Royal School of Technical Military Instruction, Rue de la Vallée Ste. Gabrielle.

The quarrel occurred after one of the weekly inspections by the General-Commandant, when Hector, accoutered with the black shiny sword-belt and cartridge-belt; armed with the sword, bayonet, and the heavy little brass-mounted, muzzle-loading musket, commonly displayed, when not in use, with two hundred and ninety-nine similar weapons in the long gallery running above the class-rooms—when Hector with his fellow-pupils of the First Division had performed a series of military evolutions in the presence of Miss Harriet Smithwick, admitted with other persons standing in the parental and protective relation to the young neophytes of the School, to the dusty patch of tree-shaded grass at the lower end of the smaller exercise-ground, where Messieurs the hundred-and-fifty pupils of the two companies of the Junior Corps—the great boys of the Senior possessing a parade-ground to themselves—commonly mustered for drill.

On other days, visitors and friends were received in a small entrance-yard, dank and moist in wet weather, baking and gritty in hot; inhospitable and uninviting at all times; in which enclosure M. and Madame Cornu were permitted by the authorities to purvey fruit and sweets, and a greasy kind of *galette*, with ices of dubious complexion in June and July; and syrups of *groseille* and *grenadine*, served hot—and rendered, if possible, even stickier and more vapidly cloying beverages by being thus served,—in the bitter winter months.

The good Smithwick would have enjoyed herself better if permitted to ascend to the department on the floor above the Infirmary, where Madame Gaubert presided, in an atmosphere strongly flavored with soft-soap, over long rows of shelves divided into regulation pigeon-holes, containing within an officially-appointed space of one foot ten inches square the linen of young Hector and his companions. It would have satisfied a burning curiosity from which the poor little lady had long suffered, had she been permitted to observe for herself the process of lavation that deprived her ex-pupil's shirts of every button, while leaving the dirt untouched; and to gauge with her own eyes the holes of the rats and mice that ate such prodigious mouthfuls, not only in the garments named, but in the sheets and bolster-covers, towels and napkins, which, by the amiable dispensation of a paternal Government, the boy was permitted to bring from home.

Instead, the poor fluttered spinster occupied a small share of one of the green benches set beneath the shade of the semicircle of lime-trees at the lower end of the exercise-ground; her neighbors on the right and left being the venerable Duchesse de Moulny of the Faubourg St-Honoré and Mademoiselle Pasbas of the Grand Opera Ballet. Pédelaborde, inventor of an Elixir for the preservation of the teeth to extreme old age, who in fact enjoyed a Government contract for attending to the dental requirements of the young gentlemen of the School, weighed down the bench at its farther end; and M. Bougon, principal physician of the body to His Majesty King Louis-Philippe, balanced his meager and wizened anatomy upon the other extremity. Nor was there the lack of sympathy between the occupants of the bench that might have been expected. The Duchesse had a grandson—Bougon a son—Pédelaborde a nephew—the opera-dancer a young *protégé* (in whom, for the sake of an early friend, an officer of Cuirassiers, Mademoiselle took a tender interest)—little Miss Smithwick the adored offspring of a revered employer, to observe blandly, and discreetly manifest interest in, and secretly throb and glow and tremble for; so simple and common and ordinary is Nature beneath all the mass of pretenses we pile upon her, so homespun are the cords of love, and sympathy, and interest, that move the human heart.

When the General-Commandant—for this was an ordinary informal inspection of young gentlemen in the School undress of belted blouse and brass-badged, numbered *képi*, not the terrific bi-monthly review *en grande tenue* of the entire strength of the establishment, when General, Colonel, Captains, Adjutants, the four Sergeants-Major, the six drummers, and all the pupils of the Junior and Senior Corps, wearing the little cocked hat with the white plume and gold lace trimming; the black leather stock, the blue frocked coat faced with red, trimmed and adorned with gilt buttons and gold braid, must pass under the awful eye of a Field-Marshal, assisted by a Colonel of the Staff, a Major of Artillery, and a fearful array of Civil Professors—when the General, addressing Alai-Joseph-Henri-Jules de Moulny, briefly remarked:

"Pupil No. 127, you have the neck of a pig and the finger-nails of a gorilla! Another offense against that cleanliness which should adorn the person of a Soldier of France, and the *galon* of Corporal, which you disgrace, will be transferred to the sleeve of one more worthy to wear it."

You beheld the immense bonnet of the venerable aristocrat, its great circular sweep of frontage filled with quillings of costly lace and chastely tinted cambric blossoms, its crown adorned with nodding plumes, awful as those upon the helmet of the Statue of the Commendatore, condescendingly bending towards the flamboyant headgear of the Pasbas—as the Duchesse begged to be informed, her lamentable infirmity of deafness depriving her of the happiness of hearing the commendations bestowed by his Chief upon her young relative,—what Monsieur the General had actually said?

"I myself, Madame, failed to catch the expression of approval actually employed. But," explained Mademoiselle Pasbas, as she lowered her *lorgnette* and turned a candid look of angelic sweetness upon the dignified old lady, "Madame may rely upon it that they were thoroughly merited by the young gentleman upon whom they were bestowed."

"I thank you, Mademoiselle." The bonnet of the Duchesse bent in gracious acknowledgment. "It is incumbent upon the members of my family to set an example. Nor do we fail of our duty, as a rule."

Perhaps the roguish dimples of Mademoiselle Pasbas were a trifle more in evidence; possibly the humorous creases of enjoyment deepened in the stout Pédelaborde's triple chin; it may be that the sardonic twinkle behind the narrow gold-rimmed spectacles of M. Bougon took on extra significance; but all three were as demure as pussycats, not even exchanging a glance behind the overwhelming patrician headgear with the stupendous feathers;—to see one another over it would have been impossible without standing on the bench. This is the simple truth, without a particle of exaggeration. My Aunt Julietta at this date purchased from a fashionable milliner in the West End of London——But my Aunt Julietta has no business on the Calais side of the English Channel!—let her and her bonnets wait!

The General's salute closed the review. The pupils presented arms, a superb effect of a hundred and fifty muskets, not infrequently thrilling parents to the bestowal of five-franc pieces; the six drummers beat the disperse as one overgrown hobbledehoy; the orderly ranks broke up. Discipline gave place to disorder. Boys ran, chasing one another and yelling, boys skylarked, punching and wrestling, boys argued in gesticulatory groups, or whispered in knots of two or three together.... The spectators on the painted benches behind the railing had risen. Now they filed out by a door in the high-spiked wall behind the dusty lime-trees, in whose yellow-green blossoms the brown bees had been humming and droning all through the hot, bright day of June. The bees were also dusty, and the spectators were liberally powdered with dust, for the clumping, wooden-heeled, iron toe-capped School regulation shoes of the young gentlemen had raised clouds which would have done credit to the evolutions of a battery of horse. And the yearning desires of Hector Dunoisse were turning in the direction of a cooling draught of Madame Cornu's *grenadine*, or of the thin, vinegary, red ration-wine; when to him says Alain-Joseph-Henri-Jules de Moulny:

"Tell me, Redskin, didst thou twig my respected grand-mamma perched in the front row between a variegated she-cockatoo and a molting old female fowl, who held her head on one side, and cried into a clean starched pocket-hand-kerchief?"

"She did not cry!" warmly contradicted the young gentleman thus assailed. "It is her cold-in-the-head that never gets well until she goes back to England for her holiday once a year; and then she has *migraine* instead. All the Smithwick family are like that, Miss Smithwick says; it is an inherited delicacy of the constitution."

"'Smizzique ... Mees Smeezveek.' ... There's a name to go to bed with!..." pursued de Moulny, his thick lips, that were nearly always chapped, curling back and upwards in his good-natured schoolboy's grin. "And how old is she?—your Sm———. I cannot say it again!... And why does she wear a bonnet that was raked off the top of an ash-barrel, and a shawl that came off a hook at the Morgue?"

Young Hector had been conscious of the antiquated silk bonnet, in hue the faded maroon of pickling-cabbage, sadly bent as to its supporting framework of stiffened gauze and whalebone, by the repeated tumbles of the bonnet-box containing it off the high top-corner of the walnut wardrobe in Miss Smithwick's fourth-floor sleeping-apartment at home in the Rue de la Chaussée-d'Antin. It had been eating into him like a blister all through the General's inspection, that venerable wintry headgear, with its limp veil like a sooty cellar-cobweb, depending from its lopsided rim. To say nothing of the shawl, a venerable yellow cashmere atrocity, with long straggling white fringes, missing here and there, where the tooth of Time had nibbled them away. But though these articles of apparel made good Smithwick's ex-pupil feel sick and hot with shame, they were not to be held up to ridicule. That was perfectly clear....

Hector could not have told you why the thing was so clear; even as he thrust a challenging elbow into the big de Moulny's fleshy ribs, turning pale under the red Egyptian granite tint of skin that had earned him his nickname from these boys, his comrades—who like other boys all the world over, had recently fallen under Fenimore Cooper's spell—and said, with a dangerous glitter in his black-diamond eyes:

"I do not know how old she is—it is not possible for a gentleman to ask a lady her age. But she is a lady!" he added, neatly intercepting the contradiction before it could be uttered. "*Une femme de bon ton, une femme comme il faut.* Also she dresses as a lady should ... appropriately, gracefully, elegantly...." He added grandiloquently, tapping the brass hilt of his little School hanger: "I will teach you with this, M. de Moulny, to admire that bonnet and that shawl!"

"*Nom d'un petit bonhomme!*" spluttered the astonished de Moulny. But there was no relenting in Hector's hard young face, though he was secretly sick at the pit of his stomach and cold at heart.

"I will fight you!" he repeated.

De Moulny, always slow to wrath, began to lose his temper. The outspoken compliments of Monsieur the General had stung, and here was a more insufferable smart. Also, it was a bosom friend who challenged. One may be angry with an enemy; it is the friend become foe who drives us to frenzied rage.

He said, pouting his fleshy lips, sticking out his obstinate chin, staring at the changed unfriendly face, with eyes grown hard as blue stones:

"I do not know that I can oblige you by giving you the opportunity of learning how quickly boasters are cured of brag. For one thing, I have my stripe," he added, holding up his head and looking arrogantly down his nose.

"Since yesterday," agreed Hector, pointedly. "And after to-day you will not have it. The squad-paper will hang beside another fellow's bed,—M. the Commandant will have reduced you to the ranks for uncleanliness on parade. So we will fight to-morrow."

"Possibly!" acquiesced de Moulny, his heavy cheeks quivering with anger, his thick hands opening and shutting over the tucked-in thumbs. "Possibly!" he repeated. His sluggish temperament once fairly set alight, burned with the fierce roaring flame and the incandescent heat of a fire of cocoanut-shell. And it was in his power to be so well revenged! He went on, speaking through his nose:

"As it is only since yesterday that you became legitimately entitled to carry the name you bear, you may be admitted to know something of what happened yesterday." He added: "But of what will happen to-morrow, do not make too sure, for I may decline to do you the honor of correcting you. It is possible, that!" he added, as Hector stared at him aghast. "A gentleman may be a bastard—I have no objection to a bar-sinister.... But you are not only your father's son—you are also your mother's! We de Moulnys are ultra-Catholic——" This was excellent from Alain-Joseph-Henri-Jules, whose chaplet of beads lay rolling in the dust at the bottom of the kitlocker at his bed-foot, and who was scourged to Communion by the family Chaplain at Christmas and Easter, and at the Fête-Dieu. "Ultra-Catholic. And your mother was a Carmelite nun!"

"My mother assumed the Veil of Profession when I was eight years old. With my father's consent and the approval of her Director," said Hector, narrowing his eyelids and speaking between his small white teeth. "Therefore I may be pardoned for saying that the permission of the family of de Moulny was not indispensable, or required."

Retorted de Moulny—and it was strange how the rough, uncultured intonations, the slipshod grammar, the slang of the exercise-yard and the schoolroom, had been instinctively replaced in the mouths of these boys by the phraseology of the outer world of men:

"You are accurate, M. Hector Dunoisse, in saying that your mother was received into the Carmel when you were eight years old. What you do not admit, or do not know, is that she was a professed Carmelite when you were born." He added, with a pout of disgust: "It is an infamy, a thing like that!"

"The infamy is yours who slander her!" cried out Hector in the quavering staccato squeak of fury. "You lie!—do you hear?—You lie!" And struck de Moulny in the face.

VII

Followed upon the blow a sputtering oath from de Moulny, succeeded by a buzzing as of swarming hornets, as the various groups scattered over the exercise-ground broke up and consolidated into a crowd. Hector and de Moulny, as the nucleus of the said crowd, were deafened by interrogations, suffocated by the smell of red and blue dye, perspiration and pomatum, choked by the dense dust kicked up by thick, wooden-heeled, iron toe-capped shoes (each pupil blacked his own, not neglecting the soles—at cockcrow every morning)—jostled, squeezed, hustled and mobbed by immature personalities destined to be potential by-and-by in the remolding of a New France,—the said personalities being contained in baggy red breeches and coarse blue, black-belted blouses. All the eyes belonging to all the faces under the high-crowned, shiny-peaked caps of undress-wear, faces thin, faces fleshy, faces pimply, faces high-colored or pale—were round and staring with curiosity. The Redskin had challenged de Moulny! But de Moulny was his superior officer! The quarrel was about a woman. Sacred name of a pipe! Where was the affair to come off? In the Salle de Danse?—empty save at the State-appointed periods of agility occurring on two days in the week. In the yard behind the Department of Chemistry? That was a good place!

Meanwhile a duologue took place between the challenged and the challenger, unheard in the general hubbub. Said de Moulny, blotchily pale excepting for the crimson patch upon one well-padded cheekbone, for his madness was dying out in him, and he was beginning to realize the thing that he had done:

"What I have said is true: upon my honor! I heard it from my father. Or, to be more correct, I heard my father tell the story to M. de Beyras, the Minister of Finance, and General d'Arville at the dinner-table only last night." He added: "My grandmother and the other ladies had withdrawn. I had dined with them—it being Wednesday. Perhaps they forgot me, or thought I was too deep in the dessert to care what they said. But if my mouth was stuffed with strawberries and cream, and peaches and bonbons, my ears were empty, and I heard all I wanted to hear."

The crowd was listening now with all its ears. That image of de Moulny gormandizing tickled its sense of fun. There was a general giggle, and the corners of the mouths went up as though pulled by one string. De Moulny, sickening more and more at his task of explanation, went on, fumbling at his belt:

"As to remembering, that is very easy. Read me a page of a book, or a column of a newspaper twice—I will recite it you without an error, as you are very well aware. I will repeat you this that I heard in private, if you prefer it?"

Hector, between his small square teeth, said—the opposite of what he longed to say.... "There can be no privacy in a place like this. I prefer that you should speak out, openly, before all here!"

There was a silence about the boys, broken only by a horse-laugh or two, a whinnying giggle. The piled-up faces all about, save one or two, were grave and attentive, the hands, clean or dirty, generally dirty, by which the listeners upon the outer circle of the interested crowd supported themselves upon the shoulders of those who stood in front of them, unconsciously tightened their grip as de Moulny went on, slowly and laboriously, as though repeating an imposition, while the red mark upon his cheek deepened to blackish blue:

"How Marshal Dunoisse originally prevailed upon Sister Térèse de Saint François, of the Carmelite Convent of Widinitz in Southern Bavaria, to break her vows for him, I have no idea. I am only repeating what I have heard, and I did not hear that. He went through a kind of ceremony with her before a Protestant pastor in Switzerland; and three years subsequently to the birth of their son, induced a French Catholic priest, ignorant, of course, that the lady was a Religious,—to administer the Sacrament of Marriage." De Moulny stopped to lick his dry lips, and pursued: "By that ceremony you were made legitimate, *per subsequens matrimonium*, according to Canon Law." He syllabled the Latin as conscientiously as a sacristan's parrot might have done. "There is no doubt of the truth of all this; my father said it to M. de Beyras and the General, and what my father says *is* so—he never speaks without being sure!"

Hector knew a pang of envy of this boy who owned a father capable of inspiring a confidence so immense. But he never took his eyes from those slowly moving lips of de Moulny's, as the words came dropping out....

"Having made Madame his wife, and legitimatized her son by the marriage, Monsieur the Marshal instituted legal proceedings to recover the dowry paid by Madame's father, the Hereditary Prince of Widinitz, to the Mother Prioress of the Carmelite Convent when his daughter took the Veil. Monsieur the Marshal did not think it necessary to tell Madame what he was doing.... Her determination some years later, to resume the habit of the Carmelite Order—provided the Church she had outraged would receive her—was violently opposed by him. But eventually"—de Moulny's eyes flickered between their thick eyelids, and he licked his lips again as though Hector's hot stare scorched them—"eventually he permitted it to be clearly understood; he stated in terms, the plainness of which there was no mistaking, that, if the Church would repay the dowry of the Princess Marie Bathilde von Widinitz to the husband of Madame Dunoisse, Sœur Térèse de Saint François might return to the Carmel whenever she felt disposed."

Hector was sick at the pit of his stomach with loathing of the picture of a father evoked. He blinked his stiff eyelids, clenched and unclenched his hot hands, opened and shut his mouth without bringing any words out of it. The Catholics among the listeners understood why very well. The Freethinkers yawned or smiled, the Atheists sneered or tittered, the Protestants wondered what all the rumpus was about? And de Moulny went on:

"Here M. de Beyras broke in. He said: 'The Swiss innkeeper spoke there!' I do not know what he meant by that. The General answered, sniffing the bouquet of the Burgundy in his glass: 'Rather than the Brigand of the Grand Army!' Of course, I understood that allusion perfectly well!"

The prolonged effort of memory had taxed de Moulny. He puffed. Hector made yet another effort, and got out in a strangling croak:

"The—the dowry. He did not succeed in———?"

De Moulny wrinkled his nose as though a nasty smell had offended the organ.

"Unfortunately he did, although the money had been expended by the Prioress in clearing off a building-debt and endowing a House of Mercy for the incurable sick poor. I do not know how the Prioress managed to repay it. Probably some wealthy Catholic nobleman came to her aid. But what I do know is that the reply of the Reverend Mother to Monsieur the Marshal, conveyed to him through Madame Dunoisse's Director, ran like this: *'We concede to you this money, the price of a soul. Sister Térèse de Saint François will return to the Convent forthwith.'*"

Hector groaned.

"It was a great sum, this dowry?"

"My father says," answered de Moulny, "the amount in silver thalers of Germany, comes to one million, one hundred-and-twenty-five thousand of our francs. That will be forty-five thousand of your English sovereigns," he added with a side-thrust at Hector's weakness of claiming, on the strength of a bare month's holiday spent in the foggy island, an authoritative acquaintance with its coinage, customs, scenery, people and vernacular. "The money," he went on, "was bequeathed to the Princess Marie Bathilde von Widinitz by her mother, whose dowry it had been. My father did not say so; possibly that may not be true."

Hector's brows knitted. He mumbled, between burning anger and cold disgust:

"What can *he* have wanted with all that money? He had enough before!"

"Some men never have enough," said de Moulny, in his cold, heavy, contemptuous way. "What did he want it for? Perhaps to gamble away on the green cloth or on the Bourse! Perhaps to spend upon his mistresses! Perhaps to make provision for you...."

"I will not have it!" snarled Hector.

"Nor would I in your place," said de Moulny with one of his slow nods. "I like money well enough, but money with that taint upon it!... Robbed from the dying poor, to—bah!" He spat upon the trodden dust. "Now have you heard enough?" He added with an inflection that plucked at Hector's heartstrings: "It did not give me pleasure listening to the story, I assure you."

Hector said:

"Thank you!"

The utterance was like a sob. De Moulny jumped at the sound, looked about him at the staring faces, back at the face of the boy who had been his friend, and to whom he had done an injury that could never be undone, and cried out wildly:

"Why did you challenge me just now for a *gaffe*—a mere piece of stupid joking—about the bonnet of an old woman who snivels in a pocket-handkerchief? Do you not know that when once I get angry I am as mad as all Bicêtre? I swear to you that when I listened to that story it was with the determination never to repeat it!—to bury it!—to compel myself to forget it! Yet in a few hours...." He choked and boggled, and the shamed blood that dyed his solid, ordinarily dough-colored countenance, obliterated that deepening bruise upon the cheekbone. "I apologize!" he at last managed to get out. "I have been guilty of an unpardonable meanness! I ask you, before all here, to forget it! I beg you to forgive me!"

Hector said, in pain for the pain that was written in de Moulny's face:

"De Moulny, I shall willingly accept your apology—after we have fought. You must understand that the lady of whose bonnet you spoke offensively is my old English governess, once my mother's *dame de compagnie*.... If she dried her eyes when she looked at me it must have been because she was thinking of my mother, whom she loved; and—I must have satisfaction for your contempt of those tears.... And—you have refused to fight me because of my birth, you have told me of my mother's sin, and of the sacrilege committed by my father. Do you not understand that this duel must take place? There can be no one who thinks otherwise here?"

Hector looked about him. There was a sudden buzz from the crowd that said "No one!"

De Moulny said, with his eyes upon the ground: "I understand that I have been a brute and a savage. The meeting shall be where you please. I name my cousin Albert de Moulny for my second, unless he is ashamed to appear for one who has disgraced his name?"

It was so terrible, the bumptious, arrogant de Moulny's self-abasement, that Hector turned his eyes elsewhere, and even the most callous among the gazers winced at the sight. Albert de Moulny, red and lowering, butted his way to the side of his principal, savagely kicking the shins of those boys who would not move. Hector, catching the alert eye of Pédelaborde, a fat, vivacious, brown-skinned, button-eyed youth who had the School Code of Honor at his stumpy finger-ends, and was known as the best fencer of the Junior Corps, gave him a beckoning nod.

"*Sapristi!*" panted the nephew of the man of teeth, as he emerged, smiling but rather squeezed, from the press of bodies, "so you are going to give the fat one rhubarb for senna? Ten times I thought you on the point of falling into each other's arms! I held on to my ears from pure fright!—there has not been an affair of honor amongst the Juniors for three months; we were getting moldy! By-the-way, which of us is to prig the skewers from the Fencing Theater? De Moulny Younger or me? I suggest we toss up. As for de Moulny Elder—he is a bad swordsman—you are better than decent! I say so!... It rests with you to cut his claws and his tail. He is stronger than you.... *Saperlipopette!* he has the arms of a blacksmith, but there are certain ruses to be employed in such a case—I said ruses, not tricks!—to gain time and tire a long-winded opponent. For example—*saisissez-vous*—you could stamp upon one of your opponent's feet during a *corps à corps*, thus creating a diversion———"

"I am no blackguard ... whatever else I may be!" said his principal sulkily.

"—Or if you felt in need of a rest," pursued the enthusiast Pédelaborde, "you could catch your point against the edge of de Moulny's guard, so as to bend it. Then a halt is called for straightening the steel, and meanwhile—you get your second wind. It is very simple! Or—you could permit your sword to fall when his blade beats yours.... De Moulny would never do a thing like that, you say? not so dishonorable! *Oh! que si!* And I said these devices might be practiced in ease of need—not that they were in good form. For example! You *could*, if he lunges—and de Moulny's lunge is a nasty thing!—you could slip and overbalance. Fall to the ground, I mean, point up, so that he gets hit in that big belly of his. It's an Italian mountebank-trick, I don't recommend it, French fencing keeps to the high lines. But—*tiens, mon œil!*—to skewer him like a cockchafer, that would be a lark!"

"Your idea of a lark makes me sick!" broke out Hector, so savagely that Pédelaborde's jaw dropped and his eyebrows shot towards his hair. Then:

"Messieurs The Pupils! RETURN TO YOUR STUDIES!" bellowed the most bull-voiced of the three Sergeants of the Line, appointed to assist the Captain-Commandant in the drilling and disciplining of the young gentlemen of the Junior Corps.

The deafening gallop of three hundred regulation shoes followed as Messieurs the Pupils surged across the parade-ground, mobbed a moment at the wide pillared entrance to the Hall of the Class-Rooms, then foamed, a roaring torrent of boyhood, up the iron-shod staircase into the gallery where the accouterments were racked, the brass-mounted muskets piled with a clattering that woke the echoes in every stone-flagged passage and every high-ceilinged room of the big, raw, draughty building.

Hector had prophesied correctly. Before evening roll-call a further, deliberate, purposefully-flagrant breach of propriety on the part of de Moulny had caused him to be relieved of the responsibilities, with the *galon* of Corporal. The duel was fought before *reveille* of the following day.

Perhaps half-a-dozen cadets were present beside the principals and their seconds. Deft Pédelaborde had purloined a pair of foils from one of the wall-cases of the School of Fence. The combat took place according to the most approved conditions of etiquette, at the rear of the Department of Chemistry, whose thick-walled, high-windowed rows of laboratories harbored no possible observers at that hour. Everybody wore an expression of solemnity worthy of the occasion.... Pédelaborde was on his best behavior. As he himself said afterwards, "As good as bread."

The buttons were ceremoniously broken off the foils. The opponents, stripped to their drawers, were placed: ... Hector looked at the big fleshy white body of de Moulny, the deep chest and barreled ribs heaving gently with the even breathing, and a shudder went through him. He was remembering something that Pédelaborde had said. And his blade, when measured against that of his antagonist, shook so that Pédelaborde could barely restrain a whistle of dismay.

"My man has got the *venette!*" he thought, as de Moulny Younger gave the word, and the duelists threw themselves on guard. Yet palpably the advantage was with his man. If not like Hamlet, fat and scant of breath, de Moulny Elder was too much addicted to the consumption of pastry, sweets, and fruit to be in hard condition. The contrast between his sallow impassive bulk, its blonde whiteness intensified by the vivid green of a vine whose foliage richly clothed the wall that was his background, and the lithe slimness of Dunoisse, the slender boyish framework of bone covered with tough young muscle and lean flesh, the unblemished skin colored like the red Egyptian granite, was curious to see.

A cat glared and humped and spat upon the wall behind de Moulny, brandishing a hugely-magnificent tail. Another cat growled and cursed hideously, below upon the grass-fringed flagstones. The rankness of their hate tainted the cool clean air. De Moulny, who loathed vile smells, and was qualmishly sensible of his empty stomach, sniffed and grimaced.... And a pale rose-and-golden sunrise illuminated the lower edges of long fleets of pearl-white, pearl-gray-mottled clouds, traveling north-westwards at the bidding of the morning breeze. The square tower of St. Étienne and the magnificent towering dome-crowned dome of the Pantheon beyond, shone out in vivid delicate aquarelle-tints of slate-blue and olive-green, of umber and warm brown.... The squat laboratory annexe, bristling with furnace-shafts, that made one side of the oblong, walled enclosure where the boys had met to fight; the big barrack-like buildings of the School, were touched to a certain beauty by the exquisite pure light, the clear freshness of the new day. And as the sparrows of Paris began to chirp and flutter, her cocks to crow, her pigeons to preen and coo-coo, and her milk-carts to clatter over her historic paving-stones—not yet replaced by the invention of Macadam—the horrible thing befell.

You cannot fence even with the buttoned foil, either for play or practice, without being conscious that the primitive murderer has his part in you. These boys, coming to the encounter half-heartedly, yielded ere long to the fascination of the deadliest game of all. The strangeness of the unmasked face, and the bare body opposed to the point, wore off. Hector and de Moulny, at first secretly conscious of their immaturity, painfully anxious to comport themselves with dignity and coolness in the eyes of their fellows, mentally clinging with desperation to evasive Rules, forgot their inexperience, and rose above their youth, in the heat and strength and fury of that lust to slay.... And by-and-by de Moulny had a jagged bleeding scratch upon the forearm, and Hector a trickling scarlet prick above the collar-bone, and now they fought in earnest, as Man and other predatory animals will, each having tasted the other's blood.

De Moulny's wide, heavy parry, carried out time after time with the same stiff, sweeping pump-handle movement of the arm, had warded off the other's sudden savage attack in quinte. He disengaged, dallied in a clumsy feint, made a blundering opening, delivered one of his famous long-armed lunges. Hector, in act to riposte, trod upon a slug in the act of promenading over the dew-wet flagstones, reducing the land-mollusc of the rudimentary shell to a mere streak of sliminess; slipped on the streak, made an effort to recover his balance, and fell, in the seated position sacred to the Clown in the knockabout scenes of a Pantomime, but with the right wrist at the wrong angle for the ducal house of de Moulny.

Your schoolboy is invariably entertained by the mishap of the sitter-down without premeditation. At Hector's farcical slide and bump the spectators roared; the seconds grinned despite their official gravity. De Moulny laughed too, they said afterwards; even as the broken point of the foil pierced the abdominal bulge above the tightly-tied silk handkerchief that held up his thin, woolen drawers. A moment he hesitated, his heavy features flushing to crimson; then he said, with a queer kind of hiccough, staring down into Hector's horrified eyes:

"That spoils my breakfast!"

And with the scarlet flush dying out in livid deadly paleness, de Moulny collapsed and fell forwards on the blade of the sword.

VIII

The Penal Department of the Royal School of Technical Military Instruction, so soon to become an institution where the youth of the nation were taught to fight for Liberty, Equality, and Fraternity under the banner of the Second Republic of France,—the Penal Department was a central passage in the basement of the Instructors' Building, with an iron-grated gate at either end, and a row of seven cool stone cells on either side, apartments favorable to salutary reflection, containing within a space of ten square feet a stool, and a window boarded to the upper panes.

In one of these Pupil 130, guilty of an offense of homicidal violence against the person of a schoolfellow, was subjected to cold storage, pending the Military Court Martial of Inquiry which would follow the sentence pronounced by the Civil Director-in-Chief of Studies. Pending both, the offender, deprived of his brass-handled hanger and the esteem of his instructors, nourished upon bread and water—Seine water in those unenlightened days, and Seine water but grudgingly dashed with the thin red vinegary ration-wine—had nothing to do but sit astraddle on the three-legged stool, gripping the wooden edge between his thighs, and remember—and remember....

And see, painted on the semi-obscurity of the dimly-lighted cell, de Moulny's plume of drab-colored fair hair crowning the high, knobbed, reflective forehead; the stony-blue eyes looking watchfully, intolerantly, from their narrow eye-orbits; the heavy blockish nose; the pouting underlip; the long, obstinate, projecting chin; the ugly, powerful, attractive young face moving watchfully from side to side on the column of the muscular neck, in the hollow at the base of which the first light curly hairs began to grow and mass together, spreading downwards over the broad chest and fleshy pectorals in a luxuriance envied by other boys, for to them hirsuteness meant strength, and to be strong, for a man, meant everything....

He would hear de Moulny grunt as he lunged. He would straighten his own arm for the riposte—tread on that thrice-accursed slug: feel the thing squelch under his foot and slip: land in the ridiculous sitting posture, bump! upon those inhospitable paving-stones, shaken, inclined to laugh, but horribly conscious that the point of the foil he still mechanically gripped had entered human flesh....

That bulge of the big sallow body over the edge of the tightly-tied white silk handkerchief! Just there the steel had entered.... There was a little trickle of the dark red blood....

"That spoils my breakfast," he would hear de Moulny say.... He would see him leaning forward with the forlorn schoolboy grin fixed upon his scarlet face.... And then—there would be the facial change, from painful red to ghastly bluish-yellow, and the limp heavy body would descend upon him, a crushing, overwhelming weight. The foil had broken under it.... Oh, God! And de Moulny would die.... And he, Hector Dunoisse, his friend, who loved him, as Jonathan, David, would be his murderer....

He leaped up in frenzy, oversetting the stool.... Came podgy Pédelaborde in the twenty-ninth hour of a confinement that seemed to the prisoner to have endured for weeks, in the character of one whose feet are beautiful upon the mountains. Undeterred by the fact that he possessed not the vestige of a voice, the dentist's nephew had recourse to the method of communicating intelligence to one in durance vile, traditionally hit upon by the Sieur Blondel. A free translation of the lay is appended:

"*You have not cooked his goose!*
(Although at the first go-off it appeared uncommonly like it!)
They've plugged him up with tow—(I mean the surgeons)
If he does not inflame—(and the beggar is as cool as a cucumber and as strong as a drayhorse!)
He may possibly get over it.
So keep up your pecker!" sang Pédelaborde.

Upon the captive Cœur-de-Lion the song of the Troubadour could hardly have had a more tonic effect. Hector sang out joyfully in answer:

"A thousand thanks, old boy!" and a savage access of appetite following on the revulsion from black despair to immense relief, he promptly plumped down on his stiff knees, and began to rummage in the semi-obscurity for one of the stale bread-rations previously pitched away in disgust. And had found the farinaceous brickbat, and got his sharp young teeth in it even as Pédelaborde was collared by the curly-whiskered, red-faced, purple-nosed ex-Sergeant of the Municipal Guard in charge of the Penal Department, and handed over to the School Police, as one arrested in the act of clandestinely communicating with a prisoner in the cells.

The civil ordeal beneath the shining spectacles of the Director-in-Chief, assisted by the six Professors, the School Administrator, and the Treasurer, proved less awful than the culprit had reason to expect.

An imposition; Plutarch's "Life of Marcus Crassus" to be written out fairly without blots or erasures, three times, was inflicted. The address of the Director-in-Chief moved five out of the six Professors to tears, so stately was it, so paternal, so moving in its expressions. The sixth Professor would have wept also, had he not, with his chin wedged in his stock and his hands folded upon his ample waistcoat, been soundly, peacefully, sleeping in his chair.

Monseigneur le Duc had graciously entreated, said the Director-in-Chief, clemency for one whose young, revengeful hand had well-nigh deprived him of his second son, and plunged himself and his exalted family in anxiety of the most cruel. The future of the young sufferer, who, the Director-in-Chief was grateful to say, was pronounced by the surgeons to be progressing favorably—("Then he was not inflamed!" ... thought Hector, with a rush of infinite relief.)—the future of M. Alain de Moulny must inevitably be changed by this deplorable occurrence—a profession less arduous than the military must now inevitably be his. Let him who had reft the crown of laurels from the temples of his comrade reflect upon the grave consequences of his act. The Director-in-Chief ended, rapping the table as a signal to the Professor who had not wept, to wake up, "Pupil 130, you may now return to your studies, but, pending the decision of the Military Tribunal, you are Still Provisionally Under Arrest."

The verdict of the Military Tribunal was in favor of the prisoner. It was decided that Pupil No. 130, roused to choler by an expression injurious to his family honor, had challenged Pupil No. 127 with justification. Having already undergone three days' imprisonment, no further punishment than a reprimand for leaving the dormitory before beat of drum would be administered by the Court, which rose as M. the General gave the signal. And Hector was free.

But for many days after the completion of those three unblotted copies of "Marcus Crassus" he did not see de Moulny.... He hung about the Infirmary, waiting for scraps of intelligence as a hungry cat was wont to hang about the kitchen quarters, wistful-eyed, hollow-flanked, waiting for eleemosynary scraps. One of the two Sisters of Charity in charge took pity on him, perhaps both of them did.... A day came when he was admitted into the long bare sunshiny ward.... At the end nearest the high west window that commanded a view of the flowery garden-beds and neat green grass-plats surrounding the house of Monsieur the Director-in-Chief, upon a low iron bedstead from which the curtains had been stripped away, lay stretched a long body, to which an unpleasant effect of bloated corpulence was imparted by the wicker cage that held the bedclothes up.... The long face that topped the body was very white, a lock of ashen blonde hair drooped over the knobby forehead; the pouting underlip hung lax; the blue eyes, less stony than of old, looked out of hollowed orbits; a sparse and scattered growth of fluffy reddish hairs had started on the lank jaws and long, powerful chin. Hector, conscious of his own egg-smooth cheeks, knew a momentary pang of envy of that incipient beard.... And then as de Moulny grinned in the old cheerful boyish way, holding out a long attenuated arm and bony hand in welcome, something strangling seemed to grip him by the throat....

Only de Moulny saw his tears. The Sister, considerately busy at the other end of a long avenue of tenantless beds with checked side-curtains, assiduously folded bandages at a little table, as the sobbing cry broke forth:

"Oh, Alain, I always loved you!—I would rather you had killed me than have lived to see you lie here! Oh! Alain!—Alain!"

"It does not matter," said de Moulny, but his long upper lip quivered and the water stood in his own eyes. "They will make a priest of me now, that is all. She"—he jerked his chin in the direction of the busy Sister—"would say the foil-thrust was a special grace. Tell me how Paris is looking? I have not seen the slut for—how long?" He began a laugh, and broke off in the middle, and gave a grimace of pain. "*Dame!*—but that hurts!" he said before he could stop, and saw his smart reflected in the other's shamed, wet face, and winced at it.

"Pupil 127 must not excite himself or elevate his voice above a whisper in speaking. The orders of the Surgeon attending are stringent. It is my duty to see that they are obeyed."

Sister Edouard-Antoine had spoken. Hector rose up and saluted as the nun came gliding down the avenue of beds towards them, her beads clattering and swinging by her side, her black robes sweeping the well-scrubbed boards, her finger raised in admonition, solicitude on the mild face within the *coif* of starched white linen....

"They shall be obeyed, my Sister," said de Moulny in an elaborate whisper. The Sister smiled and nodded, and went back to her work. Hector, on a rush-bottomed chair by the low bed, holding the hot, thin, bony hand, began to say:

"I went out yesterday—being Wednesday. Paris is looking as she always looks—always will look, until England and Russia and Germany join forces to invade France, and batter down her forts and spike her batteries, and pound her churches and towers and palaces to powder with newly-invented projectiles, bigger than any shell the world has ever yet seen, filled with some fulminate of a thousand times the explosive power of gunpowder...."

"Go it!" whispered de Moulny. Then a spark of fanatical enthusiasm kindled in his pale blue eyes. "An explosive of a thousand times the power of gunpowder, you say!" he repeated. "Remember that inspection, and the grimy neck and black hands that cost me my Corporal's *galon*! I had been working in the Department of Chemistry that morning.... I had got all that black on me through a blow-up in the laboratory. *Nom d'un petit bonhomme!* I thought I had discovered it—then!—that explosive that is to send gunpowder to the wall. Listen——"

"Do not excite yourself!" begged Hector, "or the Sister will turn me out."

De Moulny went on: "I shall pursue the thing no further, for how shall one who is to be a Catholic priest spend his time inventing explosives to destroy men? But—one day you may take up the thread of discovery where I left off."

"Or where the discovery went off!" suggested Hector.

De Moulny grinned, though his eyes were serious.

"Just so. But listen. I had been reading of the experiments made in 1832 by Braconnot of Nancy, who converted woody fiber into a highly-combustible body by treating it with nitric acid. And I dipped a piece of carded cotton-wool in nitric, and washed it. Then I dipped it in concentrated sulphuric. The sulphuric not only dehydrated the nitric—*saisissez?*—but took up the water. Then it occurred to me to test the expansive power of the substance in combustion by packing it into a paper cone and lighting it. Well, I was packing the stuff with the end of an aluminum spatula, into the little paper case, when—but you must have heard?"

"Ps'st! Br'roum! Boum!" Hector nodded. "I heard, most certainly! But let me now tell you of Wednesday." He leaned forwards, gripping the seat of the rush-bottomed chair between his knees with his strong supple red hands as he had gripped the edge of the prison stool, and his bright black eyes were eager on de Moulny's.

"First I went and looked up at the outside of the great Carmelite Convent in the Rue Vaugirard—the place where I was taken when I was eight years old, to say good-by to my mother before she went away.... Where she was going they would not tell me—nor, though I have always received a letter from her regularly twice a year, has there ever been any address or postmark upon it by which I might be guided to find out her whereabouts. But of course she is at Widinitz, in the Priory Convent there. And it seems to me that she did right in returning. In her place I should have done the same. *He* says I say so because I have Carmel in my blood!"

A faint pink flush forced its way to the surface of de Moulny's thick sallow skin. He whispered, averting his eyes:

"You have spoken to him about...?"

"When he heard of our—difference of opinion, he naturally inquired its cause."

Hector's small square white teeth showed in a silent mocking laugh that was not good to see. "He thought I fought in defense of my father's honor. He said so. He may say so again—but he will not think it now!"

The boyish face changed and hardened at the recollection of that interview. Terrible words must have been exchanged between the father and the son. De Moulny, cadet of a family whose strongest hereditary principle, next to piety towards the Church, was respect towards parents, shuddered under his wicker-basket and patchwork coverlet. There was a cautious tap at the black swing-doors leading out upon the tile-paved passage. They parted, Madame Gaubert appeared looking for the Sister, caught her mild eye as she glanced round from her work, beckoned with an urgent finger and the whole of her vivacious face.... The Sister rose, and the face vanished. As the doors closed behind the nun's noiseless black draperies, Hector took up his tale:

"I said to him that the terms upon which he had permitted my mother to return to the bosom of the Church were infamous. He laughed at first at what he called my pompous manner and fine choice of words. He was very witty about the recovery of the dowry—called it *'squeezing the Pope's nose,' 'milking the black cow,'* and other things. All the while he pretended to laugh, but he gnashed his teeth through the laughter in that ugly way he has."

"I know!" de Moulny nodded.

"Then he reproached me for unfilial ingratitude. He said it was to endow his only son with riches that he demanded return of the dowry—the surrender of the three-hundred-thousand silver thalers.... 'You are a child now,' he told me, 'but when you are a man, when you need money for play, dress, amusements, pleasure, women, you will come to me hat in hand.' I said: 'Never in my life!...' He told me: 'Wait until you are a man!'"

Hector pondered and rubbed his ear. De Moulny cackled faintly:

"He tweaked you well when he told you to wait, I see!"

Hector nodded, grimacing.

"To pull the hair, or tweak the ear, that was his Emperor's habit, when he was in a good temper.... My father copies the habit, just as he carries Spanish snuff loose in the pockets of his buff nankeen vests and wears his right hand in the bosom—so!" He imitated the historic pose and went on: "He kept it there as he pinched and wrung with the left finger and thumb"—the speaker gingerly touched the martyred ear—"laughing all the time. I thought my ear would have come off, but I set my teeth and held my tongue.... Then he let go, and chucked me under the chin—another trick of the Emperor's. 'A sprig of the blood-royal for Luitpold's blood-pudding! That is not a bad return! We shall have a fine Serene Highness presently for those good people of Widinitz.' And he went away laughing and scattering snuff all over his vest and knee-breeches; he calls pantaloons 'the pitiable refuge of legs without calves.' Now, what did he mean by a Serene Highness for those good people of Widinitz?"

"I—am—not quite sure." De Moulny pastured upon a well-gnawed finger-nail, pulled at his jutting underlip, and looked wise. "What I think he meant I shall not tell you now—! What I want you to do now is to swear to me, solemnly, that you will never touch a franc of that money."

"I have promised."

"A promise is good, but an oath is better."

Hector began to laugh in a sheepish way, but de Moulny's knobby forehead was portentous. That mass of gold, reclaimed from the coffers of the Convent of Widinitz seemed to him the untouchable thing; the taking it unpardonable—an act of simony his orthodox Catholic gorge rose at. So, as Hector looked at him, hesitating, he gnawed and glowered and breathed until he lost patience and hit the basket that held up the bedclothes with his fist, and whispered furiously:

"Swear, if you value my friendship! And I—I will swear, as you once asked me—remember, Redskin!—as you once asked me!—to be your friend through life—to the edge of Death—beyond Death if that be permitted!"

Ah me! It is never the lover who loves the more, never the friend whose friendship is the most ardent, who seeks the testing-proof of love or friendship, who demands the crowning sacrifice in return for the promise of a love that is never to grow cool, a loyalty that shall never fail or falter....

Perhaps if the boy who was now to repeat the vow that the other boy dictated had known at this juncture all that its keeping was to involve, he would have taken it all the same. Here before him lay his chosen friend, brought to the verge of that grave of which he spoke, laid low in the flower of his youth, in the pride of his strength, by the hand of him who loved him; the bright wings of his ambition clipped, the prosaic, sedentary life of a theological student unrolled before him instead of the alluring, vari-colored career of soldierly adventure, his well-loved researches in War-chemistry *tabu* forever by that pale, prohibitory reflection of the priestly tonsure.... Do you wonder that his will was as wax in the molding hands?

De Moulny's Rosary, disinterred at the commencement of his wound-sickness from among the cake-crumbs and bits of flue at the bottom of his dormitory kit-locker by Sister Edouard-Antoine when searching for nightcaps, hung upon one of the iron knobs at the head of his bed.... He reached up a long gaunt arm to get it; gave the blue string of lapis-lazuli beads, with the silver *Paternosters* and silver-scrolled and figured Crucifix, into Hector's hands, ... bade him, in a tone that already had something of the ecclesiastical authority, kiss the sacred Symbol and repeat the vow.

"'I, Hector-Marie-Aymont-von Widinitz Dunoisse, solemnly swear and depose'—where did de Moulny get all the big words he knew? ... 'swear and depose that I will never profit by one penny of the dowry of three-hundred-thousand silver thalers paid to the Prioress of the Convent of Widinitz as the dowry of my mother, the Princess Marie-Bathilde von Widinitz, otherwise Dunoisse, in religion Sister Térèse de Saint François. So help me, Almighty God, and our Blessed Lady! Amen.'"

He kissed the Crucifix de Moulny put to his lips, and de Moulny took the oath in his turn:

"And I, Alain-Joseph-Henri-Jules de Moulny, solemnly swear to be a faithful, true, and sincere friend to Hector-Marie-Aymont-von Widinitz Dunoisse, through Life to the edge of Death, and beyond Death—if that be permitted? *In Nomine Patris et Filii et Spiritus Sancti.* Amen."

IX

The Crucifix was duly saluted, the Rosary hung back upon the bed-knob.

"Embrace me now, my friend," said de Moulny, his blue eyes shining under a smooth forehead. Hector held out his hand.

"We will shake hands as English boys do. They ridicule our French way of kissing, Miss Smithwick says."

"And we die of laughter," said de Moulny, "when we see them hand a lady a cushion or a chair, or try to make a bow. If I had not this basket on my stomach I would get up and show you how my cousin Robert Bertham comports himself in a drawing-room. He is certainly handsome, but stiff! His backbone must be a billiard-cue, *nom d'un petit bonhomme*! Yet he can run and jump and row, for if he has not the grace of an athlete he has the muscles of one. He was stroke of the Eton Eight last year; they rowed against the School of Westminster in a race from Windsor Bridge to Surly and back, and beat. They have beaten them again this year, Bertham tells me in his last letter. He writes French with a spade, as M. Magne would say."

The nerves of both boys were tingling still with the recollection of the double compact they had sealed with an oath. Now they could look at one another without consciousness, and were glad to talk of Bertham, his English awkwardness and his British French. For mere humanity cannot for long together endure to respire the thin crystal air of the Higher Emotions. It must come down, and breathe the common air of ordinary life, and talk of everyday things, or perish. So Hector listened while de Moulny held forth.

"Bertham will be Bertham of Wraye when he succeeds to the peerage of his father. It is of ancient creation and highly respectable. He is my cousin by virtue of an alliance between our houses some eighteen years back, when my grandmother's youngest daughter—my Aunt Gabrielle—married Lord Bertham, then Ambassador for England here. You know the English Embassy in the Rue du Faubourg St. Honoré? My grandmother did not approve of the union at first, the Berthams are Protestants of the English Establishment. But an agreement was arrived at with regard to my aunt's faith and the faith of her daughters. The sons, Robert and the younger boy ... but that's my grandmother's cross, she says, that she has heretics for grandsons.... My Aunt Gabrielle is a charming person—I am very fond of her. She boasts of being English to the backbone ... pleases her husband by wearing no costumes that are not from the *atelier* of a London *couturière*—

that must be *her* cross, though she does not say so!" De Moulny grinned at his own joke.

"How you talk!" said Hector, flushed with admiration of his idol's powers of conversation.

"I like words," said the idol, lightly taking the incense as his due. "Terms, expressions, phrases, combinations of these, please me like combinations in Chemistry. I do not enjoy composition with the pen; the tongue is my preference. Perhaps I was meant for a diplomatic career." His face fell as his eyes rested upon the basket that humped the bedclothes. It cleared as he added, with an afterthought:

"Diplomacy is for priests as well as statesmen. Men of acumen and eloquence are wanted in the Church." De Moulny folded his lean arms behind his head, and perused the whitewashed ceiling.

"Tell me more about your cousin Bertham," Hector begged, to lure de Moulny from the subject that had pricks for both.

"You are more interested in him than I am," said de Moulny. "He writes to me, but I have not seen him since I spent an autumn month at their *château* of Wraye in Peakshire two years ago. Their feudal customs were interesting, but their society.... Just Heaven, how dull! Even my Aunt Gabrielle could not enliven us. And he—my cousin Robert—who cannot fence, was scandalized because I do not box. Because I said: 'If you fight with your fists, why not with the teeth and the feet?' That I should speak of the *savate*—it made him very nearly ill.... He implored: 'For God's sake, never say that in the hearing of any other Eton fellows! They'll make my life a hell if you do!' Say that in English, Redskin, you who have the tongue of John Bull at your finger-ends."

Hector translated the words into the original English and repeated them for de Moulny's amusement.

"It must be a queer place, that Eton of theirs," went on de Moulny. "When they leave to enter their Universities they know nothing. Of Mathematics, Chemistry, Physics, Arithmetic, they are in ignorance. Their rowing and other sports—considered by all infinitely more important than intellectual attainments—are ignored by the Directors of the School, and yet—to these their chief efforts are addressed; to excel in strength is the ambition above all. They are flogged for the most trifling offenses, upon the naked person with a birch, by the Director-in-Chief of Studies, who is a clergyman of the Established Church. And the younger boys are servants to their elders."

"We make them so here," said Hector pointedly. "We subject them to the authority that others exercised over us, and that they in their turn will use over others."

"Subjects are not serfs. These younger boys of Eton are worse used than serfs. They call the system of torture 'fagging'; it is winked at by the Directors," explained de Moulny. "To be kicked and tormented and beaten—that is to be fagged. To carry coals to make your master's fire, to bring him buckets of water from the pump, to sweep and dust and black his boots, make his bed and sleep on the floor without even a blanket if he does not choose that you shall enjoy that luxury—that is to be fagged, as Bertham knows it. They are infinitely worse off than we, these sons of the English nobles and great landed gentlemen. And yet one thing that we have not got, they have"; de Moulny thrust out his underlip and wagged his big head, "and it is worth all—or nearly all these things we have that they have not. They are loyal to each other. There is union among them. In Chemistry we know the value of cohesion.... Well!... there is cohesion among these Eton boys. How much of it is there here? Not as much as—that!" He measured off an infinitesimal space upon the bitten finger-nail, and showed it to Hector, who nodded confirmatively, saying:

"There is no currying favor with *pions* and tattling to masters, then? Or lending money at usury to other pupils—*hein*?"

"No!" said de Moulny, with a frowning shake of the head. "There is none of that sort of thing. Because—Bertham told me!—the boy who was proved to be guilty of it would have to leave Eton. Instantly. Or—it would come about that that boy would be found dead; and as to how he died"—he shrugged his shoulders expressively—"it would be as possible to gain an explanation from the corpse, Bertham says, as to wring one from the resolute silence of the School."

Hector knew a delicious thrill of mingled horror and admiration of those terrible young Britons, who could maintain honor among themselves by such stark laws, and avenge betrayal by sentence so grim.

"But there are other rules in the Code of Eton that are imbecile, absolutely, on my honor, idiotic!" said de Moulny. "Not to button the lower button of the waistcoat—that is one rule which must not be broken. Nor must Lower boys turn up their trousers in muddy weather, or wear greatcoats in cold, until their elders choose to set the example. And unless you are of high standing in the School, you dare not roll your umbrella up. It is a presumption the whole School would resent. For another example, you are invariably to say and maintain that things others can do and that you cannot, are bad form. Bertham saw me make a fire one day, camp-fashion, in five minutes, when he had been sweating like a porter for an hour without being able to kindle a dead stick. 'It's all very well,' he said, with his eyebrows climbing up into his curly hair, 'for a fellow to light fires; but to do servant's work well is bad form, our fellows would say.'"

"Why did you want a fire?" demanded Hector, balancing his rush-bottomed chair on one hind-leg.

"To boil some water," de Moulny answered, his eyes busy with the flowery, sunshiny parterres of the Director's garden. "Up on the Peakshire hills," he added, a second later, "to heat some water to bathe a dog's hurt leg. Oh! there's not much of a story. Bertham and I had been out riding; we had dismounted, tied our horses to a gate, and climbed Overmere Hill to look at a Roman camp that is on the top—very perfect: entrenchments, chariot-road, even sentry-shelters to be made out under the short nibbled grass.... Sheep as black as the gritstone of the Peakshire hills were feeding there, scattered all about us—lower down an old white-haired shepherd was trying to collect them; his dog, one of the shaggy, long-haired, black-and-white English breed that drives and guards sheep, seemed not to know its business. Bertham spoke of that, and the shepherd explained in his *patois* that the dog was not his, but had been borrowed of a neighbor—a misfortune had happened to his own. It had got the worst in a desperate fight with another dog, a *combat à outrance*, fought perhaps in defense of its master's sheep; it was injured past cure; he thought he would fetch up a cord later, from the farm whose thatched roofs we could see down in the valley below, and put the unlucky creature out of its pain. We thought we might be able to do something to prevent that execution, so Bertham and I went to the shed, an affair of hurdles and poles and bunches of heather, such as our Breton shepherds of Finistère and the Côtes du Nord build to shelter them from the weather...."

"And the dog?"

"The dog was lying in a pool of blood on the beaten earth floor. A shoulder and the throat were terribly mangled, a fore-leg had been bitten through; one would have said the creature had been worried by a wolf rather than a dog of its own breed. And she was sitting on the ground beside it, holding its bloody head in her lap...."

De Moulny's eyes blinked as though the Director's blazing beds of gilliflowers and calceolarias, geraniums and mignonette, had dazzled them. Hector asked, with awakening interest in a story which had not at first promised much:

"Who was she?"

De Moulny stuck his chin out, and stated in his didactic way:

"She was the type of *jeune personne* of whom my grandmother would have approved."

"A young girl!" grumbled Hector, who at this period esteemed the full-blown peony of womanhood above the opening rosebud. He shrugged one shoulder so contemptuously that de Moulny was nettled.

"One might say to you, 'There are young girls and young girls.'"

"This one was charming, then?" Hector's waning interest began to burn up again.

"Certainly, no! For," said de Moulny authoritatively, "to be charming you must desire to charm. This young girl was innocent of any thought of coquetry. And—if you ask me whether she was beautiful, I should give you again the negative. Beauty—the beauty of luxuriant hair, pale, silken brown, flowing, as a young girl's should, loosely upon shoulders rather meager; the beauty of an exquisite skin, fresh, clear, burned like a nectarine on the oval cheeks where the sun had touched it; beauty of eyes, those English eyes of blue-gray, more lustrous than brilliant, banded about the irises with velvety black, widely opened, thickly lashed—these she possessed, with features much too large for beauty, with a form too undeveloped even to promise grace. But the quality or force that marked her out, distinguished her from others of her age and sex, I have no name for that!"

"No?" Hector, not in the least interested, tried to look so, and apparently succeeded. De Moulny went on:

"No!—nor would you. Suppose you had met the Venerable Jeanne d'Arc in her peasant kirtle, driving her sheep or cows to pasture in the fields about Domremy in the days before her Voices spoke and said: *'Thou, Maid, art destined to deliver France!'* Or—what if you had seen the Virgins of the Temple at Jerusalem pass singing on their way to the tribune surrounded with balconies, where while the Morning Sacrifice burned upon the golden Altar to the fanfare of the silver trumpets, they besought God Almighty, together with all Israel, for the speedy coming of the Saviour of mankind.... Would not One among them, draped in her simple robe of hyacinth blue, covered with the white, plainly-girdled tunic, a veil of Syrian gauze upon her golden hair, have brought you the conviction that She, above all the women you had ever seen, was destined, marked out, set apart, created to serve a peculiar purpose of her Creator, stamped with His stamp——"

The hard blue eyes, burning now, encountered Hector's astonished gape, and their owner barked out: "What are you opening your mouth so wide about?"

Hector blurted out:

"Why—what for? Because you said that a raw English girl nursing a dying sheep-dog on a mountain in Peakshire reminded you of the Maid of Orleans and Our Blessed Lady!"

"And if I did?"

"But was she not English?... A Protestant?... a heretic?"

"Many of the Saints were heretics—until Our Lord called them," said de Moulny, with that fanatical spark burning in his blue eye. "But He had chosen them before He called. They bore the seal of His choice."

"Perhaps you are right. No doubt you know best. It is you who are to be——" Hector broke off.

"You were going to finish: 'It is you who are to be a priest, not me...!'" de Moulny said, with the veins in his heavy forehead swelling, and a twitching muscle jerking down his pouting underlip.

"I forget what I was going to say," declared Hector mendaciously, and piled Ossa upon Pelion by begging de Moulny to go on with his story. "It interested hugely," he said, even as he struggled to repress the threatening yawn.

"What is there to tell?" grumbled de Moulny ungraciously. "She was there, that is all—with that dog that had been hurt. A pony she had ridden was grazing at the back of the shed, its bridle tied to the pommel of the saddle. Bertham approached her and saluted her; he knew her, it seems, and presented me. She spoke only of the dog—looked at nothing but the dog! She could not bear to leave it, in case it should be put to death by the master it could serve no more...."

Hector interrupted, for de Moulny's voice had begun to sound as though he were talking in his sleep:

"Tell me her name."

"Her name is Ada Merling."

Even on de Moulny's French tongue the name was full of music; it came to Hector's ear like the sudden sweet gurgling thrill that makes the idler straying beneath low-hanging, green hazel-branches upon a June morning in an English wood or lane, look up and catch a glimpse of the golden bill and the gleaming, black-plumaged head, before their owner, with a defiant "tuck-tuck!" takes wing, with curious slanting flight. The boy had a picture of the blackbird, not of the girl, in his mind, as de Moulny went on:

"True, the dog seemed at the last gasp, but if it were possible to stop the bleeding, *she* said, there might be a chance, who knew? It had occurred to her that cold-water applications might check the flow of blood. 'We will try, and see, Mademoiselle,' said I."

De Moulny's tone was one of fatuous self-satisfaction.

"A rusty tin saucepan is lying in a corner of the shed. This I fill with water from a little spring that trickles down the cliff behind us. We contribute handkerchiefs. Bertham and I hold the dog while she bathes the torn throat and shoulder, and bandages them. Remains the swollen leg. It occurs to me that fomentations of hot water might be of use there; I mention this idea. 'Good! good!' she cries, 'we will make a fire and heat some.' She sets to collecting the dry leaves and sticks that are scattered in a corner. Bertham makes a pile of these, and attempts to kindle it with fusees." A smile of ineffable conceit curved de Moulny's flabby pale cheeks and quirked the corners of his pouting lips. "He burns matches and he loses his temper; there is no other result. Then I stepped forward, bowed.... *'Permit me, Mademoiselle, to show you how we arrange these things in my country.'*" De Moulny's tone was so infinitely arrogant, his humility so evidently masked the extreme of bumptiousness, that Hector wondered how the athletic Bertham endured it without knocking him down?

"So I hollow a fireplace in the floor, with a pocket-knife and a piece of slate, devise a flue at each corner, light the fire—which burns, one can conceive, to a marvel.... She has meanwhile refilled the rusty saucepan at the little spring; she sets it on, the water boils, when it occurs to us that we have no more handkerchiefs. But the shepherd's linen blouse hangs behind the shed-door; at her bidding we tear that into strips.... All is done that can be done; we bid Mademoiselle Merling *au revoir*. She will ride home presently when her patient is a little easier, she says. We volunteer to remain; she declines to allow us. She thanks us for our aid in a voice that has the clear ring of crystal—I can in no other way describe it! When I take my leave, I desire to kiss her hand. She permits me very gracefully; she speaks French, too, with elegance, as she asks where I learned to make a fireplace so cleverly?

"'We are taught these things,' I say to her, 'at the Royal School of Technical Military Instruction, in my Paris. For we do not think one qualified for being an officer, Mademoiselle, until he has learned all the things that a private should know.' Then it was that Bertham made that celebrated *coq-à-l'âne* about its being bad form to do servant's work well. You should have seen the look she gave him. *Sapristi!*—with a surprise in it that cut to the quick. She replies: 'Servants should respect and look up to us, and not despise us; and how can they look up to us if we show ourselves less capable than they? When I am older I mean to have a great house full of sick people to comfort and care for and nurse. And *everything* that has to be done for them I will learn to do with my own hands!' My sister Viviette would have said: 'When I grow up I shall have a *rivière* of pearls as big as pigeons' eggs,' or 'I shall drive on the boulevards and in the Bois in an ivory-paneled barouche.' Then I ask a stupid question: 'Is it that you are to be a Sister of Charity, Mademoiselle?' She answers, with a look of surprise: 'Can no one but a nun care for the sick?' I return: 'In France, Mademoiselle, our sick-nurses are these holy women. They are welcome everywhere: in private houses and in public hospitals, in time of peace: and in the time of war you will find them in the camp and on the battle-field. Your first patient is a soldier wounded in war,' I say to her, pointing to the dog. 'Perhaps it is an augury of the future?'

"'War is a terrible thing,' she answers me, and grows pale, and her great eyes are fixed as though they look upon a corpse-strewn battle-field. 'I hope with all my heart that I may never see it!' 'But a nurse must become inured to ugly and horrible sights, Mademoiselle,' I remind her. She replies: 'I shall find courage to endure them when I become a nurse.' Then Bertham blurts out in his brusque way: 'But you never will! Your people would not allow it. Wait and see if I am not right?' She returns to him, with a smile, half the child's, half the woman's, guileless and subtle at the same time, if you can understand that? *'We will wait—and you will see.'*"

De Moulny's whisper had dwindled to a mere thread of sound. He had long forgotten Hector, secretly pining for the end of a story that appeared to him as profoundly dull as interminably long; and, oblivious of the other's martyrdom, talked only to himself.

"'*We will wait and you will see....* You have the courage of your convictions, Mademoiselle,' I tell her, 'and courage always succeeds.' She says in that crystal voice: 'When things, stones or other obstacles, are piled up in front of you to prevent your getting through a gap in the dyke, you don't push because you might topple them all over, and kill somebody on the other side; and you don't pull because you might bring them all down on your own head. You lift the stones away, one at a time; and by-and-by you see light through a little hole ... and then the hole gets bigger, and there is more and more light.'... There I interpose.... 'But if the stones to be moved are too big for such little hands, Mademoiselle?' And she answers, looking at them gravely: 'My hands are not little. And if they were, there would always be men to lift the things that are too heavy, and do the things that are too hard.'

"'Men or boys, Mademoiselle?' I question. Then she gives me her hand once more. 'Thank you, M. de Moulny! I will not forget it was you who built the fireplace, and helped to hold the dog.' And Bertham was so jealous that he would not speak to me during the whole ride home!"

Upon that note of exultation the story ended. To Hector the recital had been of unmitigated dullness. Nothing but his loyalty to de Moulny had kept him from wriggling on his chair; had checked the yawns that had threatened to unhinge his youthful jaws. Now he was guilty of an offense beside which yawning would have been pardonable. He opened his black eyes in a stare of youthful, insufferable curiosity, and called out in his shrill young pipe:

"Jealous, do you say! Why, was he in love with her as well as you?"

De Moulny's muscles jerked. He almost sat up in bed. A moment he remained glaring over the basket, speechless and livid with rage. Then he cried out furiously:

"Go away! Leave me! Go!—do you hear?"

And as Hector rose in dismay and stood blankly gaping at the convulsed and tragic face, de Moulny plucked the pillow from behind his head, and hurled that missile of low comedy at the cruel eyes that stung, and fell back upon the bolster with a cry of pain that froze the luckless blunderer to the marrow. Hector fled then, as Sister Edouard-Antoine, summoned from her colloquy in the passage by the sound, came hurrying back to the bedside. Looking back as he plunged through the narrow, black swing-doors— doors very much like two coffin-lids on hinges, set up side by side, he saw the Sister bending over the long heaving body on the bed, solicitude painted on the mild face framed in the starched-white linen coif; and heard de Moulny's muffled sobbing, mingled with her soft, consoling tones.

Why should de Moulny shed tears? Did he really hate the idea of being a priest? And if so, would he be likely to love his friend Dunoisse, who had, with a broken foil, pointed out the way that ended in the seminary, the cassock, and the tonsure?

The savage, livid, loathing face rose up before Hector's mental vision— the furious cry that had issued from the twisted lips: "Go! Leave me! Go!— do you hear?" still rang in the boy's ears. The look, the cry, were full of hate. Yet Alain had, but a moment before, solemnly sworn to be his friend.... When we are very young we believe such oaths unbreakable.

Came Pédelaborde, and thrust a warty hand under Redskin's elbow, as he stood frowning and pondering still, on the wide shallow doorstep of the Infirmary portico, brick-and-plaster Corinthian, elegant and chaste....

"*Hé bien, mon ami; nous voilà reconciliés?* A visit of sympathy, *hein?* It is quite proper! absolutely in rule.... But"—Pédelaborde's little yellow eyes twinkled and glittered in his round brown face like a pair of highly-polished brass buttons, his snub nose cocked itself with an air of infinite knowingness, his bullet head of cropped black hair sparked intelligence from every bristle— "but—all the same, to call a spade a spade, *saisissez?* the trick that did the job for de Moulny is a dirty one. As an expert, I told you of it. As a gentleman, *voyez?*—I hardly expected you to use it!"

"A trick.... Use it!" Hector stuttered, and his round horrified stare would have added to de Moulny's offense. "You don't mean—you cannot believe that I———" He choked over the words.

Pédelaborde chuckled comfortably, thrusting his warty hands deep into the pockets of his baggy red serge breeches.

"Why, just as *he* lunged after his feint, didn't you—*hein?* Plump!—in the act to riposte, and cleverly managed, too. Suppose he believes it a pure accident. I am not the fellow to tell tales.... Honor"—Pédelaborde extracted one of the warty hands on purpose to lay it upon his heart—"honor forbids. Now we're on the subject of honor, I have positively pledged mine to pay Mère Cornu a trifling sum I owe her—a mere matter of eight francs—could you lend them until my uncle—hang the old skin-namalinks!—forks out with my allowance that is due?"

"I will lend you the money," said Hector, wiping the sickly drops from his wet forehead. "But—I swear to you *that* was an accident—I slipped on a slug!" he added passionately. "Never dare to believe me capable of an act so vile!"

He had not had the heart to spend a franc of his own monthly allowance of two louis. He pulled the cash out of his pocket now; a handful of silver pieces, with one treasured napoleon shining amongst them, and was picking out the eight francs from the bulk, when, with a pang, the barbed memory of his oath drove home. Perhaps these coins were some infinitesimal part of that accursed dowry....

"Take it all!—keep it! I do not want it back!" he stammered hurriedly, and thrust the wealthy handful upon greedy Pédelaborde so recklessly that the napoleon and several big silver coins escaped that worthy's warty clutches, and dropped, ringing and rolling and spinning, making a temporary Tom Tiddler's ground of the Junior's parade.

"*Paid not to split! Saperlipopette!*... Then there was no slug! He meant to do the thing!..."

Honest Pédelaborde, pausing even in the congenial task of picking up gold and silver, straightened his back to stare hard after the Redskin's retreating figure, and whistle with indrawn breath, through a gap in his front teeth: "*Phew-w!*"

Those little yellow eyes of the dentist's nephew were sharp. The brain behind them, though shallow, worked excellently in the interests of Pédelaborde. It occurred to him that when next Madame Cornu should clamor for the discharge of her bill for sweetstuff and pastry, the little affair of the trick fall might advantageously be mentioned again.

X

Alain-Joseph-Henri-Jules, cadet of the illustrious and ducal house of de Moulny, recovered of his wound, much to the gratification of his noble family, more by grace of a sound constitution and the faithful nursing of the Infirmary Sisters than by skill of the surgeons, who knew appallingly little in those days of the treatment of internal wounds. He left the Royal School of Technical Military Instruction to travel abroad under the grandmaternal care of the Duchesse, for what the Chief Director gracefully termed the "reconstitution of his health." Later he was reported to have entered as a student at the Seminary of Saint Sulpice. It was vain to ask Redskin whether this was true. You got no information out of the fellow. He had turned sulky, the pupils said, since the affair of the duel, which invested him in the eyes even of the great boys of the Senior Corps, to which he was shortly afterwards promoted, with a luridly-tinted halo of distinction.

So nobody save Hector was aware that after the first short, stiff letter or two Alain had ceased to write. In silence the Redskin bucklered his pride. Hitherto he had not permitted his love of study to interfere with the more serious business of amusement. Now he applied himself to the acquisition of knowledge with a dogged, savage concentration his Professors had never remarked in him before. Attending one of the stately half-yearly School receptions, arrayed in all the obsolete but imposing splendors of his gold-encrusted, epauletted, frogged, high-stocked uniform of ceremony, adorned with the Cross of the Legion of Honor,—an Imperial decoration severely ignored by the Monarchy,—Marshal Dunoisse was complimented by the General-Commandant and the Chief Director upon the brilliant abilities and remarkable progress of his son.

"So it seems the flea of work has bitten you?" the affectionate parent commented a few days later, tweaking Hector's ear in the Napoleonic manner, and turning upon his son the fanged and gleaming smile, that in conjunction with its owner's superb height, fine form, boldly-cut swarthy features, fierce black eyes, and luxuriant black whiskers, had earned for the ex-*aide-de-camp* of Napoleon I. the reputation of an irresistible lady-killer.

The handsome features of the elderly dandy were thickened and inflamed by wine and good living, the limbs in the tight-fitting white stockinet pantaloons, for which he had reluctantly exchanged his golden-buckled knee-breeches; the extremities more often encased in narrow-toed, elastic-sided boots, or buckled pumps, than in the spurred Hessians, were swollen and shapeless with rheumatic gout. The hyacinthine locks, or the greater part of them, came from the *atelier* of Michalon Millière, His Majesty's own hairdresser, in the Rue Feydeau; the whiskers owed their jetty gloss to a patent pomade invented by the same highly-patronized tonsorial artist. The broad black eyes were bloodshot, and could blaze under their bushy brows at times with an ogre-like ferocity, but were not brilliant any more.

Yet, from the three maids to the stout Bretonne who was cook, from the cook to Miss Smithwick,—who had acted in the capacity of *dame de compagnie* to Madame Dunoisse; had become governess to her son when the gates of the Convent clashed once more behind the remorse and sorrow of that unhappy lady; and in these later years, now that Hector had outgrown her mild capacity for instruction, fulfilled the duties of housekeeper at No. 000, Rue de la Chaussée d'Antin,—the female staff of the ex-military widower's household worshiped Monsieur the Marshal.

"Do you think papa so handsome?" Hector, when a very small boy, would pipe out boldly. "He has eyes that are always angry, even when he smiles. He gnashes his teeth when he laughs. He kicked Moustapho" (the poodle) "so hard in the chest with the sharp toe of his shiny boot, when Moustapho dropped a macaroon he did not want, that Moustapho cried out loud with pain. He bullies the menservants and swears at them. He smells of Cognac, and is always spilling his snuff about on the carpets, and tables, and chairs. Me, I think him ugly, for my part."

"Your papa, my Hector, possesses in an eminent degree those personal advantages to which the weakness of the female sex renders its members fatally susceptible," the gentle spinster said to her pupil; and she had folded her tidy black mittens upon her neat stomacher as she said it, and shaken her prim, respectable head with a sigh, adding, as her mild eye strayed between the lace and brocade window-curtains to the smart, high-wheeled cabriolet waiting in the courtyard below; the glittering turnout with the showy, high-actioned mare in the shafts, and the little top-booted, liveried, cockaded, English groom hanging to her nose:

"I would that your dear mother had found it compatible with the fulfillment of her religious duties to remain at home! For the Domestic Affections, Hector, which flourish by the connubial fireside, are potent charms to restrain the too-ardent spirit, and recall the wandering heart." And then Miss Smithwick had coughed and ended.

She winked at much that was scandalous in the life of her idol, that prim, chaste, good woman; but who shall say that her unswerving fidelity and humble devotion did not act sometimes as a martingale? The *bon-vivant*, the gambler, the dissipated elderly buck of the First Napoleon's Court, the ex-Adonis of the Tuileries, who never wasted time in resisting the blandishments of any Venus of the Court or nymph of the Palais Royal, respected decent Smithwick, was even known, at the pathetic stage of wine, to refer to her as the only woman who had ever understood him.

Yet when her sister (her sole remaining relative, who lived upon a small annuity, in the village of Hampstead, near London), sustained a paralytic stroke, and Smithwick was recalled to nurse her, did that poor lady's employer dream of providing,—out of those hundreds of thousands of thalers wrested from the coffers of the Convent of Widinitz,—for the old age of the faithful creature? You do not know Monsieur the Marshal if you dream he did.

He generously paid her the quarter due of her annual salary of fifteen hundred francs, kissed her knuckly left hand with the garnet ring upon it, placed there by a pale young English curate deceased many years previously—for even the Smithwicks have their romances and their tragedies—told her that his "roof" was "open" to her whenever she desired to return; and bowed her graciously out of his library, whose Empire bookcases were laden with costly editions of the classics, published by the Houbigants and the Chardins, Michaud and Buére (tomes of beauty that were fountains sealed to the illiterate master of the house), and whose walls were hung with splendid engravings by Renard and F. Chauveau, a few gems from the brushes of Watteau and Greuze, Boucher and Mignard; and one or two examples of the shining art of the young Meissonier.

The luxurious house in the Rue de la Chaussée d'Antin was less wholesome for good Smithwick's going. But I fear young Hector regretted her departure less than he should have done. True, the meek gentlewoman had not been able to teach her patron's son very much. But she had at least implanted in him the habit of truth, and the love of soap-and-water and clean linen. Last, but not least, she had taught him to speak the English of the educated upper classes with barely a trace of accent, whereas the Paris-residing teachers of the tongue of Albion were in those days, and too frequently are in these, emigrants from the green isle adjacent; Miss Maloney's, Misther Magee's, and Mrs. Maguire's; equipped with the thinnest of skins for imagined injuries, and the thickest of brogues for voluble speech, that ever hailed from Dublin or Wexford, King's County or the County Cork.

Not a servant of the household but had some parting gift for Smithwick—from the blue handkerchief full of apples offered by the kitchen-girl, to the housemaid's tribute of a crocheted lace *fichu*; from the cook's canary-bird, a piercing songster, to the green parasol—a sweet thing no bigger than a plate, with six-inch fringe and an ivory handle with a hinge, to purchase which Monsieur Brousset, the Marshal's valet, Duchard the butler, and Auguste the coachman had clubbed francs.

The question of a token of remembrance for faithful Smithwick was a thorn in her ex-pupil's pillow. You are to understand that Redskin, in his blundering, boyish way, had been trying hard to keep inviolate the oath imposed upon him by de Moulny. The monthly two louis of pocket-money were scrupulously dropped each pay-day into the alms-box of the Carmelite Church in the Rue Vaugirard, and what a hungry glare followed the vanishing coins, and to what miserable shifts the boy resorted in the endeavor to earn a meager pittance to supply his most pressing needs, and what an unjust reputation for stinginess and parsimony he earned, when it became known that he was willing to help dull or lazy students with their papers for pay, you can conceive.

He possessed the sum of five francs, amassed with difficulty after this fashion, and this represented the boy's entire capital at this juncture. A five-franc piece is a handsome coin, but you cannot buy anything handsome with it, that is the trouble. The discovery of the scene-painter Daguerre, first made in 1830, was not published by the Government of France until 1839. Otherwise, how the faithful heart of the attached Smithwick might have been gladdened by one of those inexpensive, oily-looking, semi-iridescent, strangely elusive portraits; into which the recipient peered, making discoveries of familiar leading features of relatives or friends, hailing them with joy when found, never finding them all together.

A portrait, even a pencil miniature with stumped shadows, its outlines filled with the palest wash of water-color, was out of the question. There was a silhouettist in the Rue de Chaillot. To this artist Hector resorted, and obtained a black paper profile, mounted and glazed, and enclosed in a gilt tin frame, at cost of all the boy possessed in the world.

That the offering was a poor one never occurred to simple Smithwick. She received it with little squeaking, mouselike cries of delight, and grief, and admiration; she ran at the tall, awkward, blushing youth to kiss him, unaware how he recoiled from the affectionate dab of her cold, pink-ended nose.

You could not say that the organ in question was disproportionately large, but its owner never managed to dispose of it inoffensively in the act of osculation. It invariably got in the eye or the ear of the recipient of the caress. A nose so chill in contact, say authorities, indicates by inverse ratio the temperature of the heart.

Hector got leave from the School, and went with the poor troubled Smithwick to the office of the Minister for Foreign Affairs in the Boulevard des Capucines, where for ten of her scanty store of francs she got her passport signed. Stout Auguste drove them in the shiny barouche with the high-steppers in silver-mounted harness, to meet the red Calais coach at the Public Posting-Office in the Rue Nôtre Dame des Victoires, whither one of the stablelads had wheeled Miss Smithwick's aged, piebald hair-trunk, her carpet-bag, and her three band-boxes on a hand-truck. And, judging by the coldness of the poor soul's nose when, a very Niobe for tears, she kissed the son of her lost mistress and her adored patron good-by, the heart beneath Smithwick's faded green velvet mantle must have been a very furnace of maternal love and tenderness.

"Never neglect the necessity of daily ablution of the entire person, my dearest boy!" entreated the poor gentlewoman, "or omit the exercises of your religion at morning and night. Instruct the domestics to see that your beloved papa's linen is properly aired. I fear they will be only too prone to neglect these necessary precautions when my surveillance is withdrawn! And—though but a humble individual offers this counsel, remember, my Hector, that there are higher aims in life than the mere attainment of great wealth or lofty station. Self-respect, beloved child, is worth *far more*!" She was extraordinarily earnest in saying this, shaking her thin gray curls with emphatic nods, holding up a lean admonitory forefinger. "Persons with gifts and capacities as great, natures as noble and generous as your distinguished father's, may be blinded by the sparkling luster of a jeweled scepter, allured by the prospect of dominion, power, influence, rule...." What could good Smithwick possibly be driving at? "But an unstained honor, my beloved boy, is worth more than these, and a clean conscience smooths the—way we must all of us travel!" She blinked the tears from her scanty, ginger-hued eyelashes, and added: "I have forfeited a confidence and regard I deeply appreciated, by perhaps unnecessarily believing it my duty to reiterate this." She coughed and dabbed her poor red eyes with the damp white handkerchief held in the thin, shaking hand in the shabby glove; and continued: "But a day will come when the brief joys and bitter disillusions of this life will be at an end. The bitterest that I have ever known come late, very late indeed!" Had Smithwick met it in the library that morning when the Marshal bade her adieu? "When I lay my head upon my pillow to die, it will be with the conviction that I did my duty. It has borne me fruit of sorrow. But I hope and pray that this chastening may be for my good. And oh! my dearest child, may God for ever bless and keep you!"

The mail-bags were stowed. The three inside passengers' seats being taken, poor weeping Smithwick perforce was compelled to negotiate the ladder, must climb into the *cabriolet* in company with the guard. With her thin elderly ankles upon her mind, it may be judged that no more intelligible speech came from her. She peered round the tarred canvas hood as the bugle flourished; she waved her wet handkerchief as the long, stinging whip-lash cracked over the bony backs of the four high-rumped, long-necked grays.... She was gone. Something had gone out of Hector's life along with her; he had not loved her, yet she left a gap behind. His heart was cold and heavy as he brought his eyes back from the dwindling red patch made by the mail amongst the vari-colored Paris street-traffic, but the hardening change that had begun in him from the very hour of de Moulny's revelation stiffened the muscles of his face, and drove back the tears he might have shed.

"Holy blue!" gulped stout Auguste, who was sitting on his box blubbering and mopping his eyes with a red cotton handkerchief, sadly out of keeping with his superb mauve and yellow livery, blazing with gold lace and buttons, and the huge cocked hat that crowned his well-powdered wig. "There are gayer employments than seeing people off, my faith there are! Who would have dreamed I should ever pipe my eye for the old girl! It is a pity she is gone? She was an honest creature!" He added huskily, tucking away the red cotton handkerchief: "One could do uncommonly well now with two fingers of wine?"

He cocked his thirsty eye at penniless Hector, who pretended not to hear him, and turned away abruptly; saying that he would walk back to the School.

"That is not a chip of the old block, see you, when it comes to a cart-wheel for drink-money," said Auguste over his shoulder, as the silver-harnessed blacks with much champing and high action, prepared to return to the stables in the Rue de la Chaussée d'Antin, and the silkstockinged footman mounted his perch behind.

"It is a learned prig," pronounced the footman, authoritatively, adding: "They turn them out all of one pattern at that shop of his."

"Yet he fought a duel," said Auguste, deftly twirling the prancing steeds into a by-street and pulling up outside a little, low-browed wine-shop much frequented by gold-laced liveries and cocked-hats. "And came off the victor," he added, with a touch of pride.

"By a trick got up beforehand," said the footman pithily, as he dived under the striped awning, in at the wineshop door.

"Nothing of the sort!" denied Auguste.

"Just as you please," said the footman, emerging with two brimming pewter measures, "but none the less true. M. Pédelaborde's nephew, who taught the *coup* to M. Hector, told M. Alain de Moulny, long after the affair, how cleverly he had been grassed. It was at the Hôtel de Moulny, my crony Lacroix, M. Alain's valet, was waiting in the ante-room and listened at the door. Money passed, Lacroix says. M. Alain de Moulny paid Pédelaborde handsomely not to tell."

"That is a story one doesn't like the stink of," said Auguste, making a wry mouth, draining his measure, handing it back to the silk-calved one, and spitting in the dust. "But the knowing fellow who taught M. Hector the dirty dodge and blows the gaff for hush-money, that is a rank polecat, my word!"

A crude pronouncement with which the reader may possibly be inclined to agree.

XI

The months went by. Hector ended his course at the School of Technical Military Instruction with honors, and his examiners, in recognition of the gift for languages, the bent for Science, the administrative and organizing capacities that were distinctive of this student, transferred him, with another equally promising youth, not to the Academy of Ways, Works, and Transport, where the embryo artillery and engineer officers of the School of Technical Military Instruction were usually ground and polished, but to the Training Institute for Officers of the Staff. An annual bounty tacked to the tail of the certificate relieved that pressing necessity for pocket-money. Redskin, with fewer anxieties upon his mind, could draw breath.

The Training Institute for Officers of the Staff was the School of Technical Military Instruction all over again, but upon a hugely magnified scale. To mention the School was the unpardonable sin: you spent the first term in laboriously unlearning everything that had been taught you there. On being admitted to the small gate adjacent to the large ones of wrought and gilded iron, you beheld the façade of the Institute, its great portico crowned with a triangular pediment supported upon stately pillars, upon which was sculptured an emblematical bas-relief of France, seated on a trophy of conquered cannon, instructing her sons in the military sciences, and distributing among them weapons of war. Following your guide, you shortly afterwards discovered two large yards full of young men in unbuttoned uniforms, supporting on their knees drawing-boards with squares of cartridge paper pinned upon them, upon which they were busily delineating the various architectural features of the buildings of the Institute, while a Colonel of the Corps of Instructors sternly or blandly surveyed the scene. Within the Institute, studies in Mathematics, Trigonometry and Topography, Cosmography, Geography, Chemistry, Artillery, Field Fortifications, Permanent Fortifications, Assault and Defense, Plans, Military Administration, Military Maneuvers, French, English, and German Literature, Fencing, Swimming, and Horsemanship in all its branches were thoroughly and comprehensively taught. And once a quarter the pupil-basket was picked over by skilled hands; and worthy young men, who were eminently fitted to serve their country in the inferior capacity as regimental officers, but did not possess the qualities necessary for the making of Officers of the Staff, were, at that little gate by the side of the great gilded iron ones, blandly shown out.

For, sane even in her maddest hour, France has never—under every conceivable political condition, in every imaginable national crisis, and under whatever government—Monarchical, Imperial, or Republican, that may for the time being have got the upper hand—ceased laboring to insure the supply to her Army, constantly renewed, of officers competent to command armies, of scientists skilled in the innumerable moves of the Great Game of War. Nor have other nations, Continental or insular, ever failed to profit by France's example, and follow France's lead.

The Marshal's son was not dismissed by that dreaded little exit. The fine flower of Young France grew in the neat parterres behind those lofty gilded railings. Sous-lieutenant Hector Dunoisse found many intellectual superiors among his comrades, whose society stimulated him to greater efforts. He worked, and presently began to win distinction; passed, with a specially-endorsed certificate, his examinations in the branches of study already enumerated and a few more; served for three months as Supernumerary-Assistant-Adjutant with an Artillery Regiment at Nancy; did duty for a corresponding period in the same capacity at Belfort with a corps of Engineers; and then received his appointment as Assistant-Adjutant to the 33rd Regiment of Chasseurs d'Afrique, quartered at Blidah.

Money would not be needed to make life tolerable at Blidah, where mettlesome Arab horses could be bought by Chasseurs d'Afrique at reasonable prices, and the mastic and the thin Dalmatian wine were excellent and cheap. Algerian cigars and pipe-tobacco were obtainable at the outlay of a few coppers; and from every thicket of dwarf oak or alfa-grass, hares started out before the sportsman's gun; and partridges and Carthage hens were as plentiful as sparrows in Paris.

Yet even at Blidah Dunoisse knew the nip of poverty, and there were times when the pack that de Moulny's hand had bound upon his shoulders galled him sore. For—the stroke of a pen and one could have had all one wanted. It needed no more than that.

For in Paris, at the big hotel in the Rue de la Chaussée d'Antin, in the book-lined, weapon-adorned, half library, half smoking-room that was Redskin's private den, and had been the boudoir of Marie Bathilde; there lay in a locked drawer of the inlaid ebony writing-table, a white parchment-covered pass-book inscribed with the name of Hector Dunoisse, and a book of pretty green-and-blue checks upon the Messieurs Rothschild, 9, Rue d'Artois. The dip of a quill in the ink, and one of the bland, well-dressed, middle-aged, discreet-looking cashiers behind the golden grilles and the broad, gleaming rosewood counters, would have opened a metal-lined drawer of gold louis, and plunged a copper shovel into the shining mass and filled the pockets of young Hector; or more probably would have wetted a skillful forefinger and thumb—run over a thick roll of crackling pink, or blue, or gray *billets de banque*, jotted down the numbers, and handed the roll across the counter to its owner, with a polite bow.

"So you think there is a curse upon my money, eh?" Monsieur the Marshal had said, upon an occasion when one of those scenes that leave ineffaceable scars upon the memory, had taken place between the father and the son.

Hector, spare, upright, muscular, lithe, ruddy of hue, bright of eye, steady of nerve, newly issued from the mint and stamped with the stamp of the Training Institute, and appointed to join his regiment in Algeria, turned pale under the reddish skin. He was silent.

"You have used none of it since you heard that story, *hein*? It would defile the soul and dirty the hands, *hein*?" queried Monsieur the Marshal, plunging one of his own into the waistcoat-pocket where he kept his snuff, and taking an immense pinch. "Yet let me point out that the allowance you disburse in pious alms and so forth——" Hector jumped, and wondered how his father had found out, and then decided that it was only a good piece of guessing, "may not be any portion of your mother's dowry. I was not poor when I recovered those three hundred-and-twenty-thousand silver thalers from the Prioress of the Carmelite Convent at Widinitz. I wished to be so much richer, that is all!"

"Poverty," said his son, breathing sharply through the nostrils and looking squarely in the Marshal's swollen, fierce-eyed, bushily-whiskered face, "poverty would have been some excuse—if anything could have excused so great an——"

"'Infamy,' was the word you were going to use," said Monsieur the Marshal, smiling across his great false teeth of Indian ivory, which golden bands retained in his jaws, and scattering Spanish snuff over his white kersey, tightly-strapped pantaloons, as he trumpeted loudly in a voluminous handkerchief of yellow China silk. "Pray do not hesitate to complete the sentence."

But Hector did not complete the sentence. The Marshal went on, shrugging his shoulders and waving his ringed hands: "After all, it is better to be infamous than idiotic. You hamper your career by playing the incorruptible; you are put to stupid shifts for money when plenty of money lies at your command."

"Do I not know that?"

"You have won honors, and with them a reputation for parsimony—are called a brilliant screw,—name of a thousand devils!—among your comrades. You coach other men for pay; you translate foreign technical works for military publishers; you burn the candle at both ends and in the middle. It is all very honorable and scrupulous, but would those who have sneered at you think better of you if they knew the truth? You know they would not! Instead of being despised, you would be laughed at for playing Don Quixote. That is one of the books I have read," Monsieur the Marshal added, pricked by the evident surprise with which his son received this unexpected testimony of his parent's literacy. "One can get some useful things out of a book like that, even though the hero of it is mad as a March hare. It is one of the books with blood and marrow in them, as the Emperor would have said: books that—unlike those of your Chateaubriands, Hugos, Lamartines, the devil knows who else!—are the literature that nourish men who are alive, not wooden puppets of virtue and propriety whose strings are pulled by priests—sacred name of——"

The Marshal went on, as his son stood silent before him, to lash himself into a frenzy of rage that imperiled the seams of a tight-waisted high-collared frock-coat of Frogé's own building, and gave its wearer what the Germans term a red head; with such accompaniments of gasping and snorting, rollings of the eyes and starting of the forehead-veins as are painfully suggestive of bleedings and sinapisms; cuppings and hot bricks; soft-footed personages with shiny black bags, candles, wreaths of white, purple and yellow *immortelles* inscribed with "*Regrets*," and all the plumed pomp and sable circumstance of a funeral procession to the Cemetery of Père La Chaise. He wound up at last, or rather, ran down; sank, puffing and perspiring and purple, into an easy chair.... Hector, who had listened with an unmoved countenance and heels correctly approximated, bowed and left the room, across which a broad ray of sunshine fell from the high, velvet-draped windows, across the inlaid ebony writing-table near which the Marshal lay back, wheezing and scowling, and muttering.... The thousands of shining motes that danced in that wide golden beam might have been wasps; the old man about whom they sported was so goaded and stung. Who wants to watch the Marshal in his hour of rageful humiliation.... He fumed and cursed awhile under his dyed mustaches, and then hit on an idea which made him chuckle and grin. He wheeled round, and splashed off a huge blotty letter to his bankers, and from that day the sum of One Million One Hundred and Twenty-five Thousand Francs stood to the credit of Hector Dunoisse upon Rothschild's books, and stood untouched.... One did not need much money out in Algeria, the temptation to dip into the golden store was barely felt, the malice of the Marshal was not to be gratified just yet awhile.

Though perhaps it was not altogether malice that inspired that action of Monsieur. His son forgot to question before long; forgot that old desertion of de Moulny's and its fanged tooth; forgot that check-book dimming with dust that drifted through the keyhole of the locked drawer in the writing-table, whose key was on his ring.

For there came a day when the boy—for he was little more—rode out at the Algiers Gate in command of a squadron of Chasseurs d'Afrique, under orders to reinforce the Zouaves garrisoning a hill-fort in Kabylia, threatened with siege by a rebellious Arab Kaïd who had thrown up his office, and his pay, and declared war against the Francos.

The rustle of the white cap-cover against his epaulet as he turned his head, the jingle of the scabbard against his stirrup, the clink of the bridle, made pleasant harmony with the other clinking and jingling. The air was cool before dawn, and the blue shadow of mighty Atlas stretched far over the plain of Metidja. In the deep-foliaged sycamores; from the copses of mastic, the nightingales trilled: turtle-doves were drinking and bathing in the mountain-rills, Zachar lifted a huge stony brow upon the horizon.... A slender young trooper with a high, reedy, tenor voice, sang an Arab song; his comrades joined in the chorus:

"Thy Fate in the balance, thy foot in the stirrup, before thee the path of Honor. Ride on! Who knows what lies at the end of the long journey? Ride on!

"Life and Love, Death and Sleep, these are from the Hand of the Giver. Ride on! Thy Fate in the balance, thy foot in the stirrup, before thee the path of Honor! Ride on!"

So Dunoisse rode on; the feet of his Arab mare falling softly on the thick white dust of the Dalmatie Road. And the great mysterious East rose up before him, smiling her slow, mystic smile, and opened her olive-hued, jeweled arms, and drew the boy of twenty to her warm, perfumed bosom, and kissed him with kisses that are potent philters, and wove around him her magic spells. And he forgot all the things that it had hurt him so to remember, for a space of two years.

XII

When his two years' service with the Cavalry were ended, he was transferred, with his step as lieutenant, but still in the capacity of Assistant-Adjutant, to the First Battalion, 999th Regiment of the Line, Paris; quartered in the Barracks of the Rue de l'Assyrie.

With the return to the familiar places of his boyhood, those things that Hector thought he had forgotten began to revive sufficiently to sting. A brother-officer spoke to him of de Moulny, who had quitted St. Sulpice a year previously, under a shadow so dark, it was discreetly hinted, that only the paternal influence had saved him from expulsion.

Hector did not blaze out in passionate defense or exoneration of his whilom comrade and friend. He said, briefly and coldly: "Those who say so lie! I used to know him!" And dropped the subject, as the chatterer was glad to do. For that duel fought by two schoolboys with disbuttoned fencing-foils six years before, was to be the first upon a list that grew and lengthened, and kept on growing and lengthening.... Unless you were desirous of cold steel for breakfast, there were subjects that must not be trifled with in the hearing of Assistant-Adjutant Hector Dunoisse.

The Catholic Church: Religious, particularly nuns; more particularly nuns of the Carmelite Order: ... instances of foul play in trials of strength and skill, particularly shady *coups* in fencing, slim tricks in the Game of the Sword. With other cause of offense provoking the *quid rides?* you never were quite sure where they might crop up.

And the fellow was a fighter—loved risk, enjoyed danger....

Was the grass more slippery at one end of the paced-out ground than the other? There was no necessity to toss up unless Monsieur, the other principal, insisted on observance of the strict formality—Dunoisse rather preferred slippery grass. Was the sun in the eyes of Monsieur the other principal? Change about by all means—Dunoisse rather enjoyed facing the glare that made you blink. The gusty wind that might deflect your pistol-bullet, the blowing dust that drifted into your eyes, mouth and nostrils, and that might provoke a cough or sneeze, just at the wrong moment for the swordsman; these conditions, justly regarded as unfavorable to continued existence, were rather courted than otherwise by this young officer of the Staff.

At Blidah, it had been told about, that an Arab sorceress had given the sub-Adjutant a charm, insuring success in the duel. Only, to insure this, the holder of the amulet must embrace the contrary odds and court the handicap. This story trotted back to Paris at Dunoisse's heels; it was told behind ladies' fans in every drawing-room he entered. Women liked it, it was so romantic; but men sneered, knowing the truth.

The truth, according to Pédelaborde, that is....

Like a poisonous thorn, that implied accusation of foul play made by the dentist's nephew on that morning when Redskin had visited the convalescent de Moulny in the Infirmary of the School, had rankled in the victim's flesh since it had been planted there. Honest Pédelaborde had not been idle in spreading the story and ornamenting it. Nor, if the truth had been known, had de Moulny been the only hearer who had paid him to tell it no more.

Mud is mud, though in contrast with the foulness of the hands that plaster it upon your garments, the vile stuff seems almost clean; and a slander listened to is a slander half-believed. The Pédelabordes invariably find listeners; there are always paying customers for offal, or those who deal in it might find a more sweetly-smelling trade.

XIII

Dunoisse had not long returned to Paris when he received one of those rare communications from his mother, bearing no address, forwarded by the hands of the priest who had been the director of Madame Dunoisse. Lifeless, formal notes, without a throb in them, without a hint of tenderness to the eye incapable of reading between the rigid lines:

"J.   M.   J.—x.

"MY SON,

"I am told that you are well, have returned from Algeria in good health, that your services have earned you distinguished mention in the dispatches of your Colonel, and that your abilities seem to promise a career of brilliance. Giving thanks to Almighty God and to Our Blessed Lady, and praying with all my heart that the highest spiritual graces may be vouchsafed you in addition to those mental and bodily gifts which you already possess,

"I am,
"Your mother in Christ
"TÉRÈSE DE S. FRANÇOIS.

"I love you and bless you! Pray also for me, my son!"

A picture burned up in living colors in the son's memory as he read. Hector saw himself as a fair-haired boy of six in a little blue velvet dress, playing on the carpet of his mother's boudoir. She sat in a low Indian cane chair with her year-old baby on her lap; a tiny Marie Bathilde, whose death of some sudden infantile complaint a few months later, turned the thoughts of the mother definitely in the direction of the abandoned way of religion, the vocation lost.

Even the magnificent new rocking-horse, with real hairy hide, and redundant mane and tail, and a splendid saddle, bridle, and stirrups of scarlet leather, could not blind the boy's childish eyes to the beauty of his mother. She was all in white; her skin had the gleam of satin and the pinky hue of rose-granite in its sheath of snow; she was slender as a nymph, upright and lissome as a tall swaying reed of the river shore, with a wealth of black hair that crowned her small high-bred head with a turban of silky, glistening coils, yet left looped braids to fall down to the narrow ribbon of silver tissue that was her girdle, defining the line of the bosom as girdles did long after the death of the First Empire. And her child upon her knee was as pearly fair as she shone dark and lustrous, though with the mother's eyes of changeful gleaming gray, so dark as almost to seem black.

The boudoir opened at one side into a dome-shaped conservatory full of palms and flowers, where a fountain played in an agate basin, and through the gush and tinkle of the falling water and the cracking of Hector's toy-whip, Monsieur the Marshal had come upon the pretty domestic picture unseen and unheard. He stood in the archway that led from the conservatory, a stalwart handsome figure of a soldierly dandy of middle-age, who has not yet begun to read in pretty women's eyes that his best days are over. His wife looked up from the child with which she played, holding a bunch of cherries beyond reach of the eager, dimpled hands. Their glances met.

"*My own Marie!—was this not worth it?*" Achille Dunoisse had exclaimed.

And Madame Dunoisse had answered, with a strange, wild, haggard change upon her beautiful face, looking her husband fully in the eyes:

"*Perhaps, if this were all——*"

And had put down the startled child upon a cushion near, and risen, and gone swiftly without a backward look, out of the exquisite luxurious room, into the bedchamber that was beyond, shutting and locking the door behind her, leaving the discomfited Adonis to shrug, and exclaim:

"So much for married happiness!"

Then, turning to the boy who sat upon the rocking-horse, forgetful of the toy, absorbing the scene with wide, grave eyes and curious, innocent ears, Monsieur the Marshal had said abruptly:

"My son, when you grow up, never marry a woman with a religion."

To whom little Hector had promptly replied:

"Of course I shall not marry a woman. I shall marry a little girl in a pink frock!"

How rife with tragic meaning the little scene appeared, now that the boy who had flogged the red-caparisoned rocking-horse had grown to man's estate.

Those frozen letters of his mother's! What a contrast they presented to the gushing epistles of poor old Smithwick, studded with notes of exclamation, bristling with terms of endearment, crammed with affectionate messages, touching reminiscences of happier days in *dear, dear Paris*, always underlined....

The prim sandaled feet of the poor old maiden were set in stony places since the death of the paralytic sister, to nurse whom she had returned to what she invariably termed her "native isle of Britain."... Even to Hector's inexperience those letters, in their very reticence upon the subject of poor Smithwick's need, breathed of poverty. The straitness of his own means galled him horribly when he read in Smithwick's neat, prim, ladylike calligraphy confessions such as these:

"The annuity originally secured to my beloved sister by purchase having *ceased at her death*, I am fain to seek employment in genteel families as a teacher of the French language, with which—no one knows better than my dearest Hector—I am *thoroughly conversant*. I would not willingly complain against the lot which Providence has appointed me. But *so small are the emoluments* to be gained from this profession, that I fear existence cannot be long supported upon the *scant subsistence* they afford."

The pinch of poverty is never more acutely felt than by the open-handed. In Africa Dunoisse had been sensible of the gnawing tooth of poverty. In Paris it had claws as well as teeth.

To have had five thousand francs to send to poor old Smithwick! To have been able to invest a snug sum for her in some solid British concern—those Government Three per Cents, for instance, of which the poor lady had always spoken with such reverence and respect. Or to have bought her a bundle of shares in one of the English Railway Companies, whose steel spider-webs were beginning to spread over the United Kingdom about this time. What would her old pupil not have given! And—it could have been done so easily if only he could have brought himself to fill in one of those checks upon Rothschild. But the thing was impossible.

His gorge rose at it. His religious principles were too deeply rooted, his honor stood too high, or possibly the temptation was not strong enough? There was little of the primal Eve about poor old shabby Smithwick. When white hands, whose touch thrilled to the heart's core, should be stretched out to him for some of that banked-up gold; when eyes whose luster tears discreetly shed only enhanced should be raised pleadingly to his; when an exquisite mouth should entreat, Hector was to find that one's own oaths, no less than the oaths of one's friends, are brittle things; and that in the heat of the passion that is kindled in a young and ardent man by the breath of a beautiful woman, Religion and Principle and Honor are but as wax in flame.

XIV

He scraped a few hundred francs together and sent them to poor old Smithwick, and received another letter of disproportionately-measured gratitude for the meager gift that might so easily have been a rich one, if....

He learned from a very little paragraph at the end of the grateful letter that his faithful old friend had broken down in health. That she had been seriously ill "from the effects of over-anxiety and *a too strenuous battle* with adversity," ending with pious thanks to Providence—Smithwick was always curiously anxious to avoid references of a more sacred nature—that, "through the introduction and recommendation of a *most generous friend*," she had obtained admission as an inmate of the Hospice for Sick Governesses in Cavendish Street, London, West, "*a noble charity* conducted upon the *purest Christian principles*, where I hope, D. V., to spend *my closing days in peace*."

Were they so near, those closing days of the simple, honorable, upright life? Gratitude, respect, old association, a chivalrous pity for the woman, sick, and poor, and old, conspired to make the first step on the Road Perilous easier than her pupil would have imagined. He got upon his iron-gray Arab, Djelma, dearest and most valuable of the few possessions owned by this son of a millionaire, and rode to the Rue d'Artois with the leveled brows and cold, set face of a man who rides to dishonor.

Upon the very steps of Rothschild's, a brother-officer of the Regiment of Line to which our young sprig of the Staff was attached in the capacity of Assistant-Adjutant, met and repaid Dunoisse an ancient, moss-grown, long-forgotten debt of three thousand francs.

"You come *fort à propos*—for you, that is! Here, catch hold! Sorry I met you! You're not, I'll bet you this whacking lump!" Monsieur the Captain joyfully flourished the stout roll of *billets de banque*, from which he had stripped the notes he now thrust under Dunoisse's nose. "Wonder where I got 'em? Inside there"—a thumb clothed in lemon-colored kid jerked over the shoulder—"from one of those powdered old cocks behind the gilt balusters. My old girl has stumped with a vengeance this time. I told her my tailor was a Chevalier of the Legion of Honor, and had sent me a *cartel* because I hadn't paid his bill." One is sorry to record that Monsieur the Captain's "old girl" was no less stately a person than Madame la Comtesse de Kerouatte, of the Château de Pigandel, Ploubanou, La Bretagne. "She swallowed the story, and see the result. Don't shy at taking the plasters. You can lend me again when I'm broke! Pouch! and *va te promener!*"

So Dunoisse gratefully took the tendered banknotes and with one of them an outside place on the blue Havre diligence, rattling out of Paris, next morning, behind its four bony bays, ere the milkwomen, and postmen, and newspaper-carts began their rounds.

The salt fresh wind stinging his red-brown skin, the salter spray upon his lips, the veiled and shawled and muffled ladies, and cloaked and greatcoated gentlemen, already extended on the deck-seats and deck-chairs of the steam-packet *Britannia* of Southampton—patiently waiting to be dreadfully indisposed in little basins that were dealt out by the brisk, hurrying, gilt-buttoned stewards as cards are dealt at whist; the glasses of brandy-and-water being called for by robust Britons, champing ham sandwiches with mustard on their upper lips, and good-fellowship beaming out of their large pink, whiskered faces; the tumblers of *eau sucrée* being ordered by French travelers, who invariably got toast-and-water instead; the swaying crates of luggage, the man-traps made by coils of rope on wet and slippery decks, the crash of waves hitting bows or paddle-wheels, the shrieks of scared females, convinced their last hour had come,—recalled to Dunoisse his boyish visit to what poor Smithwick had invariably termed "the shores of Albion."

He remembered with gratitude the self-denying hospitality of the poor sisters: the little home at Hampstead, the golden-blossomed furze of the Heath, came back to him with extraordinary vividness. Down to the piping bullfinch, whose cage hung in the little front parlor-window, and whose *répertoire*, consisting of the first bar of "Home, Sweet Home," the boy had endeavored to enlarge with the melodies of *"Partant Pour La Syrie"* and *"Jeanette et Jeannot,"* every detail stood clear.

And here was England, upon a pale gray February morning, under skies that wept cold heavy tears of partly-melted snow. Black fungus-growths of umbrellas were clustered on the quay; the thick air smelled of oilskins and wet mackintoshes. And so across a dripping gangway to a splashy paved incline that ended in a Railway Station, for instead of coaching through Hants and Surrey to Middlesex by the scarlet "Defiance" or the yellow "Tally-Ho!" you traveled by the Iron Road all the way to London.

You are to picture the splay-wheeled, giraffe-necked locomotive of the time, with the top of the funnel nicked like the cut paper round a cutlet-bone; the high-bodied carriages, with little windows and hard hair-cloth cushions; the gentlemen passengers in shaggy hats with curly brims, high-waisted coats, with immense roll-collars, and full-hipped trousers strapped down over shiny boots; assisting ladies in coal-scuttle bonnets, and pelerines trimmed with fur, worn over gored skirts, swelled out by a multiplicity of starched, embroidered petticoats, affording peeps of pantalettes and sandals, to alight or to ascend....

Pray understand that there was no jumping. Violent movement was not considered genteel. Supposing you to be of the softer sex—it was softer in those days than it is now!—you were swanlike or sprightly, according to your height, figure, and the shape of your nose, and your name almost invariably ended in "anna" or "ina" or "etta."

My Aunt Julietta was sprightly. She had a nose ever so slightly turned up at the end, and a dimple in her left cheek. Her elder sister, one of her elder sisters—Aunt Julietta was the youngest of six—her elder, Marietta, was swanlike, with a long neck and champagne-bottle shoulders, and the most elegant Early Victorian figure you can conceive; a fiddle of the old pattern has such a waist and hips.

Both my aunts traveled by this very train, in the same first-class compartment as the Assistant-Adjutant of the 999th Regiment of the Line. The young ladies were, in fact, returning from a visit to the elegant and hospitable family mansion of Sir Tackton Wackton, Baronet, of Wops Hall, Hants; whose elder daughter had been their schoolfellow and bosom-friend at the Misses Squeezers' Select Boarding-School for young ladies at Backboard House, Selina Parade, Brighton. It was the first occasion upon which they had braved the dangers of the Iron Road unprotected by a member of the sterner sex. Consequently, when, in the act of picking up and handing to my Aunt Julietta a sweet green velvet reticule she had accidentally dropped upon the platform, the black-eyed, dark-complexioned, military-looking young foreign gentleman, in a gray traveling cloak and cap, who performed this act of gallantry, peeped up the tunnel of her coal-scuttle bonnet, with evident appreciation of the wholesome apple-cheeked, bright-eyed English girl-face looking out from amongst the ringlets and frills and flowers at the end, both the young ladies were extremely fluttered. And as they passed on, Aunt Marietta whispered haughtily, "How presumptuous!" and Aunt Julietta responded: "Oh, I *don't* think he meant to be *that*, my dear! And *how* handsome and distinguished-looking!" To which my Aunt Marietta only responded, with the disdainful curl of the lip that went with her Roman nose: "For a foreigner, passably so!"

Later on, by one of the oddest accidents you could conceive possible, my aunts found themselves in the same first-class compartment as the foreign-looking gentleman; and as the Southampton to London Express clanked and jolted and rattled upon its metal way (rail-carriages being unprovided at that early date with springs, pneumatic brakes, and other mechanical inventions for the better ease of the public), the courtesy and consideration of their well-bred fellow-traveler, who spoke excellent English—combined with his undeniable good looks—created an impression upon my Aunt Julietta, which by the time the Express had rattled and jolted and clanked into the junction of the provincial garrison town of Dullingstoke (near which was situated the family mansion of my grandparents), had developed into an attachment of the early, hapless, unreciprocated order.

"If only," thought my sentimental Aunt, "the train could go on for ever!"

But the train stopped; and there was the family chariot, with the purple-nosed coachman on the box; there was the boy who had cleaned the knives, now promoted to page's livery, at the noses of Chestnut and Browney, waiting to convey my aunts to the shelter of the paternal roof. They collected muffs, reticules, and parcels.... The military-looking young foreign gentleman handed them out, one after the other, and bowed over their respective hands with a grace that caused Aunt Marietta to exclaim, "My dear!" and Aunt Julietta to return, "Did you ever?" as the family chariot drove away, and the Express, with much preliminary snorting, prepared to start again, and did in fact start; but brought up with a jerk, and clanked back to the platform to pick up a passenger of importance, who had arrived behind time.

A dazzling scarlet mail-phaeton, pulled by a pair of high-spirited, sweating, chestnut trotters, had brought him to the junction, sitting, enveloped in a huge shaggy box-coat with buttons as large as Abernethy biscuits; covered with a curly-brimmed, low-crowned shiny beaver hat that might have belonged to a Broad Church parson of sporting proclivities, by the side of the smart groom who drove.... Another groom in the little seat behind sheltered him from the rain with a vast green silk gig-umbrella, just as though he had been any common, ordinary landholder of means and position, with a stake in the Borough Elections, a seat on the local Bench, and the right to put J.P. after his name; and commit local poachers caught by his own gamekeepers in his own plantations, then and there, in his own library, to the District Lock Up for trial at the Weekly Sessions.

But the guard,—a functionary in the absurdest uniform, a cross between a penny-postman's and a military pensioner's, knew better. So did the porters, encased in green velveteen corduroy, as worn by the porters of to-day; so did the station-master, crowned with the gilt-banded top-hat of a bank-messenger and sporting the crimson waistcoat of a beadle. With a Parliamentary Down-train waiting outside and shrieking to come through, while a Composite of horse-boxes and cattle-trucks and coal-trucks bumped and jolted over the Main Line metals; with the Up-Express from Southampton panting to be green-flagged and belled upon its metal road to London, he waited, his gilt-banded top-hat respectfully in hand, to receive the distinguished passenger, who did not hurry, possibly in virtue of his bulk, but waddled down the platform with a gait you felt to be peculiarly his own, involving a short turn to the right as he stepped out with the right foot (encased in the largest size of shiny patent-leather boot), and a short turn to the left as he set down the left one, as though inviting the whole world to take a comprehensive, satisfactory stare at a great and good man, and be the better for it.

Impatient passengers, projecting the upper halves of their bodies from the carriage-windows, saw nothing much in him. But to these, awed porters and reverent officials whispered behind their expectant palms,—on being conjured to say what the deuce the delay was about?—that the gentleman who had caused it was a Government Contractor, tremendous influential and uncommon rich; so much so as to be able to break the Bank of England by the simple process of drawing a whacking check upon it. When the hearer laughed heartily at this, or snorted indignantly, the officials and porters amended that, perhaps to say the Bank of England was a bit too strong, but that everybody knew the gentleman was a Millionaire, and regularly rolling in his thousands.

He rolled now towards the compartment of which the foreign gentleman who had assisted my aunts to alight was now the only occupant; and allowed himself to be respectfully hoisted in, and tenderly placed in a corner seat, with his valise and hat-box beside him. He filled up the compartment—compartments were narrower in those days than they are now—as completely as a large, shaggy bear might have done, when he got upon his legs again, and stood at the window, beaming so benevolently upon the admiring crowd assembled on the platform that the station-master, upon whom had not fallen one drop of gold or silver manna out of the smiler's jingling trousers-pockets, felt impelled to say: "Lord bless you, Mr. Thompson Jowell, sir! A safe journey up to London and back! Guard, be extra careful this trip!" And the guard, who had not been tipped, touched his tall hat respectfully; and the porter, who had reaped nothing but honor from carrying Mr. Thompson Jowell's hat-box and valise; and the other porter, who had rammed scalding hot-water tins into the carriage, that the large feet of the popular idol might be warmed thereby, threw up each his muffin-shaped cap, and cried "Hooray!" And the train started,—so suddenly, in the mistaken zeal of the engine-driver, that Thompson Jowell was shot with violence into a distant corner of the carriage, and so violently bonneted by collision with the rack above, that only his large, red, projecting ears saved him from being completely extinguished by the low-crowned, curly-brimmed, shiny beaver hat, that might have been a sporting parson's of the jovial Broad Church brand.

He took the hat off after that, revealing his little pear-shaped head of upright, bristly gray hair, and his forehead that slanted like the lid of a Noah's Ark over all the jumbled beasts inside, and goggled with his large, moist, circular brown eyes upon his fellow-traveler over the voluminous crimson silk handkerchief with which he mopped his damp and shining face. He unbuttoned his greatcoat and threw his long bulky body back in his corner with a "whoof!" of relief, and put up his short, thick legs upon the seat, saying to Dunoisse, with a jerky, patronizing nod:

"Plenty of room, sir, if you're inclined to do the same. These new-fangled hot-water tins draw a man's corns consumedly!" Adding, a moment after Dunoisse's smiling refusal: "Please yourself, and you'll please me. 'Hang manners! Give me comfort!' says Mister John Bull…. You're French yourself, I take it?"

"Sir, since you do me the honor to inquire," returned Dunoisse dryly, for the goggle-eyes of Mr. Thompson Jowell were curiously fixed on him, "I received my education at a public school in Paris."

"Thought as much!" said Mr. Thompson Jowell, smiling in a satisfied way, crossing his extra-sized patent-leather-covered feet, and revolving the thumbs of the large ringed hands that were clasped upon his protuberant waistcoat. "I mayn't comprenney the parly-voo, but I know the cut of a Frenchman's jib when I see one. You might take in another man, I say, but you can't deceive me. Sharp, sir, that's what my name is!"

"I am gratified," returned Dunoisse, without enthusiasm, "to make Mr. Sharp's acquaintance!" And pointedly unfolded and began to read *The Times*, leaving Thompson Jowell uncertain whether he had or had not been insulted by a person whom he designated in his own mind as an "upstart Crappaw."

But the paper presented little of interest, and presently, from behind its shelter, Dunoisse found himself watching his companion, who had drawn from various inner pockets of the large shaggy box-coat various little bags, containing pinches of divers brands of oats, together with divers other little parcels containing short-cut samples of straw and hay. From the inspection of these, by the nose and teeth, as well as by the organs of vision, he appeared to derive delight and satisfaction so intense, that the upstart Crappaw in the opposite corner, who had had dealings with Contractors in his own benighted, foreign country, could no longer be in doubt as to his calling.

Those black eyes of the ex-Adjutant of Chasseurs d'Afrique were extraordinarily observant, and the brain housed in the small well-shaped head, under the crisp close waves of his black hair, had not been forged and tempered and ground at the Training Institute for Officers of the Staff for nothing....

This man who had been addressed as Mr. Thompson Jowell, and who had said his name was Sharp, repelled Dunoisse and interested him, as a big and bloated spider might have disgusted and attracted an entomologist.

So, when the train, jolting and rattling and clanking in the Early Victorian manner, through the chilly, dripping country, at the terrific speed of twenty miles an hour, slowed up and slid groaning into a station close to a great permanent Military Encampment in the vicinity of Bagshot Heath, where, drawn up upon a deserted siding were a long row of open trucks, loaded with trusses of hay and straw, all unprotected from the pouring rain by any kind of covering whatever; and Mr. Sharp, moved to irrepressible ecstasy by this sight, was fain to get up and thrust his big hands deep in his jingling trousers-pockets to have his laugh out more comfortably; a sudden impulse of speech swayed the hitherto silent foreigner in the opposite corner to lean forwards, and say:

"You seem elated, sir, by the spectacle of all this spoiled and soaking forage?"

The person addressed, who was bending himself in the middle in the height of his enjoyment, straightened with a jerk. His big underjaw dropped; his nose, aggressively cocked, and with a blunted end, as though in early youth it had been held against a revolving grindstone, appeared to assume a less obstinate angle; his large face lost its ruddy color. Muddily pale, with eyes that rolled quite wildly in their large round orbits, he stared in the dark face of this bright-eyed, alert, military-looking, painfully-observant foreigner. For it occurred to him, with a breaking out of shiny perspiration upon the surface of his forehead and jowl, and a stiffening of the already bristling gray hairs upon his head, that this might be the devil.

Thompson Jowell was orthodox to the backbone, and firmly believed in the individual existence of the personage named. He glanced with nervous suspicion at the small, arched, well-booted feet of his fellow-passenger. Had one of the dark-faced stranger's well-shaped gray trousered legs ended in a cloven hoof, Thompson Jowell would have said his prayers, or pulled the communication-cord that ended in the guard's van. He was not quite certain which. As it was, he felt sufficiently reassured to be overbearing. He snorted, and resumed his seat with as much dignity as was compatible with the jolting of the Express. He thrust his knees apart, leaned his large hands upon them, stared the inquisitive stranger hard in the face, snorted again, and said:

"Perhaps you will be good enough to explain, sir, what you meant by that remark?"

"I shall be charmed to do so," returned Dunoisse. "It will afford me gratification. What I meant was that you laughed: and the spectacle of waste and destruction that presumably provoked your laughter did not appear to me, a stranger and a foreigner, provocative of merriment."

"Now look you here, young sir!" said Thompson Jowell, getting very red about the ears and gills, and jabbing at the speaker with a stout and mottled forefinger. "Foreigner or no foreigner, you have an eye in your head, I take it? Very well, then, look at me! I am not the sort of person to be called to account for my laughter—if, indeed, I laughed at all, which I don't admit!—by any living man—British or French or Cannibal Islander—unless that individual wants to be made to laugh on the wrong side of his own mouth. Jack Blunt, my name is—and so you know! As regards those truckloads, they have been delivered on a certain date According to Contract, they have been paid for on Delivery, also According to Contract, and whether the troop-horses of Her Majesty's Army like the hay when they get it, or whether they would prefer plum-cake and macaroons, damme if I care!"

With which the speaker threw himself back in the corner and folded his thick, short arms upon his voluminous waistcoat, which was of velvet, magnificently embroidered, and into the bosom of which cascaded a superb cravat of blue satin, ornamented with three blazing ruby breast-pins. He breathed hard awhile and frowned majestically, and then relaxed his frown in pity for the evident confusion of the snubbed foreigner; who said, without the humility that one might have expected:

"Sir, that you and other men of your standing and influence in this country do not care, is in my poor opinion a national calamity."

The brows of Thompson Jowell relaxed at this implied concession to his greatness. He closed his eyes and puffed out his pendulous cheeks, and said, nodding his pear-shaped head, the beaver hat belonging to which was in the rack above it:

"Aye—aye! Well—well! Not badly put by half!"

"A national calamity," pursued Dunoisse, "when one reflects how large a sum of the nation's money went into the pockets of the Contractor who delivered the consignment, and further, when it occurs to one how impossible it will become for any expert to determine whether straw and hay so drenched and spoiled was not rotten and fermenting previous to delivery, and the exposure that must inevitably set up both conditions. And further still, when it is extremely possible that the neglect to cover the trucks was of design; and that the person—Quartermaster-Sergeant or Railway Official—whose duty it was to take this precaution, had been—for all men are not as scrupulous, sir, as yourself, and some are capable of such roguery—bribed by the Contractor or his confidential agent, to omit it!"

This being an exact summary of what had taken place, the above sentences, coined in Dunoisse's somewhat precise and formal English, and uttered with the short, clipped inflection that characterized it, came pelting about the large and tingling ears of Thompson Jowell like stinging flakes of ice. He gasped and rolled his eyes at them in apoplectic fashion, and wagged his head and shook it from side to side, until the speaker stopped.

"No, no, young sir!" said Thompson Jowell at that juncture. "Don't tell me! I won't listen to you; it's past crediting; it couldn't be! Frenchmen might be guilty of such doings, I can credit it; Italians very likely, Germans uncommonly-probably, Roosians without doubt! But when you go to tell a true-blue Briton such as I am, that Englishmen with British blood running in their veins and British hearts a-beating in their bosoms could be capable of such doings, I tell you by Gosh the thing's impossible! I won't listen to you! Don't talk to me!"

He fell back gasping at the end of this splendid tribute to the virtues of his countrymen. And, of such queerly conflicting elements are even liars and knaves composed, they were real tears that he whisked away with his big, flaming silk handkerchief, and the trembling of the hand that held it was due as much to appreciation of his own eloquence, as to alarm at the uncanny sharpness with which this disturbing young foreigner, with the cold black eyes and the admirable command of English, had put his finger on the ugly truth.

Dunoisse, far from suspecting that he had at his mercy the identical Contractor whose methods he had sketched with such brilliant fidelity to nature, pursued:

"Rogues are everywhere, sir. We have plenty of them in France, and, unhappily for other countries, we do not enjoy the monopoly. And—the person I reverence and honor, with one exception, above all living women, is an English lady. Respect for her great nation—and yours!—is not lacking in me, the adopted son of another nation, no less great; with whom England has striven in honorable war, with whom she is now most happily at peace. Yet though I admire I may criticise; and plainly say that the lamentable spectacle that has furnished our discussion, plainly points, if not to willful neglect, to lack of forethought and foresight upon the part of certain officials who should,—in the interests of the British Army,—have been trained to think and to see."

"I don't agree with you, young sir," said Mr. Thompson Jowell, hooking his large splay thumbs into the armholes of his superb velvet waistcoat in a bullying manner, and folding his pendulous chin into fresh creases on his cravat after a fashion he employed in the browbeating of clerks and agents. "I disagree with you flatly, and—my name being Tom Plain—I'll tell you for why. You called that spoiled hay and straw—my name being John Candid, I'll admit it is spoiled!—'a lamentable spectacle.' To me it is not a lamentable spectacle. Far from it! I call it a beautiful illustration, sir!—a standing example of the greatness of England, and the Immensity of the resources that she has at command."

"Name of Heaven, why?" cried Dunoisse, confounded and surprised out of his usual self-possession by this extraordinary statement.

"Aha! Now you're getting warm, young sir," said Thompson Jowell, triumphantly. "Keep your temper and leave Heaven out of the question, that's my advice to you. And let me tell you that Great Britain is not so poor that she can't afford to be at the expense of a little loss and damage, and that the high-bred, wealthy, fashionable gentlemen who hold commissions in her Army have other fish to fry and other things to attend to than keeping an eye on Quartermaster-Sergeants, Forage and Supply Agent's clerks and Railway Officials. And that the coroneted noblemen who sit at the head of Departments in her War Office are too great, and grand, and lofty to dirty their hands with common affairs and vulgar details—and it does 'em honor! Honor, by George!" said Thompson Jowell, and smote his podgy hand upon his gross and bulky thigh, clad in a pantaloon of shepherd's plaid of the largest pattern procurable. "My name's John Downright—and what I say is—it does 'em honor!"

"I have to learn, sir," said Dunoisse, with recovered and smiling urbanity, "that the criterion of a gentleman lies in his incapacity for discharging the duties of his profession, any more than in his capacity for being gulled by knavish subordinates and cheated by thievish tradesmen."

"Now take care where you're treading, my young sir!" said Thompson Jowell, frowning and swelling portentously. "For you're on thin ice, that's what you're on. My name's Jack Blunt, and I tell you so plumply. For I am a Contractor of Supplies and an Auxiliary-Transport Agent to the British Army, and I glory in my trade, that's what I do! And go to the Horse Guards in Whitehall, London—and ask my Lords of the Army Council, and His Honor the Adjutant-General, and His Excellency the Quartermaster-General whether the character of Thompson Jowell is respected? Maybe you'll get an answer—maybe you won't! And call at the

Admiralty—perhaps they don't know him at the Victualing Office!—and the Director of Transport never heard of him! They might tell you at the Treasury that the Commissary-General bows to him! I'm not going to boast!—it ain't my way. But if you don't hear in every one of the high places I've mentioned, that the individual inside this waistcoat"—he smote it as he spoke—"is an honor to Old England and such a sturdy stem of seasoned British oak as may be relied on to uphold the Crown and Constitution in the hour of need with the last penny in his purse, and the best blood of his bosom, call me a damned liar!"

"I shall not fail in the event you mention to avail myself of the permission accorded me," returned Dunoisse politely, "in the spirit in which it is given."

"Ha, ha! You're a joker, I see!" said Mr. Thompson Jowell. "Excuse me, young sir," he added, "but if you have quite finished with that newspaper, it will save me buying one if you'll kindly pass it over!"

With which the great man deftly whipped the unperused *Times* from the seat where it had been laid aside by its owner, and ignoring the political articles and Foreign Intelligence (under which heading a brief paragraph announcing the decease of the aged paralytic Hereditary Prince of Widinitz, might, had the glance of his fellow-traveler fallen upon it, have seemed to him of more than passing interest), dived into those thrilling columns that deal with the rise and fall in value of wheat and oats, hay and straw, beans and chaff, and other staple commodities of the Forage Trade, and record the fluctuations of the Stock Exchange; became in virtue of such elevations and depressions, immersed in perusal; and spoke no more either on the greatness of Great Britain, the greatness of Thompson Jowell or any other kindred subject. And the Waterloo Road Terminus being reached, a luxuriously-appointed brougham, drawn by a handsome horse, and ornamented, as to the door-panels and harness, with repetitions, illuminated or engraved, of a large and showy coat-of-arms recently purchased at Heralds' College, received the glorious being, and whirled him away through murky miles of foggy streets to his shabby little office in The Poultry.

Here, in a shady alley of low-browed houses near the Banking House of Lubbock, amidst dirt and dust and cobwebs and incrustations of City mud, upon the floors that were never washed, upon the windows that were never cleaned, upon the souls of those who spent their lives there, the vast business of Thompson Jowell, Flour, Forage, and Straw Contractor, Freightage- and Auxiliary-Transport Agent to Her Majesty's Army, had grown from a very little cuttle-fish into a giant octopus, all huge stomach and greedy parrot-beak; owning a hundred scaly tentacles, each panoplied with suckers for draining the golden life-blood of the British ratepayer from the coffers of the British Government; and furnished, moreover, with sufficient of that thick and oily medium, known as Humbug, in its ink-bag, to blind, not only the eyes of the people and their rulers and representatives to its huge, wholesale swindlings; but in some degree to becloud and veil its own vision, so that foul seemed fair, and petty greed and low cunning took on a pleasing aspect of great-minded and unselfish patriotism.

Cowell, the Beef-Contractor, and Sowell, who undertook to supply such garments as the Government generously provided to its soldiers free of cost; scamping materials in fashioning the one sparrow-tailed full-dress coatee and pair of trousers,—so that stalwart infantrymen found it incompatible with strict propriety to stoop; and legs and arms of robust troopers were so tightly squeezed into cases of coarse red or coarse blue cloth as to resemble nothing so much as giant sausages,—were persons of influence and standing. Towell, who turned out shirts, of regulation material something coarser than bed-ticking, paying wan workwomen fourpence per dozen—the worker finding buttons, needles and thread—and receiving for each garment two shillings and sevenpence, filched from the soldier's pay; Rowell, who found the Cavalry and Artillery in saddlery of inferior leather and spurs of dubious metal; Powell, who roofed the British forces as to the head, with helmets, busbies, shakos, and fatigue-caps; Bowell, who stocked its surgeons' medicine-chests with adulterated tincture of opium, Epsom-salts that never hailed from Epsom; decoction of jalap, made potent with croton oil; inferior squills and suspicious senna; and Shoell, who shod the rank-and-file with one annual pair of boots (made principally of brown paper), were, taken together, a gang of—let us write a community of upright and worthy individuals; but, viewed in comparison with Dunoisse's acquaintance of the railway, they paled like farthing rushlights beside a transparency illuminated by gas.

A day was coming, when Britannia, leaning, in her hour of need, upon that sturdy stem of seasoned British oak, was to find it but a worm-eaten sham; a hollow shell of dust and rottenness, housing loathsome, slimy things, crawling and writhing amidst the green and fleshless bones that once wore Victoria's uniform; housing and breeding in the empty skulls of brave and hardy men. Dead in their thousands, not of the shot and shell, the fire and steel and pestilence that are the grim concomitants of War: but dead of Privation and Want, Cold and Starvation—through the rapacity and greed, the mercenary cunning and base treachery of those staunch and loyal pillars of the British Crown and Constitution: Cowell, Sowell, Towell, Rowell, Powell, Bowell, Shoell, and, last but not least among those worthies, Thompson Jowell.

XV

Arrived at his dingy little office in The Poultry, halfway up the narrow, shady alley of low-browed, drab-faced houses near the Banking House of Lubbock, you saw Thompson Jowell, recruited by a solid luncheon, bending severe brows upon a pale-faced, weak-eyed clerk, who had grievously offended, and was up for judgment.

"What's this? Now, what's this, Standish?" the great man blustered. "You have been doing overtime and ask to be paid for it? Lawful claims are met with prompt settlement in this office, as you have good cause to know. But, lookee here!" The speaker puffed out his pendulous cheeks in his characteristic way, and held up a stout, menacing finger before the wincing eyes of the unfortunate Standish. "Don't you, or any other man in my employment get trying to make money out of ME! Because you won't, you know!" said Mr. Thompson Jowell. "D'ye see?" and jabbed at the thorax of the unfortunate Standish with the finger, and then rubbed his own nose smartly with it, and thrust it, with its fellows, into his large, deep trousers-pocket as the livid victim faltered:

"You were good enough, previously to the Christmas holidays, sir, to send for me, and say that if I cared to——"

Thompson Jowell solemnly shook his little pear-shaped head, and goggled with his large, round brown eyes upon the scared victim, saying:

"Not 'cared to,' Standish. Be accurate, my good fellow, in word as in deed!"

"You hinted to me, sir——" stammered the unfortunate.

Thompson Jowell swelled to such portentous size at this that the clerk visibly shrank and dwindled before the awful presence.

"I am not accustomed to hint, Standish!"

"You intimated, sir, that if I was willing"—gulped the pallid Standish—"to devote my evenings to making up the New Year's accounts and checking the files of duplicate invoices against the office-ledgers, you—you would undertake—or so you were good enough to give me to understand—that I should be the better for it!"

"But if I mentioned overtime," returned his employer, thrusting his short fat hands under his wide coat-tails, and rocking backwards and forwards on the office hearthrug, a cheap and shabby article to which the great man was accustomed to point with pride as illustrative of the robust humility of his own nature, "I'll eat my hat!" He glanced at the low-crowned, shiny beaver hanging on a wooden peg beside his private safe, in company with the shaggy box-coat and a fur-lined, velvet-collared cloak of sumptuous appearance, adding, "and that's a meal would cost me thirty shillings. For there's no such a thing as overtime. It don't exist! And if you proved to me it did I wouldn't believe you!" said Thompson Jowell, thrusting his thick right hand deep into the bosom of the gorgeous waistcoat, and puffing himself out still more. "For your time, young man! in return for a liberal salary of Twenty Shillings per week, belongs to Me—to Me, Standish, whenever I choose to employ it! As for being the better for having done the work you say you have, you *are* the better morally, in having discharged your duty to a generous employer; and if you choose to injure your constitution by stopping here o' nights until eleven p.m. it's no affair of mine. John Downright my name is!—besides the one that's on the brass doorplate of these offices, and what I say is—it's no affair of mine! Though, mind you! in burning gas upon these premises up to I don't know what hour of the night, you've materially increased the Company's quarterly bill, and in common justice ought to defray their charges. I'll let you off that!—so think yourself lucky! and don't come asking me to remunerate you for overtime again. Now, get out with you!"

Unlucky Standish, yellow and green with disappointed hopes and secret fury, and yet admiring, in spite of himself, the clever way in which he had been defrauded, backed towards the narrow door, and in the act collided with a visitor, who, entering, straightway impregnated and enlivened the dead and musty atmosphere with a heterogeneous mixture of choice perfumes, in which super-fine Macassar and bear's grease, the fashionable Frangipani and Jockey Club; Russia-leather, a suspicion of stables, and more than a hint of malt liquor, combined with the fragrance of the choice Havana cheroot which the newcomer removed from his mouth as he entered, to make way for the filial salutation:

"Halloa, Governor! All serene?"

You then saw young Mortimer Jowell, only surviving sapling of the sturdy stem of tough old British oak ticketed Thompson Jowell, received in that fond father's arms, who warmly hugged him to his bosom, crying:

"Morty! My own boy!"

"How goes it, Governor?" responded Morty, winking tremendously, and patting his parent on his stout back with a large-sized hand, gloved with the most expensive lemon kid. "Hold on, you!" he hailed, as the ghastly Standish, seeing Distress for Rent written large across the page of the near future, was creeping out. "Come back and help us out of this watchbox, will yer?" Adding, as the clerk assisted him out of a capacious driving-coat of yellow cloth, with biscuit-sized mother-o'-pearl buttons:

"You look uncommon green, Standish, my boy—Standish's your name, ain't it?"

"Yes, Mr. Mortimer, sir. And—I am quite well, sir, thank you, sir. There's nothing the matter with me beyond ordinary."

He hung up the son's coat on the peg beneath the low-crowned, curly-brimmed beaver of the parent, and went out. Morty, retaining his own fashionable, shaggy headgear upon a skull of the bullet rather than the pear-shaped order, had forgotten the clerk and his sick face before the door closed behind him.

"Don't you worry about Standish and his looks, my boy!" said Thompson Jowell. "That's the way to spoil a good clerk, that is. Cock 'em up with an idea that they're overworked, next thing is they're in bed, and their wives—and why the devil they should have wives, when at that fellow's age I couldn't afford the luxury, beats me!—their wives are writing letters begging me not to stop the substitute's pay out of the husband's salary, because he, and she, and the children—and it's like their extravagance and presumption to have children when they can't afford to keep 'em!—will have to go to the Workhouse if you do. And why shouldn't they go to the Workhouse? What do we ratepayers keep it up for, if it ain't good enough for you, ma'am, and the likes of you and yours? My name being Tom Candid—that's what I say to her."

He had, in fact, said it to a suppliant of the proud, presumptuous class he complained of, only that morning. And now, as he blew out his big, pendulous cheeks and triple chin above their stiff circular frill of iron-gray whisker, his tall son took him by the shoulders and shook him playfully backwards and forwards in the grip of the great hands that were clothed with the extra-sized lemon kids, saying, as he regarded his affectionate parent with a pair of brown round eyes, that, with the narrow brain behind them, were a trifle bemused with liquor even at this early hour, yet wonderfully frank and honest for a son of Thompson Jowell's:

"You knowin' old File! You first-class, extra-ground, double-edged Shylock, you! You jolly old Fee-Faw-Fum, smellin' the blood of Englishmen, and grindin' their bones to make your bread—or the flour you sell to the British Government, and take precious jolly good care to sell dear!—you're lookin' in the prime of health and the pink of condition, and that's what I like to see!"

"Really, Morty! Truly, now, my dear boy?"

Morty nodded, with a cheerful grin, and Thompson Jowell's heart glowed with fatherly pride in this big young man with the foolish, good-natured face and the round, somewhat owlish eyes, that resembled his own, though not in their simplicity. But Morty's invariable and characteristic method of expressing frank admiration of those invaluable business qualities of unscrupulousness, greed, and cunning, which the author of his being, while fattening upon them, preferred to disown—was a venomed dart rankling in the fleshy ribs that were clothed by the gorgeous waistcoat. His narrow slanting forehead, that was like the lid of a Noah's Ark—furrowed as he heard. He said, with hurry and effort:

"Yes—yes! Well—well! And how did you come, dear boy?"

"Tooled the Tilbury with the tandem over from Norwood," Morty responded, "on purpose to have a good look at you. Lord Adolphus Noddlewood, my friend and chum at the Reverend's, came along too. Lots of fun on the way! Tre-menjous row with tollgate-keeper's wife at Camberwell Gate—Tollman, gone to bed, after bein' up all night, stuck his head out of upper-window in a red nightcap to tell us, if we ain't too drunk to remember it!—we're talkin', for once in our lives, to a decent woman.... (And you ought to ha' heard the names she'd called us!) ... 'Dolph, my boy,' says I to Lord Adolphus when we got into the Borough Road—and plenty of excitement there, with a leader that kep' tryin' to get into the omnibuses after the old ladies!... 'Dolph, my buck,' says I, 'I'm goin' to show you where the Guinea Tree grows.' 'Ha, ha, ha! That means,' says he to me, 'you're goin' to fly a kite among the Jews.' 'You're dead out there, Dolph!' says I. 'For one thing, the Gov' bleeds free. A touch of the lancet, and he brims the basin. For another—there isn't a Hebrew among the Ten Tribes, from Dan to Beersheba, 'ud dare to lend me a penny-piece on my tidiest signature for fear of what my father'd do when he found out they'd been gettin' hold of his precious boy! For, deep as they are, my father's deeper,' says I, 'and artful as they are, he's more artful still; and grinding and grasping extortioners as it's their nature to be, there's not a Jew among 'em that the Governor wouldn't give ninety points out of a hundred to, and beat at Black Pool—with the nigger in the pocket and a general shell-out all round! Ha, ha, haw! Whew!..." Morty whipped out a handkerchief of brilliant hue, diffusing odors of Araby, and applied it to his nose: "Piff! this here jolly old rat-hole of yours stinks over and above a bit. Why don't you burn it down?—you're inspired to the hilt, or I don't know you, dad! And take a smart, snug, comfortable office in Cheapside or Cornhill?"

"It wouldn't do! I began in this place, and have grown up here, as one might say, and have got too used to it to fancy another. And—be a little careful, Morty, my boy!" urged the father of this shining specimen, admiring the son's high spirit and volubility, yet suffering at his well-earned praise. He felt so keen a pride in this tall, bullet-headed, broad-shouldered, loosely-jointed son, that the tears stood in his round eyes as they goggled at him; and the upright gray hair upon his pear-shaped head bristled more stiffly. "Somebody outside there might be listening," he pleaded, "and that kind of joke's dangerous if repeated. Be careful, my dear boy!"

"If you mean careful of those tallow-faced, inky, chilblain-fingered chaps in the office outside this, and the room on the other side of the passage," said Morty, jerking up his coat-tails, and seating himself upon the large, important blotting-pad that lay upon the stained leather of the kneehole writing-table, that, with the iron safe previously mentioned; an armchair with loops of horsehair stuffing coming through the torn leather covering of its arms, and bulging through the torn leather covering of its back; a wooden stool adorned with a fantastic pattern of perforations; a dusty set of wooden pigeon-holes stuffed with dustier papers, and a bookcase containing Shipping-Lists, References, Handy Volumes, Compendiums, Ready Reckoners, and Guides, such as are commonly used by business men who chase the goose that lays the golden egg of Profit through the tortuous ways of Finance;—with a few more, likely to be of use to an Auxiliary-Transport Agent and Forage Contractor—comprised, with a blistered little yellow iron washstand, furtively lurking in a shady corner, the furniture of the office,—"if you mean those clerks of yours, you're joking when you talk of them repeating anything *they* hear. They know you too well, Gov! They've sold themselves to you, body and soul. For you're the Devil, Governor—the very Devil! Ain't you? Gaw! Don't tell me you ain't! I don't believe you!" said Morty, with a tinge of the paternal manner. "I won't believe you! I wouldn't believe you if you took a pair of wings (detachable patent), like what the Pasbas—there's a stunnin' creature!—sports in the new Opera Bally as the 'Sylph of the Silver Sham'—no, dammy!—that ain't it! 'Sylph of the Silver Strand'—out of your safe, and a harp and a crown out of the corner-cupboard by the fireplace"—a rusty, narrow fireplace, with a bent poker thrust in between the bars of the niggardly grate that had a smoking lump of coal in it—"and showed me," said Morty, with a gleam of imagination, "your first-class diploma as a qualified practicing Angel! And so you know!"

He poked Thompson Jowell in the meaty ribs that were covered by his gorgeous waistcoat, and though the hidden thorn rankled more and more, and though allusions to the personage mentioned seemed to savor of irreligion, the great man's brow relaxed, and he chuckled, as he rattled the money in the tills of his big trouser-pockets.

"And how goes the learning, Morty, with the reverend gentleman at Norwood? Does he seem to have his trade as Tutor at his fingers' ends? Does he push you on and prepare you? coach you and generally cram you with the things you ought to be master of? As a young fellow of means and expectations—who will shortly (or great people break promises!)—hold a Commission in Her Majesty's Foot Guards?"

"Oh, Lord!" groaned Morty. "Don't he, though?"

"This friend of yours you've brought with you is a swell, it seems?" resumed his father.

"Lord Adolphus Noddlewood ... I believe you, Gov!" returned the son, screwing up his round, young, foolish face into an expression of portentous knowingness. "Eldest son of the Marquess of Crumphorn—ain't that the tip-top thing?"

"Eldest son of the Marquess of Crumphorn! We'll look him up in the Peerage presently, or your mother shall—that's the sort of thing a woman enjoys doing," said Thompson Jowell, rather viciously, "and that keeps her from grizzling and groaning, and thinking herself an invalid."

"How is my mother, sir?" asked the son, with a shade of resentment at the other's slighting tone.

"She's pretty much the same as usual," said Thompson Jowell sourly, and ceased to puff himself out to double his natural size, and left off rattling the tills in his trousers, "or she was when I left her early this morning. A decent, worthy sort of woman, your mother," he added, snorting, "without any spirit or go in her. And as for setting off fine clothes and jewels, as the wife of a man in My position ought to—you might as well hang 'em on a pump. Indeed, you'd show 'em off to more advantage, because a pump can't retire into the background with a Dorcas work-basket and a Prayer-Book, and generally efface itself. It stops where it is,—and if it ain't a rattler as regards conversation, people do get some kind of response from it, if they're at the trouble of working the handle. Now, your mother——"

"My mother, sir, is as good company and as well worth looking at—in fine clothes or shabby ones—as any lady in the land!" said Morty. "I'm dam' if she ain't!" And so red and angry a light shone in the round brown eyes that were generally dull and lusterless, and so well-developed a scowl sat on the rather pimply forehead, from which the tall shaggy white beaver stove-pipe of the latest fashion was jovially tilted back, that Thompson Jowell changed the conversation rather hurriedly.

"Well, well! perhaps she is!" he agreed, in rather a floundering manner. "And if her own son didn't think so, who should? Run down to Market Drowsing and see her as soon as you're able. She won't come up to Hanover Square before the beginning of May. Give her compliments, along with mine, to the Honorable and Reverend Alfred de Gassey and Lady Alicia Brokingbole. There's a thorough-paced nob for you, the Honorable and Reverend! And his wife! The genuine hallmarked Thing, registered and stamped—that's what she is!"

He referred in these terms of unqualified admiration to a needy sprig of nobility who had held a commission in a Cavalry regiment; and, having with highly commendable rapidity run through a considerable fortune, had exchanged, some years previously, at the pressing instance of his creditors, the Army for the Church, and a family living which fell vacant at a particularly appropriate moment. And, having married another slip of the aristocracy as impecunious as himself, the Reverend Alfred had hit upon the philanthropic idea of enlarging his clerical stipend and benefiting Humanity at large, by receiving under his roof two or three young gentlemen of backward education and large fortune, who should require to be prepared for the brilliant discharge of their duty to their Sovereign and their country, as subaltern officers of crack regimental corps.

Not that preparation was essential in those days, when Army Coaches were vehicles as rare as swan-drawn water-chariots; and the cramming-establishments that were some years later to spring up like mushrooms on Shooter's Hill or Primrose Hill, or in the purlieus of Hammersmith or Peckham, were unknown. Ensigns of Infantry, or cornets of Cavalry Regiments, joined their respective corps without having received the ghost of a technical military education; often without possessing any knowledge whatever beyond a nodding acquaintance with two out of the three R's.... Mathematics, Fortification, French and German, were not imparted by the Honorable and Reverend Alfred to his wealthy pupils, for the simple reason that he, the instructor, was not acquainted with these. But in Boxing, Fencing, Riding, the clauses of the Code of Honor regulating the Prize Ring and the dueling-ground, not to mention the rules governing the game of Whist, at which the Reverend Alfred always won; he was a very fully-qualified tutor. And his wife, the Lady Alicia Brokingbole, youngest daughter of the Earl of Gallopaway, initiated the more personable of the young gentlemen into the indispensable art of handing chairs, winding Berlin wools, giving an arm to a lady, copying sweet poems from the *Forget-*

Me-Not or *The Keepsake* into her album, and generally making themselves useful and agreeable. Nor was the Lady Alicia averse to a little discreet flirtation, or a little game of piquet, or a little rubber of whist, at which, like the Reverend Alfred, she invariably won. It will be comprehended that, provided the bear-cub who came to Norwood to be licked into shape were rich, the said cub might spend a fairly pleasant time; and be regaled with a good deal of flattery and adulation, mixed with chit-chat, gossip, and scandal, of the most aristocratic and exclusive kind.

"She's a spankin' fine woman, is Lady Alicia," agreed Morty, with the air of a connoisseur, "though a dam' sight too fond of revokin' at whist with pound points to suit my book!" he added, with a cloud upon the brow that might have been more intellectual.

"But she's an Earl's daughter!—an Earl's daughter, Morty, my boy!" urged Thompson Jowell; "and moves in high Society, the very highest—or so I have been given to understand."

"Correct, too. Knows everybody worth knowin'—got the entire Peerage and *Court Circular* at her finger-ends," declared simple Morty. "I drove her four-in-hand from Norwood to the Row only yesterday. Gaw! You should have seen us! Bowin' right and left like China Manda—what-do-you-call-'ems?—to the most tre-menjous nobs (in coroneted carriages, with flunkeys in powder and gold lace) you ever clapped your eyes on! And you ought to hear her tell of the huntin' supper she sat down to at her cousin's castle in Bohemia—the chap's an Austrian Prince with a name like a horse's cough. Four-and-forty covers, two Crowned Heads, five Hereditary Grand-Dukes with their Duchesses, a baker's dozen of Princes, and for the rest, nothin' under a Count or Countess, 'until, Mr. Jowell,' she says, 'you arrived at Alfred, who would grace any social circle, however lofty, and poor little humble Me!' And they played a Charade afterwards, and Lady Alicia had no jewels to wear in the part of Cleopatra, 'having chosen,' she says, 'to wed for Love rather than Ambition.' And the Prince had an iron coffin brought in—or was it a copper?—cram-jam-full of diamonds and rubies as big as pigeons' eggs, and told her ladyship to take what she chose. 'Gaw! those sort of relatives are worth havin'! Shouldn't mind a few of 'em myself!' says I to Lady A."

"That's the sort of woman to cultivate, Morty, my boy!" advised Thompson Jowell, smiling and rubbing his hands. "With a little managing and cleverness, she ought to get you into the swim. The Goldfish Tank, I mean, where the titled heiresses are. You represent Money, solid Money!—but what we want—to set our Money off, is Rank! And the men of the British Aristocracy are easy enough to get at, and easy enough to get on with, provided you don't happen to tread on their damned exclusive corns. But their women, confound 'em!—their high-nosed, long-necked women—they're as hard to get on a level of chatty equality with as Peter Wilkins' flying females were; and the mischief of it is, my boy, you can't do without their good word. So cultivate Lady A! Wink at her cheating at cards—it's in the blood of all these tip-top swells—and get her to take you about with her. And one of these days we may be hearing how Lady Rosaline Jowell, second daughter of the Earl, or the Marquess, or the Duke of Something-or-other, was Presented, on her marriage with Mr. Mortimer Jowell, of the Foot Guards; and what sort of figure her husband cut at the Prince's Levée. And, by Gosh! though I don't keep a coffer full of diamonds as big as pigeons' eggs in my safe, we'll see what Bond Street can do in the way of a Tiara for the head, and a Zone for the waist, and a necklace and bracelets of the biggest shiners that can be got, for her Ladyship, Thompson Jowell's daughter-in-law! And what I say I'll do, I do! My name's Old Trusty, ain't it, Morty boy?"

His round eyes goggled almost appealingly at his son.

"And if I'm—what you say—a bit of a Squeezer as regards making people pay; and a bit of a Grinder—though that I don't admit—at driving hard bargains; and Mister Sharp of Cutters' Lane when it comes to getting the best of So-and-So, and Such-and-Such—who'd cheerfully skin me alive, only give 'em the chance of it—you're the last person in the world, Morty, who ought to throw it in my face."

He spoke with almost weeping earnestness; there were blobs of moisture in the corners of his eyes; his blustering Boreas-voice was almost soft and pleading as Thompson Jowell bid for the good opinion of his son. "Not that I reproach you," was the refrain of his song, "but you ought to be the last!"

"Old Gov!" The large young man repeated his previous action of taking Thompson Jowell by his fleshy shoulders with the extra-sized hands, encased in the lemon kid gloves, and pleasantly shaking him backwards and forwards, as though he had been a large, plain, whiskered doll.

"There's the Commission in the Guards, Morty. You wouldn't believe—having set my heart on making a first-class gentleman of my boy—what an uncommon sight of trouble I've taken to bring that sealed paper with Her Majesty's signature on it, down from the sky-high branch it hangs on! His Honor the Commissary-General kept his word in presenting me to my Lord Dalgan, His Grace the Commander-in-Chief's confidential Secretary, yesterday, and after a little general chit-chat, I felt my way to a hint, for we must be very humble with such great folks," said Thompson Jowell, rattling the tills, "and watch for times and opportunities. My Lord was very high and lofty with me, as you may suppose.... 'So you have a son, Mr. Thompson Jowell,' says he. 'I congratulate you, my dear sir, on having done your duty to Posterity. And it is your ambition that this young man should enjoy the privilege of wearing Her Majesty's uniform? Well, well! We will see what we can do with His Grace, Mr. Thompson Jowell, towards procuring the young gentleman an ensigncy in some regiment of infantry.' 'Humbly thanking you, my Lord,' says I, 'for the gracious encouragement you have given to a man who might be called by persons less grand, and noble, and generous-minded than your Lordship, an ambitious tradesman;—since you permit me to speak my mind'—and he bows over his stock in his stiff-necked, gracious way—'I dare to say I fly higher for my boy,' says I, 'than a mere marching regiment. And what I have set my heart upon, and likewise my son his, is, plainly speaking, a Commission in the Foot Guards, White Tufts or Cut Red Feathers.' Up go his eyebrows at that, Morty, and he taps with his shiny nails—a real nobleman's nails—on the carved arm of his chair, smiling. 'Really, Mr. Thompson Jowell'—and he leans back and throws his foot over his knee, showing the Wellington boot with gold spurs and the white strap of the pearl-gray trouser— 'ambition is, to a certain extent, laudable and to be encouraged. But at the same time, permit me to say that you *do* fly high!' 'Begging your Lordship's leave once more,' says I, 'to speak out—and Plain's my name and nature!— I have come to beg the greatest nobleman in the land to make a hay-and-straw-and-flour merchant's son a gentleman. A word in the ear of His Grace, the Duke, and a stroke of your pen will do it, my Lord,' I says; 'and when I find myself in the presence of a power as lofty and as wide as yours, and am graciously encouraged to ask a favor, I don't ask a little one that a lesser influence could grant. I plump for the Guards, and your Lordship can but refuse me!'"

"You clever old Codger! Rubbin' him down with a wisp of straw, and ticklin' him in all the right places.... But look here, you know!" objected Morty, with a darkening brow, "I don't half cotton to all that patter about making a gentleman of a merchant's son. Egad, sir, I'm dam' if I do like it!"

He sat upon the knee-hole table and folded his arms upon his waistcoat, a garment of brown velvet embroidered with golden sprigs, worn in conjunction with a satin cravat of dazzling green, peppered with scarlet horseshoes and adorned with pins of Oriental pearl; and blew out his round cheeks quite in the paternal manner as he shook his bullet head.

"You mustn't mind a bit of humble-pie, my boy!" pleaded Thompson Jowell, "seeing what a great thing is to be got by eating it, and looking as if you liked it. You don't suppose I'm any fonder of the dish than you are—

but it's for my son's sake; and so, down it goes! These stately swells will have you flatter 'em, stiff-necked, and fawn upon 'em, and lick their boots for 'em. They were born to have men cringe to 'em, and by Gosh, sir! can you stand upright and milk a cow at the same time? You can't, and you know it!—so you squat and whistle to her, and down comes the milk between your fingers, squish!"

"I ain't a dairymaid," asserted Morty sulkily.

"Not you!" said Thompson Jowell, beaming on him fondly. "And when your old Governor's willing to do the dirty work, why should you soil your hands?" His thick voice shook, and the tears stood in his goggle-eyes. "I'd lie down in the gutter so that those polished Wellingtons I spoke of just now should walk upon me dryshod—by Gosh, I would!" said Thompson Jowell—"if only I might get up again with golden mud upon me, to be scraped off and put away for you! Look here! You told your swell friend, Lord 'Dolph, your Governor was a generous bleeder. Well, so I am! I'll fill your pail to-day."

He whipped out his check-book, large and bulky like himself, and—Morty having condescendingly removed himself from the blotter—drew what that scion of his race was moved to term "a whacker" of a check. And sent him away gorged with that golden mud to which he had referred, and correspondingly happy; so that he passed through the larger, outer office, where seven pallid clerks were hard at work under the direction of a gray-faced elderly man who inhabited a little ground-glass-paneled sentry-box opening out of their place of bondage, with "Manager" in blistered letters of black paint upon the door,—like a boisterous wind tinged with stables, cigars, and mixed perfumery, and shed some drops of his shining store on them in passing.

"Look here, you chaps! See what the Old Man's stood me!" Morty flourished the pink oblong, bearing the magic name of Coutts'. Six of the seven pairs of eyes ravished from ledgers and correspondence, flared with desperate longing and sickened with impotent desire. Standish still kept his sea-green face downbent. And the gray Manager, peeping out of his glass case, congratulated as in duty bound.

"You're in luck again, Mr. Mortimer!... May I hope we see you well, sir?"

"First rate, Chobley! Topping condition!" Morty stuffed the check with lordly carelessness into a pocket in the gold-sprigged velvet vest, withdrawing a little ball of crackly white paper, which he jovially displayed between a finger and thumb attired in lemon kid.

"Twig this, hey? Well, it shall mean a dinner at the Albion in Drury Lane for the lot of you ... and an evenin' at the Play—if you ain't too proud for the Pit? Leave your wives at home!" the young reprobate advised, with a wink; "you're all too much married by a lot, hey, Chobley? And half-a-bottle of fizz apiece it ought to stand you in.... And see that beggar Standish drinks his share!... Catch!... Gaw!—what a butter-fingered beggar you are, Standish!".... The paper insult, flipped at ghastly Standish's lowered nose, smartly hit that feature, and rebounded into a letter-basket as Morty blustered out. The clerks looked at each other as the swing-doors banged and gibbered behind the young autocrat. They heard him hail Lord 'Dolph, heard the trampling and slipping of the tandem-horses' hoofs upon the uneven pavement; heard Morty cheerfully curse the groom,—heard, too, the final "Gaw!" with which the heir of the house of Jowell clinched the news of his good luck with his Governor; the hiss and smack of the tandem-whip, and the departing clatter of the tilbury westwards, to those regions where golden-haired sirens smile upon young men with monkeys in their pockets; and white-bosomed waiters dance attendance on their pleasure in halls of dazzling light.

Then said the gray-faced Manager, breaking the silence:

"I suppose, gentlemen, we had better do as Mr. Mortimer so kindly suggested? I presume that no one here is averse to theatrical exhibitions, or objects to a good dinner, washed down with the half-bottle of champagne the young gentleman liberally mentioned?"

"I prefer port!" said the hitherto silent Standish, in so strange a voice it seemed as though another man had spoken.

"Do you, egad?" said a fellow-clerk sniggeringly. "Perhaps you'll tell us why?"

"*Because it is the color of blood*," the pale drudge answered. He dipped his pen in the red ink as he spoke, and dived into his ledger again, and the face he bent over the closely-figured pages was yellow and sharp as a wedge of cheese.

Chobley, the Manager, had looked sharply at Standish when he had given voice to that strange reason for preferring the thick red wine. He had respectfully smoothed out the crumpled five-pound note, and folded it into a broad flat spill, and he scraped the pepper-and-salt bristles of his chin with it thoughtfully as he took his eyes away from the downcast, brooding face; and very shortly afterwards took himself, upon a sufficient business-excuse, into Thompson Jowell's room. And next morning Standish did not appear at the office in The Poultry, and thenceforwards the place upon the short-legged, horsehair-covered stool that had been his was occupied by another white-gilled toiler; and his frayed and ragged old black office coat vanished for good from its hook behind the door.

XVI

The mental picture Dunoisse had formed of the surroundings of Miss Smithwick turned out to be pleasantly remote from the reality.

The Hospice for Sick Governesses was a tall, prim, pale-faced family mansion in Cavendish Street, London, West, whose neat white steps led to a dark green door with a bright brass plate and a gleaming brass knocker, through a wide hall hung with landscape-paintings of merit and fine old engravings in black frames, up a softly-carpeted staircase to an airy, cheerful bedroom on the second floor, where with birds and fragrant flowers, and many little luxuries about her to which poor Smithwick in her desperate battle with adversity had for long been a stranger, the simple gentlewoman, grown a frail, white-haired, aged woman, lay in a pretty chintz-curtained bed, whose shining brasswork gave back the ruddy blaze of a bright wood fire, listening to the quiet voice of a capped, and caped, and aproned nurse, who sat on a low chair beside her, reading from a volume that lay upon her knee.

Dunoisse, from the doorway, to which he had been guided by an elderly woman, similarly capped, and caped, and aproned, and evidently prepared for the arrival he had announced by letter to his poor old friend, took in the scene before patient or nurse had become aware of his presence.

The voice that read was one of the rare human organs that are gifted to make surpassing melody of common ordinary speech. Soft, but distinct, through the dull roar of London traffic in the street below, every syllable came clearly. And the shabby leather-bound volume with the tarnished gilt clasps brought back old memories of Dunoisse's childhood. From its sacred pages he had been taught the noble English of Tyndale, following the traveling crochet-hook of simple Smithwick from Gospel text to text; and the words that reached him now had thus been made familiar; and they told of Heavenly pity and love for sorrowful, earth-born, Divinely-endowed humanity, and counseled brave endurance of the sufferings and sorrows of this world, for the sake of One all-sinless, Who drank of its bitter cup and wore its crown of thorns long, long before our stumbling feet were set upon its stony ways....

Dunoisse's elderly guide had turned away at the urgent summons of a bell, after knocking at the partly-open door and signing to the visitor to step across the threshold. He had waited there, listening to the soft, melodious cadences of the voice that read, for some moments before his presence was perceived. Then, his poor old friend cried out his name in a tremulous flutter of delight and agitation, and Dunoisse crossed the soft carpets to her bedside, and took her thin hand, and kissed her wrinkled forehead between the scanty loops of her gray hair. And the capped, and caped, and aproned nurse who had been reading, and had risen and closed the Book, and laid it noiselessly aside upon a table at the first moment of Miss Smithwick's recognition, said to him:

"The patient must not be over-excited, sir. You will kindly ring for assistance should she appear at all faint."

Then she went, with an upright carriage and step that rather reminded the visitor of the free, graceful gait of Arab women, out of the room, soundlessly shutting the door behind her.

"I did not tell her you were coming.... I so much wished that you should see her!... Dearest Hector! My own sweet Madame Dunoisse's beloved boy!" poor Smithwick tittered, and Hector kindly soothed her, being nervously mindful of the nurse's warning, the while she held his strong, supple, red hand in both her frail ones, and gazed into the man's face, wistfully looking for the boy.

He was not conscious of the old uncomfortable shrinking from poor Smithwick. Her nose was not so cold; her little staccato, mouselike squeaks of emotion were missing. Most of her sentimentalities and all of her affectations had fallen away from her with her obsolete velvet mantles and queer old trinkets, fallals of beads, and hair, and steel, and the front of brown curls that deceived nobody, and never even dreamed of trying to match the scanty knob behind. The honest, genuine, affectionate creature that she was and had always been, shone forth now.... For Death is a skillful diamond-cutter who grinds and slices flaws and blemishes away, and leaves, although reduced in size, a gem of pure unblemished luster, worthy to be set in Heaven's shining floor.

And now he was to learn the reason of her harsh dismissal, and to respect her worth yet more. She charged him with her affectionate humble duty to his father....

"Who, I trust, has long since pardoned me for what he well might deem presumption in venturing to judge his actions, and question his"— Smithwick hemmed—"strict adherence to the—shall I call it compact?— made with your dear mother, at the time when she conceived it her duty to resume the religious habit she had discarded under the influence of—of a passion, Hector, which has made many of my sex oblivious to the peculiar sacredness of vows." She added, reading no clear comprehension of her meaning in the brilliant black eyes that looked at her: "I refer to the

Marshal's unsuccessful attempt to obtain from His Serene Highness the Hereditary Prince of Widinitz recognition, and"—she hesitated—"acceptance of—yourself, dear boy, as the—in point of fact—the legitimate heir to his throne!"

"Can my father have conceived such a thing possible?" said Dunoisse, doubting if he had heard aright. "Can he have courted insult, rebuff, contempt, by making such an approach? Think again, dear friend! Is it not possible you may be mistaken? No hint of any such proceeding on my father's part has ever been breathed to me. I beg you, think again!"

Miss Smithwick shook her head and sighed, and said that there was no mistake at all about it. She had received her dismissal for—it might be presumptuously—venturing to expostulate, when the public prints made the matter a subject for discussion. It had been going on for some time previously; the comments of the principal newspapers of Widinitz, and of the leading Press organs of Munich and Berlin were largely quoted in the Paris journals which had enlightened Smithwick on the subject of her patron's plans. The cuttings she had preserved. They were in her desk, there upon the little table. Hector might see them if he would.... Her thin fingers hunted under the velvet-covered flaps of the absurd little old writing-box that her old pupil handed her; she followed the movements of the well-made manly figure in the loosely-fitting gray traveling-suit, with fond, admiring eyes. A blush made her old cheeks quite pink and young as she said:

"Forgive me, dear Hector!—but you have grown so handsome.... Has ... has no beautiful young lady told you so? With her eyes, at least, since verbally to commend the personal appearance of a gentleman would be unmaidenly and unrefined."

"You have lived too long out of France to remember, dear friend," said Hector, showing his small, square white teeth in a laugh of heart-whole amusement, "that young ladies, with us, are not supposed to have eyes at all!"

He forgot meek Smithwick for a moment, remembering an Arab girl at Blidah who had seemed to love him.... Adjmeh had been very pretty, with the great blue-black dewy eyes of a gazelle, and the hoarse cooing voice of a dove, despite the little indigo lilies and stars tattooed on her ripe nectarine-colored cheeks; on the backs of her slender, red-tipped hands, and upon the insteps of her slim arched feet, dyed also with henna; their ankles tinkling with little gold and silver coins and amulets, threaded on black silk strings similar to those bound about her tiny wrists, and plaited into the orthodox twenty-five tresses of her night-black hair....

Ah, yes! though at twenty she would be middle-aged, at thirty a wrinkled hag, Adjmeh was very pretty—would be for several years to come.... Who might be telling her so at that particular moment?... Dunoisse wondered, and then the conjured-up perfumes of sandal and ambergris grew faint; the orange glow of the African sunset faded from the flat, terraced roof of the little house at Blidah, the tinkle of the Arab *tambur* was nothing but the ring of a London muffin-man's bell—and Miss Smithwick was tendering him a little flat packet of yellowed clippings from the *Monarchie*, the *National*, the *Presse*, the *Patrie*....

Taking these with a brief excuse, Dunoisse moved to the window, and the cold gray light of the February morning fell upon the face that— conscious of the mingled anger and humiliation written upon it—he was glad to hide from the invalid. Recollections were buzzing in his ears like angry wasps, roused by the poking of a stick into their habitation, and each one had its separate sting. It is not agreeable to be compelled to despise one's father, and the last shred of the son's respect fell from him as he read.

The chief among the Paris newspapers from which the cuttings had been taken, bore the date of a day or two previous to that old boyish duel at the Technical School of Military Instruction. The conversation occurring between the Duke and his guests, which, as repeated by de Moulny, had produced the quarrel, had undoubtedly arisen through discussion of these.

Press organs of Imperial convictions upheld the action of the Marshal, denounced the policy of the reigning Prince of Widinitz, in rejecting the pretensions of his daughter's son, as idiotic and unnatural in an elderly hereditary ruler otherwise destitute of an heir. Legitimist journals sneered. Revolutionary prints heaped scorn upon the man, sprung from homely Swiss peasant-stock, who sought to aggrandize himself by degrading his son. The satirical prints had squibs and lampoons ... the *Charivari* published a fearful caricature of the Marshal, in his gorgeous, obsolete, Imperial Staff uniform, tiptoe on the roof of the Carmelite Convent of Widinitz in the attempt to reach down the princely insignia dangling temptingly above him, whilst the aureoled vision of Ste. Térèse vainly expostulated with the would-be marauder from clouds of glory overhead. The *Monarchie* quoted at length an article from a leading Munich newspaper. Judge whether or no the reader went hot and cold.

"We cannot sufficiently pity the son of the high-bred, misguided, repentant lady, doomed in the green bough of inexperienced youth to be the tool of an unprincipled and unscrupulous adventurer, the handful of mud flung in the face of a Bavarian Catholic State, whose rulers have for centuries rendered to Holy Mother Church the most profound respect, and the most duteous allegiance."

"Nom d'un petit bonhomme!..."

The old, boyish, absurd expletive hissed impotently on the glowing coals of the man's fierce indignation, quenching them not at all. The writer continued:

"He who thought little of dragging the pallet from under the dying peasant, whose greed has locked and bolted the doors of the Carmelite House of Mercy in the faces of the sick and suffering poor, now lays desecrating hands upon the princely mantle, covets the hereditary and feudal scepter for his base-born son, adding to the impudent dishonesty of the Swiss innkeeper the vulgar braggadocio and swaggering assurance of the paid hireling of the Corsican usurper, who dared to mount the sacred throne of St. Louis; who presumed to adulterate with the plebeian blood of a Beauharnais the patrician tide flowing in the veins of a daughter of the reigning House of Wittelsbach."

Dunoisse's face was not pleasant to see, as, perusal ended, he set his small white teeth viciously upon his lower lip, and, breathing vengeance upon unknown offenders through his thin, arched nostrils, scowled menacingly at the smug-faced, genteel houses on the opposite side of Cavendish Street. His father's boast about the "blood royal" came back to him, and that "fine Serene Highness" the Marshal had promised those good people of Widinitz. Ah! what an infamy the whole thing had been! But at least one might count it buried; forgotten like these perishing strips of discolored, brittle paper. That was something to be thankful for.

He cleared his forehead of its thunder-clouds, and turned back towards the bed, but something of the ordeal of shame he had passed through was written on his face for Smithwick, in spite of the smile with which he dressed it, as he silently laid the yellowed fold of cuttings on the coverlet near her hand.

"They—they have given you pain?" faltered the poor lady.

"It is past and over, dear friend. These paragraphs have cleared up something that was obscure to me before," said Dunoisse—"conveyed a hint of *his* that was never again made. One cannot pretend to judge him. He has always been a law unto himself."

The bitterness of the words, and the ironical smile that curved the speaker's lips as he uttered them, were lost upon the simple woman who answered:

"I have always felt that. There are characters so highly elevated above the crowd of ordinary individuals, that one can hardly expect them to be influenced by the ordinary considerations, the commonplace principles that guide and govern the rest of us——"

"Fortunately for ourselves!" interpolated Dunoisse.

"—That, my dear, we who know ourselves their inferiors in intellect, as in personal advantages, cannot pretend to judge them," finished the poor lady.

"And in proportion with the baseness of their motives and the mean selfishness of their aims," said Dunoisse, "the admiration of their more moral and upright fellow-creatures would appear to be lavished upon them."

"Too true, I fear, my dear Hector," admitted Miss Smithwick, flushing inside the neat frills that bordered her cap. "But had you beheld your father in the splendor of his earlier years, you would"—she coughed—"have perhaps regarded the devotion with which it was his fate to inspire persons of the opposite sex, with greater leniency and tolerance."

"How did his path cross my mother's?" asked Dunoisse, amused, in spite of himself, at the unremitting diligence with which the Marshal's faithful votary availed herself of every opportunity that presented itself, to spread a brushful of gilding on her battered idol. "I have often wondered, but never sought to learn."

"During the last years of the Emperor Napoleon's sequestration at St. Helena, my dear, your father, chafing at the lack of public appreciation which his great talents should have commanded, and his distinguished martial career certainly had earned, found distraction and interest in traveling as a private gentleman through the various countries he had visited in a less peaceful character. And, during a visit to the country estate of a Bavarian nobleman, whose acquaintance he had made during—unless I err—the second campaign of Vienna, as the result of one of those accidents which so mold our after-lives, Hector, that one cannot doubt that Destiny and Fate conspire to bring them about, he crossed your mother's path."

"To her most bitter sorrow and her son's abiding shame!" commented Dunoisse, but not aloud.

"There is, or was, in the neighborhood of Widinitz—I speak of the capital of the Bavarian Principality of that name," went on Miss Smithwick, "a House of Mercy—under the management of nuns of the Carmelite Order, whose Convent adjoins the Hospital—now closed in consequence of the withdrawal from its Endowment Fund of a sum so large that the charitable institution was ruined by its loss."

Hector knew well who had brought about the ruin. He sat listening, and kept his eyes upon the carpet, lest the fierce wrath and scathing contempt that burned in them should discompose the Marshal's faithful partisan.

"One day in the autumn of 1820," said Miss Smithwick—"the Prince having ridden out early with all his Court and retinue to hunt—a gentleman was brought to the Widinitz House of Mercy on a woodman's cart. He had been struck upon the forehead and thrown from his saddle by an overhanging branch as he rode at full speed down a forest road. The Hunt swept on after the boar-hounds—the insensible man was found by two peasants and conveyed to the Hospital, as I have said. The nun in charge of the Lesser Ward—chiefly reserved for the treatment of accidents, my dear, for there were many among the peasants and woodcutters, and quarrymen, and miners—and to meet their great need the House of Mercy, had been founded by a former Prioress of the Convent—the nun in charge was Sister Térèse de Saint Francois...."

"My mother. Yes?..."

Dunoisse had spoken in a whisper. His eyes shunned gentle Smithwick's. He sat in his old, boyish attitude leaning forwards in his chair, his clasped hands thrust downwards between his knees; and those hands were so desperately knotted in the young man's fierce, secret agony of shame and anger, that the knuckles started, lividly white in color, against the rich red skin.

"There is no more to tell, my dear!" said Miss Smithwick. "You can conceive the rest?"

"Easily!" said Dunoisse. "Easily! And, knowing what followed, one is tempted to make paraphrase of the Scripture story. Had the Samaritans passed by and left the wounded man to what you have called Fate and Destiny, the cruses of oil and wine would not have been drained and broken, the House of Mercy would not have been ransacked and gutted; its virgin despoiled—its doors barred in the faces of the dying poor." He laughed, and the jarring sound of his mirth made his meek hearer tremble. "It is a creditable story!" he said, "a capital story for one to hear who bears the name *he* so willingly makes stink in the nostrils of honorable men. For if I have Carmel in my blood—to quote his favorite gibe—I have also *his*. And it is a terrible inheritance!"

"Oh! hush, my dear! Remember that he is your father!" pleaded poor Smithwick.

"I cannot forget it," said Dunoisse, smiling with stiff, pale lips. "It is a relationship that will be constantly brought home. When I see you lying here, and know what privations you must have endured before the charitable owners of this house opened its doors to you, and realize that *his* were shut because you strove to open his eyes to the precipice of shame towards which his greed and ambition were hurrying him, blindly, I ask myself whether, with such Judas-blood running in my own veins, and such a heritage of gross desires and selfish sensuality as it must bring with it!—whether it be possible for me, his son, to live a life of cleanliness and honor? And the answer is——"

"Oh! yes, my dear!" cried the poor creature tearfully. "With the good help of God! And have you not been honorable and brave, Hector, in refusing any portion of—that money?" She added, meeting Dunoisse's look of surprise: "Do you wonder how it is I know? Your father wrote and told me—it is now years ago—I hope you will not blame him!—though the letter was couched in terms of reproach that wounded me cruelly at the time...." Smithwick felt under her pillow for her handkerchief and dried her overflowing eyes.

"What charges did he bring against you?" Dunoisse asked, controlling as best he could the contempt and anger that burned in his black eyes, and vibrated in his voice.

"He said I had revenged myself for the withdrawal of his patronage, and my removal from his service," gulped poor Smithwick, "by poisoning the mind of his only child! He complained that you refused to touch a franc of his money—preferring to work your way upwards under heavy disadvantages, rather than accept from him, your father, any portion of the fortune he had always meant should be yours. And"—she put her handkerchief away and nodded her head in quite a determined manner—"I wrote back and told him, Hector—that I esteemed your course of conduct, though my counsels had not inspired it; and that your mother, when she learned of your determination, would be proud of her noble son!"

Dunoisse would have spoken here, but Smithwick held up her thin hand and stopped him.

"For it seems to me, dear child of my dearest mistress, that to take what has been given to God, is the way to call down the just judgment of Heaven upon the heads of those who are guilty of such deeds," said Smithwick, nodding her mild gray head emphatically. "And, rather than live in gilded affluence upon those funds, wrested from the coffers of the Carmelite House of Charity at Widinitz, I would infinitely prefer to carry on existence—as I have done, dear Hector—until my health failed me in my attic room at Hampstead, on a penny roll a day. And she would uphold me and agree with me."

"Who is *she*, dear friend?" asked Hector, smiling, though his heart was sore within him at the picture of dire need revealed in these utterances of the simple lady.

"I speak of our Lady Superintendent.... A remarkable personality, my dear Hector, if I may venture to say so.... It was she who, finding this benevolent charity suffering from mismanagement and lack of funds, endowed it with a portion of her large fortune, induced other wealthy persons to subscribe towards endowing the foundation with a permanent income, and, finding no trustworthy person of sufficient capacity to fill the post, herself assumed the duties of Resident Matron. Imagine it, my dear!" said gentle Smithwick. "At her age—for she is still young—possibly your senior by a year or two, certainly not more—to forego Society and the giddy round of gilded pleasure to be found in London and dear, dear Paris!— for the humdrum routine of a Hospital; the training and management of nurses; the regulation of prescriptions, diets, and accounts!"

"Indeed! A vocation, one would say!" commented Dunoisse.

"She would ask you," returned Miss Smithwick, "must one necessarily be a nun to work for the good of others?"

The words stirred a dim recollection in Dunoisse of having heard them before. But the image of the Lady Superintendent of the Hospice for Sick Governesses formed itself within his mind. He saw her as a plain, sensible, plump little spinster, well advanced towards the thirties, resigned to exchange hopeless rivalries with other young women, not only rich, but pretty, for undivided rule and undisputed sway over a large household of dependents.... preferring the ponderous compliments of Members of Visiting Committees to the assiduities of impecunious Guardsmen and money-hunting detrimentals. He said, as the picture faded:

"This lady who has been so kind to you——"

"'Kind.'... The word is feeble, my dear Hector, to express her unbounded goodness," declared Miss Smithwick. "I can but say that in the midst of sickness, and dire poverty, and other distresses that I will not further dwell on, she came upon me like an Angel from the Heaven in which I firmly believe. And when I lay down my head, never to lift it up again—and I think, my dear, the time is not far off now!—that great and solemn hour that comes to all of us will be cheered and lightened, Hector, if she stands beside my pillow and holds my dying hand."

The simple sincerity of the utterance brought tears into the listener's eyes. He winked them back, and said:

"I pray the day you speak of may not dawn for years! My leave, procured with difficulty owing to threatening national disturbances which the Army may be employed in quelling, extends not beyond three days. I shall hope to see this lady, and thank her for her goodness to my friend before I go."

"I trust she will permit it. She is very reticent—almost shrinking—in her desire to avoid recognition of her...."

Miss Smithwick broke off in the middle of her sentence. She leaned back upon her pillows, lividly pale, breathing hurriedly; her blue lips strove to say: "It is nothing. Don't mind!"

Alarmed for her, repentant for having forgotten the nurse's warning, Dunoisse grasped at the bell-rope by the fireplace, and sent an urgent summons clanging through the lower regions of the tall house. Within a moment, as it seemed, the door opened, admitting the capped, and caped, and aproned young woman who had been reading to the patient upon his arrival. A glance seemed to show her a condition of things not unexpected. She went swiftly to the bedside, answering, as Dunoisse turned to her appealingly, the words shaping themselves upon his lips that asked her: "Shall I go?"

"It will be best!... Wait at the end of the passage, near the window on the landing.... This looks alarming," she answered—"but it will not last long."

XVII

She had forgotten him before the still pure air of the sick-room had ceased to vibrate with her spoken words. She saw nothing but the patient in need of her, and had passed her arm beneath the pillow and was raising the gray head, and had reached a little vial and a measuring-glass from a stand that was beside the bed, before Dunoisse had gained the door. It might have been five minutes later, as he contemplated a vista of grimy, leaded roofs, and cowled, smoke-vomiting chimney-pots, from the staircase-window at the passage-end, that he heard a light rustling of garments passing over the thick soft carpets, and she came to him, moving with the upright graceful carriage and the long, gliding step that had reminded him of the gait of the tall supple Arab women, whose slender, perfect proportions lend their movements such rhythmic grace. He said to her eagerly, as she stopped at a few paces from him:

"Mademoiselle, you see one who is gravely to blame for forgetfulness of your wise warning. I beg you, hide nothing from me!... Is my dear old friend in danger? Her color was that of Death itself."

"There is always danger in cases of heart-disease."

"Heart-disease.... She said no word to me upon the subject. But it is like her," said Dunoisse, "to conceal her sufferings rather than distress her friends."

"She has needed friends, and the help that prosperous friendship could have well afforded to bestow, believe me, sir, in these late years of uncomplaining want and bitter privation."

The voice that spoke was sweet; Dunoisse had already recognized in it that quality. Barely raised above an undertone—presumably for the sake of other sufferers within the neighboring rooms that opened on the landing, from behind the shut doors of which came the murmur of voices, or the clinking of cups and saucers, or the sound of fires being poked,—this voice had in its clear distinctness the ring of crystal; and the fine edge of scorn in it cut to the sensitive quick of the listener. He started as he looked at her, meeting the calm and clear and steady regard of eyes that were blue-gray as the waters of her own English Channel, and seemed as cold....

For they condemned him and judged him, the rich man's son, who had left the old dependent to the charity of strangers. His shamed blood tingled under his red-brown skin, as he said, with a resentful flash of his black eyes:

"That this good woman, the faithful guardian of my motherless boyhood, has suffered want, is to my bitter regret, to my abiding poignant sorrow, but not to my shame. A thousand times—no!"

He was so vivid and emphatic, as he stood speaking with his back to the window, that, with his foreign brilliancy of coloring, the slightness of form that masked his great muscular strength, the supple eloquence of gesture that accompanied and emphasized his clear and cultivated utterance, he seemed to glow against the background of rimy February fog, and London roofs and chimney-pots, as a flashing ruby upon gray velvet; as a South American orchid seen in relief against a neutral-tinted screen. His "No!" had a convincing ring; the lightning-flash of his black eyes was genuine fire, not theatrical; the woman who heard and saw had been born with the rare power of judging and reading men. Her broad white forehead cleared between the silken folds of her hair, pale nut-brown, with the gleam of autumn gold upon the edges of its thick waved tresses; the lowered arches of her brown eyebrows lifted and drew apart, smoothing out the fold between them; the regard of her blue-gray eyes ceased to chill; the delicate stern lines of her sensitive mouth relaxed. She knew he spoke the truth.

He saw a tall, slight, brown-haired woman in a plain and, according to the voluminous fashion of the time, rather scanty gown of Quakerish gray, protected by a bibbed white apron with pockets of accommodating size. A little cape of stuff similar to that of the gown covered her shoulders. Their beauty of line, like the beauty of the long rounded throat that rose above her collar of unadorned white cambric, the shapeliness of the arms that were covered by her plain tight sleeves, the slender rounded hips and long graceful proportions of the lower limbs, were enhanced rather than hidden by the simplicity of her dress; as the admirable shape and poise of the small rounded head was undesignedly set off by the simple, close-fitting, white muslin cap, with its double frill and broad falling lappets.

Her calmness seemed immobility, her silence indifference to Dunoisse. Her hands were folded upon her apron, her bosom rose and fell to the time of her deep even breathing, her steady eyes regarded him as he poured himself out in passionate denial, fierce repudiation of the odious stigma of ingratitude, but she gave no sign of having heard. She looked at him, and considered, that was all. He said, galled and irritated by her unresponsiveness:

"I should ask pardon of you, Mademoiselle, for my vehemence, incomprehensible to you and out of place here. What I seek is a private audience of the lady who is Directress of this charitable house. Would she favor me by granting it? I would promise not to detain her. Could you graciously, Mademoiselle——"

She said, with her intent eyes still reading him:

"I should tell you it is the rule of this house that no attendant in it should be addressed as 'Mademoiselle,' 'Miss,' or 'Mrs.' ... 'Nurse' is the name to which we all answer, and we try to deserve it well."

Her smile wrought a radiant, lovely change in her that evoked his unwilling admiration. The pearl-white teeth it revealed shone brilliant in the light of it, and the dark blue-gray eyes flashed and gleamed like sapphires between their narrowed lids. But the next moment she stood before him as pale and grave as she had seemed to him before, with her white hands folded on her white apron.

"You do deserve that title, I am sure," said Dunoisse, "if you minister to all your patients as kindly and as skillfully as to my poor friend there." He added: "Forgive me, that I detain you here, when you may be needed by her bedside!"

He motioned towards the door of the room he had quitted, receiving answer:

"Do not be alarmed. Another nurse is with her. She was in the adjoining room; I called her to take charge before I came to you. And—you were desirous of an interview with our Superintendent here.... She sees few people, the nature of her responsibilities permitting little leisure.... I cannot bring you any nearer to her than you are now. But if you could trust me with the message you desire to send, or the explanation you wish to make, I will give you my promise that your exact words shall be conveyed to her. Will that do?"

Dunoisse bowed and thanked her, with some shadow of doubt upon his square forehead, a lingering hesitation in his tone.

"If you were older, Mademoiselle——" he began, forgetful of her injunction, as he hesitated before her. She looked at him, and her lips curved into their lovely smile again, and her blue-gray eyes were mirthful as she said:

"I am older than you are, M. Dunoisse. Does not that fact give you confidence?"

"It should," returned Dunoisse, "if it were possible of credence."

"Compliments are a currency that does not pass within these doors," she answered, with a fine slight accent of irony and a tincture of sarcasm in her smile. "Keep yours for Society small-change in the *salons* of Paris or the drawing-rooms of Belgravia. They are wasted here."

"I know but little," said Dunoisse, "of the *salons* of London and Paris. Circumstances have conspired to shut the doors of Society, generally open to welcome rich men's sons, as completely in my face as in that of any other ineligible. You will learn why, since you are so kind as to undertake to convey a message from me to the Superintendent of this house. It shall be as brief as I can make it. I would not willingly waste your time."

She bent her head, and the high-bred grace perceptible in the slight movement appealed to him as exquisite. But he was too earnest in his desire for justification to be turned aside.

"Say to this lady whose charitable hand has lifted my dear old friend—from what depths of penury I only now begin to realize—that if she comprehends that I was a boy at a Military School, and ignorant, thoughtless, and selfish as boys are wont to be, when my good old governess was driven from the house that had been for years her home, and that her dismissal was so brought about that she seemed but to be leaving us upon a visit of condolence to a sick relative, she will judge me less harshly, regard me with less contempt than it may seem to her, now, I deserve!——"

His hearer stopped him:

"You should be told, M. Dunoisse, that all that can be said in your favor has been already said by Miss Smithwick herself. It never occurred to her to reproach you. Nor for her dismissal can you be blamed at all. But it has seemed to me that where there was ability to provide for one so tried and faithful, some effort should have been made in her behalf by you as you grew more mature, and the ample means that are placed at the disposal of a rich man's son were yours to use. She never told you of her cruel need, I can guess that. But oh! M. Dunoisse! you might have read Hunger and Cold between the lines of the poor thing's letters."

There were tears in the great sorrowful blue-gray eyes. Her calm voice shook a little.

"If you had seen her as she was when I was sent to her," she said, "you would feel as I do. True, a letter with a remittance from you came when she was nearly past needing any of the help it contained for her. But long, long before, you might have read between the lines!"

"Ah!—in the Name of Heaven, Mademoiselle, I pray you hear me!" burst out Dunoisse, catching at the carved knob of the baluster at the stair-head, and wringing it in the energy of his earnestness. "All that you suppose is true! Even before I came of age a large sum of money was placed at my disposal by my father. Over a million of our francs, forty-five thousand of your English sovereigns, lie to my credit in the bank, have so lain for years. May the hour that sees me spend a *sou* of that accursed money be an hour of shame for me, and bitterness and humiliation! And should ever a day draw near, that is to see me trick myself in dignities and honors stolen by a charlatan's device, and usurp a power to which I have no more moral right than the meanest peasant of the State it rules—before its dawning I pray that I may die! and that those who come seeking a clod of mud to throw in the face of a Catholic principality, may find it lying in a coffin!"

He had forgotten that he addressed himself to a stranger, so wholly had his passion carried him away. He awakened to her now, seeing her recoil from him as though repelled by his vehemence, and then conquer her impulse and turn to him again.

"Pardon!" He held up his hand to check her as she was about to speak. "I speak, in my forgetfulness, of things incomprehensible to you. I employ names that are unmeaning. These have no part in the message I entreat you of your goodness to bear to the Superintendent of this house. Could it not be made clear to this lady, without baring to the vision of a stranger the disgrace of one whom I am bound to respect, and would that it were possible! Could it not be understood that this money was gained in a discreditable, vile, and shameful way? Could it not be understood that I shall never rest until it has been returned to the original source whence it was unjustly plundered and wrung? Could it not be made clear that while I was yet a boy I swore a solemn oath before Almighty God, at the instance of a friend—who afterwards cast me off and deserted me!—that this restitution should be made?... Might it not be explained that I have had nothing, since I took that oath, that was not earned by my own efforts? That I could take no holidays from the Technical School where I was a cadet, because I could not afford to buy civilian clothes, and that, until by good fortune I earned rewards and prizes and a period of free tuition at the Training Institute for Officers of the Staff—that many of my comrades deserved better, I do not doubt!—I was very, very poor, Mademoiselle! Would it not be possible?"

"Yes, yes!"—she answered him, and her pale cheeks had grown rosy as apple-blossoms, and her great gray-blue eyes were full of kindness now. "It shall all be explained. You shall be no longer blamed where you are praiseworthy, and reproached where you should be honored. And—two breaches of faith—a double perjury—are worse than one, though a lower standard of honor than yours would have taken your false friend's desertion as a release. You have done well to keep your oath, M. Dunoisse, though he may have broken his."

"I deserve no praise," said Dunoisse, "and I desire none. I ask for justice—it is the right of every human soul; I beg you to repeat to this benevolent lady what I have said, and to tell her that I will be answerable for whatever charges she has been put to, for the medical attendance and support of my dear old friend, from to-day. It is a sacred duty which I will gladly take upon myself."

"Forgive me," said the listener, and her voice was very soft, "but would not this be a heavy tax on your resources?—a heavy drain upon your slender means?"

He listened, with his black eyes seeming to study an engraving that hung upon the staircase wall. She ended, and he looked at her again.

"It would be a tax, and a drain under ordinary circumstances, but I think I can insure a way to meet the difficulty.... Is it possible that I may be permitted to say Adieu to my old friend before I leave this house? It will be necessary—now!—that I should return to France by the packet that sails to-night."

He was more than ever like a slender ruddy flame as he glowed there against the dull background of marble-papered wall and foggy window-panes. His virile energy, the hard clear ring of his voice, the keen flash of his black eyes won her rare approval, no less than his reticence and his delicacy. Her own eyes were more than kind, though in the respect of his seeing Miss Smithwick again that day her decision was prohibitory. He bowed to the decision.

"Then you shall say *Adieu* and *Au revoir* to her for me," he said, and held out his hand with a smiling look and a quick, impulsive gesture. "And for yourself, Mademoiselle, accept my thanks."

He added, retaining the hand she had placed in his:

"You will not fail of your promise to repeat to Madame the Superintendent all that I have confided to you?"

"You have my word," she answered him. "But of one thing I must warn you—if you send any money, she will send it back!"

"Name of Heaven!—why?" exclaimed Dunoisse.

"Because," she said, with a slight fold between her arched brown eyebrows, "your friend has been accepted by the Committee as a permanent inmate here, and there is no lack of funds. I must really go now if you will be so good as to release me!"

Dunoisse was still jailer of the hand she had given, and his grip, unconsciously strenuous, was responsible for that fold of pain between the nurse's eyebrows. He released the hand with penitence and distress, saying:

"I entreat you to forgive me if I have hurt this kind hand, that has alleviated so much pain, and smoothed the pillows of so many death-beds." But his lips, only shaded by the little upward-brushed black mustache, had barely touched her fingers before she drew them gently from his, saying with a smile:

"There is no need for atonement, M. Dunoisse. As for this kiss upon my hand, I will transfer it with your message of farewell to your dear old governess. My good wishes will follow you with hers, wherever you may go!"

She was gone, moving along the passage and vanishing into a room half way down its length before a bell rang somewhere in the lower regions of the house, a voice spoke to Dunoisse, and he brought back his eyes, that had been questing in search of another, to see the capped and caped and aproned elderly woman, who had a round, brown smiling face, somewhat lined and wrinkled, smooth gray hair, and pleasant eyes of soft dark hazel, waiting to lead him downstairs as she had guided him up. To her he said, as she opened the street-door upon the foggy vista of Cavendish Street:

"Be so good, Madame, as to tell me the name of the Lady Superintendent here?"

The elderly attendant answered promptly:

"Merling, sir! Miss Ada Merling."

Where had Dunoisse heard that name before? He racked his brain even as he said, with the smile that showed his small, square white teeth and made his black eyes gleam more brightly:

"I must be once more troublesome, if you will allow me. What is the name of the lady to whom I was talking just now?"

The elderly attendant answered, in precisely the same form of words:

"Merling, sir: Miss Ada Merling."

XVIII

The front-door of the Hospice for Sick Governesses in Cavendish Street had not long closed behind the retreating figure of a swarthy, black-eyed young foreign gentleman when the pleasant-faced elderly woman whose duty it was to answer its bell brought to the Lady Superintendent a card upon a little inlaid tray. She took the card and smiled.

"Tell Mr. Bertham that I will come down in a few minutes. And I hope you did not call him 'Master Robert' this time, Husnuggle?"

"I did, Miss Ada, love, as sure as my name's a queer one, and him a Secretary of State at War."

"He is not Secretary at War now, Husnuggle, though he may be again. Who can tell, when Governments are always changing and Cabinets being made and remade?"

"A-cabinet-making he went as a boy, and cut his fingers cruel, and the Wraye Abbey housekeeper fainted dead away at the sight of the blood, they said!—and the head-house-maid gave notice at being asked for cobwebs, which she vowed and declared not one were to be found in the place, though answer for attics how can you? And he had my name pat, Miss Ada, so soon as I answered the door. 'Halloa, Husnuggle!' he says; 'so you've come up from Peakshire to help nurse the sick governesses?' And I says: 'Yes, Master Robert, and it's like the good old times come back, to see your handsome, smiling face again.' And you'll come to him in a few minutes?"

"The minutes have passed, Husnuggle, while you have been talking. I am going down to Mr. Bertham now."

She found him in a little ground-floor parlor, sacred to accounts and the semi-private interviews accorded by the Lady Superintendent to shabby-genteel visitors with hungry faces (growing still more wan as the tale of penury was told) and smartish visitors with impudent faces, apt to flush uncomfortably under the keen scrutiny of those blue-gray eyes. It was plainly but comfortably furnished, and a red fire glowed in its grate of shining steel, and a plump and sleek and well-contented cat dozed happily upon its hearthrug.

You saw Bertham as a tall, lightly-built man of barely thirty, with a bright, spirited, handsome face and a frank, gay, cordial manner. No trace of the pompousness of the ex-Secretary of State either in his appearance, voice or handshake: a warm and cordial grip was to be had from Bertham;

or, in default of this, a brusque nod that said: "You are objectionable, and I prefer to keep clean hands!"

He was striding lightly up and down the little parlor, with the loose ends of his black satin cravat—voluminous, according to the fashion of the time—floating behind him; and each time he covered the distance from the hearthrug to the muslin-blinded window he would stop, look impatiently at his watch, and recommence his walk.

She said, standing in the doorway, watching him do this:

"You are not in a genuine hurry, or you would not be here at all."

"Ada!" He turned with a look of glad relief, and as she noiselessly closed the door and came to meet him, he took both the womanly cordial hands she held out to him, and pressed them in his own. "It does one good to see you. It does one good even to know you anchored here in Cavendish Street, and not flying from Berlin to Paris, from Paris to Rome, from Rome to Heaven-knows-where—comparing foreign systems of Hospital management and sanitation with our own, and finding ours everywhere to be hopelessly out of date, and inferior, and wrong...."

"As it is!" she said—"And is it not time we knew it? so that we can prove those mistaken who say, *To be insular is to be strong, perhaps, but at the same time it is to be narrow-minded.*"

"Ah! Ada, Ada!" he said, and his sweet and mellow voice had sadness in it. "If we all lived up to your standard, the Millennium would have come, and Governments would cease from troubling, and War Secretaries would be at rest."

"Are you not at rest just now?" she asked, and added, even before he shook his head: "But no! You are overworked; your face shows it."

"Mary said so this morning," he answered; "but if my looks pity me, as Peakshire folk would say, I feel fit and well."

"Where is my Mary?" she asked. "Why have you not brought her?"

"Mary has flown down to Hayshire," he said, "on the wings of the Portsmouth Express. One of the crippled children at the Home was to be operated on, under chloroform, for the removal of a portion of diseased hip-bone; and though my wife shrank from the ordeal of seeing pain, even dulled by the anæsthetic, she felt it was her duty to be upon the spot."

"Dear Mary!" she said, and if Dunoisse had seen her face he would no longer have thought it lacking in warmth and color: "True, good, noble woman."

Bertham answered, with feeling in his own face and voice:

"The dearest, living!... the noblest I ever knew—but one, Ada!"

She passed the words as though she had not heard, and said, with the soft, clear laugh that had music in it for the ears of those who loved her, and this man was one of the many:

"Husnuggle was made so happy by your not forgetting her, poor good soul!"

"Her face conjured up Wraye Rest," he said, "and the yew-tree gateway between the park and the garden; and the green terraces with the apple-espaliers and the long borders of lavender-bushes; and Darth down at the bottom of the deep valley, foaming over her bed of limestone rock, and the steep paths down to the trout-pools that were easier to tread than the slippery ways of Diplomacy."

"One can always go back!" she returned, though her sigh for all the distant sweetness had echoed his, "either to my dear Wraye Rest or your own peculiar Eden of Wraye Abbey."

"Taking our respective loads of aims and ambitions and responsibilities with us," said Bertham. "My badly-housed Military Invalid Pensioners for whom I want tight roofs, and dry walls, and comfortable beds. My Sandhurst Cadets, trussed up in absurd trappings, and harassed with rules as trumpery—hide-bound with conditions quite as detrimental to health as their cut-and-dried discipline, and innumerable supererogatory belts, straps, and buckles. My Regimental Schools, where illiterate soldiers and their wives are to learn to read and write and cipher; and my Infants' Classes, where the soldier's children may be taught as well. My Improved Married Quarters, which should—but do not, more's the pity!—occupy a separate block in every Barracks in the Kingdom, where the women and their men may live in decent privacy, and not under conditions not at all distantly recalling—to our shame! and the Red Tapeism that preserves these conditions in their unadorned and ancient ugliness ought to blush the redder for it!—the primitive promiscuities of the Stone Age. With a distinct bias in favor of that period!"

His handsome face was bitter and dark with anger; his voice, though barely raised above the level of ordinary fireside chat, rang and vibrated with passionate indignation.

"It has been borne in on me, Ada, in God knows how many hours of weariness and bitter disappointment, that our Peninsular triumphs—achieved in what we are accustomed to call the good old days—are a heavy clog upon our advancement as a nation now, and a cloud upon our eyes. They were not good old days, Ada, as windbaggy orators like to call them; they were bad old days, inhuman old days, cruel old days, when Napoleon Bonaparte possessed France upon a bridal bed of bloody corpses; and ragged, underfed, untaught, unsheltered soldiers upheld, in what neglect, what misery and suffering, you and I can barely realize, amidst Famine and Slaughter and Pestilence and Devastation hideous and indescribable, the traditional glory of the British nation, the strength and fire and power of British Arms. Let us have done with the pride of those days! Let us cease to boast of them! Let us prove our advancement in Civilization, Humanity, and Science by no longer treating these our fellow-creatures as human pawns in a devilish game of chess, or as thoughtless children treat toy-soldiers; to be moved hither and thither at will, swept off the board when necessary, and jostled promiscuously into dark and stuffy boxes until we are pleased to call for them again! Since Great Britain owes so much to her Army and her Navy, let her treat the men who serve her by land and sea with respect, and decent consideration. And in so far as Governments and Administrations of the old days ignored their rights to honest, humane, and Christian usage, let us have done with those damned old days forever, and while the life is red in us, hurry on the new!"

"They cannot come too quickly!" she said, giving back his earnest look. "Surely by raising the moral tone, cultivating the mental faculties, and improving the social condition of the private soldier, he is nerved and tempered, not softened and unstrung."

"As it is we owe him honor," said Bertham, "that, with so many disadvantages as he labors under to-day, and in the face of the bad example too often set him as to moral conduct and neglect of duty by his superiors, he is what we know him to be!"

"Ah, that is true—most true!" she answered, breaking the silence in which she had sat listening to the silvery voice of which even Bertham's enemies admitted the singular charm. "May the day soon dawn when we shall see him what we hope he will become!"

"There will be a dark night before its dawning," Bertham returned, and his smile had sadness in its very brilliancy. "For England must lose much to win that more, be assured."

He added as his look met hers, seeing the slight bewildered knitting of her eyebrows:

"There is a grand old white head nodding at the upper end of the Green Council Board at the War Office, or soundly sleeping, in the inner sanctum at the covered passage-end that has always been known as the office of the Commander-in-Chief,—that Britain, in her gratitude and loyal regard and tender reverence for its great owner,—and God forbid that I should rob him of one jot or tittle of what has been so gloriously won!—has left there long years since the brain within it became incapable, by the natural and inevitable decay of its once splendid faculties, of planning and carrying out any wholesome, needful reform in our Army's organization—even of listening to those who have suggestions to offer, or plans to submit, with anything but an old man's testy impatience of what seems new. This is deplored by personages nominally subordinate, really wielding absolute power. 'Sad, sad!' they say, 'but the nation would have it so.' Yet little more than a year ago, when, as by a miracle, the strength and vigor of the old warrior's prime seemed, if only for an instant, to have returned to him—when the dim fires of the gray eagle-glance blazed out again, and the trembling hand, strung to vigor for the nonce, penned that most electrifying letter,—published a few weeks back by what the New England Party regard as a wise stroke of policy, and Officialdom as an unpardonable indiscretion,—that letter declaring the country's defenses to be beggarly and inadequate, its naval arsenals neglected, its dockyards undermanned, its forts not half-garrisoned.... What sort of criticism did it evoke? Those who were openly antagonistic declared it to be preposterous; those who were loyal treated its utterances with contemptuous, galling indulgence.... To me it was as though a prophetic voice had spoken in warning from the tomb! And even before the graven stone sinks down over the weary old white head, Ada, and the laurels are withered that lie above, the country he loved and served so grandly may be doing pennance in dust and ashes for that warning it despised!"

"And if the War-call sounded to-morrow," she said, with her intent look upon him, and her long white fingers knitted about her knee, "and the need arose—as it would arise—for a man of swift decision and vigorous action to lead us in the field—upon whom would we rely? Who would step into the breach, and wield the *baton*?"

"A man," returned Bertham, "sixty-six years old, who served on the Duke's staff and lost his left arm at Waterloo; who has never held any command or had any experience of directing troops in War, and whose life, for forty years or so, has been spent in the discharge of the duties, onerous but not active, devolving upon a Military Secretary. The whole question as to fitness or not fitness turns upon an 'if.'"

The speaker spread his hands and shrugged his shoulders slightly, and a whimsical spark of humor gleamed in the look he turned upon the listener, as a star might shine through the wild blue twilight of a day of gale and storm, as he resumed:

"If the possession of the Wellingtonian manner,—combined with an empty sleeve—all honor to the brave arm that used to be inside it!—a manner full of urbanity and courtesy—nicely graduated and calculated according to the rank and standing of the person addressed; and admirable command of two Continental languages, and a discreet but distinct appreciation of high company and good living, unite to make an ideal Commander-in-Chief, why, Dalgan will be the man of men!..."

"But surely we need something more," she said, meeting Bertham's glance with doubt and questioning.

"Something indeed!" he returned dryly. "But be kind to me, and let me forget my bogies for a little in hearing of all the good that you have done and mean to do.... Tell me of your experiences at Kaiserswerke amongst the Lutheran Deaconesses—tell me about your visit to the Sisters of St. Vincent de Paul at the Hospital of the Charité, or your sojourn with the *dames religieuses* of St. Augustine at the Hôtel Dieu. Or tell me about your ancient, super-annuated, used-governesses. I should like to know something of them, poor old souls!..."

"They are not all old," she explained, "though many of them are used-up, and all, or nearly all, are incapable; and Bertham, with a very few exceptions, sensible and ladylike as most of them are, they are so grossly ignorant of the elementary principles of education that one wonders how the poor pretense of teaching was kept up at all? And how it was that common honesty did not lead them to take service as housemaids? and how the parents of their pupils—Heaven help them!—could have been blind enough to confide the training of their children to such feeble, incompetent hands?"

"It is a crying evil," said Bertham, "or, rather, a whimpering one, and needs to be dealt with. One day we will change all that.... As to these sick and sorrowful women, the generation that will rise up to take their places will be qualified, I hope, to teach, by having learned; and the quality of their teaching will, I hope again, be guaranteed by a University diploma. And, superior knowledge having ceased to mean the temporary possession of the lesson-book, children will learn to treat their teachers with respect, and we shall hear fewer tales of the despised governess."

She returned, glancing at Bertham's handsome, resolute face, and noting the many fine lines beginning to draw themselves about the corners of the eyes and mouth, the worn hollows of the temples and cheekbones, and the deepening caves from which the brilliant eyes looked out in scorn, or irony, or appealing, ingratiating gentleness.

"All governesses are not despised or despicable. There are many instances, Robert, where the integrity and conscientiousness of the poor dependent gentlewoman has held up a standard of conduct for the pupil, well or ill taught, to follow which has borne good fruit in after-years. We have a worthy lady here, a governess long resident in Paris, against whose exquisite French I polish up my own when I have time—a rather scarce commodity in this house!... Miss Caroline Smithwick has been cast on the mercy of the world in her old age, after many years of faithful service, because she dared tell her wealthy employer that a claim he pursued and pressed was dishonest and base. The man's son thinks with her, and has chosen to be poor rather than profit by riches—and, I gather, rank—so gained. It is a wholesome story," she said, "and when he told me to-day of his intention to support the gentle old soul who was so true to him, out of his pay as an officer of the French Army,—I could have clapped my hands and cried aloud—but I did not,—for the Superintendent of a Governesses' Home must be, above all, discreet;—'Bravo, M. *Hector Dunoisse!*'"

"'Dunoisse, Dunoisse'?" He turned the name upon his tongue several times over, as though its flavor were in some measure familiar to him. "Dunoisse.... Can it be a son of the dyed and painted and padded old lion, with false claws and teeth and a name from the wigmaker's, who was Bonaparte's *aide* at Marengo and cut a dashing figure at the Tuileries in 1804? The Emperor created him Field-Marshal after Austerlitz, and small blame to him!... He ran away with a Bavarian Princess after the Restoration—a Princess who happened to be a professed nun, and somewhere about 1828, when the son of their union may have been seven or eight years old,—when the Throne of St. Louis was rocking under that cumbersome old wooden puppet Charles X.,—when the tricolor was on the point of breaking out at the top of every national flagstaff in France,—when you got a whiff of violets from the button-hole of every Imperialist who passed you in the street,—when the Catholic religion was about to be once more deprived of State protection and popular support, Marshal Dunoisse, swashbuckling old Bonapartist that he is, reclaimed the lady's large dowry from her Convent, and with the aid of De Martignac, Head of the Ministry of that date, succeeded in getting it."

"It is the son of the very man you describe," she told him; "who visited his old governess here to-day."

Bertham shrugged his shoulders, and, leaning down, silently stroked the sleek cat, white-pawed and whiskered, and coated in Quaker gray, that lay outstretched at ease upon the hearthrug. But his eyes were on the woman's face the while.

"So that was it!" she said, leaning back in the low fireside chair she had taken when Bertham wheeled it forwards. Her musing eyes were fixed upon the red coals glowing in the old-world grate of polished steel. Perhaps the vivid face with the black eyes burning under their level brows rose up before her; and it might have been that she heard Dunoisse's voice saying, through the purring of the cat upon the hearthrug and the subdued noises of the street:

"May the hour that sees me spend a sou of that accursed money be an hour of shame for me, and bitterness and humiliation! And should ever a day draw near that is to see me trick myself in dignities and honors stolen by a charlatan's device and assume a power to which I have no more moral right than the meanest peasant of the State it rules—before its dawning I pray that I may die! and that those who come seeking a clod of mud to throw in the face of a Catholic State may find it lying in a coffin!"

XIX

She must have remembered the words, for she shivered a little, and when Bertham asked her: "Of what are you thinking?" she answered:

"Of young Mr. Dunoisse, and the struggle that is before him. He is courageous.... He means so well.... He is so earnest and sincere and high-minded and generous.... But one cannot forget that he has not been tried, or that fiercer tests of his determination and endurance will come as the years unfold, and——"

"He will—supposing him a man of flesh and blood like other men!" said Bertham—"find his resolution—if it be one?—put, very shortly, very thoroughly to the proof. For—the Berlin papers of last Wednesday deal voluminously with the subject, and the Paris papers of a later date have even condescended to dwell upon it at some length—his grandfather, the Hereditary Prince of Widinitz, who practically has been dead for years, is at last dead enough for burying; and the question of Succession having cropped up, it may occur to the Catholic subjects of the Principality that they would prefer a Catholic Prince—even with a bar-sinister, badly erased, upon his 'scutcheon—to being governed by a Lutheran Regent. And that is all I know at present."

"It is a curious, almost a romantic story," she said, with her grave eyes upon the glowing fire, and a long, fine, slender hand propping her cheek, "that provokes one to wonder how it will end?"

"It will end, dear Ada," smiled Bertham, "in this young fellow's putting his Quixotic scruples in his pocket, taking the goods the gods have sent him—with the Hereditary diadem, when it is offered on a cushion!—marrying some blonde Princess-cousin, with the requisite number of armorial quarterings; and providing,—in the shortest possible time, the largest possible number of legitimate heirs to the throne. I lay no claim to the prophetic gift; but I do possess some knowledge of my fellow-men. And—if your prejudice against gaming does not preclude a bet, I will wager you a pair of gloves, or half a dozen pairs, against the daguerreotype of you that Mary and I are always begging for and never get;—that M. Dunoisse's scruples and objections will be overcome in the long-run, and that the whole thing will end as I have prophesied."

She listened with a little fold between her eyebrows, and her thoughtful eyes upon the speaker's face.

"I fear you may be right. But I shall be glad if you prove wrong, Bertham. One thinks how bravely he has borne the pinch of poverty, and the dearth of the pleasantnesses and luxuries that mean so much to young men of his age——"

"'Of his age?'.... You talk as though you were a sere and withered spinster, separated from the world of young men and young women by a veritable gulf of years!" cried Bertham, vexed.

She did not hear. She was looking at the fire, leaning forwards in her low chair with her beautiful head pensively bent, and her slender strong hands clasped about the knee that was a little lifted by the resting of one fine arched foot—as beautiful in its stocking of Quakerish gray and its plain, unbuckled leather slipper as though it had been covered with silk, and shod with embroidered kid or velvet—upon the high steel fender.

"One would like to be near him sometimes unseen—in one of those moments of temptation that will come to him—temptations to be false to his vow, and take the price of dishonor, for the devil will fight hard, Bertham, for that man's soul! Just to be able to give a pull here, or a push in that direction, according as circumstances seek to mold or sway him, to say 'Do this!' or 'Do not do that!' at the crucial moment, would be worth while!..."

"'Faith, my dear Ada," Bertham said lightly, "the *rôle* of guardian angel is one you were cut out for, and suits you very well. But be content, one begs of you, to play it nearer home!... I know a worthy young man, at present in a situation in a large business-house at Westminster, who would very much benefit by a push here and a pull there from a hand invisible or visible—visible preferred! And to be told 'Do this!' or 'Don't do that!' in a moment of doubt or at a crisis of indecision, would spare the Member for West Wealdshire a great many sleepless nights."

They laughed together; then she said, with the rose-flush fading out of her pale cheeks and the light of merriment in her blue-gray eyes subdued again to clear soft radiance:

"I do not like those sleepless nights. Can nothing be done for them?"

"They are my only chance," he answered, "of gaining any acquaintance with the works of modern novelists."

"You do not take Sir Walter Scott, or Mr. Thackeray, or Mr. Dickens, or the author of *Jane Eyre*, as sleeping-draughts?"

"No," returned Bertham, "for the credit of my good taste. But there are others whose works Cleopatra might have called for instead of mandragora.

As regards the newspapers, if it be not exactly agreeable or encouraging to know exactly how far Misrepresentation can go without being absolute Mendacity—it is salutary and wholesome, I suppose, to be told when one has fallen short of winning even appreciation for one's honest endeavor to do one's duty—or what one conceives to be one's duty—tolerably well?"

He rose, pushing his chair aside, and took a turn in the room that carried him to the window.

"One has made mistakes," he said, keeping his face turned from her soft kind look; "but so have other fellows, without being pilloried and pelted for them! And two years back, when the office of Secretary At War seemed to have been created for the purpose of affording His Grace the Secretary For War and other high officials, unlimited opportunities of pulling down what the first-named had built up, and of building up what he, with hopes of doing good, had pulled down, the pelting bruised. But—Jove! if that part of my life were mine to live all over again, with Experience added to my youthful enthusiasms, I might reasonably hope to achieve much! Happy you"—he came and stood beside her chair, looking down at the calm profile and plainly-parted, faintly-rippling brown hair with a certain wistfulness—"most happy are you, dear Ada, who have so nobly fulfilled the high promise of your girlhood, and have no need to join in useless regrets with me!"

She smiled, and lifted her warm, womanly hand to him, and said, as he enclosed it for a second in his own:

"Wrong leads and false ideals are the lot of all of us. And you were of so much use in your high office, Robert, and wielded your power so much for others' good; you strive so chivalrously now, in thankless, unpopular causes; you make your duty so paramount above your ambition in all things,—that I am tempted to paraphrase your words to me, and tell you that you have gloriously contradicted the promise of your Eton boyhood, when everything that was not Football, or Boating, or Cricket, was 'bad form.'"

"To my cousin de Moulny's annoyance and disgust unspeakable," he returned, with a lighter tone and a lighter look, though he had glowed and kindled at the praise from her. "I did indulge—at those periods when he was staying at Wraye Abbey—in a good deal of that sort of bosh. But—quite wrongly, I dare say!—he seemed to me a high-falutin', pompous young French donkey; and it became a point of importance not to lose an opportunity of taking him down. By the way, I heard from him quite lately. He gave up the idea of entering the Roman Catholic priesthood after some clash or collision with the Rules of the Fathers Directors, and is now an Under-Secretary at the Ministry for Foreign Affairs."

"He should have a notable career before him!" she commented.

"The Legitimist Party, at this present juncture, possess not one featherweight in the scale of popularity or influence. France is on the eve," said Bertham, "or so it seems to me, of shedding her skin, and whether the new one will be of one color or of Three, White it will not be; I'll bet my hat on that! So possibly it may be fortunate for de Moulny that the harness he pulls in has an Imperial Crown upon it. I need hardly say a pretty hand is upon the reins."

Her laugh made soft music in the cosy, homely parlor, and amusement danced on her sweet firelit eyes....

"Whose is the hand?"

"It appertains, physically, to a certain Comtesse de Roux, and legally to a purple-haired, fiercely-whiskered, fiery-featured Colonel Comte de Roux—by whose original creation Comte is a little uncertain—but a brave and distinguished officer, commanding the 999th of the Line."

She said, with a memory stirring in her face:

"That is the regiment—according to his old governess, for he did not tell me—to which M. Hector Dunoisse is attached."

Bertham might not have heard. He said:

"I regret not having met Madame de Roux. One would like to see de Moulny's reigning goddess."

"She is most beautiful in person and countenance. Your term of 'goddess' is not inappropriate. She walks as though on clouds."

Her ungrudging admiration of another woman's beauty was a trait in her that always pleased him.

"Where did you meet?"

"I saw her in Paris a twelvemonth back, on the steps that lead to the vestibule of the Théâtre Française, one night when Rachel was to play in 'Phédre.'"

"I thought you had forsworn all public entertainments, theaters included?"

"If I had I should not have endangered my oath by seeing Madame de Roux pass from her carriage and walk up the steps leading to the vestibule."

"You were not in the streets of Paris alone, and on foot, at night?"

She answered simply, looking directly at him:

"I was in the Paris streets that evening, on foot, certainly, but not alone. Sister Saint Bernard was with me."

"Who is Sister Saint Bernard?"

"She is a nun of the Order of St. Vincent de Paul. You know, the nursing-community. I stayed some time with them at their Convent at Paris, studying their good, wise, enlightened methods, visiting their hospitals with them, helping to tend their sick. We were returning with a patient that night I saw Madame de Roux. It was a case of brain-fever, a young girl, an attendant at one of the gaudy, disreputable restaurants of the Palais-Royal, delirious and desperately ill. No conveyance could be got to take her to the Charité; the Sisters' van was otherwise engaged. We hired a vegetable-truck from a street fruit-seller, on the understanding that it should be whitewashed before being returned to him, wrapped the poor girl in blankets, and wheeled her to the Hospital ourselves."

"By—George!" said Bertham softly and distinctly. His forehead was thunderous, and his lips were compressed. She went on as though she had not heard:

"And so, as we went through the Rue de Richelieu, and Sister Saint Bernard and I, and the truck, were passing the Théâtre Français, into which all fashionable Paris was crowding to see the great actress play 'Phédre,' a beautiful woman alighted from a carriage and went in, leaning on the arm of a stout short man in uniform, with some decorations.... I pointed his companion out to Sister Saint Bernard. *'Tiens,'* she said, *'voilà Madame la Comtesse de Roux. Une grande dame de par le monde.'* And that is how I came to know M. de Moulny's enchantress by sight.... I wonder whether M. Dunoisse has met her?"

"It is more than probable, seeing that the lady is his Colonel's wife. And," said Bertham, "if he has not yet had the honor of being presented, he will enjoy it very soon. A Hereditary Prince of Widinitz is a personage, even out of Bavaria. And whether the son of the Princess Marie Bathilde and old Nap's *aide-de-camp* likes his title, or whether he does not, it is his birthright, like the tail of the dog. He can't get away from that!"

"He does look," said Ada Merling, with a smile, "a little like what a schoolgirl's ideal of a Prince would be."

"Àpropos of that, a Prince who is not in the least like a schoolgirl's ideal of the character dines with us at Wraye House on Tuesday. The Stratclyffes are coming, and the French Ambassador, with Madame de Berny."

He added, naming the all-powerful Secretary for Foreign Affairs, with a lightness and indifference that were overdone:

"And Lord Walmerston."

"Lord Walmerston!..."

Her look was one of surprise, changing to doubtful comprehension. He did not meet it. He was saying:

"It was his wish to come. His friendship for Mary dates from her schoolroom-days, and she cherishes the old loyal affection for her father's friend in one of her heart's warmest corners. He is charming to her, always ... and I have hopes of his weight in the balance for my Improved Married Quarters; and he really sees the advantage of the Regimental Schools.... But it is not to bore you with shop that I propose you should make one of us at dinner!" His voice was coaxing. "Do! and give Mary and me a happy evening!"

She shook her head with decision, though regret was in her face.

"I cannot leave my post. Remember, this is not only a Home.... It is also a Hospital. And what it pleases me to call my Staff"—she smiled—"are not experienced. They are willing and earnest, but they must be constantly supervised. And their training for this, the noblest profession that is open to women—as noble as any, were women equally free to follow all—is not the least of my responsibilities. We have lectures and classes here for their instruction in elementary anatomy, surgical dressing and bandaging, sanitation, the proper use of the thermometer and temperature-chart, and so on, almost daily. Mr. Alnwright and Professor Tayleur"—she named a famous surgeon and a celebrated physiologist—"are good enough to give their services, gratuitously; and I must be present at all times to assist them in their demonstrations. So you will understand, there is more to do here than you would have supposed."

"Good gracious!" rejoined Bertham; "I should say so! And your band of trained attendants who are to supersede—and may it be soon!—the gin-sodden harridans and smiling, civil Incompetents who add to the discomforts and miseries of sickness, and lend to Death another terror—are they—— I suppose some of them are ladies?"

"The ideal nurse ought to be a lady," she answered him, "in the true sense of the word. Many of these girls are well born and well bred, if that is—and of course it is—the meaning of your question. Some of them are frivolous and selfish and untrustworthy, and these must be weeded out. But the majority are earnest, honest, and sincere; and many of them are noble and high-minded, unselfish, devoted, and brave...."

There was a stately print of the Sistine Madonna of Raffaelle hanging above the fireplace. She lifted her face to the pure, spotless womanhood of the Face that looked out from the frame, and said:

"I try to keep up with these last-named ones, though often they put me to the blush."

"You put to the blush! Don't tell me that!" He spoke and looked incredulously.

"They have to learn to save their strength of mind and body, and not put out too much, even in the Christ-blessed service of the sick and suffering," she said, "lest they should find themselves bankrupt, with no power of giving more. And sometimes the more ardent among them rebel against my rules, which enforce regular exercise, observance of precautions for the preservation of their own health, even the relaxation and amusement which should break the monotony of routine; and then I long to kiss them, Robert, even when I am most severe!"

There were tears in the man's bright eyes as he looked at her. Her own eyes were on the Raffaelle print; she had forgotten him.

"What I should like best would be to endure long enough to see them outstripping and outdoing the poor example of their humble fellow-student and teacher, developing nursing as a higher Art, and spreading the knowledge of the proper treatment of the sick, until not one of the poorest and the roughest women of what we are content to call the Lower Classes, shall be destitute of some smattering of the knowledge that will save the lives of those she loves best in bitter time of need."

Her face was rapt. She went on in a clear, low, even tone: "I should like to live to be very old, so old that I was quite forgotten, and sit quietly in some pleasant corner of a peaceful English home seeing the movement grow. For it will grow, and spread and increase, Robert, until it reaches every corner of the world! And to that end every penny that I possess; every ounce of strength that is mine; every drop of blood in my veins, would be cheerfully spent and given.... Do I say would?... Will be! if it please God!" Her eyes left the picture and went to Bertham's absorbed face. "I have been holding forth at merciless length, have I not?" she said. "But you and I, with Mary, constitute a Mutual Society for the Talking-Over of Plans; and, though I sometimes tax your patience, I am always ready to lend ear. As for your dinner, it is a delightful temptation which I must resist. Beg Mary to tell me all about it afterwards!"

"Your would-be host and hostess will not be the only disappointed ones," Bertham said, and rose as though to take leave. "Lord Walmerston is one of your admirers, and"—there was a gleam of mischief in the hazel eyes—"Prince Louis-Napoleon Bonaparte was urgent for an opportunity of meeting you again."

"Indeed! I am very much honored." Her calm eyes and composed face told nothing. But her tone had a clear frosty ring of something colder than mere indifference, and the curve of her lips was a little ironical. Seeing that touch of scorn, the twinkle in Bertham's eyes became more mischievous. He said:

"The Prince's lucky star might shine on such a meeting, Ada. A beautiful, wealthy, and wise Princess would be the making of the man."

"*That* man!" she said, and a shudder rippled through her slight body, and her calm, unruffled forehead lost its smoothness in a frown of repulsion and disgust. She rose as though escaping from actual physical contact with some repellent personality suddenly presented before her, and stood beside Bertham on the hearthrug, as tall as he, and with the same look of high-bred elegance and distinction that characterized and marked out her companion. The spark of mischief still danced in his bright eyes. His handsome mouth twitched with the laughter he repressed as he said:

"So you do not covet the Crown Imperial of France, and tame eagles do not please you? Yet the opportunities an Empress enjoys for doing good must be practically unrivaled."

Her blue-gray eyes were disdainful now. She said:

"The position of a plain gentlewoman is surely more enviable and honorable than would be hers who should share the throne of a crowned and sceptered adventurer."

Said Bertham:

"You do not call the First Napoleon that?"

"There was a terrible grandeur," she returned, "about that bloodstained, unrelenting, icy, ambitious despot; a halo of old, great martial deeds surrounds his name that blinds the eyes to his rapacity and meanness, his selfishness, sensuality, and greed. But this son of Hortense! this nephew, if he be a nephew?—this charlatan trailing in the mire the sumptuous rags of the Imperial purple; this gentlemanly, silken-mannered creature, with phrases of ingratiating flattery upon his tongue, and hatred glimmering between the half-drawn blinds of those sick, sluggish eyes.... God grant, for England's sake, that he may never mount the throne of St. Louis!"

"Ah! Ada—Ada!" Bertham said again, and laughed, awkwardly for one whose mirth was so melodious and graceful as a rule. For the little dinner at Wraye House, at which the Secretary for Foreign Affairs and the French Ambassador were to meet the Pretender to the Imperial Throne of France, was really a diplomatic meeting of somewhat serious political importance, in view of certain changes and upheavals taking place in that restless country on the other side of the Channel, and divers signs and tokens, indicative to an experienced eye that the White Flag, for eighteen years displayed above the Central Pavilion of the Palace of the Tuileries, might shortly be expected to come down.

XX

However, being a skillful diplomat, Bertham gave no sign: though Lord Walmerston, Minister for Foreign Affairs, and the Pretender to the Throne-Imperial of France, were to spend in the Persian smoking-room over the ground-floor billiard-room of Wraye House—a half-hour that would change every card in the poor hand held by that last-named gamester to a trump.

"Who is good enough for you, Ada?" he said, with his hazel glance softening as he turned it upon her, and sincerity in his sweet, courtly tones. "No one I ever met!"

Her rare and lovely smile illuminated her.

"Has it never struck you, Robert, how curious it is that the demand for entire possession of a woman's hand, fortune and person, should invariably be prefaced by the candid statement that the suitor is not good enough to tie her shoes? As for being good enough for me, any man would be, provided he were honest, sincere, chivalrous in word and deed——"

"And not the present Head of the House of Bonaparte?" ended Bertham.

"You are right," she said quickly. "Were I compelled to make choice between them, I should infinitely prefer the butcher!"

"'*The butcher!*'" Bertham's face of utter consternation mingled with incredulity drew her laugh from her. And it was so round and sweet and mellow that the crystal lusters of the Sèvres and ormolu candlesticks upon the mantel-shelf rang a little tinkling echo when it had stopped.

"The butcher who supplies us here," she explained.

Bertham said, speaking between his teeth and with the knuckles showing white in the strong slender hand he clenched and shook at an imaginary vendor of chops and sirloins:

"What consummate and confounded insolence!"

"No, no!" she cried, for his tall, slight, athletic figure was striding up and down the little parlor, and the fierce grind of his heel each time he turned within the limit of the hearthrug threatened the cat's repose. "You shall not fume, and say hard things of him! He knows nothing of me except that I am the matron here. And he thinks that I should be better off in the sitting-room behind his shop in Oxford Street, keeping his books of accounts and 'ordering any nice little delicate joint' I 'happened to fancy for dinner....' And possibly I should be better off, from his point of view?"

Bertham's heel came sharply down upon the hearthrug. The outraged cat rent the air with a feline squall, and sought refuge under the sofa.

"Come out, Mr. Bright!" coaxed his mistress, kneeling by the injured one's retreat. "He is very sorry! He didn't mean it! He will never do it again!" She added, rising, with Mr. Bright, already soothed and purring, in her arms, "And he is going away now, regretful as we are to have to send him. For it is my night on duty, Robert, and I must rest."

"You will always send me away," said he, "when you choose. And I shall always come back again, until you show me that I am not wanted."

"That will be never, dear friend!"

She gave him her true, pure hand, and he stooped and left a reverent kiss upon it, and said, as he lifted a brighter face:

"Do you remember three years ago, before you went to Kaiserswerke—when you sent me away, and forbade me to come back until I had sought and found my Fate in Mary?"

"A beautiful and loving Fate, dear Robert."

"She is, God bless her!" he answered, with a warm flush upon his face and a thrill of tenderness in the charming voice that so many men and women loved him for.

She went with him into the hall then, and said as he threw on his long dark cloak lined with Russian sables:

"Those Berlin and Paris papers of Wednesday last.... It would interest me to glance through them in a spare moment, if you did not object to lend?"

"One of my 'liveried menials with buttons on his crests,' as a denunciatory Chartist orator put it the other day—shall bring them to you within half an hour. I wish you had asked me for something less easy to give you, Ada!"

She answered with her gentle eyes on his, as her hand drew back the latch of the hall door:

"Give me assurance you will never help to forge the link that shall unite Great Britain's interests with her enemy's."

"Why, that of course!" He answered without heartiness, and his eyes did not meet hers. "I am not the master blacksmith, dear Ada. There are other hands more cunning in the welding-craft than mine!"

He bent his handsome head to her and threw on his hat and passed out into the rimy February fog. But he walked slowly, pondering as he went, and his face wore a moody frown. For Lord Walmerston's influence and weight upon that pressing question, separate accommodation for married soldiers, and Military Schools for the men and their wives and children, was not to be had for nothing, he well knew....

She shut the door, and then the tea-bell rang, and she passed on to the dining-room, and took her place before the capacious tray at the matron's end of the long, plainly-appointed, wholesomely-furnished table.

She had declined to dine in the society of a Prince because she doubted his motives and disapproved of his character. She played the hostess now to her staff of nurses and probationers, dispensing the household tea from the stout family teapot with a liberal hand, and leading the conversation with a gentle grace and an infectious gayety that drew sparks from the homeliest minds about the board and made bright wits shine brighter.

The Berlin and Paris papers came by Bertham's servant as she went to her room to prepare, by some hours of rest, for the night-watch by a dying patient. She gave half-an hour of the time to reading the articles and paragraphs Bertham had considerately marked in red ink for her.

When she set about preparing for repose came a gentle knock at her door, and in answer to her soft "Come in!" the gray-haired, olive-skinned, pleasant-faced woman, who had admitted Dunoisse and shown him out again, appeared, saying:

"You never rang, Miss Ada, love, but I made bold to come."... She added in tones of dismay, "And to find you brushing your beautiful hair yourself when your old Husnuggle's in the house and asking nothing better than to do it for you!..."

"Thank you, dear!" She surrendered the brush, and sat down and submitted to the deft hands that set about their accustomed task, as though it were soothing to be so ministered to. Even as she said: "For this once, kind Husnuggle, but you must not do it again!"

"Don't say that, Miss Ada! when night's the only time of all the livelong day that I get my Wraye Rest talk with you."

Entreated thus, she reached up a hand and patted the plump matronly cheek of the good soul, and said, with soft, considerate gentleness:

"Let it be so, since it will make you happy. But those who have chosen for their life's task the duty of serving others should do without service themselves. Try to understand!"

The woman kissed the hand with a fervor contrasting incongruously with her staid demeanor and homely simple face, as she answered:

"I'll try, my dear. Though to see you in this bare, plainly-furnished room, with scarce a bit of comfort in it beyond the fire in the grate, and not a stick of furniture beyond the bed and the wardrobe, and washstand and bath, and the chintz-covered armchair you're sitting in, and a bookshelf of grave books, scalds my heart—that it do! And your sitting-room nigh as skimping. When either at Wraye Rest or at Oakenwode, or at the house in Park Lane, you have everything beautiful about you, as you ought; with paintings and statues and music, and carpets like velvet for you to tread upon, and flowers everywhere for you that love them so to take pleasure in them, and your dogs and horses, and cats and birds!... Eh! deary me! But I promised I'd never breathe a murmur, not if you let me come, and here I am forgetting!....."

"We will overlook it this time. And I will help you to understand why I am happier here, and more at peace than at Wraye or Oakenwode, or at the Park Lane house, dear to me as all three are. It is because, wherever I am, and whether I am walking or sleeping, I seem to hear voices that call to me for help. Chiefly the voices of women, weak, and faint, and imploring.... And they appeal to me, not because I am any wiser, or better, or stronger than others of my sex, but because I am able, through circumstances,—and have the wish and the will to aid them, I humbly believe, from God! And if I stayed at home and yielded to the desire for pleasant, easy, delightful ways of living, and bathed my eyes and ears in lovely sights and sounds, I should hear those voices over all, and see with the eyes of my mind the pale, wan, wistful faces that belong to them. And I should know no peace!... But here, even if the work I do be insignificant and ineffective, I am working for and with my poor sisters, sick and well. And on the day when I turn back and leave my plow in the furrow, then those voices will have a right to cry to me without ceasing: '*Oh, woman! why have you deserted us?—you who might have done so much!*'"

She ceased, but the rush and thrill of the words as they had come pouring from her, vibrated yet on the quiet atmosphere of the room.

"You had a pleasant talk, Miss Ada, with Master Robert?" the woman asked her, turning down the snowy sheet from the pillows, and preparing to leave the room.

"A long, grave talk, Husnuggle, even a little sad in places, but pleasant nevertheless. Now go down to supper, for it is eight o'clock."

Husnuggle went, having bound up the wealth of hair into a great silken twist, and her mistress knelt at a *prie-Dieu* beneath an ebony and olive-wood crucifix that hung upon the wall, and said her prayers, and sought her rest. When she slept, less easily and less soundly than usual, she dreamed; and the figure and face of the slight, ruddy-skinned, black-eyed man who had visited the Hospice that day, moved with others across the stage of her vision, and his voice echoed with other voices in the chambers of her sleeping brain.

The Havre packet had not sailed that evening, by reason of a boisterous gale and a great sea, and Dunoisse was spending the evening dismally enough at the T. R. Southampton, where "As you Like It" was being given for the benefit of Miss Arabella Smallsopp, advertised as of the "principal London theaters," upon the last night of a Stock Season which had been "a supreme artistic success."

Mr. Hawkington Bulph and a Full Company—which collectively and individually looked anything but that,—supported the star; and to the fatal sprightliness of the hapless Smallsopp, disguised as the immortal page, in a lace collar, drop-earrings, and a short green cotton-velvet ulster, dadoed with catskin, and adorned down the front with rows of brass buttons not distantly resembling coffin-nails (worn in combination with a Spanish hair-comb and yellow leather top-boots), must be ascribed the violent distaste which one member of the audience did then and there conceive for England's immortal Bard. But ere long his attention strayed from the dingy, ill-lit Forest Scene, with a cork-and-quill nightingale warbling away in the flies, as Miss Smallsopp interpolated the pleasing ditty, "O Sing Again, Sweet Bird of Eve!" and he ceased to see the dirty boards, where underpaid, underfed, and illiterate actors gesticulated and strutted, and he went back in thought to Ada Merling, and her pure earnest face rose up before his mental vision, and the very sound of her crystal voice was in his ears.

Even as in her troubled dreams, she saw Hector Dunoisse standing before her, with that swift play of his emotions vividly passing in his face; and heard him passionately saying that the hour that saw him broach those tainted stored-up thousands should be for him an hour of branding shame; and that he prayed the dawning of the day that should break upon his completed barter of Honor for Wealth, and Rank and Power, might find him lying in his coffin.

And then he yielded—or so it seemed to her, and took the shining money, and the princely diadem offered him by smooth strangers with persuasive courtly voices, and she saw the fateful gold scattered from his reckless hands like yellow dust of pollen from the ripe mimosa-bloom when the thorny trees are bowed and shaken by the gusty winds of Spring.

And then she saw him going to his Coronation, and no nobler or more stately figure moved onwards in the solemn procession of Powers and Dignities, accompanying him through laurel-arched and flower-wreathed and flag-bedecked streets to the Cathedral, where vested and coped and mitered prelates waited to anoint and crown him Prince. And where, amidst the solemn strains of the great organ, the chanting of many voices, and the pealing of silver trumpets, the ceremony had nearly reached its stately close, when the jeweled circlet that should have crowned his temples slipped from the aged Archbishop's venerable, trembling hands and rolled upon the inlaid pavement, shedding diamonds and pearls like dewdrops or tears.... And then she saw him lying, amidst wreaths of flowers and tall burning tapers, in a black-draped coffin in the black-hung nave. And a tall man and a beautiful woman leaned over the death-white face with the sealed, sunk eyes, smiling lustfully in each other's. And she awakened at the chime of her silver clock in her quiet room; and it was dark, and the lamp-lighter was kindling the street-lamps, and she must rise and prepare for her night's vigil.

It taxed her, for her dream-fraught sleep had not refreshed. But she ministered to her fevered, pain-racked patient with gentle unwearying patience and swift, noiseless tenderness, through the hours that moved in slow procession on to the throning of another day....

Her patient slept at last, and woke as the dawn was breaking, and the watcher refreshed the parched lips with tea, and stirred the banked-up fire to a bright flame, and went to the window and drew up the blinds.

Drab London was mantled white with snow that had fallen in the night-time. And above her roofs and chimneys, wrapped in swansdown mantles, glittering with icicles, the dawn came up all livid and wild and bloody, with tattered banners streaming through the shining lances of a blizzard from the East that shook the window-panes like a desperate charge of cavalry, and screamed as wounded horses do, frenzied with pain and terror amidst the sounds and sights of dreadful War.

XXI

Between Dullingstoke Junction and the village town of Market Drowsing in Sloughshire, lay some ten miles of hard, level highway, engineered and made in the stark days of old by stalwart Romans who, ignorant of steamrollers and road-engines as they were, knew as little of the meaning of the word Impossibility.

One of those ancient road-making warriors might have approved the fine height and shapely form of a soldier who marched at ease along the highway, wearing, with a smart and gallant air, the blue, white-faced full-dress uniform of a trooper in Her Majesty's Hundredth Regiment of Lancers, without the sword, and the plumed head-dress of blue cloth and shiny black leather, which a forage-cap—of the muffin pattern more recently approved by Government—replaced.

He walked at a brisk marching pace, and, in spite of the tightness of his clothes, broke into a run at times to quicken his circulation. For, though greatcoats were supplied at the public expense to Great Britain's martial sons; so many penalties, pains, and stoppages attended on the slightest damage to the sacred garment, that in nine cases out of ten the soldier of the era preferred to go without. Therefore the short tight coatee of blue cloth, with the white plastron and facings, being inadequate to keep out the piercing cold of the frosty February day, this soldier beat his elbows against his sides, as he ran, and thumped his arms upon a broad chest needing no padding. But even as he did this he whistled a cheery tune, and his bright eyes looked ahead as though something pleasant lay waiting at the end of the bleak, cold journey from the military depôt town of Spurham, thirty miles away; and the handsome mouth under the soldierly mustache, that was, like its owner's abundant curly hair, of strong, dark red, and curled up on either side towards such a pair of side-whiskers as few women, at that hirsute period, could look upon unmoved—wore a smile that was very pleasant.

"It's not a pretty view!" he said aloud, breaking off in the middle of "Vilikins and his Dinah" to criticise the landscape. "A man would need have queer taste to call it even cheerful, particularly in the winter-time! and yet I wouldn't swop it for the Bay o' Naples, with a volcano spurting fire, and dancing villagers a-banging tambourines—or anything else you could offer me out of a Panorama. For why, damme if I know!"

Perhaps the simple reason was that this homely spread of wood and field and fallow stretching away into the hazy distance, its trees still leafy in the sheltered hollows, bare where the fierce winds of winter had wreaked their bitter will, had been familiar to the soldier from his earliest years. Upon his left hand, uplands whereon the plow-teams were already moving, climbed to a cold sky of speed-well-blue; and couch-fires burned before the fanning wind, their slanting columns of pungent-smelling smoke clinging to the brown furrows before they rose and thinned and vanished in the upper atmosphere. Sparrows, starlings, jackdaws, finches and rooks followed the traveling plowshare, settled in flocks or rose in bevies, their shrill cries mingling with the jingle of the harness or the crack of the plowman's whip. And upon the right hand of the man to whom these sights and sounds were dear and welcome, rolled the Drowse; often unseen; returning into vision through recurring gaps in hedges; glimpsed between breasting slopes of park-land, silently flowing through its deep muddy channel between immemorial woods where England's Alfred hunted the boar, speared the wolf, and slew the red deer.... Silvery-blue in Summer, turbidly brown in Autumn, in Winter leaden-gray, in Spring jade-green, as now: when, although the floods of February had in some degree abated, wide, shallow, ice-bordered pools remained upon the low-lying river-meadows, and rows of knee-deep willows, marking the course of unseen banks, lifted bristling hands to the chilly skies, while cornricks on the upper levels were so honeycombed with holes of rats that had abandoned their submerged dwellings, that in contemplation of them the tramping soldier ceased to whistle, and pushed along in silence for at least a quarter of a mile before his whistle, "Vilikins and his Dinah," got the upper hand, and broke out again.

The popular melody was in full blast when the piercing screech of a distant train, accompanied by a clatter that grew upon the ear, stopped short, began again after a pause, and thinned out into silence; told the wayfarer that the London down-train had entered the junction he had left behind him, disembarked its load of passengers, and gone upon its way.

And presently, with a rattle and clatter of iron-shod hoofs, and a jingle of silver-mounted harness, a scarlet mail-phaeton of the most expensive and showy description, attached to a pair of high-stepping showy blacks, overtook the military pedestrian, bowled past; and suddenly pulled up at the roadside, at an order from a burly, red-faced, turn-up-nosed, gray-haired and whiskered elderly man, topped with a low-crowned, curly-brimmed, shiny beaver, and enveloped in a vast and shaggy greatcoat, who sat beside the smug-faced, liveried groom who drove, and whom you are to recognize as Thompson Jowell.

"Now then, Josh Horrotian, my fine fellow!" The great Contractor, being in a genial mood, was pleased to bend from his high pedestal and condescend, with this mere being of common clay, even to jesting. "How goes the world with you? And how far have you got, young man, on the road that ends in a crimson silk sash and a pair o' gold-lace epaulettes?"

"Why, not yet so far, Mr. Jowell, sir," returned the cavalryman with cheerful equanimity, "that I can show you even a Corporal's stripe upon my sleeve."

"And damme! young Josh, you take it uncommonly coolly!" said Thompson Jowell, puffing out his large cheeks over the upturned collar of the shaggy coat, and frowning magisterially. "Where's your proper pride, hey? Where's your ambition? What's become of your enthusiasm, and eagerness, and ardor for a British soldier's glorious career? I'm ashamed of you, Horrotian! What the devil do you mean?"

"You ask me three questions, Mr. Jowell, sir, that I can but answer in one way; and a fourth," returned the red-haired trooper, looking frankly up out of a pair of very clear blue eyes at the large face of disapproval bent upon him from the lofty altitude of the mail-phaeton's front seat, "that I can't answer in any way at all."

"I hope I don't understand you, Joshua Horrotian," said Thompson Jowell loftily. "But go on, go on! Damn you, don't fidget!" He addressed this exhortation to the more restive of the champing blacks, who had switched his flowing tail over the reins, and was snorting with his scarlet nostrils spread, and his wild eye cocked at the hedgerow, as though to be detained upon the road to the home-stable for the purpose of conversing with a common soldier was a thing past bearing by a high-bred horse.

"Whoa!" said the driving groom.

"Whoa, then, my beauty! That curb be a link too tight, Mr. Jowell," said Joshua Horrotian, betraying for the first time, by a lingering smack and twang of the broad local accent, that the county of Sloughshire might claim him as its son. "Shall I let it out a mite? He'll stand like a rock then."

Thompson Jowell nodded in answer, and the thing was done in a moment, and Horrotian back in his old place by the side-step, saying:

"You wanted to know just now, Mr. Jowell, where I'd left my proper pride, and my enthusiasm and eagerness and ardor for a soldier's career? I've left 'em yonder, sir." He lifted his riding-whip and pointed across country. "Over to the Cavalry Barracks at Spurham, where Ours have been quartered best part o' three years. With your leave, sir!"

He spat in a soldierly, leisurely way upon the sandy road, and hitched his pipeclayed pouch-belt, and shoved a finger of a white-gloved hand within the edge of his sword-belt of gilt lace with a white stripe, and went on speaking:

"It seems to me, sir, when I've casted round to think a bit—having done a bit o' gardening for mother in old days when I wasn't busy on the farm—that pride and enthusiasm and ardor and eagerness for a soldier's career are like hardy plants that will grow and put out leaf and bloom even in a soil that's as poor as ours at Upper Clays, if they're but wedd a bit and the snails and slugs picked off of 'em, and a drop o' water given in drought, and hobnailed boots, and wheelbarrows, turned aside from crushing of 'em down!"

"Well, well, my man! Where does this bring us to?" demanded the autocrat of the cocked inquisitive nose, and puffy cheeks, and goggling, greedy eyes, from his lofty perch upon the front seat of the scarlet mail-phaeton.

"It brings us to this, Mr. Jowell," said the trooper, with a fold coming between his thick broad smear of dark red eyebrows, and an angered narrowing of the blue eyes that were so clear, "that if you want a dog to respect himself, let alone his superiors, you'll give him a clean kennel to sleep in, and decent food to eat; and if he's to do a dog's work for you, you'll not curse and bully him so as to break and cow his spirit. Nay! and if you respect yourself, you'll give him, whether he's been a good dog or only a tolerable sort o' one—some sort o' nursing and care when he lies sick, if it's only the roughest kind, before he kicks his last on his straw bed. Then throw him out on the dung-heap if it's your liking; he can't feel it, poor brute! He be past all that. But where's the use of a Soldier's Funeral with a Firing Party and a Bugler, if,—when the man was living, you branded his soul with as many lines of anger and resentment and rage as there are stripes in the Union Jack, God bless it! that, him being dead, you lay as a pall of honor on his coffin? That's what I want to know!"

"You want to know too much for your rank and station, Josh Horrotian—that's what you do!" said Thompson Jowell, frowning displeasure upon him. "You're one of the Malcontents, that's what you are. If you were to tell me on your oath you weren't, I wouldn't believe you. I've met your breed before!"

"If you have, Mr. Jowell, my answer is that it's not a bad breed," retorted the trooper, with a hot flush and a bright direct look of anger. "Without trying to use finer language than my little education warrants, it's a breed that will fight to the death for Queen and Country, and hold that man a damned and despicable cur that hangs back in the hour of England's need. But when the same bad usage is meted out by the Authorities in Office to the willing and the unwilling, the worthless and the worthy, let me tell you, sir, a man loses heart. For Drill and Discipline and Confinement to Cells for defaulters, and Flogging for the obstropulous; with Ration Beef and cabbage, and suet-balls, tight clothes and tight belts, and a leather stock that saws your ears off, can't make a machine of a human being all through. There's got to be a living spot of flesh left in him somewhere that feels and tingles and smarts.... And the sooner the great gentlemen in authority find that out, the better for England and her Army," said Joshua Horrotian, with a straightforward, manly energy of voice and look and gesture that would have gone far to convince, if the right man had been there to hear him.

"Now, look you here, Trooper Joshua Horrotian," said the wrong man, "it's confounded lucky for you that these opinions of yours—and the private soldier with opinions is a man we don't want in the Army and would a great deal rather be without!—have been blown off to a person who—having a regard for that decent woman your mother—who I'm not above acknowledging, in a distant sort of way, as a relation of my own—isn't likely to report them in quarters where they would breed trouble for you, and maybe a taste of the Black Hole." The speaker held up a large fur-gloved hand as the trooper seemed about to speak. "Don't you try my patience, though! I've listened to you long enough.... Discontented, that's what you are! And Discontent leads to Murmuring, and Murmuring to Mutiny. And Mutiny to the Gallows—in your case I hope it won't!—but I shouldn't be at all surprised if it did. So beware of being discontented, Joshua!"

"I may be what you say, a grumbling soldier, though I don't recognize myself in the picture you draw of me," returned the trooper; "but if the time came to prove whether I'd be willing to lay down my life for the Old Shop, I'd be found as ready as any other man. And I have cause for discontent outside the Army, Mr. Jowell." And the speaker squared his broad shoulders and drew himself to his full height, looking boldly in the bullying eyes of the great man. "While I have been a-sogering my mother's farm has been going to rack and ruin. Some little-knowing or ill-meaning person has advised her, Mr. Jowell, for these three years past, to turn down the low-lying gore meadow-lands of hers beside the Drowse in clover and beans and vetch. Grazing cows is all they're good for, being flooded regularly in November and February, and Aprils extra-wet. And what with the cold, rainy summers we've had, and the rainy, cold summer we may look to, sure my mother has suffered in pocket, and worse she will suffer yet! For if her having borrowed money on mortgage to throw after what has already been lost beyond recall is going to bring her any good of—I'm a Dutchman!"

"Now, I'll tell you what, Trooper Horrotian," said Thompson Jowell, purple to the rim of his sporting parson's hat with something more stinging than the bitter February wind, "I don't pretend not to know what you're driving at, because Aboveboard is my name. If my distant relation, Mrs. Sarah Horrotian, is pleased to drive over from Market Drowsing sometimes on her egg-and-butter days, for the purpose of asking advice from a man who, like myself, is accustomed to be looked up to and consulted, supposing I happen to be at home at my little place"—which was a huge, ornate and showy country mansion, with a great deal of avenue, shrubbery, glass, and experimental garden-ground about it—"I am not the man to gainsay her, to gratify her long-legged puppy of a son."

"I'm obliged to you, I'm sure!" said Josh, reddening to his red hair, and angrily gnawing, in his desire to restrain himself from incautious speech, the shiny black strap by which the idiotic little muffin-shaped forage-cap of German pattern approved by Government, was sustained in a perilously slanting position on the side of his head.

"My name being Plump and Plain," said Thompson Jowell, once more extracting the large fur-gloved hand from under the leather apron of the phaeton, "I'm damned if I care this snap of my fingers"—he clumsily snapped them—"whether you are obliged to me or whether you ain't! Is that clear to you?"

The groom who occupied the driving seat beside his master laughing dutifully at this, Thompson Jowell's righteous indignation was somewhat appeased, as he proceeded:

"If the river flooded those gore-lands of your mother's, and the rainy season finished what the river began, I'm not the Clerk of the Weather Office, I suppose? Call Providence to account for the bad season, if you must blame somebody.... Though, if you do, and should happen to be struck dead by lightning as a punishment for your wickedness, don't expect Me to pity you, that's all! Granted I gave a pound or so for Sarah Horrotian's mildewed clover and stinking beans, and barley that had sprouted green in the ear, to burn for top-dressing; and let her have a bit of money at easy interest on her freehold of Upper Clays;—I suppose, as it's her property, having been left her for her sole use and benefit by her father (who was an uncle of my own, and don't my admitting that prove to you how little proud I am?), she's free to borrow on it if it pleases her. You are not the master yet, my good fellow!"

"And won't be, please God!—for many a year to come!" said Mr. Jowell's good fellow, with unaffected sincerity. "Nor will be ever, Mr. Jowell, supposing my mother not able to pay off your interest. You've foreclosed on too many of the small freeholders in this neighborhood, for me to believe that you'll be more generous and mercifuller with your poor relation, than you've been with them you've called your good friends!"

The groom who drove, forgetting himself so far as to chuckle at this, Thompson Jowell damned his impertinence with less of dignity and more of flustered bumptiousness than an admirer of the great man's would have expected.

"And poor as my mother is, and hard as she has been put to it," went on the trooper, pursuing his sore subject, "if she had dreamed that the spoiled fodder she sold you for the price such unwholesome rubbish was worth, was not to be burned for top-dressing, but dried in them kilns that are worked in another name than yours at Little Milding—and mixed with decent stuff, and sold as first-class fare for Army horses, poor beasts!—she'd have seen you at Jerusalem beyond the Jordan before she'd ha' parted with a barrow-load of the rot-gut stuff, or she's not the woman I take her for!"

"You insolent blackguard!" said Thompson Jowell, blowing at the speaker, and swelling over the apron of the phaeton until the soundness of its leather straps must have been severely tested. "You've heard of the Lock-up and Treadmill for proved defamers and slanderers, haven't you, in default of the damages such vermin are too poor to pay?"

"I've heard of lots o' things since I joined the Army, Mr. Thompson Jowell," retorted Joshua Horrotian, who had regained his coolness as the other had lost self-command, "and I've seen a few more! I've seen such things come out of the middle of Government hay-and-straw trusses as nobody, except the Contractor who sold and the Forage Department Agents who took 'em over, and the Quartermaster-Sergeant who served 'em out, and the soldiers who got 'em, would expect to find there. Not only cabbage-stumps and waste newspapers," said Josh forcibly, "which in moderation may be good for Cavalry troop-horses. But ragged flannel petticoats, empty jam-tins, and an old hat with a litter o' dead kittens inside of it, form too variegated and stimulating a diet to agree with anything under an ostrich; and I'm none too sure that such wouldn't be too much for the bird's digestion in the long-run."

The groom covered himself with disgrace at this juncture by exploding in a guffaw, which Thompson Jowell, mentally registering as to be expiated next pay-day by a lowering of wages, loftily ignored. He realized his own over-condescension in arguing with the worm that dared to lift up its head from the ground beneath his chariot-wheels, and argue with and denounce him. He changed his tone, now, and, instead of bullying, pitied the crawling thing.

"You don't understand what you're talking about, Horrotian," he said patronizingly, "and being a poor uneducated, common soldier, who's to be astonished at it? The British Government is too great and powerful and glorious and grand a Power to trouble itself about rags and jam-tins, or a hatful of dead kittens, shoved for a joke inside a truss of Army forage by some drunken trooper. Possibly next time you're in liquor, my man, you'll remember that you put them there yourself? As for any person being unprincipled enough to sell sprouted grain and mildewed hay, mixed up with sound stuff, as you suggest some persons do; what I say to you is that such people don't exist, such wickedness couldn't be possible; and if you undertook to prove to me that it is—I shouldn't be convinced! And, further, understand this; and what I say to you is what I said to an impudent, meddlesome whelp of a young foreigner I met in the train t'other day betwixt Dullingstoke and Waterloo—the British Government will BE the British Government, in spite of all the fault-finding and grumbling of mutinous and impudent upstart Rankers or their betters! And the iron wheels of Administration will keep on a-rolling, and so sure as heads are lifted too high out of the dust that is their proper element, those iron wheels I speak of will roll over 'em and mash 'em. Mash 'em, by Gosh! D'ye understand me?"

"Quite well, Mr. Jowell," returned the other composedly. "But I've good hopes of being able to roll or crawl or wriggle out of reach before those iron wheels you speak of roll my way. Mother having come round at last, I'm to be bought out of the Army come next Michaelmas, having served with the Colors—I humbly hope without a single act that might be calculated to dishonor them, or soil the reputation of an honest man and a loyal soldier!—rising five years out of the twelve I 'listed for; and, once being free, I mean to put my shoulder to the wheel in the farming-line in good earnest; and leave the officer's sash, and the pair o' gold-lace epaulets you spoke of, hanging at the top of the tree for some other fellow fortunater than I have been, to reach down."

"Go your way, ungrateful and obstinate young man," said Thompson Jowell, sternly, expanding his cheeks to the rotundity of a tombstone cherub's, and snorting reprehension. "I hope for your respectable mother's sake it mayn't end in ruin and disgrace, but—my name being Candid—I shouldn't wonder if it did!" He shook his pear-shaped head until he shook his hat over his goggle eyes, and so took it off, and blew his large cocked nose sonorously upon a vast silk handkerchief he whisked out of the crown, adding: "I suppose you are on furlough, and were bound for the Upper Clays when I overtook you marching along the Queen's Highway with your riding-whip in your hand?"

"Why, a cane might be better, for a man on leave to carry," returned Joshua Horrotian, meditatively running his eye from the stout handle of the riding-whip to the strong lash at its tip. "But though I came by the railway, I mean to go back by road. My Captain, being a rich gentleman, and having a good opinion of my judgment in horseflesh"—he said this with a flush and sparkle of honest pride—"has bought my young horse—'Blueberry'—for the troop. And I'm to ride him. He won't look so fat and shiny on the Government forage as he does on what he gets at home, but he'll do credit to the Regiment yet, or I'm no judge. Good-afternoon, sir!"

He saluted and wheeled, setting his handsome face ahead, and Thompson Jowell, in surly accents, bade the groom drive on. And as the spirited blacks broke at once into a trot, carrying their owner from the scene so rapidly that the spick-and-span mail-phaeton became behind their lively heels a mere flying streak of scarlet, he directed towards Blueberry and his owner the fervent aspiration: "*And I hope your brute may come a downer when you're charging in close order, and break your infernal neck for you!*" But he did not utter the words aloud.

XXII

Meanwhile Josh Horrotian pursued his march, but without the cheerful whistling accompaniment, decapitating the more aggressive weeds and thistles growing by the roadside with such tremendous slashes of the stout riding-whip as to leave no doubt that he executed in imagination condign punishment upon certain individuals unnamed. Indeed, so far did his annoyance carry him, that, disturbed beyond measure by the incessant chattering of the frosty wind amidst the crisp dry leaves of an elm-hedge he was passing, he bade the tameless element hold its noise, in what was for him a surly tone.

But, coming to a hog-backed stile, breaking the hedge and leading, by a narrow right-of-way over some clayey wheatlands, where the first faint green blush of the young corn lay in the more sheltered hollows, together with a powdering of fine unmelted snow, his bent brows relaxed, and the shadow that darkened his handsome sunbrowned face vanished. He whistled again as he threw a long blue leg, with a white stripe down the side of the tight trouser strapped down over the spurred Wellington boot, across the iron-bound log. For on the high bleak ridge of the sixty-acre upland, stood his mother's farm, facing away from him to the west; where the fall of the clay-lands upon the other side sloped to the deep and muddy Drowse, spanned by an ancient stone bridge that had rude carvings of tilting knights in plate-armor, upon some of the coping-stones of its parapet. The bridge crossed, a mile of country road dotted with farmhouses and cottages led to the small and sleepy borough-town of Market Drowsing, in the shadow of whose square Anglo-Norman church-tower many tall Horrotians had moldered into dust....

The sight of the low, irregular brown-and-red-tiled roof of the old home building, with its paled-in patch of garden at the southern gable-end, its great thatched barn sheltering it on the north side, and its rows of beehive-shaped ricks, each topped with a neatly plaited ball of grass, tarred to resist weather and impaled upon a wooden spike, warmed the man's heart, not for the reason that a somewhat cheerless boyhood had been passed beneath those mossy-green, lichen-yellowed, old red tiles, but because they sheltered Nelly.

"I wonder if she sees me?" he questioned with himself, as the path took a curve and the great church-shaped barn reared up its gray and ancient bulk between him and the homestead. "The little dairy-window at the house-back—this being about the time o' day she's drawing off the skimmings for the pigs—ought, if so be as she's on the look-out, to have given her a view"—his smile broadened—"of the approaching enemy."

Of course it had, long happy minutes back.... Even as the image of her rose smiling in his mind, she came running down the pathway straight into his arms, and with the joyful shock and the warm contact of her, vexations fled away, and he snatched her, not at all objecting, to his beating heart, and they took a long, sweet kiss—rather an experienced kiss, if one may say it, and more suggestive of the full-orbed sweetness of the honeymoon than of the wooing-time that goes before.

"Now, do 'e give over, Josh!" she said at last, and emerged all rosy with love and happiness from his strong embrace, and straightened her pink quilted sunbonnet, pouting a little. "Bain't you ashamed?"

"I'd like to see myself!" declared Josh stoutly, and had another kiss of her upon the strength of it, and then held her off at arm's length for a long, satisfying look.

She was very pretty, this Nelly, orphan daughter of a small freehold farmer named John Pover, who had borrowed money upon a mortgage from the great Thompson Jowell, and had, unhappy wretch, once the suckers of that greedy octopus were fairly fastened on him, been drained dry by means of extortionate interest, until he cut his throat—an absurd thing to do, seeing how little blood was left in him—leaving his freehold, farm, and stock to be gulped down, and his girl to take service as dairymaid with that grim Samaritaness, Sarah Horrotian.

She had sweet, soft, shy, dark eyes, had Nelly, and a sweet round face, the tops of its rosy cheeks dusted with golden freckles. There were some more on her little nose, a feature of no known order of facial architecture, but yet distracting to male wits, taken in conjunction with the rest; and a powdering of yet more freckles was on her darling upper lip, and the underlip pouted, as though it were jealous at having been overlooked. Her dark hair had a gleam of yellow gold on the edges of the curls that had escaped the control of the sunbonnet that now hung back upon her shoulders; and she had the round neck and plump breast of a dove, or of a lovely young woman, full of the vigor of fresh life and the glow of young hope, and the joy and the promise and the palpitating, passionate fulfillment of Love, without a bitter drop in the cup—until you came to Sarah Horrotian.

Josh came to Sarah, when the first edge had been taken off his appetite for kisses. He asked, unconsciously dropping back into his broad native accent, as he stood under the lee-side of the big barn, with his strong arm round Nelly's yielding waist, and her curls scattered on the broad breast covered by the tight blue jacket:

"Well, and how be mother?"

"I reckon much about the same. Throwing Scripture at a body," said Nelly, with a grimace that only produced a dimple, "whenever her be wopsy."

"And that's all round the clock," said Sarah Horrotian's son decidedly. He added: "Hard texts break us bones, Pretty. I learned that when I was a lad. And how's old Blueberry? Proper? That's right. He takes me back tomorrow—starting early so as not to overdo him, good beast!"

"I believe you love him better than poor Nelly," she said, with tears crowding on her long dark lashes at the thought of losing her love so soon.

"I'll show poor Nelly whether I love her or not." He pretended to bite a pink finger of the soft hand he cherished in his own. "Let's just forget tomorrow till it's here." His tongue broadened insensibly into the Sloughshire dialect as he went on: "And how be my old dog Roger? And Jason Digweed? Does he still take off his boots to clean pigsty, and then put 'em on again over all the muck? And wear no clothes at all to-house, and answer a knock at door naked as my hand; and scare expecting females into the straw, weeks before their time might be looked for? O' course he do! It wouldn't be Jason else. There's nobody can tell me anything new about *him*!"

"Med-be I might!"

He took her by the chin, and turned the coquettish face to him, and looked into the dancing eyes with a twinkle in his own.

"Now then, what is it? Speak up, you teasing witch!"

Nelly dimpled and blushed, and finally burst out laughing, smothering her mirth against Josh's blue sleeve in a very endearing way.

"Hurry up, or I shall guess!" Josh's florid face broadened in a smile, and his blue eyes twinkled knowingly. "I doubt but I do guess, though, all the same. Still, tell!"

She shunned his eyes with provoking coyness.

"I don't half like to say it out loud!"

"Whisper, then," he said gayly, "and give a man a chance to kiss a pretty neck!"

"Behave yourself! But stoop down. You be so tall."

He stooped, and she whispered, and the whisper sent him off into a guffaw of laughter.

"Ha, ha, ha! Well, to-be-sure!" He slapped his thigh and roared himself red in the face, and she laughed with him, though in demurer fashion. "Whew! that beats all! So Jason be in love, after all his cursing o' females, and wishing as the Almighty had seen fit to people the world without the help of petticoats. But who's the maid, if it be a maid, and what's her mind to him, seemingly? Will she swallow the mortal down, with a hold on her nose? or turn it up, and bid him get to windward with that mug of his, as a New Zealand idol might be jealous of? Come, give her a name! or I'll say you grudge her her good fortune!"

"You gave her your own, not so long back!"

"You don't mean yourself?"

Convinced by Nelly's blushes as by her laughter that she did mean herself; a purple hue swamped the trooper's florid countenance and a weakness took him in the knees. He rocked awhile, holding his blue-cloth-covered ribs, and then his laughter broke away with him, and wakened echoes that the barrack-room knew, but that the blackened, cobwebbed rafters of the ancient barn had not echoed to since a roaring bachelor squire of the soldier's name had held Harvest Home there in the dead old days when the Second George was King.

Nelly checked him when he reached the climax of gasping speechlessly and mopping his overflowing eyes. He crowed out:

"Well, that bangs the best! And what did you do when he made up to 'e? Comb his hair wi' a muck-fork or curtsey and thank him kindly for his damned presumption?"

"Use proper talk, else I'll tell 'e nowt," she threatened.

"I will, I vow! From now I'm the best boy in the Sunday-school,—mild as a dish o' milk, and as mealy-mouthed as Old Pooker—not that he's a bad sort, as the white-chokered corps go!"

"See you keep your word! Well then.... Says my customer to I...."

"Meaning Jason?..."

"Meaning Jason. Says he, smirking all over his face, as how I be a main pretty maid; and he have wrestled in prayer upon the matter, and med-be if I looked out wi' my bright eyes sharp enough, I should see myself standin' up before the Minister to Market Drowsing Baptist Chapel, being preached into one flesh wi' he—he—he!"

Josh drew a deep breath, inflating his broad chest to the utmost of its lung-capacity and bellowed:

"And this is the man as down-cries all women. Why, he got round mother that way, cussing of the female sex for traps and snares and Babylonish harlots, though why that kind o' talk should tickle her, hang me if I know! her being a woman herself, by way of!... But how did you meet the bold wooer?..."

"Tossed up my chin like so"—she furnished a distracting example—"and telled 'n as no living minister should mold me into one flesh wi' any mortal man!"

"Having been regularly tied up in the matrimony-knot by a parson—my blessings on his tallow face!" said Josh, with a triumphant hug, "that snowy day in January when you met me at the little iron church down the Stoke Road near Dullingstoke Junction, wi' the license buttoned in the pocket of my borrowed suit o' plain clothes, and the ring jammed on my little finger so precious tight—for fear of losing it!—that it took you and me and the beadle to get it off again!"

Upon the strength of these reminiscences he did some more hugging. She freed herself from the enclosing girdle of warm, muscular flesh and hot blood, pouting:

"Behave, and let a body finish! To that about the minister, and me never marrying, Jason he tells I as all young maids be 'ockerd at axing. 'But a'll gi' thee another chance,' says he. "Oolt thee or 'ootent thee? Cry 'beans' when I cry 'peas,' and it's a bargain!' Wi' that, he offers to kiss me!"

"The—frowsy son of a gun! Don't say you ever——"

"Likely!... I fetched 'n a smack in the face...."

"Bravo!"

"Following up with the promise that I'd rather die than wed 'n, and all the same so if he were hung wi' gold and di'monds...."

"There's my girl! What more?"

"Oh, Jason, he were cruel casted down. Quite desperate-like, and threatened me he'd 'list for a soger.... '*Why, they would wash 'e!*' I tells 'n; and he bundled away in a girt hurry, and haven't come athirt I since.... But your mother must ha' heard, her looks be so mortal glum."

"Never mind her looks! Tell her I've got a better husband for her pretty dairymaid than her pigman comes to, dang his dratted impudence!"

She rallied him in rude country fashion, its homeliness redeemed by the beauty of the speaking mouth and the dancing hazel eyes.

"You be jealous!"

"Jealous, am I?" He rapped out the fashionable oath, caught from his officers: "Egad! you rogue, I'll punish you for that!"

She seemed to like the punishment rather than not. And as she gasped, crimson under his kisses, there was a rustling inside the barn, near the great doors of which the lovers stood. One of these swung open, affording to the view of those without, had their absorbed faces but been turned that way, a segment of the vast churchlike interior, with its noble raftered roof upheld by kingposts at the gable-ends, and only lighted by the gleams of cold wintry sunshine that found entrance by the partly open door, and by the cracks between the ancient side-boards, and here and there where birds or rats had tunneled holes in the ancient brown thatch. Mounds of recently-threshed wheat occupied the granary at the higher end; with bales of sacks, cord-tied, destined to receive the hard, sound, golden grain. The lower threshing-floor was ankle-deep with the chaff of beans, and stout bags of these, newly tied, stood in rows against the opposite wall, while a great mound of the straw rose in the background. The wooden thail that had been used in the bean-threshing lay upon the floor. The man who had wielded it had yielded to the desire for a snooze, a weakness of Jason Digweed's when the beer was working in his muddy brain....

When the lovers had jested about him and his unlucky wooing, there had been a stirring in the heart of the mound of the bean-straw, and a dirty finger shod with a black nail had worked a spying-hole for an unwashed face, embedded in a matted growth of dirty hair, to rest in. Thus, unobserved, Mrs. Sarah Horrotian's pigman, fogger, cow-keeper, and general factotum, favored by the widow on account of his Dissenting principles and avowed and sturdy misogyny, could see what took place, and be entertained by the conversation.

It had fallen to fitful whispers. The man was urgent, and the damsel coy. The experience of the ambushed hater of the sex had to be drawn upon for the context of the broken sentences that reached the dingy ears under the dirty hair-thatch.

"Miss Impudence!" Josh called his sweetheart after some retort of hers.

"'*Miss!*'" she breathed, so softly that even her lover barely heard her.

"Miss Nelly Pover to the world as yet, and in the hearing of folks to-home here. But Mrs. Joshua Horrotian in snug corners when there's none to listen or pry. Eh, my beauty?" he said, hugging her.

"I don't know how I durst ha' married you!" she panted, "and me that afraid o' your mother...."

"Let me but get bought out of the Army and settled in my proper place as master of this farm," said Josh in a loud, ringing voice of cheerful hope, "and there's no one on earth you need hang your pretty head for, or ever shall, my darling!"

She turned to him then with all her coyness gone, and put both arms about his neck, and so clung to him, kissing the cloth of his jacket, the rough embroidery of his stiff collar, the hard, manly neck gripped by the leather stock, until the strong man quivered and grew pale, and leaned against the stout tarred timbers of the barn behind him, holding her to his breast. Thus he whispered with his lips at the rosy island of ear that showed among her curls, and his eyes seeking the desired haven revealed by the high partly-opened door. But she shook her head, with her face still hidden against him, and he was fain to wait and curb his passion, lest he should scare this shy and tender thing. He said, and his voice was not quite steady:

"As my girl pleases, be it. I'm hers for life or death! You know that, don't you, Nell?"

She pressed against the blue jacket, nibbling a bright brass button.

"Speak up and answer!"

No answer.

"Nelly!"

She vibrated at the low, persuasive call. You could see the waves of roseate color chasing each other from the edge of the print neckerchief upwards to the creamy nape of the soft dove's neck, where the silky little curls clustered under the sunbonnet. And then she yielded to him all at once, and he led her in under the high lintel of the great barn-door, and the wedded lovers vanished in the kindly, fragrant hay-scented gloom of the upper threshing-floor, where were the great golden mounds of tenfold wheat that Zeus and Demeter might have couched on.

XXIII

Meanwhile Sarah Horrotian, a small, determined, flat-bosomed woman of curiously heavy footsteps and rigorously determined aspect, attired in a narrow gown of rasping wincey and a blue-checked apron with a wedge-shaped bib, made plaint, groaning over the hideous wickedness of this world as she pounded with the roller at the dough upon the pastry-board. It helps the picture to add that the widow's pastry was of a consistence so tough and lasting that no human being, save one, partaking thereof, had ever been known to venture on a second helping, the exception being Digweed, the pigman.

When Sarah's only child, Joshua, then a white-skinned, red-curled, burly youngster of eighteen, already standing nearly six feet high in his deceased father's solid mahogany-topped boots and old-fashioned cords, and the baggy velveteen coat with the huge horn buttons, even when the hard, shiny, low-crowned hat hung on its peg against the passage wall—when Josh took the Queen's Shilling, it may have been an undigested slice of the widow's Spartan pie-crust, innocent of mollifying medium or shortening of any kind, that spurred him to the act, combined with Sarah's railing.

For the Lili and the Lilith, that ceaselessly chide, with shrill, weird, human-seeming voices, amongst the ruins of dead and long-forgotten cities on Babylonian plains, were as piping bullfinches compared with Sarah Horrotian.

If she had ever met with any members of the sect, she would have shone as a Muggletonian. To denounce rather than to exhort was her religion. To proclaim sinners lost eternally, and luxuriate in the prospect of their frying, to call down judgments from Heaven upon those who had offended her, was the widow's way.

News came to her from Jason Digweed, her unsavory Mercury and general intelligencer, that one Whichello, clerk and beadle to the Parish Church of Market Drowsing, whose incumbent claimed tithes from the widow, had suffered the loss of an eye, which had dropped out upon the Prayer-Book in the middle of the Litany, being a blinder all along—though Whichello had never had the ghost of a notion of it—and nearly scared Parson into fits.

"Then the Lord has not forgotten me!" said the grim little woman, folding her great bony hands upon her meager bosom. "He remembered that clutch of thirty addled Black Spanish eggs I bought of that whited sepulcher and set under our old Broody, and He has smitten, sparing to slay."

"Now, mother!..." began Josh, wriggling on the low-backed settle; "you don't really go for to say you believe a thing of the Lord like that there!"

"Silence!" said the widow, turning her long, sallow, high-nosed face, with the scanty loops of black hair upon the temples, upon her son, and freezing even his accustomed blood with the glare of her fierce black eyes. "If so be as the Almighty wills to avenge His chosen, who are you to say Him nay?"

She went out of the kitchen, shaking the crockery on the shelves with her ponderous gait, and visited her stores and sent from thence half-a-bag of potatoes and a leg of new-killed pork to the clerk's wife. "For the Lord never meant the innocent to suffer with the guilty," she knew. Later, when she subscribed half-a-crown towards the purchase of a glass eye for the bereaved Whichello, she forgot to quote her authority for the act.

Poor folk in want approached Sarah, expectant of verbal brimstone, not unhopeful of receiving more substantial aid. For the widow Horrotian, after severely-exhaustive inquiries, failing to run Deception to its earth, exuded silver in shilling drops, girding as she gave, when the well-to-do buttoned up their pockets and bestowed nothing but sympathetic words. Yet these were praised as kindly folk, when there were no blessings for Sarah. For even as her hand relieved, her tongue dropped vitriol on human hearts, and raised resentful blisters there.

One of these blisters, breaking upon a Sunday night at tea-time, led to the outlawing of Josh and his subsequent enlistment. A teapot was involved in the quarrel, which yet sprang from a milky source. For to the moral scourges with which Mrs. Horrotian lashed the quivering flesh of her only child, she never, never failed to add, as a crowning, overwhelming instance of the filial ingratitude of her son Josh, the reproach that she had nourished him at her maternal bosom—preferably choosing meal-times, and those rare occasions when guests gathered at her board, for these intimate reminiscences of the young man's helpless infancy.

To look at the woman raised doubts as to the possibility of her ever having nourished anything except a grudge or a resentment. No deal board could be flatter than the surface she would passionately strike with her bony hand in testimony to the fact alleged, causing Josh to choke with embarrassment in his mug of home-brewed ale, and eliciting from the guest—always a partisan and crony of her own—grunts, if a male: or pensive, feminine sighs, or neutral clicks of the tongue against the palate.

"As if I could help it!" Josh suddenly burst out on the epoch-making occasion referred to.

The turning of the worm was so unexpected that the widow leaned back in her chair, and there ensued a silence only broken when the minister of the local Bethesda groaned. For the Reverend Mr. Pooker, with his wife and daughter, were frequently guests at Sarah's board, the widow, nominally a member of the Established Church, having seceded to Dissent, liking her religion as she liked her tea, hot and strong, and without sugar.

"I think you spoke, young man?" said the Reverend Mr. Pooker, setting down the pot of rhubarb jam into which he had been diving, and staring solemnly at Josh. Mrs. Pooker faithfully reproduced the stare, and little Miss Pooker tried to do so, but only managed to look at the presumptuous youth with her little canary-colored head tilted on one side in an admiring manner. Not being sufficiently regenerate and elect to be insensible to the dreadful fascination of wickedness.

"I did speak!" asserted young Josh, boldly meeting the black eyes that flamed upon him out of the deep hollows under his mother's high narrow brow. "I said, 'As if I could help it!' and I say so again.... Were there no teapots handy? A teapot wouldn't ha' pitched itself in a child's face years after he's earned the right, Lord knows! to call himself a man."

"Scoffer!" thundered the great bass voice of the little flat-chested woman. "Mocker! As though I, Sarah Horrotian, would disobey the command that bids a woman suckle her children!"

"Well and nobly said, ma'am!" commented the Reverend Pooker, reaching for the seed-cake. "And let us hope that the respect and gratitood owed by a child so nerrished to a parent———"

"And such a parent!" interpolated Mrs. Pooker tenderly.

"Will not be forgotten," said the Reverend Mr. Pooker through the intervening medium of seed-cake, "by this misgeided and onrewly Young Man!"

"Very well, then!" said Josh, driven beyond patience. "All right! But why be I to thank her for doing what the Lord commanded her to do? That's what I want to know!"

Sarah Horrotian rose up at the tea-board end of the Pembroke table in the best parlor.

"Another speech like that, Joshua, and if you was ten times the son of my womb, you should go forth motherless from these doors. What! Shall the Name of the Lord be taken in vain at my table, and I not drive forth the blasphemer from my roof!"

"Dear sister in grace ..." began placid Mrs. Pooker, possibly foreseeing regrettable contingencies. But Sarah was fairly launched.

"And naked shall you go, Joshua, save for the clothes upon your back, and not a penny of my money shall be lavished upon the accursed of God and of his mother, for whom Hell gapes, and eternal punishment is most surely waiting."

"Hem!—hem!" coughed the Reverend Pooker, getting alarmed. But Mrs. Horrotian was wound up, and, as Josh knew, would go till she ran down.

"There shall you gnash your teeth in torment," boomed the awful voice of the widow. "There shall the Worm that dieth not gnaw your vitals———"

"Oh!—dang the dod-gassed Worm!" broke in the lost one, and at this hideous blasphemy the Reverend Mr. Pooker set down his refilled teacup with a bump that spilled half its contents over the saucer's edge, and the minister's wife and daughter fairly cowered in their chairs.

"I be sick to death of hearing about worms and gnashings and torment. And as for going forth o' your doors, I'll go now. So good-by, mother, for good and my parting respects to you, Mr. Pooker and Mrs. Pooker! Don't 'e cry, Miss Jenny! I shan't go to Hell a day sooner for all my mother's cursing. A pretty mother!" said Josh in boiling indignation, "to be calling down damnation on her only son across her Sunday tea-tray. Why, one o' they Cannibal Islanders she throws away good money on converting 'ud make a better shift at being civil to her own flesh and blood!"

Sarah did not recover her power of sonorous speech for some minutes after the best parlor door had slammed behind her departing prodigal, and his swift heavy steps had traversed the stone-flagged passage, and his manly voice, still vibrating with anger, had been heard telling the old mastiff Roger to go back to his kennel in the yard. Then she offered Mr. Pooker a fresh cup of tea, and when the pastor declined, suggesting application at the Mercy Seat for a better frame of mind for somebody unparticularized by name, the stark little woman gave no more sign of consciousness of the intimate and personal nature of the supplication, than if she had been asked to join in prayer for an obdurate Fiji Islander, determined on not parting with a favorite fetish of carved cocoanut-wood adorned with red sinnet and filed sharks' teeth.

But when the farmhouse was silent, and its few inmates, all save the mistress, wrapped in slumber, Sarah Horrotian sat upon a hard, uncompromising, uncomfortable chair by the dying embers of the farm-kitchen fire; and wept, as might have wept a wooden manikin, on some stage of puppets; wrenched with grotesque spasms and wiry throes of grief, holding her blue-checked apron squarely before her reddened eyes.

Ah! pity these isolated ones, stern of nature, obdurate of heart, who yearn to yield but are not fashioned for yielding. All they crave is the opportunity to relent and be tender, but it never, never comes! If someone had the courage to cling about those iron necks of theirs and pray them with tears and kisses, to be kind, they believe in their secret hearts that they could; but the waters of tenderness are dried up in them, or lost, as are forgotten and buried fountains in the great Desert, doomed never to spring to the light in crystal radiance and cool a thirsty traveler's lip. What tragic agonies are theirs, who can even see their dear ones die, unreconciled and unforgiven.... Ah! pity them, the obdurate of heart!

As for the Prodigal, who had tramped it into Market Drowsing, and bribed the under-ostler at the Saracen's Head Inn with sixpence to let him sleep in the hayloft appertaining to that hostelry after a supper of bread-and-cheese and ale, he had had a clinching interview with the tall Sergeant of Lancers at the Recruiting Office, before that stately functionary's palate had lost the flavor of his post-breakfast quart of beer.

Josh chose the Hundredth Lancers for the reason that he liked horses; and because the Sergeant, whom he hugely admired, belonged to that dashing Light Cavalry regiment. Also because there were knights in plate-armor tilting with lances in the half-obliterated fourteenth-century frescoes that rainy weather brought out in ghostly blotches through the conscientious Protestant whitewash of Market Drowsing Parish Church; and he had, from early boyhood, achieved patience throughout the Vicar's hydra-headed sermons, by imagining how he, Josh Horrotian, would wield such a weapon, bestriding just such another steed as Sir Simon Flanderby's war-horse with the steel spiked nose-piece and breast-piece, the wide embroidered rein, and the emblazoned, parti-colored housing sweeping the ground like a lady's train....

The Railway had not yet reached Dullingstoke. But the Sergeant, with his plentifully-be-ribboned captives, six other youths of Josh's own age, had marched into the town—with frequent washings-out of thirsty throats with pots of beer upon the way—and had whisked them off by the "Wonder" coach for Spurham before to Sarah Horrotian of The Upper Clays Farm came the news that her only son had joined in his lot with the shedders of blood.

Erelong, to that hopeful recruit, learning the goose-step at Spurham Baracks with the other raw-material under process of licking into shape, arrived a goodly chest containing comfortable provender of home-cured bacon, home-made cheese and butter, a stone bottle of The Upper Clays home-brewed ale, and a meat-pie with a crust of almost shell-proof consistency. In conjunction with a sulphurous tract, a bottle of horehound balsam for coughs, and a Bible containing a five-pound note pinned within a half-sheet of dingy notepaper, inscribed in the widow's stiff laborious handwriting: *"For my son. From his affectionate Mother. S. Horrotian."*

Do you know stern Sarah a little better now? Do you comprehend the craving need of strong excitement, the powerfully-dramatic bent that found a relieving outlet in the provocation of those passionate scenes that left the simpler and less complex nature of her offspring suffering and unstrung?

He was the gainer, she the loser, by that breach of theirs. Her terrible voice, her freezing glare would never overawe his soul and paralyze his tongue again. He would always have an answer for her thenceforth; her quelling days were over....

For to Josh, who had been bred in the belief that the word of Sarah was as little to be disputed as the Word between the black stamped-leather covers of the great Family Bible on the best parlor side-table, had come the revelation that his mother was merely a woman after all. She had always promised him that he would be blasted by a lightning-stroke from Heaven did he presume to defy her awful mandates and dispute her sovereign will. He had done both these things, and what is more, had done them on a Sunday, and the effect upon the weather had been absolutely *nil*. One of the balmiest, rosiest, and brightest of summer evenings he could recall had smiled upon the exile's tramp into Market Drowsing. He had thrown his curly red head back, and squared his strong shoulders as he went, looking up at the pale shining splendor of the evening star....

Full revelation of her loss of power to sway the imagination of her son did not come to Sarah Horrotian until two years later, when Josh, a full-blown trooper in Her Majesty's Hundredth Regiment of Lancers, came home, upon her written invitation, to spend a furlough at The Upper Clays.

He had acquired a power of smart repartee, a military sangfroid which Sarah found disconcerting.... His way of smiling as he pulled at a recently-acquired red whisker betokened self-consciousness and vanity, that damning sin.... It was in vain she urged him to confess himself a worm, and no man....

"That's your opinion o' your son, maybe!..." Josh played with the hirsute ornament, which his mother secretly admired, in the dandified way she abhorred, adding; "But I should call my father's son a decent sort o' beggar, taking him all round!"

"Pride goeth before a fall," said Sarah, in her deep chest-notes of warning, "and the pit is digged deep for the feet of the vainglorious."

"Ay, ay!" assented the soldier. "Perhaps I be vainglorious, a bit. But you have so poor an opinion o' me, mother, that I'm driven to have a better o' myself than I should in ordinary. Try praising me, if you want me to run myself down!"

Sarah was silenced. She shut up her mouth like a trap, and went about her work in rigid dumbness, while the voice of her soul cried out in bitterness, wrestling with Heaven for the soul of her son.

Whom to praise, whom to take pride in, whom to favor and indulge were to damn to all eternity, according to the Book from which some souls draw milk and honey, and others corroding verjuice and bitterest gall.

XXIV

This February noon, while the early sunset reddened the west and the son made love in the barn, the mother prepared stewed rabbit in the kitchen. She sliced cold potatoes into a pie-dish, with severe brows and compressed lips. And a young rabbit, disemboweled and skinned, ready for dismemberment and interment, leaned languidly over the edge of a blue plate, waiting the widow's will.

There was a heavy step upon the flagstones outside the closed half-door that kept the expectant group of fowls assembled at the outer threshold from intruding into the kitchen. The upper part of a tall man's body appeared over the half-door, blocking out the sunset. Its long shadow fell over the chopping-board and the widow's active hands. She knew whose was the step, and her hands were arrested in mid-movement. Had her grim nature permitted it, she could have cried out with joy. As it was, a dimness obscured her vision, and the roaring of the blood in her ears drowned out the click of the latch as he came in.

"Joshua!..."

"How are you, mother?"

The tall, manly, soldierly figure, towering in the oblong of open doorway against its background of flaming sunset sky, farmyard, and stubble sloping to the jade-green river crawling between its frosted sedges, stepped to her and took her large, hard hand, and kissed her underneath the high, sallow cheekbone, with a duteous peck of lips.

"I am well, thanks be to the Lord!" said Sarah, regarding him unflinchingly. He was so like her dead husband, his father, that a wild surge of emotion strained the hooks and eyes of the brown wincey gown and swelled her lean throat to choking anguish.

"That's right. But you always are well, ain't you, mother? Bobbish, if not tol-lol? And Miss Nelly?" For she had entered at the moment, bringing the radiance of youth and happiness to illumine the somewhat gloomy farm-kitchen. "No need to ask how she is, if looks speak for anything! How do you do, Miss Nelly? Let me hope as you've not quite forgotten an old friend?"

"No, for sure! and I be nicely, Mr. Joshua, kindly thanks to 'e!"

With her quilted sunbonnet shading a face that the February wind, or some more ardent lover had kissed to glowing rosiness, from the widow's hard black eyes, she put her pink hand in the hypocritical fellow's large brown one, and gave him modest welcome.

So modest and discreet, even in those rigorous eyes of Sarah Horrotian, that the extraordinary snorting sound emanating from Jason Digweed, who, heralded by his characteristic perfume of pigsties in combination with unwashed humanity, had appeared outside the half-door, startled the widow as though a geyser, suddenly opening in the brick kitchen-floor, had been responsible for the utterance.

"Bain't you ashamed, man?" she tartly demanded of the offender, "to make noises like the beasts that perish?"

"No-a!" retorted Jason. He stepped boldly across the kitchen threshold, permeating its slightly onion-flavored atmosphere with a potent suggestion of pigs, and planted his huge and dirty boots defiantly upon the spotless floor-bricks, in defiance of the mute appeal made by the rope-mat to the entering visitor. He scratched himself leisurely, within the open bosom of a shirt of neutral hue, and as he scratched he looked from one to the other of the three faces that bore degrading testimony to the daily and thorough use of water, soap, and flannel, and his little eyes burned redly under their populous thatch. It is not often that to a piggy man who has been wounded by the dart of Amor and roused to resentful frenzy by the fair one's contemptuous rejection of his love, comes so complete an opportunity for vengeance upon a triumphant rival as Jason savored now.

The soldier's rashness hastened the descent of the sword....

"Why, 'tis Jason," he began, with a tingling in the muscles of his strong arms prompting him to punch a head, and an urgent impulse concealed within the toes of his spurred Wellingtons, that had ended before now in somebody being kicked. "No need to inquire after your health, I see. A perfect picture.... Isn't he, Miss Nelly?—if so be as a chap could see the picture for the dirt upon it!"

"Let Digweed be. He is as the Lord made him!" boomed the deep rebuking voice of Sarah, "and a burning and a shining light of holiness such as I have prayed in vain the son of my womb might be!"

"The Lord made him as clean as the rest of us at the start, I reckon," retorted the soldier, rushing on his fate, "and a burning and a shining light in a mucky lantern is no better than a bad 'un at the best. Eh, Miss Nelly?"

At this homely piece of wit Nelly laughed out merrily, and Sarah, turning her long narrow face and stern black eyes on the blushing offender, bade her be silent in so harsh a tone that she began to cry.

Mightily relishing Nelly's tears and confusion, Jason perpetrated a whinnying imitation of the silly little laugh that had drawn down her mistress's rebuke upon her. But upon a sudden forward movement of the angry-eyed trooper, he hastily turned the whinny into a groan of the prolonged and gusty kind, wherewith searching pulpit utterances were ordinarily greeted at the Market Drowsing Bethesda.

"Now, look ye here, Digweed," began the trooper, upon whose rising anger the groan had anything but a mollifying effect, "if so be as you're a man, and have anything upon your tongue's end, out with it in human language, and ha' done wi' bellocking and gruntling,—or betake yourself where the company are more likely to understand ye."

The speaker slightly jerked his thumb towards the littered yard, in shape an irregular square; the long straggling mass of the farmhouse occupying the upper side, the stables, sheds, and cattle-byres enclosing it upon the right hand; a goodly row of populous pigsties flanking it upon the left, where a hollow depression was occupied, during ten months of the year, by a brown pond of gruel-like consistency, much patronized of paddling ducks and a large black maternal sow, at that moment engaged in rootling investigations upon its plashy borders.

"Let be!" sounded in the deep tones of the widow. She checked her son's impulse towards continued speech with a semaphore-like movement of the lean little arm with the great bony hand at the end of it. "If you have anywhat to say, say it!" she commanded, seeing her unwashed factotum to be in labor with speech.

"Mis'ess," said Jason, getting out the word with a violent wrench and twist, "since Babylonish luxury and scarlet doings be 'lowed on this here varm, my time 'ooll be up come Mickenmass—and I'll be ready to up-stick and bundle!" He wagged his shaggy head at his mistress, but his piggy eyes were on her son.

"Silence!" boomed the great voice of Sarah Horrotian. She put up her large hand as the soldier opened his mouth to speak. She set back the rabbit on the blue plate from which it had lapsed as though overwhelmed by the secession of the fogger. Then she folded her lean arms upon her triangular apron-bib, and confronted the shining light with judicial severity.

"Who speaks of luxury and wickedness doing on this place," she proclaimed, "must make his charge good. Out with yours, man!... Let us hear what you have to say!"

"I were gettin' my nuncherd o' bread an' chaze up to th' owd barn," said Jason, with another spasmodic effort, "leanin' my back agen th' boards to th' wind'erd zide of 'n, as I chudd, when I heern a nise-like inzide. Like so!"

The pigman primmed his lips, and brought out a long-drawn, chirping kiss. The sound plopped into the silence as a stone plops into a pond, creating rings of consternation. Two of the three faces the narrator scanned with the bilious little savage eyes under his heavy brake of eyebrow were flaming crimson. The third was pale with wrath, as Sarah exclaimed indignantly:

"Trapesers again!"

"A male man and a female woman," continued Jason, "kissing and cuddling as though the begetting of bastards were th' only biznurds they med ha' come into the world to tend."

He turned up his eyes and groaned again. The soldier's leathern stock grew strangling in its embrace. The milk-maid's bosom lifted on a gasp for air. Josh and Nelly, each in their different way, prayed that the ordeal might be soon over....

Meanwhile thunderclouds gathered upon the high sallow forehead of Mrs. Horrotian, between the scanty loops of her black hair. A suspicion sharpened and yellowed her. She reviewed possible offenders in her narrow mind a moment, then said:

"Be you swearing-certain they sinners were tramping bodies?"

Jason returned, plunging two hearers into a hot and cold bath of perspiration:

"Noa, I bain't!"

"Med-be," said Sarah, with a vinegar face of disgust, "that to-yielding girl of Abey Absalom's has been straying with some bachelor-mankind hereabouts. Both Joe Chinney and Tudd Dowsall be sinners prone to fall."

She waited for no answer:

"And to them and all such, Judgment will be meted out hereafter!"

She took the rabbit from the plate, disposed its limbs upon the chopping-board, balanced the chopper above the victim, and brought down the blade. Nelly squeaked as though the rabbit had been capable of utterance, as the mangling steel fell. The awful voice went on, as its owner with dreadful dexterity finished chopping up the victim:

"For there is a hell for chamberers and wantoners!" She solemnly laid the remains of the sacrifice in the pie-dish, strewed cold vegetables above, poured a cupful of gravy upon the whole, and added, with the salt and mace and pepper: "Nor shall fornicators fail of their place therein. Girl, open the oven door!"

Pale Nelly totteringly obeyed, showing a cavernous interior of coaly blackness, radiating fierce heat, illuminated by red and leaping reflections of awfully-suggestive flame. Both the son and the daughter-in-law knew themselves guiltless, their endearments chaste and lawful as those of Zacharias and Elizabeth. But when the high-priestess of the mysteries advanced, knelt, and with a powerful shove of her bony arm drove in the pie-dish to deepest perdition, and clashed the oven-door as though it shut upon the lost for all eternity, their knees trembled and their eyes clung together behind the widow's narrow back. Even Jason gulped and shuddered. But he recovered as the widow turned upon him, demanding:

"Was it Joe Chinney wi' Nance Absalom?"

"Noa!" returned the piggy man. And drove home the negative with a vigorous headshake.... Horror stiffened Sarah's facial muscles. Her great voice deepened to a blood-curdling whisper as she said:

"Dew and Randy be both wedded men.... Betsy Twitch the weeder be only half a widow.... Jason Digweed, do you mean to tell me the Seventh Commandment has been broken in my barn?"

For answer Jason raised a gnarled and stubby forefinger and made a malignant jab with the digit in the direction of the tall, martial figure in the blue, white-faced uniform.

"Best ask your soger son, Widder Horrotian. Med-be he'd took unto his'seln' a praper missus som'ers before he made 'e mother-in-laa to your own milkin'-wench?"

XXV

There was a moment's horrible silence in which the white-faced clock was drowned, or so it seemed to the married lovers, by the thumping of their hearts. Then the dreaded voice boomed forth:

"Joshua Horrotian!"

"Here!" said the soldier, as if the roll were being called.

"Your miserable mother has a question to ask. Are you, the son I bore, a villain, or an honest man? Is this girl whom I have sheltered under my roof, and fed o' my charity, a virtuous woman or a weak, to-yielding trollop?"

"I should ha' knocked down the chap who'd asked me them two questions," said Josh, turning a blazing crimson countenance, illumined with a pair of indignant candid eyes, upon the widow. "But I suppose, being my mother, and a professing Christian, it's your privilege to think the worst o' your own flesh and blood, no less than other folks. And so far as I can remember, you always have, I'll say that for you! And though such usage goes far to the making of a decent young fellow into a villain and a blackguard as well, I am neither of these things, I declare before my Maker!" He added, with a clinching vigor that drove home belief in him: "And this young wife o' mine is as clean of sin, if not as innocent—before Him I say it again!—as when she came into this charitable-thinking world a naked baby!"

The strangling sensation behind the leather stock had lessened, the ripe-tomato hue that had swamped Joshua Horrotian's open, florid countenance had faded to a more normal tinting. The flaming sunset of the cold, clear evening showed up his stately height and vigorous handsome proportions to rare advantage. He was only a private trooper in Her Majesty's Hundredth Regiment of Lancers, but in the eyes of the stern mother, whose love of him was intense in proportion to her rigorous concealment of it, no less than in those of his shy, worshiping wife, he seemed a king among men. But while the wife rejoiced in his beauty, his mother loathed it as a snare. She had no words in which to hid the soldier take not the Holy Name in vain. She turned her hollow eyes away from him, lest she should offend the grim Moloch she worshiped by excess of pride in this perishable shape of clay, formed from her own body. And the resonant manly voice went on:

"Here's the extent o' my defaulter's sheet where you're concerned. I've married your milkmaid wi'out asking leave of you or anybody. Why? I'll save you the trouble of asking the question I see on the end o' your tongue. Because I love her and she me! Come here-along, my Pretty!"

He held out, with his dead father's well-remembered gesture, the strong arm in the blue-cloth sleeve, and the masterful look of affection and the becoming air of pride he did this with, the widow of George Horrotian well knew. An insufferable pang pierced her when Nelly, with a little, eager cry, ran into the welcoming circle of the embrace. It closed upon the rounded waist as if it never meant to let go. And a spasm of rageful, despairing jealousy clutched Sarah as she saw; and her heart fluttered and clawed and pecked in her lean bosom like a starling burrowing in a crumbling wall. She closed her haggard eyes to shut out the sight of the hateful creature who had robbed her....

And yet, although she did not realize it, to the rigid woman who had yearned for a maid-child and been denied one, this creamy, rose-tinted, hazel-eyed orphan of a ruined farmer and his fagged-out young wife, was dear. Nelly had come into grim Sarah's life too late to bring about a softening change in it, and garland it with flowers. Indeed, she shrank with loathing from the widow's bony touch, and shivered with secret hatred at the sound of the railing voice that had driven her Josh from home before she knew him.... But such affection as Mrs. Horrotian had to spare from the son whom in her own characteristic and uncomfortable manner she idolized, was bestowed upon the girl who was now his wife.

Unimaginative as the woman was, her bitter love for both of them had brought its cruel gift of clairvoyance. The premonition of a growing tenderness between the two had sat by her sleepless pillow many a night past. The secret conviction that it was not to see his mother, but this bright-eyed, silken-haired interloper, had made, for months past, a whispering-gallery of her poor tormented heart. She had been driven by the nagging dread, against her better nature, to favor Jason's piggy wooing by tacit assent rather than by words....

And now—the thing she feared had come upon her. She was never, never to be beloved by her son as her great love deserved! and the girl she had taken in and protected had proved herself a traitress. For her she had no curse; but was not Scripture fruitful in denunciation of children who disavowed a parent's right? And yet *"a man shall quit his father and mother and cleave to his wife."* When she, the maid, Sarah Doddridge, daughter of a well-to-do yeoman-farmer of the county, had eloped with her penniless young lover, the couple had salved their smarting consciences with this text. Now, behold punishment meted out.... As she had served her mother, this son of her womb had served his.

Inexorable, awful justice of that grim idol her own imagination had made, set up on high, worshiped, and misnamed God! She weakened at the blow her memory dealt her. A harsh sound that was barely human came from her dry throat. She took hold of it as savagely as though it had been an enemy's, and rocked upon her flat, slippered feet as she wrestled with herself. Her son and her son's wife eyed her anxiously. They saw her moved in that strange inarticulate way, and a faint little hope awoke in both their hearts, and babbled that she might even melt and bless them—as parents, at first relentless, usually ended by doing in story-books and theater-plays.

But it was not to be. The bilious eye of the piggy man was upon the widow. And Jason, with extra garnishing of words, repeated that he was ready to go at Michaelmas. Such was his spirit, he added, that he'd be dalled if he served under a soger-master, on The Upper Clays or any other farm!

"Swear not!" trumpeted Sarah, turning her long chalk-white face and resentfully-flaming black eyes upon the factotum. She plucked herself from a brief descriptive verbal chart of the particular place in the Lake of Fire specially reserved for profane persons, to add:

"And as long as I am mistress at The Clays there can be no other voice in authority. While I choose, I rule!"

"Your soger son there says different," proclaimed the piggy one. "A's to be master heer, what time you buys 'n out o' th' Army, and then there's noan on earth her'll hang her pretty yead for...." He jerked a grimy stump of a thumb contemptuously towards Nelly. "Least of all mother-i'-laa, Widder Horrotian!"

"Mother!" broke out the soldier, controlling by a violent effort the urgent impulse to punch the speaker's matted head, "will you let this mangy dog make bad blood between us? Something of what he was repeating I did say to my wife. But I'll take my solemn oath, without a word disrespectful to you! You promised to buy me out of the Army, and let me manage the farm for you, and in the course of Nature—and may it be long a-coming!— a day 'ull dawn when I am master of The Clays. Then, as I hope my mother never has had or will have reason to be ashamed of me, so never may my wife. The words were harmless, twist 'em as the eavesdropper will. Upon my soul they were!"

Sarah swallowed something that might have been an iron choke-pear of the Middle Ages. She looked in her son's hot blue eyes, and said with stern composure:

"Pledge not your soul to its undoing, though I dread it be lost a'ready. My father left this farm to me, to use at my discretion. 'Tis for me to decide when my son be fit to rule. Jason Digweed here were one of th' witnesses to your grandfather's Will. He made it his own self, without borrowing words from any man, an' 'twas read out here, in th' best parlor, by Lawyer Haycock, after the Funeral. Digweed remembers the wording, I'll warrant. Speak out, Digweed. Prove to this undutiful and rebellious son that his mother does not lie!"

Thus adjured, Jason cleared his throat with a sound like the scraping of roads, and recited with relish:

"'And I Leaves this 'eer Varm wi' all of the 'Foresaid Messuages and Lands hadjoining and Distant To Sarah Ann Horrotian my Deer-Beloved Daughter Trusting to her Usings and Employings and Disposings of the Same For the Bennyfit of Her Lawful Son Joshua Who shall succeed to the Use and Enjoyment of the Property when in the Judgment of my aforesaid Daughter Sarah Ann Horrotian He shall Hev' Attaindered to Years of Discretion.'"

"You hear?" said Sarah.

"Ay, I hear," her son returned with bitterness. His chest heaved; his bright blue eyes burned reproachfully upon the haggard indomitable little woman in meager wincey brown.

"And I see, too," he added, with a bleak smile that showed the sour woman's portion in him, "as my mother is like to go back on her promise of buying me out of the Army, and setting me to manage the farm."

"If so be as the Almighty can recall His word because rebellious creatures to whom His promise was given have backslidden and become perverted," proclaimed Sarah, "His servant may do the same!"

"You pious folks have always th' Bible to back ye," said Josh bitterly, "when you'd wrong your neighbors—or betray your sons!"

"I betray no creature born. After such a down-bringing, paltry, miserable marriage as you ha' made, do ye suppose I can answer to my departed father for your discretion? Back wi' ye along to Barracks, and bide there! Discipline be the only rod for a stubborn nature such as yours. '*Behold, in My love will I chasten you and will not refrain from scourging.*'" She added, upon the heels of the text: "Nor shall a penny o' my money go to buy you out o' th' Army. Selah!"

"You ... won't ... buy me ... out?"

Sarah answered, in one short bark:

"No!"

He clenched his great fist and shouted:

"Who is the blackguard has egged ye on to this? Not—Jowell?"

Her stern conscience forbade her to deny the counsels of the Contractor. Yet, as a pious body of her type will, she evaded the answer direct:

"Mr. Jowell no more than yourself, that be gritting your teeth and clinching your fist at the mother that bore and suckled you."

Involuntarily Josh's eye went to the white-spouted brown earthenware teapot, that, as far back as he could remember, had sat in the middle of the second shelf of the oak-dresser when not in active use. The ghost of a twinkle flickered in his blue eye, the hovering shadow of a grin was on his solid countenance. He remembered the First Exodus and its cause. His mother may have read his thought. She said in clanging tones, as intolerable to her son's hearing as though an iron tray were being beaten with a poker close to his ear:

"Was it my doing that you casted in your lot with the shedders of blood? No, but your own upping pride, and wicked stubbornness. Back wi' ye to Barracks, and bide there! I ha' got no more to say!"

The fleshy, red-whiskered face that aged and bleached under her indomitable regard sent strange shudders through her, in its likeness to the pinched, gray waxen mask she had kissed upon the stiff-frilled pillow of her husband's death-bed. From the mouth that had straightened into a pale line under the flaming mustache came words, uttered in the very tones of the dying:

"And my wife?"

The broad hand shook that spread itself protectingly over the little brown head that shed its wealth of dark silken ringlets upon Josh's stalwart chest. A voice came from their ambush; no frightened whimper, but a clear and resolute utterance:

"Her goes wi' her own dear husband, as a wife ought!"

He groaned, forgetful of the triumphing Digweed, and the hard black eyes of his listening mother....

"My girl, my girl! you don't know what you be talking about, or what kind o' women you would have to live alongside."

Nelly lifted her cheek from the blue coat it nestled to, and met his look. Perhaps, if you had seen the quivering of the short upper-lip with the golden dust of freckles on it, and the brave way in which the hazel eyes laughed through a veil of tears, and the twisting of the pink fingers shyly interlacing upon her apron-band, you would have loved her nearly as much as Josh did.

"They would be soldiers' wives, like I be myself, dear heart."

"But what soldiers' wives, my girl! Trollops and jades many o' them, married in a moment of drunkenness. Honest women the rest; decent enough, but rough as hemp. And using language, the best o' them, such as 'ud scald these little ears to hear!..."

A sob broke from him with the bitter cry:

"Mother, you'll never deny my wife a shelter in the house where my dead father lived with you in love?"

Said Sarah, upright as a ramrod and grim as a steam-hammer:

"I ha' not gone to say as far."

With his manhood melting in him to the point of tears as he gave back the faithful look of the dark eyes that wooed his, he stammered:

"God bless you for that!"

"But," said Sarah, grimmer than ever, for the pink fingers had tapped his lips, and he had pecked a passing kiss on them, "as she has earned her dole of food and her penny of wages with service here, so she shall continue to do. I keep no idlers, nor shall!"

"Nor were asked to, I reckon!"

From the safe rampart of the blue cloth hug Nelly launched with the words a bright eye-dart of defiance. Sarah thundered in reply:

"Young woman, check your tongue!" She added, with an afterthought of precaution: "And show me your marriage-lines."

"My lines?..."

The trooper said, in answer to the puzzled knitting of the girl's soft eyebrows:

"The paper the parson as married us 'scribed out and gave ye, Pretty.... The certificate of our marriage 'twas. The wife always keeps that!" He added, dipping his tongue in salt pickle saved over from a brief experience of the lower troop-deck: "'Tis our cable and sheet-anchor both in the stiff gale we're weathering. Out with it, my girl!"

He looked to see her take it from the darling fastness of her bosom. A hand fluttered there, then dropped. The irises of the hazel eyes usurped the golden-brown-gray until they seemed all black.... A frightened voice said:

"Why ... I mind you taking o' that paper to keep for me...."

"Nonsense!" he broke out, so roughly that Nelly winced, and faltered:

"But indeed and 'deed 'tis true!... Pray do, do remember! Think how I had no pocket to my gown, having made 'n on the sly in such a hurry as never, up to th' garret where I sleep, working by the light of saved-up dip-ends hours after your mother had took th' flat candle-stick away...."

Sarah's gloomy front contracted ominously. Were not those dip-ends filched? Nelly went on, appealing to her moody, frowning lord:

"I were for putting the paper in my bosom.... 'Twas you said 'Nay' to that! So you took un and put 'n in th' pocket o' your pants."

"That I never!... Stop, though!..."

His mouth primmed itself into a whistle of dismay, so ludicrous that Nelly tittered through her tears. He felt in the single pocket permitted by Government, patted himself all over the blue covering of his big chest and solid ribs in the hope of drawing forth a paper crackle, finally bellowed with the full strength of his vast lungs:

"Right, by the Lord Harry! So I did; there's no denying!"

His eyes grew circular and bulging, his healthy, florid, intelligent countenance was stricken into the very idiocy of consternation, his bushy flaming whiskers seemed to droop, grow limp, and fade in color as he stuttered:

"And never thought about it after or since!... And the chap belonging to the Rifle Corps—that lent me the plain-clothes suit—if you can tack on 'plain' to a chessboard check in half-a-dozen colors—it being as many sizes too big for him! offered me the togs as a bargain, him being ordered out to Bermuda on Foreign Service.... And I hadn't the money—and he sold the chessboards to a Jew.... Whew! My eye and Betty Martin!... Who's got those pants on now?"

"Then," said his mother, in tones that cut like broken ice-edges, "you that are a married couple have no lines to show me?" She paused and delivered sentence, woman-like wreaking vengeance first upon the daughter of Eve....

"You poor, to-yielding wench, this man has deceived and ruined 'e! A woman without her marriage-lines be no wife at all!"

XXVI

Do you who read cry "Bosh!" at the preposterous notion?... Not so these unlettered, homespun Early Victorians, who never dreamed of its being possible, by the payment of a few silver pieces, to obtain a copy of the original entry in the Marriage Register pertaining to the sacred edifice where the matrimonial knot had been tied. Go, search through the literature of the period. You will find shelves of musty novels, piles of foxy old dramas reeking with this very situation. The cry:

"*Where are my lines?... Lost—lost!...*" meets invariably with the pertinent, potent answer, making Edwin beat his brow in despair, sending Angelina into syncope or convulsions: "*Then also lost, unhappy one, art thou!*"

At the moment when the interview above recorded was taking place, my Aunt Julietta, in the family mansion on the outskirts of Dullingstoke, was reading in the February issue of *The Ladies' Mentor* a sweet, sad, sentimental tale hinging on a similar loss. Only Edwin was a passionate, penniless young nobleman, reduced to win his bread by imparting to the daughters of the nobility and gentry of Great Britain lessons on the guitar; and Adelina was the third daughter of the Marquess of K——. And the marriage-lines, cherished in Adelina's *corsage* since the happy morn that united her for ever with the *being she adored*, had been picked up on the carpet of her young lady's dressing-room by Babette, the French lady's-maid, and employed as a curl-paper for the glossiest and most golden of her young mistress's ringlets, No. 3 on the left temple next the ear....

Even as Lady Adelina screamed, previously to falling into convulsions and rolling about like a fair and fragile football in book muslin, amongst the legs of the Early Victorian tables and chairs, so did Nelly cry out in anguish, falling, not into syncope or fits, but into the stalwart arms of her man— who received her in them, and as she sobbed upon his broad breast, tried, with a heavy heart under his white-faced blue-cloth jacket, to cheer and comfort her.

"Fiddlesticks! We're legally married, my girl!" he said. "Why, hang it! the knot was tied by Special License, and egad! I still owe half of the two-pun'-ten I paid for it to the chap that loaned me the cash! If the paper's lost, the yellow iron church is standing still, I suppose, at the bottom o' the Stone Road near Dullingstoke Junction. Nobody's blown it up with a mine, I take it? and sent the mealy-faced young parson up aloft before his time! Bless my button-stick, what a silly little soul it is!"

All this he said, and more. But stout as his words were, the heart of the trooper was as water within his body, and he knew, as he had never known it, even when marched in before his Colonel to receive an orderly-room wigging, the sensation of being gone at the knees. His mother's impenetrable self-command, her pale face of judgment between the scanty loops of her black hair, flaring torches of terror to evil-doers, began to daunt and quell him as though he had suddenly shrunk to a mere truant boy. She spoke, not to him, but to Nelly:

"This is an honest house. I don't say but its doors will be open to you, and its roof will give you shelter, if so be as you come and ask your husband's mother for it, with your marriage-lines in your hand. But till you can show them, get you gone out of my sight! Go with the man you say's your husband, forth out of these my doors!"

"So be it, then," said the trooper sullenly. "I'll take her back to Spurham wi' me to-morrow!"

"You'll take her to-night."

"Mother, you'll not turn us out like that!"

She had wrung the entreaty from him at last—humbled the hardened man who had braved and defied his mother! A spasm of savage triumph shook her inwardly, but to all appearances she might have been a wooden image of a woman, the pleading seemed to leave her so unmoved. She said, still speaking to Nelly:

"Get you up to chamber-over, and make a bundle of such odds as you'll need. Pack your box,—'twill be sent by the Railway to the Cavalry Barracks at Spurham, come to-morrow. You, Digweed, tie the clout on the gate as a call to th' carrier when he passes by." She added, addressing her son, as the piggy man departed with much alacrity to execute the congenial errand, and Nelly, obeying the order in her husband's eye, quitted the kitchen and shortly afterwards was heard tripping about with short, quick steps on the joist-supported whitewashed boards that served as ceiling to the kitchen and flooring to the room above:

"If you be ahungered or athirst, there's cold bacon and bread on th' dresser there; and she you call your wife can draw you a mug of ale."

He said, drawing himself up to his splendid height, and using a tone of cold civility that somehow cut his mother to the quick as his fierce upbraidings had failed to do:

"No, ma'am, I thank you!"

She found herself urging, as Nelly opened and shut drawers and cupboards overhead, and was heard to drag a box across the floor:

"You have had a day's journey, and started with but a dew-bit. You'd better take something to stay you. 'Twill be wise!"

Her bowels yearned over him, knowing him unfed. He said, as a stranger answers a stranger:

"I thank you kindly, but I could not, ma'am."

She began to tremble at the thing that she had done. She said, almost entreatingly, and with the metallic resonance quite gone out of her voice:

"'Twould be a want of common Christian kindness to let you go fasting!"

A red-hot spark of resentment burned in his blue eye. He said, measuring his words to the tap-tap of Nelly's little thick-soled shoes, descending the short carpetless stair:

"I have had my bellyful of Christian kindness under this Christian roof." He added, as Nelly appeared, wearing her Sunday cloak and bonneted, and carrying a rather clumsy bundle of soft consistency tied up in a workaday shawl:

"And I leave it with my wife, to return to it no more! Come, my girl! We'll quarter in Market Drowsing to-night, and take the route for Barracks to-morrow. Where did I put my haversack?"

His eyes passed over his mother and lighted on the regulation canvas bag lying on a shelf of the dresser near the home-made loaf and the rejected cold bacon, towards which he experienced a yearning that filled his mouth with water and plucked at his resisting pride. He picked up and slung on the pack with a vigorous movement, caught his cap from a wall-hook, took his wife by the hand, and, not without a certain manly, soldierly gallantry, led her out of his mother's house, leaving Sarah standing in the middle of the kitchen-floor with her great hands folded over her triangular apron-bib.

"Good-by, Old Broody and the rest," said the bride, so rosy a little while since, pale now and fighting with tears repressed, as some hens, accustomed to receive from her hand the supper-scraps about this hour, hurried to her with squawking, scaly-legged haste. "Who'll feed 'e now, poor things? and milk the new-calved cow to-night? Her never could bide the sight o' Jason, that there red Devon wi' the crumpey horn!..."

"Sensible beast!" said the exiled son of the house, picking up a little frilled nightcap with a Prayer-Book inside it, that had escaped from a yawning fissure in the bundle. That little nightcap in Josh's great hand transformed Nelly from a white rose into a red one, and was responsible for a sudden rise in the mercury of the trooper's spirits.

"Ha, ha, ha! Well, to be sure now! And uncommon becoming, I'll swear, though my money's on the curls without a cover! Give me the bundle, Pretty!" He stopped in the act of shouldering it to exclaim: "Halloa! We're forgetting another bit o' property we're bound to take with us! Can't you guess? My horse Blueberry.... My own good beast!... Come back-along and fetch him."

Together they retraced their steps, crossed the farmyard, and Nelly kept guard over the canvas bag and the shawl-bundle, to which the little frilled nightcap that had wrought such a bright and hopeful change in Josh's downcast face had, with the Prayer-Book, been returned; while the trooper disappeared into the warm hay-scented darkness within the stable. From which, after some "Come up's" and "Woa, there's!" accompanied by the creaking of a girth and the clanking of a bridle, he emerged, leading a handsome horse of strong and powerful build, with one white patch in the middle of his broad hairy frontlet, gentleness and courage in his great misty blue-black eyes, and so rare a purplish sheen on his gray coat, of equine health and vigor, as justified the name bestowed on him by his master.

And Nelly kissed Blueberry's velvet nose, and told him how he and she and his master were all going away to be happy far from The Clays; and Blueberry whinnied his pleasure at the news; and then the canvas bag and the shawl-bundle were strapped behind the saddle, and, with a kiss from the lips that never more need seek her own in secret, Josh—in defiance, Sarah thought—but really in oblivion of the gaunt eyes that stared at them over the starched muslin blind, and the hedge of winter-housed geraniums and fuchsia-cuttings that blocked the kitchen-window,—lifted his young wife to the young horse's back. She faltered, as her hands left his broad shoulders, and clung for a brief instant about his strong neck:

"Turn round your head a minute, dear Josh, and look at the old home, and all you've given up for the sake of your poor Nelly!"

He said, with a brief glance at the old gray stone building of the farmhouse, from whose mossy-tiled roof and small diamond-paned casements the reflected glow of the sky was fading fast:

"Good-by, old place! And if so-be as I must stick to soldiering all my life; I carry from you the two things a soldier needs the most,—supposing him a cavalryman!... a good horse and a sweet wife!"

Nelly's tears broke forth at that, but the bright drops were more of joy than sorrow. She urged as he took the bridle, and told her to sit fast:

"You're quite, quite sure you'll never repent it?"

"As sure," he said, walking with measured pace beside the now moving horse, and with a stern ignoring of the pale oval patch that showed against the darkness of the kitchen, above the muslin blind, "as that *she* will, come her dying day.... Why, I am damned if I'll put up wi' this!"

A nervous little shriek from Nelly, caused as much by the sudden appearance of the piggy man, starting up like a frowsy gnome or kobold under Blueberry's very nose, as by the resulting swerve which had nearly unseated her, provoked the objurgation.

The kobold danced a dance of triumph, accompanying his saltatory exercises upon the voice; and the burden of his song was that the soger and his lass, who had said they were wedded and could produce no bit of scrawly paper to prove their tale true, had got the dirty kick-out, and he, Jason, was main glad of it, that he were!

Dealing separately with the feminine offender, duly visited by express judgment from the skies, for trifling with the affections of a piggy man, he reverted, as the incensed soldier strove to control the restive horse, and Nelly clung in terror to the saddle and Blueberry's mane alternately, to a kind of recitative....

"She—be—an—Arr!"

Thus sang Jason, solemnly gamboling in the muck and litter, close to the edge of the oleaginous and strongly-smelling brown duck-pond previously described, which, reinforced by the oozings from many pigsties, and diluted by the melting of recent snows, filled the hollow it occupied to the very brim.

Changing the case, but not the meaning, the pigman chanted as he now advanced, and now retreated, doing wonderful things with his bandy legs, and achieving marvels with a set of features which, naturally grotesque, lent themselves with indiarubber-like adaptability to the exigencies of grimace:

"Her—be—an—Arr!"

And with a final, fatal inspiration followed up with:

"Soger's—Arr!..."

The epithet hit like a lump from the dungheap. The clumsy pirouette that accompanied it brought the pigman within the reach of retribution.

The gaunt eyes of Sarah saw the stalwart arm of her son shoot forth suddenly. The iron hand belonging to the arm seized the pigman by the rearward combination of matted hair, unwashed skin, and slack smock that served him as a scruff. As a rat in the mouth of a bulldog was Jason Digweed shaken, then hurled away with a rotatory motion, a human teetotum spinning against its will....

Splash! the brown pond received the gyrating one in its oozy yielding bosom. A horrible wallowing succeeded, accompanied by a smell of such terrific potency, that Adam and Eve, as they retreated from their forfeited Paradise, were forced, after homespun rustic fashion, to hold their noses.

Suppose you have heard the whitewashed gate with the carrier's wisp of rag tied on it, clash to behind the horse, the man, and the woman.... Even so, you have not done with them yet;—not quite yet....

Nor with Sarah, praying in the empty farm-kitchen, clamorously justifying herself before the Face of her Maker, as the white-faced clock ticked sorrowfully by the wall. Old Time has seen so many of us drive away the being we most loved and longed for. When has he ever seen that banished joy return in answer to our desperate prayer?

XXVII

Dunoisse never had sought, never would seek, news or speech or sight of the faithless friend; but now at last, without seeking, within a few days of his return to Paris, came the vision of de Moulny....

It rose before him in a flare of artificial light that made a yellow patch upon the foggy gloaming of that fateful day when the White Flag of Orleans that drooped—or dripped in rainy weather—above the stately central Pavilion of the Palace of the Tuileries began to show unmistakable signs of coming down.

Such signs as the unceasing, resistless rolling of huge, dense, continually-augmenting crowds of the people along the boulevards; through the wider of the ordinary Paris thoroughfares, murmuring as they went, with a sound like the great sea. With other crowds streaming in upon these from the suburbs. With thirty-seven battalions of Infantry, one of Chasseurs d'Orléans, three companies of Engineers, twenty squadrons of Cavalry, five thousand veterans of the Municipal Guard, and five batteries of Artillery, garrisoning the capital. With students of the Schools of Technical Military Instruction, students of Law and Medicine, students of Art, students of Music, starting the *Marseillaise* in the Place de la Madeleine. With the chant taken up by the Titanic voice of the people. With the breaking of a tidal wave of humanity over the palisades of the Chamber of Deputies; a rolling-back of this before the trampling horses of an advancing squadron of Dragoons; a similar advance upon the Ministry of Foreign Affairs, repelled by Municipal Guards; a shutting of shops, a mushroom-like springing up of Barricades, radiating from the Cloisters of Ste. Marie in the very heart of ancient Paris, extending from the mouths of tortuous streets to the gullets of narrow, crooked alleys, so as to form a citadel where Revolutionists concentrated, waiting instructions from headquarters of secret societies,—pending results of sittings of Committees of Insurrection, held by day and by night in the offices of the Republican Journals,—ready to act without these if they were not forthcoming. While by rail and by road, in answer to the urgent summons of muddy dispatch-bearers on wearied horses, or at the imperative tap-tapping of the electric needle; amidst the roaring and grinding of iron wheels and the trampling of iron-shod hoofs; a never-ending flood of armed men rolled down on Paris.

Now, upon a deputation from the Fourth Legion of the National Guard, calling upon a certain Crémieux, Deputy of the Opposition, with a petition to the Chamber, demanding dismissal of Ministers and Electoral Reform, came by the dawning of the twenty-fourth of February the rumor that this demanded change was actually To Be—a rumor meaning little to some, welcomed by others as the first indication of the scepter of St. Louis falling from a weak, relaxing Royal hand. Huge bonfires, made by students, of the heaped-up wooden benches belonging to the Champs-Élysées, had showed officers of the Staff galloping hither and thither with orders and counter-orders all through the raw, bleak night; had illuminated the crowds assembled to stare at the spectacle of Royal troops bivouacking on boulevards and public squares; and had been reflected in the shining bronze and polished steel of cannon, posted on the Places du Carrousel and de la Concorde.

But as yet, though Paris had seen the pulling-down, by detachments of the military, of the barricades choking those narrow labyrinthine streets that were the veins of the heart of her, and had winked at the building-up of these by the Revolutionists as fast as they were demolished; but, though a volley or two had made matchwood of the tables and chairs, the market-carts and omnibuses of the Barricades; though some minor conflicts between the People and the Police had ended with the tearing of tricolors and the capture of a red flannel petticoat mounted on a barber's pole, and the dispatch of a few laden stretchers to the Hospitals; though a bayonet-point or so had been reddened; though the edge of a saber may have been used here and there, instead of the flat; though a guerilla-warfare between scattered groups of Socialists with revolvers and bludgeons and small parties of Dragoons and Cuirassiers made public streets and squares perilous for peaceable citizens; though Republicans had disarmed the National Guards of the Batignolles and burned the station at the barrier, and though the *rappel* had been beaten and Legion by Legion these tax-paying citizen-soldiers were answering to the call to arms,—as yet the anticipated insurrection had not begun.

The sails of the Red Windmills that grind out Civil War hung slack, though the *piquets* of Dragoons and Chasseurs, posted at the openings of the streets and thoroughfares, had been on duty for thirty-six hours; were swaying with weariness and hunger in the saddles of their exhausted, tottering horses, their haggard faces half-hidden as they dozed behind the high collars of their long gray cloaks....

How did the spark reach the powder? Processions had been formed in token of popular delight at the announced change in the Government. Bloused workmen armed with pikes and sabers and pistols that had done duty in 1793, half-fledged boys with bludgeons or cheap revolvers, women of the Faubourgs with babies or choppers or broomsticks, the swarming life of the poorest quarters formed into column under the Tricolor or the Red Flag. Such a column came muddily rolling towards the Ministry of Foreign Affairs, filled the Rue de Choiseul with no sound beyond the trampling of feet, many of them in wooden shoes, many more naked, while the head of the column advanced upon the front of the Hotel, that, like its assailable sides and rear, was protected by a steel hedge, the bayonets of a half-battalion of the Line, hastily summoned from their barracks in the Rue de l'Assyrie, some twenty-four hours previously.

The Colonel and one or two officers who were personally acquainted with the Minister in popular disfavor had been summoned to a conference—involving dinner—in his private apartments looking on the garden—from which he was a little later to escape, disguised in a footman's livery. An Assistant-Adjutant commanded the companies of infantry that stemmed the onward rolling of those muddy waves of humanity that threatened to swamp the front courtyard—a slender, black-eyed, soldierly young Staff-officer of perhaps twenty-seven, with a reddish skin tanned to swarthiness by desert sunshine and dust-winds.

It was Hector Dunoisse. He sat upon an iron-gray half-breed Arab mare at the upper outer end of the bristling double line of bayonets and red *képis* that were flanked at either end by a squadron of Municipal Guards. The shako of a subaltern officer showed at the rear of the files, behind the Lieutenant rose the white-painted, gilt-headed railings topping the wall that enclosed the courtyard of the Hotel, carriages and cabriolets waiting there in charge of their owners' servants, the broad steps under the high sculptured portico dotted with curious groups of uniformed officials or liveried lackeys, or neutral-tinted strangers who had taken refuge there before the advancing column with its flaring naphtha torches and its Red Flag, and its raucous roar of voices....

There were even ladies amongst the groups in the courtyard. One, who wore a costly mantle of ermines, revealing between its parting folds a brilliant evening-toilette, upon whose bare white bosom diamonds and rubies glowed and sparkled; who had a coronet of the same jewels crowning the rich luxuriance of her curled and braided hair, stood apart, isolated from the rest, under the tall wrought-iron standard of a gas-lamp not yet lighted, talking to a tall, heavily-built young man wearing the chocolate, gold-buttoned, semi-military frock-coat that, in conjunction with trousers striped with narrow gold braid, formed the uniforms of secretaries and attachés of the Foreign Office. And that the young man was very much more absorbed by the conversation of his companion than the lady was in her listener was evident. For while his light brown head with its carefully massed locks and accurate side-parting was bent down towards her so that you saw his profile, the accurate tuft of reddish whisker above the black satin stock, the large handsome ear, the heavy clumsy nose, the jutting underlip and long, obstinate chin, *her* full face was constantly turned towards the packed and seething thoroughfare before the tall iron gates, and the living barrier of human flesh and horsemeat and steel that guarded them. And that face was very fair to see. Even in the uncertain gloaming, the loveliness of it went to the heart like a sword....

Now as the foggy dusk of the gray February day closed coldly in, and the muddy sea of humanity surged up against the wall of steel and discipline that Authority had built before the lofty gilt-topped railings of the Hotel of Foreign Affairs, the oil-cressets on the gate-pillars and above the central arch that spanned the entrance were lighted by the porters, the great gas-lamp in the courtyard and under the portico roared and hooted into an illumination that dimmed the smoky, flaring torches of the men who marched with the Red Flag. As the Adjutant on the iron-gray charger rode along the gleaming gray line of leveled bayonets, bidding the men close up;—as he called over the heads of the rank-and-file, giving some order to the Lieutenant, the young attaché who was conversing with the lady in the ermine mantle started and looked round. There was something in the clear, frosty ring of the voice that recalled ... a voice he had once known. His hard blue eyes met the eyes of the black-haired swarthy officer on the half-breed Arab the next instant. And—with a cold, thrilling shock of recognition, dying out in a crisping shudder of the nerves, Redskin and de Moulny knew each other again.

The fiery, sensitive Arab felt her rider's violent start, a sudden contraction of the muscles of the sinewy thighs that gripped her satiny sides drove both spurs home to the quick, behind the girths. As the Red Flag showed through the thick rank smoke of naphtha-torches held high in grimy hands, Djelma bounded forwards, snorting fiercely at the unexpected sting; reared at the checking bit, backed, still rearing, upon the goading steel points behind; lashed madly out, wounding herself yet more, and, knocking down two linesmen; then plunged forwards, kicking, screaming, and biting, into the thick of the crowd.

Those who marched with the Red Flag took the rebellion of Djelma as obedience, and resented being trampled, after the manner of mankind. Dunoisse was struck on the bridle-arm by a bludgeon wielded by a red-capped, bloused, bearded artisan. A frowsy, bare-bosomed woman aimed a savage blow at him with that deadly weapon of the lower classes, a baby. The man who carried the drum went down at a blow from the Arab's fore-foot. The empty-sounding crack of the splintered instrument, the oaths and yells and curses of the crowd were mingled in the ears of Dunoisse with the snorting of Djelma, the cries and exclamations from the thronged courtyard behind the wall of soldiers. A single shot cracked out behind him: the finger that pressed the trigger upset the Cabinet, changed the Government, toppled the rocking House of Orleans over with one touch. For instantly following the detonation of the shot a sharp, loud, bold, imperious voice cried:

"Fire!"

And, the next instant, jagged tongues of flame ran along the front line of leveled bayonets, the deafening clatter of a volley of musketry reverberated from the many-windowed façade of the Hotel, mingled with the splintering and shattering of glass; ran rattling up and down adjacent streets and neighboring thoroughfares, mingled with the echoes of shrieks and curses and groans.... Tumult prevailed, the Municipal Guard charged, striking with the flat of the saber ... the Red Flag wavered and staggered, the column broke up, its units fled in disorder to the Rue Lafitte. Pandemonium reigned there, a hundred voices telling a hundred stories of massacre deliberately planned....

XXVIII

You could not see the soldiers' faces, the smoke of that deadly volley had rolled back and hung low, topping the living wall of steel and flesh. But as it lifted, and they saw, by the light of the lamps in the courtyard behind them, the bloody heaps of dead and wounded men and women, mingled with children not a few, that made a shambles of the thoroughfare, upon whose gory stones the drum lay flattened, a hollow groan burst from the wavering ranks, and oaths and threats were uttered. Some wept, others were violently sick, as dying fellow-creatures crept to their feet to call them murderers, as fallen torches hissed and sputtered in the blood that ran down the gutters and lay in puddles on the pavement of the boulevard.

Confusion reigned in the Hotel, a Babel of voices clamored in the courtyard that was seething with excited humanity and littered with broken glass and bits of plaster knocked from the walls by ricocheting bullets. As Dunoisse returned on foot, leading his limping, bleeding mare through the dead and dying; de Roux, Colonel commanding the 999th, a plethoric pursy *bon-vivant*, who had been dining with the unpopular Minister in his private cabinet that looked upon the gardens, and had been snatched from the enjoyment of an *entrée* of *canard à la, Rouennaise* by the crash of the discharge, burst out of the Hotel, thrust his way through the huddled ranks, bore down on the supposed culprit, gesticulating and raving:

"Death and damnation! Hell and furies!——"

The purple, glaring Colonel struck his breast with his clenched hand, and though the action smacked of tragedy, the napkin, still tucked between the military stock and the gold-encrusted collar that had preserved the gray-blue uniform field-frock from spatterings of soup or splashes of gravy—no less than the silver fork the warrior yet grasped, imparted an air of farce to his passionate harangue.

—"Madman!" he spluttered out; "what crazy impulse induced you to give the word to fire?... Insensate homicide!—do you know what you have done? Take his *parole*, Lieutenant Mangin. Not a word, sir! You shall reply to the interrogations of a military tribunal, as to this evening's bloody work!"

Dunoisse, forbidden to explain or exonerate himself, saluted the blotchy, wild-eyed Colonel, and gave up his sword to his junior. You saw him apparently calm, if livid under his Red Indian's skin, and bleeding from a bullet-graze that burned upon his cheek like red-hot iron. The leather peak of his red shako had been partly shot away, the skirt of the tight-waisted gray-blue field-frock had a bullet-rent in it. His throat seemed as though compressed by the iron collar of the *garotte*, his heart beat as though it must burst from the breast that caged it. But his head was held stiff and high, and his black eyes never blinked or shifted, though his lips, under the little black mustache with the curved and pointed ends, made a thin white line against the deep sienna-red of his richly-tinted skin.

"Sacred thunder!... Return to your quarters, sir!"

De Roux, becoming alive to the napkin, plucked it from his bemedaled bosom and, realizing the fact of the fork, whipped it smartly behind his back. Dunoisse saluted stiffly, gave up his bleeding charger to his orderly, saluted again, wheeled, and deliberately stepped out of the radius of the Hotel gas-lamps, flaring still, though their massive globes had been broken by ricocheting bullets, into the dense gray fog that veiled the boulevard, where dimly-seen figures moved, groping among the dead, in search of the living....

"The Monarchy will pay dearly for this act of criminal folly!... How came he to give the order?" de Roux demanded.

And the subaltern officer, whose glance had followed the retreating figure of Dunoisse, withdrew it to reply:

"My Colonel, he gave no order. A pistol-shot came from behind us—a voice that was a stranger's cried 'Fire!' The discharge followed instantly, and the people fled, leaving their dead behind them."

"Why did he not defend himself?" de Roux muttered, glancing over his shoulder at the huge broken-windowed façade of the Hotel rising beyond the imposing carriage-entrance, the enclosing wall and the gateway and the tall spear-headed railings that backed the huddled figures and lowering, sullen faces of the unlucky half-battalion.

"Because, my Colonel, you had ordered him to be silent, and to return to his quarters. They are in the Rue de la Chaussée d'Antin. And he has gone to them by that route."

The Lieutenant's sword pointed the direction in which the slim, upright, soldierly figure had vanished. The Colonel growled:

"Why should he choose that route?..."

And the Lieutenant thought, but did not answer:

"Possibly because he hopes to meet Death upon the way!..."

Colonel de Roux, with clank of trailing scabbard and jingle of gilt spurs, stormed up the double line of abashed and drooping red *képis*. Interrogated, Monsieur the Captain in command of the company posted at the eastern angle of the courtyard enclosure, gave in substance the information already supplied.

"A pistol-shot came from behind us—a stranger's voice gave the order 'Fire!'—the discharge followed.... One would have said it was an arranged thing. One would——"

"Chut!"

De Roux glanced over his gold-encrusted shoulder at the façade of broken windows and chipped stone ornaments. The Captain, the same lively de Kerouatte who had paid Dunoisse that ancient moss-grown debt of three thousand francs upon the steps of Rothschild's, continued, as though the note of warning had not reached his ear:

"Madame de Roux would be able to corroborate. I saw Madame—previously to the deplorable accident—in the Hotel vestibule, conversing with an official in diplomatic uniform. She——"

"You are mistaken, sir!" said the Colonel, purple where he had been crimson, mulberry-black where he had been purple, and screwing with a rasping sound at his bristling mustache: "Madame de Roux is on a visit to some young relatives at Bagneres. This perturbed and disaffected capital is no place for a soul so sensitive, a nature so impressionable as Madame's. I have begged her to remain absent until these disturbances are calmed."

"A hundred thousand pardons! My Colonel, how idiotic of me not to have remembered that I had the honor of meeting Madame de Roux upon the Public Promenade at Bagneres only yesterday.... I ventured to accost Madame, and asked her whether I could have the honor to convey any message to you? Madame said 'None,' but added that she felt deliciously well. And to judge by appearances, there is no doubt but that the air of Bagneres agrees with her to a marvel!"

De Kerouatte reeled off this unblushing fabrication with an air of innocence ineffably insulting, inconceivably fraught with offense. De Roux could grow no blacker—against the congested duskiness of his face his little red wild-boar's eyes showed pale pink. They routed savagely in the large blue orbs of the speaker, guileless and unruffled as pools upon a Mediterranean shore, found nothing there; were wrenched away.... He gobbled out the beginning of an incoherent sentence—and then a messenger came with a hurried summons from the Minister, and the Colonel clanked and jingled back into the Hotel, from the gates of which pedestrians were unobtrusively gliding, while coupés, chariots, barouches, and landaus, driven by nervous coachmen and with pale faces peeping from their windows, or hidden behind their close-drawn blinds, or concealed behind thick veils, or upturned collars of cloaks and overcoats, were rolling hurriedly away.

The Colonel's gilt spurs had not long jingled over the tesselated pavement of the vestibule, before, from one of the smaller, private waiting-rooms, the figure of a lady emerged. A tall, rounded shape moving with a swaying supple grace "as though on clouds," wrapped in an evening mantle of sumptuous ermines, its snowy folds drawn close as though its wearer were desirous of silencing even the whisper of silken skirts; a thick veil of creamy lace wrapped about her head. She beckoned with a little hand, that had great blazing rubies on its slender finger and childlike wrist; and from a corner of the wide courtyard, crashing over the broken glass and shattered fragments of the carved stone wreaths that garlanded the high windows, came a little, dark brougham lined with gray velvet, a vehicle of the unpretending kind in which ladies who gambled on the Bourse were wont to drive to their stockbrokers, or in which ladies who gambled with their reputations were accustomed to be conveyed elsewhere....

A nondescript official, neither lackey nor porter, still mottled and streaky in complexion from the recent alarm of the fusillade, emerged from some unlighted corner of the tall portico into the flaring yellow gaslight, followed the lady of the ermine mantle down the wide steps, and with zealous clumsiness suggestive of the Police, pushed forward to open the carriage door. Recoiling from his assiduous civility with palpable uneasiness, the lady shook her veiled head. The intruder persisted, prevailed; and in that instant found himself thrust aside by the vigorous arm and powerful shoulder of a tall, heavily-built young man in the chocolate, gold-buttoned, semi-military undress frock that distinguished secretaries and *attachés* of the Ministry.

"You presume, my friend!" said a voice the lady knew; and she rustled to her seat, and settled there with nestling, birdlike movements, a light brown, carefully-curled head bent towards her. The scent of cigars and the fashionable red jasmine came to her with the entreaty:

"There may be peril for you in these streets.... Will you not let me accompany you home?"

"In that coat.... Not for the world!" said a soft voice through the intervening veil, and the warm perfumed darkness of the little brougham. "You would expose me to the very peril you are anxious to avert."

"True!" he said, repentant. "I was a fool not to remember! Grant but a moment and the coat is changed!"

"I would grant more than a moment," she answered in a voice of strange, ineffable cadences, "to the wearer, were the coat of the right color!" A little trill of laughter, ending the sentence, robbed it of weight while adding subtlety. But its meaning went to the quick. De Moulny sighed out into the fragrant darkness:

"Oh,—Henriette! Henriette!"

She continued as though she had not heard:

"And I hope to see you wearing it—a little later on. Good-night, my friend. Do not be anxious for my safety. My coachman will be cautious. All will be well!" She added: "You see I am becoming prudent, rather late in the day."

He said, and his tone grated:

"They will mark the day in the calendar with red."

A sob set the warm sweet air within the enchanted brougham vibrating.

"You are too cruel. I have been guilty of an act of unpardonable folly. But who would have dreamed of so terrible a result?"

"Anyone," he answered her in a bitter undertone, "who has ever set a kindled match to gunpowder, or poured alcohol upon a blazing fire!"

The light from the carriage-lamps showed his white face plainly. His hard blue eyes frightened her,—his forehead seemed that of a judge. She shivered, and her whisper was as piercing as a scream:

"Or dared a woman to commit an act of rashness. Do not you in your heart condemn me as a murderess? Your tongue may deny it, but your eyes have told me that instead of rolling in a carriage over those bloodstained stones beyond these gates, I should crawl over them upon my hands and knees. Is it not so, Alain?"

Between the thick frosted flowers of her veil, her brilliant glance penetrated. A cold little creeping shudder stiffened the hair upon his scalp and trickled down between his broad shoulders like melted snow.... Her breath came to him as a breeze that has passed over a field of flowering clover. Her lips, as they uttered his name, stung him to the anguished longing for their kiss.

"I have not condemned you!" he muttered. "Do not be unjust to me!"

She breathed in a whisper that touched his forehead like a caress:

"Had you reproached me, you would have been in the right. Well, dare me again!—to denounce the person guilty of this massacre.... I am quite capable of doing it, I give you my word!... Perhaps they would send me to Ham!... Who knows?"

A nervous titter escaped her. She bent her head, trying to stifle it, but it would have its way. She caught the lace of her veil in her little white teeth and nipped it. De Moulny saw the creamy rounded throat that was clasped by a chain of diamonds, swell within the ermine collar. He knew, as he inhaled the seductive fragrance that emanated from her, the exquisite allure of whiteness against white. Visions so poignant were evoked, that he remained spellbound, leaning to her, drinking her in. She continued, and now with real agitation:

"I shall see them in my dreams, those dead men in blouses,—if ever I sleep again!... Ah, bah! Horrible!... Please tell the coachman home. Rue de Sèvres." She added before he withdrew his head to obey her: "Unless I take the Prefecture of Police upon my way?..."

He retorted with violence:

"Be silent! You shall not torture me as you are doing!"

"Then," she said, with another hysterical stifled titter, "pray tell the coachman to take me home."

He told the man, who leaned a haggard face from the box to listen; and added a warning to drive through the most unfrequented streets and to be careful of Madame. To Madame he said, hovering over her for another fascinated instant before he shut the carriage door upon the warm seductive sweetness:

"Remember, you are not to be held accountable for a moment of madness. You never meant to pull the trigger. I swear that you did not!"

He drew back his head and shut the door. The window was down, and he looked in over it to say again: "Remember!" A whisper caught his ear:

"The pistol.... Where is it?"

He touched himself significantly upon the breast.

"I have it here. I shall keep it! You are not to be trusted with such dangerous things, impulsive and excitable as you are."

"Dear friend, such weapons are to be bought where one will, and those who sell them do not inquire into the temperament of the buyer. Tell me something, Alain!..."

He said in the passionate undertone:

"I love you to madness!... Henriette!..."

"Ah, not that now, dear friend, I beg of you!"

"Henriette, I implore you"

A small warm velvet hand alighted on de Moulny's mouth. He kissed it devouringly. It was drawn away, and next instant the sweet, sighing voice launched a poisoned dart that pierced him to the marrow:

"Tell me, Alain! If I pulled the trigger of the pistol in a moment of madness, were you quite sane when you cried out 'Fire!'?"

She pulled up the window as de Moulny, with a deathly face, fell back from it. The coachman, taking the sound as a signal, whipped up the eager horse. The little brougham rolled through the tall gateway into the frosty fog that hung down like a gray curtain over the bloody pavement, and was swallowed up in the mad whirlpool of Insurrection, to be cast up again on the shores of the Second Republic of France.

Follow, not the furtive little brougham, but Dunoisse, rejected of Death, perhaps because he courted the grim mower.... Follow him through the populous fog to the corner of the Rue Lafitte, where the scattered units of the shattered column of bloused men and wild-eyed women had assembled in front of the Café Tortoni, occupying the angle between this street and the boulevard.

A bearded man, the same who had carried the Red Flag, was addressing the people from the steps of the Café. He had been wounded, the blood dripped from the clenched hand he shook above his head, as he denounced the perfidy of Ministers, the ingratitude of Kings, and the blood-lust of the Army, who for gold spilled their brothers' lives. A sullen roar went up at each of his phrases, the vast crowd of listeners about his impromptu rostrum heaved and billowed, and whitened with furious faces constantly tossed up, like patches of foam upon a sinister sea.

Dunoisse, like a striving swimmer, battled in the muddy waves of that same sea, in the endeavor to reach the steps where raved the orator. It was too dark for the owners of those bodies between which he forced his way to distinguish that he was in uniform, and, so, realizing his desperate determination, they aided him.

But when at last he gained the steps, and the mingling glare and flare of the oil-lamps and the gas showed up the loathed gray-blue and red of the Line—though the Staff shako bore no number to identify its wearer as an officer of the regiment that had fired upon them—the cry that went up from all those hot and steaming throats was as the howl of ravening wolves:

"Murderer! Accursed! Back to your corps! Down with the Ministry! Down with the Line!"...

A hundred hands, some of them stained with red, thrust out to seize Dunoisse and tear and rend him. A hundred voices demanded his blood in expiation, his life for all those lives spilled on the paving-stones of the Boulevard des Capucines....

"Take it if you will!" cried Dunoisse at the fullest pitch of his clear hard ringing voice, "but let me speak!"

The flaring lamps threw pale patches of light and black patches of shadow on his face, but there was no fear there. He snatched off the bullet-pierced shako and showed them the peak that had been partly shot away; tugged at the Staff epaulet hanging by a waxed thread or two; lifted the full skirt of the tight-waisted gray-blue field-frock and showed the bullet-holes in the cloth....

"What is it to me what you do?" he cried. "Death comes to all sooner or later. But upon the honor of a gentleman!—on the parole of an officer!—I gave no order to fire. The shot came from behind! The voice that cried 'Fire!' was not mine. I swear it upon the faith of a Catholic!"

This was not a popular asseveration. The voice of the speaker was drowned in execrations:

"Ah, malefactor! Assassin! Down with him! Down with the priests! Death to the Army! Long live Reform!"

His voice was no longer audible.... He made signs, entreating a hearing; the bellowing, hooting, yelling redoubled. Stones flew, banging on the shutters of the restaurant, denting its barred and bolted doors, smashing unshuttered upper windows. A man with a musket leaped on the steps, and leveled the loaded weapon; the unfortunate young officer looked at him with a smile. Death would have been so simple a way out of the *cul-de-sac* in which Dunoisse now found himself. For if the People would not believe, neither would the Army. He was, thanks to this cruel freak of Fate, a broken, ruined man. Perhaps his face conveyed his horrible despair, for the fury of the crowd abated; they ceased to threaten, but they would not listen, they turned sullenly away. And the bearded man who had carried the Red Flag, tapped him on the epaulet, made a significant gesture, and said contemptuously:

"Be off with you!"

Dunoisse, abandoned even by Death, looked at the speaker blankly. He was burnt out; the taste of ashes was bitter in his mouth. His head fell upon his breast and the world grew dim about him. There was a cloud of thick darkness within his brain, compared with which the frosty fog of that February night was clarity itself.

Then the fog lifted, and he was alone. The boulevard was deserted, the chairs and little marble-topped tables used by drinkers of absinthes and vermouths, lay tumbled all about upon the stones.... Shops and restaurants had their shutters up; windows that had no shutters had been blocked with mattresses and chests of drawers. A body of mounted Chausseurs galloped down the Rue Lafitte, posted a piquet at the corner of its junction with the Boulevard, and galloped away again into the fog. Out of which came back the clatter of iron-shod hoofs, and the ring and clink of steel on steel, and drifts of the *Marseillaise* and cries of vengeance.

Dunoisse went to his rooms in the paternal hotel in the Rue de la Chaussée d'Antin, and sat in the dark, and saw a pair of cold blue eyes, and the thick-lipped supercilious smile he knew of old painted upon the shadowy blackness, and the ceaseless roaring of voices and rolling of wheels through the streets of Paris, mingled with the roaring of the blood in his ears.

He knew that this meant black ruin if the Monarchy stood, and ruin blacker still if Red Revolution swept the Monarchy into the gutter. Whose was the hand that had been guilty of the fatal pistol-shot?

He knew, or thought he knew—for the voice that had cried out "Fire!" had been undoubtedly de Moulny's. And the anguish he tasted was of the poignant, exquisite quality that we may only know when the hand that has stabbed us under cover of the dark has been proved to be that of a friend.

XXIX

The people collected their dead and their wounded and commandeered wagons, and loaded them with the pale harvest reaped from the bloody paving-stones before the great gateway and the tall gilded railings and the chipped façade with the shattered windows, behind which the unpopular driver of the Coach of the Crown sat gripping the broken reins of State.

Pallida Mors headed the grim midnight procession. And as it rolled, to the slow wailing of a mournful chant, by the light of flaring torches through the streets, upon its way to the offices of the *National* and the *Réforme*,—where lights had burned, and men had sat in conference for sixty hours past,—those who marched with it knocked at the doors of scared, unsleeping citizens, crying: "Wake! behold the deeds that are done by Kings!" And the noise of firing, and of furious cries, with the clanging of church-bells, sounding the tocsin at the bidding of Revolutionary hands, reached the ears of pale Louis Philippe at the Tuileries, and must have shrieked in them that all was over!

For all was over even before the Place du Palais Royal was filled by thousands of armed insurgents; before the Palais was stormed and gutted; before the Fifth Legion of the National Guard,—having its Major, its Lieutenant-Colonel, and several officers in command—marched upon the Tuileries; followed by the First, Second, Third, Fourth, Sixth, and Tenth: before the Deed of Abdication was signed—the Royal dwelling emptied of its garrison—the shabby one-horse hackney coach called from the stand—(the Royal carriages having been burned)—and before the Monarchy, covered with an ancient round hat, clad in worn black garments, and with only five francs or so in its pockets, had emerged by the little wicket-gateway near the Obelisk, stepped into the humble conveyance above mentioned, and passed away at full gallop, surrounded by Chausseurs and Municipal Guards, and accompanied by a running cortége of mechanics, artisans, nursemaids, gamins, ragpickers, shoeblacks, and other representatives of the Sovereign People.

With the aid of the English Admiralty, and the British Consul at Havre, Mr. Thomas Smith, his lady and their grandchildren, obtained berths on the *Express* packet-boat; and, despite the activities of the local Procurer of the Republic—not to mention certain perils incurred through the too-excellent memory of a certain female commissionaire or tout for cheap lodging-houses, Madame Mousset by name,—who by the light of her dark lantern recognized Majesty even *minus* its whiskers—the voyage to Newhaven was accomplished without disaster. Claremont received the Royal refugees; the

Tory organs of the English Press were distinctly sympathetic; even the ultra-Whig prints, amidst stirring descriptions of barricade-fighting and the carnage on the Boulevard des Capucines, refrained from the dubious sport of mud-throwing at the monarch all shaven and shorn....

The popular Reviews devoted some pages to the favorable comparison of peaceable, contented, happy England (then pinched and gaunt with recent famine, breaking out in angry spots with Chartist riots)—with feverish, frantic, furious France. In *The Ladies' Mentor*, the leading periodical published for the delectation of the sex we were accustomed in those days to designate as "soft" and "gentle," there is indeed in Our Weekly Letter from Paris a reference to "the landing of a *royal and venerable* exile upon our *happier shores*"; but beyond this, not a single reference or allusion calculated to shock the delicate sensibilities of my Aunt Julietta, or any other young gentlewoman of delicacy and refinement....

The pen of the writer of the above-named delicious epistles reverts with evident relief to the latest thing in Concert-dresses. A full-gored skirt of green velvet with a gathered flounce in pink *crêpe* up to the knee ... could anything be more genteel? The hair should be waved; brought low to hide the ears—"A *pity*," reflected my Aunt Julietta, *"when mine are so much prettier than poor dear Marietta's!"*—and wreathed with a garland of natural blooms, in the ease of young ladies ... the heads of matrons being adorned with caps of costly lace, or lappets, fastened with the artificial rose.

Pompadour fans were also the rage. One-button gloves, worn with broad bracelets of gold, or black velvet with cameo clasps, were *de rigueur*. Sleeves for day-wear were elbow-length with *volantes* of *guipure*. For evening, short and puffed. Pray remember that these were the days of swanlike necks and champagne-bottle shoulders, high, expansive brows, large melting Oriental eyes, and waists that tapered. And considering the obstinate preference of Dame Nature for turning out her daughters in different shapes, makes, and sizes, it is marvelous how all the women of the era managed to look exactly alike....

My Aunt Julietta had to hunt up the meanings of the descriptive foreign terms so thickly peppered over Our Weekly Letter from Paris, in perchance the very dictionary whence their gifted writer, then resident at Peckham, had culled them, before she could settle down to perusal of the exquisite *Lines Addressed To A Fading Violet*, which are to be found at the bottom of the second column of the adjoining page; and the delicious *Essay upon Woman's Love*, which usurps the whole of the first column. It begins like this:

"No *true* woman ever *loved* who did not *venerate* the *object of her passion*, and who did not *delight*, nay, *rejoice* to bend in *adoring worship* before the throne on which *He* sits exalted who is at once *her slave* and *the idol of her soul!*"

Even as my Aunt Julietta stopped reading to dry her gentle maiden tears, Paris was bowing before the idol of her soul. She called it Freedom; and when from a window of the Hôtel de Ville the Citizen Lamartine proclaimed the Second Republic, how frenzied was her joy!

For Paris is a spoiled and petted courtesan, who, suffering from the burden of her very luxury, welcomes a fresh possessor. The new lover may be poorer than the old; he may be even brutal, but he is new.... And while he is new he pleases, and while he pleases he will not be betrayed....

You are to imagine, amidst what burning of powder and enthusiasm, what singing of the *Marseillaise* and the *Chant des Girondins* by the multitudes of patriots in the streets, as by red-capped *prime donne* at the Opera, was carried out the refurbishing and gilding of those three ancient Jagannaths, baptized so long ago in human blood by the divine names of Liberty, Equality, and Fraternity.

And you are to suppose yourself witness—many similar scenes being enacted elsewhere—of the White Flag of Orleans being hauled down from above the gilded bronze gates and the great central Pavilion of the Palace of the Tuileries, and the Tricolor breaking out in its place.

Conceive, this being accomplished with bloodshed, and sweat, and frenzy; France neighing for a new paramour, even as the perfumed and adorned harlot of Holy Writ. He came, as for her bitter scourging it was written he should come.... From what depths he rose up, with his dull, inscrutable eyes, his manner silky, ingratiating, suave as that of the Swiss-Italian manager of a restaurant grill-room; his consummate insincerity, his hidden aims and secret ambitions; and his horribly-evident, humiliating, galling impecuniosity, it is for a great writer and satirist to tell in days to be.

The monk of old, dubbed idler and shaveling by the little-read, when he ceased from his stupendous labors for God with pickaxe and drill and saw, the crane and pulley and rope, the mortar-hod and trowel, the plumb and adze and hammer and chisel, to serve Him in the making of illuminated books of His Word, service and song; took unto him a clean unused quill, or a pointed brush of woodcock's hackles or hare's fur, and dipped it in liquid gold, or the purple that the Catholic Church has ever held sacred, when he would write the ineffable Name of the KING OF KINGS. With ground lapis-lazuli, sprinkled with diamond dust, he set down the Divine Titles of JESUS CHRIST THE SAVIOR.... Mary the Immaculate Mother gleams forth with the pearly-white sheen of the dove's breast from a background of purest turquoise. No archangel but has his initial letter of distinctive, characteristic splendor, from the glowing ruby of Michael, all-glorious Captain of the hosts-militant of Heaven, to the amethyst of Raphael, and Gabriel's hyacinth-blue....

The more glorious the Saint, the more gallant the colors that adorn the strap-borders and historiated initials of the pages. Each prophet, sage, ruler, lawgiver of Holy Writ is decked as he deserves; nor do great generals like Saul, David, and Joshua, lack the trumpet-note of martial scarlet; while Ahab, Jezebel, Haman, are spotted as with leprosy, and livid as with corruption; and no China-ink is black enough to score down Judas, the betrayer of his Lord. While to the dreadful enemy of mankind are allotted the orange-yellow of devouring, hellish flame, and the livid blue of burning brimstone; and the verdigris-green, metallic scales of the Snake of Eden diaper the backgrounds of the letters, and the poisonous bryony, the henbane, and the noxious trailing vine of the deadly nightshade wreath and garland them about.

Find me a rusted nib, worn and corroded with long use in the office of a knavish attorney, where perjurers daily kiss the Book for hire, and the life-blood of pale men and haggard women is sucked away by the fierce, insatiable horse-leech of Costs. In what medium shall it be dipped to pen the cognomen and style of the man I have it in my mind to write of?

All the blood shed in that accursed December of the Coup d'Etat of 1851 flowed quickly away down the Paris gutters; it has vanished from the pavements of the Rue Montmartre, and from the flagstones of the courtyard of the Prefecture; was drunk by the thirsty gravel of the Champ de Mars, where *battues* of human beings were carried out, but it has left its indelible stain behind....

Scrape me a pinch of dust from those dark, accusing, ominous patches; and pound therewith a fragment of the moldering skull of a British soldier (of all those hundreds that lie buried in the pest-pits of Varna, and in those deep trenches beside the lake of Devna, one can well be spared). Compound from the soil of Crim Tartary (enriched so well with French and English blood) a jet-black pigment. Dilute with water from the River Alma. And then, with ink so made, write down the name of Charles Louis-Napoleon Bonaparte, the Prince of Pretenders, who became by fraud and craft and treachery and murder, Emperor of France.

XXX

Dunoisse had anticipated as the result of that fatal volley a Court-Martial inquiry under auspices Monarchical or Republican—and in the absence of indisputable evidence that the word of command to fire had not been given by the officer accused, a sentence of dismissal of that unlucky functionary from the Army.

The sword did not fall. The Assistant-Adjutant remained suspended from his duties, and in confinement at his quarters in the Rue de la Chaussée d'Antin, exactly five days; during which Paris seethed like a boiling pot, and the events this halting pen has striven to set forth, sprang from the dragon's teeth sown in the fruitful soil of France by incapable, unjust, or treacherous hands. Various documents, clumsily printed in smeary ink upon paper of official buff, reached Dunoisse during this period of detention; and whereas Number One was headed by the arms of the Reigning House of Bourbon, Number Two displayed a significant blotch of sable printing-ink in lieu of that ornate device; with "REPUBLIC OF FRANCE" stamped in bold Roman capitals across the upper margin.

Monsieur the Marshal, despite his increasing infirmities, enlivened his son's captivity with occasional visits. The smell of blood and gunpowder, the thunder of cannon and the summons of the trumpet, had made the old war-horse prick up his ears, neigh and prance about in his cosy paddock. He pooh-poohed the notion of a Court-Martial. Absorbing immense pinches of snuff, he argued—and not without point—that a Republican Government could hardly visit with the scourges of condign displeasure an act that had materially hastened the downfall of the Monarchy.

"You will see!... It is as I say!... This arrest is a mere piece of official humbug. No doubt it was better for your own sake that you should not be seen in the streets for a day or so, one can conceive that!—these ultra-Reds have good memories and long knives, sacred name of a pig!"

The old man trumpeted in his yellow silk handkerchief, hobbling about the room in tremendous excitement, swinging the ample skirts and heavy tassels of his Indian silk dressing-gown, twirling his gold-headed Malacca cane to the detriment of the inlaid furniture and the cabinets loaded with the chinaware and porcelain that had belonged to the lost Marie-Bathilde....

"You gave the word to fire—why trouble to deny it? Upon my part, I defend the act!—I applaud it!—I admire! It was the idea of an Imperialist,—a move of strategical genius—fraught at a moment like this with profound political significance. *Sapristi!*—we shall have an Emperor crowned and reigning at the Tuileries, and you, with the Cross and a Staff appointment—you will learn what it means to have served a Bonaparte. Ha! hah, ha!"

"Sir," said his son, who had been looking out of the window during this tirade, and who now turned a sharp set face upon the father's gross, inflamed, triumphant visage: "you mistake.... I am not capable of committing murder for the furtherance of political ends or private ambitions. For this act that commands your admiration I am not responsible. I declare my innocence before Heaven! and shall to my latest breath, before the tribunals of men."

"Ta, ta, ta! Blague! rhodomontade!—pure bosh and nonsense!" The Marshal took an immense double pinch of snuff. "Be as innocent as you please before Heaven, but if you value the esteem of men who *are* men— '*credieu!*—and not priests and milksops, you will do well to appear what you call guilty. At this moment such a chance is yours as falls to not one man in a hundred thousand—as fell to me but once in my life. Make the most of it! You will if you are not absolutely a fool!"

And Monsieur the Marshal hobbled to the door, but came back to say:

"You appear not to have heard that His Hereditary Highness of Widinitz is dead. There can be no obligation upon you to refrain from appearing at ordinary social functions, but I presume you will accord to your grandfather's memory the customary tokens of respect? A band of crape upon the sleeve—a knot of crape upon the sword-hilt will not compromise your dignity, or endanger your independence, I presume?"

"I presume not, sir!" said Hector with an unmoved face.

And the Marshal departed, spilling enough snuff upon the carpet to have made an old woman happy for a day.... Later, an orderly from Headquarters in the Rue de l'Assyrie, brought from the younger Dunoisse's Chief—a purple-haired, fiery-faced personage, with whom the reader has already rubbed shoulders,—the intimation that, pending official inquiry into a certain regrettable event, not more broadly particularized in words, the Assistant-Adjutant of the 999th of the Line would be expected to return to his duties forthwith.

And within an hour of the receipt of this notification Dunoisse was the recipient of a little, lilac-tinted note, regretting in graceful terms that the writer had most unhappily been absent from home when M. Dunoisse had called; inviting him to a reception, to be held upon the following evening at the Rue de Sèvres, Number Sixteen....

That delicately-hued, subtly-perfumed little billet, penned in thick, brilliant violet ink in a small, clear, elegantly-characteristic handwriting, signed "Henriette de Roux."

Ah! surely there was something about it that made Hector, in the very act of tossing it into the fire, pause and inhale its perfume yet again, and slip it between the pages of a blue-covered Manual of Cavalry Tactics that lay in a litter of gloves, studs, collars, and razors, small change and handkerchiefs, cigars and toothpicks upon the Empire dressing-table whose mirror had framed the wild, dark, brilliant beauty of the Princess Marie-Bathilde.... The features it gave back now, clear, salient, striking, vigorous in outline as those representing the young Bacchus upon a coin of old Etruria, were very like the mother's. And their beauty, evoking the careless, admiring comment of a coquette, had stained the pavement before the Hotel of the Ministry of Foreign Affairs with blood that was to darken it for many a day to come.

The invitation, coming from such a source, could not be declined—must be regarded as an order. Dunoisse wrote a line of acceptance, dispatched it by his soldier-valet,—and went out.

A pretentious mourning-hatchment, displaying the splashy arms of Marshal Dunoisse, cheek-by-jowl with the princely blazon of Von Widinitz, upon a black-and-white lozenge over the hall-door, arrested his eye as he descended the paternal doorsteps; a replica of this egregious advertisement gave him a cold shudder as he passed through the gates of the courtyard on foot, for Djelma, though nearly recovered of her hurts, was still in the hands of the veterinary, and the poor young officer, son of the wealthy owner of well-filled stables, must walk, or ride his servant's horse.

The streets of Paris still ran thick with the human flood that ebbed and flowed, surged and swirled, roaring as it went with a voice like the voice of the sea.... Strange shapes, dislodged by Red Revolution from the bottom-sludge, floated on the surface of the muddy torrent; their terrible faces bit themselves into the memory as they drifted by, as aquafortis bites into the copper-plate. Bands of military students and Guardes Mobiles patroled the upheaved streets—National Guards fraternized with the people—the little white tents still studded the camping-grounds of the troops on the great public squares; the limes and acacias of the boulevards, ruthlessly cut down to stumps; barked by the hungry troop-horses tethered to them, showed naked in the wintry sunshine; while squadrons of mounted chasseurs and detachments of Municipal Guards patroled the thoroughfares, and Commissaries of Police bore down on stationary groups and coagulated masses of the vast crowd:

"Circulate! In the Name of the Republic!"—with little more success than when they had adjured it in the name of fallen Majesty and impotent Law, to roll upon its way.

Dunoisse went to the Barracks in the Rue de l'Assyrie, and later to the Club of the Line, prepared for a chilly, even hostile reception. He met with elaborate cordiality from his equals, condescension as elaborate on the part of his superiors.

The Dissolution of the Chamber of Deputies, the abolition of the Chamber of Peers, was in every mouth; the political convictions and personal qualifications of the members constituting the New Provisional Administration were discussed with heat and eagerness: the sporting odds given and taken upon and against the chances of the exiled Claimant to the Imperial Throne being permitted to return to France and canvass for election. Some said: "It will never be permitted," and others: "He has already been communicated with," and others even more positive announced: "He is now upon his way!"...

But not a single reference was made to the affair of the fusillade at the Foreign Ministry, though a chance hint, dropped amidst the Babel, gave Dunoisse to understand that the Conservative Republican and Democratic newspapers had not been so merciful.

Lives there the man who could have refrained, under the circumstances, from hunting through the files of the past week? It was a leading article in the *Avénement* that first caught the young man's eye, and what a whip of scorpions the anonymous writer wielded! What terrible parallels were drawn, what crushing epithets hurled at the unlucky head of the victim. More than ever, as the fiery sentences burned their way from his eyes to his brain, Hector Dunoisse knew himself the well-scourged whipping-top of Destiny, the shuttlecock of adverse chances, the pincushion of Fate.... And as though in mockery, yet another burden of shame must be piled upon the overladen shoulders: a brief, contemptuous paragraph in the *Ordre* caught the young man's eye, referring in jesting terms to that pretentious mourning-hatchment mounted over the door of the paternal mansion ... touching lightly on the vexed question of Succession, hinting that the Catholics of the Bavarian Principality of Widinitz were being stirred up by the agents of "a certain wealthy, unscrupulous impostor and intriguer" to rebel against the nomination, by the Council of the Germanic Federal Convention, of the Lutheran Archduke Luitpold of Widinitz, nephew of the departed Prince, as Regent.... And heavy clouds of anger and resentment gathered upon Dunoisse's forehead as he read.

They darkened upon him still when the night closed in, and he went home to his lonely rooms. Nor were they lightened by the hour that saw him, in the uniform of ceremony, and with that mourning-band upon the sleeve of the dark blue full-dress uniform frock, that the Princess Marie-Bathilde's son could not deny to the memory of her father, pitching and tossing in a hired cabriolet over the upheaved pavements of the Paris streets. On his way to the Rue de Sèvres, where in a stately suite of apartments sufficiently near the Rue de l'Assyrie—once forming part of the ancient Cistercian convent of the Abbaye-aux-Bois, the de Roux were established with some degree of splendor; visited by certain of the lesser luminaries of the great world, and receiving the cream of military society.

You saw Dunoisse dismiss his deplorable conveyance at the tall grilled gates of the Abbaye. In the exterior building, upon the left-hand side of the courtyard as one entered, were situated, upon the ground-floor, the apartments of the de Roux.... In a suite of poorly-furnished, stately, paneled chambers upon the floor above, Madame Récamier was slowly dying, haloed still by the unblemished virtue that had won the respect of the Emperor Napoleon—beautiful yet even in blindness and decay—clinging to life by the last strand of a friendship too pure and tender to bear the name of love.

The green Venetian shutters of that row of first-floor windows were closed, all save one; the fold of a green silk curtain stirred in the chill February breeze, a solitary lamp upon a table made a cocoon-shaped patch of light against the somber darkness within. A worn exquisite profile, pearly-pale as the new moon's, with a black fillet bound over the eyes, showed against the background of shadow—a man's hand, ivory-white, and so emaciated that the heavy seal-rings on the third finger hung there like hoops upon a grace-stick, drew the curtain and closed the shutters, as the firm elastic step of Youth and Hope sounded on the flagstones, crossed the threshold below....

Who would spy upon one of these last evenings with Chateaubriand? In July she was to follow him to the tomb.

XXXI

Dunoisse, to the ring of his dress-spurs upon the pavement, passed in by the glazed double-doors. A somnolent porter, rousing out of his chair, admitted the guest by yet another glass door to a handsome vestibule upon the ground floor, an orderly-sergeant of the 999th saluted his officer, received his cloak, shako, and sword, delivered him to a footman in light green livery with silver cords and shoulder-knots, whose roseate calves preceded him across an ante-room of stately proportions towards a high doorway, draped with curtains of deep crimson velvet tasseled with gold. Brilliant light streamed from between the curtains, warm fragrance was borne to the nostrils of the visitor with the hum of voices; the white shoulders of ladies, their ringleted heads wreathed, in the charming fashion of the day, with natural flowers, moved across the shining vista, companioned by the figures of men in uniform, or lay-wear of the latest mode and most fashionable shades of color; or displaying the severe black frock-coat and tricolored rosette of the New Provisional Government of France.

A man thus distinguished was speaking, as the footman raised the crimson curtain and signed to Dunoisse to pass beneath. A cessation in the stream of general chatter had conveyed that the speaker was worth hearing. And in the dignity of the massively-proportioned figure, crowned by a leonine head of long waved auburn hair, in the deep melodious tones of the voice that rose and fell, swelled or sank at the will of the accomplished orator, there was something that fascinated the imagination and stirred the pulse.

"No, Madame, I do not despise Rank or Wealth," he said to a seated lady of graceful shape, whose face, like his own, was turned from the doorway and invisible to the entering guest. "But though I do not despise, I fear them. They should be handled as ancient chemists handled subtle poisons, wearing glass masks and gloves of steel."

No one answered. The speaker continued:

"That Kings have been noble and heroic—that Emperors have reigned who were virtuous and honest men, can be proved from the pages of History. Their reigns are threads of gold in a fabric of inky black. The reverence in which we hold their names proves them to have been prodigies. They, by some miracle of God or Nature—were not as evil as they might have been.... For, even as the handle of the racket used by the Eastern tyrant had been impregnated, by the skill of the wise physician, with healing agents; the juice of medicinal herbs that, entering by the pores, cleansed, purified, regenerated the leper's corrupted flesh: so in the folds of the ermine mantle there lurks deadly contagion: so, in the grasp of the jeweled truncheon of State there is a corroding poison that eats to the heart and brain."

The mellow-voiced orator ceased, and the silence into which his closing sentences had fallen was broken by the announcement of Dunoisse's name. The recent speaker glanced round as it was uttered. Only to one man could that pale, close-shaven, classic mask belong; only one brain could house behind the marble rampart of that splendid forehead, or speak in the flashing glances of those gold-bronze eagle eyes. It was Victor Hugo; and the thrill a young man knows in the recognition of a hero, or the discovery of a demigod, went through Dunoisse, as amidst the rustling of silks and satins, the fluttering of fans and the agitation of many heads, curled, or ringleted, or braided, that turned to stare, he moved over the pale Aubusson carpet towards the seated figure of the lady, indicated by the footman's whisper as the mistress of the house.

How soon the demigod was to be forgotten in the revelation of the goddess....

As the writer of the lilac-colored note rose up, with supple indolent grace, amidst a whispering purplish-gray sea of crisp delicate silken flounces,—held out a small white hand flashing with diamonds and rubies—murmured something vaguely musical about being charmed;—as Dunoisse, having bent over the extended hand with the required degree of devotion, raised his head from the ceremonious salute, a pair of eyes that were, upon that particular night, hazel-green as brook-water in shadow, looked deep into his own.... And the heart beating behind the young soldier's Algerian medals knocked heavily once, twice, thrice!—as the knock behind the curtain of the Théâtre Français when the curtain is about to rise upon the First Act, and the strong young throat encircled by the stiff black-satin-covered leather stock, and the collar with the golden Staff thunderbolt, knew a choking sensation, and the blood hummed loudly in his ears.

A flame, subtle, electric, delicate and keen, had passed into him with the look of those eyes, with the touch of the little velvet hand that was fated to draw, what wild melody, what frenzied discords from the throbbing hearts of men....

And the gates of his heart opened wide. And with a burst of triumphant music Henriette passed in,—and they were shut and locked and barred behind her.

XXXII

Ah! Henriette, what shall I say of you? How with this halting pen make you live and be for others as you exist and are for me?

There are men and women born upon this earth, who, walking lightly, yet print deep, ineffaceable footprints upon the age in which they live. The world is better for them; their breath has purified the atmosphere they existed in.... Ignorant of their predestination as they are, every word and act of theirs bears the seal of the Divine Intelligence. They were sent to do the work of the Most High.

And there are men and women who appear and vanish like shooting stars or falling meteors. Their path is traced in ruin and devastation, as the path of the tornado, as the path of the locust is. And having accomplished their appointed work, they pass on like the destroying wind, like the winged devourer: leaving prone trees and ruined homes, wrecked ships, stripped fields—Death where there was Life.

Think of Henriette as one of the fatal forces, a velvet-voiced, black-haired woman with a goddess's shape and a skin of cream, such little hands and feet as might have graced an Andalusian lady,—with mobile features—the mouth especially being capable of every variety of expression—and with great eyes of changing color, sometimes agate-brown, sometimes peridot-green, sometimes dusky gray. Shaping her image thus in words, I have conveyed to you nothing. No sorceress is unveiled, no wonder shown.

In the old, old days when the Sons of Light walked upon earth with the children of men, some seraph fell for the sake of a woman like this. From the seed of that union sprang all the Henriettes.... You may know them by the tattered rags of glory that trail behind them; by the pale flickering aureole, no brighter than a will-o'-the wisp or glow-worm's light, that hovers over the white brow....

About that brow of Henriette the willful hair rose in a wave-crest of delicate spraying blackness; curled over, shadowing the pearly forehead and blue-veined temples and the little shell-like ears, as though the waves were about to break; then rolled back and twined into a labyrinthine knot of silken coilings from which two massive curls escaped, to wander at their will. It was a face of lights and shadows; in their continual play you forgot to criticise its features. But they were eloquent, from the wide jetty arches of the eyebrows, to the silken-lashed languid eyelids, purplish-tawny as the petals of fading violets over the liquid, lustrous, changeful eyes. Eyes that mocked and laughed at you even as they wooed you; and mourned and wept for you even as they tempted and lured.

"Ah! do you indeed love me?" they seemed to say. "Is it so? Then most unhappy—poor, poor friend!—are you! Because I am of those women who are born to cause much misery. For we sting to desire without intention, and provoke to pursuit without the will. And 'No' is a word we have never learned to say."

XXXIII

It seemed to Dunoisse that he had always known her, always waited for her to reveal herself just in this manner, as she rose up amidst the crisping rustle of innumerable little flounces, outstretched the white arm partly veiled by the scarf of black flowered lace—shed the brilliance of her look upon him, and smiled like a naughty angel or a sweet mischievous child, saying in a soft voice that was strange to his ears and yet divinely familiar:

"So we meet at last?"

He found no better reply than:

"You were not at home, Madame, when I paid my visit of ceremony."

"I detest visits of ceremony," she said, and her tone robbed the words of harshness.

"Do you then turn all unknown visitors from your doors?" Dunoisse queried. Her smile almost dazzled him as she returned:

"No, Monsieur ... I turn them into friends." Adding, as he stood confounded at the vast possibilities her words suggested: "And I have wished to know you.... My husband has told me much.... But in these times of disturbance, how is it possible to be social? One can only remain quiescent, and look on while History is made."

"I have been quiescent enough, Heaven knows!—for nearly a week past," said Dunoisse, "without even the consolation of looking on."

Her shadowy glance was full of kindness.

"I know!... Poor boy!" She added quickly: "Do not be offended at my calling you a boy. I am twenty-five—nearly!... Old enough to be your elder sister, Monsieur.... Have you sisters? If so, I should like to call them friends."

"I had one sister," said Dunoisse, his eyes upon a night-black curl that lay upon an ivory shoulder. "She died very young—a mere infant."

"Poor little angel!"

Henriette de Roux rather objected to children—thought them anything but little angels. But her white bosom heaved and fell, and a glittering tear trembled an instant on a sable eyelash. And so infectious is sentiment, that

Hector, who dedicated a regret to the memory of the departed cherub on an average once a year, echoed her sigh.

The silver-coated roach, contemplating the dangling bait of the angler, is quite aware that for innumerable generations the members of his family have succumbed to the attraction of the pill of paste that conceals the barbed hook. Yet he deliberately sucks it in, and is borne swiftly upwards, leaving in the round-eyed family circle a gap that is soon refilled.

That tear of Henriette's was the bait. When her sigh was echoed, it was to the feminine fisher of men significant as the slow, deliberate curtsey of the float is to the angler for the slimy children of the river. Variable as a fay in a rainbow, she smiled dazzlingly upon the young man; and said, touching him lightly upon the arm with her Spanish fan and leaning indolently back in the fauteuil that was almost completely hidden beneath the rippling wavelets of her purplish-gray flounces:

"Look round. Tell me what flower is most in evidence to-night?"

Thus bidden, Dunoisse turned his glance questingly about. A moment gave the answer. The corsage of every lady present, no matter of what costly hothouse blooms her bouquet and wreath might be composed, had its bunch of violets; the coat of every second man displayed the Napoleonic emblem. His eyes went back to meet an intent look from Henriette. She said:

"You do not wear that flower, Monsieur!"

He returned her look with the answer:

"My military oath was of allegiance to a King. And though the King be discrowned and the Republic claims my services, I know nothing of an Empire—at least, not yet."

The irony stung. She bit her scarlet lip, and said, with a bright glance that triumphed and challenged:

"Unless the winds and tides have conspired against us, the Emperor will be in Paris to-night."

"Indeed!" The reports bandied, the bets made at the Club, came back upon Dunoisse's memory. He said:

"Then Prince Louis-Napoleon has determined to risk the step?"

She answered with energy:

"He is of a race that think little of risking. The son of Marshal Dunoisse should know that.... Ah! how it must grieve your father to know you indifferent to the great traditions of that noble family!"

Hector answered her with a darkening forehead:

"My father congratulated me upon good service rendered to the cause of Imperialism—only yesterday." He added as Madame de Roux opened her beautiful eyes inquiringly: "He is of the comprehensive majority who hold me guilty of that deed of bloodshed at the Ministry of Foreign Affairs. He——"

Dunoisse broke off. She had become so pale that he knew a shock of terror. Deep shadows filled the caves whence stared a pair of haunted eyes. There were hollows in her cheeks—lines about her mouth that he had never dreamed of.... A broken whisper came from the stiff white lips that said:

"Do not seem to notice.... It is the ... heat!..."

Hector, exquisitely distressed, forced his gaze elsewhere. Long seconds passed, during which he could hear her breathing; then the voice said:

"Thanks!... You may look at me now!"

He found her still pale, but without that bleak look of horror that had appalled him. She tried to smile with lips that had partly regained their hue. She asked, averting her gaze from him:

"Your father.... What did you answer to him when he—said that—that you had rendered good service to the Imperial cause?"

"I told him," Dunoisse answered her, "that I could testify to my innocence of that guilty deed before Heaven. And that I should assert it before the tribunals of men."

She murmured in a tone that gave the impression of breathlessness:

"There will be an official inquiry?"

Hector returned:

"This evening, when I returned to my quarters to change my dress, I received a summons to appear before a Court-Martial of Investigation, to be held at the Barracks in three days' time. Perhaps with this cloud hanging over me I should not have accepted your invitation? But I thought ... I imagined ... you could not fail to know!"

She said, with a transient gleam of mockery in her glance, though her eyebrows were knitted as though in troubled reflection:

"Husbands do not tell their wives everything. And I am an Imperialist, like your father.... How should I blame you for an act that counts to us? But we will speak of this later.... Here is Colonel de Roux...."

Dunoisse's eyes involuntarily sought and found de Roux. The Comtesse made a signal with her Spanish fan. And as if a wire had been jerked, the purple-haired, blood-shot-eyed, elderly, rouged dandy, the center of a knot of ladies to whom he was playing the gallant, excused himself and crossed to his wife's side. He had been all cordiality and civility that morning in his office at the Barracks in the Rue de l'Assyrie; he was cordial and civil now, as he insinuated his arm through Dunoisse's and led him this way and that amongst his guests, presenting him to ladies, introducing men.

Limited as his opportunities had been of moving in those social circles to which his mother's rank, no less than the Marshal's wealth, would have given Dunoisse admission, he displayed no awkwardness—was not handicapped by the shyness that is the young man's bane. His perfect muscular development lent easiness and grace to his movements; the open candor and simplicity that characterized his regard and address might have been subtlety, they disarmed criticism so completely and won upon prejudice so well.

The gathering in the de Roux' drawing-room represented all ranks and classes of Society, severely excepting the exclusive circle of the Faubourg Saint Germain. There were Dukes of Empire creation with their Duchesses, there were Peers of the Monarchy now defunct. Politicians, financiers, editors, and dandies rubbed shoulders with stars of the stage, and comets of the concert-room; painters great and small, and fashionable men of letters. You saw the youngest of all famous poets with his radiant blue eyes, slim upright figure, auburn locks and beard, and unquenchable air of youth. And Chopin, animated, and glowing with the joy of life, illuminated with the fire of genius, hectic with the pulmonary disease that was to kill him a year later; and Liszt, iron gray, fantastically thin, at the height of his infatuation for Madame Daniel Stern. You saw Delacroix in the first bloom of success, and Ingrés, long established on his throne of fame, gray-haired and stout, robust and plain, commonplace until he opened his mouth to speak—lifted his hands in gesture. And above all towered the massive figure and leonine head of the man who had been speaking when Dunoisse had been announced.

But the majority of the male guests belonged to what Louis Napoleon was afterwards to dub the "cream of fast and embarrassed Colonels," and many of the women were of the dashing, dazzling, voluptuous type that de Musset had immortalized by a single word. The *lionne* of 1848 was ere long to be transformed into the *cocodette* of the Second Empire, and in the process was to lose the grace that is woman's womanliest attribute, and shed the last feather of the angel's wing.

Free from self-consciousness as he was, Dunoisse, with the taint of the blood shed upon the Boulevard des Capucines hot upon his memory, was not slow in awakening to the fact that the majority of the women present regarded him with peculiar interest; and that many of their male companions turned eyeglasses his way. Questions, answers, comments, dealing with the abhorrent subject came to his ears as he moved forwards, bruised like pelting hailstones, stabbed with hornet-stings.... Several of the ladies curtseyed ... some of the gentlemen bowed low; more than one feathered dowager styled him "Serene Highness" and "Monseigneur."... And with a rush of angry blood to his temples and forehead, darkening still further his tawny-reddish skin, and adding to the brilliance of his black-diamond eyes, the young man realized that the fact of Paris being in the throes of Red Revolution had not deprived, in such eyes as these, the newspaper-mooted question of the Widinitz Succession of its vulgar charm. And that, on the strength of the hateful episode at the Ministry of Foreign Affairs, in combination with the intrigues of the Marshal, Sub-Adjutant Hector Dunoisse had become a personage to fawn upon and flatter, to invite and entertain.

The band of crape about his sleeve began to burn him. The now overcrowded drawing-rooms seemed suffocatingly hot. Madame de Roux had become the invisible, attractive nucleus of a crowd of civilian coats and blazing uniforms.... Dunoisse, alternately tempted by the thought of escape, teased by the desire to join that magic circle, was enduring the civilities of a group of ogling ladies and grinning exquisites with what outward patience he could muster, when he encountered, through a gap in the wall of heads and shoulders, the gaze of a pair of golden-bronze eagle eyes, glowing beneath a vast white forehead crowned with pale flowing locks of auburn hair.

For an instant he forgot his boredom, his desire to regain the side of Madame de Roux, or to escape from the perfumed, overheated rooms to the space and freedom of the Club, or the familiar loneliness of his rooms in the Rue de la Chaussée d'Antin. He was grateful when a surge of the ever-thickening crowd of guests brought him within touch of the plainly-dressed, perfectly-mannered gentleman who was the elected chief and generalissimo of the Free Lances of Romance. But, as Dunoisse gained the Master's side, the tall rounded shape of Madame de Roux swept by, leaning on the arm of a white-haired general officer in a brilliant Staff uniform ablaze with decorations. She never turned her face.... The night of her luxuriant tresses, the pale oval of her cheek, the dusky sweep of her eyelashes stamped themselves anew upon the young man's consciousness, as her draperies, shimmering purplish gray as Oriental pearl through their veiling of black Spanish laces, swept across his feet. He felt once more that heavy knocking in the breast as though the curtain were going up upon the play.... And the scent of violets came to him with the breeze of her passing, strongly as though he stooped above the wet, dark, fragrant clusters in some woodland glade.... A knot of the purple blossoms had fallen from amongst her laces as she went by. They lay close to his foot. He stooped and picked them up with a hand that was not quite steady. And as he mechanically lifted the violets to his face, still looking after the swaying, smoothly-gliding figure, dwelling upon the beauty of a creamy nape upon which rested great coils of night-black hair, pierced with a diamond arrow, one heavy curl escaping, hiding in the delicate hollow between the rounded ivory shoulders, vanishing in the *berthe* of lace that framed their loveliness, he started, for Hugo spoke. The deep melodious voice said:

XXXIV

"It is the classic flower of Venus as well as the badge of Imperialism. And—he who receives it from so fair a hand and does not wear it must needs be very cold or greatly courageous." He added, as Dunoisse's brilliant black eyes met his own: "I wear no violets, you see. Yet had she offered them...."

He gave a whimsical, expressive shrug. Dunoisse found himself saying:

"These were not given to me, but dropped in passing."

The great master's laugh, mirthful, mellow, genial, responded with the words:

"Admit at least that the flowers were dropped most opportunely."

"Monsieur, if the knot of violets were purposely detached," said Dunoisse, "then they undoubtedly were meant for you!"

But he made no offer to resign the blossoms, and Hugo laughed again.

"They were not meant for me. Have no fear. I have drunk of a sweet philter that renders men proof against enchantment. I kissed my child, sleeping in its cradle.... My wife said: *God keep thee!* when I left home to-night."

The manner had a tinge of grandiloquence, the words did not ring quite true. Dunoisse, like all the rest of the world, knew that the boasted philter was not the infallible preventive.... The scrap of tinsel that would sometimes show among the ermined folds of the kingly mantle peeped out with a vengeance now.... And yet the man possessed a royal, noble nature; and a personality so simply impressive that, if he had chosen to sit upon a three-legged milking stool instead of a carved chair upon a tapestried dais, it would have seemed, not only to his followers, a throne.

He went on to speak of the beauty of the lady of the salon, thrilled Dunoisse by a hint of romance,—breaking off to say:

"But for you, who wear the uniform of M. de Roux's regiment, there can be nothing new to hear about Madame?"

Did a drop of subtle, cynical acid mingle with the honey of the tone?... Dunoisse was conscious of the tang of bitterness even as he answered:

"Monsieur, I was recalled from Blidah to join the 999th of the Line barely a month ago. And since then I have been absent on leave in England. I had the honor of meeting Madame de Roux for the first time to-night. She interests me indescribably. Pray tell me what you know of her...."

Hugo said: "Have a care! She wears the Violet in her bosom and the Bee upon her lips. And in the perfume of the flower there is delirium—in the honey of the insect a sting."

Dunoisse said, hardly knowing that he spoke the words aloud:

"Divine madness, exquisite pain!..."

Hugo returned with a sphinx-like smile and a curious intonation:

"You have the intrepidity of youth, with its rashness. Be it so! We must all live and learn. And so you are but newly from Algeria!—that explains why you have the coloring, though not why you should possess the shape and features of an Arab of the Beni-Raten—reared in one of the hawk's-nest fort-villages of Kabylia—nourished on mountain air. Ah!—so you have ridden down the wild partridge on the plains at the foot of Atlas, and felt on your eyes the kiss of the breeze of the Desert, and paused to breathe and rest beneath the thatch of some native hut shadowed by date-palms or sycamores, built beside streams that flow through hollowed trunks of trees. And women as black as roasted coffee-berries have brought you whey and millet-cakes, and platters of dried figs, and ripe mulberries in their dark hands decked with gold and ivory rings."

So vivid was the picture evoked that Dunoisse knew the yearning of home-sickness, wished himself back again in the little house at Blidah, even to be bored by the trivial gossip of the garrison ladies, even to be teased by the persistent drub and tinkle of gazelle-eyed Adjmeh's *tambur*. And the magician's voice went on:

"You have asked of Madame de Roux.... Her father was a grandee of Spain and famous general of guerilas. He was killed during the counter-Revolutionary operations in Catalonia in 1822.... My father knew him and his lovely wife, who died of grief within a few years of the death of her brave husband.... She was a Miss Norah Murphy, an Irishwoman. And when you say that you say all. For that wet green island of the mystic threefold leaf and the deep echoing sea-caves, and the haunting melodies, is the spot of earth whereon the rebellious Angels of both sexes were doomed by the Divine Decree to dwell until the Judgment Day. They are the Tuatha da Danaan—the Fairy Race of whom one must not speak unless as '*the good people*'; whose slender, handsome, green-clad men woo earthly women and lure them away. Madame de Roux possesses a strain of that blood. It is to be traced in the daughters of a family for centuries—I say nothing of the sons.... And its gifts are the voice of music, the touch that thrills; the eyes that weep and laugh together, the smile that charms and maddens, and the kiss that enthralls and beguiles...."

"They are hers?" came from Dunoisse, as if in interrogation, and then repeating the words with an accent of conviction: "They are hers!" he said, a rush of new sensations crowding in upon him, with the perfume streaming from the tiny knot of purple blossoms fading in his hand.

"They are hers," Hugo answered. "They were hers when M. de Roux met and married her: they were hers when as a bride of seventeen she found herself established as lady-paramount and reigning Queen of his regiment, in garrison at Ham. Life is dull in a military fortress, you will agree, to anyone but a gambler. For distraction one turns naturally to games of risk and chance...."

He smiled, but his smile was enigmatical:

"The most fascinating of all these is the game of Political Intrigue and Secret Correspondence. From a prisoner, interned for life within the Fortress, the young wife learned to play that game. Her teacher had been a professional player, ruined through an ill-calculated move at Boulogne—an attempt ending in grotesque failure!"

Dunoisse knew that by the ruined player was meant the Pretender to the Throne Imperial of France.

"The beautiful Henriette was an apt pupil; she quickly mastered the First Gambit. I have heard it said that the pawn sacrificed on that occasion was—the lady's husband, but whether that be truth or scandal I do not pretend to know.... But six years later her teacher crossed the drawbridge in the blouse and fustians of a bricklayer, with a plank upon his shoulder. And since then"—the pale features of the speaker were inscrutable—"his pupil has kept her hand in. For Intrigue is a game that a woman comes to play at last for excitement, though at first she may have played for love."

He ceased and began to laugh, and said, still laughing, while Dunoisse thrilled with pity, anger and yet another emotion:

"It would be strange if so lovely and seductive a woman could conceive a genuine passion for a little unsuccessful adventurer who pronounces 'joy' as '*choy*,' and 'transport' as '*dransbord*,' and who has a long body and short legs. Though, to have suffered for an idea, even as false as the Idea Imperial, adds stature to the dwarfish and dignity to the vulgar, even in the eyes of other men. Besides, he was a prisoner ... unfortunate and unhappy.... Why should she not have loved him after all?"

Dunoisse said, with tingling muscles and frowning brows:

"Monsieur, do you hold that women are incapable of chivalry?"

He had raised his voice, and the clear ringing utterance made itself distinctly heard above the buzz of general conversation. And as he spoke a silken rustle went past behind him, and a breath of violets came to his nostrils.... But Hugo was replying to the query in the grandiose vein that characterized him....

"No, young man!—since from my place in the House of Deputies I beheld the Duchess d'Orleans stand up single-handed against a whole nation in defense of the rights of a weak child." He added: "In days such as these the diligent student of Human Nature—the literary artist who would add a new gloss to the Book of Mankind, discovers a pearl every hour he lives. Have I not seen within the space of one week a King hooted from the Tuileries, a throne consumed by fire, a Constitution tumbled into the dustbin, and the New Republic of France rise, radiant and regenerate from the ashes, and the dust and blood of Insurrection? And I am here to-night because I seek, at the first signal of his arrival, to hasten to offer the hand of brotherhood to a Napoleon Bonaparte who has freed his chained eagle, fettered his ambitions, and asks nothing better than to set the torch of Liberty to the pyre of Empire." He added, as by an afterthought: "And also, I am here because I wish to look upon the face of Cain."

The unexpected peroration hissed like Greek fire upon sea-water. Dunoisse stammered in bewilderment:

"Pardon, Monsieur! You said ... the face of Cain...?"

The answer came:

"Monsieur, in the interests of the public who subscribe to the *Avénement*, I should sincerely thank you if you would point out to me that brother-officer of yours who caused the men of his command to fire upon the people assembled before the Hotel of the Foreign Ministry. Having looked upon his face, my desire will be gratified. I shall have seen Cain!"

The words of dreadful irony fell like the iron-weighted thong of the knout upon bare flesh, lacerating, excoriating.... Hector Dunoisse, livid under his ruddy skin, rent between rage and shame, held speechless by the sense of the utter uselessness of denial, could only meet the piercing eagle-eyes of the wielder of the scourge. And infinitely wounding was the dawning of suspicion in those eyes, and worse the conviction, and worst of all the scorn....

Dunoisse had imagined, when he felt himself the target of greedy, curious glances and shrill piercing whispers, that this great man, aware of the undeserved, unmerited accusation under which he writhed, had looked at him with comprehension and sympathy. Now he found himself bereft of these; the kindness had died out of the face, if it had ever really beamed there, and the vast white forehead rose before him like a rampart with an enemy behind it. His manhood shrank and dwindled. He found himself saying in the voice of a schoolboy summoned before the pedagogue for a fault:

"Monsieur Hugo, I thought you had heard all ... knew all.... Your look seemed to say so, to-night—when first it encountered mine...."

The other answered with wounding irony:

"Previously to your entrance, the well-known fact that certain ambitious Imperialist intriguers have put forward a claim of Hereditary Succession to the feudal throne of a small Bavarian principality, had formed the topic of a brief discussion in which I took my share. Upon your arrival you were indicated to me as the human peg on which these adventurers hang their hopes. I was quite unaware of the personal claim you have established upon the esteem of your fellow-beings by the wholesale butchery of the Rue des Capucines."

He added, with a laugh that was vitriol poured into Dunoisse's wounds:

"I am not ignorant that you have a certain reputation as a fencer and a duelist. It will be useless to challenge me, let me assure you!... I am sufficiently courageous to be called a coward for the sake of my children and my country, dearer even than they." He scanned the youthful, quivering face with even more deliberate intention.... "You are even younger than I judged at first," he said. "What may not be looked for from the maturity of such a formidable being!... Paraphrasing Scripture, I am tempted to exclaim: 'If you are as you are in the green tree, what may you not become in the dry!' Personally, I am, in my character of poet and dramatist, your debtor. For every classical student knows that Tiberius was magnificently handsome—that the base and bloody Caligula was of a beauty that dazzled the eyes. But—who has pictured Judas otherwise than as a red-haired, blear-eyed humpback? Who has imagined Cain as the reverse of swart, shaggy, hideous and terrible? No one until now! But when, after years of study and preparation, I compose in Alexandrine verse the drama of the Greatest of all Betrayals—rely upon it that the Judas of Hugo will be more beautiful than John!"

His laughter froze and lacerated Dunoisse's burning ears like pelting hailstones. It ceased; and, touched in spite of himself by the mute bleeding anguish in the young, haggard face, he said roughly:

"Why do you not speak, sir? Why do you not defend yourself?"

Dunoisse's palate was dry as ashes. He said with the despairing smile that drags the mouth awry:

"Monsieur, it would be useless. I have read your article in the *Avénement*. You condemned me before you heard."

The golden flame of Hugo's glance played over him like wildfire. The scrutiny endured but an instant. Then the master said, with a softening change of voice and face, holding out his hand:

"Young man, if you had been guilty of that crime you would be infinitely miserable. And, being innocent, you are most unhappy. For no living mortal, save myself, will believe you so!"

The hand-grasp was brief but significant. Next moment the giver was lost in the surging crowd of golden epaulets, flower-wreathed ringlets and well-powdered shoulders, Joinville cravats and curled heads of masculine hair.

The brilliantly-lighted rooms seemed to darken when the friendly face had turned away. Dunoisse, wearied and discouraged, began to think of taking leave. As he looked about for his hostess there was a bustle near the door. The agitation spread to the confines of the most distant room of the suite. Loud, eager voices were heard from the anteroom, the heavy crimson curtain was dragged back by no gentle hand.

A man in brilliant Staff uniform, the white-haired general officer who had gone by Dunoisse a few moments before with Madame de Roux upon his arm, appeared in the archway towards which the well-dressed mob now pressed and surged. His eyes shone—his face had the pallor of intense emotion and the radiance of unspeakable joy. He cried, in a loud, hoarse, rattling voice that carried from room to room like a discharge of grape-shot:

"Prince Louis Napoleon is in Paris! He has arrived at the Hôtel du Rhin!"

He tore his sword from the scabbard—held it gleaming high above his haggard, radiant head, and shouted in stentorian tones:

"Long live the Emperor!"

And the scented, well-dressed crowd, revivified by the utterance of that name of ancient magic, inspired by the breath of an immense enthusiasm, crazy with joy in the anticipation of what they knew not, echoed the shout:

"Long live the Emperor!"

XXXV

France is the most womanly of all the nations. A man once possessed her who caused her such misery that she adored him as a god. He wrung the tears from her eyes, the blood from her veins, the gold from her coffers. He slew her sons in hecatombs, and yet she gave, and gave. And when a dwarfish being of devouring passions and colossal ambitions rose up and said: "I bear the dead man's name. Worship me, living, now that he is no more!" she gave him all she had.

To these Imperialists, the exile who had returned was not Charles Louis Bonaparte, Prince-Pretender to the Imperial Throne. He was the Emperor. And as though he had been indeed the wearer of the little cocked hat and the gray surtout, they greeted the news of his return with a joy they themselves would barely have credited ten minutes before.

They laughed and wept tears of rapture that washed the paint from the faces of elderly belles and ancient dandies, and rinsed the old lees of vice and vanity and selfishness from their hearts. Friends and foes embraced; strangers exchanged hand-clasps and congratulations. The golden Age had come again. Napoleon was in Paris. And the hubbub of voices grew overwhelming, in the ceaseless reiteration of two words:

"The Emperor!—the Emperor!"

Hugo said, raising his magnificent voice so as to be heard plainly above the Babel:

"Messieurs the Representatives of the New Provisional Government, Monsieur Bonaparte has at length returned from England. Let us who, having confidence in his pledges, have voted in his favor, go and say to him: '*How do you do?*'"

And, followed by his fellow-wearers of black coats and tricolored scarfs, he went out quickly. Yet others pushed their way into the anteroom, and began to rummage for hats, coats, and cloaks. As the bustle of their departure reached its climax, Dunoisse was conscious of a breath of familiar fragrance. A silken rustle came behind him, and a soft voice reached his ear, saying:

"If only I dared follow them!"

It was Madame de Roux. And so bitter a spasm of jealousy clutched Dunoisse's heart that he was shocked and confounded by the revelation of his own huge folly. Then, as the wood-flower's perfume reached him in a stronger gust of sweetness, a whisper that thrilled said:

"Are *you* chivalrous?"

The voice added instantly:

"I overheard what you said just now.... Do not look round...."

Dunoisse stared straight before him. Rigid and immovable, he might have been taken for the colored image of an officer of *piou-pious*. Only his Algerian medals shook a little with the beating of his heart. And the voice came again. It said:

"Think of me what you will!... I must speak to you! Remain after the others have left.... Wait in the gray boudoir at the end of the drawing-room beyond this. Raise those violets to your face if you agree: drop them if you refuse!..."

His hand shook as he lifted the knot of drooping blossoms, pretending to inhale their vanished scent. He heard her whisper:

"Thanks!" and the rustle of her silks and laces—distinguishable to him through the swishing and billowing and crackling of a sea of feminine fripperies—passed on. And footmen with baskets of champagne and silver trays of glasses, light as bubbles, began to circulate through the crowd; and the explosion of corks, the gurgling of the foamy wine, the pledging of loyal toasts and the clinking of glasses heralded the conversion of a festival of sentiment into a lively night.

Amidst the popping, clinking and toasting, Dunoisse passed from the larger drawing-room into the smaller, less crowded salon beyond, and presently found himself in the little boudoir.

It was a charming, cosy nest with purple-gray silken hangings, its ebony furniture upholstered with velvet of the same shade, the black, shining wood inlaid with silver wreaths, fillets and ribbons in the unfashionable Empire style.

Lofty in proportion to its size, it boasted a painted ceiling of nymphs and satyrs dancing in a woodland glade, exquisite enough to have been the work of Boucher. A bright fire burned in the fireplace of steel and bronze; tall double-doors left ajar gave a peep of a bedroom, perfumed and pink as the heart of a moss-rose; the deep chairs and wide divan suggested slumber. A black-and-tan King Charles's spaniel of English breed, all floss-silk curls and blue ribbon bow, slept in a basket on the chinchilla hearthrug; there were books in ebony book-cases: a volume of the plays of de Musset, bound in white vellum, lay open upon an ottoman; the "Fleurs du Mal" of

Baudelaire peeped from a dainty work-basket from which a strip of ecclesiastically-patterned embroidery trailed; and violets in bowls of Sèvres and groups of the white narcissus in tall Venetian vases made the air heavily sweet.

It was a nest for confidences, a place for revelations and confessions. It contained no pictures beyond a few frames of miniatures, all masculine portraits by famous hands, and one fine full-length, life-sized oil-painting, within a massive carved and gilded frame of the period of the Regency; representing a voluptuously-beautiful woman, in the habit of a Cistercian nun, standing upon a daïs covered with blue-and-gold tapestry in a pattern of *fleurs-de-lis*. Behind her rose a marble altar, its Tabernacle, surmounted with a pointed arch and the Cross, towered overhead, and one white, dimpled hand of the fair woman grasped a Crucifix, and the other was outstretched in the act of taking from the altar a Crown of Thorns.... And at her feet, bare, ivory-white, daintily-small and pink-toed, were scattered kingly crowns and jeweled orbs and scepters. And from her loosened coif streamed golden tresses, and her proud uplifted eyes blazed, not with the heavenly fires of Divine Love, but with the lurid flames of Hell.... And in her Satanic pride and imperial arrogance of beauty she seemed to live; and send out subtle electric influences that dominated and swayed those who dwelt within the reach of them, not for good but for evil and misery, and the wreck of bodies and souls.

And Dunoisse looked at the portrait, and the red lips seemed to smile at him. And while they appeared to whisper "Stay!" unseen hands plucked at him, as though striving to drag him from the place; and a thin voice of warning fluttered like a cobweb at his inner ear, urging him to begone and lose no time about it. Perhaps wan Sister Thérèse de Saint François was praying for him in her cell at the Carmel of Widinitz. But all the champagne he had not tasted seemed boiling in his veins, and he gave back the smile of the proud, voluptuous, painted lips, and was drawing near to decipher an inscription on an ornamental scroll at the bottom of the Regency frame, when there was a rustle and whisper of silken draperies in the doorway, and he turned to meet the eyes of Henriette.

She was radiant now with triumph—she sparkled like a starry night in midwinter. She drew deep breaths as though she had been running, and lovely tremulous smiles hovered about her mouth. She lifted her little hands as the first bars of a waltz marvelously played upon a brilliant instrument, rang out, and the rhythmical sound of dancing feet began to mingle with the music and the gay din of chattering tongues, and said with a sign that bade him listen:

"Do you hear?—they are dancing over the grave of the Monarchy. They have turned my reception into a ball. What the Augustinian Sisters will say to me I cannot imagine!... The outer gate closes at eleven.... They may go on like this until day.... M. Chopin has volunteered to play for them.... He is mad, like everybody else to-night. Decidedly it is as well you came here without waiting." She added, a little incoherently: "What times we live in!—what events may not happen now! Oh! that waltz, how it distracts me! How can he dare to play like that?"

She pressed her small white hands against her temples, lifting from them the weight of hair, and sank down, panting a little still, upon the gray velvet divan, saying:

"Ouf!—my head aches. What was it I wanted to say?—I have forgotten! Do sit down! Here, beside me—you will not crush my dress.... We are not likely to be disturbed.... M. de Roux has gone to the Hôtel du Rhin with General Montguichet and a dozen other gentlemen—the rest are engrossed with their partners. What I wished to say to you was—Take this advice as from an elder sister. When you are summoned to answer before the Court-Martial for that—affair of the Rue des Capucines——"

He had fixed his eyes on the beautiful mobile mouth. Was he deceived? Did he really hear it say:

"Say that you gave the order for the men to fire. It will be the wisest course. Oh!—I know what I am talking about! No harm will come to you! You understand me, do you not? Only admit it—do not deny!"

Dunoisse rose up from the divan as pale under his red skin as when Hugo had asked him to point out the modern parallel of the primal murderer, and said in ice-cold tones:

"I have already had the honor to point out to you, Madame, that I did not give the order!"

He vibrated with passionate resentment. What—under the guise of sisterly kindness, was he advised to leap the cliff?

But a face brimming with sweet penitence was lifted to his. She said, summoning her dimples to play by mere force of will, bidding her eyes gleam through a soft veil of dewiness:

"Do not be angry!—it was a stupid joke. Must one always be so serious with you? And—I am a little mad to-night, as I have told you. It is excusable.... Pray forgive me!—sit down again!"

She stretched out a little hand, its delicate fingers curling like tendrils. They touched his—his heart leaped as they clung. He sat down again. And the waltz, played by the master-hand, ebbed away, dying in waves of sensuous sweetness, and a Polish mazurka, after a peal of crescendo chords that shrieked with frantic merriment, sprang short-skirted and flourishing belled scarlet heels, from the bewitched instrument, to take its place. And Dunoisse, with throbbing senses, tore his eyes from the enthralling face, and raised them to meet the proud, voluptuous, defiant glance of the nun in the portrait. And her red lips seemed to say: "*Why not?*" He asked involuntarily:

"Who is she?"

Henriette's soft voice answered, with a curious tone in it:

"Everyone who asks says 'Who *is* she?' as though she lived. But she died in 1743. The portrait used to hang over the fireplace in the Community Hall. I will not tell you how it comes to be where it is now—it is a secret. She who tramples upon those crowns and scepters was Louise Adelaide de Chartres, second daughter of the Regent Philippe d'Orléans. She became Abbess here when eighteen, and died Abbess of Chelles. She was divinely beautiful and of ungovernable passions.... The suite of immense rooms that were hers in the main building of the Abbaye are never used. They are always shut up, and no one ever goes into them alone."

She added, with a strange laugh:

"It is considered dangerous, even in the daytime, to enter without a companion. The Sisters say that shrieks and the rattling of chains are heard there on certain nights in the year, and that the floors are found to be stained with new-shed blood. They think that her soul comes back there to expiate the acts of cruelty she perpetrated upon her nuns; and her terrible excesses, in frightful scourgings, and tortures such as cannot be conceived."

Seeing Dunoisse's look still fixed upon the portrait, she went on:

"She was a witch. She bewitched her lovers,—she has bewitched you—you cannot take away your eyes. Ah! if you do not recoil from the sight of her, knowing her to be so wicked, there should be hope for me! For I—oh!—how can I tell you?..."

She was weeping,—the shining tears were making their way between the fingers of the little hands she clasped over her eyes. Her white bosom heaved with sobs. And the mazurka, played by the mighty master, jerked and shrilled and leaped in spasms of frantic merriment, and men and women, intoxicated with pleasure and heated by wine, yielded themselves to the furious excitement of the dance. And Dunoisse was at the side of Henriette, pleading with her in a voice that shook with emotion, to be calmer!—and presently found himself possessed of one of the little hands.

He won a glance, too, of eyes that shone out of a pale, tear-drenched face, like moss-agates seen through running water, and another by-and-by....

To shed real tears and be lovely still—what a gift of the fairies! They have it as a birthright, the Henriettes. My Aunt Julietta, crying her poor eyes out in the shadow of a four-post mahogany bedstead of British manufacture, with cabbage-rose-patterned chintz curtains, over a masculine profile discovered in the background of a colored fashion-plate in the month's issue of *The Lady's Mentor*, and supposed to bear a soul-rending resemblance to one who was to be for ever nameless, inspirer of an early love that had bloomed in a railway carriage, and shed its leaves as the train snorted its way out of Dullingstoke Junction—was not a pretty or pathetic spectacle. With her tip-tilted nose thickened by the false catarrh of tears—her slender frame convulsed with the recurrent hiccough of hysteria—what masculine eye would have lingered upon my aunt?

But Henriette and her sisters can ride on the whirlwind of the emotions, without disarranging a fold of their draperies,—go through whole tragedies of despair without reddening an eyelid,—sorrow beautifully without spoiling the romance of a situation with one grotesque blast upon the nose. This Henriette said, lifting a sweet quivering face and drowned eyes to Dunoisse's agitated countenance:

"Oh! let me cry,—it eases the heart!—and listen, for you must believe me!..."

Voices sounded beyond the threshold, the door-handle was rattled loudly. As the door opened, Henriette turned with a rapid, supple movement, and said, indicating the portrait above the fireplace with a steady hand:

"As you remark, Monsieur, Madame d'Orléans did not pass her time in saying Paternosters.... But it is said that she repented, and died in a state of grace."

She added:

"Perhaps she bewitched the priest who confessed her into granting absolution?... But no!... One cannot be irresistible on one's dying bed.... And Death is frightful.... I have always dreaded it!... Could you kiss lips that are turning into clay?... For me, I should never muster courage!..." A real shudder went through her. She said, as though to herself: "Oh, no, no, no! However much I had loved him, I could not touch him then!"

XXXVI

The door shut softly. Those who had sought privacy in the gray boudoir had retreated discouraged. No more intruders came near as the ball went on. Pale faces had become burning crimson, flushed faces had darkened to purple. A fog of powder, shaken from the faces and bosoms of women, hung in the scorching, suffocating atmosphere, and made haloes round the wax-lights dwindling in gilt wall-sconces and chandeliers. Yawning servants renewed the candles as they were burned out. Not one remembered those in the gray boudoir. And while they flickered low in their silver branches, Henriette said to Dunoisse:

"Do you know the fortress of Ham?"

She continued before he could answer:

"Picture it as a hollow square of granite, set in the middle of a vast, treeless, marshy plain. It has a huge round tower at two of its angles, a powder-magazine at each of the others. A sluggish canal crawls beneath the south and east ramparts, a river winds across the marshy plain, passing beneath the walls of the town. There is only one gateway, guarded by a square tower,—you enter, and are in a great courtyard surrounded by lofty walls, commanded by heavy masses of masonry, with water oozing from the blocks of stone that sparkle with crystals of salt-peter.... One building has grated windows—by that you know it is a prison. Another is the Barracks—a third is the dwelling of the Commandant."

She said, with a strange wild laugh, and a look of darkling remembrance:

"I spent my honeymoon there, as a bride of seventeen, eight years ago. You have noticed that I am very pale, have you not? It is because all my roses faded and died in that chill cavern of dripping stone. My schoolfellows at the Convent, who used to joke about 'Henriette's red cheeks,' would not have known me. Indeed, I seemed a stranger to myself.... The Tragedy of Existence had been revealed to me. I found it overwhelming.... Perhaps I find it so still, but I have mastered the art of hiding what I feel."

She was playing a scene as the Henriettes alone know how to play it. This atmosphere, vibrating with allusions, hints, references to hidden griefs, quenched hopes and inward anguish, was the natural element in which she breathed. From the quiver of her lips to the heave of her beautiful bosom, every effect was thought out and calculated; no inflection of her voice but was intended to make its effect, as by an artist of the stage. And she went on:

"When a young wife lives by the side of a husband who is not young or amiable, or even kind—in a place such as I have described, something she must love if she is not to die.... Thus Henriette learned to worship a Cause, and to devote herself, heart and soul, to an object. That was the Restoration of the Empire. She lives for it to-day!..."

Her eyes were like green jewels burning under the shadow of her dusky hair-waves. Her voice thrilled and rang and sighed. "Oh, how I thanked you for those words I heard to-night! What man except yourself would have spoken them! Yes—women can be chivalrous!—women can live and die for a conviction! My terrible confession is made easier by your belief!"

She paused and resumed:

"I aided the escape of the Prince Imperial.... I conceived the idea, thought of the disguise—provided the lay-figure that, dressed in Prince Louis Napoleon's clothes, lay upon the bed in his prison-cell, while M. Conneau kept guard over the supposed sick man. And I gloried in the success of the enterprise, and every louis I could obtain has since been spent in furthering the Imperial cause. Ah, Heaven! how poor its only hope has been!—he who should wield a scepter, he who should have dipped his hands at will in a treasury of milliards! How poor he still is, it pierces the heart to know. Yet how many have exhausted their resources in supplying that need of his: General Montguichet and M. de Combeville have been reduced to penury, Princess Mathilde and the Comtesse de Thierry-Robec are impoverished by their gifts! Noble, self-sacrificing women!—without envying I have emulated them.... You see these rubies that I wear? Who would guess the stones were false?"

She lifted into the light a radiant forehead. Had you been there to see and hear, you would have said with Dunoisse, "This is the voice—that is the face of Truth!"

And yet, if those rubies had been carried to some expert, obliging dealer in such gewgaws, say Bapst-Odier, late Jeweler to his Majesty, 111 Quai de l'Ecole,—they would—after that stately personage had screwed a microscope into his eye and submitted them to a brief but searching examination—have fetched a really handsome sum.

A fib, then?... Ah! but while Henriette told it she believed it. The tale had seemed to need that one artistic touch of the false jewels heaving on the loyal bosom of the fair Imperialist. And your successful, irresistible deceiver is that he, or she, who, for the time being, succeeds in humbugging and duping and bamboozling Self.

Thus, when Dunoisse, gripped by a sudden spasm of anger and contempt and disgust, muttered:

"And *he* stoops to take alms—to subsist on funds so gathered! Why not rather sweep the streets?" she continued, in a voice that thrilled with genuine emotion:

"The Arabs tells you that rubies are drops of the hearts' blood of lovers, shed countless ages ago, and crystallized into jewels by the alchemy of Time. Well, I would empty my veins to-day for the Empire, if need should arise!"

He looked at her and knew that she would do it. With what a spotless flame she seemed to burn. Sweet, heroic zealot!—adored enthusiast! What man, thought Dunoisse, could hesitate to pour his own life out upon the trampled sand of a political arena if by the sacrifice that white bosom might be spared the horrid wound!

"Judge, then, Monsieur, when it seemed, after long years, that the hour of Restoration might be approaching,—when the throne began to totter under the paralyzing weight of the Monarchy,—when I saw France, languishing for a new breath to animate, new blood to revivify her, stretch her weak hands towards the quacks and charlatans who crowd round her sick-bed,—judge if I did not thrill and pant and tremble for that absent one,—if I did not urge all those who recognize in Prince Louis Napoleon France's rescuer and savior, to exhaust themselves in a supreme effort to bring him to her side. And knowing him in urgent need, deceived by English guile, betrayed by the specious promises of that powerful Minister who has only feigned to befriend him—I borrowed money.... Yes, it must be told...."

She stretched out the little hand and touched the gold lace upon Dunoisse's sleeve, saying with a wistful smile:

"Borrowing degrades—even when one borrows from a woman. You see, I do not spare myself.... I borrowed from a man."

Dunoisse's small square white teeth were viciously set upon his lower lip. His black brows were knitted. His eyes were bent upon the carpet. He heard her say:

"A man who loved me.... Ah! what a coward I am, and how you must despise me! Who loves me, I should say!"

And the sentence was a knife in the heart of the poor dupe who heard. Words were wrenched from him with the sudden pain. He cried, before he could check himself:

"Who is the man?"

And then, meeting her look that conveyed: "You have no right to ask" ... he said with humility: "Forgive me! I was presumptuous and mad to ask that question. Forget that I ever did!"

She gauged him with a keen bright glance, and said with a noble, melancholy simplicity that was as pinchbeck as her abasement of the moment previous:

"You are very young, or you would never have committed so great an error. For if I loved him, I should never tell you for his sake, and if I loved *you*———"

She registered his start, and finished:

—"I should never tell you for yours. But as I have no love left to give to any man: as the fountains of my heart have long been frozen at their source—I will say this.... You and he were friends once, long years ago, before he became an Under-Secretary at the Foreign Ministry. A cloud has shadowed your old friendship.... A misunderstanding has thrust you apart. You know who it is I mean."

A cloud had almost palpably come before Dunoisse's eyes. Their black-diamond brilliancy was dulled to opaqueness, as he looked at Madame de Roux, and his lips, under the small black mustache, made a pale, straight line against his burnt-sienna skin. And from them came a grating voice that said:

"You are speaking of M. Alain de Moulny. I saw you together in the courtyard of the Hotel of Foreign Affairs a moment before the pistol-shot. And he———"

She stretched out, with a gesture of entreaty, her little hands, sparkling with the jewels that were such marvelous imitations, and yet would have fetched a good round sum at Bapst Odier's.

"Wait—wait! Do not confuse me. Let me tell you in my roundabout woman's way! He———"

She drew her brows together; moved the toe of her little gray satin slipper backwards and forwards through the silky fur of the chinchilla rug.

How little of actual fact may be held to constitute the entire truth, is a problem which confronts the Henriettes at every turn of the road.

"We had had an appointment to meet in my box at the Odéon Theater that evening. M. de Moulny was to have brought me the money there. The disturbances rendered it impossible that he could keep the appointment—the Ministry was guarded by troops—M. Guizot uncertain whether the King would support or abandon him—dispatches and messengers coming every moment, messages and dispatches every instant going out.... So I was to meet M. de Moulny in one of the more private waiting-rooms opening from the Hotel vestibule and receive the money from his hands. He is not rich—what younger son is wealthy? But where there is devotion—what cannot be achieved? He would do anything for me!"

She said, meeting Hector's somber glance:

"I have heard it said that you are indifferent to women. If so, you are lucky. We bring nothing but misery—even to those we love!"

She swept her little hands upwards through the mass of curls upon her temples, with her favorite gesture:

"I was leaving the Hotel—where my husband was dining with M. Guizot—when the great crowd of people, led by the drum and the Red Flag, filled the Boulevard, and seemed as though about to charge the soldiers, who were drawn up along the railings motionless as statues, with their muskets at the present.... Upon a gray Arab, in command of the half-battalion was a young officer who interested me much...."

Invisible, red-hot needles pricked the listener all over. Then something icy cold seemed to trickle down his spine and escape through the heels of his spurred military boots. The speaker did not look in his direction. Her downcast eyelids fluttered, a faint mysterious smile hovered upon the eloquent mouth.

"He sat his horse like a young Bedouin of the Desert, or such a warrior of ancient Greece as one has seen sculptured on the walls of the Parthenon at Athens. His skin was the ground-color of an Etruscan vase.... Cold though I am—ah! you cannot dream how cold I am!—I have never been insensible to the beauty that is male."

Under the covert of her eyelashes she stole a glance at the victim.

"I guessed who you were, of course!—you had been minutely described to me.... But it pleased me to pretend ignorance. I said, pointing you out to M. de Moulny: 'That must be the officer who has newly joined us from

Africa. His type is rare—at least in my experience. It is a reincarnation of the Young Hannibal. He has the rich coloring, the bold features, the slender shape.... De Roux must present him. He will bring me purple stuffs and golden ingots and the latest news from Tyre.' And de Moulny answered, looking at you coldly: 'He has millions of ingots, but he cannot give you them—unless he cares to break a vow.' I said: 'So, then, you know my handsome Carthaginian?' He answered: 'I used to, when we were boys at a military institute. It was he who induced me to give up my intention of entering the Army.' I asked: 'How, then, Monsieur?... Are you so easily persuaded? What means did your friend employ to alter your determination?' And de Moulny answered, looking at me oddly: '*A false step, and a broken foil!*'"

The spider-web of fascination she had woven about Dunoisse was weakened, perhaps, by the mention of de Moulny's name. He looked at Henriette with eyes that had become harder and brighter. He waited for the rest.

"Naturally, so strange an utterance roused my curiosity. I wanted to hear the story, if there is one? But M. de Moulny stuck out his underlip—perhaps you remember a trick he has;—and I thought: 'Some day you shall tell me the rest.' We talked of other things—standing there under the portico. Of ourselves, France, the political crisis that loaded the air with the stifling smell of garlic, of old clothes, of unwashed human beings—that filled it with those cries of, 'Down with the Ministry! Long live Reform! Give us no more thieves in velvet!' and drowned them in the bellowed strophes of 'The Marseillaise.' And as the crowd surged and roared and the Red Flag waved like a bloody rag in the light of their torches, I asked of M. de Moulny—I cannot tell you why I asked it.... Perhaps one is fated to say these things...."

Real emotion was beginning to mingle with feigned feeling. She lifted the chain of rubies that encircled her round white throat as though its light weight oppressed, and tiny points of moisture glittered on her temples and about her lips. She said, touching the lips with a filmy handkerchief edged with heavy Spanish lace:

"I asked of Alain, as the great crowd seemed about to rush upon the gates of the Hotel: 'What would be, at this juncture, the greatest misfortune that could befall the House of Bourbon?' He answered: 'That your young Hannibal should give the word to fire!'"

She imposed silence upon Dunoisse, who was about to break into impetuous speech, by laying a little velvet hand upon his lips, as she had once laid them upon de Moulny's. She kept the hand there as she said:

"Do not interrupt—it takes all my courage to tell this! I carry a loaded pistol upon all occasions—it is a habit I learned in Spain—in Algeria I found it of use. And I drew the weapon from its hiding-place,—I can hear my own voice saying as I did so: '*One shot might hasten the crisis.—What if I fired?*'... And M. de Moulny said: 'No, no! You must not!' *And I did!* I pulled the trigger, and before the echo of the shot had died, and the salt blue smoke cleared from before my face."

She was at his feet, weeping, clinging to the shaking hands with which Dunoisse strove to raise her, choking with sobs, burying her face upon his arm, wetting the blue cloth with real tears, entangling silken shining strands of night-dark hair in the rough gold embroidery of the Staff brassard on the Assistant-Adjutant's sleeve.

"This is my place! Let all the world come and find me here! I do not care! What is humiliation if I can atone? Make no allowances or excuses for me.... Do not say: 'It was a moment of madness!' Think of me as your enemy and your destroyer! Ah! what a heart I must have to have smiled in your eyes, as I did when we met this evening, and not have cried out at the first look: 'Pardon! Forgiveness!'—you whom I have wronged!'"

She drew some sobbing breaths, and said, lifting beautiful tear-drenched eyes like pansies in a thunder-shower:

"Hate me for the cold, calculating selfishness—bred of the base desire to save myself from the taint of all that blood—the cowardly fear of the possible vengeance of Red Republicans—that led me to say to you: '*Take the advice of a sister. Say that you were guilty of this crime!*' For it is a crime. It has defiled my soul with stains that cannot be wiped away."

The supple red hands of Dunoisse tightened upon the little hands they clasped. He said, looking in her eyes:

"The pistol-shot was yours. But *he* cried, 'Fire!'"

She moved her lips soundlessly and nodded.

"I recognized his voice.... I should recognize it through the noise of battle—above all the tumult of the Judgment Day. It claimed payment for the false step—indemnity for the broken foil. Well, let him have both, and find his joy in them!"

He laughed harshly, and his grip was merciless. Yet she bore the pain of it without crying out. His eyes had quitted her face—they were fixed upon the portrait of the nun-Princess of Orleans. And as though some subtle, evil influence had passed from those proud voluptuous painted eyes into his blood, he was conscious of the shaping of a purpose within him and the surging of a flood that was to carry all before it and undo the work of years.

"But one joy he shall not have...."

He hardly knew whether his own lips or another's had uttered the words. But he looked down and saw Henriette at his feet, between his hands. And as his eyes fell upon the creamy treasure of the fair bosom that heaved so near, Monsieur the Marshal, had he been enabled to look into the gray boudoir at that particular moment, would no longer have been able to say to Hector:

"You are an iceberg. You have Carmel in your blood!"

For the son of Marie Bathilde—carried away by a tidal wave of passion, such as had swept Sister Thérèse de St. François out from among the pallets of the Lesser Ward of the Mercy-House at Widinitz, out of her nun's cell into the wild, turbulent ocean that rolled and billowed outside the convent walls—was to yield, and take, and eat as greedily as any other son of Adam of the fruit of the Forbidden Tree.

How it matures, the first bite into the sweet, juicy pulp! He had seemed to Henriette a brilliant boy; obstinate and stiff-necked, scrupulous and absurd. Now she saw him transformed to a new being. Vigorous, alert, decisive, masterful, a man to be reckoned with, to be feared while you deceived. And on the boiling whirlpool of passion her own light fragile craft began to dance, and rock, and spin in ever-narrowing circles, as he said, with a strange smile that showed the white teeth gleaming under the small black mustache, but set no gay light dancing in the brilliant, cold black eyes:

"Have no fear. Try to believe me when I promise you, upon my word of honor, that no harm shall come to you from—this that you have done."

He stooped and kissed the little white hands, and said to their owner:

"Blood on these exquisite hands would be a horror. Well! from henceforth I take their stains on mine."

She faltered in real agitation:

"What are you going to do?"

The lovely lips were very near his own, as he said, still smiling in that curious way:

"I shall take the advice—not of a sister!"

She panted, shuddering closer.

"No, no! You must not——"

His eyes were fastened on her lips. Instinctively his own were drawn to them. His hot kiss would have burned them in another moment, but that a chill breath seemed to flutter at his ear, and in a flash, he saw the thing he was about to do in its true, ugly colors, and shame stung through and through him, and he drew back.

He had gathered of the fruit of Pleasure and plucked its gaudy flowers in the parterres where these things can be had at a price. He had emptied the frothy cup of Passion and paid its exorbitant bill. But though he may have coveted the mistress of another man, he had never yet desired his neighbor's wife.

De Roux might be a reprobate and a libertine, but he was Henriette's husband. And she was not the pure, unattainable planet, the chaste, immaculate divinity he had imagined her; but yet she was a wife. She felt the change in him—saw the fierce, eager light die out in his black eyes, and rose up, saying hurriedly:

"How good you are!—how good! I shall rely upon your promise. We must join the others now. It will not do to be missed!"

So they went out together and mingled with the spinning rout of dancers, as the neglected wax-lights burned out in their silver branches, and the waning moon peeped through the curtains of the gray boudoir. One pale ray touched the portrait of the witch-Princess of Orleans, grasping the Crucifix in the dimpled hand that had never scrupled to pluck Sin's reddest flowers—treading crowns and scepters under the dainty, naked feet so many lovers had kissed as gayly they danced downwards along the hellward path. And surely the proud, sensuous eyes leered with wicked triumph, and could it be that the smile upon the painted mouth had given place to laughter?

XXXVII

The General Court-Martial of Inquiry into the conduct of the junior Staff-officer left in command of the half-battalion of infantry detailed to guard the Ministry of Foreign Affairs upon a day to be marked with red upon the calendar, was held at the Barracks of the 999th in the Rue de l'Assyrie, between the official hours of Eight in the morning and Four in the afternoon.

One may suppose the pomp and solemnity of the affair, the portals guarded by sentries, Monsieur the Judge-Advocate and his subordinates in official robes, Monsieur the President and other stately cock-hated, plumed, bewigged personages of the General Staff, with the various officers convened as witnesses, solemnly filing in behind the Provost-Marshal and his guard—taking their seats, right and left according to rank, at the **T**-shaped arrangement of tables, covered with the significant Green Cloth; everyone arrayed in full Review-uniform, making the whitewashed mess-hall brilliant as a garden of flaunting summer flowers.

They took the votes according to the time-honored custom, beginning with the youngest person present. The Provost-Marshal and his merry men brought the Prisoner in.

Dunoisse, without sword or sash, went calmly to the place of dread at the bottom of the leg of the **T** of tables. Reporters for the Press were accommodated with a bench behind a board on trestles under the high window at the bottom of the hall. The Orders and Warrants were read, with clearing of throats and official hawking. And at each pause, from a balcony high up upon the plain bare wall behind the President's table, came the silken frou-frou of ladies' dresses and the rustling of ribbons and bonnet-plumes. And one heart among all those that throbbed there, under its covering of silken velvet and sable-fur, was sick with hidden apprehension and cold with secret dread.

There was no challenge on the part of the accused officer when the President-General asked the question: "Do you object to be tried by me or any of these officers whose names you have heard?" He bowed and replied, "No!".... He had no suspicion of prejudice or malice lurking under any uniform present. And then, erect, in a rigid attitude of respect and attentive deference, the Prisoner listened to the reading of the Charge.

This occupied time, the process of Courts-Martial very successfully emulating the pompous prolixity of tribunals of the Civil kind. And while the python-periods dragged their tortuous length from sheet to sheet of official paper, Dunoisse found himself mentally traveling back to those early days at the Royal School of Technical Military Instruction, when de Moulny was Redskin's hero and faithful Achates, Mentor and Admirable Crichton all rolled into one. And butt on occasions, it is to be added. For sometimes it is sweet to laugh at one you most sincerely love.

Thinking thus, he began to realize how in his loneliness he had clung to the memory of the old affection. How always,—always he had been hoping that the barriers of estrangement and silence might be broken down one day. That Alain might yet come to him with outstretched, eager hand, saying:

"I have withheld my friendship all these years, that I might be able to give you my esteem and my admiration. You have been tried by me as no friend was ever yet tried, tested to the utmost, and proved as none has ever been proved before you.... Was it not worth while to bear something to earn such praise from me?"

And now Dunoisse saw the god of his old boyish, innocent idolatry stripped of the false jewels and tawdry robes that had adorned him, his nimbus of gilt plaster knocked away. He began to understand how he, Hector Dunoisse, had been his whole life long the slave, and tool, and puppet, and victim of this cold, arrogant, dominating nature; and resentment glowed in him, scorching up the last green blade of lingering kindness; and hatred leaped up in a little flickering tongue of greenish flame, soon to become a raging prairie-fire of vengeance, traveling with the speed of the wind that urged it on.

He clenched his hands and set his teeth, remembering his long arrears of injuries. He saw himself economizing uniforms, doing without necessaries and comforts, slaving in spare hours to earn the money to buy books and instruments—bound and fettered always by that egregious vow.... Then a conviction started through him like the discharge from an electric battery. Malice was the missing key-word of the cipher that had been so difficult to read.

Revenge for the spoiled career had prompted everything. No pleasure foregone, luxury denied, but had paid off some item of the old score that had been carved with the end of the broken fencing-foil. That the false step had been deliberately planned, de Moulny must have always believed. He had told the story everywhere. And the taint of that supposed treachery had always clung about Dunoisse's footsteps. It had followed him through life.

Now he lifted up those glittering black eyes of his to the balcony where bonnet-plumes were nodding as their wearers whispered of him.... And he met the eyes of Henriette de Roux.

Those beautiful eyes!... Their owner had seemed to him upon that first night of their meeting a star and a goddess—something to dream of and worship from a long way off.

But before gray dawn had peeped in between the window-curtains upon the whirling crowd of weary, hot-eyed dancers, he had learned to know her better. The star was no celestial sphere, but an earthly planet, glowing with fierce volcanic fires; the dazzling robe of the divinity, now that she had descended from her pedestal, was seen to be stained with frailties of the human kind. But brought within reach, she was not less desirable. He thrilled at the recollection of that night in the gray boudoir.

Ah! those sweet lips that mingled Truth and Falsehood in such maddening philters! Ah! those bewitching eyes, how they promised, and coaxed, and cajoled! A shudder went through the man. For he saw again, more clearly by their light, the pleasant pathway that went winding downwards between banks of gorgeous, poison-breathing flowers. And a soft, insinuating voice seemed whispering, prompting; telling him that with a tithe of the great sum of money that had lain growing for so many years at Rothschild's, could be purchased the sweet, heady vengeance that is wreaked in the satisfaction of desire.

And then ... he became aware that the labyrinthine verbosities of the Charge had reached a final period, and that Monsieur the Judge-Advocate had a question to ask.

"Are you, Lieutenant Hector-Marie-Aymon von Widinitz-Dunoisse, Certificated of the General Staff, and Attached as Assistant-Adjutant to the 999th Regiment of the Line, Guilty or Not Guilty of the Charge brought against you, and which I have now read in the hearing of this Court?"

The reply left little excuse for prolonged investigations. The arraigned officer simply said:

"Monsieur, I gave the order to fire. I believed it necessary. I have no excuse to offer—no plea to make. I submit myself absolutely to the jurisdiction of the Court."

Which Court, at the end of this First Assembly, declined to continue the proceedings, the prisoner having acted with a certain degree of rashness, yet with the very best intentions, in the face of an emergency of the gravest kind. And, furthermore, having been severely reprimanded in orders by his Colonel; and placed in and kept under close arrest by the said commander, the said Court did ultimately find Further Proceedings under the circumstances would be Unjustifiable, and recommended that the said Prisoner be immediately Released, the charge against him Not Having Been Proved.

And the grave farce was ended—the solemn jest played out, amidst the rustling of draperies, and the nodding of bonnet-plumes, and the clapping of little kid-covered hands up in the gallery where the Band played on guest-nights, and where at least one heart beat with infinite relief.

Amidst a universal rising, saluting, putting on of plumed cocked hats and white gloves, after official congratulations and some bowings and hand-shakings, the Assistant-Adjutant, *plus* his sash and sword, was free to go about his business, without that haunting sense of being a marked man, under ban of the Second Republic of France. And Dunoisse put on his shako and went out into the sanded barrack-yard, walking with the step of the free. And an orderly of the Colonel's presently brought him a little lilac note, addressed in violet ink, in the small, clear character, exhaling a perfume that had haunted him, of late, persistently. And the little lilac note said:

"*Come!*"

XXXVIII

Perhaps you know how Henriette received him? She took his hands and looked long and softly in the clear-cut, vivid face, and said, while great tears brimmed her white underlids and fell softly down her cheeks:

"Oh, you are noble! Why have I not known you before? Why must we only meet as late as this?"

And presently:

"What other man would be capable of such generosity? And you ask nothing—you who might demand so much!"

De Roux was absent on official business. Dunoisse remained some hours, went away, and returned to dinner. Madame de Roux had a box at the Italiens for that evening. It was perfectly proper that the sub-Adjutant of the 999th should escort his Colonel's wife.

The opera was "Semiramide." Carnavale was in the stalls, wearing the crimson dress-coat dedicated to that special opera. On nights when "Der Freischütz" was given he appeared in apricot,—when "Lucia" was performed you saw him in pale blue. Giulia Gigi sang,—upon that night of all the nights the glorious artist reached the apex of her triumph. The great pure voice flowed forth, the soul was caught upon and carried away by wave upon wave of wonderful music; the Opera-House was filled with them; the atmosphere, saturated with mille-fleurs and frangipani, was electrical with human passion. Dunoisse looked, not at the beautiful singer, who trod the stage and sang as one inspired, but at Henriette.... Her head was thrown back, her transparent eyelids were closed, her delicate nostrils quivered, her throat throbbed and swelled. The curve of it suggested the swan dying in melody. For Dunoisse the music was she. She sat forwards upon her chair of velvet, and the diamond cross upon her bosom wakened into vibrant light and sank into soft suggestive shadow as she drew and exhaled deep, sighing breaths. Below the line of her short glove a blue vein leaped in her delicate wrist. To see it was to long to kiss it. Dunoisse's eyes could not keep away.

And Gigi sang more and more divinely, and at the end of her greatest *scena*, sweeping off the stage like a human tornado, you might, had you been sitting in the shadow of velvet curtains, in a certain box upon the Grand Tier, occupied by two people who hardly looked at the stage, have seen her seize from the grasp of a giant fireman in a shining helmet, tight shell-jacket with enormous shoulder-straps and cavalry trousers, a glittering pewter—pour down that statuesque throat of hers a copious draught of English porter, frothing, mellow, and mild; kick out her imperial train with one backward movement of a foot too solid for a fairy's, and storm back again amidst the thundering cries of "Bis!" and "Brava!" to grant the demanded encore.

Who grudges the Gigi her porter? I have seen the nightingale, that unrivaled soloist, at the finish of a marvelous series of runs and trills, a fine frenzy of jug-jug-jugging, look about him, preen his snuff-colored breast-feathers, and presently hop down to a lower branch and help himself to a snack. Why, then, should we chide the prima-donna for her draught of stout, or cavil at the grilled lobsters, risotto, or macaroni dressed with chillies and tomatoes, that her soul loves? For are not these, by the alchemy of digestion, equally with the earwig, woodlouse, or grub of the other singer, transmuted into heavenly sounds?

Henriette said to Dunoisse, as the great waves of melody broke over them:

"You said that night in the boudoir that you would not take advice from me as a sister. But I am your sister!—nothing but your sister! Let us make a compact upon that?"

Dunoisse agreed, without enthusiasm. She thanked him in a velvety whisper. Presently she said:

"If all men were as noble as you, this world would be a happy place for women. How wonderful to have met a nature such as yours! Another man would have kissed me—that night when I made my terrible confession. But I knew that I was secure,—I rested upon your honor. Let it be always thus between us. Let me always feel when I am with you that I am a soul without a body—a pure spirit floating in clear ether with my friend."

Dunoisse gave the promise with obvious reluctance. Then they talked about the music energetically. But presently, when the great gilded chandelier soared up into the artificial firmament of the domed ceiling, and the stage-lights were lowered, and the flats parted—revealing the Tomb of Ninus, by the pale mysterious rays of the calcium moon—a cheek that was warm and satiny, and glowing as a nectarine plucked from a south wall in the ripening heats of July, brushed Dunoisse's—and his trumpery promise broke its gilded string, and flew away upon the wind of a double sigh.

De Roux looked in to escort his wife home, at the conclusion of the opera. He had been winning at cards,—was smiling and urbane, and Dunoisse, looking at the dyed, red-faced, dissipated, elderly dandy, knew the sickness of loathing. De Roux had shown him civility, courtesy, even friendliness, yet he hated him with zeal and rancor. He watched the Colonel as he wrapped his beautiful wife in her ermine mantle—the same that she had worn, Dunoisse remembered, upon the evening of the bloodshed at the Hotel of Foreign Affairs. And as the almond-nailed, plump fingers of one of the Colonel's well-kept, ringed hands touched Henriette's bare shoulder, she winced and shuddered. Her mouth contracted as though to stifle a cry—her long eyes shot a glance at her friend that seemed a mute appeal to be saved from the indignity of that touch.... And so fierce was the jealous impulse urging Dunoisse to dash his clenched fist into the gross, sensual face of her possessor, that he was fain to thrust his tingling right hand deep into his trouser-pocket and clench it there until the glove split.

XXXIX

The Bonaparte, upon a strong hint received from Citizen Lamartine, did not make a protracted stay in Paris. He returned to the savage scenes of his exile, suffering eclipse behind the curtain of fog enveloping the barbarous island of Great Britain, until an early date in June. But previous to departure, he held a reception of his friends and supporters, followed by a supper, to which only intimate acquaintances were invited, at the Hotel du Rhin in the Place Vendôme. For the earlier function Dunoisse received a card.

The first-floor suite of rooms, occupied by the hope of the Imperialist Party, boasted a certain pompous splendor. There were gilded wall-decorations, velvet hangings, ormolu and marble consoles, clocks and mirrors topped with perching eagles, carpets patterned with garlands, masks, fillets and torches, high-backed settees with scrolled ends; chairs of classical simplicity, tripod-pedestals bearing vases, all the worm-eaten and moth-riddled lumber of the defunct Empire, routed out of basements, dragged down from garrets by a time-serving management eager to gratify their princely tenant's hereditary tastes.

He thought all this rococo pseudo-classicism supremely hideous, for his predilections were for the gaudy, the showy, the voluptuous, and the *bizarre*, yet he gazed pensively upon these relics of an extinct era. His bedroom had a vast purple four-poster with a canopy like a catafalque, and a dressing-table, white lace over violet silk, suggestive of an altar in mid-Lent, that gave him the horrors. And it was all as expensive as it was ugly, and every hour added to the length of the management's Python-bill. Fortunate that funds supplied him by an anonymous adherent had plumped the cheeks of his emptying purse, otherwise Paris might have been treated to a spectacle that London had witnessed before then—the pantomimic interlude of the Prince Pretender, who, lacking the needful cash to defray mine host's charges, had, *minus* his hatboxes and tin cases and hair-trunks, with grievous lack of ceremony, been hustled to the door....

He received his guests of that evening with a bland, dignified politeness, even a certain grace, despite his awkward build, stunted proportions, and heavy, sleepy air.

Badly dressed, in an egregious chocolate-colored evening coat with gold buttons, trousers of the same color, wide at the hips, and with strips of black silk braiding down the outer seams, he yet wore an air of composed assurance, smiling pleasantly under his heavy brown mustache, moving his tufted chin about in the high stock embraced by the cravat of white satin, adorned with emerald pins, flowing into the bosom of a waistcoat of green plush. Despite the star upon the chocolate-colored coat; and the crimson watered-silk ribbon that supported the Grand Cross of the Legion of Honor, there was not one of his small band of followers and adherents but looked more fit to play the *rôle* of Prince than he.

They bore themselves with imperturbable gravity, these needy adventurers, most of them blown by the wind that had seemed to fill the slack sails of their master's ship of fortune from Albion's hospitable shores.... They took the stage at this juncture like the characters in a Comedy of Masks.... You had the Pretender, the Confidant, the Councillor, the Panderer, the Doctor, the Valet, and the Bona Roba—the last discreetly kept out of sight. The Bravo was at that time in Africa, to be recalled later on. And they played their several parts, with some stately change of title and trappings on the part of certain of the actors, to the fall of the curtain upon the Last Act.

You saw the Count Auguste de Morny, ex-Member of the Chamber of Commerce,—afterwards to reign as the all-powerful Minister of the Home Department under the Second Empire,—as a sallow, well-bred rake of forty, prematurely bald, erect if hollow-chested, faultlessly dressed in the becoming blue swallow-tailed coat with gold buttons, voluminous starched cambric neckcloth, white vest, full-hipped black velvet pantaloons, and narrow-toed buckled shoes of the latest evening wear. Well-to-do, a familiar figure in Paris during the Monarchy, he held a better reputation than his legitimate brother, the man of straw.

And he walked behind the Prince-Pretender now, through a lane of curtseying ladies and bowing gentlemen, outwardly urbane, inwardly infinitely bored by all that was taking place, yet conscious of its probable result upon the Bourse, and alert for intelligence respecting the rise of certain stocks in which he was secretly a large investor.

His companion, some years his senior, and dressed in uniform fashion, was a personage infinitely more striking than the Count. The pale classic oval of his aquiline-featured face, its high brow streaked with a few silken strands of chestnut, the deep blue eyes lightening from beneath the wide arched brows, the sweet deceptive smile, the round chin with a cleft in it, are indelibly stamped upon the memory of the French people, whatever effigy appears upon the coinage of France. Colonna Walewski, son of the Great Emperor by the Polish Countess who was faithful to Napoleon in exile as in defeat, inherited his mother's fine quality of loyalty. In foul weather and fair, in disgrace as in triumph, in the heyday of the Second Empire as in its decline and collapse, the Napoleonic Idea remained the religion of Napoleon's bastard son.

His fellow-bastard, the wit and dandy, the politician and financier, less noble in grain than the brilliant soldier, the keen diplomat and the man of letters,—you will always find upon the winning side.

As for Persigny, the Bonaparte's parasite and inseparable companion,—who was to succeed de Morny as Minister of the Interior, and subsequently figure as Ambassador and Plenipotentiary at the Court of a neighboring Foreign Power,—he looked like what he was; a dissipated ex-quartermaster-sergeant of cavalry grafted on a rowdy buck-about-town. And Fleury, sensual, hot-headed, lively, bulldog-jowled, bold-eyed and deep-chested, heir of a wealthy tradesman, ruined through women and horses, he no less than Persigny had risen from the bottom sludge....

Elderly bloods, middle-aged dandies like their master, they dressed after him, aped his tone and manner, rouged their dry cheekbones and hollowing temples, set false tufts of curls among their dyed hyacinthine locks. Necessitous and creditor-ridden, even as he, they were sharp-set and keen as ferrets for chances of rapine and plunder. And the day was coming when they were to be glutted with these, and crawl after their leader from the warren, gorged, and leaving on the thirsty sand a wide, dark streak of blood.

"It was terrible crossing in the mail-packet," said Persigny in answer to the question of a sympathizer. "M. de Fleury and myself suffered abominably—the Prince not at all. There was something the matter with the railway-line. We had to walk to Neufchâtel over the ballast and sleepers in thin boots of patent-leather,—imagine the torture to one's corns!... But the Prince laughed at our grumblings—only when we missed the Amiens train did he lose his sang-froid and stoicism. And after all, that delay proved to his advantage.... There was an accident to the train we lost—thirty passengers killed,—many more wounded.... The Prince's lucky star has been once more his friend!"

The parasite's voice, purposely raised, reached the little ears shadowed by Madame de Roux's rich black tresses. She murmured as she sank in her deep curtsey, and emerged, radiant and smiling, from a foamy sea of filmy white lace flounces, to meet the gracious handshake that was accorded to special friends:

"It is true, Monseigneur? You have escaped such perils as M. de Persigny describes?"

Said the little gentleman with the sallow face and the dull, lusterless gray eyes, caressing the brown chin-tuft that was later to be dubbed "an imperial," and worn by all ranks and classes of men:

"I fancy there was something of the kind. I hardly noticed. I realized nothing but that, after all my cruel years of exile, I was on the road to Paris at last!"

He had been horribly seasick during the Channel crossing, and had bestowed heartfelt curses on the broken granite of the railway-line. He had paled and shuddered at the thought of the smash in which he might have been involved. But to come up to the Idea Napoleonic, it was necessary to be heroic. And with so grave a face and with such imperturbable effrontery did Persigny hold the candle, that the person belauded ended by believing all that was said.

Even now, to many of his friends and supporters, the shadow of the purple Imperial mantle gave dignity to the wearer of the chocolate-colored coat, green plush waistcoat, and big-hipped, braided trousers. His own faith in his Mission and his Star lent him the power to convince and to impress.

His was not a star of happy omen for England, who sheltered and befriended him with the kind of good-humored pity that is not unmixed with contempt. Plagued with the gadfly of debt, tormented by the Tantalus-thirst of the born spendthrift who sees gold lavished by other hands, and who has never funds at command to dissipate, what rage and hatred must have seethed under his smooth ingratiating demeanor, when, with one or another of his henchmen at his elbow, he sat down to the lavish table spread by the sumptuous mistress of Gewgaw House, or planned landscape-gardens with the master of Brodrick Castle.

That had been for years his fate, to fawn for bare subsistence upon those he hated. Compelled to this, the son of proud, faithless, extravagant, voluptuous Hortense must have suffered the pains of Hell. Not a hell whence Hope was altogether banished. He had hoped when he made the attempt on Strasburg; had hoped when the body of the Great Emperor was solemnly removed from St. Helena to be magnificently interred in Paris. Still hoping, he had hired a London-and-Margate steamer, a husband's boat, for himself and his party of sixty adherents; had purchased a second-hand live eagle, trained to alight upon its owner's shoulder for a gobbet of raw meat; had landed, with this disconsolate bird, at Vimereux, near Boulogne; had hugged the Column, attired in the historic uniform of the 40th of the Line; had ridden with his followers to the town Barracks, where were quartered the 46th; had ordered these warriors, *per* the mouth of a subaltern of their Regiment, to turn out upon the parade-ground; had bidden them thrill at the sight of the eagle, swear loyalty to the little cocked hat—salute the nephew of their late Emperor, and march with him to Paris.

We are acquainted with the burlesque ending of that enterprise, the pricking of the balloon by the bayonets of National Guards—the pantomimic flattening of the Pretender and his followers beneath the collapsed folds of the emptied bag, has been held up to the popular derision by innumerable caricaturists of the day. We are aware—I quote from an obscure comic publication of the period, long since dead of its own indigestible wit—how the Boulogne Picnic began with Fowl, and ended with Ham.... And yet, though the asserter of Imperial claims was jeered at as a mountebank;—even though that marionette-invasion ludicrously failed, how many grave and weightily-important personages had not the Prince-Pretender infected with his own conviction, that to him, and to him alone, had been entrusted the lofty mission of saving, elevating, ennobling, delivering France....

He murmured now, looking at Henriette between half-closed lids, with eyes that appraised every charm, and took deliberate stock of her whole armory of beauties:

"I had too much to think of, dear friend, to heed the perils of the road. But those who accompanied me, ready to share triumph as they have shared Failure,—it would have touched you to witness their emotion as they realized how nearly Death had quenched their hopes. They do not understand yet at what a price the exile has purchased repatriation. To-night will bring home to them the knowledge of this. Ah! here is M. Hugo, charged with the revelation. I fear it will be a painful one for you!"

"Sire ..." she breathed in distress. He corrected her imperturbably:

"Neither 'Sire' or 'Monseigneur,' I beg of you! Follow the example of M. Hugo—let me be plain 'Monsieur.'"

And as though to bear him out, the splendid voice of Hugo uttered resoundingly:

"Monsieur!..."

And beaming with cordial smiles, the great Conservative Republican advanced towards Louis-Napoleon, while some half-dozen other wearers of black coats and tricolored sashes pushed through the press towards the orator, who was later to array himself, with all his forces of eloquence, learning, irony, and enthusiasm, upon the extreme Left.

"Monsieur..." he began, while his Burgraves took up their position right and left of their Barbarossa, and the short gentleman in the green plush waistcoat stood still, with the little jeweled hand of Madame de Roux resting on his chocolate-colored sleeve: "Monsieur, when a few days back in the new Constituent Assembly of the Second French Republic the question was raised: 'Shall the nephew of the Emperor Napoleon be readmitted into France?' I and my comrades, having confidence in your pledges, voted in your favor. We extend to you now our welcome upon your return, not as the Pretender to the Imperial Throne, but as Bonaparte the good citizen; who seeks, not to rule men, but to represent them; not to be deified, but to serve. And in the name of Liberty and Peace and Freedom—I offer you my hand!"

The hand went out with its large sweeping gesture. The little gentleman stood stock still. His white-kid gloved fingers played with the black ribbon of his eyeglass. He said, with the drawling snuffle that characterized him, and with so subtle a burlesque of the pompous manner of the orator that those who were most stung to indignation by the mockery were unable to repress a smile:

"Monsieur ... the Second Republic of France is now established upon a basis that can never be undermined. As I am not a genius, I entertain no ambition to emulate the career of my glorious uncle,—Integrity and Honor, bareheaded, are preferable to crime that is crowned. Give me, then, the name of Napoleon Bonaparte, the honest citizen.... I prefer that to the title of Napoleon, the Emperor of France!"

He added, addressing himself to Hugo with an air of confidential simplicity that painted a faint grin upon the faces of de Morny and Walewski:

"I am told, M. Hugo, that during the recent reign of the barricades, no milk-and-butter carts could penetrate into Paris, and that her citizens were obliged to be content with chocolate made with water,—dry rolls, and *café noir*. Well!—let us see to it that not only milk and butter, but wine and honey flow during the New Era, and that the streets shall be repaved with hams and sausages. And in place of the planes and acacias that have been decapitated, let us plant fig-trees, olives and vines."

He bowed with much grace, considering his disadvantages of figure, and moved onwards, stepping deliberately as Agag, with the little high-arched feet in the wonderfully-polished boots that were no bigger than those of a pretty girl. It stamps him—who was undeniably possessed of a mordant power of irony,—as being devoid of the saving grace of humor, that he should, during the period of his American exile, have conferred upon a throbbing feminine devotee and partisan one of these shiny leather boots of his—which the possessor employed alternately as a receptacle for flowers, or as a repository for embroidery-silks; or merely as an object of peculiar veneration, preserved under a glass-case.

He said in the ear of Madame de Roux, as exclamations, comments, ejaculations, broke out on all sides, in tones of consternation, satisfaction, exasperation, not to be repressed:

"What do you say, dear friend? Is not the ax laid to the root of the Violet with a vengeance? Shall we not cultivate our cabbages henceforth in tranquillity and peace?"

He added, as with an ineffable air of conquering gallantry he handed the beautiful woman to a sofa, and placed himself beside her:

"Tell me that I have kept my promise, given that day when you walked with a poor prisoner on the ramparts of the Fortress of Ham.... 'If ever I return to France,' I said, 'I will hold this little hand upon my arm as I receive the congratulations of my friends."

"Ah! but, Monsieur," said Henriette, all pale and quivering, "your words were, '*When I return to France in triumph!*' and this——"

She broke off. He ended the sentence, saying with a shallow, glittering look:

"And this is not triumph, but humiliation. I understand!" He pulled at the flowing goatee, and added, in his mildest drawl:

"Let me remind you that the ancient Roman triumphs, as represented at the theater, invariably begin with a procession of captives and spoils. Imagine yourself at the Français, seated in a box. And consider that though it hardly befits an Emperor to play the part of a slave, unless at the feet of a lovely woman, yet the slave may be promoted to the part of Leading Citizen. And from the armchair upon the platform behind the tribune, might be wielded, on occasion, the lightnings that slay from a throne."

Even as he uttered the words, a witty woman of society was saying in the ear of a depressed Imperialist:

"Ah,—bah! Why are you so dismal? This is only another move in the eternal game of the Cæsars. Did Nero scruple to lick the dust in order that he might reign? To me, behind that leaden mask of his, he seemed to be bursting with laughter. Depend upon it, Badinguet is cleverer than any of you believe!"

"Badinguet" or "Beaky"—those were among his nick-names—the pigmy who aspired to the ermined mantle of the tragic giant, and the throne under the crimson velvet canopy powdered with Merovingian bees.

Doubtless, in the eyes of many another besides the brilliant speaker, he seemed as absurd, grotesque, mirth-provoking an object as any Punch-puppet. But later, when Punch was gilded thick with stolen gold, and painted red with human blood, he was to assume another aspect. For Life and Death were in his power. And the world laughed no more.

XL

He said to Henriette now, stroking his mustache, and giving another of those dull, inscrutable glances:

"No!—the President of the Democratic Republic of France would neither be destitute of the power to strike his enemies or the ability to shower honors and rewards upon his friends."

She dropped her white, deep-fringed eyelids, and said, almost in a whisper:

"True friendship seeks no honors, and is indifferent to rewards."

Only that morning he had received a letter from another woman, young, beautiful, and heiress to vast estates. She offered him all her wealth. He was to use it as he would. She made no conditions, stipulated for no repayment. She was perfectly disinterested, just like Henriette.

And on the previous day an elderly person with two wooden legs, who had once been a popular actress in vaudeville, and who kept the newspaper-kiosk in front of Siraudin's at the angle of the Boulevard des Capucines and the Rue de la Paix, had made a similar proposal.

"Monseigneur," she had said, as he gave her a small gratuity in passing, "deign to permit a word?" She added, as Monseigneur signified permission: "See you, they tell me you are uncommonly tight for money; do not ask who they are—everybody knows it. And I am not so poor but that I have three billets of a thousand francs laid away as a nest-egg. Say the word, and I will lend you them—you shall pay me back with interest when you are Emperor of France."

Kate Harvey and the newspaper-seller were more honest than the rest of them....

Kate had said:

"Look here, old pal, here are fifty thousand shiners it took me a heap of trouble to rake together. You shall have 'em to play with, only give me I.O.U.'s for a hundred and forty thou. And a title by-and-by, when you are Emperor,—something to make the proper folks at home twiddle their thumbs and stare."

That was plain speaking. He understood that kind of bargaining. People who asked nothing wanted most in the long run.

"Undoubtedly," he now replied to Madame de Roux, "friendship like yours seeks no return of favors. But the heart is relieved of its burden of gratitude in the lavish bestowal of these...." He added: "Not that obligations to you weigh heavily.... Yes, I have eaten the bread of your charity. That sum of twenty thousand francs—sent to me at the commencement of the insurrection—the twenty-five thousand forwarded to me here on the evening of yesterday—anonymously—like other sums that I have received from the same source.... Did you think I should not guess whose hand it was that traced the words, *'From a Lover of the Violet, who longs to see the flower take root again upon the soil of France'?*"

She faltered, careful that the denial should appear hesitating and labored:

"Monseigneur, you mistake.... I wrote nothing.... The money you speak of did not come from me!"

He shook his lank-haired head, and said in a nasal murmur:

"Do not deny it. The sheet of paper upon which the words were traced bore no signature, it is true, but the handwriting could not be mistaken. Or the perfume, that recalled so much when I pressed it to my lips."

Her beautiful bosom heaved. Her eyes seemed to avoid him.

"My lips, that were more privileged once.... Shall I tell you what words broke from them to-night when they announced you? Ask de Morny, who overheard. He will tell you that I said: 'Thank Heaven, she is not changed!'"

To be accurate, he had remarked to de Morny that night upon her entrance: "*She is still charming!*" and de Morny had answered: "*And still ambitious, you may depend!*"

It suited him that women should be ambitious. All through those years of intrigue and plotting their ambitions were the rungs of the ladder by which he climbed.

She looked at him full, and her beautiful eyes were dewy, and her white bosom rose and fell in sighs that, if not genuine, were excellently rendered. He went on:

"And yet you are changed. You were courageous and high-spirited—you have become heroic. That shot at the Foreign Ministry.... A colossal idea! When I heard of it I applauded the stratagem as masterly. '*Who of all my friends,*' I wondered, '*can have been so much a friend?*' Then your little message in Spanish was brought to me in London. I read it and cried out, to the surprise of de Morny and some other men who were sitting with me in the smoking-room of the Carlton Club: 'Oh, that I had a crown to bestow on her!' 'Upon whom?' they asked, and I answered, before I could check myself, 'Upon Henriette!'"

She breathed quickly as the instilled poison worked in her. The fiery light of ambition was in her glance. He saw it, and noted that her dress of filmy Alençon lace and the style of her jeweled hair-ornaments were copied, as closely as the prevailing fashion would admit, from a well-known portrait of the Empress Josephine.... It tickled his mordant sense of humor excessively that a lovely woman should endeavor to subjugate him by resembling his aunt deceased. But no vestige of his amusement showed in his sallow face as he went on:

"But magnificent as was the service you rendered, I am glad that you have escaped the pillory of publicity, and the possible vengeance of the Reds. By the way, that young officer who proclaimed before the Military Tribunal, 'It was I who gave the order to fire! Do with me what you will!' is here to-night. I told them to send him an invitation. His father was a valued General upon the Staff of my glorious uncle. I desired that he should be presented to me on that account. Pray point him out."

Then, as the lace-and-tortoiseshell fan wielded by Henriette's little dimpled hand, loaded with gems which surely were not paste imitations, indicated a young and handsome man in infantry uniform, who from the shelter of a doorway was gazing at her with all his eyes and his heart in them, the drawling nasal voice said:

"He loves you!... It is written in his face.... And I can even wish that he may be happy.... Have I not my share of heroism too?"

"Monseigneur," said Henriette, with an air of simple candid dignity, "in that young man you see a devoted friend who is ready to give all, and to demand nothing in return."

She had quite forgotten the kiss in the box at the Opera, and a good deal more besides. But when the Henriettes prefer not to remember an episode, it is as though it had never occurred. She continued in her soft, thrilling tones:

"Nothing save absolute trust: confidence such as he gives me. A few nights past he told me his entire history: I could not refrain from tears. He is young, as your Highness sees; handsome, as you have observed; heir-presumptive to the throne of a Bavarian feudal Principality and owner of a vast fortune. Well, the throne he is too scrupulous to claim, because of a fault in the line of succession; the fortune he has refused to accept because it was gained by what he holds to be an unjust claim. But if I lifted up my finger ... like that, Monseigneur...."

She laughed as she held the slender finger up, and challenge and meaning and promise were in her face, and the witchery of it, no less than that hint of gold piled up and hoarded, made even the Pretender's dull blood tingle in his veins. He said, with brightening eyes and a tinge of color in his sallow cheeks:

"It might yet be worth your while to lift your finger up, Madame, although I have as yet no crown to share with the woman who shall bear my name."

It was a name, at that psychological moment, that was not worth sixpence among the British bill-discounters, and at sight of which upon paper the sons of Levi and Manasseh morally rent their garments and threw figurative dust upon their heads. But it had a specious value, dangled as a bait before ambitious women; and here, he knew, was one....

To sway the mass of men you must have Money to give them. True, de Morny, Persigny and Co. could be pacified with orders for millions upon an Imperial Treasury that was non-existent as yet. But the rank-and-file of his filibusters and mercenaries must be paid in hard cash, and women always knew where to go for the shekels. Either they had independent fortunes, or their families were wealthy, or their lovers were rich and generous. Skillfully handled, stimulated by artful hints of marvelous rewards and compensations, Eve's daughters, his confederates and creditors, had never failed to serve him at his need.

That indomitable partisan and tireless intriguer, his cousin the Princess Mathilde, had poured her whole fortune into his bottomless pockets. Now, when his want was greater than ever, Mathilde was without a sou. Lord Walmerston's last subsidy of three thousand pounds, a sum of humiliating smallness, grudgingly accorded, was dwindling rapidly. And money for the expenses of the campaign of June must be forthcoming, and at once.

The attempt on Boulogne had failed, because the tin cases of gold coins slung round the necks of the adventurers for distribution had held so little, and been emptied so quickly.... Money must not be lacking for the printing of millions of handbills and posters; for the payment of hundreds of electioneering agents, touts, and canvassers; for the bribery of thousands of electors who could not be coaxed into giving their suffrage—heaps of money would be required now.

Money! If one would be elected as Representative for the Department of the Seine, and the three other Departments that were to prove so many steps to the armchair upon the platform behind the tribune of the Assembly—money, money! If one would by bribery and corruption raise that same armchair to the height of an Imperial throne—money, money,

money! Golden mortar, without which the house that Jack builds must topple at the first puff of wind, and resolve itself into a mere heap of jumbled brickbats. Money, money, money, money! And the little Corporal, at the lowest ebb of his fortunes, had scarcely been poorer than his nephew was to-day.

The uncle was not over-scrupulous, less so the nephew. His end of self-glorification justified every shameful means.

For him the harlot emptied her stocking, the wealthy saloon-keeper and ex-procuress poured out her tainted gold. To be mistress-in-chief to an Emperor, to flaunt a title in the face of prim Respectability, that was what Kate Harvey sought, and had, when his sun had risen. But the other women, lured on to bankruptcy and ruin by his dull magnetic glance and skillfully-cast bait of promises, saw hovering before their dazzled eyes— receding ever farther into the sandy desert of Unattainability—the bridal carriage of gold lacquer and mother o' pearl, surmounted by the Imperial Eagle. The carved and gilded Matrimonial Chair upon the crimson bee-spangled daïs and the Crown of Josephine....

So, with the flutter of a fan in a jeweled hand, a few brief sentences interchanged, the glance of a pair of brilliant eyes and the dull, questioning look of a pair of fishy ones, at the dark, vivid face and lithe, erect figure standing in the doorway, Dunoisse was bought and sold.

If he had only known, when a little later he was presented to the Prince by Colonel de Roux.... But there was no expression in the vacuous eyes that blinked at him, hardly a shade of meaning in the flat toneless voice that said:

"I am happy in the knowledge, Bonsieur, that a young officer, the gifted son of a noble father, who is gapable of acting upon his own resbonsibility in a moment of national emergency, has been exonerated from undeserved plame—has met with gomblete rehabilitation at the hands of his suberiors and chiefs. Did I possess the influence once wielded by my klorious ungle, you would be regombensed as you teserve."

For after this fashion did he misuse the French language: struggling as gamely as any German Professor to keep the g's from turning out the c's, the b's from usurping the places of the p's ... beset with consonantal difficulties to the ending of his life....

He bowed to the young man of high prospects and great possessions, and solemnly extended the gloved finger-tips of the small effeminate hand. Could it have been, despite his tactful negation of all influence, the hand that had shielded Dunoisse? Was it the hand that shortly afterwards obtained his promotion? One may suspect as much.

At that moment Dunoisse took the utterance for what it seemed worth. He looked into the puffy, leaden face, and as the lifeless eyes glittered back at him from between their half-closed shutters, he knew a base relief, an ignoble joy, in the conviction that Henriette could never have loved this man.

He was quite right. She did not love the man, neither did she love Dunoisse, or any other trousered human. Being a Henriette, she was the lover of Henriette.

True love, pure passion was not to be born in her then,—but long afterwards,—amidst dreadful throes and strivings unspeakable,—the winged child-god was to see the light. Across a gulf of seeming Death his radiant hands were to be outstretched to her. And they were to render her no flowers of joy, but wormwood and rue and rosemary, drenched with the bitter tears of expiation.

XLI

A few days subsequently to that reception at the Hotel du Rhin, Dunoisse found his friend in tears, and asked the reason. She evaded reply, he pleaded for confidence. Then, little by little, he elicited that Henriette's sensitive nature was wrung and tortured by the thought of that money borrowed from de Moulny.

Dunoisse asked of her:

"How much was the amount? I have earned the right to know."

Her heart gave a great throb of triumph, but her eyelids fell in time to veil her exultation. She faltered, in her haste only doubling the sum:

"Sixty thousand francs." She added, with a dewy glance and a quivering lip: "But do not be distressed for me, dear friend. The money shall be repaid promptly. I have still a few jewels left that were my mother's. She will not blame me, sweet saint! for parting with her legacy thus."

He assumed a tone of authority, and forbade her to sacrifice the trinkets. She pleaded, but finally gave in.

"To-morrow," he told her, "you shall receive from me a hundred thousand francs, in billets of a thousand; the sole condition being that you send de Moulny back his money, and that from the hour that sees me break a vow for you, you swear to borrow from no man save me!"

She hesitated, paled, faltered. He kissed the little hands, and she gave in. Had he been older, and wiser in the ways of the world, knowing that money is power, and that he who holds the key to the cashbox can dictate and be obeyed, he would have been more frugal. As it was, being what he was, he gave liberally with both hands. For there is no prodigal like your poor devil suddenly become rich.

Next day, the dusty check-book that had lain for long years forgotten in the drawer of the lost Marie-Bathilde's inlaid writing-table, as impotent for good or evil as the son of Eblis in his sealed-up jar, came out and went into Dunoisse's pocket, and so to the Rue d'Artois. No good angel in the Joinville cravat and the short-waisted, high-collared frock-coat of a somewhat rowdy young Captain of *piou-pious* met Hector on the steps of Rothschild's Bank on this occasion.

He went in. The double doors thudded behind him; the polite, well-dressed Head Cashier looked observantly through his brazen lattice at the young man with the hard, brilliant black eyes and the face like a thin ruddy flame. He bowed with profound respect, did the stately functionary, when he heard the name of the owner of a deposit account of one million, one hundred and twenty-five thousand francs, and sent a clerk with a message to the Manager. And a personage even statelier, wearing black silk shorts—you still occasionally saw them in 1848—and hair-powder,—a being with the benignant air of a Bishop and a dentist's gleaming smile,—issued from a shining cage at the end of a long vista of dazzling counters, and condescendingly assisted at the drawing of the First Check. Its magnitude made him smile more benignantly than ever.... The Head Cashier's checking thumb quivered with emotion as it rapidly counted over a bulky roll of thousand-franc notes.

But, the happy owner of these crackling potentialities departed, the Manager returned to his golden cage, sat down and indited a little note to Marshal Dunoisse. Which missive, conveyed to the old gentleman's residence by an official in the Bank livery of sober gray, badged with silver, made its recipient—not chuckle, as one might have supposed, but gnash his costly teeth, and stamp up and down the room and swear.

For the old brigand of Napoleon's army, the indefatigable schemer for Widinitz dignities, had been proud—after a strange, incomprehensible fashion—of the incorruptible honesty, the high principle, the unstained honor of his son. The Marshal had gloated over the set face of endurance with which the Spartan youth had borne the gnawing of the fox Poverty, beneath his shabby uniform. And that thumping check on Rothschild's cost him a fit of the gout. When his apothecary had dosed and lotioned the enemy into partial submission, you may suppose the old man hobbling up the wide, shallow, Turkey-carpeted staircase to those rooms of Hector's to find them vacant—their late occupant removed to a palatial suite of bachelor apartments occupying the first floor of a courtyard-mansion in the Rue du Bac. A million odd of francs will not last forever; forty-five thousand English sovereigns—smooth, slippery, elusive darlings!—do not constitute a Fortunatus' purse; and yet the sum represents a handsome golden cheese with which to set up housekeeping; though such sharp little gleaming teeth and such tiny white, insatiable hands belonged to the mouse that was from this date to have the run of Hector Dunoisse's cupboard, that in a marvelously short space of time the golden cheese was to be nibbled quite away.

Henriette had carried out her tacit understanding with Monseigneur. She had lifted up her finger, and a golden plum of a hundred-thousand francs had fallen from the shaken tree. Do you suppose de Moulny had been paid?

do you imagine that the Baal of her worship was to be propitiated with all that glittering coin?

Not a bit of it! For this Henriette, like all the others, had huge debts and rapacious creditors, the necessity of being always beautiful cost so much. And de Roux had his horses, gambling-losses, and nymphs of the Opera to maintain and satisfy and keep in good humor. And pious ladies, collecting at Church functions for the benefit of the poor, have been known ere now to slip their jeweled hands into the velvet bag, weighed down with the gold and silver contributions of the faithful, and withdraw the said hands richer than they went in.

The Empire was the religion of Henriette, and she made her collection in its interests tirelessly. If no more than a moiety of what she gathered clinked into the High Priest's coffers, he did not know that—any more than those who had emptied their purses to fill the bag, so nobody was the worse.

XLII

The reader has not been invited to contemplate, in the person of Dunoisse, the phenomenon of the Young Man of Virtue. Of kindred passions with his fellow-men, of unblemished health, hot blood and vivid imagination, he was, *per* grace of certain honorable principles instilled into a boy's mind by a poor old gentlewoman, no less than by an innate delicacy and fastidiousness, a cleanly liver: a man whom Poverty had schooled in self-restraint. Now Poverty was banished, and self-restraint was flung to the winds. And, regrettable as it is to have to state the fact, the lapse of Miss Caroline Smithwick's late pupil from the narrow path of Honor was attended by no chidings of conscience, visited by no prickings of remorse.

Dunoisse was happy. The world took on a brighter aspect, the air he breathed seemed purer and more fragrant, the sunshine brighter and the moonlight lovelier, because of this his sin.

The eyes of men and women—especially of women!—met his own more kindly; there was no sense of strangeness barring social intercourse.... Life was pleasanter as the months rolled into years.

People found him agreeable now—a charming fellow. He was asked everywhere, petted and flattered, quoted and caressed. Not only because he spent his money lavishly, but because there is a freemasonry between the votaries of illicit pleasure which does not extend to the conscientious and cleanly. Vice is a boon-companion in whose society you may lounge unbuttoned. Virtue and Integrity are the two flagrant offenses the world can never pardon or condone.

An agreeable, even brilliant man: well-bred, well-read, and in one branch at least of his profession, marvelously competent. These were among the encomiums bestowed by his world upon Dunoisse, who learned to dress in the height of the prevailing fashion; to spend heaps of money upon jewelry, cigars, wines, restaurant-dinners and little suppers, and to lose as much at cards in a single night at the Club as would have formerly kept him for a year. Other things indispensable to a young man moving in the inner circle of fast Parisian Society were mastered by him in due course—such as the art of living on terms of daily, familiar, friendly intercourse with a man hated, loathed, and envied above all men. Also, the secret of saying one thing and conveying another; the art of taking formal leave and slipping back again; and of applying to the solution of every sum of existence the Ancient Rule of Three.

For in spite of Adjmeh and one or two other brief amatory episodes, the Book of the Ways of Women had not until now been placed open between the hands of Hector Dunoisse.

When you have read that book from Preface to Finis you will have learned much, and yet not all there is to learn. For every page of the manuscript is a palimpsest. When the writing is washed off with tears of blood, the true characters start out from their concealment, the mystery of mysteries is revealed.

But no man has ever lived long enough to master that Book from cover to cover, though some, wiser or more patient than their fellows, have learned a chapter or two by heart before they died. And those deep scholars know that it is never possible to determine whether a woman be prompted to the gift of her beauty and the sacrifice of her honor by love of herself, or love of him who covets it. And also they are aware that the last chapter of the tome is never to be finished. Some Henriette adds a fresh gloss to it every day.

Dunoisse read in that Book with raptures and exultations, and fierce delight and passionate triumph. He was to read it with agonies and humiliations and galling, unspeakable shame. He was to shed secret scalding tears over the cruel pages. He was to laugh over them with the laughter that is born of despair. But the sweetness of honey came before the tang of gall, the pleasure before the torment. So it was and will be while the world goes spinning round.

Women like Henriette give out fascination as radium dispenses its invisible energies. Every tone of their voices is a call, every glance an appeal or an invitation, every rustle of their garments, every heave of their bosoms, constitutes an appeal to the senses and a stimulant to the passions of men.

She was half-a-dozen women in one; you were master of a whole harem of beauties possessing her; a jewel cut in innumerable facets lay in your hand. She could be fierce and tender, pathetic and cynical, gay and sorrowful, delicate and robust, in the space of half-an-hour. Cigarettes calmed her nerves; moonlight, music, tiny glasses of Benedictine, and minute pills of Turkish opium. Chloral and morphia had not at that date been discovered, else what a votary of the tabloid would have been found in Henriette.

She adored sweets, Chinese bezique and good cookery. Green oysters, bouillabaisse, *poulet sauté Marengo*, and peaches in Kirsch, were among her passions. But she was a pious Catholic, and observed with scrupulous rigor the fasts and feasts of the Church.

She had campaigned with the 999th in Algeria, wore a dagger sometimes in her girdle; carried a tiny ivory-and-silver mounted pistol—fellow to one de Moulny kept locked up—and was expert in its use, as in the handling of the fencing-foil and the womanlier weapon, the needle. What webs of cunning embroidery grew under those little fingers! She wrought at these, sometimes for days together. Then she would pine for exercise and the open air: ride furiously in the Bois, with her plumed hat cocked *à la mousquetaire*, and her silver-gray veil and smoke-colored habit streaming; use the jeweled whip until her horse lathered, drive home the little silver-gilt spur of the dainty polished boot until his flank was specked with blood. Or she would shoot pigeons at Tivoli, handling her gun with ease, and vying with crack masculine sportsmen in her skilled capacity for slaughter. Or she would be driven in her barouche or landau, lying back among her silken cushions, as though too indolent to lift an eyelash, languid and voluptuous as any odalisque. Returning from these excursions, she would lie upon the sofa, silent, pale and mysterious, her vinaigrette at her nostrils, a silken handkerchief bound about her brows. For a crown of diamonds she could not, would not go to theater, or ball, or supper that night! She was fit to die—wanted nothing but to be left in solitude.... But she never failed to go; and towards the end of some gay, boisterous midnight banquet she would move with that long, gliding, supple step of hers into the middle of the room, and dance you the cachucha, with coffee-spoons for castanets, if nobody could produce these.

Who could resist her then? With the proud little head swaying on the rounded throat, and the long eyes darting fiery glances as the lithe body swung, and whirled, and the white arms beckoned and waved. With the silken swish of skirts calling attention to the lovely supple curve that went from hip to knee, and from the swelling calf to the delicate rounded ankle, and bidding you note and worship the elastic arch of the Andalusian instep, under which water could run and never wet the sole....

Nor was she less bewitching, be sure, at those other moments when Dunoisse would be alone with her; when, snatching her Spanish guitar from clumsier hands, she would warble the naughtiest ballads of the cafés chantant, reproducing the cynical improprieties of Fanny Hervieu or Georgette Bis-Bis, with inimitable *chic* and go. Or she would sing a Spanish love-song, vibrating with Southern passion; or sigh forth some Irish ballad, breathing of the green isle whence Norah Murphy sailed, to conquer with her beauty a guerrilla chief of Spain, and bear him Henriette, and die of sorrow; bequeathing her daughter a passionate, emotional nature and an hereditary religion, and the memory of some kisses and cradle-songs.

The simile of the changeful fay in the rainbow was never inappropriate to her. What a charming mingling of inconsistencies, what a creature of contradictions was she.... When her Brazilian cockatoo "Coco," a magnificent bird, emerald-green as the Prince-Pretender's dress-waistcoat, with a crest of sulphur-yellow and a beak as crimson as the Colonel's own, was murdered by the Convent tom-cat, how tragic was her grief! Coco was interred in the Convent gardens, beautiful still in those days, though filched from even then for the builders' diabolical uses. And the glove-box that served Henriette's slaughtered darling as a coffin had been won at a pigeon-shooting match at Tivoli....

Those decapitated birds, fluttering on the smooth green turf in their death-struggles, had not drawn from the beautiful eyes a single tear. But Coco, who had been taught to shriek "Vive l'Empereur!" when he wanted fruit or bonbons, with loyalty quite as genuine as M. de Persigny's—Coco was quite a different affair....

Mistigris must pay the death-penalty—upon that point Coco's bereaved mistress was inexorable. The Augustinian Sisters pleaded for their darling; Madame de Roux would not budge. When she spoke of an appeal to the authorities—never reluctant at any time to impose penalties upon the Church—the Sisters caved in. At any rate, they ultimately produced a tail.... And whether the caudal appendage had really belonged to Mistigris, or had been filched from an old cat-skin belonging to the portress, touched up with red ink at the end where it had been attached to the original wearer, to impart a delusive air of freshness, was never absolutely known. When a cat strangely resembling Mistigris, but called by another name, attracted the attention of Coco's bereaved mistress a few weeks later, the retort was unanswerable:

"But see, Madame—he has a tail!"

That tail was a morsel that stuck in Dunoisse's throat. Another thing, as difficult to swallow, was the undeniable, apparent fact of the amiable, even affectionate relations existing between Madame de Roux and her fiery-faced, dyed, bandoliered and corseted mate.... A further, even more indigestible discovery, was, that although the springs of the young bride's heart had been so early frozen at their sources by etc., etc., the union of the couple had been blessed by children.

Three little girls in pigtails with ribbon bows, and Scotch plaid pelisses, ending in the dreadful frilled-cambric funnels that more adult skirts concealed, and which were known as pantalettes. Happening to come across a daguerreotyped group of these darlings—Henriette had been turning out a drawer in her writing-table—Dunoisse inquired who the children were? And was horribly discomfited at her reply:

"They are mine. Didn't you know? Do you think them like me?"

They certainly were not like her. Nor did they resemble de Roux. And she kissed the three glassy countenances, and murmured caressingly:

"My treasures!"

Adding, as Dunoisse looked round, uncertain whether the treasures might not appear in answer to this ebullition of maternal tenderness:

"They do not live with us, but with their foster-mother at Bagneres: an excellent person—married to a market-gardener. They had measles when last I heard of them, so of course I cannot go there just now. When they are well again you must see them. Ah! how I hope they will love you!... Dear, what is the matter now?"

Dunoisse did not quite know. But he was sensible of a vigorous growth of distaste for plaid pelisses in combination with frilled pantalettes, and for at least a week, pigtails, whenever encountered—and they were everywhere—smote upon his naked conscience like scourges set with thorns.

He rid himself of the absurd obsession presently, and was happier than ever. The world was a gay, bright, pleasant place when one took it easily, and did not demand too much virtue of oneself or the people of one's set.

But yet, on those rare occasions when one was hipped and blue with overmuch wine, or gambling, or pleasure, there were moments when the words of that old boyish vow, so earnestly made, so painfully kept, so recently broken, would start out against the background of half-conscious thought as plainly as the Writing on the Wall, and he would hear himself saying to a woman whose face he had nearly forgotten, that he hoped the day that should see him broach that banked-up store of thousands might bear him fruit of retribution, in bitterness, and sorrow, and shame....

What a fool he had been!—what a narrow-minded, straitlaced idiot! Why, the money had procured Dunoisse everything that was worth having in the world.

The open companionship and secret possession of a beautiful, amorous, high-bred woman; the friendship of many others, only a little less adorable, and the good-fellowship of crowds of agreeable men. Membership of many fashionable Clubs, invitations to all the best houses. His *brevet* as Major, or *chef de bataillon*, though the General Staff appointment that should have accompanied it unaccountably delayed upon the road. And to cap all, life had been made yet easier by the removal of de Roux to a distant post abroad.

For happy as Dunoisse was, it had been constantly borne in upon him that he would be a great deal happier if the reproach of this man's presence could be removed.

He hinted as much to Henriette. She looked at him with sweet, limpid eyes of astonishment. What! did he actually feel like that? How odd!

Dunoisse was secretly a little angry with her for not understanding. It showed a want of delicacy, not suspected in her before.

"Poor Eugène! So easy-going, good-humored and amiable. And you really wish him ... out of the way?"

She crumpled her slender eyebrows and pondered a while, her little jeweled fingers cupping her adorable chin. "Perhaps the Prince-President could offer him some foreign appointment," she said at last. "Monseigneur is always so good!"

XLIII

For the honest citizen Charles Louis-Napoleon Bonaparte had been duly returned in June for the Department of the Seine and two other Departments. The end of the month saw the streets up again: barricades rising one after the other; saw the military called out, saw cannon and howitzer battering down the crazy strongholds of insurrection; saw men in top-hats and frock-coats, armed with revolvers, and men in blouses armed with muskets, defending these works with desperation, as long as cartridges held out.

It was borne in upon Monseigneur Affre, Archbishop of Paris, that he should go forth and speak to the insurgents of St. Antoine. He hesitated but an instant. No doubt of the Voice that urged. So he went, preceded by the Crucifix, accompanied by his Vicars-General; and a man in a blouse walked before the Cross-bearer carrying a green branch in his hand. No one knew who the man was, or ever saw him afterwards. Catholics have whispered that the bearer of the green branch was no other than St. Antoine himself.

They shot the Archbishop from an upper window as he exhorted his flock to lay down their muskets, in the Name of Him Who bled upon the Tree. He sank down, mortally wounded, raised himself with a great effort, made the sign of absolution over a dying insurgent who was being carried past him, and fell back upon the bloody stones.... There was a great cry of horror from those who saw: the Archbishop was carried back to his palace, and passed to God upon the day following. But the green branch had triumphed: the servant of Christ had not died for nothing. The insurrection was virtually at an end.

Paris was sick of the reek of gunpowder and bloodshed. She longed for peace, and quiet, and a stable form of government—just the thing that seemed hardest to attain.

In the caricatures of Gavarni you may see the bemused and worried citizen torn by doubts as to which form of Republic, of all the countless varieties pressed upon the French nation by political quacks and nostrum-mongers, might be the most agreeable to take, and the most efficacious in its method of working. M. Prud'homme of the National Guard, no less than Jerome Paturôt of the Gardes Mobiles, and Jacques Bonhomme, his country cousin, were propitiated and soothed by the mildness of Representative Bonaparte's drugs, and the good sense and moderation of his views; while the feasibility and simplicity of the measures he advocated enchanted everyone who heard.

Candidate for the Presidency, with what modesty and good sense he expressed himself. What noble enthusiasm glowed in him, for instance, when he said:

"The Democratic Republic shall be my religion, and I will be its High Priest."

Meaning:

"The Empire shall be the religion of the French people, the Tuileries its Temple, and I will be the god, enthroned and worshiped there!"

Words like these won him the Presidential elbow-chair on the platform behind the tribune, placed in his neat white hand the coveted little bell with the horizontal handle; procured for him, who had been reduced to pawning-straits to pay the rent of his London lodging, palatial quarters in the Palace of the Élysée at the end of the Faubourg Saint Honoré.

The taking of the Presidential Oath exorcised that haunting specter, arrayed in the rags of the Imperial mantle,—adorned with the *fleurons* from the caparison of Childeric's steed of war. Banished, the grisly phantom sank down into its gorgeous sepulchre. Calumny was silenced, suspicion was changed into confidence, France reposed her ringleted head in chaste abandonment upon the irreproachable waistcoat of her First Citizen, who waited for nothing but the laying of the submarine cable between Calais and Dover, the passing of the Bill restoring to the President of the National Assembly the right of absolute command over the military and naval forces of the country, to toss the trustful fair one over his saddle-bow, leap up behind her, and gallop—with his swashbuckling, roystering band of freebooters thundering upon his heels, with the shouts and pistol-shots of indignant pursuers dying upon the distance—away into the frosty December night.

France was to lose her Cap of Liberty as the result of that furious ride of the night of the *coup d'État*, and something more besides....

But in the meanwhile she was content, suspecting no designs against her honor, and the Prince-President, established at the Palace of the Élysée, made himself very much at home.

Not that he cared about the place—he infinitely preferred the Tuileries. But by day the audience-rooms were packed with gold-encrusted uniforms and irreproachable dress-coats: and by night the whole place blazed with gaslight. *Soirées*, concerts, dinners, balls, and hunting-parties at St. Cloud or Fontainebleau, succeeded balls, dinners, concerts and *soirées*; and after the crush had departed there were suppers, modeled on the Regency pattern, lavish, luxurious, meretricious, at which the intimate male friends of the host were privileged to be dazzled by a galaxy of beauties dressed to slay; scintillating with jewels; lovely women who recalled the vanished splendors, as they reproduced the frailties, of the Duchesse de Berry and Madame de Phalaris.

His "flying squadron" he was wont to term them. They were of infinite use to him in the seduction and entanglement of young and gifted, or wealthy and influential men. With what enchanting grace and stateliness they rode the ocean, broke upon the breeze their sable flag of piracy, unmasked their deadly bow-chasers, and brought their broadside batteries to bear. How prettily they sacked and plundered their grappled, helpless prizes. With what magnificent indifference they saw their livid prisoners walk the plank that ended in the salt green wave and the gray shark's maw.

The Henriette, that clipping war-frigate, had brought much grist to the mills of Monseigneur.

Therefore could he deny her this simple favor, the speedy removal of an inconvenient husband? When the soft caressing voice murmured the plaintive entreaty, Monseigneur stroked the chin-tuft that had not yet become an imperial, and thought the thing might be arranged.

De Roux was not an indispensable digit in connection with the brain that worked in the Élysée. He was of the old school of military commander, deeply imbued, in spite of all his Bonapartist professions, with the traditions of the Monarchy defunct. His removal from the command of the 999th of the Line had been contemplated for some time.

And the General in charge of the Military Garrison at Algiers was desirous to resign his responsibilities in favor of a Home command, if one could be found presenting equal advantages in point of pay. Government, just at this juncture, could not afford to increase the emoluments of the only post that appeared suitable. But if a certain sum of money were placed, unquestioningly, at the disposal of Government, the difficulty might be smoothed away.

For money was badly needed at the Palace of the Élysée. Money, if one would make supple, servile agents of legal, civil and military officials and functionaries—judges, prefects, mayors, magistrates, commissaries of police, senators, counselors, brigadiers, generals, colonels, quarter-masters, sergeants, gendarmes, agents, printers, spies.

Money must be had if the plot that was to make an Imperial throne out of a Presidential armchair was not to collapse and fall through.

So the Élysée had become a shop on a vast scale, where anything desired of men or women with cash in hand could be bought for ready money. A dismissal or an appointment; a night of pleasure for yourself, or a day of reckoning for another; the advancement of a lover or the removal of a rival,—you ordered and paid, and got it on the nail. And the gold you paid was passed on into the innumerable pockets that gaped for it. Everyone who had a soul to sell found a buyer at the Élysée.

What Dunoisse wanted cost a heap of money. The cashier at Rothschild's had long ceased to be reverential,—every month's audit showed such terrific inroads on the diminishing golden store. His eyebrows were almost insulting as he cashed the check that purchased exile for Henriette's inconvenient husband. Dunoisse began from that moment to realize that he had wasted his patrimony, and would very soon be poor.

Yet what a satisfaction it was to read in the official Gazette of the Army, that in recognition of the eminent services of Colonel Count de Roux, the War Minister had appointed that distinguished officer to the vacant post of Commandant of the Garrison at Algiers.

"You see, the Prince keeps his promises," Henriette said gleefully to her lover. "Believe me, dearest, the Empire is an excellent investment!—a ship that is bound to come home!"

They were together in the Rue du Bac, where every room of the luxurious suite bore evidences of her taste, tokens of her presence. And she was leaning over Hector's shoulder as he read the paragraph, her fragrant breath playing on his eyes and forehead, her small white fingers toying with his hair.

"It will suit Eugène to a marvel," she went on, as no immediate answer came from Dunoisse. "He will have his cards and his billiards, his cigars and his horses, and his mistresses, and everything that he has here."

She added, with a little mocking peal of laughter:

"Except me. Imagine it!—he actually believes that I am going with him to Algiers—that horrible piratical Moorish seaport, full of negroes and Arabs and monkeys and smells. We shall have a scene when he learns that I remain behind in Paris—he has already been quite tragic over the idea of parting from 'Riette and Loulu and Bébé. He cried—imagine him in tears!—and said that he should never see them again—he was quite certain of it! And he has gone to Bagneres to-day with a cartload of toys and bonbons. Oh yes!—he is absurdly fond of the children. It is not because he did not wish them to live with us that you have not seen them at home."

Dunoisse knew a sudden sickness at the heart. She had given this very explanation unasked. So, then, those lovely lips could lie.... The warm, soft arm about his neck suddenly seemed heavy as an iron collar, the fragrant breath upon his eyes scorched. He freed himself from Henriette with a sudden movement; rose up, dropping the newspaper; and went to the open window and stepped out upon the balcony, seeking a purer air.

Thence he said, without looking round:

"He loves 'Riette and Loulou and Bébé, I suppose, as a man usually loves his children. Is there anything absurd in that? Perhaps you know?"

She leaped at him and caught him by the arm, and said, from behind him, in a voice jarred and shaken with strange passion:

"What—what do you mean? You shall tell me! Look round! Do not hide your face!"

He had meant nothing. His utterance had been prompted by a sudden stab of compunction, a feeling of pity for the man whom he had betrayed and supplanted, and was now about to exile. But when he turned and met the sharp suspicion in the eyes of Henriette, he knew what she believed he had meant. And with that new and strange expression in them, those lovely eyes seemed to look at him through the holes of an exquisite mask, hiding another face, that, once revealed, would chill the soul with dread, and stamp its Medusa-image on the memory—never to be forgotten, however long one lived.

His own face looked strangely at him from the frames of mirrors that gave back its hardened outlines and less brilliant coloring. Treachery had always been loathsome in Dunoisse's eyes. Yet of what else had he been guilty but the blackest treachery in his dealings with the husband of Henriette?

Deny it! What? Had he not taken his hand in friendship and betrayed him? Procured his removal by bribery, parted him from the woman whose truth he believed in, and from the children whom he loved?

Quite true, the man was vile. A lover of gross pleasures, a debauchee, a gambler. An unfaithful husband to a wife who played him false. False! Ah! to use that word in connection with Henriette opened out incredible vistas. Dunoisse dared not look. Long afterwards he understood that he had feared lest he should see the day of his own exile growing into vision—drawing nearer and more near.

So exit de Roux with the *brevet*-rank of General, after a farewell banquet from the Regiment and a series of parting dinners; amidst speeches, embraces, vivas, and votive pieces of plate. Madame did not accompany the new Garrison Commandant to the conquered stronghold of the Algerine pirates. The General's villa at Mustapha was to receive a grass-widower. Henriette's delicate health could not support the winds from the Sahara,—the Prince-President's own physician, much to the chagrin of his fair patient, advised against her taking the risk.

And Dunoisse breathed more freely once his whilom Chief had departed. De Roux had been the kill-joy—the fly in the honey. Life was more pleasant now, and infinitely easier; there were so many things that had had to be done under the rose.

As for de Roux, his exile was not without the alleviations and consolations Henriette had mentioned. He wrote home regularly, voluminous letters of many pages, and sent mysterious bales containing astonishing gifts;—Moorish caps, embroidered gazelle-skins, ornaments of sequins, coffee-cups in stands of golden filagree, for Madame: with ebony elephants and ivory dolls, dates preserved in honey, fig cakes stuck full of walnuts, and cinnamon-sugar walking-sticks, for 'Riette and Loulou and Bébé.

Handsome remittances always accompanied the letters. Dunoisse stipulated that the mony should be exclusively expended on, or laid aside for the benefit of, the three little pigtailed girls. It was a nice point, a question of delicacy, from which he was not to be turned aside by any subtle pleading. For you may build your nest of the wreckage of another man's home, and still retain your claim to be considered a person of scrupulous honor. But to dip your hand in his purse—that is a different thing!

So our hero, presently finding himself at the end of his resources, fulfilled a certain paternal prophecy, uttered when he was yet a student at the Military School of Technical Instruction, and called one day at the hotel in the Rue de la Chaussée d'Antin, prepared to consume a certain amount of humble-pie, provided that at the bottom of the unsavory dish the golden plums should be scattered thick enough.

XLIV

For many months he had not crossed his father's threshold. The great courtyard bore a look of squalor, grass was springing up between the flagstones; flaunting tufts of groundsel and chickweed were growing in the green-painted wooden tubs containing myrtles and oleanders and rhododendrons, that were ranged along the walls and on either side of the flight of steps that led to the hall-door.

The hall-door stood open: Auguste, now gray-headed and stouter than ever, waited with a low-wheeled open carriage that had succeeded the high tilbury with the rampant mare and the tiny cockaded groom. A quiet pair of English pony-cobs were attached to the vehicle. Hector stopped to look at them, and speak to the old servant, then went into the hall.

The trophies of arms upon the walls looked dull and rusty, the bronze equestrian statue of the Emperor was covered with a patina of encrusted dirt. The black-and-white squares of the marble pavement were in shrieking need of a broom and soap-and-water. Then, to the tap-tapping of the two ebony-handled crutch-sticks that had succeeded the gold-topped Malacca cane with the silk tassel, came Monsieur the Marshal, heralded by a dropping fire of oaths.

He was much changed and aged since Hector had last seen him, but bravely bewigged and dyed and painted still. He was wrapped in a furred driving-cloak, despite the warmth of the September sunshine; his cheeks were pendulous, his fierce eyes had baggy pouches underneath. And he stumbled as he shuffled over the marble pavement in his cloth boots that were slit with innumerable loopholes for the better ease of his corns.

He stopped short, seeing his son, and the change in him was painfully apparent. He was hurrying down the hill that ends in an open grave. His morals were more deplorable than ever. The cook, a strapping Auvergnate, was his mistress now, in lieu of an opera-girl or nymph of the Palais Royal: and he drank and played cards with his valet and butler: indeed, servants were his masters, and, from the porter's lodge to the mansard roof-garrets, dirt and disorder marked their unchecked sway.

Mild Smithwick, lying beside the sister who had been a paralytic, in her quiet grave in the Hampstead churchyard, would have turned uneasily upon her pillow stuffed with shavings, had she known of the goings-on of the debauched old idol of her earthly worship, who had long ago forgotten her.

He opened fire directly, quite in the old manner.

"Hey? What the devil?—so you have remembered us, have you? Well? Was I not right in telling you that that affair of the fusillade would end to your advantage? That the Court Martial was a piece of mummery—a farce—nothing more? There you are with promotion, and the patronage and goodwill of Monseigneur at the Élysée! Though for myself I cannot stomach that Bonaparte with the beak and the Flemish snuffle. Had Walewski but been born on the right side of the blanket—there would have been the Emperor for me!"

He trumpeted in a vast Indian silk handkerchief with something of the old vigor, and went on:

"Because all this swearing of fidelity to the Republic will end, as I have prophesied, in a coronation at Notre Dame, and a court at the Tuileries. My Emperor crowned himself without all this lying and posturing. He said to France: 'You want a master. Well, look at me. I am the man for you....' Josephine squawked: '*Oh, M. Bonaparte!*' 'Go!' he told her. 'Order your dresses!' just as he said to the Senate, 'Decree me Emperor!' While this fellow ... sacred name of a pig!"

He tucked one of the crutch-sticks under his arm, got out his snuff-box, and said as he dipped his ringed, yellow old claws into the Spanish mixture:

"His cant about Socialism and Progress and the dignity of Labor gives me the belly-ache. His groveling to the working man, and slobbering over the common soldier, make me want to kill him. His hand in his trousers-pocket and his eye on a *plebiscite*—there you have him—by the thunder of Heaven! A corporal of infantry said to me: 'If I showed M. Louis Napoleon Bonaparte my back—he would kneel down and salute it....' *My* Napoleon would have said to that man: 'Lie down in the mud, so that I may walk dryshod upon your body!' and the man would have obeyed him. But perhaps half an Emperor is better for France than none!"

He fed each wide nostril with the Brobdingnagian pinch he had held suspended while he talked, and said, snorting:

"We shall see if, for all his cartloads of wine sent to their barracks, and his rolls of ten-franc pieces scattered among the rank-and-file, he is served better than the man who scorned to flatter, and more loved than he who did not bribe.... Who said: 'Follow me, and I will show you capitals to plunder!' and when they were conquered, said: 'Help yourselves, one and all, there are fat and lean!'"

He plunged his shaking fingers back into the box, sputtered a little, and said a trifle wildly:

"Though there was a good deal of fasting going to set against the seasons of plenty. During the Retreat from Moscow in October, 1812, I had a handful of unset diamonds in my haversack, and a beryl weighing thirteen pounds, worth ninety-five thousand francs, upon my word of honor! Well, I swopped that crystal with a Bavarian aide-de-camp of the Staff for a pudding made of horse's blood mixed with bran and flour.... The man who sold me the pudding was Luitpold von Widinitz, a cousin of your mother's. It was a dirty action I have never pardoned. *Pardieu! Morbleu!* A comrade, and sell—not share! Prince be damned!... Huckster! Sutler! Tschah! Faugh! Pouah!"

He dropped the crutch he had tucked under his arm, and, recalled from his ancient reminiscence by Hector's picking up the stick and giving it to him, said, with a formidable bending of the brows:

"You came here, not out of filial duty, but upon some private affair or other. Spit it out, and have done!—I have no time to waste."

Hector obeyed.

"I have spent my mother's dowry as you always hoped I should. Chiefly upon gratifications—pleasures—luxuries, that I once pretended to despise. I have acquired the taste for these things. That ought to gratify you. With the money I have wasted, many prejudices and convictions that you found objectionable in past days have been scattered to the winds. If you are still disposed to give, I am very willing to take. I have no more to say!"

Seldom has an appeal for pecuniary aid been preferred less ingratiatingly. The Marshal glared and champed for several moments before he could reply:

"I do not doubt you are willing, sir.... *'Credieu!* Do you suppose I have not seen this coming?—though the insolence of your approach goes beyond anything that I could have conceived.... I have my informants, understand!... I am aware of your infernal folly, your crazy infatuation.... As for that de Roux woman who leads you by the nose, she is a jade who will land you in the gutter, and a harlot into the bargain. Do you hear?"

The bellowed "Do you hear?" was followed by a shower of curses. When these imprecations had ceased to rattle among the trophies of arms and bronzes, and bring down sprinklings of dust from the gilded cornices, Hector said imperturbably:

"My father may insult my mistress with impunity. I cannot call him out——!"

The Marshal took the opening.

"If you did, and sat down on your tail—sacred name of a blue pig!—with the notion of sticking me in the gizzard, as you did de Moulny Younger when you were boys—allow me to tell you—you would find yourself skewered and trussed in double-quick time!"

Never before in Hector's hearing had the Marshal made reference to that old sore subject of the false step and the broken foil. He made a flourishing pass with one of the ebony-handled crutches, slipped on the polished marble pavement, and would have fallen but for the strong red hand of Marie Bathilde's son.

Hector put the old man into the hall porter's capacious chair, picked up his great curly-brimmed hat—the hat worn by Deans at the present moment—brushed it on his sleeve and handed it back again. He felt a good deal like Sganarelle before Don Juan, the case being reversed, and the homilist the elder libertine.

Meanwhile the gouty old soldier fulminated oaths, and hurled reproaches of a nature to make listening Asmodeus smile. He was scandalized at the life his son was leading. Sacred name of a pipe! A thousand thunders! He shook his clenched hand, as he demanded of Hector if he really supposed there was no Deity Who demanded an account from evil livers, and no Hell where sinners burned?

"For priests are rogues and knaves and liars, but there is such a place, for all that! And you—living in open adultery—for you there will be Hell!"

Said Dunoisse, cool and smiling, standing before his irate parent:

"I am a better theologian than you are. Hell is for the finally impenitent, I have always been instructed; and I am invariably scrupulous to repent before I sin. If it will afford you any particular gratification, I will undertake to perform a special act of contrition," he looked at his watch, "punctually at the hour of twelve, to-night."

"You are going to her to-night?" snarled the Marshal, adding: "Tell her from me that she deceives a blackguard for the sake of a booby. For one you are, by the thunder of Heaven! who soil yourself and spoil yourself for such a drab as she!"

"What can you expect," said Hector, with the same cool offensiveness, "but that your son should follow in your footsteps? I am, as you have said, living with the wife of another man in open adultery. You were bolder, and more daring, who with your master had discrowned kings and humiliated Emperors. You did not hesitate, at the pricking of your desire, to ravish the Spouse of God."

"Your mother is a Saint!" cried the old Marshal, purple and gnashing with furious indignation. "Do not dare to mention her in the same breath with that—that——"

And the coarse old man plumped out an epithet of the barrack-room, full-flavored, double-barreled, of which Henriette, had she heard it, would have died.

"There is no need to tell me to honor my mother," said the son. "She is sacred in my eyes. But do not venture to speak to me of Him Whom you have dishonored. I have thought ever since I was a boy that it would be better for me and for you if He did not exist. For the fact of my being is an insult to Him. I am a clod of earth flung in His face by your sacrilegious hand!"

He had often dreamed of speaking such words as these, face to face with his father. Now they poured from him, thick and fast. But pity checked them in mid-torrent, at the sight of the working mouth and nodding head, and trembling hands of unreverend, ignoble age.

The old man capitulated even as the young one relented. He got out, between spasms of wheezing, in quite a conciliatory snarl:

"Well,—well! What if you have spent your mother's dowry! there is more where that came from. You are my legitimate heir,—and for me, I had rather you were a prodigal than a prig. And blood-horses and Indian shawls, wines, jewelry and cigars and bonnets,—wagers on the Turf and bets on cards, are unavoidable expenses.... I do not wish you to be a niggard. Only it seems to me that with your opportunities you might have invested well. Steel Rails and Zinc, those are the things to put money on. This will be the Age of traveling behind boilers and housing under roofs of metal. Ugh—ugh! Ough, c'r'r—*'aah!*"

He stopped to have a bout of coughing and hawking, and resumed:

"Do not suppose I blame you for having been extravagant. Though it seems to me you have managed badly. This Bonaparte is one who takes with one hand and gives with the other—is bled or bleeds. He has never tapped my veins yet, nor shall for any hint of his. But I suspect he has had money of you. That woman of yours—never mind! I will not name her, the cockatrice!—but I have had it hinted to me that she is an agent in his pay. And he pays women with compliments and promises—he has probably promised to create her a peeress in her own right when he is Emperor.... Her Grace the Duchess of Trundlemop—that is the title she will get."

Seeing Hector scowl forbiddingly at these unwelcome references, the Marshal made haste to conciliate.

"You have paid through the nose to get de Roux decanted to Algeria. You have been sweetly choused. One must live and learn. See!—I will strike a bargain with you. Do not you be stiffnecked any longer with regard to that question of the von Widinitz Succession, and I will unbutton my pockets.... You shall have money—plenty of money! All that you need to make a splash. I suppose you know that there are millions of thalers waiting to drop into your pockets once the Council of the Germanic Confederation shall confirm your right to the Crown Feudatory.... You will stand upon that right—it is patent and undeniable. And I will have the throne from under the Regent Luitpold in return for that lump of beryl the rogue once robbed from me!"

Absurd, formidable, gross old monster. Was the ravished crystal really the fulcrum of the lever with which the Marshal strove to upset a State? World-changes have been brought about by quarrels springing from causes even more trivial? The price of Luitpold's blood-pudding had remained for thirty-seven years an undigested morsel in the Marshal's system. It rankled in him to his dying day.

Though his gouty feet were tottering on the downward slope, his mental faculties were as clear as ever. He watched his son from under his bushy eyebrows as the young man gnawed his lip and drew patterns with his cane on the tesselated pavement of the hall. Hector had uttered sounding reproaches, arrayed himself on the side of Heaven a moment previously. The merry devil who laughs over human contradictions and mortal frailties, must have chuckled as he listened to the terms of the bargain now arranged between the father and the son.

Money. For the sake of the golden mortar without which the House of Hopes that Jack builds must inevitably tumble to ruin, Dunoisse reluctantly consented to become the puppet of an ambition he had scorned. The instrument of a desire for vengeance that had never ceased to rowel the old war-horse's rheumatic sides.

"So! It is understood, then, after all this fanfaronade of high-mindedness. You will meet my Bavarian agents, Köhler and von Steyregg—and you will be compliant and civil to them, do you understand?"

He lashed himself into one of his sudden rages, the gouty old lion, and roared:

"For my Marie's son shall not be slighted—kicked aside into a corner while that knave Luitpold holds the Regency of Widinitz from the Bund. I will give him a colic for the one his pudding gave me! And I will have no more accusations and reproaches!—I will not permit you who are my son to taunt me with your own begetting, and throw your mother's Veil of Profession, in a manner, at my head."

He rapped his stick upon the pavement. He was strangely moved, and his chin was twitching, though his fierce black eyes were hard and dry.

"You have said that I stole my wife from God, and it is true; though I do not know that it is very decent in you to twit me with it. And do you suppose I have not smarted for the sin I committed? I tell you I have shed tears of blood!"

A harsh sound came from his throat: he swallowed and blinked and went on talking:

"Listen to me, you who are more my son than Marie's, though you tell me that you hold her memory sacred, and denounce me as the plunderer of Christ? When her youngest child, your sister, died, Marie saw in that the beginning of Heaven's vengeance: the price that must be paid, the punishment that must be borne. And she prayed and wept—what tears!—and gave me no peace until she had wrung from me my promise that she should go back to her Convent if the Chapter would receive her.... I am an old tactician—I gave the pledge in the full belief that never would they open their doors.... And when she brought me the Prioress's letter, it was as though a spent cannon-ball had hit me on the headpiece. Then I had an idea. The dowry of three hundred thousand silver thalers. What the Church had once got her claws on I knew she would never let go.... So I blustered and raved and swore to Marie.... *'The dowry, or I keep my wife!'*"

His pendulous cheeks and chin shook as he wagged his head at Hector.

"Do you suppose I wanted the accursed dross? No! by the thunder of Heaven! I was greedy of something else. The woman—my wife—who lay in my arms and sighed, and kissed me, and wept...."

His voice cracked. He said:

"Do you think she did not know the truth? You shall never make me believe she did not. Even while I bragged and blustered about a lawsuit—even when my notary wrote a letter, I had fears and quakings of the heart. When no answer came from the Mother Prioress, I rubbed my hands and congratulated myself. Thrice-accursed fool who thought to outwit God——"

He rummaged for his snuffbox, tapped it wrong way up, opened it in this position, spilt all its store of snuff, swore, and pitched it across the hall.

"He is the King of strategists—the Marshal of Napoleon's Grand Army, compared with Him, was a blind beetle. The Prioress's answer came: 'We concede you this money,' said the letter, 'as the price of a soul.' Enclosed was a draft on the Bank of Bavaria. That night Marie left me. Without even a kiss of farewell, she who had been my wife for nine years, and borne me a boy and a girl.... Imagine if the money did not weigh on me like the dead horse I lay under all through the night of Austerlitz, with the bone of my broken leg sticking through my boot! Conceive if it did not smell to me of beeswax candles, brown serge habits, incense and pauper's pallets! Pshaw! Peugh! Piff!"

He blew his old nose and swore a little, and then went on:

"I did not send back the three hundred thousand thalers. True! they were so much dirt in my eyes.... But cash is cash, and to part with it would not have brought my Marie back again. I let the stuff lie and breed at my bank. I would have raked the kennels for crusts rather than touch it. Not that I have ever needed money. The old brigand of the Grand Army has known how to keep what he had gained. Though I have lived up to my income....drank, gambled, amused myself with women! What matter the women? Did Marie suppose I should spend my time in stringing daisy-chains when she had gone away?"

He laughed in his formidable, ogreish way, and said, still laughing:

"She knew me better, depend upon it. Though, mind you, I had been true to Marie. But a wife who is a nun is a dead wife. I was a widower—the boy motherless.... And He up above us had another score to make off me!... When the boy—Death of my soul!"

He struck one of his crutches on the marble pavement with such force that the stick broke.

"A day came when you looked at me with my own eyes shining out of Marie's face, and said: 'I have heard the story. The terms upon which you let my mother resume the Veil were vile!' Impudent young cockerel! Was it to be supposed that I should try to justify myself in the eyes of a stripling? A man to whom the Emperor used to say: 'Well, Dunoisse, let us have your opinion on such and such a plan?' So I laughed at you for a nincompoop—boasted of the pail of milk I had drawn from the Black Cow, saying to myself: 'All right! He is Marie's son, that boy! When he is a man grown, I will give him that accursed money, smelling of candles and incense, and he will give it back to the nuns.' And when time was ripe I transferred the whole lump to your name at Rothschild's. You made virtuous scruples about taking it, but you never restored it whence it came!... Now you have showed your breed—you have poured it into the lap of a light woman. And you come to me and own that, and ask for more to pitch after it!" He rapped out a huge oath. "Am I not justified in thinking you more my son than Marie's? Have I not the right to say I am disappointed in you?"

His voice was a mere croak. He went on, with his fierce, bloodshot eyes fixed on vacancy:

"Do you suppose I did not love your mother—have never longed for her—have ever forgotten her? I use her chocolate-set every morning.... Her Indian shawl is the coverlet of my bed. When I have the gout in my eyes I tie a scarf she used to wear over them, like a bandage. There is virtue in things that have been used by a Saint."

He added:

"For a Saint she is ... and though, as you say I stole my joy in her from Heaven—do you suppose, for one moment, a woman like that is going to let me be damned? She will wear her knees to the bone first; and so I tell you!... Was it not for the sake of my soul she went back to her cell at the Carmel? At the Day of Judgment one voice will be heard that pleads for old Achille Dunoisse."

One scanty teardrop hung on his inflamed and reddened underlid.

"But Saint or none, she loved me, like twenty women, by Heaven! And if she says she repents of that, again, by Heaven!—she lies!"

The solitary tear fell on his discolored hand. He shook it off, angrily. Somewhere in the middle of that gross bundle of contradictions, absurdities, appetites, vices, resentments, hatreds, calling itself Achille Dunoisse—there beat and bled a suffering human heart. And the distance that separated the father and the son was bridged by a moment of sympathy and understanding. And a pang of envy pierced it through....

For the supreme jewel that Fate can bestow upon mortal, is the love that will even yield up the Beloved for Love's sake. To this gross old man, his sire, had been given what would never fall to the younger Dunoisse.

By the radiance of this great passion of Marie Bathilde's, her son saw himself in like case with some penniless student in a Paris garret, crouching, upon a night of Arctic cold, over a fire of paper and straw. When the small fierce flame of Henriette's slight sensuous fancy should have sunk down into creeping ashes under the starved hands spread above it, what would be left to live for? His heart was sick within him as he went away.

He returned to Madame de Roux with the news that his application to the Marshal had succeeded. She threw her arms about him, in a transport of joy.

"Ah then, so you really love me?" the poor dupe asked, putting the most fatal of all questions. For it sets the interrogated he or she wondering, "Do I?" and hastens the inevitable end.

"How can you doubt it?" she queried, hiding an almost imperceptible yawn behind her tiny fingers. *"Did I not send away Eugène for you?"*

She passed by gentle degrees to a question possessing much more interest. The amount to be placed upon the books at Rothschild's to the credit of the Marshal's son.

XLV

So thickly did the deposit of golden plums lie at the bottom of the pie-dish—so handsomely did the Marshal keep his given word, that at the suggestion of Henriette, Hector did some more shopping at the vast comprehensive mart of the Élysée. General de Roux, puffing a cheroot and sweltering in his cane chair at the Military Club of Algiers, was to read in the official Gazette of the Army—a special copy, thoughtfully forwarded by an anonymous friend—that his late Assistant-Adjutant had received yet further promotion. That the Cross of the Legion of Honor had been conferred upon him by the Prince-President, with his appointment as extra aide-de-camp of the Staff of the Élysée.

Thenceforwards at Reviews, Inspections, and other public functions, you saw the keen dark face shaded by the plumed cocked hat of a Lieutenant-Colonel—the slender active figure set off by a brilliant uniform, as mounted on Djelma, or some animal even more beautiful and spirited, the lover of Henriette brought up the rear of the showy cavalcade of Marshals, Generals, foreign envoys, aides-de-camp and Staff officers, galloping at the flying heels of the spirited English charger ridden by Monseigneur.

What could the heart of man want more? At State dinners at the Élysée, shooting-parties at Fontainebleau, hunts at Compiègne, balls at the Tuileries, Colonel Hector Dunoisse cut a gallant figure. His intrigue with Madame de Roux became a recognized *liaison*. Monseigneur was so kind—the world was so charitable. Nobody dreamed of censuring, or even looking askew.

In the galaxy of beautiful women that glittered about that rising planet of Monseigneur's, Henriette shone prominently. Many men's eyes were fixed in longing on that throbbing, radiant star. The man on whom its rays were shed knew himself envied. Secure in possession of what others keenly desired, he believed himself happy at last.

Happiest when, with that little hand of Henriette's upon his arm, in some crush of gold-laced uniforms, diplomatic dress-coats, silks, satins, flowers, feathers and diamonds, he would encounter a tall, bulky, officially-attired figure topped with a heavy, ugly, distinguished face; and meet the cold, repellent, cynical stare of de Moulny's hard blue eyes.

The eyes would meet Redskin's, the head would move slightly, responding to Dunoisse's own chilly, perfunctory salutation. Once or twice they had been near neighbors at the dinner-table.... What of that? In civilized society one eats with one's enemy. Only the nomad of the desert and the savage of the jungle refuse to break bread with those they hold in suspicion or hate. And it is easy to forget a great injustice done you, by a friend you have ceased to care for; and to forgive a wrong wrought by a man off whom you have doubly scored.

For de Moulny had been paid his money, had not Henriette said so? Besides, she had never exchanged a word with him alone since that night of the fusillade.

She assured Dunoisse of this; and that their intercourse when they met was limited to the briefest utterances compatible with common civility. Then, no matter for de Moulny, now Representative for the Department of Moulny upon Upper Drame, and Secretary-Chancellor at the Ministry of the Interior. Success was his, though the woman he had desired had given her favors to another. Without the bliss that he had vainly coveted, let de Moulny go upon his way....

Dunoisse believed that Henriette loved him, as he her, with passion and fidelity. He asked nothing better of Fate than that he should be permitted to pass through life with those fairy fingers twined about his own. But sometimes when her beautiful hair was shed upon his breast and her lustrous eyes looked into his, and her lovely lips gave back his kisses, the thought of the strange face that might be lurking behind those beautiful, beloved, familiar features would strike him cold with dread.

He thrust it from him, that conjectured image, but always it hovered in the background of his mind. By the blood-red December dawn that followed on the crime of the *coup d'État* another glimpse of the Medusa visage was to be vouchsafed him. The day was not yet when it should be revealed in all its terror, and strike the man to stone.

XLVI

France had not taken kindly to the notion of a *plebiscite*. The good city of Paris had had an indigestion of proclamations—was beginning to suspect the motives of her leading citizen. And the capital roared and buzzed like a beehive of angry bees.

He needed very much to be Dictator for ten years at least, the little man with the lank, drab hair, arrayed in the uniform of a General, adorned with the red *cordon* and the jeweled Grand Cross and Star of the Legion of Honor, who sat, upon this night of November, 1851, in a velvet armchair before the blazing wood-fire in his small private cabinet upon the ground-floor, with the tips of his spurred, wonderfully polished little boots upon the bar of a sumptuous, palatial fender of solid silver-gilt. Twelve millions of francs *per annum* for nearly four years had left him deep in debt and horribly embarrassed. When he should drive out of the courtyard of the Elysée at the expiration of his tenure of office, the gaping jaws of a debtor's prison were ready to engulf him. He knew that very well.

And he waited, on the horns of a dilemma, with the son of his mother, who secretly detested him; and Fleury, now his senior aide-de-camp, and St. Arnaud, his War Minister, a lean, gaunt, dyed and painted personage who had once been an actor at a suburban theater, who had served in the Foreign Legion as a private soldier, who had seen much service, won promotion, and had now been recalled from Algeria by his friend. For the purpose of showing Parisians how warfare is conducted by civilized forces against Kabyles and Arabs and Moors.

Money, money!

As the neat white fingers of France's First Citizen twisted comic figures out of paper, taken from a little inlaid table beside him where writing-materials were, his brain was busy with this vexing question of how to get more cash. Hundreds of millions of francs had been expended during his tenure of office. The china, pictures and other Art treasure of the Crown had been converted into bullion. The diamonds of the Crown and the Crown forests had become gold in the crucible of the auction-room. And—presto! the vast sums thus realized had vanished—nobody could exactly indicate how or whither—it was a puzzle to baffle Houdin. Nor could anyone point out the winners of the chief prizes advertized in the Lottery of the Golden Ingots, which had, with much tootling of official trumpets and banging of official drums, been drawn some days before.

Money!...

There was a reception upon this particular evening: the little Palace and its courtyard blazed with gas. A double line of carriages rolled ceaselessly in and out of high gilded gates, their twinkling lamps reflected in the cuirasses of the guard-of-honor. A steady stream of fire-worshipers, anxious to prostrate their foreheads in the dust before their god and luminary, rolled up the imposing flight of red-carpeted doorsteps and through the gilded vestibule to the small reception-rooms. Stars and Orders were not plentiful; Ambassadors were conspicuous by their absence: the Minister for the United States being the only exception to this rule. But lovely women were present; the whole galaxy of the Élysée scintillated in the heavens, and there were plenty of young attachés of Legation and clerks of the Diplomatic Corps. And silks and satins, feathers and diamonds, flaunted by gorgeous cocodettes of the fashionable world, mingled there with cotton-backed velvet, paste jewelry and cheap book-muslin; and gold-laced uniforms twinkling with decorations, jostled the black coat with the tricolor rosette, whose wearer had tramped in from Montrouge or Menilmontant to save a 'bus fare, and had stowed his overcoat and goloshes with the shawls and overshoes and umbrellas of his women-kind away behind the pedestal of some vestibule-bronze or group of statuary, to avoid the fee that must otherwise be paid to one of the large, stately footmen in the Presidential livery, in return for a wooden counter and the assumption of responsibility for these discarded coverings.

It was nearly midnight, and yet the sun had not risen; the magnificent band of the —th Hussars, stationed in the splendid gilt ballroom where the Prince-President had as a child witnessed the second abdication of the Emperor Napoleon, had not yet crashed into *Partant Pour La Syrie*. It had been given out that Monseigneur was delayed by the non-arrival of dispatches, detained by urgent affairs of State. Detectives, mingling with the throng of guests in the reception-rooms, kept their ears open for unfavorable comments: their eyes skinned for the possible interception of significant glances. Of which, had they but chosen to step outside the courtyard-gates, they might have gathered store.

For to be plain, Paris was in a state of ferment and disruption. Disaffection prevailed. Insurrection was rising to its old high-water mark. And the cries were: "Down with Bonaparte! Long live the Republic! Long live Law! Long live the Constitution! Down with the Army, the paid tool of the President who wants to be Emperor in spite of all his oaths!" And the ganglion of narrow streets that made the center of the city's nervous system were being rapidly blocked by barricades built higher than before....

What wonder if at this juncture the crying need of Monseigneur for money opened a Gargantuan mouth for the bottle. Without money at this juncture, the contemplated masterstroke of policy must fall as harmlessly as a blow from Harlequin's lathen sword.

Money, money, money!...

And there were twenty-five millions of francs, belonging to the Orleans Princes, lying in the Bank of France, which by a Presidential Decree, countersigned by the Home Secretary Count de Morny, might be profitably sequestrated. And, contained in a series of great painted and emblazoned deed-boxes, occupying a row of shelves in the strong-room at the Ministry of the Interior, were the title-deeds to estates of the value of three hundred thousand millions more, vested in the hands of mere Trustees; who might argue and protest, but could, if it proved necessary, be gagged. And de Morny had just threatened to resign the Home Secretaryship if Monseigneur persisted in his intention of laying violent hands on these unconsidered trifles—an exhibition of obstinacy both ill-timed and in bad taste.

"Who the devil, my dear fellow," he asked, "will bid for cities, forests, palaces and villages, even if you put these up to auction at reasonable prices, when the titles to these properties must remain—to put it delicately—uncertain? A new Government may arise which suffers from the excess of scruples. In that case the estates will be returned to those whose property they are."

De Morny, with his insufferable air of superiority, and the grand manner which indubitably belonged to him, lounged against the mantelshelf and looked down on Monseigneur. St. Arnaud, his long, lank form arrayed in the uniform of a Marshal, encrusted with bullion and blazing with decorations, lay on a sofa, sucking at the jeweled mouthpiece of a *chibuk*. De Fleury puffed out his cheeks as he blew cigarette-smoke into the fluffy, puzzled face of a gray Persian kitten that had climbed upon the shelf of an ivory cabinet loaded with costly china, and spat as he teased it with the plumes of his cocked hat.

"Who will buy? The answer is cut and dried. No one! And this appropriation—as a first flight of the Imperial eagle—will make you infernally unpopular; not to warn you of this would be," said de Moray, "a *laches* upon my part. Every petty shopkeeper who has two thousand francs in the savings-bank—every peasant who has a little plot of land, will say to himself: 'This fellow sticks at nothing. Poor devil though I am, I may be the next to be plundered.' If you carry out this project of yours, it will not be with my assistance. I will help you take an Empire very willingly, but not to plunder a strong-box."

He looked at his watch, bowed with his easy grace, and went out. The man who was his brother, and envied him, following the tall departing figure with eyes of sickly hate.

"M. de Morny follows the cynical advice that is given in the Gospel of St. Luke," he said with a bitter sneer. "He would keep on bowing-terms with the Princes of the House of Orleans, so that, should I fail, they may receive him into their favor. His is the principle of hedge and trim. Well, we know his breaking-point! In the event of his kicking over the traces," he spoke the words in English, a familiar language to Persigny and de Fleury, "there is another upon whom I can depend."

And he exchanged a look of intelligence with Persigny, his shadow. For the ex-sergeant-quartermaster of dragoons would not fail him, he knew, upon a point of honor or at a pinch of conscience. Persigny was without these inconvenient things.

Meanwhile the door flew open again to re-admit de Morny, who insisted that the night grew old; that the reception-rooms were crowded to suffocation; that the long-delayed appearance of the President had provoked unfavorable comparisons, and created a bad impression; that he must come without delay.

"Let them wait!" he said, with a dull flash of ill-humor, in answer to the expostulations of Persigny. "Who are they, that they should not be kept waiting? Whom have we? A damnable rabble of bankers, stockbrokers, judges, generals, senators, Representatives and their wives and mistresses.... You know very well that what the English would call the 'best people' are those who do not come...."

Which was true. The private secretaries of the aged Duchesse de Veillecour, of the Faubourg St. Honoré, and of the venerable Marquis de l'Autretemps, being invariably instructed to return M. Bonaparte's card of invitation, with the intimation that their respective employers had not the honor of knowing the gentleman who had sent it,—or with no intimation at all....

"Let them wait!" he said again. "Am I not waiting? For this message from Walewski—for this ultimatum of my Lord Walmerston—for this establishment of the submarine electric telegraph between England and France. That gutta-percha covered wire stretching between the cave under the South Foreland at Dover and the cliff station at Cape Grisnez is the jugular vein of my whole system of policy. Had it not broken twice, should I not have prepared Paris with my proclamations—should I not have struck the blow?"

He stuck out his chin as he rolled his head upon the cushioned back of his armchair and stared at the painted ceiling, and went on in his droning voice:

"That is, if I had had money—sufficient funds at my disposal. That a man like me should want money at such a moment proves that the Devil is a fool."

St. Arnaud turned his long emaciated body and sagacious grayhound-face towards the speaker. The sofa creaked beneath his weight, and one of his gold spurs, catching in the costly brocade cover, tore it with a little ugly, sickening sound. He said, stroking the dyed tuft upon his chin with a gaunt pale hand glittering with rings of price:

"Monseigneur, pray do the personage you mention better justice. He really has served you better than you think!"

He had. The steam-packet *Goliath* of Dover, towing the ancient cable-hulk *Blazer*, the latter rolling fearfully, with a direfully seasick crew, and a hold containing but a few hundred yards or so of the twenty-seven miles of cable which had been smoothly paid out over the Channel sea-floor, had dropped her anchors off Cape Grisnez an hour before sunset; and the end of the wire-bound rope on which so much depended having been landed at the village of Sangatte, distant some three miles or so from Calais, communication had been established with the operators in the cave under the South Foreland lighthouse at Dover. And a gun had been fired from the Castle; and telegrams announcing the fact had been sent by the Chief Magistrate of Dover to the Queen and the Prince Consort, the Duke of Wellington, the King of Prussia, and a few other important personages. And the Mayor had then despatched a message of congratulation to the French Prince-President, which was being transmitted to Paris by means of Ampère's coil and needle, and the under-ground wire that followed the track of the Great Northern Railway Line.

But meanwhile a courier from the Embassy of France in Belgrave Square, London, chilled and hoarse from rapid traveling in the wintry weather, had arrived with the letter from Walewski. And when the neat white hands for which it was destined had snatched the envelope from the sumptuous golden salver upon which it was respectfully presented by the President's second aide-de-camp, its contents proved discouraging, to say the least.

Count Walewski had pleaded his relative's cause with eloquence. The enclosure would prove with what result.

A check for two thousand pounds, enfolded in a sheet scrawled with a brief intimation in my Lord Walmerston's stiff, characteristic handwriting, that no more of the stuff was to be had.

XLVII

"How like the man! The icy, phlegmatic islander! Two thousand pounds! A nothing! A bagatelle!"

The little gentleman removed his polished boots from the chased silver-gilt fender. He was strongly tempted to throw the check into the fire. But money is money, and he restrained himself. He folded the oblong slip of pink paper stamped with the magic name of Coutts and slipped it into his pocket note-case, gnawing, as was his wont, at the ends of his heavy brown mustache and breathing through his nose. He got up and looked upon his merry men with an ugly, livid smile, and said, still smiling:

"So be it! We take my Lord's charity and we repay it. Without doubt—it shall be repaid by-and-by—with other debts owed by me to England. Her grudging shelter, her insulting tolerance, her heavy, insolent, insular contempt."

Something in the speaker's short thick throat rattled oddly. His eyes, that were usually like the faded negatives of eyes, glittered with a dull, retrospective hate. The white hand shook as it stroked the brown chin-tuft, and a grayish shiny sweat stood upon his face.

"I am to be upheld and supported by Great Britain if I accomplish miracles—but I am to accomplish them unaided. Two thousand pounds! We are infinitely indebted to my Lord Walmerston's generosity!"

St. Arnaud, who had got off the sofa, remarked with a full-flavored oath:

"It is rating the Army cheap, by——!"

De Morny said, shrugging one shoulder and toying with his watch-chain:

"Two regiments of Russian Guards made an Empress of the Grand Duchess Catherine. Will not a couple of brigades do your little job for you? For my life, I cannot see why not?"

The tallow-candle-locked little man on the hearthrug retorted as he warmed himself:

"Catherine only strangled her husband Peter. I have the Assembly to throttle—a very different thing. To carry out my plan successfully I must subsidize the whole Army—cram the pockets of every officer according to his grade—with thousand-franc billets—descend upon the rank-and-file in a shower of wine and gold."

De Fleury agreed.

"*Sapristi!* it is as plain as a pikestaff. Those attempts of Strasbourg and Boulogne failed because enough drink—sufficient money—was not lavished upon the soldiers. This time there will have to be enough of both."

"Has it ever occurred to you," said de Morny, still in the tongue of barbarous Britain, as he dried the wet ink carefully, and glanced towards St. Arnaud, whose sallow face betrayed suspicion and growing ill-humor, at the continuance of this dialogue that he could not understand, "that, like Herr Frankenstein of the German legend, you may create out of the Army a monster that will one day prove dangerous to you?"

Persigny and de Fleury exchanged a glance unseen by their master. He said, throwing the half-finished cigarette upon the hearth:

"Frankenstein killed his monster when he found it inconvenient. That was a mistake; such a brute-force is always of use. He should have bled the creature into weakness and submission. Then he could have kept it until wanted in a cage."

"A sublime idea," said de Morny, with the shadow of a grin upon his well-bred, dissipated countenance. "But permit me to suggest that if you attempt to act upon it, you will find your work cut out."

"You have a biting vein of humor," said Monseigneur, turning his blinking regard upon the speaker. "Pursue it if it pleases you—it does not disturb me. I belong to the race of the lymphatics—the Imperturbables, whom nothing annoys."

Though he boasted, his quickened breathing betokened some degree of disturbance. His white hand was not steady as he took a handful of cigarettes from a jeweled box that stood upon the mantelshelf, selected one, and tossed the remainder of the handful into the maw of the red-hot fire, that swallowed the little paper tubes at a gulp. But his tone was mellifluous as he added, striking a match:

"Pray do not speak English so much.... M. de St. Arnaud is not familiar with the language."

"His vocabulary being limited to 'Goddam!' 'All right!' and 'How-do-you-do?'—phrases sufficient to equip a second-class actor for the part of stage Englishman in a vaudeville, but not," said de Morny, still in the prohibited tongue, and smiling pleasantly at the lanky figure in the gorgeous uniform topped by the made-up face with the dyed mustaches and the hyacinthine locks that were false in patches—"not to guide the War Minister of a great Continental Power through the rocks and shoals of diplomatic conferences with representatives of other Powers. One will not fail to remember M. de St. Arnaud's limitations. It will be well, my brother, if you will also. As for this decree, it may be necessary, but the moment is not ripe for it. It will do you injury, take my word for that!"

"My brother," though inwardly nauseated by the unwelcome counsel, took it smilingly. He assumed his favorite pose, borrowed from the great Napoleon, his short right leg advanced, his chin turned at an acute angle, his left hand thrust behind the broad red ribbon, a finger hitched between two buttons of his tight-waisted general's coat, and said with his most pompous air:

"M. de Morny, in answer to your objections to my proposed course of policy, I reply by dictating a Proclamation addressed by the President of the Republic to the French People. Be good enough to take your seat at the writing-table."

De Morny obeyed. Monseigneur cleared his throat, and reeled off:

"Our country is upon the horns of a dilemma, in the throes of a crisis of the gravest. As her sworn protector, guardian and defender, I take the step necessary to her rescue and salvation—I withdraw from the Bank twenty-five millions of francs wrung from her veins by the masters who have betrayed her—I apply them as golden ointment to stanch her bleeding wounds."

Said de Morny, with imperturbable gravity, speaking in the English language, as he selected a sheet of paper and dipped his pen in the ink:

"Article I. will provide that hereafter stealing is no robbery. Article II. should ordain that henceforth it is not murder to kill!"

The coldly-spoken words dropped one by one into a silence of consternation. St. Arnaud sat up; de Fleury dropped his cocked hat upon the carpet. Persigny grew pale underneath his rouge. Monseigneur alone maintained his urbane coolness, looking down his nose as he stroked his heavy brown mustache with the well-kept hand that, with all its feminine beauty, was so pitiless. Thus his blinking glance was arrested by the letter on the hearthrug. And a postscript that he had overlooked now caught his eye. He stooped, lifted the letter, and read, written in Walewski's fine Italian script:

"Walmerston is cooling; there is no doubt about the change in him. Better strike whilst the iron is hot, or decide to abandon the idea."

"And risk all ... or give up all. Very well, my friend!" he said, apostrophising the absent writer as though he could hear him, "I will risk all. I wait for nothing but the cable now."

Even as he said the words the privileged elderly aide-de-camp entered with the thin blue envelope that held the cablegram. He tore it open, and read:

"Town—Dover—congratulates—Prince-President—on—establishment—submarine—telegraphic—communication—between—France—and—England. William—John—Tomlinson.—Mayor."

XLVIII

It was given to William John Tomlinson to rouse the venomous reptile that lay hidden in this man out of his wintry torpor. A bitter oath broke from him as he read the message. He tore the flimsy scrawled paper and the blue envelope into a dozen pieces, and scrunched them in his small neat hand before he threw the lump of paper on the Persian hearthrug, and spat upon it with another oath, and ground it under his spurred heel.

Not one of those about him had ever seen him so moved. De Morny lifted his eyebrows in C, de Fleury and Persigny looked at each other in consternation, St. Arnaud's jaw dropped; he gulped, staring at his master with bulging eyes, as Monseigneur strove before them, in the strange emotion that possessed him, wrestling with something that plucked at his muscles and jerked his limbs, and contorted his heavy features, and wrenched the ugly jaw that the drooping mustache and the thick chin-tuft tried to hide, to the right and left as though the man had been a figure of wood and wires worked by some devil at play.

"The Mayor,..." he croaked, after a dumb struggle for speech. "The Chief Magistrate of Dover congratulates the Chief Magistrate of Paris. Damnably amusing!... Good!—very good!"

His laugh was a snapping bark, like the sound made by a dog in rabies. He went on, heedless of the faces gathered about him, speaking, not to them, but to that other hidden self of his; the being who dwelt behind the dough-colored mask, and looked through the narrow eye-slits, guessed at, but never before seen:

"You comprehend, Madame of England and that sausage of Saxe-Coburg Saalfeld, her Consort, think it beneath their exalted dignity to bandy courtesies with me.... Me, the out-at-elbows refugee, the shady character—the needy Prince-Pretender—admitted upon sufferance to West of London Clubs; exhibited as a curiosity in the drawing-rooms of English Society—stared at as some cow-worshiping jewel-hung Hindu Rajah, or raw-meat-eating Abyssinian King." He clenched his pretty hand and went on, carried away by the tide of bitter memories:

"One day, when I visited the Zoological Garden in their Regent's Park, I saw something that I shall not forget. A great hooded snake of the cobra species—they called it a hamadryad—had just been brought up from the East India Docks. When he found himself a prisoner in his iron-framed, plate-glass cage, he reared himself up in magnificent fury. His forked tongue quivered between his frothing jaws; he vibrated, poised upon his lower coils; struck again and again—and did nothing but bruise himself. Something that he could not break—a barrier adamantine and invisible, lay between him and the staring human faces he so hated. The clear jets of deadly venom that he spurted in his efforts to reach them trickled harmlessly down the glass...."

He went on:

"I saw myself at Ham when I looked at that creature in its loneliness and impotence, surrounded by the keepers who jeered and mocked.... Death in its fangs and death in its heart, and that barrier of glass between.... There were workmen with tools among those who stared at him. One shattering blow of a pick, and he would have been free—that living Terror, to kill, and kill, and kill!..."

He looked about him, and said, with his affected mildness:

"The pick-blow that cracks the glass of my cage will be the *coup d'État*, but not until I am Emperor of France will the barrier be done away with.... Do you know what Queen Victoria once said of me to Lady Stratclyffe? 'My dear, let me beg of you not to mention M. Bonaparte before Albert. He considers him hardly a person to be spoken of—not at all a person to know! And yet how can one deny him some measure of respect and consideration—as a near relative of Napoleon the Great.'"

He had another struggle with his rending devil, and said, when he had found his speech again:

"'Great!' Was he so great, that man for whose sake Victoria would accord me 'respect and consideration'? True, he humbled Emperors, browbeat and bullied Kings.... He kicked the board of Europe, and armies were jumbled in confusion. His screaming eagles carried panic, and terror, and devastation as far as the Pyramids. The East bowed her jeweled forehead in the dust before him—a nation of beef-fed islanders put him to the rout!"

His eyes, wide open now and glazed, looked upon the men who listened, unseeing as the eyes of a somnambulist. He said in that voice that was a croak:

"And he died, the prisoner and slave of England. Before I die, England shall be mine!"

Perhaps he fancied that he detected a faint, supercilious sneer upon the face of de Morny. For he turned upon the Count, and said, narrowing his eyelids, and smiling in a menacing way:

"You, my brother, take this assertion as a piece of boasting. Well, I am content that you should regard it so. Members of Christ's family held in contempt His powers of prophecy. Nevertheless, Jerusalem fell, and the Temple was leveled with the dust."

"By my faith!" said de Morny, shrugging his thin wide shoulders. "A parallel that!"

"A parallel, as you say," returned Monseigneur, who had made the astonishing comparison with the coolest effrontery. "Now, if you will give me pen, ink, and paper, I will write the answer to this letter from Belgrave Square."

They supplied him with these things, and he wrote, in his pointed spidery hand, stooping over the desk of an inlaid ivory escritoire—a dainty thing whose drawers and pigeon-holes had contained the political correspondence of Queen Marie Antoinette and the love-letters of amorous Josephine:

"Tell my Lord that I carry out my programme. Upon the morning of the second of December, at a quarter-past six punctually, I strike the decisive blow."

He signed the sheet with his initials, folded and slipped it in an envelope, and motioned to de Morny to prepare the wax to receive his signet. While the red drops were falling on the paper, like gouts of thick blood, he said, with his smile:

"It may be that this second of December will prove to be my eighteenth Brumaire."

And when Persigny inquired to which of the official messengers the letter should be entrusted for conveyance to London, he replied:

"To none of them. An aide-de-camp will attract less notice. And he must be a mere junior, an unimportant person whom nobody will be likely to follow or molest."

An ugly salacious humor curved his pasty cheeks and twitched at his nostrils as he went on:

"Suppose we send Dunoisse? Madame de Roux adores him, but there are occasions upon which she would find it more convenient to adore him from a distance. One can easily comprehend that!"

He added, as his merry men roared with laughter:

"It is decided, then. Colonel Dunoisse shall be our messenger. Pray touch the bell, M. de St. Arnaud."

A moment later the band of the —th Hussars crashed magnificently into the opening bars of *"Partant Pour La Syrie,"* and Monseigneur, imperturbable and gracious as ever, was smiling on the "damnable rabble" crowding to bask in the rays of their midnight-risen sun. And beyond the big gilded gates of the little palace Paris buzzed and roared like an angry beehive into which some mischief-loving urchin has poked a stick.

XLIX

The egg of the *coup d'État* was hatched as the train that carried Monseigneur's secret messenger rushed over the iron rails that sped it to the sea.

We know his programme, masterly in detail, devilish in its crushing, paralyzing, merciless completeness. The posting of notices at every street corner, in every public square, on every tree of the boulevards, proclaiming that crowds would thenceforth be dispersed by military force, *Without Warning*; the distribution of troops; the disposition of batteries; the arrests of the Representatives, the publication of the Decree dissolving the Assembly; the seizure of the Ministry of the Interior; the closure of the High Courts of Justice—a symbolical gagging and blinding of the Law. And Paris, rising early on that red December morning, turned out under the chilly skies to read her death-sentence, ignorant of its true nature; and to wonder at the military spectacle provided for her eyes.

For the five brigades of Carrelet's Division, cavalry and infantry, extended in *échelon* from the Rue de la Paix to the Faubourg Poissonière. Each brigade with its artillery, numbering seventeen thousand Pretorians, give additional regiments, with a reserve of sixty thousand men, being held in readiness to use cannon, saber, pistol, and bayonet upon the bodies of their fellow-countrymen and women, that France might be saved, according to Monseigneur.

The First Regiment of Lancers, to their eternal dishonor, opened the ball. Amidst cries of "Long live the Republic!" "Down with Louis Bonaparte, traitor to the people!" they charged the crowd. Men, women, and children were ruthlessly cut down: and then, from the Gymnase Theater to the Bains Chinois, took place the Great Battue.

Killing is thirsty work. Wine flowed down the soldiers' throats in rivers, as the blood of their victims rolled down the Paris gutters. And as the slayers flagged they were stimulated to fresh exertions. Food, drink, and cigars were lavished upon them. Rolls of gold were broken and shared among them like sticks of chocolate. Women were promised them by-and-by. Long after the soldiers were too drunk to stand upright they went on killing—an instance of devotion which brought tears of sensibility to the eyes of Monseigneur.

It was late, and raining heavily, when the Folkestone train clanked into Waterloo Station. The yellow gaslights were reflected in the numerous puddles on the slippery wooden platform; in the shiny peaks of porters' caps, and in the dripping oilskins of cabmen. A red-nosed Jehu, suffering from almost total extinction of the voice, undertook to convey Dunoisse to Belgrave Square, the haggard beast attached to the leaky vehicle accomplishing the journey in a series of stumbles, slides, and collapses.

"Vy does the 'orse fall down?" indignantly repeated the husky driver, to whom Dunoisse, on alighting for the second time to assist the prostrate steed to rise, had addressed this question. "Vy, becos' he can't stand hup, nor no more could you, my topping codger, after twenty hours on the job."

He drove his fare to the address given without further casualty, pocketed Dunoisse's liberal fare without any perceptible emotion, and, warning an advancing hall-porter to be careful, for he had brought him "something wallyble," jerked and prodded his drooping beast into some faint show of vitality, and rattled and jingled away.

The windows of the Embassy blazed with lights, music thrilled and throbbed upon the ear, a double line of waiting carriages extended along the railings of the Square garden,—late arrivals were even now being set down in the shelter of the awning that protected the crimson-carpeted doorsteps from the sooty downpour; police were on duty in unusual force, and the six tall cuirassiers of the Embassy were dwarfed into insignificance by a British guard of honor, betokening the presence of Royalty; stately, splendid Household Cavalrymen, whose gold-laced scarlet blue velvet facings, gleaming steel cuirasses, and silver, white-plumed helmets lined the flower-decked vestibule, and struck savage splendid chords of color amidst the decorations of the marble staircase, where Gloire de Dijon roses and yellow chrysanthemums were massed and mingled with the trailing foliage of smilax, and the tall green plumes of ferns.

The Tricolor was barely in evidence. The Imperial colors of green and gold, displayed in the floral decorations, predominated in the draperies that hung below the carved and gilded cornices, and beneath the pillared archways that led to the dining and reception rooms. The full-length portrait of the Prince-President that hung over the sculptured marble fireplace had a canopy of emerald velvet spangled with fleurons, and upheld by eagles perched on laurel-wreathed spears. And above the head of the portrait, slender gilded tubes formed the letter N, and above the initial, concealed by a garland of trailing rose-boughs, lurked another more significant device....

Thus much evidence of preparation at the Embassy for some event of profound importance was evident to the bearer of the letter from the

Élysée, before the steward of the chambers, a stately gold-chained personage in discreet black, accosted the stranger, and at the sight of a signet bearing a familiar coat-of-arms, conducted him in haste to an apartment on the rear of the ground-floor, reserved for similar arrivals; set sandwiches, cold game, and champagne-cup before him; indicated a dressing-room adjoining where the stains of travel might be removed; and disappeared, to return before the rage of hunger had been half-appeased, ushering in a handsome personage in a brilliant Hussar uniform, who greeted Dunoisse as an acquaintance, and shook him warmly by the hand.

"There has been a great dinner this evening," explained this personage, who held the post of First Military Attaché to France's Embassy. "The entire *Corps Diplomatique* accredited to the Court of St. James's, to meet the Duke of Bambridge and Lord Walmerston. His Royal Highness will be leaving directly; those Life Guards in the square and in the vestibule are his escort of honor. Magnificent men, are they not? But less active dismounted than our own Heavy Cavalry. Are you sufficiently refreshed? You will take nothing more? You are positive? Then be good enough to come with me."

And they returned to the hall, to commence the ascent of the great staircase, as a steady, continuous stream of well-bred, well-dressed people began to flow downwards in the direction of the refreshment-buffets. The slender, supple figure of the stranger, attired in plain, close-fitting mufti black, relieved only by the red rosette at the left lapel, closely following its brilliant guide, attracted many curious glances as it passed.

"The women wear magnificent jewels, and are handsome, are they not?" commented the Hussar. "These English skins of cream and roses, these thick, straight profiles, these rounded contours, these fine eyes, lacking expression and fire, but still magnificent, these superb *chevelures* would atone to most men for their lack of grace and *verve*. But to me, my dear fellow— word of honor! the little finger of a *chic* Parisienne is worth the whole of Belgravia. Pray, how is Madame de Roux? Heavens! how her presence would eclipse a roomful of British beauties! They tell me"—possibly the speaker was not guileless of a dash of malice—"de Roux is exerting himself to get transferred to a Home command. For me, I find that natural. Don't you?"

And the attaché, whose loquacious vivacity could not hide the excitement and suspense under which he was laboring, and which were palpably shared by every official encountered on the way upstairs, paused at a curtained archway at the end of a short corridor on the second floor, and said, lifting the velvet drapery that Dunoisse might pass within:

"This is His Excellency's library. Wait a moment, and I am instructed to say that he will join you here. Excuse me that I am compelled to leave you now!"

The curtain fell heavily, blotting out the handsome martial figure. Dunoisse moved forwards, and found himself in the middle of an octagonally-shaped library, furnished in the somber, sumptuous style of the Empire. Bronze bookcases, surmounted by crowned eagles holding wreaths of bay and laurel in their beaks, lined the walls, bronze-colored velvet curtains draped the windows, the walnut furniture was upholstered in bronze leather; the needed note of color being supplied by the superb Persian rugs that covered the polished walnut parquet, the single gorgeous amaryllis that bloomed in a tub of Nankin ware upon an inlaid ivory stool, and the brilliant trophies of Eastern arms that gleamed from the upper walls and covered the ceiling. A glowing fire of billets burned on the bronze dogs of the fireplace. Above the carved walnut mantelshelf, where groups of wax tapers burned in silver candelabra, hung a fine replica from the brush of David, of the painter's imposing, heroic, impossible portrait of Napoleon crossing the Alps. And Dunoisse, sinking down with a sigh of relief amongst the cushions of a capacious armchair and stretching his chilled feet towards the cheerful hearth-glow, remembered with a faint amusement how violent an outburst of indignation this picture invariably provoked from the Marshal; who with many oaths would denounce the long dead-and-buried painter as an ass and a jackanapes, incapable of imagining the conqueror of the Simplon as anything but a barley-sugar soldier, or of representing upon canvas the true spirit of War.

"He rode a mule, did my General, and left his charger to his bâtmen. The flaps of his cocked hat were turned to keep the snow out of his neck and ears; he tied them down with a peasant-wench's red woolen shawl, and wrapped himself in an old gray cloak lined with skins of lambs. Death of my life! the road to glory is not paved with sugar-plums and rose-leaves.... A fellow who looked one way and spurred his beast another as the fool is doing in that accursed picture would have found himself at the bottom of an ice-gulf before he could say '*Crac!*'"

There was something in the Marshal's roughly blocked-out word-sketch that warmed the heart and stirred the blood as the classical equestrian figure of the David portrait failed to do. Dunoisse, even in his childish days, had recognized this. He was looking at the picture between half-closed eyelids; and the spirited charger had begun to shrink into a mule, and the red woolen shawl of homely truth had covered up the laced cocked hat of ornamental fiction, when the imperative summons of a door-bell pealed through the house, and was succeeded by a sudden lull in the Babel of general conversation.

L

Dunoisse, roused by the unmistakable double ring of a telegraphic messenger, started to his feet. The undelivered letter in his breast seemed to burn there like red-hot iron. His keen ears pricked themselves for what he knew must come, if this were as he suspected, a cable from Paris.

He stepped towards the door, put aside the velvet draperies of the *portière*, and turned the handle. He emerged upon the landing, where a few persons were gathered, conferring eagerly in undertones. He moved to the balustrade of the great well-staircase, and looked down into the flower-decked, brilliantly illuminated hall, to find it packed with a solid mass of heads of both sexes, all ages, and every shade of color. Bald craniums of venerable diplomats nodded beside the more amply thatched heads of middle-age politicians or the hyacinthine curls of juvenile Guardsmen; tiaras of diamonds crowning snow-white or chestnut, sable or golden locks, blazed and coruscated, wreaths of flowers twined in Beauty's tresses made a garden for the eye. And all these heads, it seemed to Dunoisse, were turned towards the full-length portrait of Monseigneur, attired in the uniform of a General of the French Army, smiling with his imperturbable amiability above the marble fireplace.

For what were they all waiting? Leaning over the balustrade above, Dunoisse could see that a small round ventilator in the wall immediately above the picture, and hidden from the persons assembled in the hall below by the bespangled canopy, was open. Through the aperture came a hand holding a lighted taper; and in another moment, with a faint hissing sound, the initial N and an Imperial crown above it leaped into lines of vivid wavering flame.

Babel broke loose then. Questions, ejaculations, comments, explanations, congratulations, in half-a-dozen European languages, crossed and recrossed in the air like bursting squibs. And seeing officials and attachés of the Embassy beset by eager questions; and conscious that curious glances from below were raking his own dark, unfamiliar features, Dunoisse, as a wave of excited humanity began to roll up the grand staircase, retreated to the library, knowing that the *coup d'État* was an accomplished fact.

He had left the library empty, but he found it occupied. A lady and a gentleman had entered by a door at the more distant end. The lady's back was towards Dunoisse. Her male companion, a tall and handsome man of barely middle age, wearing the gold-embroidered uniform of the diplomatic corps with grace and distinction, said to her, in the act of quitting the room:

"Wait here. I will go and order the carriage, but the crush is so great that some delay is unavoidable. Mary shall come and keep you company. By that small private staircase communicating with the dining-room she can join you quite quietly and unobserved. No one will be likely to disturb you. M. Walewski will not be able to escape from the congratulations of his circle for a considerable interval, and Madame Walewski is engaged with the Duke."

The speaker withdrew by the more distant door, softly closing it behind him. And Dunoisse stood still in the shadow of a massive writing-table, flung by the light of fire and candle upon the heavy velvet curtain behind him, uncertain whether to remain or to retreat. One moment more; and then, as the tall, slender, white-robed figure of the lady turned and moved towards him across the richly hued Oriental carpets, a memory, faint as a whiff of sweetness from some jar of ancient pot-pourri, wakened in him, quickening as she drew nearer into fragrance fresh and as living as that exhaled by the bouquet of pure white roses clustering in their glossy dark green leaves, that she carried in her slight gloved hand; and by their fellow-blossoms, drooping in the graceful fashion of the day, amidst the heavy shining coils of her rippling gold-brown hair.

For it was Ada Merling.

He drew noiselessly back into the shadow, looking at her intently. A dress of costly fabric, frost-flowers of Alençon lace wrought upon cloudy tulle, billowed and floated about her slender, rounded form. Glimpses of shimmering sea-blue showed through the exquisite folds. The moony glimmer of great pearls, and the cold white fire of diamonds crowned her rich hair and clasped her fair throat, circled her slight wrists, and heaved on her white bosom. Jewels and laces could not add to her beauty in the eyes of those who loved her. To Dunoisse the revelation of the loveliness that had been gowned in Quaker gray, crowned with the frilled cap of the nurse, and uniformed with the bibbed apron, came with a shock that took his breath away.

She had not seen him, standing by the curtain. She evidently believed herself alone when she dropped her fan and bouquet on a divan, as though their inconsiderable burden had oppressed her, and moved towards the fireplace. She looked steadfastly at the replica of the David portrait of the Great Napoleon that hung above. Her name was upon Dunoisse's lips, when the sound of the unforgotten voice of melody arrested it. She spoke; and her words were addressed, not to the living man who heard, but to the deaf, unheeding dead.

"Oh, you with the inscrutable pale face and the cold, hard, pitiless eyes! who point forwards ceaselessly," she said, "scourging your dying soldiers along the road of Death with the whip of your remorseless, merciless will, do you know what *he* has done, and is doing?—the man who bears your name, and would, if he could, revive the withered glories of your Empire by dipping them in a bath of human blood.... Do you hear the shrieks, and groans, and prayers for mercy? Do you see the red tide running in the streets of Paris? Do you see the people butchered at the police-bureau and guard-houses? And seeing, do you own the slayer as a son of your House?... I cannot believe that you and he have anything in common.... You were a magnificent despot, a royal tiger, but this man is——"

"Mademoiselle!" broke from Dunoisse, as with a most painfully-embarrassing consciousness upon him that his unsuspected presence should in decency have been made known to her ere now, he moved from the shadow of the doorway.

"Who is it?"

She turned her face to him, and it was pale and agitated, and there were tragic violet circles round the great brilliant blue-gray eyes. They recognized Dunoisse, and she held out her hand in the frank way that he remembered, and he took it in his own.

"Monsieur Dunoisse!... Colonel Dunoisse I should say now, should I not?"

"I thank you," he said, "for not completely forgetting me; otherwise, I hardly know how I should have recalled myself to you."

"Why so? You have not changed," she answered, looking in the dark keen face. And then, as the light of fire and candles showed the fine lines graven about its eyes and mouth, and the sprinkling of gray hairs upon the high, finely modeled temples, she added: "And yet I think you have."

"Time is only kind to beautiful women!" Dunoisse responded, paying her the implied compliment with the gallantry that had become habitual. But she answered with a contraction of the brows:

"Time would be kind if this December day, that dawned upon the betrayal of the French Republic, and set upon the massacre and slaughter of her citizens, could be wiped from the calendar forever."

Tears sprang to her eyes and fell, and her bosom heaved under the jewels that sparkled on its whiteness.

"One should never consent to act against one's own innate convictions, even to gratify the dearest living friends," she said. "My mother, the kindest and most unselfish of women, has never ceased to regard my chosen work as a kind of voluntary martyrdom; my duties at the Home, absorbing and delightful as they are, as irksome and unpleasant. 'If Ada would go out into Society sometimes,' she says constantly, 'it would be more natural!' And so, to please the dear one—who has been, and still is, very ill, and whom I have been nursing—I accepted their Excellencies' invitation, left her sick-bed, put on my fallals and trinkets—and came here with Mr. and Mrs. Bertham to-night—to join, although I did not know it, in celebrating the perpetration of a crime, and hailing as a great and memorable stroke of statecraft a deed of infamy."

The letter in Dunoisse's breast became an oppressive burden. His eyes fell under hers. She pursued, with a deepening, intensifying expression and tone of horror and repulsion.

"For that the banquet in which I shared to-night was intended to celebrate this day that has seen the triumph of bad faith and mean deceit, and hideous treachery, over generous confidence and open trust, can be doubted by no one!... And while we ate and drank, and laughed and chatted, sitting at the table of *his* plenipotentiary, what horrors were taking place in Paris! what crimes were being committed against Law, against Honor, against Humanity, against God!..."

Her voice broke. Innumerable little shining points of moisture started into sight upon her broad, pure forehead, and in the shadow of the silken waves upon her blue-veined temples, and about her pale, quivering lips. She said, lifting her lace handkerchief and wiping the moisture away:

"I speak thus to you, who are an officer of the Army of France; who hold a post of confidence—or so I have been given to understand—on the Prince's Military Staff. It may be that you prize Success above Integrity, that the result of the *coup d'État* will justify in your eyes the measures that have been taken to carry it out. But, knowing what I know of you—having heard from that dear lady,—who is now, I earnestly believe, crowned in a more glorious life than that of earth, with the reward of her pure faith and simple virtues,—the story of your renunciation of great fortune and high prospects for the sake of principle and honor—I cannot believe this. If it were so, you would be changed, not only in outward appearance, but in mind, and heart, and soul."

She added, with an almost wistful smile:

"And I do not wish to find you so. I prefer, when it is possible, to keep my ideals intact."

"Miss Merling," returned Dunoisse, "I break no bond of secrecy in saying to you that the *coup d'État* has long been expected, both by the enemies and the friends of Monseigneur the Prince-President. But although the most minute preparations have been made to insure perfection in the military operations and the proceedings of the police; the friends most depended on by His Highness—the agents most necessary to the execution of his plan—have had no knowledge of what was to be their share in the programme until the moment for action arrived. The Prince, M. de Morny, M. de St. Arnaud, M. de Persigny, Colonel de Fleury, and M. de Maupas, alone shared the secret. And they have kept it well!"

"Too well!" she said, and her arched brows drew into straight lines of condemnation over the severity of her clear gaze. "One would have prayed for less perfection! The plot has been a masterpiece of cool Machiavellian treachery, devised with extraordinary genius, and carried out with consummate skill. It is hinted that Lord Walmerston approves and encourages, if he has not aided and abetted.".... A shudder rippled through her slight body. "Oh, I knew him subtle as Odysseus," she said, with starting tears of indignation—"but I never believed him guileful; never imagined that he could justify God-defying, cold-blooded murder as a means to an end. If this indeed be so, those who have termed him England's typical and representative Englishman"—the tone was of keen, cutting sarcasm—"must find him another description. Hell's typical and representative devil"—Dunoisse started as the fierce condemnatory sentence rang through the room—"is he whom you call master! The jailer who has turned the key upon the freedom of the people of France!"

"Miss Merling, the ways of Government and Rule are bestrewn with obstacles and beset with pearls," returned Dunoisse, "and Expediency demands many moral sacrifices on the part of those who sit on the coach-boxes of the world. As a man of honor"—the well-used word fell lightly from his lips as he slightly shrugged his shoulders—"I deplore that they should be necessary! But in the years that have passed since it was my privilege to meet you, I have learned to swim with the stream; to take Life as I find it; and not to ask a greater excess of nobility and virtue from my neighbors than I possess in myself."

His slight momentary embarrassment had passed away. He had recovered his customary ease and sangfroid, and the acquired manner of his world, self-confident, almost insolent in its cool assurance, lent its meretricious charm to the handsome face and upright gallant figure as he faced her smiling, the ruddy firelight enhancing the brilliancy of his black eyes and the ruddy swarthiness of hue that distinguished him, his supple, well-shaped hand toying with a fine waxed end of the neat black mustache.

"Nothing, Mademoiselle," he went on, "would distress me more profoundly than to think that credit was given me for opinions I have long learned to regard as prejudiced and crude, and a course of conduct subsequent experience has proved to have been so mistaken that I have long since endeavored to correct its errors by adopting an opposite policy. I——"

LI

He ceased, for a sudden burning wave of color flooded her to the temples. Her white throat and bosom were tinged with the red stain.

He bit his lip in chagrin, seeing her recoil from him. Fair women were not wont to turn their eyes from Dunoisse. He began, in much less confident tones, to exonerate himself:

"In the world of to-day, Mademoiselle, especially the world of Paris, one is compelled to abandon high ideals of life and forsake the more rigid standards of conduct. One is forced...."

She looked at him full, and the scathing, merciless contempt in her great eyes both froze and scorched him. He stammered, bungled, broke down. The clear voice said with a cutting edge of irony:

"The boy of whom my dear old friend, Miss Caroline Smithwick, spoke with so much affection; the young man of whom she was so proud, was not to be 'compelled' or 'forced' to turn from the path of truth and honor by any stress of circumstances. You have changed very much, Colonel Dunoisse, since you visited her in Cavendish Street! Good-night to you, and good-by!"

The tall, white-robed figure was sweeping to the door, when it stopped, and turned, and came back again. She said, with almost a pleading look:

"But I cannot leave you so, remembering how true and kind you were to *her*. My fault is to be over hasty in judgment, I fear." She added: "There must be many excuses that you could make for yourself, and are too proud and too reserved to offer.... Especially to one who has no claim upon your confidence; so let us part friends, even though we never meet as friends again!"

He took the white, firm hand she held out. He had thought her insular and prejudiced, narrow-minded and intolerant. Some magic in her touch wrought a change in him. He said in a far different tone:

"That I have sinned against your ideals of character and principle is my punishment. Tell me—Miss Merling—if I had been the kind of man you thought me—if I had come back to Cavendish Street and sought your friendship—would it have been denied?"

"No!" she said, looking in his face with beautiful candor. "For I saw much to admire and to respect in you—as you were in days gone by."

"The world dubbed me, very plainly—a fool for being what I was in those days," returned Dunoisse, with a slight deprecatory lift of shoulders and eyebrows. "And frankly, Mademoiselle, I had not the courage requisite to go against the world."

"If you were a fool, you were God's fool," she answered him, "and such folly is superior to the wisdom of the sages. Now, good-by, Colonel Dunoisse."

And, with a slight inclination of the head, she withdrew her hand and moved away, as the farther door of the library opened, admitting Madame Walewski, her homeliness painfully accentuated by her dazzling dress of gold brocade and famous *parure* of Brazilian emeralds; and another lady, dark-haired, sweet-faced, and of middle height, dressed in half-mourning, towards whom Ada Merling hurried, saying in a tremulous whisper as she caught the outstretched hand:

"Oh, Mary, come!....."

And then the three ladies were gone, retreating by that farther door into unknown, conjectural regions; and the velvet curtain lifted and dropped behind Dunoisse, and he turned, instinctively drawing the Prince's letter from his breast, to meet the radiant blue eyes and graceful, cordial greeting of Count Walewski, and to be presented to the Ambassador's companion, Lord Walmerston....

You saw the all-powerful Foreign Minister as a hale, vigorous, elderly gentleman, displaying a star, and the broad red ribbon and oval gold badge of a Civil G.C.B., and the befrogged and gold-laced swallow-tail of official ceremony rather awkwardly, upon a heavy-shouldered, somewhat clumsy figure, though the black silk stockings showed well-made legs, and gold-buckled, patent-leather shoes set off the small, neat feet.

Little enough remained at this period of the dandified elegance that had won repute at Almack's in 1820, and the grace that had made him famous in the waltz. The weather-beaten face, surrounded by pepper-and-salt hair and whiskers, the square-ended, sagacious nose and flexible, curving lips, might have belonged to a shrewd, humorous, Northern farmer rather than a brilliant statesman; while the jerky manner, the odd gesticulations that accompanied the hesitating, drawling speech, made the stranger to whom it was addressed ask himself in wonder whether this could really be the great orator, the dazzling politician, the famous diplomat who had steered England's ship of State through so many troubled foreign seas? until the keen, dark, glittering eyes met and held his own; and under the merciless, piercing scrutiny of their regard the querist ceased to question, and the critic found himself appraised, weighed, judged, and valued by a mind without its parallel in the science of reading men.

One phrase employed by him was to linger in Dunoisse's memory. He said, as Walewski handed him the letter from the Élysée, and he wiped his tortoiseshell-rimmed eyeglasses to read:

"You herald the event after its occurrence, Colonel."

And a moment later, folding up the sheet and returning it:

"His Imperial Highness certainly owes less to a fortuitous concourse of atoms than to his own ability, energy, and tact." He added with emphasis: "This is an immense act; its importance can hardly be overestimated. For my part, I officially recognize it, and shall adhere to my determination to support it."

Then, as Walewski, flushed with a triumph he could hardly control, murmured a gracefully-worded, low-toned entreaty, he responded:

"Ah! I understand. You wish me to write a line to His Imperial Highness, recapitulating what I have just said, to be conveyed with your own loyal congratulations by his messenger?..."

Walewski, unable to trust himself to speak, bowed assent. Perhaps the hand that held the tortoiseshell-rimmed eyeglasses knew a moment of unsteadiness as its owner's swift brain balanced the question of risks. Then, with characteristic boldness, my lord took the leap.

"Certainly, my dear Count—certainly. I see no objection at all!"

And, with a slight jerky nod of dismissal for Dunoisse, accompanied by a not unkindly glance of the hard, powerful, dark brown eyes, the stooping figure of England's great Foreign Minister moved forwards to the writing-table and penned the single, brief, emphatic line of approval, that burned the writer's boats and brought about the downfall from which he was to rise, with popularity enhanced and power redoubled, within the space of a year.

An hour or so of fevered sleep in a luxurious bedroom, ringing with the clatter of late cabs and early milk-carts upon London paving-stones, and Dunoisse was on the iron road again. As he leaned back, with folded arms, in the first-class compartment that had no other passenger, his imagination followed Ada Merling back to the Hospice in Cavendish Street. But it was to a house in Park Lane that swiftly-trotting hoofs and rapidly-rolling wheels had carried her when she had left the Embassy on the night before.

LII

An elderly servant in plain clothes had admitted her. The man's face bore traces of watching and anxiety. And at the stair-foot waited the matronly woman who bore the quaint name of Husnuggle, and the first glance at her quivering lips and reddened, swollen eyelids told the daughter that all was not well in the sick-room.

The shadow of Death brooded over the great canopied bed in the luxurious chamber, where a face that was the pallid wraith of Ada's own lay low amidst the lace-trimmed pillows; its pinched and wasted beauty framed in the dainty little muslin cap that covered the still luxuriant and glossy hair.

A nurse from the Hospice rose up from her seat near the bed-foot, made her report in a few low-toned sentences, and was dismissed to take her needed rest, as a tiny china clock upon the mantelshelf struck one. And as her daughter bent above the sick woman and kissed the fair, unwrinkled forehead between the bands of gray-brown, the sunken eyes opened widely, and the weak voice said:

"You have come back!... Is it very late?... The time has seemed long!..."

"Dear mother, I should never have left you had you not wished it so. Have you been lonely in the midst of all the pain?"

"I have been thinking!..." said the toneless voice.

"Of me, dear mother?"

"Chiefly of you, my own."

She wished to be raised a little on her pillows, and the daughter's skilled hands tenderly performed this office, and put nourishment between the pale lips. You saw Ada, moving to and fro in her filmy, trailing laces and flashing jewels, between the glimmer of the silver night-lamp and the oblong patches of gray dawn that showed between the window-curtains, like some fair ministering spirit of pity and love.... And the feeble voice resumed after an interval:

"It is you who will be lonely, child, when I am gone. Then you may think more favorably of—of the course that others follow, and welcome those natural ties, my Ada, that make the happiness of life."

Ada answered, putting up a hand to hide her tears:

"When you are with God I shall be lonely, dearest, but not sorrowful, knowing you in His safe keeping. As for marriage, urge it upon me no more, my mother! For something tells me that these natural ties you speak of, sweet and pleasant as they are, are not destined for me."

"Why not? You would make a noble wife and mother, Ada. You are young, and cultivated, and beautiful, and have so many other gifts and graces, that, were you possessed of no worldly advantages, my child, you might still expect to make what Society calls an advantageous match...."

"Mother—my mother!—let us forget the world and Society!... To-night I have heard both applaud a God-defying crime as a stroke of exquisite diplomacy, and exalt a murderer as the saviour of his country, and their plaudits ring in my ears yet.... And I have seen the change—the base, corroding, ugly change!—they can wreak upon a nature that was—how short a time ago!—brave, and chivalrous, and simple; and a character that was honorable, upright, and sincere. I have a quarrel with Society and the world, mother; let them go by! And speak to me of marriage no more, in the little time we yet may have on earth together. For without love—such love as God has created, and blessed, and sanctioned between men and women—such love as you and my father knew!—I will never take on me the name of wife, or be the mother of any man's children. Do not be vexed, dear mother!" she begged, in sweet, entreating tones.

"My daughter," the dying woman said, "I am only grieved for you.... For I have fancied—if, indeed, it was fancy?—that your heart was not quite free; that your imagination had been touched, your thoughts attracted, Ada, by someone of different religion, language, and nationality, met and known abroad. Someone, the recollection of whom—forgive me if I am wrong, dearest!—has made you indifferent to the good qualities of Englishmen of your own rank and social standing, cold to their merits and blind to their attractions——"

"Mother, are you not talking too much? Will you not try to sleep?"

"My dear, I have but little time left for talk, and in a very few hours my sleep will know no earthly waking. Answer my question now!"

Ada Merling laid down the thin, frail hand that she had clasped, rose up, and went to the window, moved the blind, adjusted the curtain, went a step or two about the room, and having, possibly, controlled some emotion that had threatened to master her, resumed her seat beside the pillow and took the feeble hand again, saying:

"Mother, there can be no concealment between us!... I have allowed myself to think too constantly of a man whom I met not quite three years ago; and who appeared to be, morally and mentally, as he undoubtedly is physically, as superior to the common run of men as Hector must have seemed, compared with the other sons of Priam; or the young David, set amongst the warrior-chiefs of Saul; or Kossuth, placed side by side with the man who rules in France to-day." She added rather hurriedly, as the mother would have spoken: "Remember that I only said '*appeared.*' For I was doomed to know the pain of disillusion, and witness the breaking of the idol I had made for myself.... I shall be better for the lesson, painful though it has been! And so, let us speak of this no more! Even to you it has been difficult to confess my absurdity. Now, will you not try to rest?"

"Presently ... presently! Tell me more!—I should have known of this sooner! If any misunderstanding has arisen between you and one who loves you—and who could fail to love you?—it might have been cleared away by the exercise of a little tact—a measure of discrimination. But you, Ada—*you* to be despised and slighted! You, to give your love to one who makes no return!... The thought is incredible ... it bewilders and astounds me. Perhaps I err through excess of pride in you, but I cannot take this in!"

"Listen to me, dear, and you will understand more clearly...."

The face of the speaker was set to the desperate effort. Unseen by the dim eyes of the listener, the pang of self-revelation contracted and wrung it; the anguish of the confession blanched it to a deadly white.

"This is not a question of being appreciated or not appreciated, valued or undervalued. Your daughter, of whom you are so proud, threw away her heart unasked; and on the strength of a single meeting, built up the flimsy fabric of her house of dreams. To-night I met the man again, and the charm was broken. I saw him, not as I had imagined him to be, but as he is! Not the young Bayard of my belief, but the *beau chevalier* of Paris salons; not as the man of unstained honor and high ideals, but as the attaché of the Elysée, the servant of its unprincipled master—the open lover of Madame de Roux."

She hid her face, but her shoulders shook with weeping, and little streams of bright tears trickled between the slender white jeweled fingers, and were lost amidst the snowy laces of her dress.

"Again, I say that I cannot conceive it!" the mother faltered. "The man was hardly known to you?..."

"I had heard him glowingly described and fondly praised by one who loved him...."

"He is a foreigner?... A Frenchman?... A Roman Catholic?..."

"He is a Bavarian Swiss by birth; French by naturalization and education, and a Catholic, without doubt."

"And had he asked you, you would have left us all to follow him?"

"Mother, you did the like at my father's call!"

"Our parents approved!"

"If they had not, would you have abandoned him?"

"I cannot reply; it is for you to answer me.... Would you, had this man loved and sought you in marriage, have changed your religion and embraced his?"

"Mother, you ask a question I need not answer. He did not love me ... he never sought me.... Were our paths, that lie so far apart, to cross now ... did he ask of me that which I might once have gladly given, I should deny it, knowing him to be unworthy of the gift."

"Ada, I must have your answer! Would you have deserted the faith of your Protestant forefathers?"

"It may be, mother, that I should have returned to the faith in which their fathers lived and died. Remember, we Merlings were Catholic before the Reformation."

"Those were dark days for England. A purer light has shown the path to a better world since then."

"Dear one," the sweet voice pleaded, "we have never thought alike upon this matter."

"To my bitter, secret sorrow," the mother answered, "I have long known that we did not; or say, since you returned from your course of study in the Paris hospitals I have seen it, and guessed at the reason of the change! For you have lived with Roman Catholic nuns in convents, Ada, and have listened to their specious arguments. Snares may have been set—may Heaven pardon me if I judge wrongly!—to lure the English heiress into the nets of Rome."

"No, no, dear mother! there were no arguments, no efforts. The Sisters treated me with the kindest courtesy, while they seemed to shun, rather than to desire, to discuss the difference of creed. I gathered at the most that I was pitied for having missed a great good, a signal blessing, an unspeakable privilege; that had fallen to their more happy lot. And when I have seen the Sisters' faces as they came from their early, daily Communion, and when I have seen the little children—the tiniest creatures—fed with the Bread of Life, in which I might not share——"

She broke off. The sick woman said reproachfully:

"Had you not the privileges of your own reformed faith? Could you not have attended the monthly Communion at some French Protestant church, to your spiritual profit and refreshment?"

"Without doubt," was the reply, "if I had needed nothing more than these."

"Then.... You bewilder me, Ada! What can you find lacking in the services of your Church?"

She said, slowly and thoughtfully:

"What?... I have thought and reflected much upon this question, and I have decided that the coldness and narrowness that have chilled my soul, and the aching sense of something being wanting, arise from the lack of belief in the Real Presence of Christ in the Blessed Sacrament, and in the deliberate, purposeful absence of love, and honor, and worship towards His Mother——"

She was interrupted by an outcry of feeble vehemence.

"You horrify me, Ada. Worship towards a created being!... A sinful vessel of common human clay!"

She rose and said, standing beside the pillow, with the light of dawn upon her hair:

"Mother, there is profanation in the thought that the vessel chosen by its Maker for that tremendous service could be anything but immaculately, divinely spotless.... Can pure water be drawn from an impure well? or good fruit, to quote the words of her Divine Son, be gathered from a tree that is evil? How could the Mother from whose flesh was formed the sinless Body of the Redeemer, be capable of sin? My God-given reason tells me it is impossible! And—can I ever forget that the Heart that poured forth its Blood upon the Cross was filled from the veins of Mary, when there is not a single Gospel that does not tell me so?"

There was no answer from the pale lips. She said with energy:

"How can we pay her too much reverence, accord her a devotion too profound, to whom Archangels bend the knee and the Son of God accorded filial obedience? Being perfect Man, He is a perfect Son; the desire of such a Son must be to see His Mother honored. From a child I felt the incomparable beauty, the resistless charm, of that Divine Maternity.... I used to steal away alone to think of It. I used to say to myself, seeing you dressed for some dinner or ball, in all your laces and jewels, 'My earthly mother is beautiful, but my heavenly Mother is far, far more fair!' and I loved to imagine myself as a little child at Nazareth who had fallen down and lay crying with pain beside the well from whence she nightly drew her pitcher of fresh water, and whom she gathered in her arms and comforted. If love of the Mother of Jesus were prayer, surely I prayed to her then!"

Still there was no response. She sighed and resumed her seat beside the pillow; and said, stooping and touching with her lips the waxen hand:

"I ought to tell you that I wished and tried, to put many questions to the Sisters. But they had pledged their word to discuss with me no question of religious faith, and they were adamant—not at all to my delight. 'But I am a heretic,' I said to Sister Édouard-Antoine. 'Am I not worth the effort to convince and enlighten?' She said: 'My dear, when Our Lord wishes to enlighten and convince you, He will do it from within, not from without!' Now I have told you all there is to tell—nothing is kept back—no shadow lies between us. Are you not content with me now?"

"I shall know peace," said the relentless voice from the pillow, "only when I have your promise—a pledge that, once given, I know my Ada will keep. Say to me: 'Mother, I will never become a Romanist, or marry any man who holds the Catholic faith!' That pledge once given will be kept by you, I know...!"

In her very feebleness lay the strength that was not to be gainsaid or resisted. Her daughter's tears fell as she whispered in the dying ear:

"Dear little mother, when you have crossed the deep, swift river that separates Time from Eternity, and the Veil has fallen behind you, you will be so wise, so wise!... Not one of the kings, and priests, and prophets who lived of old, will have been so wise as you. Think, dearest and gentlest!—if, by the light that shines upon you then, you were to see that the ancient Faith is the true Faith and the Mother Church the One Church ... would you not grieve to know your Ada shut off from peace—deprived of the true and only Bread of Life—fettered and shackled, body and soul, by an irrevocable vow?... Would you not—"

Her voice broke and faltered. But the pale head upon the pillow made the negative sign, and she went on:

"Will not you—who have submitted yourself so meekly to the will of Almighty God in accepting this cup of death that He now offers you— leave the issue of affairs—in faith that He will do all for the best—to Him? and forbear to exact this promise, which my heart tells me will bring me sorrow and pain!"

In vain her pleading. The tongue that was already stiffening uttered one inexorable word.

"No!"

"Oh, then I promise, mother!" she cried through bursting tears. "And may God forgive me if I promise wrongly, seeing how much I love you, dearest dear!"

Ah me! the dying!—how pitiless they are! What heavy fetters their feebleness can rivet on our limbs, what galling yokes their parting wishes have power to lay upon our aching necks! How they stretch us on the rack with their strengthless hands; ruthlessly seize the levers, turn the jolting wheel; and wring from us, with tears of blood, and groanings of the flesh and of the spirit, the pledge we most shrink to give! and pass content, knowing we dare not break the promise given to one upon whom the grave is about to close.

"Promise me, my son," I heard the worn-out drudge of a London insurance office say to his boy of twelve years, grasping the small warm hand in his, that was gaunt and cold, and damp with the sweat of death—"promise me that when I lie beside your mother in the cemetery you will never fail to visit our grave each Sunday; and lay upon it of the flowers that are in season, the freshest and best, as you have seen and helped me to do ever since she died! Promise me that weeds shall never grow above her resting-place; that dust and soil shall never smirch the stone we placed above her; and see that the fee to the man who mows the grass be regularly paid. Do not fail me in this, my little son!"

Little son, with wide blue eyes fixed in awe and terror upon the whitening stare of impending dissolution, sobbed out the asked-for promise, and the bankrupt died content.

He knew that on the day following the shabby funeral that was to swallow up the last remaining five-pound note of his miserable savings, his penniless child was to be taken by his sole living relative—a struggling tradesman resident in a remote London suburb—to help the uncle in his business as a tobacconist and newsvendor, clean the shop windows, carry out the papers, perform odd offices in the household, and generally fulfill the duties of an unpaid errand-boy, yet he died content!

No realization of the crushing weight of responsibility laid on those thin, childish shoulders; no thought of the desperate, fruitless effort to be made, Sunday after Sunday, to keep the extorted pledge, marred the moribund's happy complacency in the undertaking given. Almost with his final breath he whispered something about the flowers in season, and the tidy gravestone, and the weeds that were never to be allowed to grow....

"Promise me, swear to me!" pants the departing wife to the man who has been faithful to his marriage-vow, but has realized every day since the glamour of the honeymoon faded, that his union with this woman has been a terrible mistake. "Let me go hence contented in the knowledge that you will never marry again, dear! I could not bear to think of you happy in the arms of another woman. Say, now, that it shall never be!"

She is thinking of one special woman as she feebly turns the thumbscrew, and forces her victim to open his jaws to take in the iron choke-pear of the prohibitive vow. He has not the courage or the inhumanity to resist her. Nay! it is impious to refuse to grant the wish of one about to die. So he yields, and she departs; and he goes lonely and unmated for all the days that are his upon earth.

And perhaps it may be the bitter punishment of those who have exacted from us these cruel promises; that, with eyes from which the films of earth have been purged for evermore, they may be fated to see them kept.

LIII

It was a calm, bright day, that third of December, with a mild, sweet westerly wind blowing between a blue, waveless sea and a blue, cloudless sky. So warm and genial the weather, that sandwich-board-men parading the streets of Folkestone behind blue-and-red double-crown bills announcing that Performances would be given at the Town Hall of that Thrilling Melodrama, "The Warlock of the Glen," by Miss Arabella Smallsopp, of the Principal London Theaters, and a Full Company of Specially Engaged Artists, For Three Nights Only,—were fain to lean against the outer walls of public-houses—thus nefariously concealing from the public eye the colored pictorial representations of Miss Smallsopp in the *rôle* of the persecuted Countess—Mr. Montague Barnstormer as the usurping Laird, and Master Pilkington as the infant Adalbert—and hide their streaming faces in pots of frothing beer.

And so, over the salty, creaking, tarry-smelling gangway to the deck of the Boulogne packet *Britannia*. A jovial Irish priest, a pair of prim English spinsters in green veils, their lapdogs and their maid, their manservant and their courier; with Dunoisse and a honeymooning couple, made up the list of the *Britannia's* after-cabin passengers. The bride was my Aunt Julietta; Fate would have it so.

For the impression created three brief years before upon the susceptible maiden fancy of my Aunt by the very ingratiating manners and handsome personality of a young foreign gentleman, by chance encountered in a railway-train, had faded; to be replaced by the highly-colored image of a large, loud, heavily-built, sturdily-limbed young man, holding the commission of a junior Captain in Her Majesty's 444th Irish Regiment of Foot; a well-known fighting corps, distinguished in the annals of the British Army by the significant sobriquet of the "Rathkeale Ragamuffins."

You saw in Captain Golightly M'Creedy the eldest of fourteen children, begotten of an ancient warrior of Peninsular fame, a certain Lieutenant-General M'Creedy of Creedystown, County Cork, who had served twenty years in the 444th, had left three fingers and half a sword-hilt upon the field of Talavera, and wore a silver plate at the top of his skull, to testify to his having been cut down by a sergeant of French Light Infantry during the Battle of Barrosa, when in the act of capturing an eagle from the foe.

Having thus performed his duty by his country, the veteran thought, and with some reason, that his country owed something to him; and commissions for his sons Golightly, Thaddeus, and Considine being obtained by the paternal interest, these three young gentlemen—as innocent of polite education and technical information as the hairy "lepping" colts they hunted, and the half-bred pointers they shot over—were pitched into the General's old regiment, and left to sink or swim.

Goliath, Thady, and young Con, after some rasping experiences, mastered the small amount of professional knowledge that was held in those days to be indispensable to the status of an officer and a gentleman. Indeed, by the time the Rathkeale Ragamuffins, with flying colors, banging of drums, and blaring of brazen instruments, marched into the provincial garrison town of Dullingstoke, in the genteeler suburbs of which stood the family mansion of my grandparents, Captain Goliath M'Creedy had attained some degree of reputation in his regiment as a smart officer and a show man.

You saw him at this era as a strapping young Celt of thirty, with thick sandy whiskers and a thicker brogue, who could top the regulation three bottles of port with a jorum or so of whisky-punch; walk home to his quarters while men of weaker head were being conveyed to theirs in wheelbarrows; and consume vast quantities of bacon and eggs, washed down by bitter ale, at breakfast, when hardened seniors were calling for green apples and glasses of gin, and pallid juniors nibbled captain's biscuits as they quenched their red-hot coppers with soda-water. But what did my Aunt Julietta see in him, I should like to know?

Why did not her gentle affections rather twine about the Captain's younger brother, Lieutenant Thady, who sang Irish ballads with the sweetest of tenor voices, played juvenile leading parts in private theatricals, and won regimental steeplechases on his leggy Irish thoroughbred, to the admiration of the gentler sex and the envy of the males? Or Ensign Con, who had the biggest blue eyes and the smallest waist you can imagine; wrote poetry which was understood to be of home manufacture, in feminine albums—painted groups of impossible flowers and marvelous landscapes upon fans and fire-screens—waltzed like an angel, and was generally admitted to be a ladies' man.

Why should my gentle Aunt adore Captain Goliath, who gambled, and swore horribly when he lost; who loved strong liquors, to the detriment of his figure and complexion; who had fought duels and perforated with pistol-bullets the bodies of two gentlemen who had impugned his honor; who kept fighting-cocks in his quarters, and the steel spurs wherewith he armed these feathered warriors for the combat in a neat leather pocket-case; who would consume raw beefsteaks, bend pokers, and lift ponies for wagers, and win them; and spend the money in carousing with his friends; and who had once—oh, hideous thought!—backed himself to kill three rats with his teeth against the Major's bull-terrier bitch Fury, and accounted for the rodents with half-a-minute out of five to spare?...

In the lifetime of my grandfather, thrice Mayor of Dullingstoke, a peppery old sea-dog, who had settled down as far from his professional element as possible,—had amassed a considerable fortune in the tanning-trade, and had made it the business of his later years to keep his large family of daughters single—no young men were ever admitted within his doors. It is on record that no sooner had the sable border of woe upon the edge of my widowed grandmother's notepaper narrowed to the quarter-inch significant of tempered sorrow than—each of my aunts having inherited a nice little landed property under the paternal will—in addition to a snug sum, comfortably invested in Three Per Cent. Consols—the bachelor officers of the "Rathkeale Ragamuffins" began to buzz like hungry wasps about the six fair honey-pots that adorned my grandmother's tea-table.

Ordinarily of a frugal mind, she is said to have been lavish in her expenditure of plum-cake, home-made jams, preserved ginger, and best Souchong upon these festal occasions, accounting for her prodigality to a female friend in these words:

"I grudge nothing, Georgiana, that helps to get rid of the girls!"

Honest Captain Goliath, introduced at the ladies' tea-table by Lieutenant Thady—who had a knack at making acquaintances which the clumsier Captain did not possess, was at first attracted by the showier charms of my Aunt Marietta, which, you will perhaps remember?—were of the lofty, aquiline, disdainful kind. He stared at the young lady a good deal, and tugged his sandy whiskers, and breathed hard, as he paid her clumsy compliments, punctuated with "Egad!" and "By Jove!" He was rather at a loss when his long legs were inserted under my grandmother's polished mahogany. He liked the rich plum-cake, but tea was a beverage abhorred of his manly soul.

"Women's slops," the young officer mentally termed the infusion beloved of the sex, as he took three lumps of sugar, and stirred the boiling liquid so clumsily with a fiddle-headed silver teaspoon that—splash!—he overset the cup.... My Aunts Harrietta and Emmelina, who were timid, screamed aloud.... My Aunts Elisabetta and Claribella, who were sitting upon either side of Lieutenant Thady, tittered, being giddily inclined.

My Aunt Marietta, who was wearing a sweet new pink *barége*, suffered the complete ruin of a beflounced side-breadth, and, it must be owned, took the unlucky incident with a very bad grace; even permitting herself to utter the word "Clumsy," and toss her head in contempt of the crimson Captain's profuse if incoherently expressed regrets. While my Aunt Julietta, in whose lap the agitated sweep of the young man's elbow had deposited a plate of bread-and-butter, butter side down—bade him "Never mind!" in so soft a tone of kindness, accompanying the words with a glance so bright and gentle, that the utterance and the look bowled Goliath over as completely as the elder Philistine, his namesake, was, cycles of centuries ago, by the brook-stone hurled from the young David's sling.

"Indeed and indeed, Miss Juley," the Captain stuttered, "with all the good-will in the worruld a man can do no more than apologize, that has had the bad luck to do damage to a young lady's dress. And though you're so kind and amiable as to make no very great shakes of it, begad! I see your own elegant gown is spoilt entirely by the clumsy divvle—begging your pardon for the word!—that would walk from here to London—supposing you'd accept it!—to get you a purtier gown!"

The Captain dropped a glove in the hall when he went away. It had his initials marked inside in great big sprawling characters; but even without the inky "G. M'C." my Aunt Julietta would have known to whom it belonged....

Ah! in what a pure, sweet hiding-place it was lying, that clumsy hand-cover of dogskin,—while the Captain was routing in the litter of bills, and writs, and dunning-letters that strewed the table in his quarters, and cursing at his soldier-servant for losing his things. And he came to tea yet again, and one of his extra-sized feet accidentally touched, beneath the shelter of the well-spread board, a little foot in a velvet sandal-slipper; and She blushed like an armful of roses, and He crimsoned to the parting of his sandy curls. And thenceforwards the Captain's wooing proceeded smoothly enough, save for a few manifestations of jealousy on the part of Lieutenant Thady, who was inclined to resent the appropriation of my Aunt Julietta's smiles.

"For I inthrojuiced you—and you'd heard me say the black-eyed wan was the natest pacer of the sthring—and you've cut me out with her—so you have!—and begad! the thing's joocedly unfair!"

Upon which Captain Goliath extracted a shilling from his waistcoat-pocket, and suggested that the goddess of Chance be called in to decide the issue.

"I'm wit' you!" said the Lieutenant, with alacrity. "And the best two out of three takes Black Eyes!"

"Done!" agreed his senior, rubbing the edge of his coin carelessly with a stout, muscular thumb. "And the loser will have his pick of the five girrls that's left. He'll not have a pin to choose between them in the way of fortune, for the old man left them share and share alike; but the fella that gets the high-nosed wan"—in these disrespectful terms the Captain alluded to my Aunt Marietta—"will have a vixen, take my word for it! Call, now! Heads or tails?—shame or honor?"

Lieutenant Thady called "Tails," and Captain Goliath spun, and the Lieutenant lost the toss three times running, unaware that the astute Captain carried a double-headed shilling for contingencies of this kind.

A few days later, with the consent of my grandmother—now beginning to realize that the sacrifice of her best plum-cake and Souchong had not been all in vain—the Captain drove my Aunt Julietta out in the family chaise. That drive was, at the outset, a painful experience for Browney, the younger of the stout, elderly carriage pair, who was attached to the vehicle. Never had such pace been got out of him before. Never had such scientific handling of the reins, such artistic touches of the whip, been known to the experience of that respectable cob. But it is on record that he returned home at his own pace, with an engaged couple behind him; and that when my Aunt Julietta was assisted to descend by the hand of the *brave and gallant man*, to whom, as she wrote to her confidential friend, the daughter of Sir Wackton Tackton, "I have plighted the *fondest vow* that a *woman's lips* may *breathe*," she went to the sedate animal's head and thanked him for the happiest day in all her maiden life, and kissed him on the nose.

Thus Captain Goliath M'Creedy and my Aunt Julietta became definitely betrothed. And the Lieutenant, after some hesitation between blue eyes and brown, arch, coquettish ringlets and Grecian coils, "plumped," as he afterwards said, for my Aunt Elisabetta.

And Ensign Con, being ordered by his seniors to choose a bride of three-hundred a year pin-money from amongst my grandmother's remaining daughters, wrote her a note in his best round-hand, soliciting an interview upon a "mater of importanse very near my hart"; and upon the receipt of an elegant billet naming a fitting hour, set out, attired in his best; curled, pomatumed, gloved, and booted beyond anything you can imagine, to conquer Fate.

Perhaps the brain behind those cerulean orbs of my Uncle Con's was of rather soft consistency. Or it may be that the sight of my grandmother sitting in her best parlor, arrayed in her stiffest black silk gown—endued with her most imposing widow's cap and weepers—waiting, with folded mittens, to hear that yet another of the pound-cakes cast upon the waters had not been sacrificed in vain—was calculated to make havoc of stronger wits and daunt a stouter courage. Suffice it to say that, having started out from barracks with the firm intention of returning as a man definitely engaged—preferably to my Aunt Emmelina rather than to my Aunt Claribella (young ladies between whose respective persons Con had hesitated, uncertain as the proverbial donkey between the bundles of hay)—the Ensign tottered back to quarters, a blighted being, engaged to my Aunt Marietta, whose Roman profile and haughty manners had from the first stricken terror to the young man's soul.

He must have made wild work with his wooing, unlucky Con! for my grandmother subsequently confided to her bosom friend, Georgiana, that at one moment her firm conviction had been that the young man, with a maturity of taste and judgment rare in one so young, was proposing marriage to herself. In vain Con's fraternal counselors advised him to go back, explain that he had got the wrong girl, and change her! Con could not muster the pluck! And so my Aunt Emmelina, who had loved the handsome young booby, never married; and Con was a henpecked husband to the ending of his days.

There was a triple wedding, so that one breakfast and one cake might do duty for three brides, a flying visit to London to do the lions; and now you saw my Aunt Julietta, a wife of two days, starting on her honeymoon-trip to Boulogne with the idol of her soul. Be sure that she recognized the deposed idol in their handsome fellow-traveler; that my aunt's fresh English face had completely faded from Dunoisse's memory may be guessed.

But the natural chagrin of my Aunt at this discovery was to give place to pangs of a less romantic kind. She had studied French fashions in the illuminating pages of the *Ladies' Mentor*, had mastered the French language sufficiently to spell out a "Moral Tale" of Marmontel, or a page of Lamartine, or even a verse of Victor Hugo; and had compounded French dishes from English recipes. But she had never previously crossed the restless strip of Channel that divides her native isle of Britain from the shores of Gallia. And in those days nobody had ever heard of a real gentlewoman who was not very seriously incommoded, if not absolutely indisposed, at sea.

Conceive, then, my Aunt Julietta upon this smoothest of crossings, being dreadfully prostrated by the malady of the wave. Imagine her flattening her bridal bonnet—a sweet thing in drawn peach-blossom satin, with a wreath of orange-blooms inside the brim—into a cocked hat against the stalwart shoulder of her martial lord, as she reiterated agitated entreaties to be taken immediately on shore—picture her subsiding, in all the elegance of her flounced plaid poplin—a charming thing in large checks of pink, brown, and bottle-green—and her mantle of beaver-trimmed *casimir*, into a mere wisp of seasick humanity, distinguishable afterwards as a moaning bundle of shawls—prone upon a red plush sofa in a saloon cabin—ministered to by a stewardess with brandy-and-water and smelling-salts.

While the *Britannia's* other first-class passengers gathered for the one o'clock dinner about the long table in the adjoining saloon, whence the clashing of knives and forks and the robust savors of the leg of boiled mutton with caper sauce, turnips, and potatoes—the porter and ale that washed these down; the apple-pudding that followed, and the Dutch cheese that came in with the materials for gin-hot and whisky-toddy—penetrated to the sufferer, moaning on the other side of the dividing partition of painted planks.

You may imagine that the bridegroom—placed upon the right hand of the *Britannia's* commander at the head of the board, made tremendous havoc among the eatables; disposed of pewter after pewter of foaming ale; hobnobbed with the more jovial of the male passengers in bumpers of whisky-toddy; cracked broad jokes, and roared at them loudest of all; and capped the skipper's thrilling recital of how, in 1830, when First Officer, and on his way to join his steamer at Southampton, he had nearly been pressed for service in the Royal Navy, and had, armed solely with a carpet-bag, containing a log-book and some heavy nautical instruments, done battle with and escaped from the clutches of a gang of crimps and man-catchers;—by relating, with much circumstantial detail, and to the breathless interest of his auditors, the story of how he, Captain Goliath M'Creedy, had backed himself to kill "tree rass" with his "teet" in emulation of the Adjutant's "ould turrabred bull-bitch Fury," and had "shuk the squale" out of the last remaining victim thirty seconds under the five minutes. "To the chune of ten guineas and six dozen of the foinust clarrut that ever a gentleman put down his troat!"

LIV

There were not lacking signs by the wayside, as Dunoisse was whirled along the iron road to Paris, of the bloody drama that had begun upon the previous morning, and was being played to the bitter end.

Troops and bodies of police lined the platforms of the railway-stations. Pale faces, downcast looks, and mourning attire distinguished those members of the public whom business or necessity compelled to travel at this perilous time. Glimpses of towns or villages, seen as the train rushed over bridges or in and out of stations, showed closed shops and jealously shut-up houses, many of them with bullet-pocked walls and shattered windows; more police and soldiers patroling the otherwise deserted thoroughfare; and agents in blouses, with rolls of paper, ladders, brushes, and paste-pots, posting the proclamations of Monseigneur upon walls, or trees, or hoardings, or wherever these had not already broken out like pale leprous sores. And upon many country roads significant-looking black vans, surrounded by Dragoons or Municipal Guards, and drawn by muddy, sweat-drenched post-horses, traveled at high speed, followed by open laudaus containing lounging, cigar-smoking Commissaries of Police. And in the roaring, cinder-flavored blackness of tunnels, or in the cold glare of chalky, open cuttings, huge locomotives would flash and thunder past, whirling yet other prison-vans, placed upon trucks, guarded by soldiers or mobilized gendarmerie, and packed with Representatives, Judges, Editors, Chiefs of secret societies, public leaders, and popular orators, to destinations unknown. And as the dusk day-brow sank over the red wintry sunset, the roll of musketry and the thunder of cannon, answered by the dropping, irregular fire from seventy-and-seven barricades, betokened that the train was nearing Paris; and then—the flaring gaslights of the Northern Station were reflected in the polished surfaces of steel or brazen helmets and gleaming blades of sabers; and winked and twinkled from shako-badges and musket-barrels, and the thirsty points of bayonets that had drunk the life-blood of harmless women, and innocent children, and decent, law-abiding men.

Paris had never seemed to Dunoisse so crowded and so empty as when, on foot—for no public conveyance was obtainable—he returned to his rooms in the Rue du Bac. Entire regiments of cavalry, riding at a foot's pace in close column, flowed in slow, resistless rivers of flesh and steel, along the boulevards. And brigades, with their batteries of artillery, were drawn up in the great squares and public places, waiting the signal to roll down and overwhelm any organized attempt at resistance, under cataclysms of disciplined force.

No street but had its silent menace of cannon posted at the mouth of it, waiting, in case Liberty and Equality should lift their heads up from the blood-smeared asphalte, to decapitate them with a discharge of grape. But no head was lifted, and no Red Flag was raised; the iron heel of the Friend of Labor and the Lover of Humanity bore with such paralyzing, crushing weight upon the necks of men.

Save for curt words of command, the jingling of bridles, and the snorting of wearied horses, the silence in this city of shot-riddled walls and splintered windows was like a heavy hand upon the public mouth. Street-lamps were few—nearly all had been shattered by bullets—but when dusk had given place to darkness, the immense bivouac-fires of the troops reddened the lowering sky, and Paris might have been Tophet, she so reeked of smoke and furnace-heat. And by that lurid glare in the heavens dark, furtive shapes might have been seen hurrying by in the shadow of walls and hoardings, that were spies of the police, or agents of the National Printing-Office, charged with the posting of yet more proclamations; or Revolutionists speeding to join their comrades on the barricades, and share with them the last crust, and the few remaining cartridges, before drinking with them of the strong black wine that brims the cup of Death. Or they were men and women crazed with anxiety, or frantic with grief; dragging by the hand pale, frightened children, as they went to search for missing friends or relatives at that universal Lost Property Office, the Cemetery of Montmartre; crying with that dumb voice of anguish that echoes in the chambers of the desolate heart, and which the most stringent decrees of Monseigneur were powerless to silence.

"Oh, my father!... Oh, my mother!... Alas! my husband! lover! sister! brother! friend!... Am I despairing—searching by the flickering light of the tallow candle in the broken lantern, or the uncertain match-flare, amongst all these ghastly unburied heads of staring corpses, starting like monstrous fungi from the trodden, bloody soil of this consecrated place of murder—to find the face beloved?..."

More corpses, and yet more, were being made, to the echoing roll of the drums in the Champ de Mars, and piled in carts under the scared eye of the pale, sickened moon, and rattled away to Golgotha.

Turning the corner of one of the narrower thoroughfares, where a single unbroken oil-lamp made a little island of yellow light upon the murkiness, Dunoisse came upon two persons who were, for a wonder, conversing so earnestly that neither paid attention to the light, quick, even footstep drawing near. Said one of the couple, a bloused, shaggy-headed man of the artisan type, whose lantern-jawed, sallow face was lighted from below with rather demoniacal effect, by the flare of the match he had struck and sheltered between his hollowed hands, for the kindling of his short, blackened pipe:

"They made no resistance—they were butchered like sheep.... That was at midday, on the boulevard opposite the Café Vachette. Before dark, when I passed that way, the bodies were lying piled up anyhow.... The blood still smoked as it ran down the kennels—my shoes were wet with it, and the bottoms of my trousers. See for yourself the state they are in!"

He held up a foot, supporting himself with a hand against the wall behind him. His companion, a shorter, stouter figure, whose back was towards Dunoisse, stooped to look, and said in an astonished tone, as he straightened himself again:

"There seems no end to the killing, sacred name of a pig! One wonders how many they have polished off?"

The first man rejoined:

"No newspaper estimates will be published. Nor will there be any official list of killed, you may depend upon that!"

The shorter man put in, jerking his thumb towards the dusky sky that was smeared in long streaks with the red reflections of the bivouac-fires:

"Unless He up there has kept one!..."

The first man said, throwing down his burnt-out match-end on the muddy pavement:

"Fool! Do you still believe in Him when this Napoleon says He is a friend of his—when the cemeteries are stuffed with corpses, and the beds in the hospitals of St. Louis and of the Val de Grace are full of wounded men and women?" He added: "General Magnan went there in full fig with all his staff to visit them to-day.... It is like the public executioner calling to know how the guillotined are feeling without their heads!..."

The stout man cackled at this; and Dunoisse, perhaps for the sake of lingering a little in the neighborhood of one who found it possible to be merry under the circumstances, paused, and drew out his cigar-case, and said, addressing himself to the mechanic with the pipe:

"Monsieur, have the goodness to oblige me with a light!"

The haggard workman answered, tossing him a grimy matchbox:

"Here, take the last! If it does not strike, your *coup d'État* is a failure—you must turn out of the Élysée."

The reckless daring of the speaker, in combination with the alcohol-taint upon his reeking breath, proved him to be drunk. His sober companion, glancing over his shoulder, and mentally pronouncing Dunoisse to be no spy or police-agent, said, as he looked back at his companion:

"They kept up the ball at the palace last night with a vengeance!... Champagne flowed in rivers; I had it from François."

The sallow, taller man laughed in an ugly way, and said, spitting on the pavement:

"And women were to be had for the asking. Such women!..."

Envy and scorn were strangely mingled in his tone as he said, again spitting:

"Such women! Not only stunners like Kate Harvey and that red-haired, blue-eyed wench they call Cora Pearl, that drives the team of mouse-gray ponies in the Bois, and curses and swears like a trooper; but real aristocrats, like the Marquise de Baillay and Madame de Kars, playing the prostitute for political ends—you twig? There was one whose name I do not know—an ivory-skinned creature, with ropes of black hair and eyes like emeralds.... She was half-naked and covered with jewels.... The Secretary-Chancellor of the Ministry of the Interior received a warning—that was at four o'clock in the morning, when they were still supping.... Word came to him that the Ministry was to be seized ... he rose from the table, saying that his place was in the office of his Department.... And she put her arms round him before them all.... She kissed him full upon the mouth, and said '*Stay!*'"

"And he stayed?" asked the stout man eagerly.

"By my faith, my friend!" rejoined the tall man, "he did as you or I should have done in his place, you may be sure!"

The echo of the speaker's ugly laugh was in Dunoisse's ears as he passed on, and the image of the black-haired, cream-skinned woman whose kiss had stifled the voice of conscience upon the lips of the Government official rose up in resistless witchery before his mental vision; and would not be banished or exorcised by any means he knew....

So like!—so like!... Thus would Henriette have tempted and triumphed, provided that Hector Dunoisse had not been absolute master of her heart, and supposing that to tempt and triumph had been to serve that idol of hers, the Empire.... He drove away the thought, but it returned, bringing yet another bat-winged, taunting demon, who reminded him in a shrill, thin, piercing whisper that de Moulny was Secretary-Chancellor of the Ministry of the Interior....

To suspect ... oh, base! Did not Dunoisse know—had not Madame de Roux assured him over and over that intercourse between herself and Alain was limited to the merest, slightest civilities that may be exchanged between acquaintances? Had she not pledged her word—had she not kept her vow? Anger, and shame, and horror at his own disloyalty burned in Dunoisse like some corrosive poison; killing the wholesome appetite for food, banishing weariness and the desire for rest. And thus, reaching his rooms in the Rue du Bac, and dismissing to bed the sleepy valet who had waited up for him, Dunoisse bathed and changed, and instead of lying down, went out, haggard, and hot-eyed, and headachy, into the soldier-ridden streets again, in the clear, pale, frosty sunshine of the December morning; barely feeling the slippery asphalte pavement underneath his feet; hardly cognizant of faces and shapes that passed him; answering mechanically when challenged by sentries or stopped by patrols, and hastening on again, driven—though he would have died rather than own it—by the demon that had been conjured up by the tall, grimy, sneering workman who had chatted with his mate on the previous night, at the street-corner....

His destination was the Rue de Sèvres, for Madame de Roux still retained her apartments in the outer buildings of the Abbaye-aux-Bois, where cloistered Princesses once gave instruction in housekeeping, deportment, and diplomacy to the daughters of the noblest families of France, and stars of the Comédie Française drilled the youthful performers in the dramas of "Esther" and the ballets of "Orpheus and Eurydice."

The Abbaye has nearly all been swept away; the last wheelbarrowful of rubbish has been carted from the cat-haunted desert where once the stately chapel stood: they have built upon the lovely gardens where Marie de Rochechouart, beautiful, pure, and saintly, once walked with Hélène Massalska clinging to her arm. But at this date the gardens, though sadly curtailed, were still beautiful.... Nowhere in all Paris were such chestnuts and acacias, such lilacs, and laburnums, and hawthorns to be found. The branches of the loftier trees—leafless, and bare, and wintry now—seemed to Dunoisse to nod and beckon pleasantly over the high iron-spiked walls and great grilled gates that shut in the stately pile of ancient masonry.

And with the sight of these familiar things his mood changed.... His demon quitted him,—he knew infinite relief of mind when the portress, a buxom peasant of Auvergne, roused from her morning slumbers by the Colonel's ring at the gate-bell, at length made her appearance; apologizing with volubility for her nightcap; for the red woolen shawl and short, striped petticoat, bundled on over a lengthier garment of dubious whiteness; and the stout, bare feet thrust into the baggy list slippers that completed her disarray.... And Dunoisse greeted her pleasantly, responding in gallant vein to her profuse excuses, failing to notice the sharp glances with which she scanned him; unobservant of the avid curiosity that her verbosity would have concealed, while his wearied eyes drank in the scene about him; the blackbird, and thrush, and robin-haunted shrubberies of frosted laurels, and myrtles, and veronicas glimpsed through the arched carriage-way, piercing the more modern right wing of the ancient building: the beds starring the rimy grass-plat in the center of the great courtyard, gay with such flowers as the rigorous season admitted: clumps of mauve, and pink-and-white Japanese anemones; hardy red chrysanthemums; frost-nipped bachelor's buttons; and even a pinched, belated dahlia here and there....

Here at least no grisly shadow of the Élysée brooded, or it seemed so to Dunoisse. Into this quiet haven the blue official documents, the brass-bound shakos, and clanking swords of Military Authority had not intruded, bringing disorder, confusion, and terror in their train.... Lead, and Steel, and Fire—that trio of malignant forces—obedient to the potent nod of Monseigneur, had swept past the Abbaye, without pausing to exact their toll of human life. And the robin's breast, burning like a crimson star amidst the rich dark foliage of a yew-tree, the short, sweet, sudden song of the bird seemed to answer, "Happily, yes!" And the wintry yellow sunshine drew a pleasant smell from the chilled blossoms, and the wood-smoke of the portress's crackling, newly-lighted fire came fragrantly to the nostrils of the returned traveler, as he passed under the portico of the stately block of building where were the apartments rented by Madame de Roux, and rang the ground-floor bell.

The thought of seeing Henriette again absorbed and dominated him completely. And yet, even to his slight passing observation, the servant who answered the door seemed flustered and embarrassed. The man opened his mouth to speak, shut it hurriedly, and awkwardly drew back to let the Colonel pass in. But a moment later, as Dunoisse's eager footsteps were hurrying in the direction of the gray boudoir, he arrested them by saying:

"Pardon, Monsieur the Colonel! but Madame is not at home!..."

"Indeed? Madame went out early?"

Thus interrogated, the man showed confusion. He explained, after some floundering, that Madame had gone out, and had not yet returned.

"Not yet returned?..." Dunoisse repeated.

It seemed to him that the servant must be absurdly mistaken; for in the inner breast-pocket of his coat, just above his heart, nestled a little note, penned in violet ink, in Henriette's clear, delicate, characteristic handwriting. It had lain upon the vestibule-table in the Rue du Bac. He had read it and kissed it, and known assuagement of his burning torture for ten minutes, ere the twin-demons of jealousy and suspicion had swooped down on him again. It said, under the date of the day of his departure from Paris:

"Dearest,

"*Take care of yourself upon that horrible railroad. I have been miserable all day, thinking about you. It is now six o'clock. My head aches. I am denied to all visitors—I have refused all invitations. I am going to dine early and betake myself to bed.— Another day—one more night of loneliness, and then—may my Hector's guardian spirit guide him back in safety to his fond*

'Riette."

LV

Dunoisse, with a deadly sickness at the heart, drew out the little lying letter and re-read it, and turned a bleak sharp face upon the nervous servant, and asked, with a glance of the black eyes that made him wince and flush:

"Madame went out—yesterday evening—alone?"

Shame pierced him. To be reduced to questioning a servant was abominable. But he waited for the answer. It came:

"Madame was summoned, a few hours after Monsieur the Colonel's departure.... A carriage was sent to fetch her. The carriage came from the Élysée."

The words fell upon Dunoisse with the cold, heavy shock of a douche of salt water, literally taking away his breath. Could it be? Had she left home upon the eve of Monseigneur's masterstroke? Was it possible that a night, and a day, and yet another night, had passed, and found her still absent? He told himself, poor wretch, all conscious of his self-deceit, that there had been some mistake ... that one of the little girls at Bagnéres must have been taken ill ... that the mother had been sent for.... Knowing in his soul that the Henriettes never risk their beauty in the neighborhood of possible infection, he pretended to believe this lie.

He turned from the servant, and went through the empty, close-blinded reception-rooms, stumbling at the pattern of garlands on the carpet as though they had been thorny ropes set to trip him up. And he went into the gray boudoir where he had fallen captive to that luring beauty, and the stately portrait of the beautiful wicked Abbess, daughter of the evil Regent, seemed to smile at him in jeering triumph from its station on the wall.

He drew up a blind, and there were the familiar gardens bathing in the clear, cold December sunshine. He threw up a sash, letting in fresh air, and the smell of thawing earth, and the chaste, pungent fragrance of the chrysanthemums. As he leaned against the carved and painted shutter the Abbaye clock struck eight, and all the other clocks in Paris responded, one after the other, and then—his heart leaped, for there came the opening and shutting of the hall-door, and the sound of silken draperies sweeping over velvet carpets. A light footstep crossed the threshold.... He wheeled, and was face to face with Henriette....

She was in all the splendor of full dinner-dress, and her lovely person blazed and scintillated with magnificent jewels. Many of the costly gems she wore had been given her by Dunoisse, but others, costlier still, were new to him.... Her rich black hair hung in dishevelled curls—the pitiless sunlight showed her beautiful eyes deep sunk in violet caves of weariness. The *berthe* of costly lace that edged her corsage was torn, revealing charms that even Fashion decrees should be hidden.... There was a fierce red mark upon her rounded throat, and another on one white breast....

The picture was burned in upon the brain of the man who saw, as a corrosive acid might have bitten it on copper. He opened his dry mouth to speak, but no words issued thence. She said, dropping her sable-lined mantle upon the floor, dragging at one of her bracelets that obstinately refused to be unfastened:

"So—you have returned!... Then you have not been to the Rue du Bac?"

"I went," he said, showing her the little treacherous sheet—"and found your letter there...."

A rush of angry blood changed her from white to crimson. The mark on her throat vanished, and then, as the fierce tide receded, stood out once more in burning, guilty red. She tore off the bracelet, and tossed it down, and said, lifting her white arms to release her little head from the weight of the diamond coronet:

"The Prince-President sent!... It was a command. How could I disobey?"

Dunoisse answered her in tones she had never before heard from him:

"The Prince-President should know that the *droit du seigneur* went out with the Monarchy. It is not an institution that the Republic of France will wish to see revived during His Highness's tenure of the Dictatorship.... I will explain this to His Highness without delay!"

Her beautiful eyes blazed rebellion, and her bosom tossed the red mark up and down tumultuously. She cried:

"Are you mad? What right have you to demand explanations, or to give them, pray?"

"What right?" Dunoisse echoed, looking at her incredulously. "Do you ask by what right I say that you shall not be degraded by the contact of persons who are infamous—used as a bait to lure golden fish into the net of Presidential intrigue?—poisoned and contaminated by the atmosphere in which nothing that is pure can exist, and everything that is vile——"

"Ah, ah!" she said, interrupting him; "you talk in riddles and parables. Be plain with me, I beg of you! Or—permit me to be so with you!"

She sank down upon a divan with her knees apart, and said, thrusting her clasped hands down between them, joined together at the wrists as though they were fettered:

"Listen to me!... You are not my husband!... I advise you to remember it!... It will save trouble in the long-run—it will be better for yourself and for me if you will do this!"

Dunoisse returned, in tones that cut like ice-splinters:

"I have not the honor to be your husband, it is true! But as long as the relations which have hitherto existed between us continue, I forbid you to go alone to the suppers at the Élysée! As for that accursed banquet of the night before last——"

He broke off, for something in her face appalled him. She stamped her little foot and cried:

"Great Heavens! Am I a young girl, all blushes and book-muslin? And you—what are you? A soldier? Not a bit of it! My dear old fellow, you are a prude!"

She rose up, with eyes that shot lightnings, though her mouth was smiling, and pointed to the baleful picture that hung above the fireplace, that was full of dead ashes, like her unhappy victim's heart.

"Look at Madame there!... Does not she seem as though she laughed at you? You, who would drive Propriety and pleasure in double harness—who expect a woman like me—who have drunk with you the bowl of Life—who have given you myself, with all my secrets and pleasures—to behave as a young girl who goes into Society, with her eyes bandaged, and her ears stopped up with cotton-wool. You are not very reasonable, Monsieur!"

She had taken the diamond circlet from her hair, and dropped it on the divan. Now she thrust her white fingers into the heavy masses of her curls, and lifted them up from either temple. Her long eyes gleamed like green topaz from between the narrowed eyelids. And to the man who was the bondslave of her body she seemed like some fair, malignant spirit of the storm, about to rise and fly, borne on those silken, sable wings....

"I ..." he began stammeringly. "You——"

He broke off. For it rushed upon him suddenly in blinding, scorching certainty that she, and no other, was the night-haired, ivory-white wanton who had kissed de Moulny on the mouth and bidden him stay. The impulse to leap upon her and wring from her confession, and with it full revelation of all that had passed, and in what secret bower of lust and luxury the intervening time had been spent, nearly overcame him. But he fought it back. For full knowledge must mean severance, and——"O God!" the poor wretch cried in the depths of his tortured heart; "I cannot live without her, however vile she prove!"

It was strangely, horribly true. He had never been so completely dominated by Henriette in the days when he still believed the angel's wing to be folded beneath her draperies. He drank her beauty in with thirsty eyes, and thirsted the more he drank; and was, to his unutterable shame and degradation, stung to yet sharper torments of desire, because of those red marks made by a rival's furious kisses—and did not dare, poor, pusillanimous, miserable wretch! to say: "You have betrayed me! Who is the man whose brand you bear upon your bosom. You shall tell me!—even though I know!..."

As she went on talking, spreading out her hair, pressing the points of her fingers into the velvety, supple skin above her temples:

"You idiot! can one drive Propriety and Pleasure in double harness? Your mother could answer that question—that Carmelite coquette who deserted her convent for the world, and went back to the convent when she was weary of the racket. Not that I wish to insult your mother. Quite the contrary. She did as it pleased her, and I also.... Ouf! ... how my head aches!... What an hour you have chosen for a scene of reproaches and recriminations!... Still, an explanation clears the air.... Now I am going to bed, for I am 'regularly done up,' as the Prince says." She phrased the English words with exaggerated elaboration, rolling the gutturals, and making a distracting mouth over them. "But for the future we shall understand each other better, shall we not, Monsieur?"

"I thought," he faltered—"I believed!..." and could go no further. She retorted, stretching as gracefully as a leopardess, smiling with a touch of roguery, her rosy tongue peeping from between her teeth of pearl:

"You thought me an angel, who am nothing but a woman. What! would an angel have fired that shot at the Foreign Ministry?" She shrugged her white shoulders. "What! and let you bear the whole affair upon your shoulders for fear lest the Red Republicans should take a stiletto-vengeance? And pay you in kisses and the rest as I have done?"

"It was no mere sordid bargain!... You loved me!" Dunoisse cried out in misery. "You gave me yourself for love, not for fear or gain!"

"Oh! as for that," said Henriette, with a cynical inflection, "I loved you, and I love you uncommonly well to-day. But your love is not to deprive me of my liberty—that must be understood!... There, there, my poor dear boy!..."

He had sunk down upon the gray velvet divan, looking so wan and haggard, and yet so handsome in his despair and wretchedness, that her shallow heart was stirred to pity, and she went swiftly to his side. He threw an arm about her, drew her to him, and said, looking up at her with wistful entreaty, and speaking in tones that had suddenly become pitiful and childlike:

"Dearest Henriette, I will do everything you ask me—everything!... You shall not have one single wish ungratified! Only do not go to the Palace without me, I beg of you, Henriette!"

He told himself that she was yielding, pressed her to him, and hid his burning forehead and aching eyes against her. It was a symbolical action, that willful blinding, presaging what was to come.... She knelt down before him, wound her soft white arms about him, and drew his head to rest upon her bosom, so that his cheek rested on the flaming mark that so short a time back had said to him in red letters, "*She is false to you!*" She said, holding him closer, blinding and drugging him with her breath, her contact, her voice:

"Well, then, very well! Henriette is never unkind or cruel.... It shall be as you choose. Only do not thwart me or upbraid me, Hector dearest. I am of Spanish blood—you should remember it!... How hot your forehead is! Have you, too, a headache? That is from traveling all night. How I hate those jolting railway-carriages! *Fais dodo*, poor boy!"

She rocked him upon her breast, smiling to see the rigid lines of mental anguish relax and smooth out under her caresses. And as she rocked, she sang in a velvety cooing voice a little witch-rhyme of Catalonia, meaning everything or nothing, just as the hearer happened to be a Catholic or a Calvinist ... a horrible little rhyme, dealing with a cat and the cupboard of the Archbishop, set to a soothing lullaby....

Hushaby!—Honor, and Principle, and Religion. Sleep, sleep well! rocked on the bosom of Desire.

If Ada Merling had seen Dunoisse at that moment, shorn of his strength, willfully blind to his degradation, lying in the arms that had already bound and delivered him to the Philistine, she would have blessed the hour that brought her disillusion; instead of looking back upon it sorrowfully, and writing, in the locked journal of her thoughts and impressions, that was kept in a secret of her writing-table:

"There is no teacher like Experience. By suffering and humiliation we gain sympathy for the sore and despised; and acquire insight through our own short-sightedness. How often in the old home-days at Wraye, when one of the village women has wound up some sorrowful story of human passion and human error with: '*She fell in love wi' him at sight, d'ye see?* have I not interjected, quite seriously and sincerely: '*Oh! but why?* And found myself smiling when the answer would be: '*Nay, now, Miss Ada, however can I tell, when her didn't know herself, poor soul?*'"

"Oh me!... I shall never laugh again over such stories. Is that my gain or my loss?"

A space, a blotted line, and then came, in the flowing, finely-pointed handwriting:

"It must be to my gain.... That I, who am habitually reserved, who have been reared in refinement and exclusiveness, should have known a weakness such as this, shall be of use to me and for the help of others. When I am tempted to approve my own judgment as sounder, esteem my own standards of morality and conduct as purer and loftier than those of my sister-women, let me for my soul's health—let me remember that the man to whom, in the first moment of our meeting, my heart went out—and whose name, indifferent to me as he must have been, I could never, for long afterwards, hear without emotion—is worldly, cynical, sensual, and dishonorable; deeply entangled in a shameful intrigue; bound to the interests of the Power that is the plague-sore and the curse and the ruin of his adopted country; perhaps involved in its plots—stained with its guilt of treachery and bloodshed...."

At the bottom of the page came:

"Perhaps I wrong him?... It may be that I judge him unjustly, that he has been shamefully slandered—and that he is—really is—what once he seemed. Grant it, Thou God! Who hast the knowledge of all hearts, and by Thy grace canst purify the unclean and make the evil good, and change base things to noble! And if it be Thy Will that I am never to know the sweetness of earthly love, give me to know what love may be in Heaven!"

LVI

The Marshal, having plumped out with golden blood the depleted veins of Hector's account at Rothschild's, exacted his pound of flesh in the matter of the Claim of Succession. Köhler and von Steyregg, those birds of ill omen, shortly presented themselves at the Rue du Bac, bearing the elder Dunoisse's letter of introduction, addressed to "His Serene Highness the Hereditary Prince of Widinitz," and bearing three immense splashes of scarlet sealing-wax, impressed with the writer's own pretentious coat of arms....

Two such men, these agents, capacious vessels of clay, into which the Marshal's gold was continually ladled....

Köhler styled himself an Attorney and Commissioner of Oaths of Prague. One felt sure wherever his offices were, that the business of the money-lenders flowed across the threshold. You saw him as a small, pale, scrupulously-attired, flaxen-haired man, with sharp, shallow brown eyes. Three or four bristling yellow hairs at the outer angles of the upper lip served him as a mustache—one thought of a white rat when one looked at him. Von Steyregg was a vast, pachydermatous personality, whose body was up-borne on short legs, shaped like balusters, and clad in the tightest of checked pantaloons. His venerable black frock-coat had grown green through long service—the copper of the buttons peeped through the frayed cloth. His swag-belly rolled under an immense nankeen waistcoat—over the voluminous folds of a soiled muslin cravat depended his triple row of saddlebag chins, his moist, sagging mouth betokened a love of good cheer, the hue of his nose—an organ of the squashed-strawberry type one so seldom meets with at this era—testified to its owner's appreciation of potent liquors. Huge shapeless ears, pale purple-and-brown speckled, jutted like jug-handles from his high-peaked head, whose bald and shiny summit rose, lonely as an Alp, from a forest of flaming red hair. His little gray eyes were latticed with red veins. From one of them distilled a perpetual tear, destined to become a haunting bugbear to his employer's son.

Von Steyregg, who swore in a dozen languages with equal facility and incorrectness, claimed to be a Magyar of noble family. His dog's eared visiting card dubbed him Baron. On occasions of ceremony, an extraordinary star in tarnished metal, suspended from a soiled watered-silk ribbon of red, green, and an indistinguishable shade, which may once have been white, dignified his vast expanse of snuff-stained shirt-front. Though its owner declared this ornament to be the Order of St. Emmerich, bestowed by that saintly Prince upon a paternal ancestor, the reader may suspect it to have been originally a stage-property. Steyregg having failed in theatrical management at Vienna, Pesth, and elsewhere; and being, when full of wine—and it took an immense quantity of that liquor to fill him— prodigal of reminiscences of the *coulisses*, pungent and racy; related with the Rabelaisian garniture of nods, winks, leers, and oaths of the most picturesque and highly-flavored kind.

Both men invariably addressed Dunoisse as "Highness" or "Your Serene Highness." They maintained a scrupulous parade of deference and respect in their dealings with their victim—they retreated backwards from his presence—to Madame de Roux they almost prostrated themselves— kotowing profoundly as the Ministers of the Fifteenth Louis, before the dainty jeweled shoe-buckles of the Pompadour....

Of the mad tarantula-dance through which this precious pair of showmen presently jerked their puppet,—of the kennel of obloquy and shame through which they dragged him with his companion,—the writer, confessing to some degree of parental tenderness for the hero of the story, designs to tell as briefly as may be.

According to Köhler and von Steyregg, the Regent Luitpold, having obtained from the King of Bavaria permission, confirmed by the approval of the Bund, to secularize several wealthy monasteries within the principality of Widinitz, was in worse odor with his Catholic subjects than ever before. Not only had several large communities of religious been reduced to penury and rendered homeless; but certain influential farmers, tenants of these, had been ejected from their homesteads, and divers peasants, having espoused the cause of the monks with less worldly wisdom than goodwill, had been turned out of their cottages, or had them pulled down over their heads. Disaffection was spreading, discontent prevailed. The iron was hot, said von Steyregg and Köhler, for the striking of a blow in the interests of the son of Princess Marie-Bathilde.

You may imagine how eloquently the Marshal's agents dwelt upon the enormities of Luitpold; you can conceive how they advanced their plan, and pressed its various points upon the passive victim. Wreaths of verbal blossoms covered up its spotted ugliness. Was it not a beautiful and edifying notion, asked von Steyregg, that the Heir-aspirant to the feudal throne of Widinitz should take part in the great annual festival of mid-August, the Assumption of the Blessed Virgin—at which season the Lutheran Regent—loathing the smell of incense and the chanting of Litanies as another personage is reputed to abominate holy water—yet not daring to provoke his Catholic liegemen to the point of open rebellion by prohibiting the procession—invariably absented himself from his capital, or shut himself up in the Schloss. The suggestion of so open a bid for popularity Dunoisse at first scouted. But the whole plan had a spice of adventure that charmed and excited Madame.... Paris would be intolerable in August—a delicious month to travel in. Henriette had never seen Bavaria—she longed to breathe the air of its romantic pine-forests, and gaze upon its sunset-flushed snow-peaks. For two pins she would make one of the expedition, she vowed.

And Dunoisse, being keenly aware that, although no suppers would be given at the Elysée during the red-hot months of autumn, there would be *fêtes* at the Tuileries and at St. Cloud, and shooting parties at Compiègne and Fontainebleau, was extremely willing to gratify the desire of his fair friend....

Indeed, when von Steyregg and Köhler hinted that the Marshal would not welcome the addition of a petticoat to the party, the Colonel manifested for the first time in their experience, energy and decision.

"My father may please or not please," he said to them. "I do not go without Madame de Roux!"

The Marshal received the information with a fearful outburst of profanity.

"He is not to be moved, Monseigneur!" said Köhler.

"Excellency," put in von Steyregg, "the Prince, your son, is a chip of the old block. Without the petticoat he will not budge, I pledge you the word of a Magyar nobleman!" He shook his bald and flaming head, and shook off the tear that as usual hung pendulous from the weeping eyelid, as he added:

"And the lady is a highly attractive person!"

"We shall split on the rock of her attractive person!" said the Marshal with a detonating oath. And so it ultimately proved.

Neither then, nor long afterwards, when the scar of the appalling fiasco had partially healed, could Dunoisse rid himself of the impression that the expedition had been of the type of adventure that is wrought of the stuff of dreams.

In the highlands of South Bavaria, sheltered by the skirts of the Alps, lay the Principality of Widinitz, a mountainous district cloaked with beech-woods and pine-forests, jeweled by turquoise lakes, and valleys like hollowed emeralds, kept green in the fiercest heats by the mountain-torrents and glacier-rivers and streams of melted snow....

That August journey was one of unclouded pleasure. The handsome officer and the lovely lady in the luxurious dark green traveling-chariot, that was lined with pale green satin and drawn by three powerful grays, were taken by the hosts and hostesses of the picturesque, vine-draped and rose-covered posting-inns where they slept, or halted to change horses, to be a honeymooning couple. One may imagine how the princely coronet that gleamed above the coat-of-arms emblazoned on the door-panels of the green chariot (a touch of von Steyregg's) and engraved upon the silver plating of the harness (a happy inspiration of Köhler's) swelled the totals of the bills. As for the Marshal's agents, sharing with the Colonel's valet and Madame's maid the big brown landau that lumbered at the heels of four stout beasts in the wheel-tracks of the green chariot, they were supposed to be the major-domo and the chaplain of the distinguished pair.

Köhler traveled light in the matter of baggage. A battered hat-box and a venerable portmanteau contained his indispensable necessaries of the road. An old campaigner in the field of fortune, von Steyregg's coat-tails invariably did duty as his carpet-bags and valises. Upturned, these well-stuffed receptacles served as cushions, upon which the Baron lolled magnificently, patronizing the subservient valet and the blushing maid who secretly admired large, overbearing men with flamboyant hair. True, von Steyregg's hyacinthine locks left off long before they reached the summit of his cranium, but you cannot have everything, thought the maid.

"We are not real," Henriette would say to her lover. "We are two sweethearts out of some fairy-tale of M. Anthony de Hamilton or Madame d'Aulnoy.... That old woman in the red cloak is not a wood-gathering peasant, but a witch; that black face peeping at us through the bushes does not belong to a charcoal-burner or a lignite-miner, but to some spiteful gnome or kobold.... You are the Prince of the Enchanted City in the Sleeping Forest. And I am your Princess, my dear!"

Dunoisse sighed, knowing that whether he were a Prince or not would depend upon the disposition of the liegemen of Widinitz; upon the goodwill of His Majesty the King of Bavaria; upon the approval of the Diet of the Germanic Confederation, and the clinching decision of the Special Tribunal known as the Austrägal Court. And that, even if these powers were unanimous in confirming the claim of Succession made by the son of Marie-Bathilde, the question of Henriette's ever becoming the legal partner of the throne, which in that event would be his, opened up another vista of possibilities, amongst which Divorce loomed large ... whilst Death, his black robe discreetly draped about his grisly anatomy, hovered unobtrusively in the background.

Nom d'un petit bonhomme! If de Roux should die, that regrettable loss to the Army of France would be, it seemed to Dunoisse, the way out of the tangled labyrinth of difficulties and anxieties.

His eyes avoided Henriette's, lest she should read his thought in them. But hers were raised to the rosy snow-peaks that lifted above the dark, shaggy green of the pine-forests, her sensitive nostrils quivered, her lips were parted as she drank the fragrant air.

How crystal-pure she seemed.... And yet it was but seeming.... A picture, shown upon the background of a murky Paris street-corner, by the flare of a smoky lamp, rose up in Dunoisse's memory; and the ugly, haunting laugh of the tall, sardonic workman who had chatted with a comrade on that unforgettable night of the return from London, sounded in his ears. And when Henriette asked, turning to him with the tenderest solicitude in her lovely face:

"Why do you shiver, dearest? Are you cold?" her lover answered, with forced gayety:

"A footstep must have passed over the place where my grave is to be made. You know the old saying?"

"Quite well," she told him, adding with an exquisite inflection of tenderness. "But it would be 'our' grave, Hector.... For I could not live without you, you know that very well! Dearest, why do you start?"

For the muscles of the shoulder against which she leaned, had given a sudden jerk, and the man's head had pivoted from her abruptly, as though pulled by a wire.

"Did I start?" he asked, looking back at her rather vaguely. "If so, it was because I fancied—not for the first time—that I heard someone laugh in there!..."

He pointed to the covert of pine-scrub, larch, yellow-berried mountain-ash, and tall brake-fern that edged the forest road, and went climbing with them still when the slower oaks and beeches were outstripped and left behind. It was Henriette's turn to shiver now. Hector was so strange—so very strange—she told herself, at times!...

Another man, much less handsome, not half so sweet-tempered, amiable, devoted, and clever, would have made a pleasanter companion upon these wild, rugged mountain-roads.... His blue eyes would have had a provoking challenge always, for those of his friend.... Cynical jests, sharp witticisms, would have alternated with daring compliments, bold hints, and subtle allusions, upon his projecting, fleshy lips. Yet de Moulny, a year or so back, had been a submissive, humble lover. In those days he had yielded to and been ruled by the will of Henriette. In these days, delicacy and shyness no longer characterized his wooing. He demanded, exacted, extorted favors that others had obtained by service and suit, and sighs.... She said to herself, as a mysterious smile hovered about the exquisite lips, and the long, dark lashes swept the cheeks that no sun, however ardent, might kiss to russet, that Alain was no fool! He had found out that what women liked best in a man was hardihood, and assurance touched with brutality. He had learned the secret of success with the sex.

Now, Hector....

When a Henriette begins to compare her lover, to his disadvantage, with other men, she has already wearied of him. His day is over and past.

Thenceafter, nearer and ever nearer, draws the fatal crisis. No fresh turning in the beaten road they travel together, but may lead to a definite parting of the ways.

LVII

So the company of adventurers traveled through the new, strange, lovely country, feasting and making merry, spending the Marshal's money royally; and of such queer warp is the cloth of Human Nature woven, the grotesque homage of Köhler and von Steyregg ceased to be quite intolerable in the estimation of Dunoisse.

When the inns and posting-houses began to display the arms of the von Widinitz, the coroneted casque *argent*, with its *panache* surmounted by the heron, *overt, sable*, Köhler, being nimbler of the pair, leaped out of the brown landau, climbed the steps of the green chariot, and offered homage to the pretender to the feudal dignities.

"Now your Serene Highness is upon your own territory," said he, and would have grabbed Dunoisse's hand to kiss, but that its owner put it in his pocket. Von Steyregg was standing up in the vehicle that followed, waving a huge, dingy silk handkerchief, and shedding tears of loyal enthusiasm from both eyes.

"How Monsieur the Baron loves His Serene Highness!" said Henriette's maid to her mistress at hairbrushing time that night. "Fancy, Madame, he rocked him in his arms as an infant, and taught him to ride his little horse. Monseigneur would go nowhere without his good M. von Steyregg, who plunged into a boiling torrent (into which Monseigneur's nurse had accidentally dropped him) and saved him at the risk of life. It is incredible, such devotion! It makes one weep to hear Monsieur the Baron talk!"

And the maid made good her words with a snuffle or two; and the mistress even wept a little in sympathy. Tears came at call to those beautiful eyes of Henriette's.

Thus, daily drawing nearer to the scene of destined humiliation and well-earned disgrace, the green chariot and the brown landau rolled on, until at high noon upon the Vigil of the Assumption, after a three hours' drive through ancient oak and beech-forests, when a hundred unseen church-bells were tripling the Angelus, the gray walls and gates of the towers of Widinitz rose before the travelers, venerable in their setting of ivy only less ancient, whose rugged stems grew thick as the body of a man.

It was a city in a forest, with the tops of more trees waving over the ivied walls of it. Oak and beech followed the chariot and the landau to the drawbridge, fell back as the vehicles crunched over the gravel-covered timbers, started up under the gateway, and marched with them through the streets that were bordered with runnels of clear water. Signs of preparation for the morrow's solemnities were not lacking. Men leading donkeys burdened with panniers of white or reddish-colored sand, were distributing this medium in astonishing patterns over the principal thoroughfares. Others, who followed, were strewing them with pine-branches and the glossy leaves of laurel and bay. Lamps, as yet unlighted, twinkled among the boughs. Venetian masts of the Bavarian colors supported garlands of many-colored streamers. The Market Place was a blaze of color, with temporary altars erected at the opening of every street. And nearly every householder, with his family and servants, was engaged in decorating his dwelling with carpets, bunting, and wreaths. Said von Steyregg, as he tumbled out of the brown landau, and ran with servile hurry and flapping coat-tails, to open the door of the green chariot when it finally stopped under the sign of "The Three Crown" inn: "One would think, Highness, that the news of your intended visit had reached Widinitz before you." His tear hung trembling upon his eyelid as, with an egregious affectation of respect and reverence, he assisted his principal to descend.

"It is in honor of Our Lady's Feast to-morrow, all that you see," explained the landlord, a short man in claret-colored kersey knee-breeches, blue yarn stockings, snowy shirt-sleeves, and spotless apron, who had come out to receive the strange guests. He possessed a suite of private rooms, worthy of persons of such distinction. He pointed out one or two of the lions of Widinitz before he ushered them in—the Schloss, a square building of red granite with pepper-box towers, topping a green hill that breasted up upon the northern side of the Market-Place. Another steeper hill rose upon the southern side of the great white square that was spangled with silver, dancing fountains; and the towers and roofs and steeples of the city proper covered this like a fungus-growth. The ancient Gothic pile of the Cathedral crowned the summit; the smaller, fortress-like building adjoining, the host pointed out as the Archbishop's Palace, an episcopal habitation, reared on the foundations of what had been a Roman camp.

"Sprung, your Excellencies, or our most learned Professors lie," explained the voluble landlord, "from the ruins of a temple where the Old Slavonians used to sacrifice white cocks and new mead to Svantovid, their god of War. God or no god, the gentleman had a sufficiently queer name, as your Excellencies will agree; and as to white cocks, the broth of one is—according to the old nurse-women of our principality—a certain remedy for tetters. Heathen they were that drank sickly mead in preference to sound wine!—but thanks be to Heaven and St. Procopius, who converted them, we that are come down from those old sinners know better to-day; and the vineyards of the Wid yield a liquor that has no equal in Bavaria."

And the landlord proudly pointed to a third hill that cropped up westwards; at the foot of which eminence a jade-green trout-river, spanned by three bridges of white marble, rushed foaming between rocky banks that were covered with vines, laden now with the glowing purple clusters from which an excellent red wine was made by the vine-growers of the principality.

Flasks of this sterling vintage figured upon the guest-table of the Inn of "The Three Crowns," when the newly-arrived travelers sat down to dine, the occupants of the green chariot being served in their private apartment: the Marshal's agents, for humility or for the sake of freer elbow-play than is licensed by strict good manners, preferring to eat at the common ordinary, spread in the coffee-room, together with Madame's maid and the Colonel's man.

Here, down both sides of a long table, were ranged perhaps a score of decent citizens of the sterner sex, indicating the nature of their several professions, trades, and occupations, in the fashion of their attire, as was the custom then; and engaged in discussing what, for the ninety-nine per cent. of Catholics among the company, was the single meal of the fasting-day.

Judge, then, how frigidly received by the faithful were Steyregg's Gargantuan praises of the fish, flesh, fowl, and pastry which were set before himself and his partner, and of which both ate copiously, washing down their meal with plentiful libations of the juice of the local vine.

The pickled sturgeon with mushrooms and cucumbers, to which Madame's tirewoman discreetly restricted herself, proved a mere whet to the gross Baron's huge appetite. Half a ham and the greater moiety of a pasty of eggs and capons, hurled to the ravening wolf concealed behind his dingy shirt-bosom, left him with a niche quite available for tartlets, and a chink remaining for cream-cheese.

He said at length, piling a block of this delicacy on a rusk, bolting the mouthful, and sending a generous draught of the strong red wine hissing on the heels of it:

"Now, having fed, I may say my *Nunc Dimittis*. After such a meal"—he produced and proceeded to use a battered silver toothpick—"I feel myself the equal of Prince, Regent, or Archbishop, I care not which!"

A clean-shaven, fresh-faced, gray-haired citizen, clad in a long-tailed coat and buckled knee-breeches of speckless gray-blue broadcloth, with a starched and snowy shirt-frill jutting from his bosom and rasping his triple chin, looked up from his dish of fricasseed eggs at this boast of von Steyregg's and said, a trifle sourly:

"The late Prince, sir, being with the departed, presumably has done with eating and drinking, although our Regent, being of the Lutheran persuasion, is at liberty to feed as freely upon the Vigil of the Assumption, as upon all other prescribed fasting-days.... But of his Lordship, the Archbishop, I dare to say that like any other respectable religious, he is, with his clergy, in strict retreat at this moment; and if anything beyond pulse—or dry bread and water—have passed his lips to-day, I will undertake to eat this book of mine!"

He indicated, amidst some tokens of amusement manifested by other abstainers at the table, a Missal that was propped up against the cruet at his side; then wiped his lips, threw off a glass of water, whisked the napkin-end from the bosom of his spotless waistcoat, and beckoned the waiter, asking what was to pay? The man named fifty pfennigs, the client threw down a mark and asked for change. But before the base metal could be transferred from apron-pouch to pocket, von Steyregg, completely deserted by his guardian Angel, tipped the wink to Köhler—who was diligently cramming plum-pie with whipped cream—and rose up, stretching out an immense protesting, mottled hand. His tear hung in his eye, his strawberry nose and flabby mouth quivered with emotion:

"Take up that coin, sir, I beg of you! Nothing is to pay, for you, or any other citizen of Widinitz who occupies a chair at this board together with my companion and myself on this auspicious day. You have told me that your Prince is no more; I say to you that, being dead, he cries from the tomb—'*Resurgam!*' For in an heir of his blood and name he shall live again; the youthful phœnix but waits the signal to emerge full-fledged from the parental pyre of flaming spices.... What? Do you doubt! O! man of tepid faith, I will prove it you! His Serene Highness is, at this moment, with Her Excellency, deigning to partake of refreshment in the private room overhead!"

"*Wie? Was?*" ejaculated the tradesman, staring at von Steyregg with bulging eyes, as the big fist banged the table, and the cutlery and glasses danced about, while the fifty pfennigs change leaped from the plate held by the startled servitor, and ran into a corner and hid as cleverly as little coins can. "*Ach so!*" the astonished man added, bringing down his eyebrows with some difficulty. "What you tell us is very surprising, if it be true!"

"And all tales are not true!" put in the oracular barber, who had been polishing off a plate of pickled sturgeon; while von Steyregg held forth.

"Decidedly," added a bookbinder, who was lingering over a bowl of cabbage-soup and black bread, "one is wise not to believe everything one hears."

"My friends, I state the fact, upon the honor of a Magyar nobleman!" von Steyregg asseverated. He appealed to Köhler, who replied: "Undoubtedly," and went on munching, looking sharply this way and that out of his round brown twinkling rat's eyes. "You hear the eloquent testimony of my associate," the self-styled Baron went on. "You see these highly-respectable persons," he pointed with a flourish to the abashed valet and the blushing maid, "who in their varying capacities have the honor to serve His Serene Highness the Prince-Aspirant of Widinitz,—traveling *incognito* under the style and cognomen of Colonel von Widinitz-Dunoisse,—and the noble and lovely lady"—a cough momentarily checked the flood of the Steyreggian eloquence, and then it rolled turbidly on again—"whom I mentioned just now. They are here, as I have said, partaking, after the fatigues of their journey, of marinaded trout, ragout of veal, salmi of grouse, and *quelquechoses*. Your privileged eyes will behold them presently, when they descend to distinguish your boulevards and promenades by taking the air upon them.... To-morrow, when the Procession of the Feast takes place—in preparation for which anniversary your streets are even now being strewn with pine-branches and oak-leaves, your public and private buildings adorned with banners and hung with lamps—your maidens are twining garlands, your infants of both sexes learning hymns—to-morrow all Widinitz will behold its hereditary Sovereign participating in the solemnity; and draw, I trust, parallel between Gothic intolerance—I name no names!—and noble, princely piety! Excuse me, my good sirs," the Baron added, and ostentatiously wiped his lachrymose eye, "I am not easily moved to emotion, but the inward chords cannot but respond to the conception of a spectacle so poignant and so memorable. You must pardon me this single tear!"

A murmur of ambiguous meaning traveled round the table. The plump tradesman whom von Steyregg had first addressed pushed back his chair and rose, picked up his Missal, tucked it under his arm, took his soft felt hat and thick, tasseled walking-cane from the waiter's hands; and then said, turning to the Magyar nobleman:

"*Würdig Herr*, you have paid for my dinner, and I am bound to be civil to you. But this is a Catholic State all said and done; the Lutherans are the peppercorns sprinkled through the salad, and if any other man than you had told me that this gentleman could take part in Our Lady's Procession, having filled his belly full of fish, flesh, and fowl upon the Eve of the Feast, I should have called him a liar! knowing that no person is permitted to take part in the solemnity who is not in a state of grace. By that is understood fasting, or at least abstinence, upon the Vigil, with confession, absolution, penance duly discharged, and Communion crowning all; added, a proper spirit of devotion to the most chaste Mother of God, Who, let me tell you!

is honored in this State. I might add that the recommendation of a priest is usually required, and here in Widinitz the sanction of his Lordship the Archbishop. But perhaps your principal has a dispensation which releases him from these trifling obligations?"

Teeth showed, or bits of German boxwood strung on silver wires; or gums that lacked even these substitutes, in the faces that were set about the table. The Pagan Steyregg, flustered by wine and confused by theological terminology, rushed upon his fate. Of course, he declared, his principal had a dispensation and Madame also.... Every member of the party was furnished with the requisite in case of need.... It was not customary for persons moving in exalted social spheres to travel without, he begged leave to inform the company. Whose entertainment was to be charged, he emphatically insisted, upon His Serene Highness's bill.

The table was vacated, the room emptied without any special demonstration of gratitude on the part of those who had participated in His Highness's bounty. The guests dispersed, to tell their wives or housekeepers, or to forget to do so, not one remaining save the portly citizen with the finely-starched shirt-frill. He said, once safely outside the coffee-room door, pausing to offer his snuff-box to the landlord, whom he encountered on his way from the cellar, bearing a flask of Benedictine and a bottle of special Kirschwasser:

"You have queer guests upstairs, or I have been listening to a lunatic within there!"

The speaker, dusting the pungent brown powder from a first finger and thumb, pointed the indicatory digit in the direction of the coffee-room. The landlord said, holding the Kirsch between his eye and the light:

"Heretics, who come to witness our procession of The Assumption as they might visit a theater-play. Well! one can only pray for their conversion, and charge their impiety among the extras on the bill."

His expression portended a total of appalling magnitude. He added:

"They give the surnames of von Widinitz-Dunoisse. He does, that is! And we have learned enough since His late Serene Highness was gathered to his fathers to know what rascally impudence tacks the two together."

The citizen said, putting away his snuff-box, and flicking some of the brown grains from his shirt-frill:

"His secretary, steward, pimp, or parasite—whatever the bigger of the two rogues in there"—he signed with his chin towards the coffee-room—"may be to your man upstairs, styles him the Prince-Aspirant, Serene Highness, and what-not. One would say, to hear the braggart, that this son of Napoleon's old marauder had the King of Bavaria, the Federative Council, and the General Assembly at his back!" He added: "As for the lady who accompanies him, she is styled Excellency. One can only hope she is his wife?"

"*Meinherr*, not so. Upon this point I may pronounce authoritatively." The landlord of "The Three Crowns" looked extremely wise. "Married Her Excellency may be; that is extremely probable!... But it is not to the fellow who will pay for this!"

"*Ach, ach!*" ejaculated the sleek citizen, shaking his scandalized head, "this is truly deplorable!" He added, knowing an instant's doubt of the intuition of the innkeeper: "But how are you sure? May you not mistake?"

"Because," said the host, whose chatter and round vacant face had beguiled Henriette into believing him a simple child of Nature, "because the *Herr* Colonel (who for all his fine figure and good looks is a mere *Duselfritz*), because the Colonel—when Madame holds up her little finger—obeys without questioning—that is why I am sure! The legal partner of a man's bosom may nag or cajole him; she does not issue orders or commands. It is the mistress, not the wife, who gives herself such masterful airs. Again, my *Frau* tells me that Madame's nightcaps are of real Valenciennes, with little moss-rosebuds set inside the frills; and, says my dear one—no respectable married woman would, for a mere husband, thus bedeck———"

"Prut—prut! it would be well, my good friend," interrupted the respectable tradesman hastily, "to remember that this is a peculiarly solemn season, and———"

But the host went pounding on:

"Moreover, all the gold plate of Madame's dressing-case is engraved 'H. de R———.' But to my mind the thing that convinces most is that the *Herr* Colonel (who is a *Quatschkopf* as well as a *Duselfritz*) should let her order up this from the cellar just to taste!"—the speaker lovingly blew a cobweb from the fat neck of the Kirsch bottle—"though Kirsch of fifty years old is four thalers the bottle, and he has said to her how he hates the stuff! Would any husband, even of a week or so, tolerate such prodigality in a wife?"

"*Nu, nu!*" said the portly citizen, completely convinced. "What should be done," he cried in great agitation, "to rid the town of such a scandal? Think! My wits are upside down!"

He wrung his hands. The innkeeper, that simple child of Nature, rubbed his nose with the knuckle of his thumb, and said:

"What if you, *Meinherr*, who supply the Palace with groceries and are so highly respected, should drop a hint to his Lordship in writing? Retreat or no retreat, I'll bet you a flask of my best the Archbishop takes measures, and promptly, too! Here, as it chances, is my cook's errand-boy with his basket. Look you, I will put a new-caught trout from the Wid inside it, and your bit of paper under that. The Father Economus will be sure to spy it; the rest we may confidently leave to Heaven!"

Meanwhile the Marshal's agents, having fed largely and drunk to correspond, rang the bell, summoned the innkeeper, and issued orders. Then von Steyregg mounted to the private room, scratched the door after the manner of the confidential attendants of royal personages, and appeared, contorted with bows, before the Colonel and Madame, hoping that the entertainment set before them had not been utterly unworthy of personages so exalted! "It is not, Your Serene Highness, as though you were at your own Schloss over yonder," he said, spreading his thick hands and shrugging his big shoulders. "Ere long let us hope that Destiny and Your Serene Highness's lucky star will restore you to your own! Meanwhile, I have ordered a barouche, with four outriders, being the best equipage the establishment can furnish. It is but fitting that Your Highness should utilize the earliest opportunity following your arrival to make a Royal Progress—I would say, a little tour of inspection—embracing the chief objects of interest in the town."

Dunoisse, inwardly sickened by this prospect, made objections, but Henriette overruled them all. That idea of a Royal Progress was pleasantly titillating. The Eve in her snatched at the apple tendered by the serpent von Steyregg. The barouche came lumbering to the front door before the dispute ended in Madame's favor; she glided away to "make herself beautiful," leaving a mollifying glance and smile behind with her vanquished opponent. So, petulantly fuming, Dunoisse made ready to accompany her, mentally thanking Heaven that the Staff uniform of ceremony (in which the Baron suggested his victim should array himself) had been left behind in the Rue de Bac.

If the four stout, long-maned, and amply-tailed nags attached to the barouche had not proved pink-eyed and cream-colored; if the vehicle itself had not been so conspicuously yellow; if the blue-and-scarlet livery of the coachman and the brace of badly-matching footmen, who hung to the back-straps and occupied the board behind, had been less tawdry and belaced with grease; if the red-nosed elderly outriders had not been so obviously bemused with potent liquor, and their beasts less spavined, broken-kneed and cracked in wind, that so-called progress through the capital of his ancestors' hereditary principality might have proved less intolerable to the unlucky scion of their race. But with Köhler and von Steyregg on the front seat, both bare-headed and bare-toothed, oozing with respect and deference, the Baron's bosom heaving with loyal enthusiasm beneath the metal starfish previously described; some luckless subject of mediæval justice newly flayed, and paraded upon the hangman's cart for the popular obloquy, might have felt as raw and smarting as did Dunoisse.

A straggling cortège of beggars, spectacle-hunters, servant-maids in their high crimped caps and silver breast-chains, loafers and idlers of both sexes accompanied the yellow barouche. Vocal dogs and an Italian organ-grinder with a pair of monkeys brought up the rear of this motley following. Every now and then von Steyregg would plunge his hand into a stout linen bag, which he nursed upon his knees, and scatter small change among these gentry. You may imagine this largesse received with yells, cheers, and scrambling. Black eyes and gory noses were distributed at each fresh shower.

The Town Hall and the Museum, occupying an entire side of the Market Place, the Church of the Pied Friars, and the Tower of the Clock with its life-sized brazen woman spinning at the top of the weathercock, occupied but passing notice from the distinguished visitors. The yellow barouche, with its huzzaing tail of ragamuffins, breasted the State Street, while the holiday strollers that thronged the sidewalks stood still to stare, and heads were projected from upper windows. And reaching the Cathedral Square that crowned the hilltop, the noble party alighted at the west porch of the stately building and passed in.

Not for years had Dunoisse set foot across the threshold of the House of God; the cult of devotion and worship, the high belief in glorious things unseen, the fulfillment of the obligations of the Catholic faith, had long ceased to be indispensable or even necessary to the man; he looked back upon the piety and fervor of his boyhood with a wonder that was largely mingled with contempt. Now, as he mechanically dipped two fingers in the miniature font that was supported by a sculptured shield bearing the casque with the *panache*, surmounted by the sable heron of Widinitz, made the Sign of the Cross, and bent the knee before the solemn splendors of the High Altar—gleaming upon the vision from the distant end of the huge echoing nave—he glanced at Henriette in wonder at the contained and modest reverence of her demeanor; and, seeing her sink down gracefully amidst her whispering flounces and bow her lovely head as though in adoration, felt the muscles of his lips twitch with the ironical desire to smile.

"Wonderful!" he thought, more nearly approaching to a critical analysis of her than he had ever permitted himself. "Whether she believes or not, she never dispenses with the outward observance of religion! She is an enigma, a problem to baffle Œdipus! One would say she and not the son of my mother had Carmel in the blood!"

For how strangely amorous license and devotional fervor commingled in the nature of this woman, who should know better than this man....

How often, waking in the perfumed, darkened chamber from the deep, dreamless slumber that falls on the indulged and satiate senses, had not Dunoisse found himself alone, and realized, with a creeping chill of awe mingled with repugnance, that she was kneeling, a white-robed figure veiled in shadowy hair, before the ivory Crucifix that hung above the *prie-dieu*, praying....

Ah! with what abandonment of sighs and sobs, and tears!... Ere she would rise, traverse the velvet carpet silently as some pale moonray, and glide, mysteriously smiling, into her lover's arms.

"Why should I not pray?" she had said to him once. "After all, Christ died for sinners, and I am a sinner.... And even devils believe, they say. It is only men who deny!"

Dunoisse had long joined the ranks of the deniers. He had determined that for him yonder shining, jeweled tabernacle should thenceforth house no Unspeakable Mystery, shelter no Heavenly Guest. Nothing beyond an amiable superstition, an innocent, exquisite myth, embodying a profound religious truth for two hundred and sixty millions of Christians; modified or rejected by the Lutheran, Reformed, and Presbyterian Churches; ignored by Confucianist, Taoist, and Buddhist, abhorred by the Hindu, the Mohammedan, and the Jew, should henceforth be enshrined there. He had come to the conclusion that it was better so.

The light of faith had been quenched in the man's heart by his own deliberate act of will. He had said to his soul, unwitting that he had thus spoken:

"If I believed, could I continue to live as I am doing, storing up sharp retribution, dreadful expiation, inconceivable anguish for the world to come? Not so! Therefore I will forget such words as Death and Judgment. For these poignant, embittered, passing joys, I am content to barter the hope of eternal bliss."

And yet, upon those rare occasions when, as now, Dunoisse found himself in the House of his Maker, the still air, fragrant with the incense of the most recent Sacrifice, oppressed him, and the very silence seemed eloquent as a voice of Divine reproach....

For you may slough your skin of State-patronized, easy-going Protestantism as easily as you can change your political convictions, and presently, with Modern Buddhism, or Spiritualism, or Platonism, Christian Science, Agnosticism, Mormonism, or Hedonism, be covered and clad anew, but Catholicism penetrates the bones, and permeates the very marrow. You cannot pluck that forth; it is rooted in the fibers of the soul.

Dunoisse followed his Fate up the great echoing nave of the Cathedral, ushered by the gyrating von Steyregg. Penitents of both sexes, waiting their turn in lengthy rows outside the occupied confessionals, glanced up from their beads, as, in a whisper that rattled amidst the carved rafters of the lofty roof, the agent announced:

"Here lie Your Serene Highness's illustrious forefathers!" And ostentatiously dried his sympathetic tear with a vast flapping handkerchief of Isabella hue.

Certainly the sacred fane was populous with departed von Widinitz, from Albertus I., First of the Line, and his spouse, the chaste Philippina; to Ludovicus, the latest departed, whose Bathildis had predeceased him by a generation or two.

You saw them represented from life-size to the quarter-bust, in brass, bronze, lead, marble, porphyry, granite, alabaster—every conceivable medium known to sepulchral Art. And to Dunoisse's peculiar torment, those tricksy sprites, von Steyregg and Köhler, united in discovering between the cast or sculptured countenances of these worthies and the moody visage of their harassed descendant resemblances of the striking kind. To hear the knaves appeal to one another—warrant, justify, and approve the claim of a thirteenth-century nose to its modern reproduction—to witness them scouring aisles or rummaging chapels in full cry after a chin, or mouth, or ear, or forehead; to see them run the elusive feature from metal or stone to living earth; and congratulate one another on the fortunate issue of the chase; would have provoked a smile on the countenance of a Trappist. Their sacrifice laughed even whilst he writhed.

The ceremony of leaving cards upon the Archbishop of Widinitz followed. A trap-mouthed, blue-shaven ecclesiastic of the humbler sort, who wore a bunch of keys at the girdle of his well-darned cassock, opened the oaken, iron-studded door, and took the proffered oblongs of pasteboard without enthusiasm, intimating that His Lordship did not receive strangers upon days of solemn retreat. With this janitor von

Steyregg parleyed vainly, maintaining a brisk exchange of arguments at the top of the Palace doorsteps, whilst his principals waited at the bottom in the yellow barouche.

A sportive Fate at this juncture breaks the thread of the narrative with a Pantomime Interlude. For as, more in sorrow than in anger at the obstinacy of the janitor, the Baron shook off his tear upon the inhospitable threshold, and turned upon his heel—a little white-headed, berry-brown urchin—a bare-legged messenger, arrayed in a tattered shirt and the upper half of a pair of adult breeches, carrying a reed-basket in which reposed a fine, fat, silvery trout, newly-caught and tempting,—dived between the legs that so strikingly resembled balusters, and dodged into the Palace with a flourish of dirty heels.

If a portly Magyar of noble rank, in the act of rolling down a steepish flight of limestone steps, could possibly be regarded as a mirth-provoking object, one might be tempted to smile as von Steyregg, recording each revolution upon his person with grievous bumps and bruises, performed the horizontal descent. Henriette screamed, Köhler beat his bosom, the tag-rag and bobtail roared with glee, while Dunoisse, compelled to share in their amusement despite the sickness at his heart, jumped out of the carriage and picked up the groaning Baron, restored him his battered curly-brimmed hat, the comb, hairbrush, and piece of soap which had escaped from his coat-tails in the course of transit, thrust him into the vehicle, and bade the coachman return to "The Three Crowns."

LVIII

What the Father Economus said when he found the grocer's billet under the red-spotted trout we may not hear. How the Archbishop received the warning must be equally a matter of conjecture. Hasten on to the smarting conclusion of the Day of Disgrace that dawned so fairly, that shone so brightly, that promised such a harvest to those who failed to mark how upon the southwest horizon huge formless ramparts of blue black cumuli were steadily building, while faint mutterings of distant thunder presaged the breaking of the storm....

The four adventurers had supped together upon the best the inn could furnish. Now, seated at ease about the relics of the banquet, in the dining-room of the private suite occupied by His Serene Highness and Her Excellency, they discussed the Plan of Campaign. Fragrant vapors of choicest Habanas enhaloed them, by permission of Her Excellency, who held between her exquisite lips a Turkish cigarette. And as they smoked and talked, the contents of a capacious China Bowl of Maraschino Punch (compounded by Köhler, who was a clever hand at such delicious chemistry) sank lower, inch by inch....

You may picture Steyregg, revived by much food and a great deal of liquor; his cuts and scratches plastered with diachylum, the Alpine summit of his bald occiput adorned by a compassionate chambermaid with patches of brown-paper steeped in vinegar, retained in place by a linen bandage of turban-shape, reading from a folio sheet of coarsely printed rag-paper, blackened with ancient Gothic capitals (and filched from where it had fluttered, held by a pin, upon one of the notice-boards exposed in the porch of the Cathedral), the Programme for the following day.

"We begin," he boomed, after much preliminary throat-scraping, "by Your Serene Highness's permission—if the Herr Attorney-Oath-Commissioner will snuff the candles I shall be able to see better!—we begin with Deputations from the various Trades-bands and Companies of Handi-craftsmen carrying banners.... Follow...."

The gross man expanded his chest, and rolled out:

"The Charity-Children of both sexes, the boys carrying green branches, the girls bouquets of flowers. Succeed....

"Confraternities of Sodalists, male and female, headed by Persons on Horseback in Roman and Silesian costumes, representing St. Lawrence with his gridiron and St. Hyacinth with his ax.

"A triumphal Car, with a Tableau of St. Helena in Roman Imperial Habit, instructing St. Macarius, Bishop of Jerusalem, where to Dig for the Relic of the True Cross....

"The Four Mendicant Orders of Religious of both sexes, with tapers.

"The Boys of the Dominican Orphanage bearing tapers.

"The Girls of the Carmelite School strewing flowers.

"The Image of Our Lady of the Assumption, attended by Sisters of the Order of the Immaculate Heart."

Dunoisse started in his chair. A burning heat raced through him, and yet he shivered, oppressed by a deadly sickness of the soul.

"The Secular Clergy," read von Steyregg, and cleared his throat. "The Archbishop and Chapter. The Sacred Canopy, borne by six Noble Officers of the Garrison in Full Uniform."...

Dunoisse, with an ashen face, rose up at the foot of the table.... It had been revealed to him as by a lightning-flash, over what a bottomless abyss he hung.... Henriette appeared to notice nothing.... von Steyregg pursued:

"In this unhappy document, Madame, I have suggested an alteration. As here provided, the Mayor and Corporation, the Garrison—in uniform of review—with the towns-people, peasants, children, and beggars were to have brought up the rear of the procession. But my amendment (forwarded in writing to the Archbishop, since that prelate has rudely closed his doors against us), is, that His Lordship and the Chapter should be followed by— grant but a moment!—I will set it down...."

He sucked a black-lead pencil, scrawled on the wide margin of the official programme, and read as he scrawled:

"His Serene Highness, Hector-Marie-Aymont, Prince-Aspirant of Widinitz, carrying a taper, and attended by the *Wohlgeboren* Herr Attorney-and-Oath-Commissioner Ottilus Köhler, and the *Hochwohlgeboren* Herr Baron, Rodobald Siegfridus Theodore von Steyregg, Knight of the Most Pious Order of Saint Emmerich." He added, blowing like a seal, and mopping his great moist countenance with a crumpled table-napkin:

"Take the word of a Magyar nobleman, Your Serenity, that taper of yours will have cooked the Regent Luitpold's goose for him, all being said and done!"

But His Serene Highness, who had dropped heavily back into the chair, was leaning upon his folded arms, staring with an air of deep abstraction at the polished surface of the dessert-covered mahogany, and might have heard or not.

"Dull dog that you are, my Prince!" said von Steyregg mentally, "this charming Eve of yours is worth a million of you. Were she Princess-Aspirant of this phlegmatic State, it would be a hop, skip and jump into the saddle. With you, had you not a Steyregg at your elbow—*Ps'sst!*—the whole adventure would fizzle off like a damp squib—I would bet my head on it! Now, what picture you are gaping at—with your eyes fixed and your jaw dropping—I would give this glass of punch to know."

He tossed it off with a flourish and a wink at his rat-faced confederate. The flourish, the wink, were lost upon Dunoisse.

For as a hanging man may see, in the last struggles of asphyxia, the dreadful details of the crime that led to his execution limned in lifelike action and color on the swirling fire-shot blackness, so rose before the mental vision of the son of Marie-Bathilde a picture of the Cathedral, with the great procession of the morrow—headed by the white-robed bearer of the Crucifix, amidst wafts of incense and intoned Litanies, rolling down the nave of the Cathedral and out through its west door upon the streets.

Ah! was Henriette deaf, that she did not hear the chanting voices, and the slow, measured tread of the lay folk, and religious, and the pattering footsteps of the children, as, with reverent demeanor and hushed, rapt faces they moved before or followed the image of the Mother of God?

Did she not see the Canopy of wrought cloth-of-gold, adorned with tassels of pearls, fringed with innumerable little golden bells that tinkled as its bearers bore it onwards? Was she blind to the Figure that stumbled along in its shelter, robed in white linen, bloodstained and torn and dusty, bending almost double under a Cross of roughly-shaped timbers, and wearing a Crown of Thorns?...

The haggard black eyes sought hers in desperate interrogation. But Henriette was dreamily playing with a silver fruit-knife as she listened to von Steyregg. Her own eyes were hidden under their long lashes; her face told no tale, as the intolerable voice of the agent trumpeted:

"As regards a favorable answer from this arrogant prelate, Your Excellency, I will guarantee it within the hour—or two—having, in His Serene Highness's name, as his business-representative, undertaken that compliance with his desires will be made profitable in the pecuniary sense by a donation of One Thousand Thalers to the Restoration Fund of the Cathedral. Ahem!"

He winked his left eye, which the sliding turban threatened to extinguish, folded up the official programme and threw it on the table, saying:

"This reading dries the throat consumedly. With Her Highness's—I mean with Madame's permission, I will take another drop of punch!"

He filled a bumper and proposed a toast: "To the Success of The Adventure!"

Köhler drank the sentiment with enthusiasm. Henriette sipped, smiling at her moody lover, who pushed his glass away. And a resonant, cultured voice said from the doorway:

"Permit me to beg pardon of the company for having entered unannounced!"

The heads of the adventurers turned as by a single impulse. The landlord, who had knocked unheard, and ushered in a stranger under cover of the toast-drinking, was seen to be posed, in an attitude of rigid respect, beyond the threshold. The person who had spoken, a short priest with singularly bright gray eyes shining out of a pale, thin-featured face;—who was wrapped, despite the sultry heat of August, in a voluminous and shabby black cloak, and did not seem at all embarrassed,—was standing just within the door.

He said, and the great volume of his voice seemed to fill the room and flow outwards through the French windows that opened upon a stone balcony overhanging the Market Place:

"May it be understood that I am here as the mouthpiece of the Archbishop of Widinitz?... May I presume that I shall be patiently listened to?... I will be as brief as is compatible with clearness. Pray remain seated, all of you. No, sir, I am obliged!..."

For Henriette had risen languidly and curtsied deeply. Von Steyregg had hoisted himself to those baluster-shaped legs of his. Köhler had got up with his mouth full of almonds and raisins: and Dunoisse, with the polished grace that distinguished him, was offering the little priest his chair.

The ecclesiastic scanned the dark, handsome face and the soldierly, muscular, supple figure with a degree of kindliness. He said, as he waved the offered seat away:

"What I have to say, Colonel Dunoisse, will be best said standing. Your intention to visit this town was not previously notified to the Archbishop. He was not consulted in the matter of your intentions and views. Otherwise you might have been spared the commission of a grievous error, which cannot but create antagonism, prejudice, and contempt in the minds of those whom you would most desire to ingratiate———"

He broke off, for von Steyregg smote upon the table, and bellowed, while the decanters and glasses jingled, peaches hopped from the center dish, and the thumper's turban fell off and rolled under the board:

"'Contempt,' sir, is not a word to be used in connection with His Serene Highness. I, Rodobald von Steyregg, Baron and Knight of the Sublime Order of St. Emmerich, protest against its use!"

Having protested, Steyregg dived for his turban, replaced it on his head, and snorted defiance. The small pale priest regarded him with a faint, lurking smile, and said calmly:

"Sir, the Archbishop received a letter from you this evening. I am charged with the answer to the document herewith."

He turned to Dunoisse and continued:

"Colonel Dunoisse, the fact of your near alliance by blood with the reigning House of Widinitz is incontestable and undeniable. Did not the Salic law obtain in this principality, upon you would undoubtedly devolve the Hereditary Crown."

His great voice seemed to be a palpable presence in the room. While he spoke, not by any means at the full pitch of it, the wires of a spinet that stood against the wall vibrated audibly; and the crystal pendants on the chandeliers and mantel-vases tinkled with a gentle musical sound. While another sound, of which Dunoisse had been faintly conscious for some time, and which might have been the muttering of distant thunder; or the humming of innumerable bees; or the purring of a cat of Brobdingnagian proportions, was stilled as though the unknown forces that combined to cause it had caught an echo of the powerful tones, and held their peace to listen.

As the priest went on:

"Undoubtedly, but the fundamental law as it stands strictly excludes the female line and the males derived from it. And were it possible to change this law, even at the eleventh hour, I am deputed to say to you that the procedure would be strenuously opposed *by the person who would in that event stand as the direct dynastic successor to the hereditary authority!*"

"My mother!"

Dunoisse, through whom the words had darted with a shock and thrill resembling the discharge from an electric battery, thrust from him the chair on which he had hitherto indifferently leaned, and turned upon the speaker a face that had suddenly grown sharp and pinched, saying in a voice that was curiously flat and toneless:

"You are in communication with my mother, sir? You have been deputed by her to say this to me?"

The priest bowed assent, and continued calmly:

"For, though it be true that the Almighty, in His Infinite wisdom, has chastened us Catholics of Widinitz by placing over us a sovereign of the Reformed Faith; and, though we cannot but deplore the rigor with which the Regent has treated certain communities of religious hitherto resident in the principality; we are bound to own that in other respects we have been treated with clemency and justice. In addition, the domestic life of our Regent is free from scandal...."

Dunoisse's ears burned like fire. The little priest's great voice went on:

"We recognize in His Serene Highness a chaste spouse, a wise father, a prudent governor. How ill-advised should we be to prefer to a ruler such as this a bad Catholic, an individual whose personal history affords a lamentable example of ungoverned passions; who, dead to all sense of shame, blazons his infamy before the eyes of the conscientious and the decent——"

Dunoisse interrupted, saying with stiff lips:

"May I take it that these personalities are leveled at myself?"

The little priest returned, with extraordinarily quiet dignity:

"The rebuke, Colonel Dunoisse, is meant for you. I do not deal in personalities."

He added, in a voice that sent keen, icy thrills coursing down the spines of his listeners:

"The Archbishop replies to the proposal contained in your agent's letter emphatically in the negative. He says to you, Colonel Dunoisse, with the voice that speaks to you now: 'You have offered us a price in money for the privilege of participating in the morrows procession. You have not scrupled to present yourself as a partaker in the solemnities of our Blessed Lady's

Festival. You shrink not at the thought of approaching Him Who is borne beneath the Sacred Canopy, unconfessed, unabsolved—in a state of deadly sin. Shameless, unabashed, you would display yourself to the scandal of Christ's servants, accompanied by the partner of your lamentable errors—with your acknowledged mistress, the unfaithful wife of another, flaunting by your side!"

Henriette, pale as death, leaped up from her seat as a woman might who had swallowed some deadly alkaloid. Dumbly, as though the poison veritably stiffened her muscles, she writhed, fighting for speech—wrenching at the velvet ribbon that confined her swelling throat.

"You!—you!—you hear these insults?" she at last stammered, pointing a quivering hand at Dunoisse, whom the words seemed to have deprived of the powers of speech and motion. "Are you deaf, sir, that such things are spoken, and you stand there silent as one of those statues in the Cathedral? Are you dumb or paralyzed that you do not order this man to leave my presence? Cannot you see," she raved, "that this is no messenger from the Archbishop? Some fanatical priest,—some presumptuous secretary,—has dared—has——! Just Heaven!—if my husband had been here, he would have thrown the creature from the room!"

But Dunoisse remained speechless and frozen, under the fiery torrent of her upbraidings. It was von Steyregg who, in absence of any demonstration from his principal, seized his opportunity to be effective and picturesque. He strode haughtily to the door, and, opening it, turned with majesty to the intruder, trumpeting:

"With your person, sir, respecting your cloth as I abhor your sentiments, I will not soil my fingers. But unless you instantly remove yourself from these apartments, private to His Serene Highness and Her Excellency, I will—I will ring for the landlord and have you carried out and put upon the street!"

"That could hardly be," said the little gray priest mildly, "for I am the Archbishop of Widinitz...."

He showed one lean finger outside the folds of the shabby cloak. Upon the digit a great sapphire gleamed darkly.... And a silence of unspeakable consternation fell upon the conspirators, that was suddenly broken by a half-brick, deftly thrown, that crashed through a pane of one of the French windows, shivered a crystal chandelier full of twinkling wax-lights that hung above the supper-table; and plopped into the punch-bowl, dispersing shivers of Oriental ware and gouts of fragrant liquor into every corner of the room....

LIX

The crash broke the spell that clogged Dunoisse's faculties. He cried out in savage anger, and tore open the swinging, splintered window, and dashed out upon the balcony, stopping short in sheer astonishment at the spectacle he beheld below.

For the vast white square of the Market Place, that was centered by four crystal, springing fountains, and backed by an August sunset of pale green and clear rose and glorious flaming orange-red, was full of heads of women and men, some bare, some covered, so closely packed that an acrobat might have walked on them without leaping a single gap. And the faces belonging to those Teutonic heads and the vari-colored glittering eyes enameled in all the faces, were intent upon the room to which belonged the window with the shattered pane. And at the sight of Dunoisse the vast assembly sent out its breath as at a single hissing expiration:

"*S's ss!*"

Beyond that, nothing more. But the very restraint of the vast crowd was worse than sinister. Plainly these lumpish Teutons were not there to waste valuable time in threats. Their silence menaced and appalled beyond all Gallic yells and execrations. And as Dunoisse stood speechless, staring down into all those tigerish eyes, a strong thin hand gripped his shoulder, and the Archbishop's voice said in his ear:

"You witness the terrible effect of your own insane rashness—the sacrilegious presumption of your agents...! Present yourself upon the streets to-morrow—attempt to join in the procession—and the people will tear you to shreds! Be silent! I will speak to them!"

He plucked Dunoisse back into the room with one imperative hand, unhooking the shabby black cloak with the other. He shook it deftly from his shoulders, removed his soft felt hat, threw it aside, and stepped out upon the balcony, revealed as a small slight figure in a worn black cassock, red-piped, red-buttoned, and sashed, his high-domed baldish head covered with a purple skull-cap, the sacred symbol hanging by its golden chain upon his breast. And at the sight of him a change came over all those waiting faces, and a feline purr of satisfaction came from the great crowd.

The Archbishop said, in a mild and gentle tone, addressing the assemblage:

"My children, we are not ignorant of the cause of this demonstration. You are gathered here to protest, by force if necessary, against what justly appears to you a sacrilege of the most flagitious kind——"

In every attentive face there showed upon the instant a gaping hole. A roar of assent responded that shattered the leaping columns of the Market Place fountains into a rain of glittering fragments. Scared doves rose in bevies from the housetops, wheeling in circles under the rose-flushed sunset sky. The Archbishop went on, in a voice of astonishing resonance and power:

"My children, be at peace! No indignity such as you have had reason to fear will be offered to the Divine Presence of Our Lord in the Most Blessed Sacrament, or to the Immaculate Virginity of His Holy Mother!"

He lifted his hand.

"Therefore, I say to you, profane not the Eve of the Feast with violence! Disperse without casting one other stone. Be assured, Colonel von Widinitz-Dunoisse will not walk in the procession unless in a state of soul conducive to edification. I bid you now go home!"

The Archbishop might have been obeyed, but that a lean tall man in seedy black, with burning cavernous eyes in a lean, parched, yellow face, leaped up upon the bronze balustrade of one of the Market Place fountains, and cried, in a voice that cracked like a breaking stick:

"He has scattered money among you, and some of you have stooped to gather it! For shame! Do you not know whence those accursed coins were taken? Then I will tell you. From the dowry of the Carmelite Sister Thérèse de Saint-François! From the funds of the House of Mercy over whose closed doors the ivy is growing! From the Treasury of Christ!... Then hurl back the defiled and tainted coins with contempt and indignation! Drive forth the thief's son with his harlot! Purge the town of them! Kill—a-a-a!"

The lean man threw up his hands at this juncture, and fell back frothing in epilepsy. But he had spoken words that had the effect of oil poured upon a slackened furnace. The hubbub of voices that ensued reduced even the Archbishop to dumb show. Stones began to fly, no longer leveled at the room behind the balcony, where the high-domed head and pale, worn profile of the prelate were descried, as he parleyed with the unwished-for visitors.... The lower windows suffered attack; and with the larger missiles came hopping the coppers and silver bits that had been scattered from Steyregg's bag. Those who grudged parting most threw hardest of all.... The crash and tinkle of breaking glass went on until every window-frame in the frontage of "The Three Crowns" presented a central void befringed with splinters—until the landlord, hysterical with loss, rushed out bareheaded into the Market Place, and, falling upon his knees, solemnly swore that if the work of destruction did but cease, the loathed intruders should then and there depart from his house.

His piercing accents reached the beleaguered garrison in the room behind the balcony.... The Archbishop turned to Dunoisse, and said, slightly shrugging his shoulders:

"Compliance will be your only possible course."

Dunoisse was about to expostulate, but Henriette panted at her lover's ear:

"Yes!—let us go from this dreadful place! Oh!—mad that I was to have set my foot in it!"

Then Dunoisse rang the bell. With its broken rope in his hand, he shouted to the scared and chalk-faced waiter:

"Bring the bill! Order both carriages! Instantly! Do you hear?"

The affrighted man gasped out:

"Sir, they are ready!"

And almost instantly, as it seemed, the green chariot and the brown landau, horsed, and heaped with unlocked and unpacked portmanteaux, empty valises, and the garments and articles of toilet that these had contained, were rattled out of the posting-yard and brought to the front-door of "The Three Crowns."

No bill appeared. The banknotes and gold Dunoisse would have thrust upon the landlord the man refused, perhaps out of conscientiousness, perhaps in fear of further damage to his property.... Throwing the money down upon the table, Dunoisse grasped his hat and cane, and offered his arm to Henriette. She placed her little hand upon it, and shrank in terror as a savage, ominous growl came from the angry throng outside.

"They shall not harm you!" Dunoisse muttered between his teeth, and urged her forwards.

"They will not harm you, Madame!" the Archbishop said, who had quitted the room a moment previously, and now returning, gravely offered his own arm to Henriette upon the other side. She cast him a swimming, eloquent look of reproach that said: "My touch pollutes,—you yourself have said it!" Then, as another growl came from the Market Place, she gulped her resentment down, and set her little frightened clutch upon the red-piped cassock-sleeve....

And so, protected by the Church that had denounced her, Henriette went forth, her livid lover bulwarking her frail charms upon the other side. At sight of her it was as if the great cattish crowd crouched before springing. It wagged from side to side, and the eyes in it flickered yellow and green. But the blood-thirst that parched those hot and savage throats was checked when the red-buttoned black cassock and high domed head were recognized by her side. The crowd fell back into its former stolid immobility, and Dunoisse opened the carriage-door, instead of the shrinking hostler, and the Archbishop handed in Madame de Roux, and, to the astonishment of all, followed her. Dunoisse took his seat in the vehicle at a sign from the prelate, who then gave the postillions—who had slewed round in their great boots, the better to view a sight so unusual—the signal to move on....

And then, at a walking pace, through a lane that continually opened in the great mass of grim-faced people, and as continually closed behind the green chariot and the brown landau—containing only the scared valet and the quaking maid—(the Marshal's agents having mysteriously disappeared), both vehicles passed through the Market Place, down the Promenade, and rolled under the portcullis of the Peace Gate. Only when their wheels resounded on the gravel-covered drawbridge did the Archbishop give the signal to pull up. Bareheaded, Dunoisse lent aid to his descent, stammering out some broken phrases of gratitude.

"Sir, I have done no more," said the Archbishop, "than was enjoined on me by my calling and profession. See to the lady, who has suffered much alarm. And—I have not yet given you the message from your mother. She has a dispensation to receive you. She will expect you at dark, at the Convent of the Carmelites in the Old Town. It must be reached by a different route, but that need not concern you.... Put up for the night at 'The Heron' posting-house, fourteen miles from here; you will remember the inn—you passed it on your journey. I have sent on a servant with swift horses in advance of you,—you will mount and ride back with the man; he will guide you in perfect safety! As for Madame, you need be under no apprehension—the landlord of 'The Heron' is a trustworthy person.... Dear me! What have we here? How truly deplorable a spectacle!"... Was there a twinkle of amusement in the bright gray eyes that regarded it?... "These two gentlemen who approach in such haste," said the Archbishop, "I take to be those members of your party who preferred to remain behind!"

Despite the water that dripped from their garments, proving them to have been ducked in one of the fountains of the Market Place, and the adhering filth that proved them to have been subsequently rolled in the kennel, the two bounding figures were recognizable as Köhler and von Steyregg. For—having concealed themselves in the cellar of "The Three Crowns," with the intention of remaining there *perdu* until darkness should favor their departure from Widinitz—the confederates had been discovered amongst the vats and barrels by a hireling; plucked thence and, thrust by the maddened landlord and his willing servitors forth upon the pavement, but a few minutes after the departure of the Colonel and Madame....

You saw the pair, running the gauntlet of thumps, buffets, clouts, and whacks, down the lane that kept opening in the crowd in front of them and closing up behind.... The suggestion of a citizen that they should be tumbled into the city fosse met with some approval, but the majority were against the proceeding. In that case the Archbishop might have intervened, instead of taking snuff and looking the other way....

The fugitives gained the rear carriage, and leaped in, each at a door, the impromptu harlequinade provoking roars of laughter. Neither had a hat, or breath to lavish. Steyregg had parted with an entire coat-tail. His Order was missing from its soiled, watered ribbon—a loss which caused him infinite torment. Köhler was collarless and bleeding from the nose.

The accommodation offered by "The Heron" posting-house, upon the forest-road fourteen miles from Widinitz, subsequently appeared to both the worthies too near the city to be healthy. Therefore, without taking formal leave of His Serene Highness or Her Excellency (so lately the recipients of their heartfelt homage), the Baron and the attorney hired a post-chaise; and, racked by grievous bodily aches and pains, it may be conjectured, as well as twinges spiritual and mental, pushed upon the road to France.

"And so," said von Steyregg, upon the day that saw the return of the precious pair to Paris, "because of Prince Cocky-Locky's *béguin* for Madame Henny-Penny, a plot of the first order is fudged, dished, and done for. Devil take the woman!"

Köhler returned, straightening a brand-new paper collar with a conquering air:

"She is a *chic* type, so no doubt he would be agreeable. Which of us is to tell Old Fireworks of the fiasco? That will have to be done!"

Von Steyregg retorted irritably:

"Tell—tell! Why the deuce are you so set on telling? Will he stump up a single shiner, once he knows of the mess?"

Köhler made a neat circle with his left thumb and forefinger, and winked through it. Both men, it will be perceived, had left their graceful phrases and courtly manners behind in Widinitz, with Köhler's original paper collar and his partner's left coat-tail. To the mute admission of the wink, von Steyregg returned:

"Very well, then! We have made a bit out of this—at least, you have——"

Köhler interpolated:

"Go it!"

"I am going to go it," said von Steyregg blandly. "I have not seen my native Hungary for a long time, and the heart of the true Magyar, even amidst the most beauteous scenes of foreign countries, ceaselessly yearns for home. Impart the news of the disaster to Monseigneur if you feel disposed to be kicked!—or leave the too-painful duty to his puppy of a son!"

He turned, revealing an aching void where there had been a coat-tail.

"Tell me one thing before you hurry back to your native Hungary, you yearning Magyar," said Köhler brutally. "Who was it kiss-kissed the people of Widinitz on to break the windows of the inn of 'The Three Crowns,' frighten Madame de Roux into hysterics, provoke Monsieur the Colonel into a display of determination, duck both of us in one of the public fountains, and toss me in a horse-blanket? For all his mealy mouth, *I* say the Archbishop!"

Von Steyregg said, rolling a bloodshot eye in rapture:

"Undoubtedly, the Archbishop! Assuredly, the Archbishop!" He heaved an elephantine sigh. "With a confederate like that priest to back me, I could break the bank of every gambling-hell in Europe. What a waste that he should be an honest man! *Au revoir*, dear friend! You shall visit me at my baronial castle in beloved Hungary, as sure as I am a Magyar of the pure blood!"

"Farewell for ever, old comrade!" said Köhler, with emotion, as he hailed a passing cab.

LX

That wild night-ride through the beech-forest back to Widinitz, and the interview with his mother at the Convent of the Carmelites, was ever to Dunoisse the most unreal, the most strange of all those adventures that seemed as though woven upon the loom of Sleep.

He remembered his lost mother as so tall—yet, when the dark woolen curtains hanging behind the double grating that halved the Convent parlor had been drawn back, revealing the two brown-robed, black-veiled figures—the shape that had put its veil aside with a little, shrunken hand, and called him by his name—had appeared to be barely above the stature of a child.

Not in the haggard, ashen-gray face, closely framed in the conventual folds of white linen—its features pinched and drawn, its eyes almost extinguished as though with constant weeping—was there anything left that recalled in the remotest degree the lovely, beloved mother of the old, unforgotten days....

Only the voice, so soaked with tears, so changed from that of her son's remembrance, retained tones that well-nigh wrought Dunoisse to a wild outbreak of weeping, though sometimes in the dim and sunken eyes there shone a transient ray of the dear light of old.

If she had shrieked, it would have pierced the heart less than her immobile and rigorous quiescence. Yet her trembling could not be controlled by any act of will. Between the visitor who stood upon one side of the double grille, and the brown-robed, black-veiled figure seated upon the other, a current of hot air might have been rising, the shape so quivered and vibrated and shuddered before his eyes.

Ah! could he have realized the wild conflict of emotions surging under the white *guimpe* and the coarse brown habit.... But if the weak body of Sister Térèse de Saint François was shaken as a reed, her determination was immovable; her word was not to be gainsaid.

Never, never!—though the Plenum of the Federative Council should throw all its "Ayes!" into the scale that confirmed the females of the house of Widinitz and their heirs in the dynastic succession, would the nun-Princess consent to her son's occupying the throne.

Saying the word so softly in her threadlike, feeble voice, her "Never!" reared between Hector and the hereditary dignities a Titanic wall of rock, that no tempered tool might pierce, no fulminate shatter and blast.

So it was quashed and ended, the vexed question of the Claim of Succession. And Dunoisse drew breath with almost a sensation of relief. Of reproach there was not a shadow in her voice or expression. She had not heard—possibly she had not heard?—that her son had not lacked a companion on his journey. Those scathing reproaches of the Archbishop's were not to be voiced again by Sister Térèse. She spoke of the Marshal—asked of his health? Their son felt himself flushing guiltily in the sheer inability to reply with authority. Who knew less of Achille Dunoisse, well or ill, jaundiced or jovial, gouty or in good fettle, than the son he had begotten? Tardy Conscience, waking from a nodding sleep in the saddle, dug both spurs rowel-deep in Dunoisse's smart sides. His eyes shunned the sunken eyes that questioned with such desperate eagerness, belying the sparse, meager utterance, the carefully colorless tone. He stammered a conventional reply.

"You will give him a message from me, when you return to him," she said, and dropped the faded curtains of her eyelids between them.... "Tell him that I who know him to be infinitely generous and noble at heart"—Dunoisse barely restrained a start of incredulous surprise at the new idea of nobility in connection with the Marshal—"tell him that I was never led by any act of his to doubt the disinterestedness of his regard. And say to him, that what he wildly dreams may one day be brought about, cannot and will not! That in the parched and dried-up skeleton you have seen here at the Convent there is no beauty left to covet. Entreat of him to think of his wife and your mother as one who has passed forever beyond the gates of this world.... For I have chosen to be dead whilst living," said the thread-thin, trembling voice, "that by the Divine Mercy not only I, but others—may not taste of the Death that is eternal." She added, almost inaudibly: "My strength is not great, Hector. I have suffered much lately.... Take my blessing now, and go."

She rose from what was now revealed as a wooden stool, and as her son knelt down before the inexorable grating, she thrust a slender, wasted finger between the iron wires of the lattice, and lightly traced the Sign of the Cross upon his brow. How its touch thrilled him—the withered little finger that Achille Dunoisse had kissed with such exuberant rapture! Her son would have pressed his lips to it, but that she drew it quickly away. He said in a tone of bitter sadness, for the slight involuntary recoil had wounded:

"Ah!—you do well to shrink from me, my mother!—could you know all!..."

She put up her little shaking hand, and swiftly pulled her close black veil down, and breathed from behind its screen:

"I do know all.... It is not for me to judge you—whose veins were filled from mine...."

"Mother!" broke from Hector hoarsely, for her terrible humility appalled him. It was as though she had bared her scarred shoulders in his sight, and bent her frail strength to the scourge. She silenced him by a gesture, and continued, in a whisper so faint that it barely reached his ears:

"But if you can—atone!"

The veil was lifted, the sunken eyes met Hector's.... What infinite tenderness shone in their dark gray depths. She said, in the voice that fluttered like a cobweb in the wind: "For there is but one road to peace, and that is the Way of Expiation. My feet have stumbled amidst its thorns for many years now.... Farewell! Pray for me! Tell your father I——"

Dunoisse had no more words of her. The little figure had swayed and wavered, the watchful Sister in attendance had stepped forwards and thrown an arm about it and pulled the curtain-rope with her disengaged hand. And the black woolen drapery had fallen, with a rattling of metal rings,—and Dunoisse as he stumbled from the parlor, blinded by rushing tears, knew that he had looked his last, in this world, upon his mother....

But the details of that brief meeting remained as bitten in with acid on the memory of the son. An elderly woman, who served the Sisters as portress of the Convent's outer gate, contributed a touch or two to the unforgettable picture; speaking, in tones of genuinely affectionate reverence, as she guided the stranger, by the light of the evil-smelling tallow candle in her iron lantern, through divers stone-flagged passages previously traversed, of Sister Térèse de Saint François.

"Who has been our Mother Prioress now ten years, and a holier and wiser never ruled the Convent. And how she wept, dear, humble soul! when the decision of the Chapter was made known to her at Vienna. She implored the Mother-General, upon her knees, to spare her the shame of being sent back to rule her superiors in piety and obedience ... but no! it had to be.... Thenceforth—until her strength gave out—the tasks that were too heavy for the most energetic were performed by the Mother-Prioress, who was the weakest of all. And to this day, when compelled to rebuke a sister for a fault, she will first beg her forgiveness; or, when any specially heavy penance will be enjoined upon another by the Father-Director, she will meet such a one as she comes from the confessional and whisper: '*Tell me what it is, so that I may perform it with you!...*' One might truly say our Mother has a zest for mortification, and an appetite for fasting that is never satisfied." The portress, whose rosy cheeks and plump figure testified to a discreet enjoyment of the good things of the world, sighed and shook her black-capped head as she added: "The *gnädiger Herr* knows that Saints are not made without suffering. Our Lord decreed it should be so. And—come the Last Day—if I can catch on to the skirt of our Reverend Mother's habit—I dare to say I shall stand a better chance than most. Good-night, *gnädiger Herr*!—or rather good-morning!—for in another hour it will be day." And the portress curtsied Dunoisse out into the clammy grayness that heralded dawn, and closed and locked and barred the Convent door. And as the stars paled and the wan moon reeled northwards as though sickened at the spectacle of all the deeds that are done by men under Night's sable canopy, Dunoisse and Remorse rode back through the shadowy forest roads, to the inn of "The Heron," where waited Henriette.

She had not been to bed. She had paced the single guest-room of the posting-house all night, waiting in passionate impatience for her lover's return. When she heard his step upon the uncarpeted stair, she ran to the door and opened it, and shut it when he entered; and threw herself before it, and opened the flood-gates of her fury, that had been pent up all those hours....

"So!... You have returned!... I presume I am expected to be grateful! I, who have spent a night of horror in this miserable place with a pair of frightened servants for my sole protectors and companions...."

"Are not von Steyregg and Köhler———?" Dunoisse began. She answered before he had completed the sentence:

"They have taken what conveyance they could procure, and posted on to Paris; and had I been wiser I would have accompanied them.... '*Had I been wiser*' do I say?..." She laughed angrily, plucking at the ribbon of velvet that confined her swelling throat. "One grain of sense would have saved me from the fatal error of accompanying you to that den among the mountains—that hot-bed of bigotry and intolerance—whence we have been—like a pair of lepers!—cast out." Her teeth chattered, she struck her mouth with her little clenched fist as relentlessly as though it had been an enemy's. "But you insisted," she resumed—"I yielded to your persuasions.... Oh!—how hideously I have been repaid!"

His haggard eyes regarded her with a dreadful recollection in them. In her disarray and abandonment—the dishevelled hair, with its drooping curls and loosened coils, the pallor of fatigue that warred with the burnt flush of feverish excitement; the hinted lines and indicated hollows in the passionate, mutinous, changeful face that the merciless daylight revealed as it showed the crumpled silks and soiled laces of the dinner-dress that had been so fresh and dainty a few hours before—she was the Henriette of that morning of his return to Paris—save for the branding mark upon her throat. While in her disillusioned eyes he seemed almost plain, not at all heroic—desperately uninteresting—a poor creature stripped of all his princely garniture.... And she cried, in a voice unlike her own:

"For you have made me blush for you! Why could you not have gone out upon the balcony and spoken to the people? Where were your courage—your manliness—your strength?"

Dunoisse might have answered her: "With you!" but he bowed his head in silence under the lashing hailstorm of her reproaches. The springs of energy were dried up in him; he felt like an old man. She pursued, while her beautiful eyes shot baleful lightnings, and her little teeth gritted savagely:

"How can a woman of spirit love a man who is not manly? You will have yourself to thank for whatever happens now!... Where have you been all this night? What have you done? Into what new kennel of degradation will you next drag me? Or having gone so far, will you abandon your undeniable right, and seek no longer to obtain recognition of your Claim of Succession from the Council of the Federation? That you intend to do so I am quite prepared to hear!"

She paced the painted floor of the meagerly-furnished, bare inn guest-chamber, dragging the woolen rugs awry with her trailing silken flounces, spurning the spotted fawn skins with the toes of her little satin shoes. Dunoisse murmured, as he sank down wearily into the uncomfortable arms of a three-cornered elbow-chair of green-painted pine, upholstered in Berlin-wool cross-stitch, and turned his eyes from her:

"Dearest, my mother has put her veto on the affair—it is for her to decide—and I am bound to respect her wishes." He added, in a breaking voice: "Would to Heaven they had been known to me before!"

"Your mother!—your mother!" she raved. "Is no one to be considered—no one obeyed but she? You fool!—your wife might meekly submit to be thrust aside because of your duty to your mother.... But not your mistress!—not a woman like me!"

She was beside herself—a beautiful fury—her lovely face distorted—her mouth wrung crooked with the bitter flood of invective, insult, upbraiding, that came pouring from it. He rose, and said, in a tone that was hostile and menacing, while the cold light in his black eyes chilled and daunted her:

"When you speak of my mother, Madame, you will do so with consideration, and respect, and reverence. Let that for the future be understood."

She laughed harshly, setting his teeth on edge with a sensation that was sheer loathing of her. She said, shrugging her shoulders, driven on to the verge of self-degradation by her resentment, and her contempt, and her weariness; willing to break her spell over the man forever, if only she might wound him sufficiently deep:

"With all my heart, Monsieur! But at the same time, accord to me a measure of the consideration, respect, and so forth you lavish so abundantly upon Madame there! I may lay claim to it, I fancy.... After all, we are in the same galley; though, let me point out, *I* was not chained to the bench by an irrevocable vow." She added, as Dunoisse stared at her speechlessly: "Good Heavens! it is inconceivable that nobody has ever told you, when people are so malicious! Have you never heard that I was a novice in the Convent of the Vergen de la Soledad at Cartagena when de Roux saw me, and fell in love with me, and begged me to run away with him?..."

A strange sound came from the man's throat. She pursued, cynically smiling in his horror-stricken eyes, playing her little hand as though she held a fan:

"Listen!... My father was killed when I was an infant. My mother died when I was five years old. The Sisters of the Soledad brought me up with the idea that I might perhaps become a religious.... I dreamed of the vocation, and prayed much...." Her pearl-white teeth gleamed between the mocking curves of scarlet. "Then—my dreams changed," she said, "and my prayers became shorter. Except the Chaplain who confessed the nuns and the pupils, and the Bishop who visited us for Confirmations, no man ever set foot inside the Convent walls. Yet we elder girls constantly talked and thought of lovers, from little Dolores, who was twelve and had a hump, to great Carlota, who was seventeen, and ah! so beautiful.... And you may imagine whether or no Henriette had her visions too!... Yet I was quite content to be a nun.... I had had the White Veil of Reception from the Bishop on my sixteenth birthday ... my behavior gave great edification to the Sisters, and his Lordship, and the clergy ... everybody said, *'That young girl will one day become a Saint!'* And one night, a week later, I got over the garden-wall because a band was playing on the Calle Major—I walked down the middle of the great, crowded street, in my little old cast-off black alpaca Convent frock and blue ribbon.... I had left the habit and the White Veil folded on the pillow of my bed.... A French officer accosted me and asked my name. It was Eugéne—I thought him splendid!—perhaps he was—compared with the Bishop, and the Chaplain, and the gardener.... And—I never went back to the Convent of the Soledad. De Roux married me. Another man might have been less honorable.... Perhaps it would have been wiser to have waited, you may think?" She laughed jeeringly. "Some odd chance might have brought you to Cartagena. Some lucky wind might have blown you over the Convent garden-wall!"

The tale was a trumped-up one at least as regards the novice's habit and the White Veil—yet her gift of deception lent it such reality that shame and horror struggled in the heart of the man who heard. To kill her—and himself—was an almost ungovernable impulse, but he drove the nails of his clenched hands deep into their palms, and moved stiffly to the door, and Henriette shrank away.... If he had seized her by the throat,—struck her and cursed her,—marred her beauty with merciless bruises,—stabbed her, even,—he would have won her back again, though only for a time.... But in conquering the mad desire to wreak such brutal vengeance on the woman, he lost her irretrievably.... And so went from her out into the clear morning sunshine, and fled blindly, hunted by all the devils she had roused, into the dew-wet forest, and flung himself face downwards amidst the tall golden bracken at the knees of a graybeard oak that spread its giant boughs and browning foliage as though to afford sanctuary to such hunted, desperate creatures,—and wept, with groans and chokings—what bitter, scalding, shameful tears....

LXI

But he dried them, and controlled himself, and returned to "The Heron" inn, and from thence traveled with his fair companion back to Paris. Some sort of a truce was patched up before the ending of the first day's journey—a week, and Monsieur the Colonel and Madame were upon almost their old terms of familiar, easy intimacy. Returned to Paris, the tenor of the old life was resumed as though the rupture had never happened. But the exquisite glamour of their passion had vanished; the rose-colored mist no longer veiled the crude realities of life. A heavy shadow brooded between the pair, and, gradually assuming substance, thrust them, with every day that dawned, a little farther apart. There would be days when their cooling passion would blaze up again as fiercely as a bonfire of straw.... There would be weeks when their intercourse would be limited to the baldest commonplaces that may be exchanged between a politely-indifferent husband and a civilly-contemptuous wife. The easy-going *camaraderie* that had existed between Henriette and de Roux would never reign between Henriette and her lover. For to attain that level of complete mutual understanding, all rights must be abrogated—the last claim resigned—the last shred of self-respect cast upon the winds. Dunoisse knew that very well.

How much of self-respect remained to him as it was, he did not venture to question. Nor did he own to himself that his life was lived in fear. But sometimes the burnt-in memory of that November night of his return from London would ache and throb, and at other times he would hear the voice of his mistress saying:

"You will have yourself to thank for whatever happens now!"

Do you wonder that a man bedeviled and obsessed after this fashion should grow moody and suspicious? That he should hear the snaky rattle of warning from under every clump of flowers or tuft of grass? That he should see in every man upon whom his lovely friend bestowed her smiles a possible rival? And does it surprise you that, after a succession of violent scenes of jealousy, Henriette should have seized an early opportunity of confiding her disillusions and anxieties to the sympathetic ear at the Élysée?

When it came to stretching a point to oblige a pretty woman, who was useful to him, that woman could depend upon the goodness of Monseigneur.

"Jealousy, dear friend," said he, with his most oracular manner, "is a vice as incurable as crib-biting in a horse, once contracted. It was Othello who ought to have been smothered!... Desdemona would certainly have consoled herself with the attentions of M. Cassio...."

"Ah! but suppose Cassio in his turn had been bitten by the green-eyed monster," suggested Henriette, to whom Dunoisse had read the tragedy of the lady and the Moor.

"To smother Cassio," said Monseigneur, with his somewhat ponderous humor, "would have been what literary critics term an 'anticlimax.' I should suggest service with the Foreign Legion for the gentleman in question,—if you are quite certain that as soon as he has gone you will not wish him back again?"

As Henriette crumpled her beautiful eyebrows in doubt, bit her red lips, and hesitated, he added:

"Besides—would it be wise to banish from your side a young, attractive man who has brilliant expectations?... This question of the Widinitz Succession—are we to hear no more of that?"

She faltered:

"I fear not, Monseigneur!... You cannot imagine the strength of his prejudices.... He is quite convinced that to put himself at the head of the Catholic electors of the Principality would be an insult to Heaven, because his mother happened to be a professed nun. Ah! how I weary of his eternal arguments."

"Indeed!" said Monseigneur, with a curious inflection. His dull eyes had a faded twinkle in them as they rested on the lovely speaker's face. She crimsoned to the wreath of roses nestling in their leaves within her bonnet,—pulled down the flowered lace veil with a petulant jerk of the little hand. Monseigneur hastened to soothe the sensibilities he had ruffled.

"Take my advice," he said, "who have so often taken yours, and found it excellent. Do not hurry on a crisis. Wait!—and let me think out some effective, easy method of relieving the tension of affairs."

His tone was mellifluous as that of a dentist who thinks that the toothache may be eased without extraction—the doubtful molar saved. She thanked him in silvery tones, made her deep reverence, and glided from the apartment where Monseigneur had received her; the private cabinet upon the ground-floor of the Élysée, where the Prince-President saw his intimate associates, interviewed his official spies and agents, and carried out experiments in musketry with the inventor, Major Minié.

You are to understand that he had lunched early that winter day, and was taking his cigar and coffee and Benedictine at a little table by the fireside. He smoked and sipped, with his dainty little feet upon a velvet footstool, and his big head lolling back against the padded velvet back of his easy-chair.

The question of how to dispose of Henriette's inconvenient lover occupied this hour of leisure. The young man had had a good deal of money, a considerable amount of which had found its way to his own bottomless pockets. He was the only son of a wealthy father, and might be well worth plucking again by-and-by. Even the abandoned claim of the Widinitz Succession might prove a profitable investment—a veritable gold-mine, to one who possessed the art of making stubborn natures malleable. A German Serene Highness who should be devoted to one's interests would be a useful tool, it occurred to Monseigneur....

He had, to do him justice, an exquisite discrimination in the selection of human instruments suitable for his hand; a knack of getting the best from them by stimulating their jealousies; he displayed an extraordinary cleverness in getting rid of them when blunted.... He never kept them long enough to be worn out.

It was his pride that at first sight he invariably detected in a man the qualities that would best serve him. In this handsome ex-Adjutant of the 999th, for whom Madame de Roux had had such a violent fancy—who had paid through the nose to obtain the transference of her husband to a post in Northern Africa, and who had forked out again for his own appointment as *aide-de-camp* upon the Staff of the Presidency—Monseigneur had never seen anything out of the way.

True, the man's career at the Training Institute for Staff Officers had been brilliant. But a reputation for brilliancy is easily gained. As a Chasseur d'Afrique he had served with distinction in the wars of Algeria—when transferred to the Line he had excellently discharged his regimental duties. Of hundreds of other men the same might be said....

The subject of his reflections was on duty that morning.... Monseigneur stretched out the neat, small hand that held his cigar, and touched a little golden chiming-bell. Dunoisse appeared in obedience to the summons, crossed the deep-piled carpet with long, light, noiseless footsteps, and placed, with a respectful hand, clad in the regulation white kid glove, a pile of letters on the little coffee-table, beside the elbow of Monseigneur.

Monseigneur, generally skeptical as regarded things unseen, firmly believed in his guiding genius. That invisible personage, he was subsequently convinced, dictated the question he suddenly put to Dunoisse;

an interrogation that broached his own long-cherished purpose, and gave a clue to the deep and dark and secret workings of his strange, cold, snaky mind.

"Monsieur—supposing that France had determined to espouse the interests of the Sultan of Turkey, to the point of becoming his ally in war—waged with Russia in alliance with a certain insular maritime Power, upon the debatable ground of Eastern Europe—how should she proceed so as to insure to her Army the maximum of advantage with the minimum of loss?... Do not answer hastily I beg of you.... Reflect before you reply."

Dunoisse thought for a minute, and gave the answer, clearly and promptly, and very much to the point. It shortened Monseigneur's breathing inconveniently, and brought a shiny gray dampness out upon the dough-colored surface of him, as though a snail had crawled there and left its track of slime. But it was not his habit to betray emotion. Those years spent in captivity had taught him self-control.

His small, flat eyes, usually so devoid of luster, assumed the shallow glitter of aluminium. He said, composedly, urbanely, stroking his heavy brown mustache:

"The most plausible theories sometimes evaporate when one tries to set them down on paper. You would oblige me very much, my dear Colonel, by putting yours in black upon white...."

Dunoisse bowed, and said he thought it would be possible to oblige Monseigneur. His theory, set forth in half-a-dozen pages of small, neat manuscript, illustrated by plans, and maps with dotted lines traced in divers-colored inks upon them, was laid before Monseigneur on the very next day.... Monseigneur studied these papers with close attention; rolled them up, retied, and locked them away in a secret hiding-place. And said, regarding his own features in a Venetian mirror that hung above the *secrétaire*, a precious article in pearl and ebony, that had held the toys and *bibelots* of Marie Antoinette, and the love-letters of Josephine:

"My friend, you have been saved by your lucky star from committing an irreparable error. This young man is a genius of the first water. Even to gratify the wish of a still singularly-charming woman, you would be mad, my friend, to part with Colonel Dunoisse!"

Thenceforwards, Dunoisse's active duties as assistant *aide-de-camp* gave place to the more sedentary occupations of Military Private Secretary, with a step in rank, a salary raised in accordance with his elevation in the estimation of his employer. It being presently discovered that he was master of Arabic, Turkish, Albanian Greek, German, Russian, and English, and possessed besides of a fair command of the Slavonic dialects of Roumania and Bulgaria, the office of Private Military Interpreter was created, and conferred on him by Monseigneur.

There was a little study, looking on a corner of the leafy gardens of the Palace, which communicated by a hidden door with Monseigneur's private cabinet. Dunoisse was installed in this snug den, into which none of the associates of Monseigneur ever thought of penetrating. And with his notes, and maps, and works of reference about him, was given a free hand, and bidden to carry out his plan.

And now at last the studies prosecuted in spare hours at the Training Institute for Staff Officers; those years of dogged, diligent acquirement of knowledge, began to bear fruit.... At last the man had found the severe, arduous employment that gave full play to his brilliant faculties. His face grew strange to his associates and friends, as his task absorbed him more....

Masses of papers, methodically filed and docketed, accumulated about Dunoisse. A vast correspondence in many European and several Oriental languages was carried on by him. He became the center of a vast web of intelligence, the active brain of a formidable working system that centralized in the little room adjoining the private cabinet with the bullet-chipped cornices; crossed the Alps and leaped the Carpathians; threw a spider-line from Odessa to Bucharest—linked Sevastopol with Batum—and traveled back again *viâ* the great roaring world-fair of Constantinople to the cabinet at the Élysée.

Men of many nationalities, tongues, and colors, and convictions, came and went, by day and night; gave their information, received instructions, verbal or otherwise, took their money, and departed. But they never came or went in couples, nor was the business of one known to the next. A Roumanian, one Michaëlis Giusko—formerly an assistant-lecturer and teacher of the Slavish languages at the Training Institute for Staff Officers, and a Barbary Jew, Israel Ben Hamon, with whom Dunoisse had studied Arabic in North Africa, became presently his assistants, bound to secrecy under oath.

Giusko had been found starving in a Montmartre garret; the Barbary Jew Dunoisse had accidentally encountered upon one of his periodical visits to Paris, to treat with the paper-merchants for the sale of rags from Tunis and the Levant. Both men were bound to their junior by ties of gratitude; the Israelite because his wife Miriam, now dead, had been saved by Dunoisse, when a young officer of Chasseurs d'Afrique, from robbery and outrage at the hands of some drunken Zouaves at Blidah; the Slav because all hope had left him, and he had been upon the point of suicide, when his old pupil had appeared before his gaunt and desperate eyes. But though both were trustworthy, neither of these men was to be trusted completely, according to the secret instructions of Monseigneur.

Nor had Dunoisse, who day and night sat spinning at the colossal web of Monseigneur's private purpose, and hatching out the egg of that potentate's secret plan, any definite knowledge of the breed of basilisk that would presently chip the shell.

LXII

Balls, dinners, concerts, receptions, and hunting-parties at the Tuileries and at Versailles, St. Cloud, and Compiègne, succeeded in dazzling rotation. Round the little study where Dunoisse wrought and planned and labored, driven on by a very demon of work, the active, busy, vari-colored life of the palace hummed and buzzed and swirled. Strains of music, gay or voluptuous, and sounds of fast and furious revelry came, midnight after midnight, to the ears of the solitary toiler—sometimes sounds more sinister than these.

The screams of a woman.... "Help! Mercy, for the love of Heaven!..." dying away into incoherent prayers and moans. The noise of a scuffle—the scraping of feet—the hoarse panting and muffled ejaculations of men engaged in desperate struggle—the thud of blows falling on something soft. Desperate outcries of "Murder! Treachery!... Monseigneur promised!... Monseigneur swore that I should be set free!" The revolver shots in the leafy palace garden, followed by a heavy silence not even broken by a groan. The man who heard never interrupted his labors for a moment. If the Prince-President chose to make the Élysée a place of execution, why,—stranger things had been done at the time of the *coup d'État*. And the vices of potentates are privileged.... That woman's voice crying for help was not the voice of Henriette.

She was as beautiful as ever. At the most splendid State functions, in the vicinity of her most brilliant rivals, her charms shone with undiminished fire. Men paid her court as ardently as ever, and her accredited lover was still a man keenly-envied. But in despite of this, and although his pressing duties at the Élysée debarred him from his place at her side in Society, Dunoisse had ceased to be jealous. So powerful an anodyne is absorbing mental labor, the shrill rattle of warning that used to sound from under every tuft of flowers or clump of grasses brushed by her draperies in passing, had fallen silent. Her paramour no longer dreaded a possible successor in every young and handsome man on whom she shed her smiles.

The green-eyed demon even left off taunting Dunoisse with de Moulny, still Representative of the Right for Moulny upon Upper Drame, and Secretary-Chancellor at the Ministry of the Interior; where the Count de Morny had been succeeded by M. de Persigny—less affected than his predecessor with scruples, you will remember, regarding the contents of a certain stately row of steel deed boxes that were crammed to bursting with palaces, cities, forests, villages, and farmsteads, and emblazoned with the arms of the House of Bourbon.

Rivers of plundered gold, derived from the sale of these great family estates, flowed away between Dunoisse's fingers. None of it stuck to them, much to the surprise of Monseigneur. For Dunoisse wanted money; and the chief reason at length become known to his patron, who had a peculiar knack of getting at the secrets of men.

To repay the three hundred thousand thalers that had been the dowry of Sister Térèse de Saint François had been, ever since the hour of their meeting, the abiding steadfast purpose of her son.... He saw her sometimes in dreams, when he went home in the gray dawn from the palace, and threw himself down, half dressed, upon his bed to snatch a little fevered sleep. And he would seem to hear the tear-soaked, toneless voice saying that the only road to Peace was the thorny Way of Expiation.... He would feel again the light, thin touch upon his forehead, and would wake, crying "Mother!" as the black curtain blotted her from his sight. And at other times, when the man was bound to the revolving wheel of his endless labors, the diligent pen would be arrested as her dim wistful eyes came hovering between his vision and the page. Then he would drive her away, and fall to his work with desperate assiduity. For never, Dunoisse knew, would he be happy until he had earned and repaid every centime of that accursed dowry. That debt discharged, there would be a turn of the tide. De Roux would die; his widow would become the wife of her lover; there would be happiness, children, a home.... For these he spent himself, allured by the glitter of Monseigneur's golden promises as other victims had been—would be until the end.

And in the fever of toil that consumed him, the man aged and wasted visibly. His black eyes lost their fire, his vivid coloring faded, his hair, no longer thick and glossy, showed broad streaks of gray. Lines graved themselves between his eyebrows, crow's feet appeared upon his temples. The wings of the nostrils were pulled downwards by the unrelaxing, constant tension of the muscles of the mouth, as month after month Dunoisse sat diligently incubating the egg of Monseigneur.

It hastened matters sensibly, that physical decadence—that wreck of the man's good looks upon the rocks of merciless mental toil. Society was charitable—Monseigneur was all kindness—but the betrayed husband and the supplanted lover are fair game, always: has it not been so since the beginning of the world?

Whispers began to circulate.... In the smoking-rooms of the great Clubs, in the social circle at the palace of the Presidency, Dunoisse's rare appearances were provocative of the smart *double entente,* and the cynical witticism; flagged darts that, thrown without discretion, presently found their way to the raw quick under the thickened skin. The very day that showed the stupendous task all but accomplished, brought home to Dunoisse—by the medium of an unsigned letter in a delicate feminine hand—the knowledge that, in the estimation of his world, at least—he was held to have been supplanted by de Moulny. The closing sentence of the anonymous writer reproduced, almost in the very words, the unforgettable utterance of Henriette at the inn of "The Heron":

"You only have yourself to thank for what has happened now!"

It seemed the very voice of his Fate speaking, and Dunoisse grew pale as ashes, and laid the letter down. He had been much weakened by his unremitting labors, and the drumming of the blood in his ears and the violent beating of his heart made him deaf to the quiet opening and closing of the door. But a voice spoke to him, and he looked up, with the sharp-fanged fox of desperate jealousy gnawing under his uniform, as it had possibly gnawed under that of de Roux, and became aware that Monseigneur had entered, and was looking at him with a somewhat sinister smile. He said—as Dunoisse stumbled to his feet and saluted—looking narrowly at the haggard handsome face, and smoothing his thick brown mustache with the little hand that was so like a pretty woman's:

"So! We draw near the end! We have at last the goal in view, according to the report I received from you this morning." He added, as Dunoisse bowed in assent: "Accept my sincere congratulations upon the excellent service you have rendered, General-of-Brigade von Widinitz Dunoisse."

His glance, as keen as dull and lusterless, had recognized the writing of the letter lying on the blotting-pad. He had calculated, and rightly, that to grant the coveted step at the moment of revelation would inconceivably intensify the torment of its sting. He did not delay to receive the halting thanks of the victim. He went on in his cool, mellifluous tones, showing a docketed paper in his hand:

"You mention at the close of your summary of the work that has been accomplished, that without diligent and painstaking revision of the maps of Eastern Europe at present in use at our Military School, and employed at our War Department, the coping-stone of perfection must be lacking still." He added, "This, I will own, surprises me, our Government Survey Department being considered—I believe with justice!—as pre-eminent in skill and accuracy. How, then, do you suggest that the maps should be improved?"

"Monseigneur, the network of intelligence being complete," answered Dunoisse, "a minute sanitary survey of the ground most likely to become the scene of militant operations should necessarily follow. Fever-breeding districts must be plainly labeled 'Pestilential,'—doubtfully-salubrious regions must be indicated for what they are.... No detail should be neglected. Special qualifications—precise scientific knowledge will be necessarily required of the Staff officer who is deputed to carry out this mission." He added, "For upon the health of the Army depends its fighting-power. One cannot win battles with sick men!"

"An excellent apophthegm," Monseigneur pronounced, with that peculiarly amiable smile of his. He tapped his teeth thoughtfully with the paper in his hand. "As regards the Staff officer who is to be despatched on this—would you call it a perilous mission?"—He went on, Dunoisse having admitted it to be a decidedly perilous mission—"I know of but one individual possessing the necessary, indispensable qualifications, and he is yourself!" He added, turning the poisoned poniard in the wound: "Fair eyes will weep at your departure, my dear Dunoisse—lovely lips will call me cruel. But undoubtedly—you must be the man to go!"

LXIII

So Dunoisse, with a step in rank in lieu of the promised heap of gold, and the suspicion rankling in him that his banishment had long been contemplated, went back to the Rue de Sèvres and found Henriette and de Moulny there together.

It was early upon a chill October evening. They were talking low and earnestly before the fire that glowed in its polished steel basket. The rose-shaded lamp threw a tender light upon the pair. And the portrait of the nun-Princess of Orleans, treading with dimpled, naked feet upon scattered crowns and scepters, looked down upon them with her triumphant harlot's smile.

There was a silence, poignant and tense. They had risen upon Dunoisse's entrance—both faces wore a set, artificial smile of greeting. He looked from one to the other and waited, the venomed sentences of the anonymous letter rankling in his sickened mind. He noted, dully, that Henriette wore a loose, flowing robe of creamy white, the skirt edged, the low neck and loose sleeves bordered, with a Greek key-pattern in dull gold; and that de Moulny's tall, official figure—arrayed in the unrelieved magpie-garb of black-and-white that Fashion had but recently decreed as the only evening wear for the ultra-fashionable civilian—bulked gigantic in the small boudoir that was no longer gray, but pranked it gayly, as one of Monseigneur's own pages, in a coat of green-and-gold. His own face was sharp and hard as though sculptured in Egyptian granite, and his black eyes were glittering and chill. And it seemed as though the silence would last unbroken forever.... The Sèvres clock upon the mantelshelf ticked, the wood-ashes fell from the grate with a little rustling sound.... Dunoisse could hear de Moulny's deep, even respiration and Henriette's agitated, hurried breathing. It seemed to him that his heart did not beat—that he himself did not breathe at all. And then the spell was broken by a woman's soft utterance. Henriette said:

"Dear friend, your arrival is opportune. M. de Moulny has called upon me to entreat that I would use such influence as I am—perhaps mistakenly—credited with possessing—to effect a reconciliation between you both.... The misunderstanding that has divided you so long shall be cleared up, shall it not—as he wishes?" She added, looking from one man to the other with softly-beaming eyes: "I too wish this, so very greatly.... Will you not be friends, to please me?"

De Moulny's deep voice said:

"Have we ever been enemies?"

And he held out to Dunoisse his large, thick, white hand with the fleshy, round-tipped fingers; and, as a man in a dream will unquestionably accept some inconceivable, impossible situation, Dunoisse took the hand in his. It loosely grasped and was withdrawn. Then, there had followed some moments of conventional, ordinary, social commonplace. They had discussed the Message to the Senate, and the protest of the Count de Chambord against the contemplated restoration of the Empire; the probable results of the *plebiscite*, and the superior becomingness of the Marie Stuart style of *coiffure* to a roll *à la Chinoise*. And then de Moulny had taken his leave, and, freed from the hateful oppression of his presence, Dunoisse could think clearly again.

Ah! could it be—without any bridging of the wide gulf of silence and neglect by any explanation—without any clearing up of that trifling matter of the command to fire, that had followed the pistol-shot at the Foreign Ministry nearly four years previously—could it be that Redskin and Alain were reconciled? With the anonymous letter festering in his memory—with the knowledge of impending banishment gnawing at his heart—Dunoisse answered No, no, no! to the question.... And then, a sudden, unexpected surge of joy lifted the poor dupe off the shoals of Disillusion, and swept him—how willingly!—back into the deceptive deeps beyond.

He broke to Henriette the news of the Eastern mission. She paled ... cried out ... threw herself half-swooning—bathed in tears, upon his breast. Cruel, cruel Monseigneur!... Her beautiful bosom heaved as she inveighed against the implacable tyrant at the Élysée. She vowed she would not submit to such a heartless abuse of authority.... She would go to the Prince, she declared—throw herself before him—plead upon her knees for a reversal of the pitiless appointment. And Dunoisse dissuaded her with difficulty from adopting such a course; inwardly blessing the power she reviled, for the discovery that, after all, he was loved....

And indeed, during the few, the very few, days that intervened between the reconciliation with de Moulny and Dunoisse's departure, Henriette's passion, that shriveled rose of Jericho, soaked in warm tears from lovely eyes, regained its pristine color, bloom, and fragrance. The ancient glamour was upon all earth and heaven, and the cup once more offered by those exquisite hands to the thirsting lips of her lover brimmed with the intoxicating wine of old.

LXIV

Their parting.... Ah! what pen could do justice to their parting, when, upon a certain fateful morning, some eight days subsequently to the decision of Monseigneur, Dunoisse tore himself away from Henriette and his revived and radiant happiness, and left Paris, *en route* for Eastern Roumelia, and the debatable ground one day to be contested by the forces of the Sultan and the Czar.

Not without pith of meaning is the old saw that warns the traveler never, once having started, to retrace his steps. But the overworked pointsman's blunder that sent the engine of the South-Eastern express crashing into the rear-wagon of a goods-train outside the station of Joigny—a disaster without resultant loss of life to any portion of the human freight—must be held responsible for Dunoisse's return.

His route had officially been pricked out *viâ* Marseilles and Constantinople. Owing to the lapse of hours that would intervene before the next Southward-going mail could be boarded, the bi-monthly steamer plying between the ports above named must certainly sail without Dunoisse. Somewhat bruised and shaken by the shock of the accident, and furthermore possessed with an intense nostalgia for Paris and Henriette, her lover yielded to the tempting, urgent voice; left his baggage—soldierly in its economy of bulk—in charge of the officials at Joigny—and burdened with nothing more cumbrous than a traveling-bag—took the next train for home.

The city clocks were striking twelve when he left the terminus of the Rue Mazas and rattled in a hired *coupé* over the Bridge of Austerlitz. It was a windless night of numbing cold, and the long double line of the quays, and the sluggish river winding between them, and the arcs of the bridges spanning the wide, turbid flood, were only indicated by their lamps, twinkling brightly as a jeweler's emeralds and topazes out of wrappings of fleecy cotton-wool. No bivouac-fires reddened the foggy sky; no troops occupied the public places or patroled the streets; no blood-bedabbled corpses were being carted to the cemetery; yet Dunoisse was irresistibly reminded of the night of his return from London, on the morning that had followed the master-stroke of Monseigneur. Perhaps that association threw the first splash of cold water on his enterprise.... But he told himself for the hundredth time that he was going back to Henriette, who loved him; and that her joy at the unexpected sight of him would clear away all shadow of doubt and misunderstanding from between them for evermore.

It seemed a long drive. You are never in such a red-hot hurry as when you are speeding to the wreck and ruin of an illusion upon the jagged rocks of a test. But at last it was over. He dismissed his cab at the street-corner, in the interests of the joyful surprise he had in view—and reached the familiar gates on foot. No need to use the little pass-key, carried in Dunoisse's waistcoat-pocket, and admitting by the smaller portal, framed in the corner of the larger one, for—thanks to some neglect of the portress—the little door stood ajar; it swung inwards at the first touch.... And thus Dunoisse stepped noiselessly into the dark, foggy courtyard, passed under the tall, stately, familiar portico—conjectured rather than seen in the draping veil of fog—and drew out the latch-key of the de Roux's hall-door. But that door was also open—upon this night of wonders every obstacle seemed to dissolve like foam or mist-wreath under the touch of the man who was hurrying to prove his mistress faithful. For, stripped of all ornament or pretense, you have in these five plain words the reason of Dunoisse's return.

The servants had gone to bed, or had been given leave to spend the night elsewhere. A small lamp burned feebly in the deserted vestibule, like Faith trying to keep itself alive in a soul that has learned to doubt. The drawing-rooms were in darkness, their wood fires mere cores of red under gray crusts of ashes. Beyond, the green-and-gold boudoir, with a brilliant fire and many lights, gleamed like some transcendent emerald at the end of a tunnel of ebony blackness. She was not there. But the door of the bedroom that was fragrant and pink as the heart of a blush-rose—that stood a little ajar....

Moving with long, swift, eager strides over the velvety carpets, Dunoisse reached the open door of the bedroom. With a heart that throbbed as madly as on the first night that had seen him cross its threshold, he looked in, and saw Henriette.

In sharpest contrast with the brilliancy of the green-and-gold boudoir, the rose-colored bedroom, save for the blazing wood-billets that dispensed a dancing light and a delicious warmth, was all in shadow. At an angle, facing towards the fire, stood a low, broad ebony couch without a back or foot-piece, covered in rose-color matching the shade of the draperies of the windows, the walls, and the tent that in the graceful fashion of the era, sheltered the bed. And Henriette lay—in beauty revealed rather than covered by a thin diaphanous robe of lawn and lace—outstretched upon the couch beside the fire, her shoulders raised upon its rose-colored cushions, her lovely head thrown back and drooping as in the chaste abandonment of sleep, toward the shoulder whose curving whiteness shone pearly between the tresses of night-black hair that streamed across it and downwards; partly veiling the white arm, and the delicate hand that rested, palm upwards, on the leopard-skin that was spread before the hearth.

Surely, surely, she was very pale.... But never had she seemed more alluringly, irresistibly fair in the eyes that drank her in, and could not slake their thirst in gazing. And surely she was very still.... The colorless lips, parted in a faint, mysterious smile, gave forth no sighing breath; the pulses at the base of the rounded throat did not throb perceptibly—the full, goddess-like bosom that gleamed through the mist-thin fabric of her robe did not rise or fall with the deep even respiration of natural, wholesome slumber. But not until Dunoisse had crossed to her side—bent down and set his burning kiss upon those smiling lips, did he realize that they were icy cold; that the teeth were rigidly clenched behind them, and that the half-open eyes were fixed in a glassy stare. And in the poignant horror of the discovery he cried her name aloud, and snatched the inert form into his embrace—lavishing frantic caresses and adoring words upon her—imploring her to revive ... to look at him ... to answer ... if only by a sigh.

In vain his prayers. The silent heart against which his cheek was pressed gave back no throb; not the slightest answering pressure might be won from the nerveless arms he laced about his neck—not the faintest nerve-thrill told of life in the beautiful body, whose most secret chords were so well used to respond to the urgent call of Passion. She was cold, white and silent as the dead.

Could this be Death indeed?... Dunoisse drove the haunting query desperately from him. He remembered with relief a flask of cognac that he carried in an inner pocket of his traveling-cloak; and tried, out of the silver thimble-cup that was screwed as a cap over the stopper, to pour a little of the spirit between the small, set teeth. When her head rolled helplessly on his supporting arm—when the liquid, finding no entrance, flowed away at the corners of the pale, stiff lips, adding a coarse spirituous tang to the delicately-fragrant atmosphere of the bedroom, the dreadful doubt assailed Dunoisse more fiercely. Baffled, sick with despair, he laid her back upon the couch, freed himself tenderly from the long strands of night-black hair that clung to his rough traveling clothes and tangled in his buttons—struck a match and lighted, with what a shaking hand!—the rose-tinted wax candles upheld by porcelain Cupids on the mantelshelf. Holding one of the candlesticks on high, he sent a questioning glance about in search of smelling-salts or some more powerful restorative. And not until then did the tell-tale disorder of the place yield up its ugly secret. He knew all.

The disorder of the luxurious bed ... the little table of two covers that stood near its foot, bearing a plate of caviare sandwiches partly consumed, a cut *pâté* and two champagne-bottles, one prone and empty, the other partly full, gave testimony there was no disproving. Even without the clinching evidence furnished by the heavy, fur-lined overcoat that sprawled over the back of a chair—the masculine stock that curled about an ivory hand, loaded with rings of price—the black satin cravat that lay upon the lace-draped toilette table, its twin diamond pins, linked by a chain of gold, winking and gleaming like mocking goblin-eyes. And was not that a man's white glove, lying where it had been dropped upon the rose-colored carpet?... Mechanically Dunoisse crossed the room and picked it up. And it was no glove, but a crumpled note, penned in violet ink, in Henriette's clear, delicate characteristic hand, on her white, satin-striped paper. And it told all, crudely and without reserve, to the poor dupe whom it flouted and mocked.

"Unruly Monster,—

"Yes! 'tis true! Don Quixote has departed. Naturally I am inconsolable!—but since you profess yourself convinced of the contrary, you may come at the usual hour. The servants will be disposed of—the doors will be open.... When we meet, perhaps I may be——

Thy Henriette."

LXV

He turned upon her with her letter in his hand; with fierce upbraidings struggling for utterance at his twisted lips; with a heart full of bitter hatred ready to outpour upon her. She quelled his madness—she struck him speechless—he tried to curse her, but could find no voice.

For a nameless, awe-inspiring change, had crept over her. The shell-white features were now pinched and drawn. Beneath the broad white brow the partly-open, coldly-glittering eyes were sunk in caves of bluish tinting. Hollows had appeared beneath the cheekbones; while about the mouth, whose drawn, livid, parted lips revealed the little clenched pearly teeth, that disquieting shadow, cruelly suggestive of dissolution and corruption, showed in a broad band; and beneath the swelling curves of her bosom a deep, abdominal depression now sharply marked the edges of the lower ribs. And thus Dunoisse, familiar with Death as a soldier may be who has met the grim King of Terrors on the battle-field, and in the camp, and on the pallets of field-hospitals, told himself that beyond all doubt Death was here.

And so it was that he could not curse her for a harlot. She was dead, and Death is pure.... She was dead, and Death is meek and helpless; at the mercy of the smallest, most despicable, weakest thing that walks or crawls or flies.

Looking upon Henriette, you would never have guessed that here lay a wanton, stricken down at the height of a delirious orgy of forbidden pleasure. Rather you thought of a snow-white seagull, lying stiff and frozen on a stretch of sunset-dyed seashore, or a frail white butterfly, dead in the heart of a pink, overblown rose.

So the madness burned itself out in the brain of Dunoisse as he stood looking at her. The blood in his veins ran less like liquid fire, the cold sweat dried upon his skin, the roaring in his ears lessened—he could now control the twitching of his muscles that had ached with the desire to kill with naked hands a man abhorred—to batter out all semblance of its luring beauty from the white, white face against the rose-hued background. If the prone figure had given sign of life!—but its pallor as of snow—its rigidity and breathlessness remained unaltered. And presently, looking upon her, lying there; laughter and tears, love and anger, forever quenched in her; disarmed of her panoply of conquering gifts and graces by pitiless Death, a bitter spasm took him by the throat and a mist of tears came before his eyes. He trembled, and for lack of power to stand, sat down upon the foot of the sofa, near where the stiff little feet he had so often kissed peeped out beyond the border of her robe of lawn and laces. His haggard eyes were fixed upon the cold and speechless mouth. And in its rigid silence it was eloquent.

"Dear friend," the dumb voice seemed to say ... "sweet friend, whose pleadings won me to deceive—and whom I have in turn deceived—the heroic virtue of Fidelity having no part in the pliable, silken web of my nature—listen to me, and be, not pardoning—but pitiful!..."

"God knows," said Dunoisse sorrowfully, "how I pity you, Henriette!"

"Born with the fatal gift of maddening beauty—endowed with the deadly heritage of irresistible fascination," went on the silent voice, "ask yourself how it was possible for your Henriette to pass through life untainted by the desires—unbranded by the scorching lusts of men? Be fair to me, dear friend. Question—and give answer."

Dunoisse asked himself the question. There was but one reply.

"Look around," said the voice, "and you will see my prototype in liberal Nature. The bird that builds too low; the rose that does not hang her clusters high enough; the fruit whose very ripeness calls the wasps to settle and feast. Yet who says to the bird, 'Build higher! Another year you will not lose your eggs so!' Does anyone bid the rose change her nature and lift her perfumed blossoms far out of reach of plundering hands? What if one cried to the peach, 'Do not ripen, stay crude and sour because thus you will not tempt the yellow-and-black marauder.' Would not the pious tell us that to expect Heaven-taught Nature to alter her ways at our bidding were to be guilty of mortal sin? Then, what of us Henriettes—born to yield and submit, give and grant and lavish? Are we much more to blame, do you think, than the bird, than the rose, than the peach?"

"Oh, my poor, frail, false love!" said Dunoisse, "how wise Death has made you!" For his bitter anger and resentment were vanishing as the silent voice talked on:

"We drink in the sunshine of admiring glances at every pore," said the voice. "We thrive on smiles and compliments. All young and handsome men—even those who are neither young nor handsome—are our comrades or servants—until the moment arrives when the comrade becomes tyrant, and the servant commands! Then, what tears we shed!—for our dearest dream is always of pure passion—unrewarded fidelity. We are continually planting the gardens of our hearts with these fragrant, homely flowers, and Man is always tearing them up, and setting in their stead the vine of nightshade, deadly briony, sad rosemary, bitter wormwood and sorrowful rue. And as long as the world shall last, the cruel play goes on...."

The half-open, glassy eyes were dry, but the silent voice had sobs in it. And it said:

"We give all we have for love, and the love is never real, only pinchbeck of flattery and kisses; or the cruel love of an urchin for a kitten—of a baby for a tame bird.... You who sit by me to-night, dear friend, have never loved me!... Have you ever sought to find my Soul within the house of flesh that caged it? Have I not seen you smile in mockery when I knelt down to pray?"

"You are wrong—absolutely wrong, Henriette!" he wished to say to her. But a scalding wave of guilty consciousness broke over him. He dropped his shamed face into his hands and groaned.

What had he ever sought of her but sensuous pleasure? She spoke truth—their intercourse had never risen for an instant above the commerce of the flesh, to the plane of things spiritual—he had never even thought about her Soul. Now he seemed to see it, a wandering flame no bigger than a firefly's lamp, or the phosphorescent spark the glow-worm carries—wandering through the illimitable spaces of Eternity,—looking in vain for God. Whose very greatness made it impossible for the tiny, flitting thing to find Him....

"Forgive me, Henriette!" he faltered, pierced to the quick.

"There is more to forgive," the still voice rejoined, "even than you believe. When you found me lying cold and stark in the midst of toys and trifles—when you read the letter that proved me treacherous and vile—think! was it genuine grief that you felt, or the savage wrath of baffled appetite? And even now——"

"Have mercy! Spare me that at least!" he begged. For he knew that in another instant she would bare his own mean, petty self before him—she would tell him that even then a strife was going on in him between a cowardly cur who wanted to steal away and leave her ... and a man of common honor and ordinary decency who said: "*It is my part to stay!*"

For both of these men knew, fatally well, that when the morrow's sunshine should find her lying there—when the outcries of her terrified maids should summon eager, curious strangers to gather about and stare at their dead mistress; when the scandal of the manner of her death should leak out; the world and Society, that had so good-naturedly blinked at her liaison with Dunoisse, would not spare him his well-earned wage of contumely. There could not fail to be a Medical Inquiry ... the Police would be called in to clear up suspicious mysteries.... Also, de Roux would be recalled from Algeria ... there would be a duel ... consequences much more unpleasant than a duel.... For Monseigneur would not look with complacency upon the return of an emissary proceeding to the East upon a special mission.... Worse still, that stealthy return from Joigny might be held to have been prompted by a sinister motive. Men had been imprisoned—men had been hugged headless by that Red Widow the Guillotine upon less suspicion than Dunoisse had tagged to himself by the mere fact of his secret return.

The porcelain clock upon the mantelshelf struck one and the half-hour, as Dunoisse sat thrashing the question out—to go or stay with her? And presently he raised his wrung and ravaged face, and got up and stood beside the sofa, looking down at Henriette....

"Poor soul!" he said. "You knew me better than I knew myself. I am a purblind idiot, Henriette, who, having profited by your unfaith—looked to you to be faithful. Now I am paid in my own coin—it is my pride that suffers—not my love. For as you say, and rightly!—I have never loved you. Yet, love or none, because that other man has fled and left you, and because that viler self that lurks within counsels me to follow—I stay beside you here."

LXVI

When the porcelain clock upon the mantelshelf had chimed the hour, a cautious footstep had crossed the flagged pavement of the foggy courtyard. Dunoisse had not heard it—he had been listening to that speechless voice. But now that the stealthy footsteps traversed the parquet of the vestibule—stumbled over an unseen ottoman in the darkness of the large drawing-room—threaded the next, and crossed the threshold of the green-and-gold boudoir, he heard it, with a creeping icy chill, and a rising of the hairs upon his scalp and body. He remembered that he had not shut the courtyard gate, or the hall-door behind him, upon this fatal night of revelation.... It occurred to him that some prowling night-hawk of the Paris streets might have entered in search of food and plunder, or that the intruder might prove to be a *sergent de ville*, or the watchman of the quarter, or even a gendarme of the city patrol.... But when a large, powerful, well-kept white hand, with fleshy, round-topped fingers, came stealing about the edge of the partly-open door, and pushed it cautiously inwards—Dunoisse, with a savage leaping of the blood, knew—even before a tall, bulky figure loomed dark upon the threshold, seen against the brilliance and glitter of the boudoir—that the man who had left her had returned.

That the man was de Moulny he had never for one instant doubted. Now the muscles of his folded arms tightened across his breast like cords of steel, his keen face was set like granite, and a cold, fierce light of battle blazed in his keen black eyes. It was good to Dunoisse that this hour should have come, setting Redskin face to face with his old, treacherous enemy, stripping all pretenses from their mutual hate. The loaded pistol in the inner pocket of his coat gave him the advantage—supposing de Moulny unarmed.... But he knew how to equalize the chances.... They would toss for the shot, or throw away the Colt's revolver. Men can kill men with no other weapons than their muscular naked hands.

In the first moment of his entrance, de Moulny—newly out of fog and darkness—blinking from the radiance of the boudoir, did not observe that the bedroom held any occupant besides the rigid, white form upon the rose-colored sofa. His light blue, strained and slightly bloodshot eyes went to that directly. His jutting underlip shook, a question was written large upon the pale, heavily-featured countenance. "*Has she moved or breathed since I left her?*" it seemed to ask, and the negative of her immobility wiped a latent expectation out from it. And then——

Then a purposely-made movement of Dunoisse jerked de Moulny's head round. A sudden reddish flame leaped into the pale eyes as they took in the slender, upright figure in the rough gray traveling surtout, standing at the foot of the couch with folded arms.... And though de Moulny did not palpably start, yet his big jowl dropped a hair's-breadth. A slight hissing intake of the breath betrayed his perturbation and surprise.

"Th'h'h!".... And then in an instant the old de Moulny was back, arrogant, cool, self-possessed as ever. His blue eyes were hard as polished stones as they met the black eyes of Dunoisse. He said, pouting his fleshy lips, sticking his long obstinate chin out, looking arrogantly down his big thick nose in the old familiar manner:

"An unexpected return invariably leads to unpleasant explanations. But in the present case I design to make you none, further than that I came here by appointment." His smile was intolerable as he added: "Not for the first time. And I will meet you when you please, and where you please. You have your choice of weapons, understand me—from ordinary dueling-pistols to a buttonless foil!"

Dunoisse, lividly pale and sharp-faced, looked at his enemy, showing his small square teeth almost smilingly, breathing through his nose rather loudly, just as Redskin had done upon the day of the boyish quarrel at the School. Even as then, he was conscious of being a little sick at the pit of his stomach: the sight of de Moulny, big and blond and brutal, his light-brown, curled hair and reddish whiskers glittering with fog-beads, his hard eyes bloodshot with the night's excess, his immaculately-cut black frock-coat buttoned awry, its collar turned up to shield the bareness of his thick white bull-neck from the chill night air, its lapels dragged over the breast to conceal the absence of a cravat, his usually irreproachable trousers and polished boots dabbled with the mud of the streets, affected Dunoisse with a physical nausea as well as a malady of the soul.... To the picture of the libertine confronted by the grim mower in the midst of his garden of stolen pleasures, was added a touch of absurdity in the little white-papered, red-sealed chemist's parcel, held with a certain air of fastidious helplessness between a finger and thumb of one of the large, white, carefully-tended hands. And as though Dunoisse's glance at this had reminded de Moulny of its destined use, he said, holding his head high, speaking through his nose, deliberately:

"Monsieur, since we have arrived at a complete understanding, it appears to me that delicacy and good taste should counsel you to retire, and leave me to minister to the very evident need of our lovely friend." Meeting no response from Dunoisse, he added, with his insufferable smile, glancing towards the still sleeper on the rose-hued sofa:

"She swooned in my arms.... These delicate sensualists live hard—to put it brutally. '*One must pay the piper*,' as the English say,—in the end,—for being perpetually attuned to concert-pitch.... And the servants had all been sent out of the way!... Imagine my predicament!... A senseless woman on my hands, and not another woman within cry.... Thus it was, that in my present, slightly compromising state of *déshabille*, I sallied out to fetch a surgeon—an excellent, discreet, and reliable person, who—as luck would have it—has gone into the country to operate upon a patient, and until to-morrow is not expected to return.... Failing him, I knocked up a chemist, who supplied me with these drops—warranted infallible"—he held up the little parcel—"adding some advice *gratis* as to treatment of the sufferer, involving—unless I err—friction over the region of that conjectural feminine organ, the heart...."

De Moulny, seeming bigger and more blond and brutal than ever, moved with his long, padding elastic step,—recalling the gait of a puma—to the sofa. Dunoisse, even quicker than he, interposed, and said, baldly and simply, speaking between his close-shut teeth, and looking straight in the other's stony eyes:

"If you touch her I shall kill you! Take care!..."

"Oh, as to killing!" de Moulny said with a shrug.... But he did not carry out the intention expressed in that long, catlike stride. He moved to the hearth, where the wood-fire was glowing with a comfortable warmth that tempted him, and said, daintily picking up his splashed coat-tails, as he lolled with his heavy shoulders against the mantelshelf:

"Permit me to point out that your utterance savors of the dog in the manger. You have failed to revive Madame—and I am not to try. You would rather Death laid his bony hand upon that eminently lovely person than that I did.... Well!... Be it so!"

He shrugged with an elaborate affectation of indifference—even feigned to yawn. Dunoisse answered hoarsely, turning away his sickened eyes from him:

"Death has already touched and claimed her. She is Death's—not mine or yours!"

De Moulny's big jowl dropped. He shot into an erect attitude, dropped his coat-tails and made, rapidly and stealthily, the Sign of the Cross. His widely-open eyes, their distended pupils swallowing up the pale blue irises, seemed to leap at the white shape upon the sofa; and then relief relaxed the tension of his muscles, and his thick lips curled back in an almost good-humored smile. He said, in Alain's old way:

"*Nom d'un petit bonhomme!*—but you are mistaken, my excellent Dunoisse!—fortunately most damnably mistaken, as it turns out! Even from where I stand, the quiver of an eyelid,—the stirring of a finger—the faintest heaving of the bosom I am not to touch, may occasionally be perceived. Use your own eyes, and they will convince you." He went on jeeringly as Dunoisse, shaken by the furious beating of his heart, dizzy with the shock of the unexpected, and dim-eyed with newly-stirred emotion, moved unsteadily to the couch, and, stooping, noted the signs, faint but unmistakable, of reviving vitality in Henriette. "Aha! I am now enlightened as to the secret of your phlegm—your apathy—your air of fatalistic composure!—'*Dead*,' not a bit of it! She will live to dance over de Roux's grave and yours, my good sir, and possibly mine.... But if she had been," went on the big, blatant voice, with a scoffing gayety in it that set the still air of the rose-colored bedroom vibrating as though unholy wings had stirred it, "with that solid common-sense which she has found stimulatingly refreshing,—in contrast with the moonstruck vaporings of a person who, being present, shall go unnamed—I should have made myself scarce in double-quick time. For to be compromised with a living woman is sometimes sufficiently embarrassing, but when it comes to a———"

"Be silent—be silent!" said Dunoisse in the thick, quivering voice of overmastering anger. "Have you no sense of decency?—no manhood left in you?" he demanded, "that you mock and jeer at a woman who cannot even answer in her own defense? Our meeting cannot be too soon!—my friends will wait upon you in a few hours. Meanwhile, relieve me of your presence!" He pointed to the open door.

De Moulny, maintaining his position on the hearthrug, hunched his shoulders as though a shrug were too elaborate a method of conveying indifference. His solid jowl was doggedly obstinate, and a red light shone behind his pale blue eyes. He said:

"You have anticipated me—forestalled me, General, in pointing out that—to quote the old adage, 'Two are company.'... Might I suggest that you should prove your own claim to decency and so forth by effacing yourself from a scene where—to put it obviously—you are *de trop*...! The equally obvious fact that your presence here will not conduce to Madame's complete recovery, does not seem to have occurred to you. Face the situation. You took her from me—I won her back from you. A shameful struggle," said de Moulny brutally, "a paltry triumph." His thick lips rolled back in the contemptuous smile. "But be that as it may, the fact to be confronted, we have shared a strumpet, you and I!"

The words seemed so like a brutal blow in the white face against the sofa-cushions, that Dunoisse could not restrain an indignant ejaculation. De Moulny resumed, with the same intolerable coolness:

"Since neither of us will give place, one must listen to the other.... Whether Madame there hears matters very little to me.... There is very little of either delicacy or decency in the present situation. We might with truth be likened," said de Moulny, "to a couple of dogs growling over a bone."

He threw out his big arms and drew the air into his broad chest greedily.

"'F'ff! There is a certain relief in discarding conventionalities—in being, for the nonce, the natural man. For years, without a spoken word,—as men used before language was invented to swaddle Truth in—we have hated one another cordially, my very good Dunoisse. You had robbed me of a career—and though—when a rogue had come to me babbling the story of that trick of fence that did the business, I had stuffed his jaws with banknotes not to tell—one does not forgive a theft of that nature.... I think you upon your side resented—with a good deal of reason—a silly oath I had exacted—an oath you had at last the common sense to break. *Nom d'un petit bonhomme!* I should have broken it ages before you did.... But at least you learned the art of succeeding without money.... There is not one man in a million who understands that!..."

He stuck out his hammer-head of a chin in his old way of reflection.

"I should have let you alone if you had not—for the second time—come between me and my desire. That day at the Ministry of Foreign Affairs, when the pistol-shot.... Aha!" cried de Moulny, Dunoisse having winced at the allusion, "I see our disputed possession has told you the pretty little tale.... But it may be, with some embroidery of imagination (if she overhears what I say she will thank me for putting it so charmingly).... Possibly with some divagations from the rigid rectilinear of truth! For it amounts to this, that de Roux had borrowed from the regimental money-chest; the money had to be replaced, if unpleasant consequences were to be averted. And knowing me to be the most recent and infatuated of all her worshipers, Madame applied to me to make up the sum."

His smile was an insult as his cold eyes went to the face upon the sofa. And an indefinable change seemed working under the rigid features, as one may see to-day in the partly-masked face of the anæsthetized patient outstretched upon the operating-table, a reflection of the torture caused by the surgeon's dexterous knife.

"Perhaps she lied—as women will—and really wanted the money for her bonnet-maker or her Bonaparte," went on de Moulny. "Still, I knew de Roux to be not afflicted with scruples—he had scraped by the ears out of even more questionable affairs. And I saw my chance, and got together the money.... One was a poor devil in those days—and thirty thousand francs meant much. And she took them—and threw me over. As one might have expected," said de Moulny, dourly, "if one had not been a fool!"

"She repaid—" Dunoisse began in a strangled voice; and then it rushed on him that she had kept the money. His eyes fell in shame for her. De Moulny went on:

"Pass over that affair of the order to fire. Did it do otherwise than make your social reputation—smooth your path to possession of the woman I desired...? By Heaven!"—the speaker's pale eyes gleamed, and he clenched his white hand unconsciously,—"when you lied with such gorgeous effectiveness before the Military Commission of Inquiry, I could have bitten myself, as patients do in rabies—knowing that I had been forestalled again! After that, your road lay open—your names were bandied from mouth to mouth all over Paris.... Your intrigue was Punchinello's secret; *she* made no mystery of it when we met. But"—the brutal smile curled the fleshy lips—"perhaps it may interest you to know that I was given to understand that your proprietorship was from first to last a question of Money. And that, supposing all those Widinitz millions had been mine to pour into de Roux's insatiable clutches—Henriette would have been sold to a man she loved, instead of to a romantic weakling whom she despised and laughed at ... even from the first ... do you hear, my good Dunoisse?"

A hoarse sound came from Dunoisse's dry throat. It deepened the ugly smile upon the sensual face of de Moulny. He said, opening and shutting one of his big white hands, with a mechanical, rhythmic movement as he went on, slowly, deliberately, pouring himself out:

"Why do men love women?" He added with an accent of utter contempt: "They are either fools or jades! Play with them—use them as tools—they can be edged ones.... But to love them—to set the heart on them—to stand or fall by their truth or treachery—that is not for a man of sense. When I loved Henriette—she fooled and flouted me.... When I had ceased to love, and only desired her—when the day came that saw hundreds of millions stored up under my hand at the Ministry of the Interior, I knew that my time had come—do you comprehend?" He rubbed his heavy chin reflectively. "She was more charming than ever—she wanted to find out how far I would go to get what I wanted—I suspected her of spying for the Count de Morny—I had long known her to be a tool of the Prince.... So I did not show her the keys of the Orleans strong-boxes—I did not even let her know where they were kept; but I made other concessions to her, concessions that I knew were harmless...." The pale, glittering self-satisfaction in his eyes was intolerable, as he added: "They served me excellently!—and for the time being pleased her just as well!..." He added, meeting Hector's glance of loathing: "Possibly you think me a scoundrel?... I am completely indifferent to your opinion. To pursue.... She persuaded me to join the circle at the Élysée. We met at the suppers there.... You must know I am a *gourmet* and a sensualist. Those suppers were everything one could imagine of a Regency. The corruption—unimaginable. The license—complete...." It was as though de Moulny smacked his lips as he added: "Yes!—the Élysée is the shortest road to Hell I know of.... But it was not until the night preceding the *coup d'État* that I—attained the supreme end I had had so long in view."

He breathed heavily, and blinked his pale eyes in luxurious retrospection. Dunoisse drove his nails deep into the palms of his clenched hands, restraining the almost irresistible impulse to dash his fist in the evil, sensual face.

"Be reasonable, my excellent Dunoisse," he heard de Moulny saying, in almost coaxing accents. "Quit the field—accept the situation—remove from the path the obstacle of yourself.... For Henriette de Roux has long been very weary of you!... Only her exquisite womanly insincerity—the characteristic softness of her nature—have prevented her from forcibly breaking her connection—has held the hand that would otherwise have administer to you the final *coup de grâce*." He added, with his smooth brutality:

"Endeavor to understand that your foreign expedition has been arranged for you!—to conceive that the anonymous letter you previously received was considerately planned in the notion of opening your eyes. And receive from me the very definite assurance that where you once were ruled I am the ruler; and what you once imagined you possessed I hold and possess, and keep while it pleases me. For Henriette de Roux is my vice," said de Moulny, dully flushed now, and with his heavy face quivering. "No other living woman has such fragrance and savor, such daring originality in the conception of sheer evil.... You have never appreciated or understood her! You were the peasant set down to the *pâté* of truffles—the village fiddler scraping out a country reel upon a priceless Stradivarius—the thistle-eating ass who sought to browse on tuberoses and orchids!... What?... Have I roused the devil in you at last?"

For Dunoisse, with the savage, sudden lust to kill, thrilling in every nerve of his supple body, had leaped at the bull-neck, as a slender Persian greyhound might have launched its sinewy strength at a great mastiff; and locked together in a desperate grip, Alain and Redskin struggled for possession of the prize.

The slowly-dropping, envenomed taunts, the gross sensual hints, the vaunted luxury of possession had kindled and fanned Dunoisse's own cooling passion to a white-hot furnace-flame. What did it matter if Henriette were vile, as long as she remained what this man appraised her—a perfect instrument for fleshly joy? She was his by right of ownership—no other man on earth—least of all this big blond brute, conceited, fatuous, arrogant in very depravity—should have and hold her but Hector Dunoisse.

So Redskin and Alain struggled for possession of her, panting and swaying to and fro amidst the delicate toys and plenishings of the rose-colored room; crushing frail chairs and spidery whatnots under the weight of their grappling bodies; grinding the costly trifles swept from tables and consoles into powder under their reckless, trampling, muddy-booted feet.

A vivid recollection of the duel at the School leaped up in Hector as he listened to de Moulny's thick panting, and saw the savage, livid face, its paleness now blotched with red, coming nearer and more near.... And suddenly he realized that his antagonist was the stronger.... The supple muscular strength once distinctive of Dunoisse had deteriorated; possibly from excess of pleasure—from excess of labor it may be.... He nerved himself for a supreme effort, but the superior force and greater weight of his antagonist were surely gradually crushing him backwards across the sofa-foot, with those big white hands knotted in a strangling grip about his throat.

Choking, he freed one arm, and with fiery circles revolving before his eyes, and a deafening sound as of many waters in his ears, felt for the revolver in the inner pocket of his gray surtout. He meant to use it.... He would have used it, in spite of his determination, but that with lightning quickness his enemy divined his intention, and captured within his own the weaponed hand.

"Truly, old friend," said de Moulny's voice, thickly and lispingly, "one must needs be prepared for tricks when one happens to fight with you...." He crushed the imprisoned hand within his own, smiling evilly, and as Dunoisse, almost with a sensation of relief, felt the cold circle of steel forced home against his own temple, de Moulny spoke again:

"Do you comprehend, my excellent Dunoisse, what plan has just occurred to me? It is very simple—just a little more pressure than this upon your trigger-finger—and you will have committed suicide.... When they find you—(an ugly spectacle)—the revolver will be grasped in your dead hand—there will not be the slightest suspicion of foul play attaching to any other person. Nothing will be involved beyond the minor scandal of Madame's discarded lover having shot himself in her room———"

He laughed silently, puffing short whiffs of breath through his clumsy nose, his bulky body yet heaving with the exertion of the struggle, his big muscles still taut with the effort of keeping the upper-hand. His eyes were very cold, and smiled cruelly. He said, looking into the fierce black eyes that stared up at him out of the discolored face of the strangling man:

"——But as I wish to spare her an ugly spectacle, and further, because I am original in my methods of reprisal...."

The Colt's revolver, strongly thrown, crashed through the thick rose-colored glass of the one window that was not closely curtained, and, without exploding, was heard to fall upon the soft damp earth of a flower-bed underneath. And the choking grip upon Dunoisse's throat relaxed— the weight of his enemy's bulky body ceased to crush him....

"Get up," said de Moulny coarsely, "and—since you will not take your dismissal from me—take it from Madame there. Look!... She is coming to herself!... In an instant she will speak!"

It was true. Long shudders rippled through Henriette's beautiful, helpless body. Her bosom heaved with shallow, gasping breaths. The eyes between the parted eyelids rolled and wandered blindly. She moaned a little, as though in pain.

"Awake, my white leopardess!" said the voice Dunoisse so hated. "Unclose your petals, my blood-red, fragrant flower of Sin! Mock your lovers no more with that white sculptured mask of chastity, my imperial Messalina!... Say to this poor wretch, awaiting your sentence in anguish: *'Another lover is preferred before you.... You have had your night of rapture.... Depart! and let me see your face no more!'*"

She only moaned, and feebly beat her head from side to side upon the cushions. Her eyelids trembled. Spasms, like shadows, passed over the ivory face.... Her mouth hung a little open, as her lungs drank the cold foggy air that poured in through the shattered window.... And a new idea struck de Moulny. He looked at Dunoisse, standing white and haggard and shame-stricken on the other side of the sofa. And he said, in a changed, less smoothly brutal tone, and without his hateful smile:

"This is a strange, unusual method of settling a dispute for possession, but unconventionality pleases me.... Understand, I am ready to abide by the issue, be it what it may—nor have I any objection to pledge myself by an oath...." He glanced at the wall beyond the bed-foot, where Dunoisse knew well there hung an ivory Crucifix. The figure was covered with a drapery of black velvet. And at the sight the banished light of mockery came back into de Moulny's hard blue eyes.

"Ah, no! There shall be no oath, my good Dunoisse," he went on, almost gently.... "Both of us have proved the brittleness of such things!... But listen, and if my plan appeals to you, accept it.... When——" He rose up, and turned his eyes to the sofa. He asked himself, musingly, with cold considering eyes studying what lay there: "Was I mistaken, or did I hear her speak?"

She had only moaned, and muttered something incoherent. De Moulny went on:

"Long years ago—when one whose name is too sacred to be uttered within these walls—lay in a swoon as deathlike and protracted as this"—his big hand motioned towards the sofa—"the first name she uttered upon her recovery, was that of her youngest son.... And I knew then—though she had never made any parade of difference between us,—that of all her children she loved me best. Then listen. Whose name this woman speaks, his she shall be, soul and body! Is that agreed, my virtuous Dunoisse?"

The cold blue eyes and the burning black eyes met and struck out a white-hot flame between them.

"It is agreed!" said Dunoisse in a barely audible voice.

"Her husband is out of the running,—a scratched horse," said de Moulny, sneering and smiling.... "He has battened on the sale of her beauty, and climbed by the ladder of his shame. Therefore, should those pale lips frame *Eugéne*—it counts less than nothing.... We stand or fall by their dropping into the hair-weight balance of Destiny a 'Hector' or 'Alain.'"

A silence fell. The ashes of the dying fire dropped upon the tiled hearth with a little clicking echo.... Three rivals waited by the moaning figure on the sofa in the disarranged, disordered bedchamber.... De Moulny, and Dunoisse, and Another Whose Face was hidden by a veil....

"*Ah, Jesu Christ!...*"

The Name came from the pale lips of Henriette in a sighing whisper. Then silence fell again like a black velvet pall.... Dunoisse and de Moulny, the fire of lust and anger dead ashes between them, looked with awe and horror, each in the other's face. And stronger and clearer upon the strained and guilty consciences of both, grew the impression of an unseen Presence, awful, condemnatory, relentless, all-potent, standing between them in the rose-colored room.

De Moulny spoke at last, in a shaking whisper, a strange light burning behind the eyes that were like polished blue stones:

"Do you hear?... She is God's, this woman for whose body and soul we have disputed.... Christ has claimed her!... She is no longer yours or mine!..."

He thought he spoke to Dunoisse, but Dunoisse had already left the Rue de Sèvres behind him. With despair eating at his heart, and Remorse and Shame for traveling-companions, he had resumed his interrupted journey— he was speeding to the Pestilential Places of South-Eastern Europe to carry out the secret mission of Monseigneur.

LXVII

Have you forgotten a trooper of Her Majesty's Hundredth Regiment of Lancers, who, being secretly married to his mother's milkmaid, and detected by a pigman in the administration of divers conjugal endearments—sanctioned by Church and State, but unpardonable in the hollow eyes of Sarah Horrotian—was, by maternal decree, incontinently driven—with his young bride and his good horse Blueberry—forth from the gates of Upper Clays Farm?

The wedded pair supped and slept that night at Market Drowsing, in a garret of the Saracen's Head Inn. So many thirsty callers were attracted to the bar of this hostelry by the news—disseminated as soon as told—of the rupture between Sarah Horrotian and her son, that the landlord, for the accommodation above-named, refused payment.

"For—my part I praise 'e for the step you've taken! All same," the landlord added, with a touch of the Sloughshire caution, "theer be no need for 'e to go telling Widow Horrotian as much. For her puts up her shay and pony here regularly on market-days—and custom is custom, be it large or small."

At dawn, fortified by slaps on the back and a good many handshakes, as well as cold bacon, bread and butter, tea for the bride and ale for the groom; man, woman, and horse took the road for Dullingstoke Junction, whence Mrs. Joshua Horrotian was to proceed by rail to the cavalry depot town of Spurham, and await at an address supplied by her husband, his slower arrival by road.

It was a raw, cold, weeping day. A numbing wind blew between its sleety showers. As they paused on the bridge that spanned the swollen river to look their last at the farm perched on the high bleak ridge of the sixty-acre upland, a scarlet mail-phaeton rattled past behind the flying heels of its pair of spirited blacks. The trooper, recognizing the squat and bulky figure buttoned in beside the driving groom under the phaeton's leather apron, wrapped in a dreadnought cloak and sheltered under the vast green silk umbrella dutifully held over him by the servant who occupied the back seat; reddened to the rim of the idiotic little muffin-shaped forage-cap of German pattern approved by Government, but Thompson Jowell gave no sign.

"Damn my tongue!" had come from Josh in almost a mellow tone of retrospective ruefulness.

"Whatever for, dear Josh?"

Nelly turned on her love rounded eyes of alarmed astonishment. He answered, wiping with the back of his sinewy hand a splash of Jowell's mud from his sunburnt cheek.

"Because I doubt I ha' made me another enemy with it, and that's one too many, Pretty—as things are just now." He whistled a stave of "The Ratcatcher's Daughter" with defiant melodiousness, then broke off to say with a broad, irrepressible smile:

"To think of my having twitted of him wi' buying spoiled hay and mildewed barley, and pitched them kilns that are worked in a name that isn't his'n at Little Milding—along of the empty jam-tins and dead kittens and so on that ha' been sarved out to us chaps in the Government Forage trusses—at his head. Egad! I can hardly believe it o' myself!"

With her bonnet thrust back and falling on her shoulders, and the sweet rosiness hunted from her cheeks by the revelation of his terrible presumption, she panted softly:

"Dear Josh, you never!..."

"Ay! but I did though," the soldier retorted, "as true as I live!"

"And him that great and rich and powerful," she breathed. "Whatever will he do to 'e? By way o' revenge, I mean—come he gets the chance."

"Why, he med make more bad blood between me and mother—if so be as that's to be done," said Josh, meditatively tapping Blueberry's shining neck with the end of the bridle he held—"or drop a word at Headquarters that 'ud sow salt in my bed." He added: "By jingo! if—as seems likely—I be doomed to spend my long life sogering, I've done none too well by myself. Or you, poor girl, I doubt!"

His tone of pity hung bright drops on her dark eyelashes. She murmured, stroking the blue cloth that covered the broad shoulders:

"How can e' fare to say that? Haven't 'e married me? And the long life you talk of will be ours, dear love!—not yours to live alone."

"The harder for you, maybe!" he said, bending his brows and setting his strong jaw doggedly. "If I were free of the Service, to earn enough to keep you in comfort would be an easy job for hands as strong as mine. But with 'em tied to the lance, carbine and sword—and my legs bent round a horse's belly—all I am worth in the opinion of my betters is one-and-tuppence a day. You ha' got to go into decent lodgings somewheres," pursued the trooper, "till I can get the ear of the Officer Commanding our Squadron—and my Captain being his friend, and a free-spoken, kindly young gentleman—med be he'll take an interest in our case. If so, the fact o' my having gone and got married without leave—and I could punch my own head for a fool's for having done it!—might be blinked at and got over like,—though it comes next to Insubordination and Neglect of Orders on the long list of a soldier's sins. In which case—inquiries being made and satisfactorily answered—you'll be allowed fifteen pence a week. It ain't a handsome income," commented Josh, "when you remember it's supposed to find 'e in house-room and food and firing, but at any rate it'll eke out what we have. Even if I'm disappointed about the Captain's buying Blueberry, I've a pound or so put by in the little green purse you netted, against a rainy day. And if this bain't the kind o' weather that calls for it I'm a Dutchman! No!—don't you begin to talk about your blessed little savings," the soldier added hastily, "laid up out o' the four pounds odd to-year my mother's paid 'e!... There may come a use for them, before you know!"

She faltered, with the banished roses crowding back into the sweet oval cheeks, and the shy hazel eyes shunning his warm blue ones:

"And shall I have to live in lodgings always?"

"Why," said Josh, setting his strong face ahead as he marched steadily by the side of Blueberry, "if I have luck in getting a good word from Captain Bertham, you may be took upon the strength of the Regiment as a Squadron Woman by-and-by. Which means you'll live wi' me in Barracks, and share a room with eight or ten married couples and their families, and maybe a bachelor or two thrown in, in case we're too private and decent-like among ourselves.... West Indian slaves, I'm told, are allowed separate huts by their masters when they're married. But an Army blanket or a patchwork counterpane hung on a clothes-line," said Joshua Horrotian, with a resentful light burning in his wide blue eyes, "is good enough—according to the grand gentlemen who sit in Cabinet and call themselves the Government—to hide the blushes of a soldier's wife!" He added, with a latent grin hovering about the mouth that was shaded by the bold dark red mustache: "Not that it 'ud take an over-and-above sized one to hide Mrs. Geogehagan's. She bain't a blushing sort—though I've seen Geogehagan's ears as red as two boiled lobsters when she've took it into her head to pull 'em—the masterful catamaran!"

"Whatever for?"

The trooper's solid shoulders shook a little. The grin was no longer latent as he replied:

"For the preservation of Discipline—or because the Corporal had stopped in Canteen when he'd ought to ha' been helping her peel the taters or wash the babbies.... 'Give me your ear!'—she says to 'n—and he gives it, as meek as a mouse. Ha, ha, ha!" He ceased his laughter to say in a tone not at all mirthful: "And mind you!—she's the sort of woman you'll have to live alongside of, if you're lucky. As for the rest.... But there!—I've took oath to cure myself of griding and grumbling.... 'Discontented,' that's one o' the things Mr. Jowell called me yesterday, and for all I know the man may be right." He filled his big chest with the keen air and puffed it out again, as though he blew away his discontent with it. "Look here! Let's make-believe, as the children say, that all's for the best that's happened. I'm game if you are!"

"And sure to goodness," Nelly put in, as the big hairy-backed hand gave the upward twist to the dark red mustaches, and the firm mouth it shaded curved in the old smile, "what wi' Jason's ragging and your mother's nagging, I could no ways ha' bided to The Clays for long."

"No more you could, now I come to think of it!"

In cheering the drooping spirits of his bride he had heartened himself; and now he turned a brightened face to Nelly's, and said in tones that had the old hearty, buoyant ring: "True love drove our nail, Pretty, and Good Luck may clinch it. I said to that big gentleman I angered yesterday wi' my plain talk—as how I'd leave the crimson silk sash and the officer's gold epaulettes a-hanging at the top of the tree for some cleverer fellow than me to reach down. But wi' you standing at the bottom to cheer me on," said Josh, with a great revival of energy and spirits, "damme if I don't have another try for 'em! So remember,—the toast for my next mug of beer—which must be a half-pint, seeing as I'm a married man and can't afford luxuries—should go: 'Here's to Promotion—and may it come soon!' Hup! will 'e, Blueberry!" The soldier added as the young horse obediently quickened his pace. "You're our best friend just now, it strikes me. For if so be as the Captain's pleased wi' you and buys you—there's his money to put with the rest into the stocking—not to mention his good word for your master's wife. Look at his ears, Pretty," adjured Josh, beaming and patting the glossy gray shoulder. "Don't the twitch and set of 'em seem to answer, that what he can do he will?... Talk about Dick Whittington's Cat—and Puss in Boots, this here horse o' mine is worth a shipload o' such miaulers. When we get to Dullingstoke,—and it's not but three miles farther,—suppose you hear the bells o' the little yellow iron church in the Stokes Road begin to ring out 'Turn again, Joshua Horrotian, Regimental Sergeant-Major!' don't you be surprised!"

LXVIII

But although the twitch and set of Blueberry's ears did not fail of their significance—though the young horse was duly purchased by the kindly Captain for Josh's troop, and the good word of the officer was not wanting in the interests of the clandestinely-married couple—the day that was to confer upon Nelly the privileges of the barrack-room and the right to revolve in the select if limited social circle where Mrs. Geogehagan reigned in virtue of her rank as Corporal's lady—did not dawn for many, many months.

The sweet came before the bitter. Though the rose-colored glasses through which couples wedded for love invariably view the scenery of the honeymoon, could hardly disguise the fact that the lodgings—a two-pair-back in a dingy street of rickety houses in the purlieus of the Cavalry Barracks at Spurham—were squalid, dingy and dubiously clean. Yet the neighborhood presented advantages. Regimental visitors were frequent. Healths were pledged with these in foaming pots of ale and stout from one or other of the prosperous taverns in which the neighborhood abounded. And not infreqently the parting guest—counting on the liberality of a man who was not only newly-married, but had the price of a horse in his pocket—appealed to Josh for a loan, and got it. Do you call the lender spendthrift and the borrowers shabby spongers? They would have ministered to their comrade's need—supposing their pockets had been full, while his were empty. 'Twas a way they had in the Army when Queen Victoria was young and pretty.... 'Tis a way they have still, though her grandson reigns in her stead.

You are asked to imagine the palpitating wonder and delight of Nelly's first plunge into the giddy round of garrison-town pleasures. The Circus presented charm but not novelty—because every year when the plums were ripe, and the Fair was held at Market Drowsing, Banger's Royal Terpsichorean and Equestrian Grand Gala Entertainment encamped upon a marshy patch of waste in the town suburbs, and foreign-complexioned men with earrings, carrying whips of abnormal length, came to The Upper Clays to bargain for oats, hay, mangold-wurzel, and cabbages—the last-named commodities constituting the elephant's favorite bill-of-fare. Free admissions to the sawdust-strewn, horsey land of enchantment within the big creaking tent of patched canvas were granted upon these occasions—not to stern Sarah, in whose gaunt eyes spangled females capering in pink tights upon the backs of ambling piebalds, represented the peculiar progeny of the Babylonish Whore—but to her maid and man. For Jason's chapel-going never cured him of the horseriders. In the secret estimation of the piggy man the New Jerusalem was but an immensely-magnified, unspeakably more glorious Banger's. Not but what the lithe and supple gentleman in a sheath of glittering scales—who doubled himself into snaky knots while spewing fire—was hardly the sort of personage one might expect to meet with up here....

You are asked to be present in imagination upon the gallery benches of the Theater Royal, Spurham, upon the never-to-be-forgotten occasion when Josh took his bride to the Play. The blood-curdling melodrama of "The Ruffian Boy" constituted the principal item of the programme. Miss Arabella Smallsopp of the Principal London Theaters having been specially engaged to appear in the character of "Ethelinda," the Baron's Bride.

To look down from the gallery—sitting perched up there so high—and beside a husband so big, so manly, and so handsome in his uniform that the old lady in the squashed bonnet and nose to match, who sold you winkles, oranges and nuts, cried "God bless him!" as he rated her for giving short measure in the latter commodity—was in itself an experience thrilling enough to make you gasp even supposing the extraordinary mixture of paint, varnish, gas, drains, damp clothes, and heated humanity that was supplied to the patrons of the gallery in place of air, had not tickled your nose and stung your throat and eyes, making you cough and sneeze and blink....

Only two defacing smudges marred the shining page whereon Memory recorded the history of that evening. Incident No. 1 occurred shortly after a row of heads and shoulders, with musical instruments of various kinds attached to them, which Josh explained to be the Orchestra, had sprung up like mushrooms at the bottom of a big black ditch, below the line of smoky tin-screened lights twinkling at the bottom edge of a great Curtain—with a palace in an astonishing garden, and a lake full of swans, and groups of dancing ladies painted on it; marvelously beautiful, but wi' so mortal few clothes on as to make a body ashamed to look.

It was just before a lank gentleman with upright hair had popped into a seat raised above the level of the previously-described heads and shoulders, and briskly rapping with a little black stick upon a desk, had caused the Orchestra to burst into a jumble of Popular Airs, described by a waggish young man on the back benches as a "musical bluemange," beginning with "My Heart's in the Highland," continuing with "The Marseillaise"—for some reason or other vociferously applauded—and ending with "Rule, Britannia" and "Britons Strike Home."

A young female—not so very young neither—Mrs. Joshua Horrotian couldn't help but notice!—in spite of her vividly red-and-white complexion, and a profusion of light ringlets, tumbling out of a smart bonnet of pink satin trimmed with green ostrich feathers—a gaudy, tawdry young woman of the class we were then, as we are now—content to call unfortunate—closely followed by a tall, lean, pimply-faced young trooper in the beloved blue, white-faced uniform of the Hundredth Lancers—came squeezing her way between the row of knees on one side and the row of shoulders on the other—and plumped herself down in the vacant place by Joshua Horrotian's side.

To the stolid vice of the country-side Sarah's late milkmaid was no stranger. Abey Absalom's too-yielding girl, Betsy Twitch the weeding-woman, were not the only specimens of female frailty to be found in the neighborhood of The Upper Clays. Fairs and public holidays, stirring up the muddy dregs of Market Drowsing, showed, while the naphtha-lights still flared amongst the booths—while unsteady revelers staggered homewards between the hedgerows—spectacles sordid, brutal, and obscene enough to have been worthy of the brush of some bygone Flemish painter of revels and kermesses....

Nelly had known from childhood that certain men and women habitually committed sin together; sin for which the women were locally denounced as "right down bad uns," or "demmyrips," or purely as whores—while the men reaped no blame whatever. She was too simple to dream of injustice—she sometimes wondered why, that was all.

The first glance had told Nelly that Pink Bonnet was a "bad un." The whiff of cheap musk that emanated from the tawdry garments—the smell of spirits that breathed from the leering painted lips, had sprung the rattle of warning, before—in a voice brazen and hoarse with drink, excess, and midnight brawling, Pink Bonnet addressed Joshua Horrotian as "her ducky," and asked him to "stand a drain."

Never, never! would Nelly forget the turn that creature gave her—not if she lived to be ever so old....

With Josh, as red as fire, or the coat of the infantryman sitting in front of him, saying in a sheepish, bashful voice, not at all like his usual robust one:

"Excuse me, Miss!—I'm a married man!"....

Why Pink Bonnet, on the receipt of this intelligence, should become vociferous and abusive, calling Josh a low, imperent soger, and a great many worse names, Mrs. Joshua could only wonder. Indeed, so forcible and lurid became her language, that cries of "Order!—Or-*der*!" rose up about them; and the row of backs of heads in front became a row of faces, full of round, staring eyes and grinning mouths. And then a huge man in a Scotch cap and shirt-sleeves looked over a wooden partition at the back of the gallery, and presently came striding down the narrow gangway, followed by a chimney-pot-hatted policeman. And Scotch Cap said, beckoning with one immense finger: "Come! Out o' this, Polly, since you dunno' how to behave yourself!" Upon Polly's launching into a torrent of sulphurous invective, the policeman added, warningly: "You ought to know by this time, my gal, that cussing makes it worse!" And as Polly—still fulminating threats of ultimate vengeance, wreaked upon somebody's eyes, heart, and liver, was hustled out and vanished, followed by her tall, pimply-faced companion, Nelly whispered to Josh, as a vast breath of relief heaved the big ribs that pressed against her side:

"Her were quite a stranger to 'e—weren't her, Josh, love?"

And heard him answer, as he wiped the standing sweat-drops from his high, tanned forehead, with a big hand that shook a little:

"I never saw her before in all my born days."

LXIX

But of course Josh knew Pink Bonnet—with the peculiarly intimate knowledge that is entertained by the soldier for the garrison prostitute. He pitied himself for the rough cross-chance that had brought her to the theater—with the man who had taken the place he had indifferently vacated—and set her down, blazing with gin and jealousy, on the bench, cheek-by-jowl with the man who had thrown her over to marry a cleanly maid.

Ah, poor young wives! How little they dream of the muddy secrets hiding behind the clear, candid eyes they gaze in so trustfully—how little they suspect what lips the beloved lips have kissed! If you told them: "This hand that strays in your hair has tangled in the tresses of the harlot," they would laugh you to scorn, or scorch you with their burning indignation; so unshaken is their faith in the manly hearts of whose swept and garnished chambers none ever held the key before them—whose most hidden secrets they believe they have been told. Alas! the poor young wives!

As for the husbands of the wives, by a law immutable as the foundations of the world we tread on, Pink Bonnets must be paid for in the end. Find me a smart to outdo that of lying to the dearest who never dreams of doubting you! thought the trooper, in homelier phrase than this. Sickly heats coursed through his thick veins, and the taste in his mouth was bitter as Dead Sea waters. The big, tawdry theater, packed full with eager pleasure-seekers, gave a sense of emptiness that frightened him.... Nelly nestling by his solid side, seemed miles and miles away.... For the shadow of an old, wellnigh forgotten sin had come between them, and was pushing them apart. To counteract the mental conviction of guiltiness he repeated to himself all the trite clauses of the Code of Manhood, and employed, in imaginary defense of conduct denounced by an unspecified accuser—all the clinching arguments he knew.

"Ye wouldn't have a man live aught but a man's life would ye?"

Followed by:

"'Tis true I ha' run wild a bit—drank a bit,—betted a bit—frequented loose women, and the rest of it!—but so have all the young chaps I ever knew or heard of. Why should I set up to be better than the rest?"

Then:

"Women ye see—they be made different from men! 'Tis easy for them to run straight—that is, for the good ones. They can resist temptation better than us—being so much weaker and less sensible than we!"

The Curtain went up as the unseen person with whom Josh argued—and who never answered any of his arguments,—was getting the best of it, to the trooper's mind, Mrs. Joshua clutched the big blue cloth-covered arm with a little squeal, as the Interior of the Robber's Cave amongst the Rocks was revealed by the combined light of a calcium moon and a brazier with rags dipped in spirits-of-wine blazing in it. Anon, to his band of cloaked, bearded and villainously slouch-hatted myrmidons, entered—to tremulous music from the fiddles, down the rocks, Giraldi Duval the Ruffian Boy.

Never was such an out-and-out scoundrel. For certain unspecified reasons it was comforting to Joshua Horrotian to have somebody to disapprove of just then. The light and trivial sins of a whole regiment of British soldiers, would, if piled into the balance against the crimes of the Ruffian, have certainly kicked the beam.

It was necessary to assure Mrs. Joshua, holding on to the stout blue arm and shivering deliciously, that the whole thing was make-believe. That the Ruffian—unloading pocket after pocket of stolen jewelry and bags of guineas—bragging of his enormities, and quaffing draught after draught from an immense gilt goblet painted red inside—was a respectable gentleman "off." That he had not just drunk a stranger's blood with his thirsty dagger in mistake for the beauteous Ethelinda's; and that Innocence and Virtue as personified by that fair creature—whose scorn had driven the Ruffian to raving madness—though doomed to suffer hideous things in the course of the evening (unless the playbill deceived people who had paid their money for places) would certainly triumph in the long-run.

How enchanting Ethelinda was, when the Castle Hall, having hurried on from both sides and fallen down in the middle—and a brace of retainers in black wigs having brought on a table and two chairs—she appeared in pale blue satin, spangles, curls, and feathers, leading the Baron's children—Ethelinda being the Baron's lady, it was even more possible to cry out upon the Ruffian—and telling the faithful Catherine and her dearest prattlers all about her latest escape from Giraldi's unhallowed hands.

The Baron was sure that in spite of the valor of a husband's arm, the Ruffian would have another shy at running off with the lady; and so he did, in the very next scene, dressing up in old Margaretta's cloak and hiding in her cottage; and terrifying Ethelinda into vowing never to quit her Baron's castle again, even though myriad summers decked the land with flowers and feathered songsters upon every tree tempted the ear with joyous songs of love—until the Ruffian should have yielded up his ghost upon the gallows.

Depend upon it, our forerunners of the forties were not half so ignorant and unsophisticated in matters dealing with Dramatic Art as we suppose them to have been. They knew, as well as we do, that Life, as represented on the stage in that era, was impossible, unreal, and absurd.... But just because it was so unlike Life they loved it. They preferred Action to Art—and got it.... They reveled in impossible, absurd sentiment, and high-flown hyperboles. Impromptu love-matches, extravagant, gaudy crimes, and greased-lightning repentances gave them the purest joy. When you went to the theater you left Reality behind you. You expected the combined smells of paint, glue, and varnish to be wafted over the footlights. The last thing you wanted was the odor of new-mown hay.

The Gothic Chamber in the Baronial Castle was another thrill—the evening was a succession of them—with more of the tremolo passages from the fiddles in the Orchestra, heralding the advent of the Mad Lady—whose daughter—you have of course forgotten—had been immolated by the Ruffian in mistake for Ethelinda. To see the poor thing trailing about looking ghastly in white draperies, staring glassily at nothing in particular, and blowing lamps out with deep sighs, drew pitying tears from Mrs. Joshua, and even caused Josh to sniff and gulp and surreptitiously wipe his eyes. Both were certain she would be seen more of presently; and so she was—coming on in the very nick of time—just as the Ruffian, armed with a drawn sword, had burst from behind the tapestry in Ethelinda's bedchamber—to terrify him into rushing off, just in time to meet the Baron, with *his* drawn sword, in the Gothic Gallery.

Clish—clash! went the broadswords in the dark—stage darkness at that era being but a shade or two less obscure than a November afternoon.... Chains, repentance, vengeance for the Ruffian, union, joy, felicity for the Baron and Ethelinda. And the Drop came down upon a general picture, to rise again and sink once more, and rise—ere the tidy semicircle of legs of both sexes had quite disappeared from view—amidst round upon round of clapping; piercing whistles——the pounding of approving sticks, enthusiastic umbrellas, and urgent boot-heels, and reiterated shouts of "Bravo!" and "'Core!"

The interlude of "The Lancers" followed, and then the great queen curtain fell amidst the strains of "God save the Queen," and then the sensations of the evening were over. All save that last one at the very end.

It happened when the packed gallery-audience, howling like Siberian wolves from sheer high spirits and good temper—swept down the long steep flight of stone stairs and out into a muddy side-street, and filling this mean alley from wall to wall, crushed out at the upper end of it, to encounter the turbid flood of humanity roaring from the gullet of the Pit Entrance that gaped just beyond the gilded portals by which the gentlefolks who came in carriages and wore Evening Dress, and didn't seem to enjoy themselves half as much as folks who sat in cheaper places—were admitted to the Grand Tier.

There was a good deal of joking, laughter, squeezing, and jostling, and some pocket-picking beyond a doubt.... The shiny chimney-pot hats, smug whiskered faces, and bright brass collar-numbers of policemen bobbed up and down amongst the crowd—there were several ugly rushes, accompanied by oaths and screaming; and Josh and Nelly, carried off their feet by one of these, were swept up some steps leading from the gilt-pillared portico previously referred to, as some well-dressed Circle and Box people were coming down them, headed by a tall and handsome young gentleman, who, with a gallant air of being in charge of something particularly precious and breakable, was bending down to whisper to the young lady who leaned upon his arm....

Josh hadn't the faintest intention of bumping into the lady, a slender, pretty young creature in a white velvet mantle—trimmed beautifully with swansdown—and who was wearing a garland of pale blush roses on the loveliest fair hair you ever did see. But as the trooper ruthfully stammered his apologies, the gentleman—becoming aware of the blue, white-faced uniform, brusquely interposed, saying in a tone by no means pleasant to hear:

"You infernal scoundrel! how dared you jostle the young lady? What do you mean by it, you blackguard, hey?"

Josh answered with a sullen frown:

"I've said a-ready, sir, as I didn't go to do it, and that I'm as sorry as man can be!"

The gentleman retorted, in a cold savage way, speaking between his set teeth:

"If you had meant it, you dog, you would have been soundly thrashed for your insolence. As it is—take that!"

That was a sharp blow across the trooper's mouth from the lady's fan, carried in the white-gloved hand of her gallant. The ivory sticks broke, and the blood sprang, and Nelly cried out; and then, as the gentleman hurried the young lady down the steps—at the bottom of which a brougham waited—with a liveried servant holding open the door:

"You didn't hurt the man, Arthur, did you?..." Nelly heard the young lady ask, and the answer came brusquely:

"No! though the blackguard deserved it.... Broken your fan though! Pity!... Never mind!... You shall have a prettier from Bond Street, when I get back from Town...."

Then the carriage door banged, the crowd seemed to melt away, and Mr. and Mrs. Joshua Horrotian were hurrying through the muddy ill-paved gas-lit streets, home to their lodgings. From whose dinginess the rosy glamour of the honeymoon had quite, quite fallen away....

As Josh, by special permit, was not due in Barracks before next day's Revally, the newly-wedded couple supped on cold scraps put by from dinner,—or pretended to, for the trooper's cut lip hurt him, and Mrs. Joshua couldn't have eaten a mouthful, seeing him so cast down—not if you had tempted her with Turkey Soup—as understood to be consumed by the Lord Mayor of London out of a gold spoon—and Roast Venison—and betook themselves to rest. Nelly had comforted the swollen lip with old linen rags and hot water; but the swollen heart of its owner was not to be eased, even by her gentle touch.... Long after her soft even breathing had convinced him that his young wife slept, the man lay open-eyed and wakeful; staring at the narrow line of watery moonlight that outlined the edges of the square of dirty blind....

And presently he knew that Nelly had not been sleeping; for he heard her sob out in the darkness the question that could not be kept back.

"Oh, Josh, dear love! Why ever did he do it? Why should even a grand, rich gentleman have the right to treat my husband so?"

She hardly knew the hard, stern voice that answered:

"You ask why he called me dog,—and struck me? Being th' dog's wife, med-be ye have a right to know! 'Twas because the gaslight showed my soldier's cloth and buttons.... We're housed like dogs, and fed like 'em— and take our pleasures come-by-chance as dogs do—and are sometimes whipped as dogs are.... Why shouldn't he call me dog? He was in his right—I was in my wrong! There's little else to say!..."

She sobbed out some indignant, incoherent words of protest. He filled his vast chest with a long, deep quivering breath, and sent it slowly out again, and said, still sternly, but less bitterly:

"In th' old days, dear lass, when, as I've heard tell, Leprosy were common in England, smitten folks went about th' roads and byways, sounding bell and clapper to warn wholesome people out of their tainted way. In some such manner—as I have no learning to word as should be—my uniform, that ought to be my honor, is my shame, in the eyes of my superiors and even many o' my equals. And gentlefolks like *him* and his, shrink from the rub o' the soldier's sleeve as if it carried th' pest. Now you and me'll speak no more of this, my Pretty. Let it be buried deep—and covered up—and hid away."

She promised amidst tears and wifely kisses, and thenceforwards the sore subject was touched upon no more. But Nelly was to learn that there are some things that, however deep their grave be dug, and though whole tons of figurative earth be heaped above them, cannot be kept buried. Long after the trooper's wounded lip had healed and the small scar left by the ivory fan had paled and vanished, she saw the bleeding scar.

LXX

Blueberry's purchase-money had long been spent—Josh's hoarded pound or so had melted, crown by crown, out of the green netted purse,—the last shillings of Mrs. Joshua's small store of savings had been swallowed up by those three shrieking needs of Humanity—more particularly Humanity reared under the inclement skies of Great Britain, for Food, Fire, and Shelter—before capricious Fortune relented in some degree towards the poor young lovers; permitting the missing certificate of their marriage at the yellow iron church at the bottom of the Stoke Road near Dullingstoke Junction, to be discovered within the covers of that sacred volume, the trooper's "small book," tucked snugly away in a fold of the parchment binding.

A copy of this talisman being forwarded by Josh's friendly Captain to Sarah Horrotian, with a request for a written testimony to the respectability of the young woman who had married her son, elicited from the widow an inky chart indicating vanity, light-mindedness, lack of religious fervor, ingratitude to benefactors, and carelessness in making-up the market-butter, as the principal rocks and shoals upon which the esteem of an employer would be most likely to suffer wreck. Beyond these categorized failings, in Christian justice (since the young woman was proven virtuous and no to-yielding trollop) Sarah had no more to add.

Perusing her epistle, Josh's troop-Captain whistled plaintively. For the crime of getting married "off the strength" was in those days, as it is in these, the blackest sin upon the soldier's list of minor offenses. Confronted with a problem of no ordinary toughness, the Captain betook himself and his difficulty to the Adjutant, an elderly officer of astuteness and experience, who, while maintaining a well-earned reputation as a rigid disciplinarian, had a heart in the right place. Over cigars and brandy-and-water the case was thrashed out....

"'Man is, as I understand you, in the very devil of a tight hole," said the Adjutant, knocking a two-inch ash off a long, dry, deadly-looking Trichinopoly cheroot. "Only thing possible for you to do for him under the circumstances would be *im*possible—for a conscientious officer—you quite understand? So I take it you'll simply wash your hands of Horrotian and his love-affairs—instead of sending in the mother's letter as testimony of character—and applying to Headquarters for permission for your beggar to get spliced. Having obtained that, you would—supposing you to be the kind of man I quite understand you not to be—put in the Certificate of Marriage—previously being careful to upset the ink-bottle over the place where the parson filled in the date!... Understand, I speak unofficially, when I say that in ninety-nine cases out of a hundred the mild deception would pass muster. Specially in the present case—the C. O. being uncommonly groggy about the eyesight; and objecting to spectacles on the grounds of their giving away a man's age. Officially speaking, if such a course of conduct were brought to my knowledge, I should instantly report it—do you understand me? And the consequences would be serious—consumedly serious, my dear fellow! For Rule and Routine are not skittles to be bowled over by privates who have kicked over the Regulations and married without the permission of their Commanding Officer. And Favoring is a thing to be avoided—I'm sure you'll understand!"

The Captain understood perfectly; and, though he rather overdid it with the ink-bottle—causing not only the date, but the names of the contracting parties to vanish under a sable lagoon of carefully dried writing-fluid—the charitably-conceived plot was successful, from beginning to end.

Those iron wheels of Administration—sorely hampered, even in these modern days, with that entangling medium known as Red Tape—did at last revolve without crushing the last hope of an ill-clad, hungry girl who was soon to be a mother. The hand of Official Authority was extended to Mrs. Joshua Horrotian with a weekly stipend of fifteen pence. By grace of the Officer Commanding the Squadron, Nelly—no longer of the depressed sisterhood of dowdy Paris yearning outside the sentried gate of that grim Paradise, the Cavalry Barracks—was admitted; privileged to bear her remunerated part in the getting-up of officers' linen, the lavation and mending of troopers' undergarments, as in the sweeping and scrubbing of passages and floors. Yet another day dawned that saw her an inmate of the long, bare barrack-room, where Mrs. Geogehagan—in virtue of her social status as Corporal's lady—resided with her husband and her young family, in a neat three-sided villa of patchwork quilt, at the upper, fireplace end....

When the pale-faced, shabbily-dressed, shy young woman was brought in with her light box and her meager bundles, by her husband, the room seemed already full of soldiers and their wives and children. The din of voices beggared description. Moggy Geogehagan was crying herrings at the top of all.

It is not to be supposed that the herrings were actually in evidence; but the raucous shriek with which Moggy—ere wooed and won by her Corporal—had vaunted these marine delicacies—fresh and saline—was justly famed throughout her native city of Dublin. It leaped three streets, to waken shattering echoes in the alleys beyant them—the suburbs knew it—

you heard Moggy coming, leaving a trail of fish and headache behind her all the way from Donnybrook to Irishtown....

The troop-room was entered from the upper end of a long, slate-flagged, ground-floor passage, smelling of potato-peels and boiled cabbage, and with coal-bunkers at the more distant end, under the iron-shod, iron-railed staircase. The walls were whitewashed, with patterns of damp bricks showing through; and had no other ornament than iron shelves and hooks, from which depended shining arms and various soldierly accouterments and trappings; the floor was of bare boards, clean-scraped and well-scrubbed. Long rows of cot-bedsteads, made in telescopic fashion so as to occupy half the space during the day that they took up when expanded by night, were ranged along the walls, with rolled and strapped up mattresses upon them; and not all the beds were screened off by rope-suspended counterpanes, or cast-off horse-rugs, from the rake of the public eye. Down the middle of the room ran heavy wooden tables on iron trestles, affording accommodation—on the backless benches that appertained to them—for eight married men with their wives and children; and the two bachelors who occupied opposing couches at the draughty end nearest the door.

Three or four men, and perhaps half-a-dozen women were sitting on the benches. Moggy Geogehagan herself, a short black pipe in her mouth, superintended the cooking of some pap for a regimental baby, in a small tin saucepan on the hob. Geogehagan—a stoutish, baldish trooper, with large red ears—Nelly could not but suspect the fundamental reason of the excessive development of these organs—was sitting on a three-legged stool, engaged, by the aid of a lighted candle, in dropping sealing-wax on the end of a new clay pipe.

There was a momentary lull in the deafening Babel. Then:

"Hooroo, Jude!" said Mrs. Geogehagan, with graceful brevity, rising up to the full extent of her six feet odd of stature, setting her vast elbows akimbo, and surveying the scared intruder with the eye that did not squint while the other swiveled round to make sure that her cookery was not burning. "Will any gintleman or lady presint condescind," she pursued in a tone of raking irony, "to be afther inthrojuicing me to the bit av' gintility that's dhropped in to pay us a marning call?"

"With your good leave, ma'am," put in Josh, with a more submissive tone and less confident air than Nelly would have ever expected of him, "this is my young wife, who—as I've explained to you already—has had the good fortune to be entered on the Regiment's Married Roll, after nigh on two years of delay. And I take the liberty, among comrades, to hope she's not unwelcome to any here present?—knowing of no reason why she should be!"

He looked about him, and there was an assenting murmur, and the seated men got up to shake hands, and the women, after a moment's hesitation, did the same. All save one, more tawdrily dressed than her companions, and with a great many light yellow curls, who kept her face turned persistently away.

"Gi' me your hand, Mrs. Horrotian, ma'am!" said Mrs. Geogehagan, advancing with great ceremony and stateliness. She added, as Nelly complied—in a soaring shriek that made Mrs. Joshua jump and flush nervously:

"Jems!"

"Is it me you're wantin', Moggy?" said bland James Geogehagan.

"It is!" said Mrs. Geogehagan severely, "an' the Divil mend your manners. Rare up on the ould hind legs av' you, and bid this dacent young wife av' Horrotian's welcome to the Rooms." She added, as the Corporal complied: "For we may bless ourselves there's men in the Rigiment that has more dacincy than to stand up for-ninst the clargyman or the priest wid a wagtail av' the gutther! I say ut in the brazen face that's lookin' at me now!"

There was no mistake about the face that confronted the indomitable Mrs. Geogehagan, ambushed in a forest of egregiously-curled light ringlets, with blazing eyes set in it, and flying the scarlet flag of battle in cheeks that wore the brownish stains of ingrained rouge. Nelly's hazel glance went to it timidly; and then—even if the pink bonnet—sadly the worse for wear—had not hung on a peg driven into the whitewashed wall behind, she would have recognized it with the same sinking of her heart. For it belonged to the flaunting woman who had accosted Josh upon that unforgettable evening at the theater; the patchouli-reeking, gin-perfumed creature who had thrust a red, ringed hand under the trooper's stiff, reluctant elbow, and had called him ducky, had asked him to stand drink.... Oh! how glad was Mrs. Joshua that hand had not been offered like the rest!... Never could she have demeaned herself to touch it, not for diamonds and gold....

Meanwhile it had been dawning in the slow brain of the tall, thin, pimply young trooper who had been Pink Bonnet's companion upon that memorable night, and was now sitting affectionately in her pocket, that the utterances of Mrs. Geogehagan were leveled at his wife. He had applied for permission to marry, and the inquiries of the Commanding Officer had been satisfactorily answered. There were persons who made quite a capital living—in those days as in these—out of whitewashing the feathers of the grimiest of soiled garrison doves.

You saw Trooper Toomey, yellow in the face and scowling, lumbering up at the nudge of an imperative elbow, from the form he had bestridden, with the air of a man nerving himself for a fight.

"Look a' here, I'm blasted if I'll stand this!"—he was beginning, when Mrs. Geogehagan cut him short.

"Toomey, me fine man," she said almost mellifluously, "av ye show them dirty teeth av yours at me, 'tis taking lave of your mouth they'll be with the dhrive in the gub I'll land you,—so shut ut—an' sit ye down!"

Thus cautioned, Toomey snapped his lank jaws together, threw his long leg across the form, and sat down sullenly, leaving Pink Bonnet to enter the arena alone.

In high, shrill accents she demanded to be informed without reserve whether she, the speaker, was or was not the lawful married wife of a low-bred white-livered 'ound what was afeared of standing up for her against them that for all their back-talk and sauce—was nothing but Irish Scum—and would, if all was knowed that might be knowed!—be held unworthy to sweep up the dust of her feet, or to eat off of the same table with her!...

"Hooroo, Jude!—an' is that the talk you have?" retorted Mrs. Geogehagan, with overwhelming irony. "Married you are, bedad!—an' proud av it as a mangy bitch wid a new tin collar. As for Toomey there!—sure, pay-cocks wid their tails spread is less consayted, I'll go bail!" She broke off as the Dinner Call sounded; plunged at the hanging tray above the long table, and began—as did several of the other women—to rattle down the plates and basins, crockery mugs and wooden-handled knives, in an orderly jumble upon the upper end of the board, while the sulky Toomey, seizing upon two very large, very bright, and very deep tin dishes, and hanging a tin pail over his arm, hurried out to the cook-house to get the mess for the Room. And in his absence, such men as had been taking it easy without their belts, coats and stocks, put them on again, and the women tidied their hair.

You subsequently beheld Mrs. Geogehagan in her glory, serving broth, boiled meat, cabbage and potatoes, in strictly equal helpings, into the various bowls and platters assembled on the board. This onerous task being completed to the general satisfaction, the men chose their portions first, and were succeeded—according to the husband's seniority of rank—by their wives. Then Mrs. Geogehagan, standing beside her Jems in front of the short form that stood at the upper end of the table—pronounced a pithy grace, which ran—unless my memory trips—something after this fashion:

"May Christ and the Four Evangels bless this mate!... Bad scran to that villain av' a throop-cook! Sure, the praties is burraned agin!"

LXXI

The door was thrown open by an Orderly Sergeant during the progress of this, Mrs. Joshua's first meal in Barracks, and a gruff bellow of "Attention!" caused a cessation of the clashing of knives, and a general uprising about the table heralded the entrance of the Officer for the Day. He was a blushing subaltern, fair-haired and nicely-mannered, who said a pleasant word of welcome to Mrs. Joshua, and, being preceded out of the room by the Sergeant, earned a favorable comment from Mrs. Geogehagan by not forgetting to shut the door.

After dinner the men adjourned to the Canteen for malt liquor, and the women strolled out, or gossiped among themselves. Tea-time meant for nearly all of them a snack of bread and cheese, washed down with beer—the fragrant leaf being eight shillings a pound in those days. Yet Moggy Geogehagan never failed to dhraw a raking pot upon the fire-cheek. She would as soon go without duds, she proclaimed, as widout her dhrop av' tay. To porther, consumed in the pewter pots with a cauliflower head on, Moggy was, as was her Jems, exceedingly addicted. Sometimes under the influence of the beverage the worthy couple quarreled. And upon these occasions—probably feeling the need of maintaining herself in an upright position—the Corporal's huge helpmeet would ask him for the loan of his ear.

Helping to undress, wash and tuck the children into their truckle beds, and washing-basket cradles, gave the young wife quite a homelike feeling. It was at Roll-Call—when every trooper not on duty stood to his bed and answered to his name—that the cheeks of Sarah's ex-dairymaid began to tingle and burn.

She had screened off her bed and her husband's with an old curtain and her shabbiest shawl, by the aid of clothes-line and corking-pins, nails and hammer.... Now, when the Sergeant had followed the officer out, and Josh—having been warned for First Relief of the Guard—had hurried on his greatcoat, belt, and pouches,—taken his lance, sword, sling-carbine, plumed cap and gloves from the iron shelf and the hooks in the wall immediately above the bed-head,—stuffed a hunk of bread into his pocket, kissed her and jingled out with another man detailed for duty—it dawned on Nelly—silent in the midst of all these women and their men—who laughed, quarreled, kissed, sang or cursed freely and unrestrainedly, and without the slightest regard for the convenience of their neighbors or the feelings of the diffident stranger—that she and Josh had got to go to bed to-night, and every night for years to come, in the midst of this deafening din; under all these curious, or indifferent or evil eyes....

You are to imagine the two great foul-smelling tubs brought in—and the imperative trumpet-call "Lights out!" turning the perpendicular crowd into a horizontal one—the smelly, noisy gaslit hell—for it seemed nothing less to Nelly—into another of stifled laughter and whispered words ... of blackness, and stench, and worse.... You may suppose the homely domestic Virtues ranged side by side with the fouler vices on the huckaback-sheeted, brown-blanketed, straw-stuffed palliasses. Be a little sorry for the country girl, accustomed to retire at curfew—rung even to this day in remote English villages—with her flat candle-stick to her clean and quiet chamber over the great farm kitchen; and sleep in lavender-smelling linen, lulled by the rush of the Drowse under its three bridge-arches, unawakened by the crying of the hunting owls as they moused along the rick-eaves and raided the sparrows' nests....

The great tubs were not the only things that reeked in the long, stuffy, vile-smelling room. Things were said that scalded the ears of the young wife, things were done of which she had never dreamed....

If she had had her man's strong arm about her, she would have hidden her face in his breast, and, with his hard hand covering her little ears, have sobbed herself to sleep. But she was alone—in a void of dreadful darkness, populous with goblins hideous and grim.... Realizing this, and being well advanced upon the road that ends in a full cradle or empty arms, an hysterical access seized the poor young thing.

Her sobs, her cries and writhings—for strange, sharp, piercing pangs began to be added to the mere mental tortures—at length attracted the attention of those who waked, and roused those who snored.... Iron bedsteads creaked, relieved of heavy bodies—a candle-end flared in a lantern at the Corporal's end of the room.... The stalwart figure of Moggy Geogehagan, arrayed in an ancient watch-coat, with her head tied up in a red-spotted handkerchief, and a blue yarn stocking tied round her neck—a certain cure for cowlds!—was illuminated by the candle's yellow flicker, demanding to be infrorumed av the rayson av the outrajis hullaballoo?

Receiving no reply, the indomitable Moggy strode to the quarter whence the crying came. You saw her lift the hanging shawl and disappear behind its meager screen. From within her voice proceeded, pitched in a key less raucous than was usual:

"'Tis her Woman's Hour that has come too soon upon the poor young crayture!... Let a brace av dacent women that are mothers, come quickly widin to me here!"

Ah! they were no longer troll-wives, grim female goblins of a strange nocturnal underworld! With one touch of the magic wand of Sympathy, brandished in her big red fist, did Moggy Geogehagan transform them into beings of warm human flesh and blood.

They left their beds and gathered round the flimsy tent of shawl and counterpane that housed the timid sufferer. Brawny women and scrawny women, little women and big women; women half-naked and not at all ashamed; women who habitually retired to rest as fully clothed as any Boer's *vrouw*. Pity and Compassion, hidden in these rough natures as silver in lead, or gold in quartz, or the ruby in its rough brown matrix of corundum, came shining to the light. The sheep with the goats, the "dacent" with the disreputable—they vied with each other in doing what they could. Even Pink Bonnet rose to the emergency, vindicating her oft-vociferated claim to be a woman, after all....

There was a gaunt bare whitewashed room with a rusty stove and a double row of moldy pallets in it, that was termed—with irony none the less grim because unconscious—the Barrack Hospital. No place was set apart where the soldier's wife might be tended in sickness, or bring forth her babe in peace; but thanks to Moggy Geogehagan and the two dacent women, and the rest that made a living wall of themselves between the poor young mother and the strange male eyes she dreaded so—the pale, rainy dawn that climbed over the high spiked walls of Spurham Cavalry Barracks, brought with it a new young life.

Thus Joshua Horrotian, coming back, yawning and shivering, at the expiration of his allotted term of hours On Guard, was met upon the threshold of the troop-room by the lady of the villa near the fireplace, big with news that made him stare.

"'Tis a grand boy, God bless it!—though he kem before he was joo, bedad!" trumpeted Mrs. Geogehagan, opening a chink in the clean, but yellowed flannel petticoat that had something that squirmed inside....

"And God bless you for a good woman, Mrs. Geogehagan!" stammered Joshua Horrotian. He added: "But oh! my poor girl! To ha' gone through her trial under the eyes of a crowd o' strangers, was cruel hard on her!"

"Hutt!" said Moggy scornfully, hushing and rocking the baby. "'Tis as well to get used to the worrust at firrust. What's natheral can't be desprit," she added, quoting a favorite proverb of her land. "And she has sinse, and pith in her, begob she has! 'Scrame out!' I sez to her in the nick of the danger—'if ye'd ever rise from that bed, scrame out, and not in!' And scrame she did till the hearers blessed themselves. Pass me your arrums to rack, an' take the child!"

But Josh, looking dubiously at the sleeve of his great-coat, whereon the lice of the guardroom crawled, hesitated to obey....

"Phyaugh!" said Moggy, with a toss of the head—adorned with the red-spotted handkerchief—that brought a quantity of coarse black hair, mightily resembling the tail of her husband's charger—tumbling down her back. "What matter for the like av thim ginthry! All the *weeneen* asks is an honust man for his dadda, and a dacent young crayther for his mammy—such as her widin there,"—she jerked her head towards the distant end of the troop-room—"wid a breast av milk to bate the Queen's" (who was popularly understood just then to be rearing a royal bantling after the natural method). "Hould out your han's, I bid ye," commanded the golden woman, "and take and bless your son!"

Joshua obeyed, for she would have cried herrings upon him in another minute.... And as he took the squirming bundle, he sniffed, and something splashed upon the yellow flannel petticoat. But Moggy had turned her back on him, and was racking the arms away.

LXXII

At St. Paul's Cathedral, beside the glorious bones of England's elder idol, the Admiral of the empty eye-socket and the vacant sleeve, the grand old white head of England's soldier-hero was laid to rest. The Army was Chief Mourner, the Nation followed him to the tomb. Britons had heartily hated him as Minister—as military leader they adored him. Nothing was remembered in that parting hour but what they owed to him. His funeral wreaths were hardly withered when,—with some noise of cheering from the Officers' Mess at lunch-time, echoed from the Sergeants'—who were having dinner—caught up by a squad dismissed from drill, and vociferously joined in by heads that were thrust from troop-room windows, it was made known at the Barracks of the Hundredth Lancers that the gentleman who had got himself elected President of the French a year or so previously, had now proclaimed himself Emperor of that nation. Upon the subject Mrs. Geogehagan was as bitterly sarcastic as Mrs. Geogehagan alone could be.

"Hooroo, Jude!" said she. "Cook him up wid a crown on! Sure there will be no houldin' him now—such will be the proide and consayt av the cobbler's dog!"

"And will it do us any good—the gentleman's being made an Emperor?" asked Mrs. Joshua Horrotian, who was sitting on her bed, nursing the infant Sarah, while little Josh, now a sturdy red-haired toddler of two years old, was dragging a headless wooden horse about the well-scrubbed floor.

"Why, none as I can think on," somewhat moodily returned Mrs. Joshua Horrotian's husband, who sat upon a bench not far off, engaged in doing what he would have technically termed "a bit of sogering"—represented in the polishing of divers chain-straps, buttons, badges, and belt-buckles to the brightest point of brilliancy attainable by the use of scraps of "shammy" and whitened rag.

"Unless," he added, "being well-disposed towards our country and our people, he med-be were to ask us to go snacks with 'n in a European War. With the Pruskis or th' Ruskis—that be showin' their teeth just now at the Turkeys—there baint much to choose between Foreigners anyway," said Joshua oracularly. "Not but what," he continued, with an afterthought, "they French Frogs be foreigners, too. And us have fought 'em in the Duke's day—and learned 'em the taste of a beating. 'Twould be oddish, now I come to think of it," said the trooper musingly, "for we to take 'em for Allies at this time o' day! And howsomever friendly this new Emperor may call hisself, there baint no gettin' away from the truth of his being the nephew o' the man as we boxed up in St. Helena—and his being, by reason o' that, a poor, out-at-elbows, shabby kind o' beggar—till his luck took the turn. 'Taint in Nature to suppose he's as uncommon fond of us as he makes out. I'm dodgasted," said Josh, employing the Sloughshire imprecation, "if I should be in his place! What be ye thinking of, my Pretty?"

For Nelly was looking at him across the baby, with a dubious wrinkle between her hazel eyes.

"Could I love 'e, I do wonder," she breathed in the ear he leaned to her, "supposing you'd went and killed a live man!"

"It wouldn't be a man, Pretty—it would be an enemy!" explained the trooper in all sober faith.

"But a man for all—of live flesh and blood!" Her sweet underlip turned downwards like a grieved child's. The trooper said, after a slight reflective pause:

"Why, dash my button-stick! I never thought of the beggar in that light. Howsomever, the chances are that th' boot might be on t'other leg—as far as the killing went. Halloa! Why, what's this for?"

He had been leaning forwards, looking at the baby, and his handsome head was very near the bosom whence it drank. So, pierced by the stab of that light careless reference to the grim chances of War, Nelly had thrown her strong young arm about her husband's neck, and snatched him to her, panting:

"Oh, if he ever dared!... The wicked—wicked——"

Mrs. Geogehagan, squatting on her own bed mending her Corporal's overalls, cried herrings in reprobation:

"Wickud, is ut? Sure, and wouldn't his wife—whoever she was, poor craythur!—an' whatever outlandish, quare kind av lingo she might use to spake her mind in, be after havin' an aiqual right to say the same av your man?"

Mrs. Geogehagan went on to say that Active Service, meanin' liberal Bounties, and more Pay, and the chances of Promotion, the jooty of every raal soldier's wife was to lep out av her skin wid joy at the wind av the worrud av a War.

The intelligence being shortly afterwards conveyed to Moggy that "ould Boney's nevey" was seeking a consort among the marriageable daughters of

European Reigning Sovereigns, she cried more herrings on the outrajis impidence of the man.

"A mane little jumped-up spigareethahaun!... Offerin' himself to ivery King's daughter in Creation before the sate of his throne is warrum!... Begob! we'd have him axing Queen Victoria herself to stan' up before the priest wid him—supposing herself wasn't suited wid a betther man!"

His Imperial Majesty's repeated failures to secure a suitable alliance caused Moggy exquisite gratification. She relented towards him a little upon his officially-announced determination to follow the dictates of his heart, and tread the flower-strewn path of connubial happiness, indicated by the implacable hunting-whip of Mademoiselle de Montijo. Public Securities went down two francs; Court jewelers, dressmakers, tailors, modistes and florists, wine-merchants and confectioners, danced like happy motes in the golden rays of Imperial Patronage; and Marquises, Dukes, and Counts of Napoleon I.'s creation—who had crept out of dark forgotten corners when the Empire came in again—cleaned the dust off their forelegs, and spread their crumpled wings, and buzzed like joyous bluebottles about the tables being spread for the Wedding Banquet. Most of the nobles of the defunct Monarchy danced to the tune Monsiegneur played them. But the ancient Duchesse de Viellecourt and the venerable Marquis de l'Autretemps, and the younger scions of the Old Régime—these would not shake a leg for him, however he might pipe.

But Paris was very gay indeed, blazing with new uniforms and newer bonnets,—bristling with lances, bayonets, and expectation.... The bustle and clamor were prodigious, the rattle of drums and the blare of trumpets, the squealing of feminine sightseers crushed in the crowd—the cursing of male citizens whose toes had been pounded by rifle-butts, made thick the air. Swarms of foreigners, avid to behold the pageant, filled the hotels and boarding-houses to bursting—you may imagine the accent of Albion predominant in the salad of mingled pronunciations—you may suppose the gold of the Briton clanking royally into the Gaul's trouser-pockets and tills.

Upon the carriage of the Imperial *cortége*,— (each drawn by six white horses) the arms of the Bourbons had been effaced in favor of the Imperial Crown. Over which the golden letters "N" and "E" had been tastefully emblazoned on a chaste cerulean blue background.... *The* carriage was drawn by eight prancing steeds, adorned with nodding plumes. And its domed roof was topped with an Imperial Crown of dimensions that caused the vehicle to sway and to wobble; so that the Eagle perching at each corner, and the Loves and Graces painted on its panels of mother-o'-pearl and golden lacquer, shuddered as though palsied with ceremonial stage-fright.

Sixteen colossal gilt eagles perched on the hoary towers of Notre Dame, brooding with outspread wings of blessing over the nuptial solemnities. Everything that could be draped, was draped with green velvet powdered with golden bees. The nave was carpeted with green. The Canopy above the Imperial Throne, and the Matrimonial Chair upon the dais (covered with a white carpet spotted with black, to represent ermine)—was of crimson velvet, bee-besprinkled. Above the Canopy was another Imperial Crown, on which sat another eagle—apparently of solid gold.

Referring to the Imperial Wedding number of the *Ladies' Mentor*—into which entrancing periodical Mrs. Geogehagan,—acting during a delicate domestic crisis as nurse to a new baby of the Colonel's lady—occasionally got a peep—it appears the Empress—already admitted to that title by the civil ceremony, was dazzling and *spirituelle* in a dress and train of white *velours épinglé*, and a diadem of superb diamonds, with a veil of *point d'Angleterre*. The Emperor,—admitted to be at considerable disadvantage in point of height as compared with his stately bride,—wore the Grand Cross and Collar of the Legion of Honor, with many other Stars and Orders, above the uniform of a French General of Division,—ending in white doeskins, high boots with four-inch heels, and spurs.

Five Cardinal-Archbishops and ten Bishops tied the sacred knot between them. Hooroo, Jude! Mrs. Geogehagan blessed herself to think of that. And so, attended by Ladies of Honor, Ministers, Marshals of France, and other State dignitaries, with Foreign Envoys and Minister Plenipotentiaries, the wedding-guests and a tag-rag and bobtail of Notabilities, Personages, and gilded and upholstered Functionaries—the splendid procession returned to the Tuileries.

Nothing—observed the Imperial Press organs—could be more proper than the attitude of the people. Not a single hostile expression was heard by the official reporter along the route. A statement of the purest verity, for although the troops and the salaried hoorayers shouted "*Vive l'Empereur! Vive l'Impératrice!*" at certain fixed intervals, the frozen silence of the people as that leaden, puffy face of Monsiegneur's passed by in the great creaking gilded coach beside the snow-white face of the beautiful Empress—was unbroken and profound.

He had become, perforce, accustomed to these silent acclamations, as, nodding as mechanically as any China Mandarin, he would be carried through the streets of the capital he had besmeared with blood. For though he had gagged the Assembly—swept the boulevards with discharges of grape, ridden down and sabered Frenchmen and Frenchwomen in broad daylight—locked the doors of the High Court of Justice—faked a *Senatus Consultum*, forged signatures to the Ballot Papers of the *Plebiscite* by the cartload; refurbished old Napoleon's dusty throne—mounted the seat—clapped his wings and cockadoodled the Prince of Knaves into the Emperor of Traitors—he could not make his people cheer.

Students and grisettes, artisans and their sweethearts, might exclaim at the beauty of the Empress and the splendor of her jewels. Not one woman envied her—not one man would have changed places with *him*. Wherever his puffy face and leaden eyes turned, as he bowed from side to side with the mechanical courtesy of a clockwork puppet or the Mandarin of China—not a hat was raised—not a handkerchief waved,—not a voice wished him long life or happiness. The regard that met his was as bleak, and cold, and nipping as the bitter January day.

He could intern those who had offended him in distant provincial townships. In cells of civil prisons, in dungeons of Military Fortresses, he could immure others, for the term of their natural lives. He could sentence yet others to be hugged to death by the Red Widow, or have them shot; and he did constantly. But none the more could he make the people cheer.

There were faces more exalted that as coldly regarded his pretensions. To wit, those Reigning Monarchs, parents of marriageable daughters who had declined the honor of his hand. Also the young Emperor of Austria, and the King of Prussia, and more formidable than all these put together, the grim Colossus of the icy North.

By Nicholas Romanoff, Autocrat of all the Russias,—who lived as plainly as the humblest of his soldiers, and died on a sack of leather stuffed with hay—the Tsar to whom Monsiegneur—when merely Monsiegneur—had made secret and ineffectual overtures with a view to the dismemberment and division of the Ottoman Empire—the brand-new Imperial Majesty of France was treated with a distant civility that galled and stung—as possibly it was meant to do.

England, the ancient, tried, and proven ally of Russia, was presently to bind herself in monstrous alliance with the crowned adventurer. The chaste Victoria was to dance at his Embassy—visit his capital—kiss him upon both cheeks—strange pasture for lips so stainless!—and call him "Sire my Brother."

But to Nicholas—until he became "Sire my Enemy," he was never to be anything but "Sire my Friend."

LXXIII

In the summer of the fateful year of 1853, a city of canvas tents sprang up, like a growth of giant mushrooms, on Chobham Common, and the evolutions of the troops encamped thereon, converted that usually bare and arid expanse of heath into the semblance of a vast market-garden crammed with perambulatory beds of the gayest and most flaunting flowers. Ere long a Grand Military Display took place under the eyes of British Royalty and various Foreign Crowned Heads—not to mention a hundred thousand representatives of the British Public, whom coaches, carriages, brakes, vans, gigs, market-carts, shandrydans, nags, and the humble efforts of Shank's Mare had brought to the scene of action.

Do you hear the trumpets crying and the bugles calling, and the batteries of the Royal Artillery thundering from the sandy heights overlooking the arena of mimic warfare? while withering volleys of blank cartridge from a line of white-duck trousered Infantry two miles long, shattered the glass of windows at Bagshot Hall (and, it is said, at Farnborough) and—to the profound relief of the Special Artists employed by the illustrated newspapers—caused the subsequent charge of the Cavalry Brigade commanded by H.R.H. the Duke of Bambridge, to be executed under cover of a dense and impenetrable cloud of smoke, jagged through with spurting jets of fire.

The same sort of thing—strange to record—was taking place on the other side of the Channel. Upon the extensive green billiard-table of the Bruyeres, sufficiently near the French Military barrack-camp of Helfaut, the training-maneuvers of some ten thousand representatives of every service branch of the French Army were duly succeeded by a Grand Inspection, carried out by Monsiegneur the Marshal de St. Arnaud, Minister of War. A sham battle followed in the presence of the Emperor and Empress, fresh from a triumphal tour throughout the North of France.

You are to suppose the heavy brazen field-guns belching and bellowing, whole miles of Minié rifles blazing and cracking, the crowds of spectators scattering for their lives as the Chasseurs de Vincennes advanced in column at the gymnastic pace of one hundred and eighty steps a minute, and the mounted Chasseurs charged, thundering over the wet soggy ground. Decorations were distributed to distinguished commanders, and a few smart sous-officiers in brand-new uniforms. Louis David painted the beautiful Empress in the braided tunic of a Hussar, wearing a beaver with a military plume, and mounted on a handsome charger. What earthly brush, asked the Imperial Press organ in a gush of inky rapture, could do justice to the grace of the Emperor?

In sober truth, the little, big-headed man with the long body and the short legs, was a finished master of the equestrian *haute école*. Few men in France could handle a horse better; and as he passed along the lines upon some splendid animal, he would turn its head towards the eagle-topped standard of each regiment, compelling his beast to bow and caracole as its rider did homage to the avuncular emblem. This circus-rider's trick, no matter how often repeated—never failed to elicit a genuine shout of "*Vive l'Empereur!*"

And what of the Northern potentate, England's old friend and ally, for whose warning and instruction these remarkable international demonstrations of military power had been devised and carried out? Physically the biggest man in his vast Empire, there was no moral littleness about Nicholas. He was wary and subtle and diplomatic, but he was not cunning or sly. He was a galloping terror to dishonest, peculating officials—it is on record what retribution followed his hawklike swoop upon the Imperial Dockyard at Cronstadt, where stores and materials of war—being conveyed in at one of the three gates, and duly registered by the clerks of the Receiving Department, were by a second gate, *convanient*—as Mrs. Geogehagan would have said—smuggled out again, and brought back *per* medium of the third; once more to be debited against, and paid for by the Russian Government. Also, there was at this date—sweeping the streets of Sevastopol in company with other persons, distinctively attired, shaven in sections, and adorned as to the legs with irons—a convict who had—previously to the Tsar's last visit to that important naval stronghold—shone glorious in bright green cloth, belaced cocked hat, and golden epaulets, as Governor of that place.

For—though this Tsar would have dearly liked to be sole master of Europe—though he would have gladly renamed the Bosphorus and built a new St. Petersburg at the mouth of the Dardanelles—though it would have gratified him to add Afghanistan and India to his dominions—though he was often unscrupulous in the spreading of nets for the catching of able men—though he would sacrifice soldiers in hundreds of thousands, did he deem it necessary for the safety of his State and his religion—though he punished Treason—real or imaginary—with the knout and imprisonment, Siberian exile or death—one cannot deny him to have been a high-minded and honest-souled, if prejudiced and narrow gentleman; who strove, according to his lights, to be just towards men, and upright before God.

There was not a drop of coward's blood in him—those who hated him most were ready to admit that. He would, in his grandson's place, have gone out from the Winter Palace alone to meet the strikers who carried the ikons, on that 18th of January, 1905. He threw all Russia into mourning, but he would never have marked upon the Calendar that red St. Vladimir's Day. Nor, having converted a peaceable demonstration into a general massacre of children, nursemaids, discontented workmen, and harmless citizens—would he have sat shuddering and shaking in his guarded palace, and left his mother to play the man.

Though getting somewhat stout, stiff, and elderly by this time, Nicholas was still what Mrs. Geogehagan, seeing his portrait in the illustrated newspapers borrowed from the Mess by the Colonel's lady—approvingly termed "a fine upstanding figure av a man." After the Peace of 1815, being then a handsome young Colossus of twenty, he had cut a dashing figure at the various Courts of Europe.... English Society had adored and *fêted* him—adipose elderly dowagers who had at that date been famous dancing beauties, boasted of having been his partners in the then newly-imported waltz.

In the *Memoirs* of the late Dowager-Duchess of Strome—who as Lady Margaretta Bawne, was a Maid of Honor to Princess Victoria, and subsequently Lady of the Bed-chamber to the young Queen—you will find in the chapter headed "How We Danced when I was Young" a vivid description of a waltz experienced with the superb Grand Duke at one of Almack's Balls.

"It was," says the venerable *raconteuse*, "like dancing with a human cyclone. After the first glissade and twirl my sandals quitted the floor—seldom to revisit it until the stopping of the music put a termination to the furious revolutions of the dance. During the ordeal—witnessed by an admiring crowd comprising several Crowned Heads and half the notabilities of Europe—I lost my slippers—my coronet—my combs—and finally my consciousness—which returned to me—in a shock of alarmed modesty—with the resounding salute imprinted on my cheek by His Imperial Highness at the final arpeggio."

Lord! how we had flattered and praised and quoted him—the huge hard man whom, for some occult reason, we now stigmatized as "The Northern Barbarian." He had ceased to dance when he commenced to reign—unlike Sire my Friend, who gyrated for the admiration of his Court—as he made his charger caracole for the approval of his Army. The Emperor who, unarmed and unattended by even an *aide-de-camp*, had quelled an insurrection among his Guards by giving the order to pile arms in that bellowing Minotaur voice of his, would have ridden over—not before—those soldiers who did not cheer.

He had no reason to be pleased with the Ruler of the Ottoman Empire—whose tottering throne he had bolstered in 1833 and again—in alliance with England and the two leading Powers of Germany—in 1840. A Firman issued by the Sultan, according to the Latin Church the Key of the great door of the Church at Bethlehem, and a Key to each of the doors of the Altar of the Sacred Manger—and bestowing upon France the permission to inlay on the floor of the Grotto of the Divine Nativity an arrogant Silver Star,—doubtless emblazoned with the Imperial Eagle—had kindled the Autocrat of all the Russias—in his anointed character as Supreme Head of the Orthodox Church—to flaming indignation. Nor had the diplomatic representative of Great Britain at Constantinople—by terming the resulting dispute "a wordy war of denominational trivialities"—cast else but oil upon the roaring flame.

Later, when Moslem troops under Omar Pasha were dispatched by the Sublime Porte—acting under advice from a certain suspected quarter—to operate against the Greek Christian rayahs of Montenegro—a pretty euphemism for the plundering and burning of farms and villages—the torture of men—the violation of women and the cutting of children's throats—the Barbarian of the North dispatched a small installment of fifty thousand troops into the Danubian Principalities—picketed the shaggy horses of his Cavalry with their noses against the frontiers of Moldavia—ascertained that upon a certain date the foundries of Rostof and Taganrog would infallibly carry out their contract to deliver a mere trifle of nine hundred thousand iron projectiles of all sorts and sizes—and sat down to play the game.

With movings of Divisions and Brigades, and marchings and counter-marchings. With Imperial Inspections, Reviews, and sham fights on a scale as colossal as himself. With repetitions of that effect of the vast market-garden of perambulatory beds of the most brilliantly-hued flowers, when a hundred thousand troops of all arms were maneuvered at the Camp of Krasnoé Sélo. Replying to great Naval Demonstrations at Spithead and Queenstown, Havre, and Brest and Toulon, culminating in combined visits of the French and English fleets to Turkish waters, with ominous increase of activity at Cronstadt and Revel, and menacing, ominous movements of steam and sailing-squadrons in the Baltic and on the Black Sea.

LXXIV

The well-oiled machinery of his Secret Intelligence Department—that kept him informed of every movement not only of those Powers who were his enemies, but of those who might one day become so—had long ago placed on the Barbarian's table, proofs that the grain, forage, and salted-provision merchants of the Levant were finding a customer upon a Brobdingnagian scale in Sire my Friend at the Tuileries. That the freightage, railway charges, and import-duties upon these had been reduced to a mere nothing by Imperial Decree, and that immense cargoes were daily shipped to Marseilles and Toulon, to be stored in huge Government magazines that were being built on all sides as though in preparation for war. A little later came the news that the salted-provision, forage, and grain-merchants of Roumelia, Bulgaria, Wallachia, Transylvania and Galicia were basking in the patronage of the same liberal buyer; whose granaries and storehouses had sprung up like mushrooms on the Turkish coasts of the Black Sea. As also depots of horses, cattle, timber and wagons; the contractors who had supplied these things being bound by Secret Contracts under divers penalties....

"Not to supply grain, stores, requisites, and material to Us," said the autocrat, shrugging a gentle shrug of calm, suave indifference, and blowing his nose in his copious, characteristic way. "Does this Bonaparte suppose the resources of my Empire to be so small that it would be possible to cripple ME by taking these precautions? Really, he lacks intelligence—or is very badly informed."

And as a Barbarian may smile, knowing All the Russias, Poland, the Grand Duchy of Finland, and the vast grain-producing area of the Caucasus his to draw upon—(even had his State magazines and the huge storehouses upon the coasts of Mingrelia and Guria not been bursting with flour, groats, biscuits, hay, and straw) the Tsar smiled, leaning back in the big battered, chipped, ragged-armed chair that he liked best, and chewing at the feather-end of a disreputable old quill pen.

He was closeted with Gortchakoff in the Imperial study in the Winter Palace. You saw it as a big plain room, full of heavy writing-tables and bureaus. Laden bookcases full of works on Drill, Tactics, and Fortification climbed to the scagliola ceiling-frieze, and between these were stands, supporting glass cases containing colored wax models of Cavalry and Infantrymen, stiff as life, and fully accoutered, whilst battle-paintings executed by native artists—wherein the Russian Forces were depicted in the act of conquering enemies of various nationalities amidst seas of carmine blood and clouds of flake-white smoke—hung on the walls above. In an adjoining room, furnished with soldierly simplicity, the ruler of seventy-four and odd millions of men slept on a narrow camp-bedstead, with no other covering than a single rug, and in winter his fur-lined cloak. And—perhaps because his huge hereditary dignities came to him through the tainted blood of scrofulous, insane, and degenerate Romanoffs—the innumerable handkerchiefs with which the despot stanched his constitutional catarrh were scattered, thick as the leaves of Vallombrosa, on the tables, chairs, and floor.

Gortchakoff, ex-Imperial *aide-de-camp* and Governor-General of Western Siberia, diversely represented by our Illustrated Papers—much to the confusion of Mrs. Geogehagan—as a mild, plump, spectacled, smiling personage, and a gaunt, grim, trap-jawed Fee-Fo-Fum—had, as newly-appointed General-in-Chief of the Southern Forces—been summoned to take leave of his master before setting out—as simply as a junker returning from furlough—per telega and by relays of post-horses, for the frontiers washed by the Pruth. Now, at the close of the Imperial utterance recorded, to which he had listened in a bolt-upright attitude of respectful attention, he coughed dryly; and pulling a document from a sheaf of tied and docketed papers, placed it before the Tsar, whose head—even as its owner sat in his chair—overtopped his own.

Nicholas sniffed several times as he perused the document, which was worn in the folds and incredibly greasy; was written in the Little Russian dialect of Bessarabia, and proved to be a contract between a certain Kirilov, an Akerman dealer in timber, and the official representative of Sire my Friend, who signed himself in a bold, free, looping hand:

"H. M. A. Von Widinitz-Dunoisse. General of Brigade of the French Army. Acting Head of the Eastern European War Survey and Army Supply Department of the Imperial Government of France."

"By St. Peter and St. Paul!" said the Tsar, blowing his nose noisily; "this Bonaparte has imagination. 'Not to furnish supplies to the Chiefs of the Army of Great Britain, or assist her military forces in any way whatsoever!...' Let me see the date of this!"

It bore date of three years back. A paper precisely similar—save that it was written in the Slavish Latin of Wallachia, and that the contracting party was a wealthy Boyard of that country—who bred and sold sheep, cattle and horses on a vast scale—was only three months old. The spectacles of Gortchakoff glittered like diamonds as he saw this fact sink through the calm blue eyes of the cold-faced handsome Tsar, into the big brain ramparted by the lofty forehead. Not long would Nicholas remain in doubt as to the breed of chicken that would soon chip the shell of the egg of Monseigneur.

"August.... Dated on the 30th of August at Kustendje," said Nicholas, reaching out his hand to take a fresh pocket-handkerchief from a little pile of these necessaries. He added: "A vessel of our Black Sea Steam Navigation Company touches at that port once a fortnight, taking mails and passengers for Varna and Constantinople." He added: "The railway between Paris and Marseilles is nearly completed.... This Dunoisse would be in touch with the Tuileries, easily—passably easily. He would be kept informed of the march of political events.... And Sire my Friend, was at Dieppe in the beginning of July—Lucien Buonaparte the guest of the Queen of England at Windsor.... The Secret Treaty of Alliance was signed.... The combined Fleets were anchored in the Bay of Besika. And yet, in the event of war, the ally of France is to be denied assistance!... What does it mean? Let me think!..."

He had so much of the Oriental Satrap about him, that even his terrible Grand Wazir was no more than a piece of furniture when he desired to commune in private with the other man who dwelt within himself. The short daylight died as he sat, huge and massive and silent, profoundly thinking. The great Winter Palace leaped into a blaze of brilliancy, but the core of it, the study where the Tsar sat plunged in meditation, became so dark that you could not even distinguish the gleam of Gortchakoff's spectacles as the late Governor-General of Western Siberia stood, stiff and immovable as a statue of ebony, beside his Little Father's chair.

"Umph! Are you there, Peter Michailowitch?" said the deep voice out of the heart of the blackness, and the Prince answered with chattering teeth—for no one daring to enter unsummoned the room where the Tsar sat closeted with the newly-appointed General-in-Chief of his Southern Forces—the fire in the great stove of gilded porcelain had died to a pale red glow. "I have thought it out, and the man is even less of a gentleman than I have esteemed him. He would play the old game of the ape who made the cat pull the chestnuts out of the fire—the confidence-trick of the London swell mobsman.... Listen! England is to pay for her triumph at Trafalgar and the defeat of Waterloo through this alliance with Sire my Friend. She is to be drained of her blood and of her gold until she sinks down dying—and then he will offer me Great Britain with her East Indies, and the Danubian Provinces of Turkey in exchange for Constantinople, Asia Minor, and the Holy Land—he will be anointed Emperor of Palestine upon the Savior's

Sepulcher, and if the child prove a son—create him Crown Prince of Bethlehem——"

"Supposing you, Bátiushka," deftly put in Gortchakoff—who called him Little Father simply as a soldier or a peasant would have done—"choose to accept his terms?"

"That will I never, so help me God and Our Blessed Lady the Virgin!" said Nicholas, rising to his colossal height and crossing himself as he bowed in the direction of the ikons. He added: "This is an able man, this General Dunoisse, who spins his web for him. Of course, he is of their Training Institute for Staff Officers.... I should like to have that man." He added, simply and Orientally: "I will have him. Get him at any price!"

"He is not to be bought, Bátiushka," was the answer.

"Absurd, Peter Michailowitch!" said the autocrat. "All men are to be bought. This one as well as the others." He added, as a stray gleam of light from a wind-blown lamp in the great courtyard evoked no responsive twinkle from the Prince's spectacle-glasses: "Unless you mean that he is dead?"

"Look, Sire, when there is light, at the signature to the later document," said Gortchakoff. "It is the feeble scrawl of a dying man. This officer had undergone many hardships in the past three years—surveying and traveling alone—or with only a peasant to guide him—he knew the country from the Balkans to the Sea of Azov—he had the Danubian Principalities at his fingers' ends—he was, as Bátiushka says, a man worth any price. But—the day after the last contract was signed he left Kustendje for the delta of the Dobrudja. He had made his way up there from Varna on foot—and he had the fever of the country upon him"—Gortchakoff shrugged—"but he did not stay for that. He pushed on into the Dobrudja, taking the road that goes by the Chain of Lakes—and then the wilderness opened and swallowed him. And—that is now three months ago, and he has not been spit up yet."

"Akh!" said Nicholas, who was to lose thousands of men in the poisonous marshes, as on the waterless steppes of that same region. "But I should not make sure that he is dead, even now. Men who do not value life are difficult to kill. My Russian soldiers hold it cheap when it comes to a question of obeying the orders of their Emperor.... They will prove themselves in 1854 what they were in 1812. And though Austria desert me and Prussia play the knave, I have Three Allies," boomed the great bull-voice through the chilly darkness. "Pestilence, and Hunger, and Cold—that never yet failed to serve a Russian Tsar. As for England—I tell you, Peter

Michailowitch!—between Louis Napoleon Bonaparte and her Army Contractor"—it would appear that this remarkably well-informed Barbarian had even heard of Jowell—"she will yet climb her Calvary with her Cross upon her shoulders—we shall see her crucified between two thieves!" He rose, and said, clapping his General-in-Chief quite genially upon the shoulder: "This room is cold, and I have a deputation from the Peace Society of England waiting to address me. Come and listen to these Quakers—they seem very honest men!..."

He received the three representatives of the English Society of Friends courteously and kindly. He heard the Address with tolerance and patience. Somewhat after this fashion he replied:

"I do not desire War, but since England and France have sided with the enemies of Christianity; and, without warning to Russia have sent their fleets to Constantinople and thence into the Black Sea—to encourage the Turks and impede our battleships in the protection of our coasts—it would appear that both these Western Powers seek War. I will not attack—but I shall act in self-defense! Now, since I think you have not met my wife and daughter, will you come and be introduced to them? It will give them very great pleasure, you may be assured."

LXXV

In August and September a marvelous comet flamed over the British Isles. There were great strikes in the Cotton Districts of the North, and haggard eyes of starving idlers, and hot and steaming faces of begrimed and furious rioters were lifted to the wonder at great open-air meetings; or from the crush that thronged the yards about the burning mills, and kept the engines back.

Livid sufferers, writhing in the deadly grip of Cholera in foul uncleanly tenements of provincial towns, or squalid garrets and reeking cellars of common lodging-houses in great sooty London, would raise themselves upon their beds of noisome rags—in some brief respite from hideous spasms—to stare at that strange menace through the broken skylight or the iron street-grating. But Mrs. Joshua Horrotian never lifted her head from her work. For little Josh and the baby Sally were both dead and buried, and their mother was stitching her fingers to the bone to pay for the mourning and the tiny double funeral; and never even glanced up, when Moggy Geogehagan—who in defiance of Barrack Rules was hanging half out of the window—bade her come and look at the quare ould kind of gazabo did be hangin' up in the sky.

It was not the Blue Gripes—as the rank-and-file had learned to call it, out at Buenos Ayres and on Service in East India—it was not the Cholera that had left this mother's arms empty and in her heart a vast and dreadful blank. It was something you called with a shudder and under your breath— "The Bad Throat"—an invisible, impalpable Something that rose up in the night beside the crowded cots in the damp, foul, insanitary, whitewashed sepulchers that were called Barracks—and gripped little children oftenest, yet sometimes grown men and women—in a strangling clutch so that— with awful suddenness—they died.

We know, at this date, the name of the unseen demon to be Diphtheria. We exorcise it with trap-drains and Sanitary Precautions—we fight it with gargles of chlorine and Jeyes' Fluid, moppings out of mercurial perchloride and—in the more serious cases—injections of the antitoxin. But in spite of all that Science has done for us, we cannot keep out the grim invisible intruder. And still it is the old story of the strangling clutch and the swift death that follows, although we have grown so wise....

This new Barracks—it was rumored, when the Route came for the Hundredth Lancers to remove to another Cavalry Depot—had had a bad name for ever so long. "Children did not thrive," it was said—meaning that they died like poisoned flies there. So, before the remove, Joshua Horrotian and his wife had concocted, indited, and dispatched a letter to the widowed Sarah, his mother, asking her to give the babies shelter and house-room at The Upper Clays, at least until wholesome lodgings could be found.

When the answer came, it was a bald, bare, bleak refusal. You read the stiffness of the widow's back in it, and the cramped clutch of the hard, bony fingers on the seldom-used pen. You saw the gaunt black eyes glooming in their hollow caves under Sarah's tall, narrow forehead between the scanty loops of black hair that was growing gray.

What you never would have guessed was that Sarah's mouth twisted with anguish as she penned the sentences of denial; and that her hard eyes were dim with tears. For the woman's bowels yearned over her unseen grandchildren. She would have been kind—pardoning even as the parent of the Prodigal in Scripture. But the Prodigal should first have come and laid his hands between her hands, and said, "Mother, I have sinned!"

So the invisible spider-thing that spins a yellow web in the children's throats, so that they are suffocated slowly under the eyes that love them, killed both the little ones in a few hours. Tracheotomy—resorted to by a few daring Continental operators at this date—the Regimental Surgeon had never heard of. So it was as I have told.

The girl was gone, with a gasp or so and a brief convulsion. The boy fought manfully for continued life. He thought he had a bone in his throat, and kept begging his mammy and his daddy to take it away because he was choking. When they die—believing that you could have helped it if you had only chosen—quite a special brand of vintage goes to the brimming of your Cup of Despair.

And the woman had loved with such excess of maternal passion these children begotten by the man her husband, that when they went they seemed to take with them his share of love as well as their own.

She had "gone numb" as Mrs. Geogehagan expressed it. The power to think, or feel, or see anything beyond the open grave with those two little white deal boxes at the bottom of it, was denied.... She grew thin, and dowdy, and slovenly; and her husband moodier and more sullen and lowering of aspect, as day succeeded day. No promotion had come to the trooper since his clandestine marriage with Sarah's milkmaid—the single good-conduct badge now vanished from his sleeve of coarse blue cloth. For he drank now, in bouts, and by fits and starts. Drunkenness, the soldier's common vice, would not have prejudiced him in the eyes of his commanding officers, in those days, when the nightly feat of topping up the regulation three bottles of Mess Port with copious libations of whisky-toddy, and staggering back in jovial curves to quarters, was accomplished by many a brave and honorable son of Mars. But in his cups Joshua was betrayed by his countenance and his unrulier tongue.

According to Mrs. Geogehagan, the Oracle of Troop Room No. 4, it was the big black scowl Horrotian did be having on the face av him, no less than the unsaysonable spaches he'd let fly when he was carryin' a dhrop too much—that prejudiced the non-commissioned officers, and caused so many sable entries to be made on the Troop Defaulter's Sheet, to bear fruit in Extra Fatigue Duty, C.B., and Punishment Drill.

A hint from Moggy Geogehagan was a slog from a cabbage-stump. Roused from her stupor of bereavement by such an application, Mrs. Joshua ventured—during the course of a Sunday walk with her husband—to repeat this utterance to him.

"My face!" the trooper echoed bitterly. "You found no fault with it when ye married me five years ago. What has happened to it since? The bit o' glass in the lid o' your workbox shows it much the same, I reckon.... And if 'tis sullen and rebellious as you say—and makes me enemies among the officers and men—who stamped that look upon it? Med-be you'll tell me you don't know! Ay! but I know! I have the name on my tongue's end this minute. And speak it I would, if I was to be shot the next! 'Tis Jowell!—Thompson Jowell, and may the Almighty damn him for it!—that can take his pleasure in grinding, and hazing, and trampling of me down!"

"Oh, hush!" cried Nelly in terror, and below them the lips of the sea said "Hus's'sh!" against the shingle—for the Garrison town that boasted the insanitary Cavalry Barracks being situated on the Chalkshire South Coast, their Sunday stroll had led them to the low white cliffs that overhung the beach. There were fortifications here, and the grassy slope they sat on was fragrant with wild thyme, and short-stalked June clover, and gay with yellow dandelions and coltsfoot, and the air breathed salt from the heaving bosom of the sea. The sky was clear fresh blue, with floating scarfs of gossamer mist upon it. Sheep grazed near, and, with pyramidal heaps of whitewashed forty-pound shot between them—three great iron cannon of the Coast Defense—imposing enough outside, but rusty-throated as that old clamorous Fear of Invasion by the Bonaparte on the other side of the Channel—looked between the rounded breasts of their weather-worn embrasures—placidly out to sea.

"Believe it or not, as you like," the trooper went on with increasing heat and indignation, "since I married ye I have kept a guard upon my hasty temper—and often bitten my tongue nigh through, rather than speak words that might ha' been hurtful to us both. I ha' lived decent, and cleanly, and orderly, and sober——" He flushed a dark red and boggled at the last word, but the faded prettiness of Nelly's face was turned from him seawards, looking wistfully beyond the white horses that rose and fell upon the horizon, towards the grayish haze that people said concealed the Coast of France.

"Till lately," the trooper amended, "neither officer nor non-commissioned officer o' mine has had just cause to complain o' me. But I am breaking under what I have to bear, an' maddening under it fast. I am hounded, and drove and put upon—I say it afore the Face of my Maker, as no Christian man should be!"

His pent-up wrath made him choke and stammer. He unhooked his stiff collar with a shaking hand, and loosened his stock, and threw it on the grass. His wife gave him her handkerchief, and he mopped his streaming forehead with it, and went on talking, gesticulating with the great brown fist in which he held it—and sometimes pounding the fist upon the sod.

"Do ye ask me how I know 'tis Jowell that's my enemy—that's undermined my credit and blackened my good name—and lighted this furnace of hate in me that burns without quenching day and night? Can I doubt it when I never take my turn to draw troop-rations without being asked by that black dog Mullett," (a Squadron Quartermaster Sergeant who was particularly responsible for many of those sable entries in the Troop Defaulters' Book) "to look and make sure the Government hasn't cheated me in the quality o' the Commissariat flour and meat, and so on?—when I can't feed my horse without being asked whether I've found any empty jam-tins, old hats, or dead kittens trussed up in the Forage Contractor's hay?"

One may here endorse the trooper's statement, Mullett being really one of Thompson Jowell's merry men. Mullett soared to be Regimental Quartermaster-Sergeant presently, and would have retired, and opened a snug public-house immediately after the War of the Crimea, but that another kind of opening presented itself, and he was tumbled in, in company with honester men, and covered up; to wait the Great Reveille.

"Lord knows," pursued the angry speaker, "as how I wish my silly tongue had been cut out, before I taunted a man powerful enough to ruin me—with what my betters are too sensible even to hint at—the fact that for the Nation's honest money, Mr. Jowell, and others like him, sell bad, poor, rotten goods! But the vengeance he've took—and still takes—is mean, and low, and cowardly!" said the trooper, emphasizing each adjective with a tremendous blow of the huge brown fist upon the mild green face of Mother Earth. "And if some day I be drove to tie a loop of whipcord to the trigger o' my carbine an' hitch my toe in it—Jowell will be the man as blew my brains out—though the Military Commission of Inquiry and the Jury of the Coroner's Inquest may call it Suicide!"

"Oh! my dear husband—no!"

Nelly shut her eyes, and shuddered at the ghastly picture the rough words conjured up before her. Her numb heart beat a little quicker at the discovery that she still had something dear to lose that Death might rob her of.

"Send I don't meet that man," pursued the trooper, with a dark frown and a gesture of his strong right arm that augured ill for Jowell, "when my heart is bursting with the wrongs he's heaped on me, and I've a weapon in my hand! The dog he've given a bad name to might swing for him yet, med-be! Meantime, supposing it be true as my mother believes—that 'tis possible to call down Judgment on the wicked merely by wishing it with all one's heart and soul—and since through him I've lost my own two children, I'll wish—for that bad man has got an only son and sets his eyes by him—may the sins of Thompson Jowell be visited on him by means of that same son! Send I may live to see young Jowell in rags; an' with an old boot on one foot and an old shoe on t'other, asking—and asking in vain—for a handshake from an honest man! As for his father, may the Hand That's Above us scourge him with rods of shame and retribution! May he drink of the cup that I ha' drunk of, and drink it deep and long! So be it. Amen! Come, let's be stepping back-along to Barracks."

They never called it Home.

LXXVI

The Tsar was genuinely puzzled to know—War having been declared between himself and the Sultan—why he could not crumple those thirteen vessels of a Turkish Convoy bound with troops, arms, and ammunition for a certain important port on the coast of the Black Sea without provoking such a deafening outcry from Gallia and Britannia; and, indeed, what the Daily Press of both these countries persisted in calling the "outrage" of Sinope, seems at this distance of time no more than a provoked and unavoidable measure of defense.

A Comic Illustrated Paper of the date represents the Sultan as a curled darling in short socks, strap-shoes, petticoats, and pinafore, sniveling, with his little fist in his weeping eyes—the while he blubbers out to grinning, knickerbockered Russia:

"Hoo—boohoo! You've broken my nice new Fleet!... Wait till I tell Nursie France and Auntie Britannia—they'll give you a good spanking, you—boohoo!—naughty Boy!"

For some reason there was hurry. The Holy Standard was unfurled and the Sacred Shirt displayed; the Moslem, who had suddenly become so dear to us, plunged, with renewed vigor, into hostilities; the Russian Ambassadors quitted London and Paris; but weeks before Great Britain and France leagued themselves with the Infidel against Christian Russia, and War was proclaimed by the Lord Mayor of London from the steps of the Royal Exchange, Her Majesty's Foot Guards received orders to proceed to the East, and the Second Battalion of the Cut Red Feathers marched out from St. George's Barracks; and the Third Battalion of the White Tufts marched out from the Tower; and the First Battalion of the Bearskins Plain marched out of Windsor—slept a night at Wellington Barracks; and with bands playing "Cheer, Boys, Cheer," "We are Going Far Away," "Oh, Susannah! Don't You Cry for Me!" and "The British Grenadiers," they were off and away for Gallipoli *via*—why *via* Malta?

You may conceive the cheers, the tears, the shaking of the earth by the even tread of battalions of marching men; the waving of hats and pocket-handkerchiefs; the wives, and children, and sweethearts crying and clinging to husbands', and fathers', and lovers' arms. You may imagine the roaring trade done by the venders of oranges, whelks, polonies, pettitoes, and other portable refreshments; and the generosity with which these were pressed upon the rank-and-file; and the lavishness with which the thirst of the

British soldier—great even in piping times of peace—was assuaged by copious draughts of foaming beer and liquors even more potent....

The Bearskins Plain got the best send-off, for from Bird Cage Walk to Buckingham Palace, and along the Strand to Waterloo, many thousands of people were gathered to give them God-speed, and the Mall was made gay with bunting and streamers. Jowell, Sewell, Cowell, Towell, Bowell, and Co., of whose cunning, and greed, and rapacity most of these departing warriors were presently to perish—filled an official window in Pall Mall with gorgeous waistcoats and patriotic enthusiasm.

"Noble fellows! God bless 'em!" they cried, and shed tears and waved their pocket-handkerchiefs. They slopped over with patriotic sentiments as the champagne slopped over their glasses; while they told each other how soon those steadily-marching legs would bring their owners back. The whole thing was extravagantly simple. The British Army had but to proceed to the East—quite an enviable trip now the spring-time was approaching—show itself—conquer by the mere show; and return to be thanked and praised.

They were to return so soon, and the climate of Eastern Europe was believed, even in March, to be so warm and genial, that nothing in the way of extra covering had been issued to England's darling sons. Sire my Friend, had equipped the French Army with a complete outfit of serviceable winter clothing. Stout and easy-fitting boots protected its feet, great-coats of heavy waterproofed material were supplied it against the nip of cold or the exigencies of wet weather. Even the Infidel had purchased for his troops, fifty thousand ample capotes of leather lined with sheepskin; but Britannia relied exclusively upon the glow of martial ardor for the generation and preservation of caloric. Hence it came about that whole battalions of the legs that were presently to march away, marched in the trousers of white duck, in which they had returned from service in Bermuda, China, and the East Indies. And the rest in a shoddy summer cloth of dirty bluish gray.

It is odd how universal was that conviction that the Expedition to the East was to be nothing beyond a flying visit. When the cheering broke out at the Officers' Mess House—the Rathkeale Ragamuffins being at that moment quartered at the Victoria Barracks, Dublin; my Aunt Julietta,— who dined with the children at one o'clock, and frugally supped upon cold mutton and the remains of the rice-pudding or custard in the petrified or gelid state, whilst her Golightly was enjoying his seven courses, cheese, and dessert in the society of his peers—my Aunt, learning that the dreaded summons had come, greeted the reappearance of her lord with an outburst of hysterical emotion. Upon which Captain Goliath, whom you may suppose well primed with Mess Port, and subsequent whisky-toddy; jested at her wifely tears, and made light of her tender terrors.

"I tell ye there's no danger!—they'll simply send us out and order us back again. We'll never get a *shass* at them—more's the pity!—much less a prod. They're cowards, rank cowards! They'll turn tail and run at the first British cheer we're after giving them. We're simply being sent out—do you hear me?—to be sent back again. Sure, now, when ye married me, Juley, me own darling!—you didn't suppose ye were taking anything but a soldier, did ye now? Killed is it? *Killed!*... Nonsense, ma'am!—there'll be no killin' at all, at all! Compose yourself, Mrs. McCreedy—for your own sake and the baby's! Don't you hear me saying that they'll simply send——Will You Be Quiet And Listen to What I'm Telling You!" bellowed Captain Goliath, at the full pitch of a remarkably powerful pair of lungs.

But my Aunt Julietta, unwilling to lose so favorable an opportunity, here went into hysterics after the latest recipe published in the pages of *The Ladies' Mentor*, and screamed, cried, and laughed so vigorously, that—had not the alarmed and flustered Captain seized and applied the Cayenne pepper-castor in mistake for my Aunt's silver vinaigrette of Red Lavender—unfavorable results to the expected olive-branch of the McCreedy stem might have supervened.

But my Aunt—in paroxysms of sneezing—recovered sufficiently to scold her clumsy hero; and the Captain departed; to return towards the small-hours in a condition which his military body-servant erroneously described as "fresh."

Ah, poor gentlewoman! how my Aunt winced at the coarse pleasantries of the man, and the hiccupping genialities of the master! How many times since she pledged to the *idol of her soul* the *fondest vows*, etc., had not that idol proved himself a mere lump of sodden, heavy clay.

She dismissed Private Fahy, ungratified in the wish—audibly expressed—for a hair of the dog that had bit the Captain—and herself undressed her prone and wallowing warrior; got him to bed, and while he snored, knelt beside the pillow his hoggishness defiled, and prayed to Heaven—pure, simple, loving creature!—that War might spare him to his wife and children, for many a long year to come!...

For the rest she was as "callum as you please, and as brave as a *liness*" to quote the Captain; when he gave her his parting hug on Kingstown Harbor Quay.

The month's installment of a Serial Tale then running in *The Ladies' Mentor* contained a harrowing description of a similar leave-taking between husband and wife. But it seemed to my Aunt Julietta that the *gallant* and *high-souled* Colonel Reginald de la Vaux and his *young* and *sensitive* bride said too much—and said it too coherently to be quite real.

They ought to have gulped out trivialities until the last minute, such as: "Don't forget the whisky-flask!—it's in your great-coat pocket." "Not me, egad! trust a British soldier!" and "Do, now, remember, love!—*always* to change wet socks!" Then, as the Fifes and Drums squealed, and company after company marched up the gangway, and the Colors were displayed on the quarter-deck, they should have choked and grabbed each other. And with the rasping scrub of a wet mustache upon her mouth, and the smell of wet umbrellas and oilskins in her nostrils, and the strains of "The Girl I Left Behind Me," and "Cheer, Boys, Cheer" in her ears; and the tears rolling down her cheeks as heavily as the rain dripped from the eaves of her bonnet—as the big steamer moved slowly, remorselessly away from the quay amidst cheering and good-byes—my pretty Aunt was left standing in a puddle—much to the detriment of a smart pair of velvet boots.

Heaven knows how long the poor soul would have stood there, but that her children's nurse—a Sloughshire girl, married to a private of the Rathkeales—who made one of a group of disconsolate dripping soldiers' wives—perching amongst piles or crates and timber-balks and coils of tarry rope to see the last of their men—ran to her, crying wildly: "Oh, ma'am!—ma'am!... my Tom!... Will he ever come back, do you think, ma'am?... Shall I ever see him again?..." And my Aunt wakened out of her desolate stupor, and took the weeping creature's cold wet hand, and kissed her swollen cheek, and told her: "Of course you will, Mrs. Kennedy! They're only sending them out to the East to send them home again!"

Ensign Mortimer Jowell—who for two years now had held Her Majesty's Commission, did not sail with his regiment. A common, infantile complaint, characterized by a rubious rash and yclept the measles—had stricken the only hope of the House of Jowell down on the very threshold of Active Service, much to his indignation and chagrin.

The young man's bosom-friend and brother-officer Ensign Lord Adolphus Noddlewood, marched in the uniform of a private of the Cut Red Feathers, from the train to the Docks between two of the men of his own company, thus avoiding a sheriff's officer who—armed with a writ issued by Nathan and Moss of Giltspur Street—had been sent down to arrest this gay young nobleman.

But Morty, frying with fever and boiling with vexation, must perforce remain a prisoner in the huge palatial four-poster in the luxurious bedroom of the suite of private apartments which the fond father had caused to be specially decorated and furnished for his only son at the Jowell mansion in Hanover Square. Instead of farewell banquets washed down with the golden, creaming nectar of Sillery and Épernay—followed by bumpers of the Port of Carbonell—the young man perforce must subsist on blameless slops of chicken-broth and barley-water—must be regulated with saline doses of the cooling, nauseous, fizzy kind....

His mother presided over the medical regimen; administered the medicines, turned the pillows—pounded into feather-pancakes by her boy's aching bullet-head—read him the newspaper-accounts of the departure of his comrades—washed him—scolded him—bore with his fevered grumblings; and—reverting to the days when the big young man was a mere topknotted youngster in plaid frocks, diamond socks, and strap-shoes—heard him say his nightly prayers.

In those early days referred to, young Mortimer—proving himself a true sapling of that sterling stem of stout old British oak, his father,—had been wont to derive profit of the solid, terrestrial description from these orisons, by tacking on to the supplementary petition for parents, requests for toys and treats particularly desired.

"Please God bless my mother, and make her buy me that new engine I saw in So-and-So's shop-window"—was naturally followed by fulfillment.... Faith is the first of the theological virtues.... What Christian mother would have her boy grow up an atheist? Arguing thus, the poor lady would purchase the engine; and Morty's prayers would be without addenda for a night, or maybe two. But before a week was over the maternal head, this infant Samuel would be praying for a new gun or a new puppy—and the thing would begin all over again....

To do Morty justice, he loved the meek, sad woman, despised by Jowell as being devoid of "spirit" and "go." She never dreamed—when her darling went to Rugby—how many pugilistic encounters his promise of never forgetting his daily prayers was to cost a boy whose dogged obstinacy of nature led him to shun the concealment offered by blankets, and persist in saying them out of bed.... It is on record that the boys Morty pounded presently followed his example; while the boys who pounded him had suffered so many contusions in the course of the contest, that they had no urgent desire to provoke a renewal of war.

Do you hear the embarrassed, clumsy accents of the large young Ensign, mumbling that simplest, noblest, and most Divine of all petitions? Do you see that sorrowful, plain, dowdy woman, sitting in the shadow of his sumptuous brocade bed-curtains, cherishing the big, powerful, hot young hand?

"'But deliver us from evil.'... And make me a good boy—no! hang it!—I mean a good man and a good officer.... And make me well quick, and let me get to our fellows Out There—before all the fun of the fighting's over!—And don't let my mother fret and worry herself—and bring me back safe home to her again. For Christ's sake, Amen!"

That brought the tears, hard as the mother tried to stop them—pattering, hot, and quick, and heavy, on her brown silk lap. She held the big hand until his tea came—fed him with strips of toast soaked in the blameless infusion—ere she crept away to compose herself in the solitude of her own huge palatial bedroom, before going down to preside over her silver teapot—set at the end of a vast expanse of dining-table spread with the customary complements of the distinctive British meal. The redness of her poor eyelids could not be concealed by any innocent application of cold water and Johann-Maria-Farina, and, at the sight of them Thompson Jowell—who came home early from the City in these days of his son's sickness—dropped upon the hearthrug the newspaper he had been perusing, and—nimbly as the Zoological Society's Rhinoceros might have quitted his private pond in the Regent's Park Gardens—floundered out of his armchair.

"What the devil's this, ma'am?" he blustered, staring at his wife with eyes rendered even more froggishly prominent than usual by apprehension. "You're not going to tell me the boy's taken a turn for the worse, and is in danger?" He added, as she reassured him on this point: "If you had, I wouldn't have believed you! Tom Tough, my name is—when it comes to a question of constitution—and my son takes after his old Governor! But, Lord!—you've given me a start."

He broke off to swab his face, and the hand that wielded the silk bandanna handkerchief, shook quite as though the great Contractor had been a being of common flesh and blood. It was to shake more, erelong. For, as though that curse of Trooper Joshua Horrotian had had real power to bring Misfortune down—strange ill-chances and cross-happenings, eventuating from the dubious business-methods of the parent Jowell, were to place in very frequent jeopardy the one person, of all living beings—whom the man desired should go scot-free. For all the gold that War would pour into his coffers, Jowell would not have risked a hair of the head of this beloved son....

He had always thriven upon disaster. Mildewed harvests brought him golden ones, even as the murrain among cattle and the rot among sheep glutted the storehouses of Cowell with barrels of Prime Salted Beef, and tins of First Class Preserved Mutton, for the nourishment of the British Army. And the skins of the diseased beasts above-named, being sold to Shoell, at a friendly lowness of price, were converted into Boots and Saddlery and so on....

Towell and Sewell, buying whole cargoes of Damaged Cotton—salvage from the spinning-mills that were always being set on fire and flooded with water—and the waste of countless Woolen Manufactories—the first to be woven into soldiers' shirting, the second to be manufactured into shoddy cloth of gray or blue or brick-dust-red to upholster martial bodies withal—flourished on the same principle of Give as little as you may and Take all you can get.

Bowell, who took over obsolete or damaged medical stores and necessaries from Britannia's Hospitals and Infirmaries and Workhouses, and sold them back again without a blush upon his tallowy countenance; Powell, who bought thousands of tons of waste and spoiled paper from the Horse Guards and the Admiralty and other Government offices—where paper is wasted and spoiled—and transformed it into cardboard wherewith to strengthen busbies, shakos, helmets, and cocked-hats, and render them proof against bullets and grape, stroke of saber or cut of sword—were in like manner enriched at the mere cost of discomfort to many men, and a man's life here and there.... But until the War broke out, and the Genius of Jowell spread its leathery bat-wings and soared—none of these enterprising spirits had ever dreamed what wealth, beyond the dreams of avarice, might be gathered and piled up, at cost of misery to thousands, and innumerable lives. When they realized this, they bowed their foreheads in the dust before the roomy patent-leather boots of Jowell, and mumbled them. He grew great in their eyes, and greater still. The sun rose to light his path, and set because he had done with it for the present.... They whispered to each other—behind their ringed and stumpy hands—that he was the devil, the very devil, sir! And as the earthly Vicar and representative of that dark potentate they worshiped him, having forgotten GOD.

LXXVII

Morty—after an eclipse somewhat protracted—being at length emancipated from the shadow of the brocade bed-curtains, having changed his skin, shaved, and attired himself—by parental request—in his Mess-uniform, came down to the five o'clock dinner—a feast comprising every delicacy most beloved of the young man.

Morty was in great spirits. The solemn butler—who had presided over the sideboard of an Archbishop—condescended to smile at his jokes, and the three powdered footmen openly sniggered. All the female servants were gathered on the upper landing listening and giggling and admiring. Jowell, too, was in great form.

He had—like other bulky birds of the carrion-feeding kind—who display excitement when there are preparations amongst humans for hostilities—been clumsily flying from place to place, making Contracts and Arrangements. He would be at the Horse Guards one moment—at the Admiralty the next, at Plymouth, Southampton, or Portsmouth before you could turn round. He had seen all the fine sights his boy had missed.... The Queen's Review of the Baltic Fleet, and the Embarkation of the Guards, as of the first Drafts of Regiments of the Line—and he described these stirring sights to his wife and son in the characteristic Jowellian way.

"It brought tears to My Eyes—it did, upon my word!" he assured his hearers, in reference to such and such a demonstration of patriotic enthusiasm. And whether he spoke the truth or not, the water certainly stood in those bulging orbs of his, as he bade the archiepiscopal butler bring forth his most ancient white-sealed Port, wherein to pledge his newly-recovered son.

"To my dear boy's health! Good luck to him, and God bless him!" he proposed, goggling fondly at the large young figure in the scarlet Mess-Jacket, through the tawny-golden wine. The next glass was swallowed to the toast of "The Queen, our Army and our Allies!" while the third was "Here's to the Flour, Forage, Freightage, and Transport Trade. Large Profits and No returns!"

He chuckled so over this cryptic sentiment (which Cowell, Shoell, Sewell and Co. would have perfectly understood and enthusiastically applauded)—that he choked in his wine, and gasped and crowed so awfully that his wife—upon her way to the door, which Morty, with his recently-acquired gloss of good manners rather too obviously upon him, held open—was fain to pause behind her husband's chair and pat him on the back. And then she kissed her son, whispering. "Not too much wine, my dearest!" And with a wistful smile at her one joy, went away to sit and knit at stockings for him, in a gorgeous gilded desert of drawing-rooms, opening one out of the other.

Left alone, Morty chatted with his sire, and found him well-informed and interesting. He knew so many things at first-hand. For instance, how many picked squadrons went to the Cavalry Division that was under orders for the East, and what vessels these warriors and their steeds would sail in. For as the British Government possessed but three available transports, Britannia may be said to have leaned with confidence, at this juncture, upon the bosom of Jowell. Who—it not being desirable that lofty officials should soil their fingers with such vulgar transactions—not only acted as the Government's middleman or agent, in the hire and charter of such vessels of the Regular Screw Steamship Company; the Eastern and Occidental Steamship Company; and the Antipodean Company, as had been marked down for War-Service—and reaped very considerable profit and enrichment from such mediation—but for the conveyance of the heavier munitions of War; the Forage, the Commissariat Stores, and the horses of the Cavalry and Artillery—had been privileged to place his own private fleet of sailing-vessels and steamers at the service of an appreciative country.

It is to be whispered here, that the knowledge of ships and maritime matters indubitably possessed by Thompson Jowell had been gained by that great man in his earlier years, while serving in the humble capacity of private in a Regiment of Marines....

The private soared to become Quartermaster-Sergeant, and married the penniless orphan daughter of a Naval Surgeon. Being of a bilious temperament, and invariably deadly sick when upon sea-service, Thompson Jowell made haste to retire, upon a nest-egg that he had accumulated by the sweat of the brow of a true-born Englishman.... Which nest-egg, being invested in the shop, stock, and goodwill of a ship's chandler and drysalter—later expanding into a rope walk (taken over for a bad trade-debt), and in process of time engulfing the business of a bankrupt forage merchant—was in time to hatch out the Great Contractor, the glory of his age.

He was in a beaming, radiant mood upon this particular afternoon. Smiles garlanded his large visage, even his rummaging, sniffing nose was cocked at a less aggressive angle, say forty-five instead of sixty degrees.... As the wine warmed him—though he could drink enough of his old tawny port to float a jolly-boat, without overheating or muddling the hard, sharp little brain enclosed in his pear-shaped skull—the strings of his tongue were loosed, and he spoke to his son and heir as to a second self, unreservedly.

He had attended at the newly-created Transport Office at the Admiralty, and had secured fresh Contracts—and he had been to the Victualling Office—(also a sub-department of the first-named Institution) and there he had received such gracious usage at the hands of the presiding genius, Mr. Commissary-General Blunder, that it had brought the tears into his eyes again.

Pray take a glimpse of Mr. Commissary-General Blunder, whose name was later to be spelt by prejudiced Press correspondents and critics of the Commission of '56 with an initial to be found much later in the alphabet.

Comparatively obscure, previously to this period, you found him suddenly become all-powerful in half-a-dozen Departments. He was indubitably an official of great experience, having been present at the later Peninsular battles of the Duke's time, in the character of a Director of Wagon Trains—unhappily abolished during the days of the Prince Regent, and not yet replaced by any organized means of Land Transport. Now you saw him as a little dry, meager man of seventy, his baldness covered with a black, scratch-wig, his sharp black eyes looking out over angular cheekbones, scrawled with strange characters as though in official red-ink. Topped with the cocked-hat of a Brigadier-General, his little round pot-stomach buttoned up in the epauletted gold-laced swallowtail of Full Dress, he was barely a stately or imposing figure. But later, he was to reveal himself as a powerful Necromancer, who with so many strokes of a pen would create a squadron of paper horses, clap these unsubstantial beasts between the legs of as many solid, British troopers, and make the Nation pay for them in good hard money. Or, with a wave of the same inky wand he would command forage and rations, shirts and great-coats and blankets to be compounded and formed out of impalpable air; so that real horses and real men might feed upon these shadows and be clothed with them.

Newly endued with the power to pay away vast sums of Government money, it is little wonder that Mr. Commissary-General Blunder seemed to Jowell a being almost divine. By dint of perching him upon the piled-up bodies of his forty Commissariat staff-clerks, the Contractor saw him—and conveyed to his son the impression that he too saw him—as a giant rather than a dwarf.... Hearken to Thompson Jowell, enlarging in his idol's praise....

"Comes into the Office—hangs up his hat himself—cracks a joke with the head of his staff of clerks—a Man Like That—who has authority, in case of need, to communicate direct with Foreign Governments—and can dip his hand in the Treasury as if it was his own breeches' pocket.... 'The weather's warum, Colonel Jinkins,' says he, in his sing-song Northern drawl—by the New Order they have military ranks according to grade, and, by Gosh! you should see 'em in their uniforms!—'but by the latest adveece from the East we're to have it warumer still!' Says Jinkins: 'Glad to hear it, Sir, and so is Mr. Thompson Jowell, unless I'm mistaken?' Says I: 'My name being John Bull—it can't be too hot for me!' 'Glaed to find you in such speerits, Mr. Jowell,' says His Honor, taking a pinch of snuff and speaking as dry as chips and shavings—'for when I saw you I was afraid you were going to aesk me for some of the Government's money.... What?... You are?... Waell!—since we caen't stave you off, sign your name to this Contract Demand Dischaerge Receipt, and I'll make you out an Order on the Treasury.' Wuff! goes the sand over the wet ink—none of your new-fangled blotting-paper at the Crown Offices. 'There you are, Mr. Jowell!... Thirty-Five Thousand Pounds!' And between me, and my boy, and the bedpost," said Thompson Jowell, nodding over his wine at his son and heir, "that's a mere flea-bite to what I am a-going to get out of this here Eastern Expedition—long before the end!"

"Gaw!" ejaculated the Ensign, who had inherited the paternal reverence for money. He added, with a tongue somewhat thickened by the frequency with which, in defiance of his mother's warning, he had applied to the decanters. "You jolly old Croe—what the dooce was the tremendously wealthy feller's name who was ordered to be burnt alive?—don't I wish I was in your jolly old shoes, that's all!"

"You are in 'em, Morty, my own boy!" said the father, goggling at the younger Jowell tenderly. "Don't think that what I do is done for myself—for I am a bloody humble man!" His little slanting forehead—so like the lid of a Noah's Ark hooked tightly down over the jumbled beasts inside—the Lamb and the Dove being uppermost at that psychological moment—was full of anxious lines and corrugations. He mopped his overflowing eyes with his table-napkin, and his voice shook and wobbled with emotion as he went on:

"What I do is done for you—what I get is got for you! Remember that!" said Thompson Jowell, leaning forward over his dessert-plate until his vast expanse of shirt-front bulged—why are the shirt-fronts of great financiers invariably badly got up?—and two or three diamond studs unshipped their moorings, and the son caught a glimpse of the hairy bosom the hardy parent scorned to shield with a flannel vest. "Win distinction in the Field—out there!" Jowell waved a gross fat hand in the direction of the London Docks. "You can do it—it's in your blood!—if you told me that it wasn't I shouldn't believe you!—and I shall see you General Sir Mortimer Jowell, K.C.B., before I die, please Heaven!"

"Gaw, Governor! how you pile it on," responded the young man, who was not at all inclined to underestimate his own capacity for heroism. "You ambitious old Codger," he elegantly pursued, "Military Knight Commanderships of the Bath don't grow on every gooseberry-bush.... Why," said Morty, opening his round brown eyes and shaking his bullet head at his parent, "even a first-class tip-top hero like our C.O."—the young man referred to the gallant Colonel of the Cut Red Feathers—"hasn't got that yet! And perhaps he don't deserve it?... Oh, no!... Certainly not!" said Morty in a tone of sarcasm. "Not by no manner of means!..."

"And why hasn't he got it? Not because he ain't brave enough, or enough of a tip-top swell," Jowell wagged his bristly head of upright gray hair sagely at his heir-apparent, and punctuated his periods by sips of the tawny port, "but because he hasn't Money enough to back him. And whose fault is that but his own? Look at his position—think of his chances and opportunities!—and tell me whether he mightn't be as rich as a Jew if he made use of 'em? Don't you go to tell me he couldn't—because I know best!"

"And so do I!—and hang me, if it don't do him honor! I mean," said Mortimer in a tone of disdain that mingled verjuice with the bumper Jowell was in the act of emptying, "his refusin' to cabbage from the men's rations, and firing, and clothing, and uniforms.... Everybody knows it's done, and Government winks at it," pursued the Ensign, getting very red about the gills, but looking straight out of the eyes that were so oddly clear and honest for a son of Jowell's, into the muddier, more prominent orbs that goggled back at him. "But I'm confounded glad *he* sets that fine old face of his against it! and in his place I'm dam' if I shouldn't do the same myself!"

Jowell hastily set down his glass, and fell back in his armchair with a hot and clammy dew breaking out upon his large, and just now queerly-mottled countenance. He puffed and blew like a stout, shaven walrus for some moments before he could speak. Then he said—and the short, thick hand that held a choice cigar he had just taken from a chased casket of precious metal emblazoned with the large and ornate coat-of-arms that had been bought at Heralds' College, shook as he said it:

"But if he had a son, he'd alter his notions about Cabbaging. Not to tell you a lie, my boy!—and my name's Jack Candid—and has been all my life long—I'm a Cabbager myself! Lord!—if I hadn't made use o' my opportunities for Cabbaging—you'd be a private in the ranks, or serving out flour and treacle in an apron behind a chandler's counter, and your mother'd be at the washtub—or charing for a livelihood at eighteenpence a day...."

His thick voice shook and his surface grew more unwholesomely mottled, and his popping eyes whirled in their circular orbits. That this beloved son—in whose interests so many nefarious and tricky schemes had already been concocted and carried out—for whose ultimate aggrandizement Thompson Jowell had planned a crowning masterstroke of villainy that—the man's conscience not being dead in him—jolted him up on end o' nights with his heart thumping and every hair upon his body prickly with fright—should thus have turned and rent him, pierced him to the quick through his pachydermatous hide.

As for Morty—the adage that evil communications corrupt good manners may be reversed in his case with some appropriateness. This big, chuckle-headed young man was sloughing his skin in more senses than one. Since he had mingled daily and hourly in the society of men of honor and high-breeding, the Honorable and Reverend Alfred no longer appeared to him as a model to copy or even a person to tolerate. New ideals had risen up before the eyes of Jowell's son.

The Colonel, who, like many another commanding officer, preferred to be a comparatively poor man, rather than use his prerogative of plunder, seemed to Morty more enviable than the parent who had piled up enormous riches by means he dimly realized to be dishonest and mean.... True, Jowell was never weary of assuring his boy that he, Mortimer, would never be ashamed of his old Governor. But Morty was, secretly, not at all certain on this point.

"I'm not the man to boast, Morty, my boy," the father went on as the son wriggled in his chair with growing uneasiness. "Ben Bragg never was my name or nature, but many another man in my place would have Cabbaged without as good an object. You have been my object—ever since you were born. To be a Millionaire—and I am one, I tell you plainly! isn't enough for me—being my boy's father. I've made up my mind to be as rich as Coutts and Gurney rolled together—and by the Lord! I see my way clear. Draw close—fill up your glass, and listen."

He pushed away the painted porcelain dessert-plate from before him so clumsily that it fell from the shining, slippery mahogany to the floor and was shattered; and went on, jabbing a thick stumpy finger at his son, to emphasize notable points; and sometimes banging a gross fist upon the table, so that choice hothouse fruit and crystallized dainties piled up in costly dishes escaped from their receptacles, and the lusters of the chandeliers trembled overhead.

"This here Eastern Expedition of the Army is the Big Thing I have been a-waiting for. It has put in my way opportunities such as I have only dreamed of up to now. If I didn't grab 'em, other Contractors would—and small blame to 'em. That's why I sank money in that fleet o' nine sail and steam vessels, every one of 'em hired out to Government for Transport at up'ards o' Two Hundred Pounds *per* day."

He puffed and blew and snorted in his walrus-fashion, and, between wine, and the sense of his own importance, seemed to increase in bulk as he went on; punctuating his sentences with jabs of the podgy finger, and sometimes scratching in his stubby growth of hair with it, or tweaking at a gross and purple ear.

"I'm paid for the use o' the ships, and I'm paid for the stuff that goes into 'em. Hay at Twenty Pounds per ton—thousands o' tons—and thousands o' barrels of Flour. Maybe some of the trusses of hay are packed round a core o' cow-parsley, and road, or common-trimmings—them that talk of old hats and empty jam-tins are liars, and I'll prove it in their teeth! Likely you'll happen on a barrel o' breadstuff here and there that's sour or blue-moldy in the middle.... Fraud I scorn," said Jowell, breathing noisily, "but Business is Business with me as other men. The bad with the good—the rotten with the sound—that's the secret of successful dealing. Push the decanter over, will ye? David Drychops is my name this evening! Thanks, my own dear boy!"

He filled a bumper and drank with greedy, spluttering noises, and went on, sucking at his fleshy lips, that were moistened with the sweet red wine:

"Lord! if you knew as much of the tricks of the trade as I do!—you'd think your old Gov. a Angel without wings.... I tell you—and my name's Nick Know—millions o' golden pounds'll be paid, before this here War is over, for Rot, and Rubbish—and nothing more. War Scares are got up—that's what they are—to give opportunity for Cabbaging on the Grand Scale to Nobs and Bigwigs—War Office and Admiralty Bigwigs—whose names—if I whispered 'em—'ud take away your breath. And me and the other Contractors—men as they are lofty to, and patronize—are in their secrets, and up to every move and dodge of the game they couldn't play without us—and their hands—white as they keep 'em—and with gems engraved with family crests that are heirlooms shining on 'em—are not a whit cleaner than what ours are—and there's the naked truth!"

Fate spurred him on—who had never even to himself, or that gray confederate Cowell, spoken thus openly—to this unbosoming, else his son might have died believing him a worthy kind of man. In his urgent need for the love and respect and admiration of this hulking young scion of the house of Jowell, he emptied himself, to the foiling of his passionate desire.

"Take the case of a brand-new Government Transport I am a-loading with my own and other Contractors' stuff at Portsmouth Dockyard," he babbled on recklessly. "By Gosh! if you could see the inside of the barrels and crates and cases her holds are chock-full of—to the tune of Five Hundred Thousand Pounds! Thousands o' barrels o' salt beef and pickled pork that were laid down in brine before the Battle o' Waterloo. Ay!—and thousands o' tins of preserved meat that 'ud blow your head off with stink and stench—if they were ever to be opened!—and cases—thousands o' cases o' dead worms that were born of biscuit and lived on biscuit—and died when there was no more biscuit to live on—and ankers of Prime Jamaica Rum made of burnt sugar-and-water and Spirits of potato and beet—not to talk of the crates full of Shoell's Army Boots that *are* boots—till you get down to where they're nothing but odd sizes, and spoiled uppers, and scraps of old leather—and the Winter Clothing and comforts from Sewell's Factories—watch-coats and guernsey frocks; coatees and trousers; woolen vests and drawers and socks atop, and Dunnage underneath—and nothing but Dunnage! Like the Medical Stores that are the sweepings of every Hospital in the United Kingdom. All packed under loose shot, and empty shell, and supplies of munitions for the Ordnance—to prevent 'em being too easily got at, d'ye twig?... Whoof! I'm short o' breath!" snorted Jowell, fanning his large red face with his crumpled napkin. "Old Billy Blowhard, and no mistake about me!"

He had really talked himself into an apoplectic and congested condition, and now was fain to break off speech and muster a second wind, while his son, whose large ears were humming with these revelations, regarded him with a circular stare of surprise. But even as Morty's mouth opened for speech, Thompson Jowell put up a coarse, ringed hairy hand and stopped him; and plunged back into the subject ere his son could get out a word.

"Don't you say what you're a-going to say!—and tell me that you don't mind Government and the Nation being Cabbaged from—but as an officer holding the Queen's Commission you're damned if you like the notion of the British Army being served up on toast. I tell you—and my name's Sure and Certain in the present instance—the British Army—God bless it!—won't be a ha'porth the worse for anything on board the Transport I've told you of—even if anything on board of her was likely to be wanted—which won't be the case—mark me! For this here Eastern Expedition will be back by the beginning of October at the latest; and—I tell you with all my cards on the table—this Two-Thousand-Six-Hundred-Ton steam-screw Transport I am a-talking of is as crank as a child's tin boat.... Built of unseasoned Baltic pine she is—not a plank of honest English oak in her—

the man who contracted with the Admiralty to supply the timber is a friend of mine—d'ye twig? She won't weather out a Black Sea gale, by Gosh she won't! If Old Moore and Mother Shipton and Zadkiel's Almanac told me she would I should call 'em liars! A crank ship!—a damned crank ship!" said Thompson Jowell, thrusting his great crimson face and starting eyes near his son's, and speaking in a husky whisper. "Nobody would be so wicked as to count on her Going Down—people don't do such things!—if they owned to me that they did I wouldn't believe 'em! But now the cat is out of the bag—and tip us your fist, my boy!"

He squeezed his son's large, unresponsive hand, and, reluctantly releasing it, went on, in the flux of confidential talk that had seized and overmastered him: "And remember that you have a Brilliant Career before you—that's what you have! Through you I mean the name of Jowell to strike root deep in the Old Country and spread wide and tower high. I ha' lived small—here and at that little place of ours in Sloughshire—and haven't launched out in a Scotch Castle and a Deer Forest and a Salmon River when I might—perhaps you've thought? What I say is—Wait until you come back from this campaign, and then you shall see a thing or two! Why have I bought up the village, field by field, and cottage by cottage, and whole streets o' freehold shops and dwelling-houses in Market Drowsing Town? Because I mean you to be returned Member of Parliament for the Borough—and you shall sit in the Upper House among the other nobs as Baron Jowell by-and-by! There's a pretty estate of ten thousand acres of park and stubble, covert and woodland, will be on the market presently—and a sixty acre o' clay upland freehold within a mile o' Market Drowsing—with a homestead and some good gore meadows—suitable to build a Stud Farm and Kennels on—as I've a mortgage on and mean to have by-and-by. And, by Gosh, my boy!—the County shall cap to you as Lord Lieutenant before you're forty," said Jowell, stretching the coarse hairy hand across the table. "Here's my hand again on it—and so you know!"

"Haw, haw, haw! You're going to go it, Governor, ain't you?—with a vengeance!" said the son, with heartiness rather forced. He added, repressing a hiccup, for his potations had half-fuddled him: "But what's this sixty-acre you're talking about for a Stud Farm within a mile of Market Drowsing?... Gaw!—you don't mean to say you mean my Cousin Sarah's bit o' land?"

"She's not your cousin—if Burke took his Bible oath she was I wouldn't believe him!" said Thompson Jowell, his large cheeks purpling as he bent his brows upon his son. "She's a Poor Relation of mine—and what is it to you how I get land? If you're to be a Nobleman, Land is what you want—and Land is what you must have. Trust your old Gov.!—my name's Stephen Staunch where you're concerned, ain't it? And now tell me—when do you leave for the East, and what's your barkey? Is she a regular good 'un? *The British Queen*, dy'e say?... She's a clipper of a ship," said Jowell, rummaging in a hairy nostril. "One o' my own—I bought her from the Newfoundland Emigration Labor Company for a mere song, better than new! She sails on the 18th from Southampton, with a draft of the Hundredth Lancers; six officers, and seventy Rank-and-File, and the Admiralty Agent, the Honorable Mr. Skiffington. My Hay in the fore-hold, troop-horses in the after-hold," said Jowell, smiling and winking knowingly. "Dunnage under the horses—barrels of Cowell's salt beef under the Dunnage—it ain't my lookout if it gets spoiled—and Cowell wouldn't object, I rather fancy!... And now we'll adjourn to the drawing-room," said Jowell, scraping back his chair, and getting up on his short, thick legs, and gripping his son affectionately by the elbows—his inferior stature not permitting him to reach the Ensign's broad shoulders. He ended, looking with moist, smiling tenderness in the owlish, rather tipsy young face, as he shook Morty to and fro. "And we'll have a little music.... You shall tip us 'Vilikins And His Dinah'—if anybody told me Robson could sing it better I wouldn't believe 'em. And I'm damned if I haven't half a mind to give you 'Marble Halls.'"

Morty obliged with "Vilikins"—the newest thing out in ditties of the comic order, and Jowell was as good as his word with the operatic selection to which he referred. "I Dreamt that I Dwelt in Marble Halls" is a melody with many turns and flourishes, and Jowell executed them conscientiously, not sparing one....

If Britannia, leaning with complete confidence at this juncture upon that stout and sturdy stem of tough old British oak, had peeped in and beheld the great Contractor—gathered with his family about the grand piano in the most sumptuous of the telescopic drawing-rooms—and beating time all wrong as he murdered the tune with simple, whole-hearted enjoyment,— she might have withdrawn her helmeted head in the conviction that here Was an honest man.

Though in Morty's muddled mind some degree of dubiousness was created, as to the exact description of "Marble Halls" merited by a man who was cramming a crank-built transport of Baltic oak with rot and rubbish to the tune of Five Hundred Thousand Pounds. He was secretly wondering whether—in the estimation of his demigod, the Colonel of the Cut Red Feathers, a cool stone cell in Newgate Jail might not meet the case?—when Mrs. Jowell—at his own request—tried to sing 'Home, Sweet Home'—and broke down in the second bar. He was wondering still, when three silver bedroom candlesticks arrived on a tray so massive, that the footman who bore it staggered. He was wondering yet, as his parents accompanied him up the broad, shallow staircase, and parted from him on the threshold of his palatial, gorgeous bedroom, with blessings and kisses and tears.

He could not have done with wondering. The scene closes upon him, standing—in an Oriental dressing-robe of sumptuous fabric superimposed above the long-tailed garment of the night, before his colossal, gilt-plate-laden dressing-table—saying, as he regarded his own foolish, tipsy young face in the great glittering mirror:

"Well, Blow Me Tight, if I don't believe the Governor is the very devil!" He added, as he crowned himself with a tasseled nightcap and blundered into bed: "And he may be a regular tip-top business man—but I'm hanged if I cotton to such games. No, sir! I'm dam' if I do like 'em! I'm Blest if I do—so there!"

LXXVIII

You are to imagine how Morty's mother sobbed and kissed and blessed him, over and over at parting; and how earnestly the poor woman begged of her darling never to forget his prayers, or go out fasting in the chill morning air, and always to wear flannel next to his skin—and you are to learn that the big young man had left the poor soul shut up in the biggest of her suite of gilded drawing-rooms, and was in the act of clanking down the doorsteps to the brougham that was to convey him with his father to the railway station, when he suddenly turned—and galloped clattering back.

He strode through the hall—burst into the drawing-room—sending all the crystal dillywangles on the vases and chandeliers into tinkling fits of agitation—called with the old, old voice of the child to the woman sitting there in stony, despairing silence:

"Mummy!"

—and fell down at her trembling knees; butted his bullet-head against her thin, aching bosom, and hugged her again and again.... She thanked her Maker all her life afterwards for that unexpected burst of love and tenderness.... Her boy was to call her once more—out of the jaws of Death—and she was to hear him—even though thousands of miles of dry land and bitter water separated mother and son....

As for Thompson Jowell, that fond parent traveled down with his boy to Southampton, and benefited him with parental advice and fatherly counsel by the way. He repeated over and over again that Morty was to be sure and win distinction; and trust to his old Governor to back him up. And the young man, touched to melting by the evident solicitude and affection—responded in his characteristic vein of clumsy raillery, punctuated by heavy pats on the back, and filial pokes in the fleshy ribs that were covered with a waistcoat of gorgeousness even more pronounced than usual, made of an embroidered Turkish shawl. He told Thompson Jowell that he was a regular Out-and-Outer, a capital Brick, a Rare old File, and a stunning old Nailer, and Jowell never guessed that Morty's habitually-stated conviction that his parent was the devil—the very devil!—was not forthcoming because Morty had once felt it to be so nearly true.

Later on—in that new-born sensitiveness of his—Morty found himself wishing that he were the son of a man several sizes smaller. As, for instance, when Thompson Jowell stood with his short legs wide apart on the hearthrug of the Officers' Mess Cabin on the poop-deck, and rattled the big tills in his trousers-pockets, and patronized the Colonel and the half-dozen officers of Her Majesty's Hundredth Lancers who were going out with this draft.

It hideously irked Morty—not ordinarily thin skinned—to find that, as in the case of the Admiralty Agent the Honorable Mr. Skiffington—who was going out in the *British Queen* to watch over the maritime interests of Britannia at Constantinople, two of the after-cabin staterooms had been, by the removal of the bulkhead between them, knocked into one for his reception; and that in consequence, some of the ladies—as several of the male cabin passengers—were grievously incommoded and squeezed.

Nor was this the least objectionable of the many ways in which Jowell's paternal tenderness for his boy manifested itself. Consignments of special luxuries had been provided for the after-cabin table. Nay, every one of the rank-and-file upon the troop-deck was to be allowed per day, throughout the voyage, and at the Good Fairy Jowell's expense, an extra half-pint of porter. In addition to this, Jowell explained to the Colonel, he had taken the liberty of augmenting the Mess wine-list with twelve dozen of the tawny port, from his own cellars. And he caused shudders to course down the spine of his son, by calling the steward, and ordering bottles of this precious vintage to be uncorked there and then, that all might taste of his bounty. And, as his oppressive patronage and condescending geniality extended to the ladies present—as he counseled those who were parting from their husbands, fathers, or brothers, to drink of his liquor that they might be nerved to bear the ordeal; and pressed yet others who were going out with the regiment to partake that they might face the trials of the voyage with a better heart—he seemed to Morty to swell and grow so that his upright hair appeared shooting through the cabin skylight, and the shadow of his bloated body banished the bright spring sunshine from the place.

One ought to love and honor one's father, it was the duty of a Christian as well as of a gentleman, but—Gaw!—when the Governor was facetious with the Colonel's wife—and when he tipped the company a speech—and was alternately patriotic and pathetic—it made at least one person present go hot and cold.

"By Gosh! ladies and gentlemen, if these Roosians think they can beat us, let them try it!" he said, over and over. He became intolerable in his looseness and prodigality of words. His son, whom he had so often assured that he should never find cause to be ashamed of his father, found it now; and was dyed in crimson blushes to the roots of his hair, as Jowell addressed his fair hearers and his gallant friends.

He told them that this here War was a War of Right and Justice—a War about to be fought by Old England shoulder to shoulder with her Natural

Allies. And that Heaven—Thompson Jowell confidently answered for Heaven—would not fail to nerve the arms of those who were taking the part of the weak against the strong. Talk of Uncle Tom—Cousin Turk being a-many shades nearer the true British color, ought to be as many degrees nearer the true-born Briton's heart.... Thompson Jowell laid a podgy paw upon his own, and dropped the "h" as he enunciated the word. If anybody told him otherwise, he added—his name being Peter Plain—he wouldn't believe him, by Gosh! he wouldn't. But all present were Englishmen and also gentlemen. And—Britannia—Thompson Jowell had answered for Heaven and now he answered for Britannia—Britannia confidently looked to all his gallant friends—might the speaker call them his dear and gallant friends?—somebody said "Oh Lord, yes!" to this, and Thompson Jowell thanked him in a stately way, and lumbered on to his peroration. Britannia looked to every one of his dear and gallant friends here present to uphold the reputation of British Arms. England, he added, was not absolutely ignorant of the name of Jowell. He bowed his tier of chins, above their stiff frill of gray whiskers, in the direction of the sarcastic voice that cried "Hear, hear!" And ended, with overflowing eyes turned upon his boy, and real emotion surging behind his magnificent Turkish-shawl waistcoat:

"May she hear more of it before this War is done!"

Jowell hugged and kissed his boy at parting, ignorant of the secret shrinking with which Morty received these caresses—bade God bless him and take care of him! and the tears rolled openly down his large whiskered face as he thrust a bulky roll of banknotes into his hand.

And then he tore himself away, and Morty—conscience-stricken in the realization of his own unfilial relief at the sight—saw the bulky back of him—topped with a low-crowned curly-brimmed hat that was of straw in deference to the hot May weather—waddle down the bouncing gangway—saw the great red face slewed midway for a last glance, and a clumsy farewell flourish of a big gross hand that gripped a gold-topped stick. And then the Great Man was lost in the huge crowd surging and roaring at the quay-edge as completely as though the grave had swallowed him up.

And with much churning of oily-looking salt water and vomitings of sooty-black coal-smoke and cindery flavored white steam by an excited paddle-wheel tug-steamer; amidst waving of male hats and feminine handkerchiefs, cheers and good-byes from the throngs upon the quays—with a return of hurrahs from the troopers crowding at her bulwarks and thrusting their faces through the ports of her main troop-deck—with chorusing of "Auld Lang Syne" and "Cheer, Boys, Cheer, Old Russia's All

Before Us!"—the second line having been adapted by an anonymous genius to fit the case—*The British Queen* dropped her moorings, and was towed away down the River on her watery way to Gallipoli, *via*—why on earth *via* Gibraltar?—receiving the customary compliment of eighteen guns from the Platform, and leaving the usual deposit of red-eyed, shabbily-clothed soldier's wives and children, crying on the sunshiny, cheerful quay.

Had Moggy Geogehagan been numbered among those disconsolate women left weeping on the quayside, she would have had no tale to tell me in Ballymullet Workhouse, where her days were ended. But, indeed, had "the lots gone agin' her," she declared—and it was not possible to doubt her, for there was fire in the glance of her eye, and energy in the thump of her staff-end on the tiled floor, even at eighty-nine—she would have made her way out to where Jems was fighting with the Ridgimint—on her own four bones.

But here she was, on *The British Queen*—and near her Mrs. Joshua Horrotian. When the Call was sounded for the drawing, and the folded slips of official paper that had an inky scrawl of "Go" inside them, or a blank more eloquent still, were tossed—as was the ancient custom in this Regiment—upon the sheepskin of the kettledrums yet vibrating from the Charge—Nelly had waited her turn in a mounting fever of anxiety that had melted the last icicles away from her poor heart. Joshua Horrotian had hardly known the bright-eyed, rosy-cheeked creature, who had run to him, panting and trembling, and thrown glad arms about his neck, and shed tears of bliss upon his bosom, crying, "I'm to go!—I'm to go!" For until you are about to lose the last remaining joy, you never realize how rich you are, or how poor you may yet live to be if God takes that also.

After dinner that evening, while the light airs from the nor'-west were pushing *The British Queen*—long since parted from her tug—towards the Bay of Biscay, and glowing cigar-ends were patroling the quarter-deck singly and in couples; and the tinkle of a piano-played waltz came cheerfully from the Officers' Mess Cabin, and the strains of "Annie Laurie" and "A Life on the Ocean Wave" proceeded from the troop-deck as the forecastle—where troopers and tars fraternized in high accord—Morty heard one semi-visible stroller say, in answer to some remark of a companion:

"By Jove no! But with me it's like this!—I don't object to a man who smells of Money—but a man who stinks of it, I simply can't stand!"

It was the male voice that had cynically cried "Oh Lord, yes!" and "Hear, Hear!" when Jowell was speechifying. And a feminine voice responded:

"He *meant* well, dear, I'm *sure*! But *what* a dreadful man!"

Morty knew whom the officer's wife was discussing with her husband. And whilst he burned and smarted, he admitted perforce the truth of their utterances. His father did stink of Money. His father undoubtedly must appear to persons of any breeding and refinement a really dreadful man. Why, his own son—

Later, when Morty was in bed in the comfortable lower berth of the state-room that had been expanded, to the compression of the young man's fellow-passengers—and *The British Queen*, having left the glassy Solent far behind her, was beginning to roll amidst the restless surges of the Atlantic so that cabin doors banged, cabin crockery rattled, timbers groaned and creaked—and heavy rushes of footsteps on the deck were followed by the flumping of tightened canvas and the noisy coiling away of ropes—Jowell's son—who, like his great parent, was of queasy sea-stomach—found this question cropping up again.

The Governor stank of Money. That was why his son, who had learned since he joined the Cut Red Feathers to refrain from quenching his thirst with brandy-and-water early in the morning, and to eschew cravats and waistcoats of violently contrasting hues—who had left off sleeking the stiff brown hair upon his bullet-head with perfumed bear's grease and besprinkling his person with the combined essences of Frangipani and Jockey Club—found respiration difficult in his father's company. But—was it only Money the Governor stank of?... The air of the big dining-room at Hanover Square had been heavy with the odor of roguery on that night when Thompson Jowell had laid his cards, as he had said, upon the table, and owned up to playing—from first to last, an infernal dirty game!...

"I'm a bit of a Cabbager myself!" Morty could hear him saying it. And—"The bad with the good—the rotten with the sound—that's the secret of successful Contracting!"

It was jolly—confounded jolly to be a British Guardsman and know yourself the son of a father who had become a millionaire—and meant to become yet richer—by diddling the British Army. It was enough to drive sleep from any honest, decent pillow, and this is a feeble pen if it has not conveyed that Morty Jowell was an honest, decent young man. Vulgar and dull and clumsy perhaps—but sound at the core, and wholesome-natured, as his mother's son could hardly fail to be.

The rolling of the vessel increased, and, from the adjoining cabin, occupied by the Honorable Mr. Skiffington, the Admiralty Agent—whose experience of the ocean had been gathered in the course of two or three Naval Reviews at Spithead and half-a-dozen trips across the English Channel—groans of the most piteous description now began to be heard. So Morty sat up, hugging his knees and frowning at the pale eye of the state-room port-light—which, sometimes hidden by its short green velvet curtain, or revealed—as the drapery swung aside with the ship's rolling—seemed to wink in a derisive way.

"Gaw! how this dam' ship rolls!—and, talkin' of stinks—how smelly she is!... Horses and soger-men and tar and bilge—piff!—and somethin' else to top up." He sniffed, becoming more and more sensible of having inherited the queasy paternal stomach.... "Somethin' I've smelt at those kilns at Little Milding—where the Governor dries his sprouted oats and mildewed hay." He added, in an aggrieved tone:

"My forage 'ud taste a deal sweeter if it had been bought with cleaner money. That's what I say, and to that I shall stick. And I'm ready to lay any fellow ten to one in tenners—and the Governor's given me a hundred of 'em!—I shall come across that core of cow-parsley in every truss I get!"

Here Morty succumbed to the malady of the ocean, groaning just as dismally as the Admiralty Agent. You may imagine corresponding sounds breaking out in neighboring cabins—indeed, for some hours the stuffy, crowded troop-deck had been littered with the bodies of those who had fallen victims to this insidious complaint.

And as the weather worsened, and hatchways, companions, and even scuttles were kept closed, that smell that Morty Jowell had said "Piff!" at—and that was reminiscent of the kilns at Little Milding, where fermenting hay was dried—mingled more potently in the hotch-potch of weird smells that distinguishes a troopship full of seasick soldiers.

It came in overpowering gusts from the fore-hold, that was close-packed with the Government forage-trusses. It came in blasts more overpowering still—being mingled with an appalling equine odor—through a square black hole in the lower deck—a yawning hole that had not been padded with sacks of straw like the corresponding aperture in the deck above it—when by means of canvas slings and tackle from the mainyard, the horses had been lowered into the after-hold.

Descending into the stifling blackness of this place, you presently made out by the significantly-haloed light of a couple of wire-guarded ship's lanterns, rows of frightened hairy faces ranged along the sides of the hold, and looking at you across the spars that kept their owners—slung in canvas belts from hooks in the over-deck beams—in the stalls that were padded with straw and bundles of tow.

The central space between the rows of frightened hairy faces was packed to the upper-deck with more of Jowell's forage-trusses. Dunnage was beneath the hoofs of these unlucky four-legged passengers, and layers of Cowell's beef-barrels were underneath this. And when the ship rolled in stress of heavy weather, and the barrels shifted, the legs that got between them were frequently mashed to jelly, adding to the deadly qualms of nauseau torments more cruel still.

Sire my Friend accommodated the horses of his Cavalry, Artillery and Transport on the spar-decks of troop-ships—or at worst in the 'tween decks; sheltering them in the first instance beneath canvas, or housing them under temporary sheds of planks. But Britannia, at the instance of her evil genius Jowell, stowed—in nine cases out of ten—these luckless brutes upon the ballast.

Every day on board *The British Queen*—as on board those other transports speeding in the cause of Humanity to the East with men and horses—shots were heard far down in these submarine hells; and every night hairy bodies—sometimes dreadfully disfigured and distorted—were hauled up with rope-tackle and hove overboard. For your horse, whose anatomical structure renders it next to impossible to vomit, is capable of going mad; and does it under given circumstances, with conspicuous thoroughness. Therefore the faces of the men who went down into these places, looking pale or red as the case might be, came up again livid or purple; and the oaths they swore grew more sulphurous every day. For between good men and good horses there is love.

What time *The British Queen* was staggering, close-hauled, through the shattering yellow-green seas of the Bay of Biscay O! two hundred miles from England—and it blew a great gale through heavy squalls of rain—and the hatches were battened down, and every soul on the troop-decks, and every military officer in the poop cabin and several of the ship's officers and crew, were dog-sick and helpless; even stout Blueberry nearly gave up hope of seeing the light of day again, and breathing something sweeter than the atmosphere of the after-hold.

For the comrade on his off-side was screaming in the convulsions of tetanus; and the mare on his near-side was dead like many another, with her long neck and helpless head banging him, flail-fashion, whenever the smelly, stifling stable you were pent up in stood on its front end—or swinging the other way and banging Corporal Geogehagan's horse—and even the sailors who had come down at intervals to pump the tainted water from the tanks and serve out the musty hay had left off coming.

Then, in the middle of one unforgettable, fateful night, was heard aboard *The British Queen*, and heard in every conceivable tone of human and animal terror, fear, and anguish—the dreadful cry of Fire!

LXXIX

Upon a fine June morning some eight days later, Jowell, in his dingy office in The Poultry, London, in the narrow alley of sordid houses hard by the Banking House of Lubbock, received a telegram from the Admiralty. A moment later the gray-faced Chobley, busy in his little glass case opening out of the office where the seven pallid clerks bent over ledgers, was summoned by a strangled shriek that came from the whistle of the speaking-tube, and entered the Contractor's private sanctum. A moment later he rang the bell.

For a dreadful, white-and-blue faced jabbering Something that wore the clothing of Thompson Jowell had come staggering at the manager, shaking a slip of flimsy yellow paper; and, jabbering out an unintelligible word or so, had fallen down in a fit.

"Fetch a doctor from somewhere, will you!" said Chobley to the sea-green Standish's pallid successor, as he knelt over the bulky, stertorously-breathing body that sprawled upon the shabby ink-stained carpet, fumbling at its shirt-collar stud. He had been enlightened by a glance at the telegraphic message from Whitehall, and added, working away:

"There has been bad work at sea. The forage aboard *The British Queen* worked and took fire—at least, the message says so. Ship was a blazing hulk in half-an-hour from the outbreak—they took to the boats, such of 'em as they could get at. A Dundee brig bound for Lisbon picked up three of 'em—a Southampton-bound barque and a schooner for Port au Prince, St. Domingo, overhauled the rest. Eighty-nine souls were saved, twenty-three drowned or burned—including the Veterinary Surgeon and the Colonel of the Regiment. And all the horses except one—I should like to know how that one managed to save himself," said Chobley rather gruesomely, "from being frizzled with the rest in the after-hold?"

Avid of more horrors, Standish's successor queried:

"And Mr. Mortimer?"

"Why," returned the manager, still busying himself about the neck of the prone, insensible figure, "Mr. Mortimer has been picked up, with the rest, aboard the ship's boats. It's the shock of hearing that his son was in danger lays the Governor snoring and choking here. For *The British Queen* and everything aboard of her was insured—pretty heavily insured; and there's no loss to us resulting from the casualty—rather the reverse!"

Chobley, the leaden-complexioned, meant a great deal the reverse; and the clerk knew it as he went away for the doctor; and the manager—having loosened his employer's collar and cravat, opened the window to admit what passed in The Poultry for fresh air. And presently Jowell recovered sufficiently to be hoisted up from the carpet, and got into his chair; and damn them for calling in the medical man.

He went home early to Hanover Square, and—saying nothing of his own indisposition—broke the news of Morty's peril and deliverance—escape-end first—to his boy's mother. And then—sending one of the large powdered footmen for the immense gilt Church Service, usually borne after him upon Sundays in the country by one of these privileged menials, as the great man waddled up the aisle of Market Drowsing Parish Church—he mounted his glasses and read, occasionally pausing to take off and wipe these aids to vision—the Prayer for Those at Sea.

His wife, subsequently entering his library, found him thus employed, and was secretly thankful. It seemed like a first answer to all her petitions for him. He looked up as she came in, and found no fault with her red eyes on this occasion, his own being, if possible, redder.

He spoke gently to her, and finding him in this unusual mood, and being anxious to improve the occasion, she bade him take comfort and be thankful, for their dear son was under the protection—forbid that I should quote the words irreverently!—of a Heavenly Father's Hand.

At which Jowell blew his nose—cocked at quite a subdued angle—and agreed with her, adding:

"All the same, the boy has got a good 'un Down Here. No man can call me Ben Blinker at any time, but where my son's concerned I'm William Wide Awake, Esquire. As to the hay firing of itself—I don't believe it! To palm off hay green, or hay half-cured, upon Her Majesty's Government's Contractors would be a Fraud. People don't do such things—they ain't capable of it!" said Jowell virtuously. "Some drunken sailor dropped a lighted candle-lantern into the fore-hold, or some trooper smoking on the sly on stable duty stuck his pipe in amongst the straw and left it there—and if I had him here," said Jowell ogreishly, "I'd make him smoke on the wrong side of his mouth, by Gosh, I would!"

He added: "And you're a good woman, Maria, by Gosh, you are!" And in testimony to this excellence he bought her, the very next day, an immense cameo brooch, representing the triumph of Venus, and set with many blazing brilliants of great price.

Wounds of the soul, neglects of years, are healed and made as nought in the belief of men like this man, by a trinket purchased at the jeweler's. Disloyalties and treacheries are blotted out—harsh words, ill-usage and infidelity atoned for. The wives who receive these gewgaws know sorrowfully well why they are given.

All unsolicited gifts bestowed by men like Jowell are sops to the shrill-voiced Conscience chiding behind their waistcoats. Thus, the man gave to his wife because she had so much to forgive; he sent a draft for a great sum to his son, not only because his own dishonesty had placed that beloved one in peril, but because he had so greatly swindled the sons of other men. That half-pint of porter shed upon the troopers and their wives in the 'tween-decks did them good, perhaps! But how they paid for it in the end!

Young Mortimer Jowell escaped, not without risk of life, upon that night of terror. For when columns of stifling smoke lanced through with yellow flame came pouring up the fore-hatch—and the ineffectual hoses had ceased to play upon the conflagration—while the burning vessel ran with lashed helm before the westerly gale to keep the fire forward, while the boats were being hurried off the skids and launched and loaded—a big young man in night-shirt and trousers—a young man who had been knocked senseless by a tackle-block falling from the blazing mainyard—was being lowered by the Captain of *The British Queen* into the last boat of all—when a horizontal, swordlike tongue of flame licked through the smoke now rolling up the mizzen-hatchway, proving how fearfully the fire gained below—and the rope was severed by it as by a saber-stroke—and the half-naked senseless wretch fell into the raging sea. And would have been drowned undoubtedly, had not a hulking, red-headed trooper of the Hundredth Lancers, when a dripping head rose in the yeasty smother close to the boat's side—reached forth his hand and grabbed its owner by the scruff, and hauled him so near that other hands could help to drag him into comparative safety.

And presently, his scattered wits returning, young Morty Jowell became aware that he was bitter cold. Next, that sea-water was washing over him; next that he was not on board a ship, but a comparatively small ship's boat, dancing like a walnut-shell in the tourney of monstrous seas. And then—opening his raw and stiffened eyelids—he became aware that he, half naked, wet and shivering, was one of a crowd of fellow-creatures, chiefly male, equally unclad, perished and soaking. And that, as the boat was pitched from ridge to ridge of huge and watery mountains—there were to be had brief, appalling glimpses of a burning ship with showers of incandescent fragments falling from her rigging, and clouds of firefly sparks drifting away to leeward—painted in hues of rose and apricot, clear dazzling scarlet, peacock blue and springlike, exquisite apple-green upon the background of pitch-black tempestuous, rainy night—and that the shrill song of the gale in their frozen ears was mingled with the roar of the greedy flames that crunched her bones. And that those dreadful shrieks that ripped and tore through the other noises were the cries of horses burning in her after-hold, and men burning on the blazing decks of her.... For the Captain of the unlucky vessel, the Veterinary Surgeon of the Hundredth Lancers—twenty troopers and the Colonel—had—the long boat having been rendered useless—remained on board *The British Queen*.

One other terrific picture was bitten in as with corrosive acid on Mortimer Jowell's memory. It was when—her mainmast having fallen with a tremendous crash, and her ballast having shifted from her unguided, furious wallowings amidst the liquid mountains—*The British Queen* canted over with a tremendous list to port.... They saw her decks then as one sees a stage with a steep rake, all smoking and charring and crawling with tongues of liquorish fire. Also, they saw, and groaned aloud with ineffectual pity—for they had but one oar, and, had the boat been capable of holding another passenger, could not have moved to the rescue—doomed human beings huddled in her starboard mizzen channels, that were as yet not burned away.

And they recognized, in less time than one takes to write it, in a fiery object that burst screaming up upon her after-deck, a maddened horse, whose mane and tail were on fire, whose legs were flayed and bleeding, and whose sides and flanks were garnished with blazing patches of tow.

There was a piteous cry at that sad sight, and a woman swooned. Strange things had been seen that night, but none more strange and terrible. How the brute had freed himself from that fiery hell below may not even be conjectured, but there he was, as I have said....

He pranced down the deck with heraldic, rampant gait, screaming and snorting; reared, with his bloody forelegs stuck out stiffly, and leaped into the sea. And a man sprang up in the boat and pointed with a scorched and naked arm; and yelled out something that was drowned in the shriek of the gale and the bellowing of the fire. What he yelled was:

"That's my horse! I'd know him among a thousand! And, by G——, he's swimming. Keep up! Don't ye give in, my brave old Bluberry!"

He could not have heard, but he did not give in.... He was breathing yet, with his long neck thrown across the charred and floating wreckage of the fallen mainmast when the wild gray dawn broke, and the brig *Maggie o' Muirhead* and the St. Domingo schooner overhauled the red-hot hulk of *The British Queen*.

The Captain and a trooper were rescued, living, from her mizzen channels, the perishing castaways in the boat were saved. Sailors are superstitious. Not being desirous of a mutiny in his forecastle, the master of the *Maggie* yielded to the pressure brought to bear by his crew. And they got a bight of a line round Blueberry, and hauled the horse aboard; dosed him, all limp and sprawling—with tincture of ginger—kept by the mate for stomachic chills—in hot water; doctored his burns with linseed oil—and presently he floundered up on those raw legs of his, and tried to be himself again.

Thenceforth he consorted with the ship's goat until the *Maggie* reached Lisbon; and, though he bore the scars of that wild night's work all the rest of his life, and the hair, where it grew again upon his flanks, came white in patches, he lived to carry his master through the Charge of the Light Brigade at Balaklava, and die at the long last of cold and famine at the Cavalry Camp on the slopes above Kadikoi.

Said Morty, coming up to a red-headed trooper on the forecastle-deck of the *Maggie*: "Look here! I've just found out it was you who saved my life. And I'm obliged to you—tremenjous!—and though all the money I'd got was burned on that dam' ship, my father—Mr. Thompson Jowell—owner—will give you anything you want! See?"

And the speaker, attired in a cast-off pair of trousers of the master's and a pea-jacket lent by the *Maggie o' Muirhead's* second mate—and wearing a list slipper of the steward's on his right foot, and a half-boot contributed by another philanthropist, on the left one—held out his large hand to his savior with genuine eagerness.

"Blast your father!" said the red-headed trooper, so suddenly and so savagely that Morty jumped in his odd foot-coverings. "Can he give me back *my* boy? And do you think—if I'd been let to have a chance o' choosing—I'd ha' put out my hand—knowingly—to save his son? Wait till next time, that's all I ha' got to say!—you wait till next time, that's all!"

And Joshua Horrotian turned his back on the heir of his enemy, and spat over the bulwarks of the forecastle-deck in loathing, and then a thought occurred to him that brought his head round again.

His wish had been granted. He had lived to see Jowell's son, half-clad and penniless, with an old boot on one foot and an old shoe on the other—asking—and asking vainly for the hand he had denied.

It was merely an odd chance. That experimental curse of Josh's had had nothing to do with it. And yet—supposing Some One Above had heard—the granting of that ill wish had not spared misfortune to the wisher. The wife and the horse were safe, though; and Corporal and Mrs. Geogehagan were in one of the boats that had been picked up by the St. Domingo schooner. One would do well not to grumble at one's luck, reflected Joshua Horrotian.

LXXX

The Tsar was right. Men who desire Death very keenly and bitterly, who seek the grim tyrant in his very citadel, find him difficult of access, as a rule.

Something that had been a man came staggering back out of the poisonous swamps of the delta of the Dobrudja, and—more dead than alive—reached the port of Kustendje on the Black Sea, what time Protestant England and Catholic France had allied with the Moslem against Christian Russia; and Lord Dalgan, Commander-in-Chief of the British Forces, and H.R.H. the Duke of Bambridge, were being entertained by Sire my Friend, at Paris.

As though the out-at-elbows refugee, the borrowing adventurer, the temporary occupant of the Presidential armchair had never existed, you are to see him Sire my Friend as the Ally of Great Britain, the gracious patron and protector of the Sick Man. He had had his will; his plot had blossomed in this gorgeous flower of International War—the Allied Fleets were in the Black Sea—France was rent with the shouting of trumpets and the screaming of bugles; she quaked with the tramping of cavalry, the ceaseless passing of batteries of artillery, and trains of wagons and ammunition-carts. And day by day his crowded transports steamed for the East from Toulon and Brest and Marseilles.

He was happy. The Northern potentate who would not call him brother—the Army he had bribed with stolen millions to enthrone him—which he feared, and which openly ridiculed him—the English Sovereign and her Consort, who had despised and condescended to him—these were destined to drink of a cup that had taken years to mix.

England's trust in him entertained him hugely. She took the leap, with all its tragic possibilities, like a generous horse ridden by a reckless sportsman at a killing fence; ignoring the deadly possibilities of the stake, and the barbed wire, and the back-breaking deep ditch beyond.

To gratitude, good faith, rectitude, loyalty to vows a stranger—all must smart sooner or later, who had trusted this man.... Thus, France paid in the end in other things than her virtue for that furious midnight ride upon the saddle-bow. But her new owner amused her; and she was prosperous, or seemed to be.

For this was the era of great Booms in zinc, and charcoal, and foreign bonds, and American steel rails. It was also the age of folly, flummery, flippancy, and frolic. The ponderous classicism of the Empire style, the rococo ugliness of the Monarchy, both were kicked into the dustbin on the arrival of the Second Empire. Gaudy colors, *bizarre* fashions, gay, sparkling music, *chic* saucy women, men who amused themselves—where Sire my Friend reigned, these reigned. Ashtaroth, Belphegor, and Belial were worshiped at the Tuileries and Compiègne. But the High-Priest of their mysteries improved Paris if he corrupted her—that must be allowed.

After Nero, he was possibly the greatest designer of landscape-gardens, the most gifted layer-out of streets and promenades, that has ever existed. He inspired Haussman. He dreamed in avenues wide enough to maneuver cavalry in; he thought in boulevards down which whole batteries of artillery could sweep. He who had been immured in a prison loved Freedom, Air, Light, Space—and he gave these good things to his capital. Also he gave her the Cocodette.

The *lionne* of 1848—of her we know something.... She was passionate, wayward, exquisite, and unprincipled. In three words, she was Henriette. But in exchanging her for the cocodette of the Second Empire, France paid in the resultant loss of beauty. With her limbs eased in the steel cage of the crinoline that hid the fault; with her little hat tilted above her mountains of bleached hair; with her fringe, her panniers puffed above the artificial deformity that later became the bustle—with her huge and tasteless lockets and chains, belts and dog-collars of precious metal—she is a type of the decadence of the Age of Sire my Friend.

The cocodette was giddy of brain, false from the love of deceit, impure without passion, hideous in the extreme; and knew not her absurdity or her ugliness any more than the Frenchwoman of to-day—whom her English and American sisters ape, in their hobble or harem skirts, and their waste-paper-basket hats, trimmed with patches of brocade, whole fowls, and lumps of velvet. Elegance has fled—Grace has departed—Good Taste conceals her face—Beauty has ceased to exist, in France, since Religion was abolished. How should it be otherwise when from His peculiar country, men have driven out God?

When the Athenians lost the sense of loveliness that lies in the pure vigorous line, that was the commencement of Greek degradation. In like manner the boneless ugliness called The New Art was a symptom of disease and decay. Buildings without angles are as faces without noses. Design that is all curves marks exhaustion in the brain that conceived it, and impotence in the hand that executed—nothing more.

But Sire my Friend was pleased, and extremely well contented. In the popular acclamations accorded to H.R.H. the Duke of Bambridge and the Commander of Britannia's Forces, their host had had his share. Also, the Empress's Monster Ball at the Élysée—given in honor of these distinguished visitors—had come off successfully. Though M. Chose, Secretary to the venerable Duchesse de Viellecourt, and Mademoiselle Mirepoix, amanuensis of the aged and purblind Marquis de l'Autretemps, had returned their respective employers' cards, with the intimation that neither enjoyed the acquaintance of M. and Madame Bonaparte.

All through Good Friday, and its night, and the following day, sleepless workmen toiled at the Palace of the Élysée; and there rose under their cracked and bleeding hands a vast and flimsy edifice, of unseasoned wood and hurriedly-laid brick.... One may regard it as a typical and apt representation of the Second Empire, when, its walls of wet plaster covered with satin draperies, their gaping cracks concealed with gilded moldings, huge mirrors, trophies of arms and garlands of real and artificial flowers, it stood at length complete and challenged admiration.

Christ hung upon the Cross—the Tabernacles stood empty of the Blessed Sacrament—the faithful crowded the black-draped churches—priests, gaunt with fasting, succeeded one another in the pulpit; but still the workmen toiled like busy ants, and still the great ballroom went on growing—in honor of the bluff Protestant Duke, who in his own way, with a high hat and a black coat, hot-cross buns, a service in church, and salt fish at dinner, held sacred that Day of Days.

The Soul of Man's Redeemer, breathed forth on Calvary, passed downwards on the way to Purgatory, with the saved thief trotting in His footsteps like a dog. He descended to those regions where souls under penalty lie writhing in the torture of purifying fires. His tidings of pardon and salvation fell like cooling dews upon their expiatory anguish, ere He rose like the sun upon the spirits of the Blessed, walking before His dawn in the calm fields of Paradise. But before he ascended to His Throne of Glory He came to comfort a little knot of sorrowing men and women gathered together in a bare chamber at Jerusalem—and to rejoice His Mother with the sight of her risen Son.

But the honored guests of the Empire attended a Review on the Champ de Mars, and inspected the Barracks of the famous Regiment of Guides, and dined at the Tuileries in state, and entertained Ministers of the Crown, Foreign Ambassadors, Nobles of the Empire and distinguished members of the Senate, royally at the British Embassy; and the Monster Ball went off like an Arabian Night before they departed—amidst the united strains of massed bands playing the British National Anthem, and *Partant Pour La Syrie*—and cries of "*Vive la Reine Victoria!*" "*Vive le Duc!*" "*Vivent les Anglais!*" for Marseilles. They and their Staffs were banqueted there by Marshal de St. Arnaud and his Staff—while the great screw-transports, chock-full of men and horses, guns and stores of all kinds, were scurrying away from Toulon and Brest and Marseilles as fast as steam could carry them—*en route* for the Dardanelles.

And presently—both French and English Commanders-in-Chief with their Staffs having sailed for Constantinople—Sire my Friend could draw unhampered breath. Despite his boast of belonging to the genus of Imperturbables, his pulses had been unpleasantly quickened by something that had happened. For a moment he had seen the basilisk that Time and opportunity had hatched out of that egg of his, in danger; he had known the torture bred of long-meditated, almost-consummated vengeance that is about to be foiled. But all was well!—prompt measures had been taken.... Still, it was inconvenient that the man had lived to return....

LXXXI

The inconvenient thing had happened on the night of the Ball at the Élysée. Sire my Friend had dined early in private with the Empress—the dinner at the English Embassy taking place upon that night—and now at seven of the clock, the fairyland of imitation marble halls and green gauze grottos filled with real and artificial flowers and illuminated with blue and pink and yellow Chinese lights, not being appointed to open before nine-thirty, he was smoking in his peculiar snuggery at the Tuileries, one of a suite of low-ceiled rooms on the ground-floor between the Pavillon d'Horloge and the Pavilion de Flore, containing a splendid collection of arms, many priceless miniatures, and exquisite articles of furniture and bijouterie and priceless Sèvres that had belonged to Marie Antoinette. And with him were the Duke de Morny, Persigny—also elevated to the Peerage—and the Commander-in-Chief of his Eastern Forces, Marshal de St. Arnaud.

Time and an excessive indulgence in the pleasure of the senses had not added to the personal attractions of Sire my Friend. He looked—despite the artistic make-up of his valets and dressers—sick and sleepy, sluggish and old. His person was soaked with scent; the side of the middle and the top-joint of the first finger of the right hand were dyed yellow with perpetual cigarette-smoking. It had played havoc with his digestion, and his nerves, and his throat.... And the bevy of enameled, dyed and bewigged *roués* surrounding him, looked not one whit better for world's wear than their master. They bored him by grumbling—perpetually grumbling.... He had poured out money in floods upon them, and yet they were not content....

De Morny had had a million—Persigny a million—de Fleury the appointment of aide-de-camp in chief and half-a-million—Kate Harvey a quarter-of-a-million and the title of Comtesse de Belletaille. Only some few who had loved and served him disinterestedly may have been forgotten in this hour of his prosperity.... And how many of the Henriettes were left to chew the cud of broken promises and disappointed hopes....

To more than these he had been prodigal of promises, liberal of vows, forgetting that these are birds that sooner or later come back to roost. That oath of the Carbonari was presently to haunt his pillow, dog his steps with the assassin's soundless footfall; explode bombs—in the hour of his triumph—that strewed his fated pathway with the dying and the dead.

He sat and smoked and ruminated, upon this April night of '54, much as he had done upon that November night of '51, when he had received news of the laying of the Channel Cable. There was one now that reached from Marseilles to Constantinople; he could dictate his will by the mouth of his Ambassador to the Sublime Porte without delay or hindrance; by tugging at the fiery rein of the live wire he would presently be able to make his Army curvet or demivolt without exposing himself to the discomforts of a campaign beyond seas. And the burden of his hidden thought was that his Star had again befriended him. For when the time came to broach the great secret, his followers would believe the master-plan was solely his. There was no one now to start up before him and claim the credit. Months back he had information.... Today decisive intelligence had confirmed the report. The officer who had devised the undertaking, the emissary who had been dispatched to carry out the indispensable survey and make the secret treaties, was dead.

Dead.... Thenceforth Dunoisse's vast capacity for toil, his discretion and silence; his powers of concentration, his geographical, topographical, and scientific knowledge; his consummate powers of arrangement and organization, his command of tongues, were lost to his master at the Tuileries. He was—his great task complete—to have had high military rank and a great guerdon in money. He had been asked to name his price, and he had stipulated for One Million One Hundred and Twenty-Five Thousand Francs. Sire my Friend smiled, knowing this to be the exact amount of a fortune its owner had squandered—remembering who had helped Dunoisse to scatter the glittering treasure to the four winds of the world. He wondered whether Madame de Roux had heard of the death of her old lover? She came to Court but seldom now, and then only to those unimportant functions to which the stars of lesser social magnitude were invited. The violent colors and *bizarre* fashions of the Second Empire did not suit her style of beauty—only ugly women looked really well in them!—or she was getting a little *passée*—the poor Henriette! She had a new *liaison*—an intrigue with one of the Generals of the Army of Algeria, recently appointed to the command of the Fourth Division of his Eastern Forces. It was said that she was to accompany Grandguerrier on the campaign. Pleasant for de Roux, who was still at Algiers—very pleasant! The dull eyes of Sire my Friend almost twinkled as this occurred to him. He smiled, caressing the chin-tuft that had become an imperial.

Said de Morny, Duke and Peer of France, gracefully masking a yawn with three long, slim fingers:

"Sire, if Your Majesty has anything amusing to impart to us—and your smile conveys the idea that you have—we entreat you not to withhold it.

We are all dull, drowsy, and damnably out of spirits!... These imported fogs of Britain have chilled us to the bone!"

His Imperial Majesty exhaled a cloud of smoke, leaning his long thick body back in the well-cushioned corner of an Oriental sofa. He wore, as customary upon gala occasions, the levee uniform of a General of Division, adorned with many blazing Orders and Stars. His short legs—clad in white kid knee-breeches fastened with diamond buckles, white silk stockings, and high-heeled pumps of white patent leather, also diamond-buckled—were crossed, and as he ruminated he stroked one well-turned ankle with his dainty womanish hand. He glanced at the hand appreciatively as he dropped his cigarette-ash on the costly carpet. Then, barely lifting those sick, faded eyes of his to the face of de Morny, he answered in his drawling, nasal tones:

"Since my smile must be translated into words, it had at that moment occurred to me how consummately foolish our British guests would look, did they know why they were embarking on this Eastern Expedition." He caressed his high instep with musing approbation. De Morny said:

"*Sapristi!* I presume they are no more ignorant than ourselves that this is a war without an adequate reason. Monseigneur the Duke of Bambridge, if he be ever to succeed the Earl of Dalgan at the War Office, must see some Active Service—that is undeniable. M. de St. Arnaud requires a dress-rehearsal with volleys of real ball-cartridge, in his *rôle* of a Marshal of France. Also, your Army is plethoric—its health requires blood-letting. Beyond these reasons—none that I can see.... Unless you, Sire, by personally leading your hosts to battle, intend to follow the glorious example of the Emperor Napoleon the First?"

Sire my Friend detecting a supercilious smile upon the face of the speaker, bestowed on him between his narrow lids a glance of fraternal hate. De Morny—now President of the Legislative Council—carried the diplomatic swallow-tail of dark blue velvet, heavily encrusted with silver oak-branches and palm-leaves, upon his tall, well-bred figure, with the grace and ease that were distinctive of him. He wore the broad red ribbon of a Grand Officer of the Legion of Honor beneath his single-breasted waistcoat of white cashmere. His white lawn cravat was a dream of perfection. His long, well-made legs, encased in silver-striped, faultlessly-cut trousers of white cashmere, and buckled pumps of black patent leather, nearly as small as those of Imperial Majesty, were fraught with offense to Sire my Friend, always sensitively conscious of the shortness of his own.

For this reason that stumpy Jove did not rise to hurl the thunderbolt. He leaned back, with an exaggerated affectation of indolence, and said deliberately:

"As a fact, my dear fellow, I weary of the achievements of my glorious uncle. I am not disposed to emulate them at all! One is not born into the world for the purpose of copying one's predecessors.... I prefer to strike out a line extraordinary—astounding—marvelous—above all, original and new!"

De Moray merely bowed, but the bow was to Sire my Friend superlatively offensive. He rose up, forgetful of his disadvantages of stature, and said, looking round upon the dyed heads of hair and painted elderly faces surmounting the brilliantly laced and bedizened uniforms—and as of habit, assuming his Napoleonic attitude.

"These English are bound to the East to carry out my Mission—to fulfill the destiny presaged by my Fortunate Star. You, my brother, who found it inconvenient to know me when that Star was below the horizon, have since accused me to your confidants of abrogating to myself the credit of successes that others have helped me to achieve. You taunt me perpetually with the desire to emulate the First Napoleon. Well! I shall show you soon—very soon—some things accomplished that he could not do. I will avenge at one blow the catastrophe of the Moskva, the defeat of Waterloo, and the humiliation of St. Helena. How? Did you ask how? By all means you shall learn!"

He laughed, and that outrageous mirth did such violence to the sense of hearing that even de Moray shuddered, and St. Arnaud made a clicking sound of dismay with his tongue against his teeth. The speaker resumed, looking glassily about him:

"My uncle would have declared War against the nation he designed to crush and conquer. His nephew, wiser than he, will share with her the apple of amity, cut, Borgia-fashion, with a knife poisoned only on one side! Needed only to further my plan that Russia should pick a quarrel with Turkey. The old question of her authority over the Eastern Christians—the smoldering grudge in the matter of her claim to precedence of admission to the Church of the Holy Sepulcher—served me excellently! And I have championed the cause of the Sultan—I take the field against the Northern Power, with England my Ally!"

He lifted the drooping lids of those eyes of his, and they were dim and lack-luster no longer. They blazed with a radiance that was infernal and malign. He said—and the breathless silence of his hearers was intoxicating joy to him:

"And, blinded by that stiff-necked pride of hers, she will walk into a death-trap, planned and devised and perfected by the man she has despised!

Russia shall have supremacy over the Danubian Principalities. I may even cede her Constantinople—I am not quite certain.... But Great Britain shall be France's footstool and East India her warming-pan!"

He fancied de Morny about to interrupt, and said, turning upon him with a tigerish suavity:

"Proofs—you require proofs! Assuredly, you shall have them. Be good enough to follow me. This way, Messieurs!"

He led the way to a room at the end of the suite, the walls of which were hung with maps, plans and diagrams, and lined with bookshelves and presses; whose tables were loaded with models of public buildings, steam-boilers, and engines of artillery; and where the gilded cornices and moldings were chipped with rifle and revolver bullets, as had been those of the smaller cabinet at the Élysée. Lamps burning under green shades illuminated this place of labor. He took a Bramah key from under the setting of a signet ring he wore, unlocked a press and racked back the sliding doors in their grooves with a gesture of the theater. The alphabetically-numbered shelves were loaded with papers. He said, indicating these:

"You see there the fruit of three years of unremitting labor, performed in secrecy. To-night there is an end to secrecy. I hardly thought the hour would come so soon!"

He took from a compartment of the shelves two square sheets of yellow, semi-transparent tracing-paper, and turned to face his audience exactly as an actor would have done upon the stage. He was master of the situation—he was making the great disclosure just as he had mentally rehearsed it. Not for nothing had he trusted in his Destiny and his Star.

"The sealed orders you, M. de St. Arnaud, were to have received from me upon your departure for Marseilles to-morrow," he said, addressing the Commander-in-Chief of his Eastern Army, "would have made you sole participator in my secret. Yet I feel no hesitation or reluctance at enlarging the circle of my confidence," he added, as he encountered the satirically-smiling glance of de Morny. "To betray me would be an act of madness. For—insignificant as I may appear—I am the Empire! Remember that, Messieurs!"

He delicately laid one of the semi-transparent, crackling papers upon the lamp-illumined Russia leather surface of a writing-table near him. A pencil tracing of just such a map of Eastern Europe as was habitually in use at his Ministry of War, and in his Military Institutes—only that the tracing was enriched with added lines, diagrams and notes, in red and blue and various-colored inks. He said, as his followers crowded to look at this—and now there was a shiny gray dampness on his cheeks and forehead, and he secretly dried the palms of his hands with his delicate handkerchief:

"These numbered circles and squares in colored inks represent depots of timber, cattle, salted provisions, forage, and grain, established by me—under private names of ownership—at Sinope, Bourgas, Varna, Kustendje, and other places on the shores of the Black Sea. So that, in the case of an Army of Invasion marching from Varna towards the frontiers of Bessarabia, or maintaining a siege, shall we say?—of any fortified harbor on the coasts of the Crimea——You are surprised, M. de Morny? That is gratifying indeed!"

De Morny had given vent to a long shrill street-boy's whistle, about as expressive of astonishment as it could be. But he did not possess the quality of reverence. He sang, in English, thrusting his hands into the pockets of his wide-hipped, silver-striped, white cashmere pantaloons, and executing a *cancan* step cleverly and neatly:

> "That's the way the
> milliard went!
> Pop! goes the weasel!"

and ceased as Sire my Friend went on, rolling his handkerchief—dampened with his hidden agony of exultation—into a ball between his palms:

"Immense contracts for the further supply of cattle, provisions, cereals and fodder to France, have been signed by the heads of the principal firms in the Levant and Eastern Europe. Much of the land-transport throughout the Danubian Principalities had already been chartered by Russian agents—a partial check, I will admit, to my views in this direction. Yet thousands of wagons, arabas, telegas, and other vehicles; hundreds of teams of horses, yokes of bullocks, strings of baggage-mules, are at my sole disposal—their proprietors having received liberal payment on account, and having before them the hope of treatment still more generous. Do I weary you? Am I prosy? Do stop me if I bore you!" entreated Sire my Friend.

Nobody stirred or spoke. He went on, savoring his triumph, tasting each sentence as a morsel of some delicate dish:

"Without spies, informers, interpreters, and agents of all grades, an Invading Army is blindfold and helpless. Thus, the assistance of pachas, boyards, consuls, attachés, secretaries, postmasters, innkeepers, will be ours, having been secured on liberal terms. Every Commissariat-clerk, commercial traveler and correspondent who could be bought to serve my purpose has found in me a ready purchaser. And every Turk or Tartar has made oath upon the beard of the Prophet—every Jew is sworn upon the Ark of the Tabernacle—every Bulgarian is pledged upon the Blessed

Sacrament—not to supply the English with wood for gabions or shelters, with provisions, grain, fodder, horses, wagons or carts. Wherefore, if they need these things, they must draw supplies from Great Britain, or from Italy. And, failing these sources——"

The speaker shrugged again, and said with a sardonic affectation of humility:

"For the unworthy successor of my glorious uncle, it seems to me that I have hit upon a very good idea!"

He smiled upon them, saying it, and between that swelling sense of achievement, and his inward laughter at having thus duped and distanced those who thought they swayed and guided him, he seemed to increase in stature and gain in dignity. Even de Morny was momentarily bankrupt of a gibe to throw at him. De Fleury could only gape and goggle at him. St. Arnaud said, in a voice broken by surprise and admiration:

"My master—my Emperor, you are greater than Napoleon the Great!"

Persigny went over and knelt down upon the carpet before him. He bent over and kissed one of the little diamond-buckled pumps fervently, as a Dervish might have kissed the Holy Stone of Mecca. He said, in a voice that shook and wobbled:

"I say that you are neither my master or my Emperor. From this moment you are my god!"

"Absurd!" said Sire my Friend. But he smiled as Nero might have smiled upon Tigellinus, and said, still smiling:

"Wait—wait! I have not told everything! You have yet to look at the second chart!"

He laid it down upon the first, which it exactly resembled, save that the numbered rounds and squares indicating the depots were missing, and that along the conjectural route of the Army of Invasion certain areas were staked off with green or blue or vermilion dots, and labeled "Malarious," or "Insalubrious," or "Salubrious," as the case might be, and others "Pestilential," in a tremulous, uncertain handwriting that told its story to at least one pair of eyes there. Looking up with a vexatious expression of cynical intelligence on his well-bred, rakish countenance, said de Morny:

"And your man, your administrative, polyglot genius who planned and carried out"—he tapped the first chart with a polished finger-nail—"this masterpiece of organization, and later made this survey of Death's garden—what has become of Dunoisse?" He added: "For this is

Dunoisse's handwriting—and two years ago he went East upon your business, and has not since been heard of. Did he die out there in Death's garden? or—as the possessor of an inconvenient amount of secret information—have you quodded him in some snug dungeon at the Fortress of Vincennes, or the Prison of Mazas? Or have you had him shot, or scragged him, before putting him to bed in quicklime blankets? *Kif—kif— burrico!*—a quietus, either way!"

Horribly meaningful as the words were, the gesture accompanying them was even more significant. It brought a dull, scorched flush into the pasty cheeks of Sire my Friend. But he maintained his boasted imperturbability, and answered, with his quiet smile of menace:

"It pleases you to be offensive. Pursue your vein if you imagine it will serve you—I am indifferent to your opinion of me! As for General Dunoisse—who, as you rightly guess, acted as my instrument in carrying out these comprehensive arrangements for Commissariat and Transport— who completed this sanitary survey of the debatable ground—that unhappy officer expired of fever in the swamps of the Dobrudja, some months ago. These charts were brought me by his confidential secretary—one Michaëlis Giusko—to whom the dying man entrusted them." He added, in answer to de Morny's smile: "Your perspicuity is not at fault.... Lest his silence and discretion should fail us at this crucial moment—M. Giusko is in safe keeping—where, there is no need to say!... As for this second chart of the Unseen Dangers, by following its guidance our Army will not encamp within insalubrious or pestilential areas. While our Allies—unless they have taken similar precautions—are likely more or less to suffer!" He ended meditatively, stroking his imperial:

"We share with them the Borgian apple—we take the half that is not poisoned. The whole thing is simple. It is not we who die!"

He opened his eyes widely and looked upon his followers. It seemed to them that through those blazing windows they saw down into Hell. As he said again how simple the thing was, a rattling oath of the canteen and the barrack-room escaped from de Fleury, that caused the green shades of the table-lamps to shiver in their gilded sockets. Persigny's teeth were chattering, though the April night was almost sultry. De Morny broke out peevishly as he wiped his clammy face:

"*Zut!*—there is no doubt you have got them in the treacle! But why did your Majesty not wait to tell us this until Lord Dalgan and the Duke had left for Marseilles? I am sick in my stomach with funk, absolutely!—at the thought of doing the civil to them and their men to-night!"

"Be uncivil, then," advised his Imperial master. "Between your compliments and your insults there is so subtle a distinction that neither the Duke or Dalgan will be the wiser, you may be sure!"

St. Arnaud roared at this mordant witticism. De Morny was about to launch a return-shaft, when there came a gentle, significant knocking—not upon the door through which they had previously passed, but another, communicating with the outer gallery.

"Enter!" commanded Sire my Friend, for the knocker had given the prescribed number of taps that heralded his Private Military Secretary.

And the door opened, and there entered, gently closing it behind him, the very man who had died in the marshes of the Dobrudja months before.

LXXXII

He was so strangely altered, aged, bleached and wasted, that for some moments Sire my Friend and the other owners of the curled and made-up heads that had pivoted round upon his entrance regarded him in the silence that is born of dismay. The color of old wax, or of a corpse some days dead, an atmosphere of such chilly isolation surrounded this pale spectral figure, that even de Moray, that cool smiling skeptic, knew the shudder of superstitious terror, and felt his thin hair stiffen on his scalp. A worn and shabby Staff uniform of the date of the Presidency hung in folds upon the intruder's lean and stooping body. His black eyes burned in caves hollowed by protracted mental labors and immense physical exertions. His black hair, long uncut, and mingled with streaks and patches of white, hung in tangled elf-locks to his tarnished epaulets, and drooped in a heavy matted plume upon his brow. To the gaunt hollows beneath his haunted eyes he was raggedly bearded with this piebald mixture. And as he stood before them, intermittent gusts of fever seized and shook him, until his teeth chattered audibly, and his bones seemed to rattle in his baggy, withered skin. As, in one of these gusts, he coughed, and pressed to his parched lips a yellowed cambric handkerchief that was presently bloodstained, de Fleury—reassured by this incontestable proof of mortality—took courage and called him by his name:

"Dunoisse!"

"Dunoisse!... A thousand welcomes, *mon cher* General!" Sire my Friend, instantly assuming his urbane and benignant air, stepped towards the shabby scarecrow with graciously extended hand. But the scarecrow raised its own, and waved Imperial Majesty back with a gesture so expressive of warning, if not of menace, that the action sent a shudder through its witnesses. Again they doubted if this were not some ghostly visitant from the world that is beyond the grave.... And again the hacking, tearing cough came to convince them that this was no spirit, but merely a dying man.

Said Sire my Friend, after that slight pause of consternation:

"My good Dunoisse, you have dropped on us—literally from the heavens. As a fact, we had heard on excellent authority that you were—ill—and that the pleasure of welcoming you must be—indefinitely deferred. Upon this account excuse what may strike you as lack of cordiality in our greeting!" He added, and his growing confidence permitted an outcrop of anger upon the smooth polish of his accents. "And explain to us—the rules denying unknown officers access to the Emperor's private apartments being even more stringent than those which protected the President from such intrusion—how you gained admittance here?"

For all answer, the shape he spoke to lifted its left hand, and showed, hanging loosely on a wasted finger, a signet ring. Sire my Friend, recognizing the token conferring upon his Equerry General, Private Secretary, and Military Secretaries, access to his person at all hours, shrugged his chagrin; and tapped his daintily-shod foot impatiently upon the floor.

"Of course! Naturally! Pardon my forgetfulness!" he said urbanely. "I myself bestowed that Open Sesame upon you, when your skill, and intelligence, and ability prompted me to promote you to a confidential post upon my Staff. And later—when my reliance in your discretion and fidelity led me to place in your most able hands the task which you have so superbly completed—you took the ring with you when you left Paris for the East." He added, discerning that the black eyes burning in their shadowy caves glanced at the faces of his merry men with doubtfulness:

"Have no fear! These trusted friends who shared with me the secret of the intended *coup d'État* participate in knowledge of this later—measure of diplomacy.... You have arrived at the very moment of disclosure.... Therefore speak out quite freely, my very good Dunoisse!..."

Dunoisse opened his cracked lips, and said, in a voice so faint and hollow that it might have answered from the sepulcher of Lazarus when the Voice bade the dead come forth:

"I will speak out freely. To do so is my right. None can dispute it."

He waited, gathering strength, clenching his fleshless hands, breathing painfully; and a glistening upon his sunken parchment temples and the burning patches of red upon his hollow cheeks betrayed the terrible emotions that rent and tore the wasted body that housed a suffering soul.

"I have spread your nets," he said, in the voice that had lost its clear, sharp ring, and was feeble, and flat, and broken. "From the Balkans to the Pruth I have set your springes—dug your pitfalls—sharpened your hidden stakes. I have put it in your power to precipitate a crisis. To meet events and grapple Fate I used all the strength and all the skill I had."

He drew a shaken breath and went on:

"I have subsidized scores of men into this service—no man knowing his neighbor for a fellow-conspirator—every man secretly bound by the oath that is most sacred in his sight. Turks, Greeks, Tartars, Jews, Armenians,

Bulgarians, and Wallachs—all have been pledged not to give aid to Russia, or England the Ally of Russia, in the great War that was presently to be waged with France and the Ottoman Empire—over the Debatable Ground...."

A rush of fever dyed his sallowness to dusky crimson. The heat that radiated from his burning body struck upon the bodies of the other men.

"I served you," he said, fixing his sunken, glittering eyes upon the face of Imperial Majesty, "to the very gates of Death. Believing myself to be dying, I placed—in the hands of two men who had sought me out and found me—the original charts that proved my task completed, and the tracings of those charts. One, at least, of my messengers could not fail to reach you——"

De Morny said, pointing to the writing-table, where the squares of shiny tracing-paper, covered with spidery diagrams and dotted lines in red and blue and green and vari-colored inks, lay in the yellow radiance cast by the green-shaded lamp:

"There are the proofs that one of your messengers did reach his destination. We had been looking at those marvelous charts the moment before you came in."

De Morny, Duke and Peer of France, might have been a mouse squeaking in a corner or one of the love-birds and wax-bills—dainty feathered creatures for which Imperial Majesty possessed an amiable *penchant*—twittering in its gilded window-cage. For Dunoisse neither saw nor heard him, but folded his thin arms upon his hollow breast, and spoke with his haggard eyes on the face of Sire my Friend.

"I came back to civilization to learn the truth of you. I was not the keeper of your secret, the agent of your power, set to pit craft against craft and insure victory by wise precaution!—I was your dupe, your accomplice, and your tool. Judas! Oh, Judas!" said Dunoisse, in a dry, fierce rustling whisper that was like the sirocco passing through a field of withered maize-stalks. "How is it that I believed you—knowing you besmeared with blood, and rotten to the soul with deceits and falsehoods? How should *I* not be among the number of those you have flattered and swindled and betrayed?"

The silence of sickening consternation was on each of those who heard him. Their crests of false curls drooped; the paint faded from their faces under the lashing hail of his words. They were crimson or leaden or sea-green according to their various temperaments—the complexion of Sire my Friend having undergone this last and most unbecoming change. And Dunoisse went on speaking, almost without a gesture, as a man whose bodily weakness compelled economy of breath and action.

"I was to have had a great reward of you for my services. One million one hundred and twenty-five thousand francs, to be definite! Keep your stolen money! Could I buy back self-respect with the price of blood? As for you, you have won your Empire—have brought about the War you schemed and plotted for; you will take the field with Turkey and your Ally of England, shoulder to shoulder—side by side!... Ah!—you read Machiavelli at the Fortress of Ham to good purpose!... You grew more than violets upon the ramparts, Monseigneur! You matured plans for revenge.... And you will have your honeyed vengeance," said Dunoisse, in that distinct, rasping whisper. "And gall will mingle with the sweetness as you suck it. For those old associates of yours—those men of the Reform and Carlton Clubs of London—will say of you: 'By God!—this Emperor of France is a damned scoundrel!' And, by God!—they will be right!"

The sentence, spoken in English, cut like a tandem-whip. As it hissed through the stagnant, perfumed, tobacco-laden atmosphere of the room, the speaker drew his sword. Sire my Friend recoiled and cried out at the sharp hiss of the steel, and de Fleury, brave as a bulldog, sprang before his master instantly. But Dunoisse only balanced the weapon a moment with the deftness of a master of fence, ere, with an effort that taxed his feebleness to the utmost, he snapped the tarnished steel across his thin knee, and said, as he threw the pieces down clattering at the dainty buckled feet of Imperial Majesty:

"My military oath of allegiance was to the President, not to the Emperor. I will serve you no longer, be that understood! And—though the work I have done has been fatally well done!—in so far as it be possible, I will unmesh the net I have woven.... Therefore be warned, Monseigneur!"

With this, as a man might shake off from his hand some venomous insect, he dropped the loosely-fitting signet ring upon the carpet, ground it with a sudden, savage impulse underneath his heel, and went out, leaving them staring and short of breath.

A moment later, Sire my Friend, whose complexion of sea-green had suffered change to a congested purple, staggered and clutched at nothing, and fell down frothing in an epileptic fit.

By the advice of Persigny—who had seen him before in that pitiable condition—they moved the furniture away from his vicinity, and left his devil to use him at its will. And presently he came to, staring and shuddering, with a bitten glove between his teeth; and was very feeble and exhausted, and full of fears lest the Empress had seen him thus afflicted. But by-and-by, when reassured, and restored, and renovated, he was able to interview the Chief of his Secret Police, and give orders for an arrest....

He was peculiarly benevolent, urbane and smiling, an hour later, when, to the united strains of "God Save the Queen" and *"Partant Pour La Syrie,"* he entered the fairyland of blue-and-white striped awnings, blue carpets, gold-tasseled hangings of pink satin, and elfin grottos of green gauze, full of palms and hot-house roses, illuminated with pink, blue and yellow Chinese lights. Leading the beautiful Empress—who rested her gloved hand on the happy arm of the Duke of Bambridge—followed by the French and British Commanders-in-Chief, with their Staffs, his brothers and his uncle, he looked—or might have with the addition of a few more inches—every inch an Emperor.

And not only an Emperor, said the Imperial Press Organs—a philanthropic lover of mankind, who—supported by Great Britain, the nursing-mother of infant nations—was about to carry out a war in the cause of Freedom, Justice, and the Rights of Man against Irresponsible Despotism.

Amidst the general joyousness, the depression of de Morny—that usually light-hearted cynic—was curiously apparent. Lord Dalgan noticed this, and commented upon it in his exquisite, polished French:

"By my faith, Monseigneur!" returned de Morny, in the English language, "I cannot deny it, I am confoundedly hipped to-night! Absolutely, I am like the Princess in the Suabian fairy legend—there is a rose-leaf under my twenty-ninth feather-bed. Why? I am envious—absolutely envious! I have seen a poor man throw away one million one hundred and twenty-five thousand francs for the privilege of enjoying a luxury that I, who am a rich man, cannot afford."

"Really! And what is that costly form of indulgence?" asked my Lord.

De Morny answered, with a curious smile on that well-bred, rakish face of his:

"The luxury of telling the truth!"

He could not afford it, though he would have liked it.... It was not yet convenient to break with Sire my Friend....

And so the Monster Ball spun and whirled itself out, dancing becoming public after the departure of the Imperial Party and their guests. At three in the morning when even young and handsome faces looked fagged, and old ones witchlike and ghastly; when the real flowers were faded, and the imitation ones dusty and limp; when the elfin grottos were revealed as garish shams which no respectable fairy would have dreamed of being seen in—when the innumerable colored lanterns hung from trees and twinkling amongst shrubberies looked pale and mean and sickly in the light of coming day; a prison-van, bolted on a railway-truck—having a carriage containing an Imperial aide-de-camp and two Commissaries of Police in front of it, and another full of gendarmerie behind it—was being whirled by a special engine into the Northern Department of the Somme.

At the station where the van was unbolted from the railway-truck an escort of Lancers waited; also a one-horse brougham, an open brake, drawn by a pair; and a couple of spare horses. These being harnessed to the van, the aide, after exchanging a sentence or two with the commander of the cavalry escort, stepped into the brougham, followed by the police-officers, who modestly took the front seat. Then at a curt word of command the party put itself in motion, and clattered and clinked and rolled away.

And presently the prison-van, with its wheeled and mounted guardians, passed—with a challenge from a sentry and the giving of a countersign at each—over two drawbridges, and clattered and rolled—the prisoner judged by the damp chill and the hollow echo—under a heavy archway of stone. And then, with the grinding of heavy iron wards in locks, and screaming of solid iron bolts in stony groovings, the van came to a halt; the steps were banged down, the door was opened; and the yawning jailers who had traveled with the prisoner unlocked his narrow cell.

Dunoisse was invited to get out. He moved his cramped limbs with difficulty, and descended the iron steps in the gay sunshine of an April morning, which painted long blue shadows on a lofty wall centered by a massive gateway with a square watch-tower, across the stones of a flagged courtyard.

Two huge round towers flanked the south and west angles of the courtyard. A block of buildings was upon his right hand that looked like a Barracks. Another, smaller, on his left, was probably the dwelling of the Commandant. A gray-haired, stout man in the undress uniform of a field-officer of the Line came out of the house, saluted the Imperial aide, and returned the salute of the officer of the escort. He had a blue paper in his hand.

He said, addressing the prisoner after a brief colloquy with the Imperial Staff officer:

"You will be confined here during the pleasure of the Emperor."

Dunoisse knew that meant for life. He lifted his haggard eyes as he asked the question:

"Where am I?"

The answer came:

"You are in the Fortress of Ham."

LXXXIII

"Camp near Varna,

"*June.*

"My dearest Mother,

"We arrived Here all Safe, and are Incampt with the Division on a Scrubby Plane by a Lake full of Leaches about 2 milse inland of Varna, Which is the Beastliest Town you ever Saw. It is Full of English, French, Turks, Bulgarians, Jews, Infadels, and Herraticks. Every now and Then a Fire brakes out which Marshal St. Arnod the French Commander-in-Chief says is Dew to insendiary Greekse. Yesterday it Was the House next our Powder Maggazine, but luckily the Wind Changed, and we Lost neerly all our Stores of Barly, Biskits, Tea, Suggar, Coffy, Flower and so on. N.B.— How does He know it was insendiary Greekse?

"Tell my Father that the Army is short of Otse and Forridge. Though we have Not quite 4,000 Beests of Transport to move an Army of 27,000 Men!!! We Have Hardly Annything to Give them, And the Noise they make is something Friteful, and every day Lotts of them die. The Cavalry Horses are Fed at preasent, that is all One can Say. I am quite Well, so you must not be Fritened when you Read in the Paperse that Colera has broken out among the Troops."

Young Morty Jowell, seated on the end of the tent-cot before his folding trestle-table, laid down the pen at this point, and dispiritedly rubbed his nose. Looking from where he sat, he could see under the lifted canvas of the hospital-marquees the rigid shapes of smitten soldiers lying in rows on the cut rushes that covered the bare ground.... For Spring and Summer had conspired with Sire my Friend to the undoing of his Allies of England. Spring had spread beds for the soldiers of the deep wet moss, starred with purple iris and the blue bead hyacinth. Summer had woven her nets of wild sweet roses, filled her deep vineyards with deadly bait of grapes, peaches, and figs. The bees had made for them of the yellow azalea-blossoms, the fragrant, poisonous green honey that breeds fever and delirium. They had eaten of this, and of the tempting fruit, and sickened; and Pestilence had risen up and breathed her blue miasma upon them, and gripped them in her iron cramps, and they had died. The dead were being buried as Morty wrote on:

"Odly enuf, the French on the Hites have got it Though their Camps are better Plaiced than what ours Are. They have sent 3 Divisions into the

Dobrudja, where 90 thowsand Russians are being held in Chek by Omar Pasha. They are putting Whole Regiments on their Transports and sending Them out to Sea.

"Yesterday I saw the loveliest Girl I ever saw in my Life out Riding on the Road to Aladyn on the Finest Brown Horse I ever Saw in my life. She comes from the Bashi's Camp. None of the Officers know her Naim, but all of them call her Golden Cloak, bicause of her Hair, which is the most Wonderful I ever Saw in my Life. A man of Ours told me Her Father is a Colonel of Bashis and that her mother was a Georgian Princess. I Never saw such Hair or such Eyes in All my life.

"I am your loving son,
"MORTIMER.

"P.S.—I forgot to tell my Father that the Trooper who saved my life in the Reck of *The British Queen* is my Cousin Sarah's Son, Joshua Horrotian. When I thanked him and asked him to Shake Hands he Rifused. I Think it is bicause of Something My Father Has Done about his Mother's Propperty. Tell my Father I do Not want a Hunting Box and that I had rather die a Beggar than That enny man should be Wronged for me. Mind you tell that to my Father. And tell him I have Not yet Had His Anser to a Certain Letter he knose of. And that I Mean it Every Word.

"M. J.

"P.P.S.—You must Not supose that Bicause she Comes from the Bashis' Camp she is Not a Lady. If she is Not One I never Saw one in my Life.

"M. J.

"P.P.P.S.—Love and Thanks for the Caises of Good Things which were Hily apreciated.

"M."

That is, by the rank-and-file. For Morty, mentally burdened by the paternal confidences as to cabbaging, declined to partake of the luxuries sent out to him in huge consignments by special deliveries, week and week about. You saw the Ensign turning these over to the men of his company, and living on Service rations of fresh or salt pork, biscuit, rice, and rum. To those who asked why, he explained that he preferred this Spartan form of nourishment; at those who chaffed he grinned or scowled. And presently the big tin-lined cases from Fortnum and Mason's, or Goodey and Cates, left off coming, as did those that had been dispatched from the emporiums of these purveyors to hundreds of other wealthy young officers, and to the caterers of countless Regimental messes. Entombed at the bottoms of holds, beneath shot and empty shell; piled up in warehouses with mountains of other good and useful things, doomed never to be drunk or eaten, worn or used, they lay until the ending of the War brought about their exhumation. And long before then, flinty biscuit had become a luxury, and salt pork was not to be had every day.

You may gather that from the very outset of the Eastern Campaign the names of Cowell, Sewell, Powell, and many others of the fraternity had not infrequently reached Morty's ears in conjunction with expressions of disapprobation. Nor, despite all the consideration shown him by his comrades, could references to Thompson Jowell, couched in terms the reverse of admiring, fail to find utterance in the presence of the great man's son. For when he was not present as a Forage and Supply Contractor, you met him as an Auxiliary Transport Agent. He was here, there, and everywhere.... He had a finger in every pie.... Before very long, it seemed to his son, that whenever men talked together in lowered tones, with angry faces, the name of Jowell was certain to be the burden of their discourse.

"S'sh!" someone would say hastily, as Morty's tall shadow fell across the threshold of the mess-tent, or drew near over the sandy parading-ground.

"Why?... Who?..." the man who had been holding forth would ask, without looking up.

"*His* son!"... the man who had "S'sh'ed!" would say:

"Oh!"

Morty grew to hate that branding interjection. And that prophecy of Jowell's, that he would never be ashamed of his old Governor, was falsified every day.

Sometimes he would begin to fear that he hated the man who had begotten him. This acute stage of his complaint was reached when it began to be known that the Allies would winter on the Black Sea. For forage, and clothing, and provisions, and all that the Army needed, it was said, was being sent out in the great Government transport, *The Realm*, from Portsmouth Dockyard.... What wonder that the boy, unwilling sharer in the grisly secret that made the stiff gray hair of Thompson Jowell bristle on his head o' nights, was galled and tortured! His apprehension had ridden him as though he had been another Sindbad, throttled by the hairy incubus of the immortal story. Then he had hit on a plan for getting rid of this dreadful Old Man of the Sea.

He had taken his courage in both hands and written boldly to his father, maintaining at the same time a caution that made him shudder at himself. For lest Jowell's murderous secret should leave bloody finger-marks on every page, it was necessary to be ambiguous. Yet he had conveyed his meaning clearly, and the final sentence, with all its crudity, had the ring of steel on stone.

"Sinse I Caim out Here I Have Bigun to understand Better than I did Bifore What you Meant by What you Said that Night at Dinner. And if you Do this Thing that you have Planned to do, I will never come Home Agane or call myself by your Naim, or take another Six-pens of your Money. As God lives, I won't, so now you Know! My mother shall hear the Truth and Chuse between us! It is Hard on a Fellow To have to rite like this to His Father, but You Have Brought it on yourself!"

There was a postscript:

"Remember I will never come Home or Call myself by your Naim, or Take another Peny of your Monney. Don't do it, Gov.! Don't do it for God's saik. He might Forgive you. I Never shold, I Know!

"M."

You are to imagine Thompson Jowell perusing this composition with eyes that whirled in their shallow round orbits, and a complexion that underwent strange changes, deepening from fiery red to muddy purple, and from muddy purple to pale sea-green.

The letter had been directed to his place of business in the City. When he blundered up out of his office-chair, crumpling it in his shaking hand, he was dizzy, and there was a singing in his ears. That his boy should even dream of turning against his old Governor was preposterous and absurd, if appalling. The letter was a bit of high-flown nonsense. Nothing would ever come of it! But yet he shook in every limb, and his shirt was damp upon his back.

It was his Fate, that, priding himself as he did upon the doggedness of will and tenacity of purpose that had combined with unscrupulousness in the making of his fortune, he could not recognize in his son the first-named qualities. He had begotten his own judge. Though he blinked the fact, it was presently to come to him, after a method unexpected, terrible, and strange.

The dizziness passed off; Jowell waddled on his thick short legs to the rusty fireplace, thrust the letter deep into the heart of the handful of coal that burned there, and held it down with the poker until it blazed up and was reduced to a grayish crisp of thin ash. Then he got a glass of water from the yellow washstand, went to his cupboard, and deliberately swallowed two Cockle's pills.

Whenever Conscience woke up, and clamored behind the gorgeous waistcoat of the great Contractor, he was accustomed to silence her by the administration of a bumping dose. Purged of repentance and relieved, we may suppose, of scruples, his reply to Morty's letter was a masterpiece in its way.

For it reminded the son, indirectly, of all that the father had done for him, and temptingly enlarged upon all that he meant to do.... At the end came the pregnant intimation that Mortimer was not to flurry himself about affairs that were no concern of his. And that—in a particular instance not more definitely specified, Sturdy Stephen Standfast was the name of his old Gov.

"For he don't mean that letter! Not a word of it!" snorted Thompson Jowell, quite himself as he blotted the reply to Morty's letter on the morning after the two Cockle's pills. He added: "Throw his old Gov. over!... By Gosh! he ain't capable of it. By Gosh! if an Angel came down from Heaven"—one would like to hear Jowell's conception of Heaven—"and told me he was, I wouldn't take its word."

When it comes to a tussle between Old Standfast and Young Standfast, one may be pretty certain as to which is going to win.... Having marked out, in his blundering boyish way, a line of conduct, Mortimer Jowell meant to follow it unswervingly. Hence the answer to the letter was a blow to all his hopes. He wrote no more to his father, though the dowdy woman regularly received his ill-spelt letters! And being of a kindly, affectionate disposition, he was profoundly wretched, in anticipation of the coming hour when he must keep his word.

Gnawing suspense and mental anxiety, combined with the effects of a deadly climate, might have hurried the Ensign to the grave on the heels of many another brave young officer, had not Love, with all its distractions, fears, and longings, acted as a tonic, and braced the patient up.

The Mounted Irregulars whom Morty had learned to refer to as the Bashis, were encamped in what had been a vineyard by the roadside on the way to Aladyn. Their chief, reported to be the father of Golden Cloak, Morty knew by sight as a bronzed, fiercely-mustached, soldierly man of perhaps forty-five. Splendidly mounted, dressed in the dark blue single-breasted tunic with green facings, light blue red-striped pantaloons, long spurred boots, black sheepskin kalpak and gray cloak, you would have taken him for an Osmanli commander of regular horse—had it not been for the blue, silver striped shawl worn round his kalpak, in combination with his unstudied off-hand manner of administering chastisement to his ragged, strangely bedizened, variously-weaponed troopers, with the flat of the naked sword.

It was torture to know that the bright cynosure hailed from that rowdy camp of brigands.... Morty, who had never previously known concern as to the reputation of any young woman, was uneasy upon this score. He found the cool, cynical attitude of his brother officers intolerable. For Golden Cloak had flashed by, a shining meteor borne on a brown-black storm-cloud—and left behind a champion and a slave.

She had ridden her magnificent Kabarda, with its costly shabrack of blue cloth, gold-embroidered, and gold and scarlet bridle, astride, after the graceful fashion of Peruvian ladies. She was small, pale, slight in stature as a child.... Her tiny features, pure as pearl, illuminated with black Oriental eyes, flashing and melting under the arches of meeting eyebrows, were crowned by a little black lambskin kalpak, in which was set an aigrette of flashing diamonds. The miraculous cloak of shining curls covered her to mid-thigh.... But he could see that she wore a Hussar tunic of dark blue, with golden frogs, green welts, and trimmings of black lambskin, and that her girdle was of gold lace, crimson-striped. Also, that her ample trousers of light blue cloth ended in high boots of scarlet leather, golden-spurred.

There was a sand-wind blowing under a blistering sun that day, and at first young Mortimer had cursed it heartily. With equal heartiness he was to bless it, presently. For as she galloped past, it had snatched the lambskin kalpak from her head, and dropped it in a puff of scorching dust at his feet. He had pounced on it greedily. Golden Cloak had reined up her splendid beast, and wheeled, and ridden towards him....

"Beg pardon! You dropped this!"

Young Mortimer had held up the dainty headgear towards her, saluting with the best grace he knew how to muster. She had answered in English.... Heavens! what lisping, quaintly-flavored English!...

"It is mine."

"Please!... Won't you take it?"

He had tendered the kalpak, wondering why she stretched forth no hand to receive it. Instead she had blushed and frowned, shaking her head. And as the boy had faltered, abashed by her loveliness, downcast by what seemed her disdain, a gust of the dusty wind had lifted the golden mantle, shedding it on either side of her slim young body like a pair of glittering wings; and Mortimer Jowell, standing in the soft black dust of the road between the vineyards, had known an overwhelming shock of grief, surprise, and horror; for Beauty had no hands.

The Lancer tunic had wide short, braided sleeves that ended well above the elbow. From these two slender white arms projected, ending in the stumps of little wrists.... The reins of her fiery horse were buckled to a leathern strap that went about her middle. She guided him by the sway of her slender body to right or left; stopped him by leaning back, maintained her seat by the clasp of her supple limbs about his shining barrel. There was perfect accord, complete sympathy, between the rider and the steed.

But oh! the pity of it! Young Morty had not been able to speak, lest he should stammer, and choke, and blubber. He had stood in the middle of the road, gaping stupidly, holding the dainty headgear, which he made no effort to restore.... She had flushed red. Perhaps she had thought—who knows what she thought of the dull young English officer? But the horse had drawn nearer, trotting through the thick black dust, with dainty mincing steps, whisking its superb tail and tossing its mane, spreading its scarlet nostrils, cocking its wild eye backwards at its rider, less in mischief than in play.

It had moved abreast of Morty, almost touching him with its glossy shoulder, and stopped. The rider had bent low, shedding a torrent of curls over the holsters at the saddle-bow, covering even her dainty boot with the hem of her golden cloak. Evidently she expected the Englishman to replace the kalpak on her head. But he did not. She gave him a furious glance, caught the cap in her little teeth, snatched it from his hand, rose in the saddle, and was gone like the wind itself.

"Gaw!" cried Mortimer in stupefaction, for it was the darting flight of the swallow rather than the gallop of a horse. And then the thick red blood had rushed from his heart and dyed his healthy round face to the forehead.... She was afflicted, this lovely girl, and he had stared at her! Smarting, he went back to camp, more out of conceit with Morty Jowell than he had even been before, and yet supremely, idiotically happy. For her hair had swept over him, bathed him, drowned him for one divine moment in fragrance and beauty. And he could never forget that moment, not if he lived to be an old, old man, he knew.

Now he finished his letter to his mother, addressed and stamped it, took sword and revolver from the tent-rack, and went for another walk upon the road to Aladyn. Not with the idea of meeting her. You are not to imagine it. He was merely looking for a native wagon-driver who would take his letter to the post. Presently one came along, straddling with unclean bare feet upon the foot-board of his creaking wagon, scratching the populous head under his sheepskin cap with one hand, the other being engaged in goading his ill-fed bullocks with the end of a sharpened stick. And to him Morty said in his brand-new Turkish, not being up to the Bulgarian:

"Ohay *arabaji*! How much casho will you aski to carry a *mektub* to the *Posta Khanê* in Varna? Understandi? *Yok?*"

But the native shook his shaggy head, scowling upon his interlocutor in a manner the reverse of friendly, and upon Morty's drawing anew upon his stores of Turkish, responded with a Rabelaisian gesture of contempt which brought the wrathful blood to the rim of the Ensign's forage-cap.

"You uncivil beast. Ain't we here to fight for you?" he demanded; but the *arabaji* only prodded his lean bullocks and creaked upon his way. Morty would have dearly liked to follow him, and punch his shaggy head, but that a long way off he saw her coming, and his heart thudded against his scarlet coat, and his stock was suffocating.... Because she must not pass him by, believing that he had been a boor, coarse and unfeeling. She must stay— she must hear what had to be said. And he had no words, but intensity of feeling lent gesture eloquence. He stretched his hands, palm upwards, towards her, then brought them to his lips, and folded them upon his breast.

"You who are so stricken, yet so beautiful—you to whom my heart has gone out—whom I loved at sight—pardon me!—pity me! Oh! do not pass me by without one word!"

The gesture said all this, though he did not know it. She checked her fiery Kabarda in mid-canter, and rode slowly up to him. He grew dizzy as the breeze brought him the remembered perfume of her hair. And she said, slowly, fixing her great dark eyes upon the simple face of Mortimer Jowell:

"You wish to speak to me?" She added, as he looked away, stroking the delicate withers of the thoroughbred: "You wish to tell me that you did not know, I think, and that now you do know, you are sorry—yes?"

He gulped the lump in his throat and nodded, finding courage to look at her. She said—and an Asiatic lisping of the consonants and lengthening of the vowels lent charm and strangeness to the words—

"You are an *agha* in the Army of the Ingiliz?"

He answered at a venture that he was. She said, and the small pale face had a delicate vivacity:

"I like the Ingiliz. I have their blood through my father! He is Kaimakam of the Bashi of the Brigade of Adrianople, and comes of a noble family of London. He is of the Jones."

"Beg pardon!" stuttered Morty, thinking that he had not heard clearly, "but would you mind saying that again?"

Golden Cloak repeated, folding her slender arms proudly upon her round young bosom:

"He is a Jones of London, my father. That is a name of honor in your country—yes?"

"Gaw!" said Morty, forcing enthusiasm, "I should rather think it was!"

The diamond aigrette of her cap sparkled in the hot sunshine as she bent her golden head royally. A smile played about her little lips, scarlet as pomegranate-buds.

"There are many of my father's name in London?"

Morty said truthfully:

"Bless you! there are thousands of 'em in the Post-Office Directory!"

"Some day I will go," she said, "to Ingiland, and make acquaintance of my relatives. For now, I am with my father.... He has no one but me.... I could not bear to leave him.... I have been with him always, since my beautiful mother died." She added, and the tiny nostrils quivered:

"I know that she was beautiful because my father has her portrait. She was a Christian Princess of Georgia, daughter of the Eristav of Kakhetia. He was a noble Prince of the Bagratides, descended from the Great Sarbad. The price paid by that family in expiation of murder is double the blood-fine of the lower class!"

She showed her little gleaming teeth in so proud a smile as she made this statement that Morty stammered out:

"Uncommon gratifying, and—and jolly for them, I'm sure, Miss!"

She did not look at Mortimer Jowell. Her great gazelle eyes were fixed upon a heron that was fishing in a little river that wound through the deep green vineyards beside the dusty road. The bird rose with a loud, melancholy *honk*, clapped its wings, and flew away diagonally, its long legs stuck out straight behind it, its crop thrust forwards, its slender neck curved back between its wings. A shaggy dog rushed out of a little hut that was only a reed-mat thrown over two poles, barking at the heron—a gypsy-girl thrust her tangled head out and nodded to Golden Cloak, showing grinning white teeth in a face burned black by the Bulgarian sun. The nightingales were jug-jugging in the poplars that edged the rivulet, the walnut and apricot-trees seemed full of lesser warblers, the frogs kept up a subdued bass of croakings, the black-backed, white-bellied swifts wheeled screaming through the pure, clear burning air. And it was to the boy as if he had never before seen these things, or guessed their beauty and significance. And they, and the hot blue sky that roofed them, and the thick black dust his boots and the delicate feet of her horse were bedded in, were of Golden Cloak and belonged to her, as the setting belongs to the gem. And, clear and plaintive as some shepherd's flute, her small, sweet voice went on speaking of the dead mother:

"She died when I was born. Her family were angry when she ran away to be always with my father. They held him accursed because he had abjured Christianity and embraced the faith of Islâm. But it was her fate. Can a woman resist her fate? And besides, my father is not a good Mussulman at all!"

The great blue-black eyes were on Mortimer's. They drew and drew him....

"Not long afterwards my father was sent upon an expedition into Mingrelia. It was the month of *Nissân*—the time when the people make strong wine of green honey and *jundari*—what you call, I think, the millet? The Bashi stole much of this, and became more than ever 'lost heads.' They entered the villages of Christians, they plundered, burned, and killed men, women, and children without mercy. And my mother rode up with my father, as one of his *chawushes* cut off the hands of a young girl.... To my father she said that night: '*The child of our love will be born handless.*' And it was so. And when they brought me to her, she lifted the shawl that covered me, and died!"

The proud little face broke up. Great tears sprang from the beautiful eyes and ran down, splashing on the golden braidings of the Hussar tunic, falling like scattered pearls on her black sheepskin of the saddle-holsters. She shook her head, and jerked them off. Then, trembling at his own audacity, Mortimer Jowell produced from his cuff a spotless cambric handkerchief, and would have dried those sacred tears, had not the fiery Kabarda reared so suddenly, that the too-daring Ensign, catching the bridle in fear for Golden Cloak, was swung off his feet.

"Let him go," she said, high in mid-air, unconcerned and now smiling. Adding, as Morty obeyed, and the horse came gently to the ground: "Do not be angry, Urvan, this is another friend!" Then: "Urvan is a little jealous, he sees me speak to so few people.... And next to my father and my nurse, Maryanka, a Tartar woman who has been with me since my birth, he is my protector.... My father trusts me with him.... He would be dangerous to anyone who tried to do me harm.... You cannot think how he loves me!... Even like this he loves me!"

And with a gesture that wrung the boy's soft heart she showed her piteous stumps. And Morty blurted out, desperately:

"So do other people love you! Don't *I* love you? Gaw!—I'd lie down in the dust and let that beautiful beast of yours trample me to mash if it would give you what you want! I swear I would!"

"Ah! You are generous!" she said softly. "I saw it in your face. Tell me your name, that I may always remember it!"

He said, with a boldness that appalled him:

"When you have told me yours!"

"It is Zora. You do not like it?"

He blurted out: "I adore the name. I worship the girl it belongs to! I'm blest if I don't, so there!"

She leaned from her saddle impulsively, and the golden cloak fell over him and covered him. He looked up, drowning in the light of her glorious eyes, and his boyhood fell away like a cast garment. He had come into his kingdom. He knew himself a man....

They were to meet but once again upon the dusty road to Aladyn. The next letter of the yellowed bundle docketed "From my dearest son" is dated:

"BRITISH CAMP,

"KALAMITA BAY,

"*September 14.*

"MY DEAREST MOTHER,

"The Hole Army has landed after a Saif and Prosperus Voyag across the Black Sea to the Crimea. We—I Mean the English—saled in 7 Collums each of 30 vessels every 2 or 3 Vessels being toad by a Steemer. The Fiteing Force that convoid us was 10 Line-of-Battle Ships besides 50 gun Frigats, 2 screw and 13 small steemers. I herd an Ngineer say to his mait the Smoak was for all the World like the Pit Country. The French and Turkish Fleats we overhawled shortly after saling, the French had 15 Line-of-Battle ships and 3 War Steamers, the Turks 8 Line-of-Battle ships and 3 War steemers. I did not count the transports. But the site of the Flotilla at Sea was tremenjus, and Must have made the Ruskies at Sevastopole shaik in their shose. At Nite with all the Red, Blue, and Green litse hung from the masts it was a good deal like Vauxhall Gardens. N.B. Without the Cold Ham and the Champain, there being Preshus little to Eat on Bord.

"*Day after Landing.*

"What do you think of the Froggeys having the Impudens to Move our Boy in the Night from the Plais where It had been ankered by the Admiral of the Flaggship and the Quartermaster-General, thus Bagging the Hole Bay for their Opperations. Nice I don't Think! We were all Landid without our Tents and Lots of the men without their Napsacks being too week to carry them and lay down on the Beech in the Poaring Rane and you never heard a Grumball, and Colera bissy among them too. Me and my Captain Lord Leighminster and Lieutenant Ardenmore (Whisky) slep in a Cornfield near the Beech and Woak in a puddel 6 in. deep, and the Duke and his Staff past the nite under a Bullok Waggon and seamed rather to Injoy it than Not.

"But if you had seen the jumball we were in, French and English all mixt up together! The Ruskies would have had an Easy Whack if they had made a Sortee.

"*4 Days after Landing.*

"We are Moving Against the Russian Position on the River Alma which means Apple, and now my darling Mother on what Perhaps may be the Eave of Axion I must tell you that I Love her with All my Hart. What I shall Do if she will Not Marry me I don't Know, so perhaps it Wold be Best for Me to get Shott. N.B. It is the girl they called Golden Cloak at Varna. Her Father's Regiment is with the Turkish Army 2 milse down the Cost. Her Christian name is Zora. She told me I might call her by it....

"The Pity is———" *Scratched out.*

"It is Sad to Think———" *Scratched out.*

"Perhaps the Cheaf reason I Love her So is Because She has No Hands."

LXXXIV

The snuff that got the best stories out of Moggy Geogehagan at Ballymullet Workhouse was a pungent, ginger-colored mixture, and an ounce cost fourpence-halfpenny. You sneezed when Mackiboy, who kept the general shop, took the lid of the tin off, but Moggy consumed vast pinches of this luxury without turning a hair. Naygurhead was her weakness when it came to smoking-tobacco. Her dearest treasure was a little old, inconceivably foul, black pipe that had belonged to Jems Geogehagan.

When the Allied Armies landed in the Crimaya, the scene upon that crowded beach was beyond all description. Every voice was swearing, the language was enough to split a stone.... You ate what you could get, or went without, according as luck would have it; and lay down anyhow and anywhere, to snatch your forty winks.

Between the crying of the trumpets, and the calling of the bugles, the shouting of men trying to find their lost regiments, and the noise of the starving beasts that clamored for their fodder, you were awake the greater part of the time you were sleeping. The hullaballoo made you think of the Judgment Day, with Donnybrook Fair thrown in.

At the beginning of the March upon the Alma, according to Moggy, the Hundredth Lancers with two other Light Cavalry Rigiments forrumed the Advance, and when the Armies were halted, and the Commanders-in-Chief rode along the Front, and Lord Dalgan—a grand, fine, bould-lookin' ould gintleman to look at—dressed in a dark blue frock an' gray throusers, an' a plain undhress cap with a gould band, made a spache to the French in their quare lingo, their Commander-in-Chief, Marshal de St. Arnaud—a long, thin, painted gentleman, all over gould and jools—returned the compliment by addressing Her Majesty's troops in their native tongue.

"Angleesh Soldats!" the Marshal is reported to have said on the occasion: "'Ow do you do? I 'ope you vill faight vell to-day!" Upon which, from the safe anonymity of the ranks, a Hibernian voice retorted:

"Arrah, Froggy! Don't you know we will?"

Staff officers rocked in their saddles. Massed regiments were grinning. No one had the least idea as to the identity of the offender. But long after, when Jems Geogehagan was at his dullest, men remembered what he had once said to the French Commander-in-Chief.

The March of the Three Armies was a cure for sore eyes, the greatest sight consaivable. It was for all the worruld an' a Chaney orange like three great snakes sthreelin' along. A Red Snake, and a Light Blue Snake, an' a Dark Blue snake, wid golden scales, an' diamond hair standin' stiff along the backs av' thim. And the Blue Snakes were always between the Red Snake and the sea. The rowl of the Artillery batteries, and the tramplin' of horse and fut, and the sounding of the trumpets an' the crying of the bugles made you think again of the Day of Judgment. An'—more by tokens!—the Last Day was soon to dawn for many that was there.

The roads were more thracks than roads; the counthry Moggy considered to be not unlike the Curragh of Kildare, with a dash of Galway, a sinsation of Bagshot Heath, and a taste of Shorncliffe. There was rowling open plains to begin wid; you could see the Fleets movin' as the Army moved, the big line-av-battle ships standin' well out—so as to get the good av their long-range flankin' batteries—and the smaller war-steamers keepin' inshore, ready at the wind of a worrud to dhrop in a shell from their pivot-guns. But when the bush-covered slopes began to heave up like solid waves about you, and in front of you, begob! the say might have dhried up! For all you'd have known there was no Army in front of you at all, at all! but for the dead and dying bastes, and the sun-sick and cholera-smitten men it had sloughed as it traveled on. *"Don't leave us!"* the sick cried out in a lamentable manner, and good rayson they had to cry, poor craythers! For the ambulances having been left behind at Varna, to lave them was to lave them to be aiting by the buruds av the air and the bastes av the wild. So thim among the women that was able—and many was sick, God pity them!—gave up their places on the wagons to these unfortunates, and footed it beside the thrains.

They bivouacked under a dhry sky that night, and marched in the gray of the morning, losing the road and climbing the hills in the tracks the plunging batteries had made. The bush that clad these hills was tamarisk and broom, and furze, and oak-scrub; thorny red-and-yellow berried barberry, wild grape-vines, and a shrub wid shiny leaves and the smell av thim like bog-myrtle. The scent of crushed thyme and worrumwood rose up about your feet, as you tramped on. The sun shone white-hot in a sky of harebell blue.

It was high noon of a scorching hot day when you heard the Fleet's guns firing. Powerful the banging was. They were shellin' the Russian Artillery posted on the heights. Then came volleys av muskethry, crackin' and rattlin'. Clouds of salty-tastin' powdher-smoke came driftin' down upon the wind. And the sun bein' in your teeth, your shadow and the shadows of the women marchin' with you, and the carts, and the bastes, and the men that dhrove them, loomed thremenjous on the vapor that riz behind you like a wall. But when the big grass garrison-guns the Inimy had cocked up on the rock-ridges above the river began convarsin'—and the French and English Artillery answered wid shrapnel an' rockets an' grape—you walked in a white fog laced wid tongues of fire, an' round-shot as big as melons trundlin' through it—expectin' you'd be raising the whilleleu wid the Holy Souls in Purgatory the next minute, or dhrinkin' tay wid the Blessed in Paradise. The screaming of the bugles split the reek, and pierced the smother; and—in one lull—came the sound of the Zouave drums beating the *pas de charge*.

You know it.... It begins with a low faint throbbing that grows upon the ear and fills it, drowning out all other sounds. It is a hurricane from Hell that blows armed men, like red, and blue, and golden leaves before it, urged by the simultaneous desire to strike, stab, crush, overwhelm, destroy and conquer other men....

The fighting was over, when the women with the seven-mile-long wagon-train, loaded with sick and dying, drawn by gaunt horses, emaciated mules, and starving bullocks, climbed the rise where the Tartar village was still smoldering and reeking. Dismounted field-guns, shattered limbers, dead and mutilated men and horses and bloody mash that had been men and horses, showed where the Inimy's canister and grape had done its business upon the batteries of our Artillery. Cooking-fires were already lighted, fatigue-parties were digging grave-trenches, the distant trumpets were calling the Cavalry back from the pursuit. It was for Moggy and for many of the women with the wagon-trains, the first sight of a battle-field.

But not until—word having been brought down that the Cavalry would encamp a mile south of the Katscha, and that their women were to follow them—not until their smaller train of vehicles separated from the rest, and began to roll over the ridge, and down the steep banks to the river-ford—did they realize the grim meaning of War....

The trodden slopes that were strewn with shattered Minié rifles and smashed muskets, Highland bonnets, bearskins and shakos, and dead and dying men in kilts and plaids and red coats, lying in queer contorted attitudes (as if a giant child had been playing at soldiers, and had given the green board a spiteful kick and gone away)—were covered with a low shrub like billberry, seemingly laden with a plentiful crop of red fruit, yet they were not berries but blood-drops. The grasses wept—the earth was soaked—the river in the glen-bottom ran blood.

Realizing this, there was an outcry; and pale women huddled at the back of Moggy Geogehagan, as scared ewes will seek refuge behind some aged and weather-beaten herd-mother. Said Moggy, crying herrings for shame upon these tremblers:

"Hooroo, Jude! Are ye women or girshas that do be squaling an' squaiking? Sure what's natheral can't be desperate, an' what's more natheral than blood? Her that will lie by her man this night will do as I do. Sthrip off, pluck up, an' leg through this wid me."

And the brave wife of Jems whipped off her brogues and footless blue yarn stockings, tucked up her petticoats, and led the way down, striding bare-shinned through the bloody bilberries. The Woman from Clare followed, after came flocking the rest.

LXXXV

Upon the rise beyant the sthrame that ran red, where yet other Tartar peasants' huts were charring and smoking, brass-bound firelocks were mingled with the scattered Miniés and the broken Brown Besses; and the Highland plaids, and the red coats were infinitely outnumbered by the gray.

Up above on the hills, scored with rifle-pits, bristling with batteries, these gray coats lay in swaths and mounds as though the Divil had been makin' hay there. And the wearers of the gray coats were pale, flat-faced men in black leather metal-spiked helmets, or white linen forage-caps. Clane-shaven men, wid sizable mouths on them, and little noses, as like wan anodher as pays out av the same pod. Catholics, too, sorrow a doubt on it! The open shirts beneath their unbuttoned coats showed, strung round their thick white necks, medals of the Mother and Child, and Crosses with the Image of the Crucified. The dead had died, grasping these. The dying strove to kiss these—making the Sign with fumbling, groping fingers—gasping out broken sentences of prayer.

And then it flashed on Moggy that this was the Inimy—could be nobody but the Inimy. The Barbarian, with teeth like prongs of hay-rakes—who dressed in sheepskins, relished tallow-candles and soap, and worshiped devil-gods—had never existed at all.

This was a shock, but nothing to the revelation of some seven hours later, when—as Moggy squatted over a fire of dried weeds and Commissariat cask-staves, toasting her man's supper of salt pork on the end of a broken ramrod—under the black canopy of a starless night, came down the sickly, tainted wind the mournful cry:

"*Oi-oi-oi!*"

Even as Rachel, Russia mourned for her sons and would not be comforted. The huge, beaten army of Menschikoff, retreating down the great trunk road towards Sivernaia, had left a shattered brigade of Imperial Guards and a regiment or two of cavalry encamped upon the Belbek. And that piercing "*Oi-oi*" is the wail of the mujik, who, soldier though he be, is always a peasant at heart. It was the Cossack of the Eastern Caucasus who cried: "*Ai-ai-ai-dalalai!*"

"Mary be about us! What's that?"

The woman rose up from her task, dropping the frizzling meat upon the dull red embers. She plucked back the shawl that hooded her, listened intently, and said, with her hollowed hand yet cupping the cocked ear:

"*Musha yarra!* Is it savigees they do be callin' thim?... May I never break a pratie more av they're not keening their dead like dacent Irish. Do ye not hear thim? Och! och! your souls to glory!" she cried. "What are we fighting yees for at all, at all? For a dirty baste of a Turk that spit on the Holy Crucifix, an' shaves his skull as naked as me hand!"

They grew to like the snub-nosed, flat faced Ivan or Piotr in the coarse gray overcoat. The man of dogged imperturbable endurance, who lived on thin kvas and black bread. Who stood up in blocks as big as Trafalgar Square to be shot at. Who advanced on the bayonets or faced the batteries with the bravery of unquestioning obedience; and regarded his Little Father, the Tsar, as the Vicar upon earth of the Great Father in Heaven.

The Ivans and Piotrs, aware of their Tsar's weakness for lightning journeys and anonymous visits of inspection, believed him to be constantly with their Army, though unseen. Over many a bivouac-fire they whispered of a huge officer who sometimes rode with the Headquarters Staff, but oftenest marched with their battalions; a man whose impassive stolid face, with the stony blue, prominent eyes bulging under the spiked black leather helmet, was reproduced in the official colored print that hung in every barrack-room. He had captured the imagination of his people in the Cholera year of '46, when he thrust his way through the panic-stricken people surging round the Church of Our Lady of Kasan.

You know the story.... Reports had been spread that all sufferers taken to the hospitals were poisoned there. Panic reigned. Revolution was imminent. And Tsar Nicholas drove into the square in his little one-horse droschky—leaped out and mounted the church steps with those long, quick strides of his—turned, and threw open the gray great-coat, showing the glitter of the Orders he wore. Beneath the rim of the spiked helmet his sullen eyes blazed at his people.... His puffy cheeks had lost their crimson and were deadly pale.... He bellowed at the full pitch of that extraordinary voice of his: "Russians, to your knees!" and down they went.... No wonder they believed in their Tsar, those Ivans and Piotrs.

Later they arrived at the pitch of interchanging civilities with the British invader. Sentries who were posted within hailing-distance on the banks of the Tchernaya, would swop pipes or lumps of black bread for bits of biscuit—exchange confidences oddly couched in a jargon of their own. They agreed that the Frantsos were bono, the Ruskies were bono, the Anglichanin were bono; but that the Turk was no bono at all.

Referring to the Child of Islâm, the Piotrs or Ivans would expectorate, and hold their noses, as though those organs were afflicted with an unpleasant odor; while Thomas Atkins or William Brown would affect to run away in terror, squalling: "Ship, Johnny! Ship!"

This inevitable climax never failed to provoke laughter. It recalled how—briskly as some colony of whistling marmot-rats into whose rows of tenanted holes an Army naturalist had poured water—the nimble Asiatic had evacuated the Northern redoubts on the day of the Balaklava Attack.

Hopped out at the rare av the earthworks like flays, they did, whin the Inimy turraned the guns upon thim.... You might have knocked Moggy Geogehagan down with a feather when she saw the blaggyards lep....

Purty as a picther the battle was, with the green hills set round it like a frame, and the blue sea lyin' on your right hand, so calm you saw the white clouds sailin' in it.... Nothing Moggy had ever clapped her two eyes on would aiqual it, barrin' the glimpse they had had of the place they called Sevastopol—a wondrous city, with great quays and populous docks edging the bright blue bay-water, white marble palaces, and yellow churches with green domes, glittering blue and green and silver ridgimints paradin' in the public squares, and sparkling fountains springing in the sunshine—as the Red Snake and the two Blue Snakes, turning inland, crawled up the rugged heights that tower beyond the Farm of Mackenzie, and streamed down the steep defile in an endless river of dusty, dry-throated, weary, sore-footed beasts and men.

The Red Snake had led the way that day, Moggy remembered.... Riding without scouts, or advance-patrols, quite like a knightly Crusader of ancient story, the "bould ould gintleman," with his Headquarters Staff and escort about him, had butted into the tail-end of the great Army of Russia as it ebbed away, like a great gray wounded python, towards Simferopol.

Faix an' troth! an' a battle there would have been to bate Banagher!—supposin' the bould ould gintleman to have starruted two hours airlier, as the Frinch Commandher-in-Chief had coaxed him to do. As it was, there was a bit av a skirmish between the throops that did be convoyin' the baggage-wagons av the Inimy, and our Cavalry.... When the said wagons were delivered to the sturdy hands that had captured them, Jems tasted the joys of loot.

True, his share was only a marbled paper bandbox containing some elderly field-officer's auburn wig, and a daguerreotype of Mdlle Pasbas of the Imperial Opera, Petersburg. But as plunder, these things were prized above rubies by Corporal Geogehagan.

Often and often…. But at this point the listener would urge Moggy to speed on to the great keening-match in which the wife of Jems so grandly maintained her own against the overweening pretensions of the Woman that hailed from Clare.

You must know that on the inland side of the Valley, bottomed with coarse grass, where the Light Brigade were encamped, rose a hill that had served as a signaling-station for the Russian coastguard; and from its summit the squadron-women watched the battle throughout the livelong day.

It was when these watching women saw a cloud of men in blue and crimson and gold and scarlet—mounted on black and brown and bay horses—sweeping down the Valley towards the Cossack squadrons that had clumped in a dusk mass behind their guns on the banks of the green Tchernaya—crushing down the vines and the tamarisk-bushes and oak-scrub, falling under the plowing fire from the Russian batteries posted on the Woronzoff Ridge and the Fedioukkine Heights, vanishing in the smoke to wheel and return upon their own bloody path—that the Woman from Clare screeched out, and clapped her hands, and dropped as though she had been shot.

She had long been a thorn in Moggy's side, by rayson of the gabbin' an' blather she made, claiming to be descinded from the Seven Champions of Gortgorla in Ballynahinch Knockmalone…. Wild as an aigle and brown as the say-weed, she was; and eyes like two blazing yellow torches under the red thatch of hair she had. Her man was a young color-sergeant in Lord Cloneen's famous Hussar Regiment, and she knew him to be end-file rider on the right of the single squadron that brought up the rear.

Watching from her eyrie with those piercing yellow eyes of hers, she had seen the shell burst, and the plumed busby fly, and the little gay-colored speck that was all her joy tumble out of the saddle, as Houlahan's riderless horse swept on, borne by the rest.

Fell wid a screech she did, an' then riz up, an' the eyes of her might have been sewn in wid red worsted…. Her blue Galway cloak flapped like wings as she cried, tossing up her lean freckled arms:

"Och! my grief for the sthrong men! the fine big sthrapping men that do be lying dead below the hillside! Blood on the sod, an' the yellow fat laughing from the deep belly-wounds! Father av Heaven! Was it for this that their fathers begot and their mothers suckled them? Christ and Mary pity the wounded, comfort the dying, help for the souls av the departed, even if they passed widout a prayer!"

She clapped her hands and swayed herself, gathering all her forces, and not an Irishwoman there but clapped and rocked with her. She cried:

"Och vogh! my grief! for my own grand young husband Michael Houlahan! For the hoofs of the horses are tangled in his bowels an' his brains are spilt like curd upon the ground! Man that I always knew you— why did I turn from you—last night when we lay togedher undher the wet tent av the sky? 'Sleep,' I said, 'Sleep! that ye may be sthrong to meet the morrow!' An' he turned from me an' slept, wid the cowld raindrops on his cheek.... Och! vogh, vogh! Ochone!—for my own man, Michael Houlahan! Darlin', darlin', why did you die? Why did I deny you, avourneen, jewel of my heart! that sought to lave a son of your race behind you? A graft to bear, a seed to spring in the womb! Blessed Saints, pray for the desolate widow of Michael Houlahan! Holy Souls! pity——"

The strained voice of lamentation cracked—just in time. For Moggy Geogehagan could bear no more. For all she knew Jems Geogehagan was killed like the rest of them—and here was this unconscionable woman monopolizing the good offices of every One of Thim Above.

She tore out a handful of her coarse black hair, cast it from her with a superb gesture, clapped her hands, and took up the theme. Ordinary language was far too poor to do justice to the merits of the departed. She gave him all the grandest words she knew.

"Woman!" she began, with a clap of her hands and a toss of her head. "Away wid you! I am extenuated wid your lamentations! What call have you to be bragging of your Mike Houlahan? Sure, beside the man that was Jems Geogehagan your Mike Houlahan showed no bigger than a flay! Of a configuration that excogitated the beholder wid revelations av martial splindhour, where was his aiqual? What modher's son iver got the betther av him? Whilleleu! Och, och! whatever will I do at all?"

She shrieked like a locomotive, reveling in the glory of her wretchedness, and drew her ten nails down the length of her face. The woman from Clare had collapsed by this time into a blue rag-bundle. The other women came crowding about Moggy—laying hands upon her—pointing, vociferating.... With the power that was upon her in that great hour, they fell off her elbows, she said, like a bundle av sthraws....

"Whoo! My bitther black curse upon the vagabone that kilt Jems Geogehagan! May he die like a dog in a ditch, the big murdherin' rogue! May he——"

But every throat set up a cry and every finger pointed in one direction, and a rush of the crowd swept her down the steep hillside. You may conceive how the women greeted that straggling party of unhorsed, dejected men, some of whom were wearing bloody head-bandages, others of whom limped painfully, as, supported by their comrades, they made their way back to the camp of the Light Brigade. And the irrepressible cry broke from Moggy, as Jems ambled towards her, grinning foolishly:

"The divil baste your hide! What call have you to be alive, and me raising the widdy's cry for you? Give me your ear, you sorrow o' the worruld!"

But when she saw that his round face was white and drawn, and that his left arm dangled helplessly; and that a bright red stream was running from the deep sword-thrust in his side, the woman's heart got the better of her. She uttered a great maternal cry of love, and tenderness, and sorrow, and caught him, fainting, in her brawny arms.

LXXXVI

Dunoisse had been arrested on the steps of the English Embassy upon the night of the Monster Ball at the Élysée. Not a moment too soon, it may have been, for the safety of the chicken that had hatched out of the basilisk-egg.

Having himself suffered the slow torture of imprisonment, who should know better than Sire my Friend, how to refine and embroider upon the sufferings of a prisoner? Dunoisse was assigned to the care of the Commandant of the Fortress under minute and particular instructions, which were, by that official, scrupulously carried out.

Solitude and Silence were the regimen prescribed for the captive. Save the Commandant, or the priest who would on rare occasions be admitted to administer religious consolation—no one might speak to Dunoisse, or answer when spoken to, save by certain strictly-regulated signs. Pens, pencils, ink and paper, newspapers and books—manuals of devotion excepted—were sternly prohibited. In order to guard against communication between the prisoner and the soldiers of the garrison, blinds were nailed over the windows of the barracks looking on that restricted space upon the ramparts, where Dunoisse was permitted to take the air.

The room allotted to him in the prison of the Fortress was one of a suite of three that had in 1840 accommodated a certain political gamester, ruined by the failure of an ambitious *coup* at Boulogne. Luck had turned; the penniless plunger had swept the board, and broken the bank. Now, lifted and borne high upon the tidal wave of Fortune, he could look down upon Powers and dignities by whom he had been despised.

The cage that had held the Imperial bird—repaired at the time of his incarceration—was now dilapidated and leaky. The floor of uneven bricks was damp and chilly, the plaster of the ceiling was tumbling down. The paper hung upon the walls of weeping stone in folds and festoons—the rusty iron sashes of the thickly-barred windows would neither shut or open. With the fever and ague of the Dobrudja still upon him, Dunoisse, denied the comfort of fire or extra bedding, invalid nourishment, medical attendance, or the commonest human intercourse; would have died, or sunk into a lethargy of inertia ending in death, but for one thing.

Habitual criminals, when subjected to the system of solitude and silence, either become imbecile or are rendered tenfold more brutal, degraded, and dangerous than they were before. Under the same process, men and women of wide education and high intelligence condemned by the laws of Government for political offenses—although the alternative of idiocy or insanity be open to them as to the felon or the murderer—usually emerge from the ordeal—presuming they survive?—confirmed in their convictions, strengthened in determination, fortified by suffering for endurance of greater ills. The enthusiast has become a fanatic, the propagandist has become a leader. The cause for which the man or the woman has suffered becomes flesh of the flesh and bone of the bone.

That intention of atonement—vague, unspecified—that determination to unmesh the net that he had woven—upheld and supported this man. Otherwise the fatigue-party of four soldiers with spades, the box of tarred planks, and the blanket of quicklime would have been called into requisition—and Sire my Friend would have been disappointed of a reprisal he had planned.

He had not given Dunoisse the room for nothing. On the stone lintel of the low, barred window was scratched, perhaps with the point of a nail or a pair of scissors, a fragment of erotic verse beginning:

"O *charmante Henriette! Mon ange, ma belle!...*"

Dunoisse knew the handwriting for that of his late master. Reminiscent of that old intrigue, it had few stings for him, who had done with intrigue forever. There were other inscriptions, in the same hand—philosophical, heroic, amatory, cynical—upon the mantelshelf, upon the balustrade of the staircase, upon the parapet of the ramparts where the prisoner was allowed to exercise. Two beds of earth were here, containing some straggling untended annuals. A few sickly violets were trying to bloom in the shadow of the chill gray stone. Beneath the rampart, fosse and marsh were flanked by the canal that was edged by tall straggling poplars, standing ankle-deep in the grim green-black waters that wind snakily across the plain. Beyond the canal rose the *demi-lune*—beyond this mass of comparatively modern masonry was yet another fosse. And then, the interminable marshes spreading to the misty horizon, and beyond these—the world.

What was taking place out there? Were nations striving against nations? Were Fire and Iron, Lead and Steel, Death, Famine, and Pestilence playing their parts in the dreadful Theater of War? Were those secret treaties, those signed contracts, those imposed oaths, bearing fruit, not in the defeat of an enemy, but in the destruction of an ally? Had those vast sums of poured-out gold purchased for Sire my Friend the vengeance that would be sweeter to him than victory? To pace upon those ancient stones, tainted by his dainty, mincing footsteps—and wonder—and be kept in ignorance of what was common knowledge to the drummers of the garrison, the scullions of the Commandant's kitchen—was torture to Dunoisse.

Treachery.... Ever since that night of his unexpected return to the Abbaye, the thought of treachery had held and obsessed him. It had flavored his food. He had tasted it in his drink. Unknown to himself, the traveler's cold accusing glance had stricken terror to the soul of the Greek or Slav or Turkish innkeepers who had overcharged him, the peasants who had robbed him, and the knavish servants who had stolen the fodder from his horses, and the rugs from their backs. The nomad Tartar who refused payment for shelter in his flea-ridden tent of felt, and a share of the rancid boiled mutton smoking in his sooty caldron because it would, to his untutored mind, be a sin to barter for silver the sacred privilege of hospitality, was puzzled by that chilly, questioning look.

Suspicion had rankled in the man like a poisonous thorn or an eating ulcer. Seated near some pretty woman in a public conveyance or a public place, he would wonder with whom the charming stranger was deceiving her husband or playing her lover false? Drawing rein before some Wallach peasant's hut of turf and reeds at eventide, as the bronzed, black-eyed maiden drew the woolen threads from the distaff stuck in her wide, embroidered girdle, the look the traveler cast on her would question: "Are you as pure as you appear? Does this virginal exterior cover a spotted conscience?" And when his dog fawned upon him, he would think, even as he caressed it: "Ah, but suppose I fell, attacked and worried by other dogs, would you defend me against them, or would you not rather aid the pack in tearing out my throat?" And as the thievish innkeeper had quailed, and the innocent young woman or the pure young girl had trembled beneath that chill regard of his, the dog would quail and tremble too, and slink guiltily away. And the heart of the man would contract in a bitter spasm, and drops of sweat would start upon his forehead. For to the generous it is anguish to suspect.

One does not know what would have been the end of this man—to whom no man might speak—who was not even permitted to dibble in the earth of Sire my Friend's old flower-beds lest he should scratch a message on the arid soil that might meet some friendly eye; who might not even feed with crumbs—saved from his scant meals—the doves upon the ramparts—lest some written communication from that tabued world outside, cunningly attached to a leg or hidden beneath a wing, should reach him in his captivity. Perhaps inertia would have ended in collapse, mental or bodily. But that in his crying need of friendship, he found a Friend at last.

The Breviary and Vulgate, with the *Imitatione Christi* of Thomas à Kempis—left in Dunoisse's cell by some cynical whim of his Imperial jailer—proved to contain within them fountains of healing for his sick and suffering soul. Unguessed, undreamed-of beauty and delight and sweetness had lain hidden in the narrow columns as in the closely-printed pages. The casual reader became a student, the student a scholar, long before he knew.... And the Denier denied no longer. Dayspring banished the darkness; Faith revived in him—he could pray again. How strange it is, that only when the meanest and humblest of our fellow-creatures turn from us, do we seek the companionship of One Who is King of Kings.

At Christmastide—for the snow lay on the marshes and the ramparts—the fosse and the canal were frozen—and the church bells of the distant town had rung the carillon of Nöel at midnight—they admitted a confessor to the prisoner in his cell.

"What is the news, my Father? What has happened in the great roaring world whose voice has never reached me since these walls of Cyclopean masonry rose up about and penned me in? War had been proclaimed when I was arrested.... Has there been War? Is there War now?" Dunoisse asked.

But the priest made answer to his eager questions:

"My dear son, to gain admittance here I have pledged my word that I will not discuss with you any worldly matter. Let me, while I have the opportunity, give you news of the Kingdom of God."

Dunoisse, so long a willing exile from that Kingdom, had been by slow and painful stages finding his way back there. Now, with the aid of the Church, he cleansed his sin-stained soul in the lustral waters of Confession. He was absolved. He received the Bread of Life.

It seemed to him at the supreme moment that a burning ray of Divine Light penetrated and illumined him. He saw himself clearly as he had never seen himself before. He understood how he had fallen from his old ideals, and strayed from the way of cleanliness and honor. He realized that Sympathy had been the missing link between himself and his fellow-men. He had loved one man. He had worshiped one woman with an overwhelming, guilty passion. Both friend and mistress had deceived him; and for this reason he had reared a wall of icy doubt between himself and the rest of Humanity.

You might have smiled, could you have seen him at this juncture trying to love his silent jailers, guessing at their hidden lives, wondering about their wives and families, probing without the aid of words, to reach their conjectural hearts.

And it seemed to him that they looked more pleasantly upon him. Probably it was so, for his black eyes had lost their piercing hardness, and his smile was no longer bitter and edged with scorn. Yet he suffered more, for the melting of the ice within his bosom had freed the springs of our common nature. He yearned for human kindness and human companionship. He thirsted for the voice and the grasp of friendship. He longed inexpressibly—and none the less that he knew himself to have forfeited the right to this—for some pure woman's devoted love.

He looked out over the ramparts as the snows vanished, and a rosy tinge that spoke of coming spring stole over the leafless copses, and young green grass-blades peeped in the sheltered hollows; and the yellow aconite and the pale primrose bloomed, and the tall scraggy poplars of the thawing marshes showed the black knots of bud. He had never been beloved, it seemed to him.... Doubtless his mother had loved him—poor old Smithwick, dead many years ago, had certainly loved him. Adjmeh might have loved him—as some pampered pretty animal loves the master who tends and feeds it. Henriette had entertained a sensuous, fanciful passion for him. But Love he had never known, in its fullness, as it may exist between woman and man.

Once he had met a woman with a noble, earnest face and calm, pure, radiant eyes, and had gone upon his world's way and had forgotten her. They had met again, on the night of the *coup d'État*, at the French Embassy in London. And her glance had pierced to the quick through his armor of selfishness, and vanity, and lust. She had not spared him reproach, though at their parting she had softened and relented. She had said in effect: "Though you are nothing to me now, I might have loved the man you used to be!" What had he not lost by that change? What might he not have gained had he chosen, instead of the easy road of pleasure, the stony path of rectitude! Dimly he began to realize what an inestimable treasure of tenderness, what an inexhaustible mine of shining loyalty, and glowing faith, and pure passion, had lain hidden in the heart of Ada Merling, for the lover who should prove himself worthy of the supreme boon.

Had the lover come? Was the great gift bestowed, or yet withheld? Dunoisse wondered as he paced his daily hour upon the Fortress ramparts, followed by the two warders who were bound to keep him in sight. Was she wedded or free? He asked himself this question over and over. And, by the stab of pain that followed when he said: "She is a wife!" he knew....

He loved her. Happy for her that Fate had sundered them, if by any remote chance she might have loved a man so little worthy of her as Hector Dunoisse. But she never would have ... she never could have.... He tried to follow her in thought as she went upon her selfless way. He saw her pure, sweet influence shed on other hearts to soften, and uplift, and cheer them. He saw the poor relieved by those generous hands. He heard the sick, healed by her skilled and gentle ministrations, blessing her. He dreamed of her—with a cruel pang—as endowing some true man with the priceless treasure of her love. He pictured her with their children rocked in her arms and nourished at her bosom. He imagined her growing old, and moving down the vale of years, leaning on the stalwart sons and matronly, handsome daughters, who should look up to her even as they aided her, in perfect confidence; and whose children, inheriting their tender reverence for that dearest mother, should love and trust her, too. And a great yearning swelled in his desolate heart, and his aching, mateless soul rushed out across the void to her....

"Ada!..."

In the anguish of his loneliness he lifted his arms to the wild, gray sky of March, and, in a voice that was like the wailing of the bitter wind across the marshes, cried on the beloved name:

"Oh, Ada!—Ada!..."

And—spun to the merest spider-thread of sound by infinite distance, her unforgettable voice answered ... beyond doubt or question answered:

"*I hear you.... Oh, where are you?*"

LXXXVII

He could not doubt that she had heard and answered. There was no explanation possible. It had happened, that was all. You may rub shoulders, in the course of a morning's walk down one of the big world's crowded thoroughfares, with a hundred men and women who are genuinely convinced of the impossibility of such communication between the minds and souls of those who, separated by countries, or continents, or oceans, are not even aware of one another's whereabouts. But the hundred-and-first will be initiate. She or he will have felt the tightening of the invisible spider-thread, experienced the thrill, known the familiar touch upon the brow or breast—heard the beloved voice speaking at the inner ear. And, like Dunoisse, having experienced, they will refrain from questioning. It has happened.... When the time comes, it will certainly happen again....

Not long after, during an attack of fever, Dunoisse dreamed that he awakened in the chill gray dawn of a February morning to see Ada Merling sitting by his bed. It seemed so natural to have her there, and so divinely sweet and comforting, that he lay for a long time gazing at her, dwelling on each dear, remembered trait and lovely feature, breathing her atmosphere, drinking her in. She wore in this his vision of her, not the gray nurse's dress of Cavendish Street, but a plain black gown, though the frilled white muslin cap of his remembrance sat close and sober, as of old, upon her rich, brown, waving hair, and the cambric apron made a splash of white upon the blackness of the dress. The lines of the pure features were a little sharpened, the eyes larger, the sensitive, clearly-cut lips were closely folded. She looked sadder ... older.... Even as he realized this she smiled; and such a radiance of beauty kindled in her, and shone forth from her, that he cried out in rapture and awakened; and in his weakness shed tears on finding himself a prisoner and alone.

But the dream, following the answer on the ramparts, left a clear impression. She was living, and yet unwedded, and she had not forgotten him—not quite forgotten him! The conviction of this gave him new strength to live. Later on he received another intimation, not from the living world beyond the ramparts and the poplared marshes, but from the other World that is beyond the Veil.

It came to him one day at dusk with a crisping of the hair and a shuddering of the flesh that was not terror—rather wonder and awe, and solemn gladness. The day had been dark and rainy. His lamp had not been lighted, the scanty fire burned low in the rusty grate. Dunoisse sat thinking, leaning his elbows on the table where his silent servitor had set his meager supper. And suddenly the recollection of his mother as he had last seen her rose up in him. The whisper of her woolen draperies seemed to cross the rough brick floor, her thin light touch was between his eyebrows, tracing there the Sacred Sign. And almost without conscious volition her son rose up, placed a rush-seated chair opposite his own at the poorly-furnished table; filled a goblet with pure water, cut bread, laid it upon a plate, sprinkled a Cross of salt upon it, and set it for his unseen guest.... Then he resumed his own seat and ate, comprehending that she wished it. And as he ate he talked, in low, soft murmurs, as though answering.... Depend upon it, one never pours out one's hidden self so freely as when one speaks with the beloved dead.

And then he found himself rising up, bidding God-speed and farewell to the guest unseen, in a solemn form of words quite strange to him. And then he knew himself alone.

Upon the following morning, being unexpectedly visited by the Commandant, he said to the official:

"Sir, I already know what you have come to tell me. My mother died yesterday."

The Commandant started, and dropped a paper. It was a telegraphic message from the Minister of the Interior, conveying, and bidding him impart the news. He asked the prisoner:

"How did you hear this?"

And Dunoisse smiled so strangely in answer that the Commandant's next official report contained the sentence quoted hereunder:

"*No. X.—the officer confined during His Imperial Majesty's pleasure—is undoubtedly becoming insane.*"

"*Zut!*" said de Morny with a shrug, when Sire my Friend showed him this communication. "That is what you wanted, is it not?" He added: "You have used the man, and broken the man! When you need him again—he will not be available. Brains of such caliber as his are not often found under a Staff-officer's cocked hat. Leave him shut up—and they will find them plastered on the wall one morning.... Heads are softer than walls; madmen always remember that!"

He shrugged again, and the shrug and the cynical inflection dismissed the subject of discussion. But not many weeks subsequently the Commandant again visited Dunoisse, and said to him abruptly:

"You are free."

"Free!...."

Dunoisse trembled in every limb, and caught at the table to save himself from falling. So well had the instructions of Sire my Friend been carried out, that all hope of being delivered out of his bondage had abandoned him. It was almost appalling to learn that he might now ask questions. He faltered out:

"How long have I been here?" and was told:

"About six months."

Six months!... If they had said six years, Dunoisse would have believed them. Could it be possible that such slow, interminable agonies as he had drunk of, such painful resignation as he had fought for and won, had been packed into so short a space of time as half-a-year? He asked for a mirror he had been denied—and they brought him one. He looked in it, and saw a face bleached to the tint of reddish ivory, framed in white hair that fell in waving locks almost to the shoulders. The long straggling mustache and beard were of white with streaks of blackness. From the deep caves under the arched black eyebrows the bright black eyes of Hector Dunoisse looked back at him. But they looked with a gentleness that was new. And the smile that hovered about the sharply-modeled lips had in it a sorrowful, patient sweetness that the smile of Dunoisse had never had previously. It was partly this change that had caused the Commandant to report the prisoner as insane.

Dunoisse's watch and chain, with his penknife, pencil-case, and razors were now restored to him, with his clothes and a portion of the considerable sum of money that had been taken from him at the time of his arrest. A military barber of the garrison trimmed his hair and reduced the mustache and beard to more conventional proportions. Attired in a well-worn suit of gray traveling clothes, hanging in folds upon his stooping emaciated figure, you saw the late prisoner take leave of the Commandant and step into a closed carriage that was waiting in the courtyard, with an officer of police in plain clothes seated by the driver on the box. When the carriage rumbled out under the great square gate-tower erected in the fifteenth century by the Count of St. Pol, the man inside had an access of nervous trembling. He shut his eyes, and presently the shadow passed, and he could look upon the free, fair world again.

It was the end of October; the gaunt poplars had shed their yellowed leaves, and the haws were scarlet on the bushes. Mists hung over the marshes—the odor of decaying vegetation came to Dunoisse with each free breath he drew.

He could no longer judge of time, and the watch they had returned to him had not been wound up. It seemed to him a drive of many hours before the carriage stopped. He was told to get out, and obeyed. He found himself in a graveled enclosure outside a railway-station. His meager baggage was deposited. The carriage was driven away. It was so marvelous to have a porter come and pick up his battered valise and light portmanteau, and so overwhelming to be asked where the latter was to be labeled for, that Dunoisse, standing on the Paris departure platform, could only stare at the interrogative porter, and answer after a bewildered silence:

"I really do not know!"

He knew a few moments later. For a gray-painted express rushed, with a winnowing and fanning as of giant wings, through the station. The train was full of English soldiers, their unbuttoned coats testifying to the heat of the closely-packed compartments. Their fresh-colored faces crowded at the windows; they left behind with their cheers and fag-ends of comic songs an impression of rude health and pathetic ignorance, above all, of extreme youth.

Dunoisse, unnerved by captivity, rendered dizzy by the sudden shock of revelation, reeled back and collided with a person who stood behind him, and proved to be a humpbacked, withered little old man, in charge of the station newspaper-stall. The little old man—who wore a black velvet cap, and had a ginger-colored chin-tuft, and spoke French with a curious hissing accent—received his apologies with a smiling air.

"A nothing! A mere touch!... Monsieur was momentarily startled by the passage of the monster. For months those expresses from Boulogne have been thundering through here. Full—as Monsieur saw—of soldiers, French soldiers at the beginning.... Regiments of the Line from Helfaut, batteries of Artillery from Lille, and St. Omer, and other fortresses; then English, English, nothing but Englishmen.... *Via* Paris for Marseilles and Toulon, to be shipped for the Bosphorus and the Black Sea."

The prattle of the newspaper stall-keeper had never before been listened to so greedily as by this white-haired, haggard, shabbily-clothed traveler. The little man went on, plainly reveling in the sound of his own queer voice:

"They were fine men at first, some of them giants. Now they are boys—mere infants, one might say!... Conscripts, one might say also; but that they are without the conscription in England. Food for the Hungry One all the same. For Death is a glutton, Monsieur, not a *gourmet*. All he asks is—enough to eat."

He added with his whinnying laugh:

"And he gets enough. For of all those train-loads of British that have rolled through here since January, not one has come back, Monsieur.... Possibly there have been returns by sea, but by this route we have seen none of them. We have French invalids in incredible numbers, *en route* for the Northern military hospitals and convalescent camps. They are not beautiful to see, those men who are recovering from fever, and dysentery, and cholera; and"—he wrinkled his nose expressively—"they are excessively unpleasant to smell! But—with the exception of the bodies of wealthy officers, who have died out there and are being forwarded, embalmed, for interment in their family mausoleums—as I have said, Monsieur—there are no English at all. With regard to these last, my peculiar humor, in connection with my trade of bookseller, has suggested a little pleasantry.... They went out to the East in cloth, gilt—and they return in plain boards! Monsieur will pardon my humor? Occasionally one must laugh at Death, who laughs as no else can!"

The haggard black eyes of the white-haired traveler had never quitted the face of the speaker. The hunchback gave another irrepressible little skip, and went on:

"Seriously though, Monsieur, it is incredible what a fatality has dogged the footsteps of these English. From the moment of disembarkation at Varna, new misfortunes, fresh calamities, have fallen on them every day. I ask myself why, and there is no answer but one! They are brave, but stupid, these sons of foggy Albion! And yet there are two great secrets they have mastered perfectly. How to fight, Monsieur—and how to die!"

"Go on," urged Dunoisse, with feverish eagerness. "Tell me more—tell me everything you know!"

"Assuredly!" cried the hunchback, smiling widely. "But where," he added, with irrepressible curiosity, "has Monsieur buried himself all these months that he is ignorant of what the whole world knows? I have not a single paper left to sell, if Monsieur would give me ten francs for it, But I possess a memory and a gift of eloquence. Listen, then, Monsieur!"

He gave another little goatlike skip upon the asphalt, and went on eagerly, fearing to be interrupted; pouring out words, weaving an invisible web about him by the rapid gestures of his supple, bony hands. And Dunoisse realized, as the grim recital continued, in how far his own deep-laid schemes had been successful; and in what respects they had been set at nought by the grim Power that men call Destiny. With incredible fatuity or appalling dishonesty, those officials who controlled the Commissariat and Transport Departments of the British Eastern Expedition had poured out the troops of England upon a foreign soil without clothing, provisions, forage, or beasts of burden sufficient to supply, support, and transport an army of twenty-eight thousand men. They had relied almost exclusively upon the resources of the country. Thanks to a well-laid plan, the country had been found without resources: the Allies had been condemned to a stagnant immobility, as injurious to discipline as dangerous to health.

Sickness had raged among them like a wolf in a sheepfold. Nor had the Army of France escaped. That chart of the Pestilential Places had availed it nothing. Even while on the voyage from Marseilles to Gallipoli cholera had broken out virulently among the French troops. Encamped upon the heights north of Varna, the deadly exhalations rising from the smitten British camps had infected them. They had suffered as severely as the white Tufts, and the Bearskins Plain, and the Cut Red Feathers, whose tents were pitched upon the sylvan shores of the Lake of Death, and amidst the blossom-starred, poison-breathing meadows and fruit-laden orchards of Aladyn.

He heard of the Russian evacuation of the Danubian Principalities, and of the Council of the Allied Generals, resulting in the Invasion of the Crimea. He learned how the buoy, set to mark the landing-point of Britain's forces, had been moved mysteriously in the night. And he knew by whose command the thing must have been done, instantly. And when, after the story of the great battle of Infantry and Artillery that had trodden out the grapes of the vineyards on the banks of Alma and reddened her chalky shallows with the wine of life, came intelligence of the death of St. Arnaud—he realized with a strange, awful thrill, that the master whose service he himself had abjured, had been deprived by Death of his chief confidant and most unscrupulous instrument, and that in this, Fate had been upon the side of England. For the new Commander-in-Chief, Marshal Boisrobert, though willing enough to oblige his master at the Tuileries, lacked the supple skill in lying, and the keen relish for bloodshed, which had distinguished the late intimate of Sire my Friend.

He heard next of the Flank March, and the passing of the ridge of the Tchernaya, and how the harbor of Balaklava, guarded at its narrow, constricted entrance by its two stupendous cliffs of calcareous marl, had become the English base. He was told of the Russian attack, and the battle on the Upland, and the magnificent Light Cavalry charge that had thrilled the watching world to wonder, and admiration, and pity, and wrath, but a few days before....

"There was loss upon our side, naturally. But upon the side of the British it is astonishing what slaughter!" pursued the newsvendor. "And what numbers of wounded there are to be dealt with Monsieur may conceive. In litters, or upon the backs of mules and horses, they are being conveyed to the coast, where the transport-vessels wait to receive and carry them to the Bosphorus. On board—Heaven knows whether they will get any medical aid or surgical treatment until they arrive at the Hospital Barracks of Scutari.... And even there—since the English Army owns no trained nurse-attendants, or sanitary organization—and the building covers some six miles of ground and accommodates—according to the published reports—fifteen thousand men—the greater number of these poor devils are likely to spit up their souls unaided! For what can one young, high-bred English lady, aided by a handful of Catholic Sisters of Mercy and Protestant *religieuses*, do to assuage the sufferings of thousands? Why—nothing at all! Not even so much as *that*!"

He shrugged again as he snapped his fingers, and then added, with one of his curious little skips upon the pavement:

"I can picture that young lady, for I, like all my family, have the gift of imagination. She is flat-chested, Monsieur, as are all the English Meeses. She has hair like tow, blue eyes, round, pale, and staring—a nose without charm or character—projecting teeth, bony red hands, sharp elbows, and large flat feet. She is clothed in garments of colors that shriek at you—she carries an English Protestant Bible and a bottle of smelling-salts in her reticule—and a red guide-book under her arm. She is immensely rich and execrably sensible, *avec un grain de folie*. A little cracked, like all the rest of her tribe. And she will be confident in herself and in her mission to-day, but to-morrow, Monsieur!—to-morrow she will have a crisis of the nerves, and resign her commission from the British War Office. And—I predict it confidently—take a berth on the next passenger-steamer bound for her island of——"

The close of the sentence was snatched from the speaker's lips by the hurricane-passage of another of the gray-painted expresses, crowded with English troops. It flashed by and was gone. With the thin hair upon his big head yet stirring with the wind of its passage, the hunchback said, pointing to the lowered indicator of the up-train signal:

"The Paris mail is due in another moment.... Monsieur is traveling by that train?"

But Dunoisse, hardly knowing why, responded with another question.

"The English lady who has gone out to the great Hospital of Scutari to nurse the British wounded.... Oblige me by telling me her name?"

The deformed newspaper-seller answered, not knowing that he spoke with the mouth of Destiny:

"Merling, Monsieur; Mademoiselle Ada Merling.... Just Heaven!... Is Monsieur ill?"...

For a mist had come before the burning eyes of the man who heard, and his heart had knocked once, heavily within his breast, and then ceased beating. Another moment, and the thin red stream within his veins, rushed upon the ceaseless, hurrying circle of its life-journey, bearing a definite message to his brain....

His star of pure, benignant womanhood, his light of hope and healing had risen in the pestilence-smitten, war-ridden East. Well, he would follow her there. And, if she would hear him, he would tell her all, and ask one word of pitying kindness to carry with him on the path he meant to tread.

Dead Marie-Bathilde had pointed it out with her little shrunken finger. He seemed to hear her saying: "For Peace is only reached by the Way of Expiation."

To have Carmel in the blood is no light heritage. Thenceforth the feet of Hector Dunoisse were to be set with inflexible purpose upon that way of thorns and anguish. He lived but to atone.

LXXXVIII

About this time a new voice began to be heard in England, a big insistent voice that the deafest ears could not shut out. It spoke with candid fearlessness and direct simplicity. It painted, with rough, sure touches, in the very colors of life, pictures that were living and real. It gave praise where praise was due. It pointed out neglects and denounced abuses, having begun by drawing the attention of Britannia to the fact that the sick among her troops—and we had brought the Cholera with us from England—had been landed without blankets or nourishment at Gallipoli.

Looking back through many yellowed, time-faded columns of this date, one sees the formless, weltering confusion upon which the Cimmerian darkness that is dear to Officialdom heavily brooded, pierced by a ray of pure dazzling light. And presently the thick mists were to be scattered—the bat-winged demons of Ignorance, Incapacity, Meanness, Neglect, Indifference, and Carelessness, Mismanagement, Corruption, Greed, and Venality, exorcised and—if not absolutely banished—at least deprived of power to work unlimited misery and ruin upon Humanity, by the timely intervention of that beneficent Genius, the Influence of the Daily Press.

What time the Brigade of Guards were encamped upon the grass-slopes of Scutari, near the great Cemetery where the wild dogs and the nightingales sang all the night through, a little blue striped tent had sprung up on the flank of the Cut Red Feathers. Between 2 and 6 a. m., Tussell, War Correspondent of *The Thunderbolt*, was occasionally to be found inside, writing, upon a saddle, and by the light of a tallow dip stuck in an empty whiskey-bottle, the letters that were presently to wake all England up.

When the cases containing the new Minié rifles were opened, and the weapons they contained served out to the Cut Red Feathers and their neighbors, the Bearskins Plain, in lieu of the old smooth-bore Brown Bess, this intrusive person—destined to earn an unfading halo of popularity by telling unpleasant truths with force and vigor—happened, by the merest accident, to be upon the ground.

The odor of cabbaging was rank in the nostrils—not only of young Mortimer Jowell—as the contents of the cases were distributed. For only the top layers consisted of Miniés. Removing these new and serviceable weapons of warfare, the Armorer-Sergeant and his minions laid bare—what a heterogeneous collection of obsolete and discarded firelocks, bearing the marks of no less than fifty different corps!

Roars of Homeric laughter went up from the ranks as the men stood at ease and handled the interesting relics. And Morty's C. O. promptly returned Brown Bess to her original owners, conferred the Miniés upon certain Regimental sharpshooters, tumbled the rusty relics back into their cases, and returned them whence they came. And the War Office—which had contracted with Crowell for the supply of the new rifles, maintained a Rhadamanthine silence—and Crowell, a member of the great fraternity not previously mentioned, preserved a discreet opaqueness.... Of his blunt iron swords that would not cut through Russian helmets and great-coats; of his soft-iron, short-handled picks and mattocks, that bent and buckled and broke in the frost-bitten hands of the soldiers toiling at the trenches before Sevastopol—Tussell, War Correspondent of *The Thunderbolt*, told us later on.

The myrmidons of other Fleet Street rags, following Tussell's lead, presently took to telling the truth in ladlefuls. There was no silencing them. They would write home. And Jowell, Cowell, Sowell, Crowell, Dowell, Bowell, and Co., danced and popped like chestnuts on a red-hot shovel as they perused the columns containing their latest revelations. And when one ink-smeared varlet presumed to weigh in with a copy of the official statement regarding the *personnel* of the Medical Department of the Eastern Expedition—which afforded for the comfort and relief of twenty-seven thousand men of all arms, two hundred and four medical officers; including one chief Apothecary and three dispensers of medicines—and provided no ambulance-corps, beyond the stretcher-carrying bandsmen—and revealed the fact that three out of the four Divisions of troops landed in the Crimea had been without their knapsacks since the day of disembarkation—even Officialdom wriggled uneasily in its well-stuffed chair at the War Office Council Board; and Britannia, lulled to hypnotic slumber by the mellifluous voice and snaky eye of Sire my Ally, drowsily wondered whether it would not be as well to think about waking up?

Those Letters from the Seat of Hostilities, how eagerly they were devoured by the British Public! How they were welcomed, discussed, denounced, and praised! And presently, when sorrow and bereavement came knocking at the doors of people of all ranks and classes, and every hour added to the huge roll of Deaths issued from the War Office—even Routine and Red Tape were powerless to silence those voices that clamored in Britannia's drowsy ears....

"Wake up!" they cried, "wake up! for your sons are dying! On the stinking, earthen floors of the hospital-tents—on the naked, filthy planks of the hospital-ships, they lie unhelped, unfed, unclothed, unpitied! Doomed to be the food of vermin, flies, and maggots!—sealed as the victims of

Fever, Gangrene, and Cholera, unless you wake and come speedily to the rescue!"

And so, with a tremendous start, Britannia WOKE UP.

Over the United Kingdom broke a cyclone of indignant grief and generous emotion. Not a woman but was enveloped and carried off her feet. From the seamstress in the attic to the Queen in her palace the wave spread, the thrill was communicated, the magic worked its wonder.... Do you remember when that cry of pity came from the heart of Victoria? She was more a sovereign in the true sense of the word, at that moment, than any Queen that had ever reigned before her on the throne of England.... She atoned for a thousand faults, she reached the hearts of her people once and forever, with those outstretched, womanly hands of sorrow and compassion and love.

Perhaps you can see my grandmother rushing to her store-cupboards, filling boxes with pots of home-made jam, pound-cakes, bottles of calf's-foot jelly, potted meats, and pickled shalots. Imagine how my Aunts—typifying the younger generation of Britain's daughters—pitched *The Ladies' Mentor*—always gracefully reticent about the War—behind the fire—tore up their Berlin-woolwork patterns—threw the green baize cover over the canary's cage—boxed the King Charles spaniel's ears—had hysterics—came out of them—and set to scraping lint with a vengeance. The most rigorous spinster knitted waistcoats and socks and undervests. Professed man-haters compromised on helmet-caps and muffetees.

My Aunt Julietta bottled broth, scraped lint, cut out and made Hospital shirts in a kind of sacred frenzy. Her Captain Goliath was not amongst the wounded, but any day—who knew?... Her round face grew puckered, and her pretty eyes dim by dint of searching through War Office Casualty Lists. She pictured her hero on outpost-duty on the snowy plains, knee-deep in the freezing slush of the muddy trenches—many a time when he was sheltered by a roof of ragged canvas, and warmed by a scanty fire of grubbed up-roots. She dreamed of him as starving when he had cleared his tin platter-full of hot fried biscuit and scraps of salt pork, it may be. And how often she saw him brought back dead and bloody from a sortie, when he was roaring some stave of an Irish song over the punch-bowl, I leave you to guess. Yet for all that, the Captain took his manly share of peril, privation, suffering and hardship with the best of them; and a day dawned when—oh! with what tears of anguish, and delight, and rapture—my Aunt got him back again....

You have heard how the call came to the less heroic daughters of England.... To Ada Merling, dreaming one gold October noon under her Wraye Rest cedars, it came, as of old, to the virgin Joan of Arc. If Tussell of the roaring bull-voice and the pronounced Hibernian brogue was her St. Michael, who shall wonder?... God chooses His Messengers when and where He wills.

For as the Sainted Maid was chosen, consecrated, inspired, and sped, nearly five hundred years before upon the errand that was to end in the deliverance of her dear land of France; so certainly the path this woman was to tread was pointed by a Hand from Heaven; so surely the words she was to utter, the deeds that were to be done by her—were prompted and helped by the Angelic Messengers of God.

One wonders whether any foreknowledge of her high fate, her great and wonderful destiny, the sufferings she was to alleviate and soothe; the sorrows she was to pity and console; the crying wrongs she was to redress; the prim and mean and narrow Officialism her generosity was to put to shame,—may have been vouchsafed her, ere that sunset hour?

I do not think she ever dreamed of what was coming. Her path was set about with homely duties; her mild, beneficent influence was exercised in a comparatively narrow sphere. She would have smiled if it had been told her that a time was at hand when the demands upon her trained skill, her fertile brain, her vast genius for organization were to be varied and innumerable; when the road before her was to widen out into a vast Field of Battle where nations strove with nations in bloody combat; where the smoke of cannon blotted out Heaven, and Earth shook with the roll of iron-shod wheels and the trampling of iron-shod hoofs, and was furrowed deep with trenches and honeycombed with mines, and mines yet more; though the picks and shovels of the haggard men who dug them tunneled their dreadful way through the festering bodies of the buried dead, whom Famine and Pestilence—no less than steel and shot and shell—had slain.

With her to decide was to act, swiftly and certainly. To Bertham, once again in divided, incomplete authority at the War Office, the quivering butt for every shaft launched at Officialdom, she wrote in words like these:

"It is asked whether there is not at least one woman in England who is fitted by knowledge, training, character, and experience to organize and take a Staff of nurses to the East, in aid of these suffering soldiers? I know that I am capable of undertaking the leadership. If you think me worthy, say so, and I will go!"

Twenty-four hours before, as the Emergency Sitting had ended, and friend and foe had passed out into the cool of the Westminster night air, a pale man with long black hair and a markedly sarcastic cast of countenance, had said in Bertham's hearing to a colleague of the Opposition benches:

"The Government needs three remarkable men to save the country at this crisis. It has not got them, and that *Thunderbolt* fellow knows it has not! Therefore he appeals to the nation, on the principle that if nine tailors go to the making of one ordinary son of Adam, nineteen millions of average Britons of both sexes may produce a reliable Prime Minister, a capable Commander-in-Chief, and an efficient Secretary at War!"

Disraeli's gibe failed to wound. Bertham was devoid of the base quality of vanity. Single-handed he had striven against colossal and venerable prejudices, moss-grown abuses, corruption wide-spreading as unsuspected and unseen. He had fought a good fight against overwhelming odds, and he knew it. As he walked home with his long light step and through the graying gaslit streets, he repeated the beginning of the wit's poisoned sentence:

"'We need three remarkable men to save the country. We have not got them.'" And then he added: "But we have one woman who might help us! Why have I not thought before of Ada Merling? I will write and ask her now!"

No answer came to his letter. We may know she had not received it. She was hurrying to London, to beg him to let her go. Ignorant of this, unable to endure suspense longer, he went next morning early to the house in Cavendish Street, and found that she was there.

She had arrived on the previous night. She expected him—came hurrying into the hall at the sound of his voice, speaking to the servant. And her air seemed so gallant, her eyes were so beautiful and calm and courageous, that the sick heart of Robert Bertham lifted on a wave of hope as he looked at her, and said, taking her hand in his courtly way:

"In this my hour of sorrow and humiliation I have turned to you, dear Ada. Give me your answer. Decide—not as friendship dictates, but as reason counsels, and let your great heart have the casting-vote. It is tender to those suffering men, I know!"

She had answered in that voice of warm, human kindness:

"It would break for them, if it could not serve them infinitely better by keeping in working-order. But you speak of your letter. Has not mine?—no!—mine must have traveled up in the very train by which I came. You will find it on your table when you go home presently, asking you to lay upon me if you think fit, this burden of duty. Ah! if you do, God knows that I will bear it faithfully as long as He gives me strength."

So she had entreated to be let help when her help was the one thing needful! A passionate gratitude dimmed his brilliant eyes as he looked at her. He had no words, who was usually eloquent. But he took her white, strong, slender hand, and stooped low over it and reverently kissed it. Then he threw on his hat in his careless, breezy fashion, and, hardly speaking, and with his face turned from her, went upon his way.... And so out of the story, taking with him the love and respect of all true men and women, for one of whom, in the best and most chivalrous sense of the words, it may be written:

"*He loved and labored for his fellow-men!*"

LXXXIX

In the Paris mail, as in the Southern Express speeding to Marseilles, Dunoisse, *per* medium of the newspapers, plunged once more into the arena of worldly affairs.

At Marseilles he learned of the combined attack of Soimonoff, Pauloff, and Dannenberg in concert with Menschikoff; and of the great battle that had raged two days previously, upon the scrub-bushed slopes that rise to a plateau from the yellow marl cliff, honeycombed with the cave-dwellings of the ancient Tauri, and topped with the gray line of battlements, broken by round towers, that are known as the Ruins of Inkerman. And of the War Council resulting in the decision that the Allied Forces should winter in the Tauric Chersonese.

At the Docks of Marseilles the landing-quays were paved with sick and wounded French soldiers, just landed from two Imperial Government transports, newly returned from the seat of War. Lying upon straw and bedding, awaiting the arrival of the hospital-ambulances, they were very patient, even cheerful—with the smiling spirit of their gallant nation—despite the ravages of cholera, and fever, and dysentery, and the dreadful wounds too many of them bore. Those thus disfigured or mutilated were the merriest. Those whom sickness had robbed of the joy of real fighting regretted their bad luck, and to the pitying exclamations or horrified looks of strangers they had one reply:

"It's bad, Madame, or Monsieur! but when you lend soldiers to the Sultan of Turkey to play with, you must expect to get them back a little chipped and damaged. We are pretty to look at, compared with those who are coming presently, sacred thunder! But what would you have? It's the Fortune of War!"

The steamer by which Dunoisse took passage for the East was crowded to overflowing with French and English officers going out to fill up gaps created by Alma and Balaklava casualties. Newspaper correspondents of both nations, Greek and Turkish merchants, were aboard her. Also, a Queen's Messenger, a Spanish dancer going out in charge of an aunt to fulfill an engagement at the Imperial Opera House of Constantinople, and some ladies of the French and British Diplomatic Staffs, returning to their winter villas at Pera and Therapia.

Great Indiamen crowded with English troops; gray-painted, red-flagged, and numbered transports with drafts of French, thronged the Mediterranean sea-ways. Ship-loads of invalids of both nations passed, with a crowding of haggard, unshaven faces at the taffrail, and troop-deck gun-ports; and a waving of caps in thin hands, and a feeble, unsteady cheer. A few homeward-bound warships towed Russian prizes, and carried Russian prisoners, red-bearded, flat-faced men in gray caps and ragged gray greatcoats, on their way to the hulks at Toulon, or Sheerness, or Devonport; who squatted in the 'tween decks or upon the forecastle under sentry guard, and played with noisy laughter and good-humored horse-play a childish game of cards, in which the forfeits consisted of raps upon the nose.

Among his countrymen and countrywomen, Dunoisse had at first feared recognition; but, thanks to the change wrought in him by sickness and mental suffering, the eyes of people whose names and faces were familiar to him, glanced at him indifferently and moved away.

They gossiped in his near vicinity as freely as though he were deaf or ignorant of their language. One day it was mentioned in his hearing that de Moulny, Secretary-Chancellor of the Ministry of the Interior during the Presidency, had abandoned the diplomatic career, received Holy Orders, and gone out to the Crimea as chaplain-in-charge of one of the war-hospitals at the French base of Kamiesch. Upon another occasion a knot of French officers discussed with mordant relish the funeral of St. Arnaud....

The obsequies of the Imperial favorite had taken place, with all the pomp of military and official state, at the Chapel of the Invalides, at the end of October. The galleries had been packed with tearful ladies in black and bugles.... Ambassadors had held the ends of the pall.... The entire Army had acted as chief mourner.... And a representative of the Emperor had conveyed to Madame la Maréchale the following touching message from his Imperial master:

"*I simply transfer to you, Madame, the sentiments I entertained for my departed friend.*"

Which noble and touching utterance, for some reason, tickled these Gallic warriors hugely. But he was droll, they said, that fellow Badinguet! Depend upon it, he would presently compose an epitaph which would make everybody laugh like mad.... One of the gossipers suggested that "*Morte la bête mort le venin*" (which is a polite version of "Dead dogs cannot bite") would look well in gilt letters upon the memorial tablet dedicated to the virtues of the deceased.

Another quotation occurred to Dunoisse as he stood leaning on the bulwark not far from the chatterers:

"*I am taken in mine own toils; I am fallen in the pit I dug for others: Death hath pierced me while I sent forth my swift arrows against the lives of many men.*"

Though those men had died, and other men would die, there was no help for it! That was the word brought by those silent ghastly messengers who came drifting down from the seat of War.

As the steamer threaded her way amidst the swirling currents of the Cyclades, their accusing shapes began to start up, in some eddy of water and sunshine, or water and moonlight, under the steamer's side, and vanish in the flurry of her paddles and reappear in her wake, drifting away....

Sometimes they were animals of draught, and Commissariat and burden, who, despite the bloating of long immersion, had plainly died of want. Or they were shapeless forms, swathed in canvas, of sick or wounded soldiers who had died upon the homeward-bound transports, and had been consigned to the deep, sewn up in hammocks too scantily shotted. Or they came in little knots and groups of red coats and blue coats, consorting and intermingling, parting and drifting on in silent, passionless acquiescence with the will of the winds and tides.

These were the dead, French and Turkish, but chiefly English soldiers who had sailed from Varna in September, and had been thrown overboard during the transit of the Black Sea. They were heralds of the hospital-ships that, packed from stem to stern with unspeakable misery and suffering, would soon be hurrying down the Bosphorus on their way to Scutari.

Young soldiers, raw recruits upon their way to Gallipoli, peeping rosy-gilled or pale-faced through the gun-ports on the troop-decks, would jerk back their heads in consternation as they encountered an eyeless grin of greeting from one of these stark voyagers, of whom the great bossy-mailed turbot, and the giant sturgeon of the Black Sea, grown dainty with full feeding, had merely taken toll, and passed on to the ravenous sharks and the huge rays and octopi of the Ægean, and Ionian, and Mediterranean seas.

"Hail, comrade! Soon shall you be as I am, food for Death the Insatiable!" the silent one would say, and with the wave of a rigid arm, pass on. And the recruit, with a sick heart under his coarse red jacket, would crack a brutal jest, or the older man would comment, spitting into the oily water:

"Poor beggar, he do look bad, sure*ly*! Well, War or Peace, that's what we all will come to at the last!"

Whilst the Zouave or Voltigeur would shrug, pipe in mouth, and say, grimacing at the foul exhalations of corruption, and the fœtid odors of the sludge:

"He stinks, our friend there, sacred name of a pig! and he is not quite so handsome as when his sweetheart last embraced him, but what of that? It's the Fortune of War! Our Army of France has been pruned; ten thousand out of seventy-five thousand brave fellows have spit up their souls of cholera and dysentery. *Saperlipopette*! it's the Fortune of War!"

And the wheeling cloud of gulls that came with and followed the visitors would scream as though in derision, and settle again to their feast in the transport's wake. And the Voltigeur, or Chasseur, or Zouave would toss off a glass of Cognac and return to the game of dice or cards. But Dunoisse leaned upon the taffrail of the steamer, and stared at the floating dead men with eyes that were full of horror. It seemed to him that the empty sockets glared at him, that the stark hands pointed at him, that the lipless mouths cried to him: "Thou art Cain!"

Had he not been going to *her* he could not have borne it.... He said to himself that, of all women living, Ada Merling alone would pity and understand.

Said a ruddy-haired, high-colored, handsome young British giant to another, graver, older man, and both were officers of a crack Dragoon Regiment going out to fill up Balaklava chinks in Redlett's Heavy Brigade:

"That white-haired polyglotter in the shabby togs, who answers you and me in English, and talks Parisian French with the French fellows, and Greek with the Cypriote currant-merchant who makes such a hog of himself at the cabin *table d'hôte*—and is civil in Spanish to the opera-dancer and her aunt from Madrid whenever he can't avoid 'em—and swops Turkish with the Osmanli Bey who's been Consul for the Porte at Marseilles—is a queer kind of chap, uncommonly! Do you know, I've seen him looking at those floating soger-men as if he'd killed 'em all!"

Answered the speaker's senior officer, lighting a large cheroot:

"Why should he look as if he had when he hasn't, and couldn't have? My dear Foltlebarre, you're talking bosh!"

"Bosh, if you like, Major," agreed the ruddy-haired boy good-humoredly; "but such a melancholy customer as that white-haired chap I never yet came across!" He broke off to cry: "By Gad! what a thundering big Government transport! That must be *The Realm*, going out with the forage and stores and winter clothing to the tune—a fellow I know at Lloyd's told me—of five hundred thousand pounds. They've been keeping her back in Docks at Portsmouth on the chance of the war being over before the winter, and now they're rushing her out for everything she's worth!"

She was a great three-masted screw steamship of two thousand six hundred tons, and as, with her Master's pennant flying from her main top-gallant mast, and the red Admiralty flag with the foul anchor and the Union Jack canton bannering splendidly from her mizzen halyards—she bustled by—hurrying under full steam and every stitch of canvas for her pilotage through the Dardanelles—she was to the inexperienced eye a gallant sight. But the experienced eye saw something else in her than bigness. And the senior officer who had been invited to admire her, being a keen and experienced yachtsman—shook his head.

"My own opinion—supposing you care to have it!—is that your friend at Lloyd's—take it he belongs to one of the firms of underwriters who've insured her?—is likely to find himself in the cart. For I've seen some crank Government tubs in my time, and sailed in 'em—very much to my disadvantage. But never a cranker one than this, give you my word of honor! Why, she sits on her keel with a crooked list to port that a bargeman couldn't miss the meaning of. And she has no more buoyancy than a log of green wood. Look at our skipper shaking his head at the Second Officer as he shuts his glass up. Lay you any money you please he wouldn't like to have to chaperon her through a November Black Sea squall! By Jupiter! you were right just now, and I beg your pardon, Foltlebarre!"

He had been following the course of the "thundering big transport" through a Dollond telescope, and the face of the white-haired man in the shabby togs, as he leaned upon the taffrail of the passenger deck forward, had come into his field of view.

He said, after another look: "It's a disease, the existence of which is denied by the Faculty, but he has got it! That man is dying of a broken heart!"

You were right, Major, who were doomed yourself to die so soon in the freezing mud of Balaklava. But the end did not come for many, many years.

A dark-blue haze hung over the Sea of Marmora. Rain fell, soaking those passengers who, owing to the crowding on board the vessel, had been compelled to sleep on deck. Dunoisse was one of these, and, little fitted as he was to endure hardship, he suffered. The cough returned, and with it fever and pain. But he forgot both when a wind from the southwest lifted the fog, rolled it up like a curtain, and showed the cypress-canopy of the great Cemetery of Scutari hanging like a thunderous cloud against the rose-flushed eastern sky. And as the steamer entered the Bosphorus, the dusk shape of Bûlgurlû Daghi, girt about the flanks with snow-white mosques and glittering palaces and fairy gardens, rose into view; and on the grassy slopes that climbed from the water's edge—where the Brigade of Guards had camped, and where the black and yellow striped tents of the German Legion now dotted the hillside—you saw, as you see to-day, the great quadrangle of yellow stone, flanked with spire-topped square towers—that had been the barracks of the Turkish Imperial Guard.

One traveler drank the vision in with a sense of revived hope and a wonderful thrill of expectation. And as though his unuttered thought had communicated itself to another, an English infantry officer standing near him turned to another man and said, gravely pointing to the building on the green hillside:

"She is there!"

And the heart of Dunoisse echoed with unspeakable gladness:

"She is there!"

XC

For days the dark malodorous blue fog had hung over Stamboul. Now the southwest wind had rolled it up like a curtain and carried it away into Syria, and the great imperial city of marble domes and snowy minarets tipped with golden crescents, cypress-groves, and fountains, bagnios and beggars, sylvan vistas and screeching stinks, lay basking in golden November sunshine under a sky of purest turquoise. The scarlet and yellow tinting of the vines and creepers that draped the walls and the balconies of the black and red and white and yellow houses, alone told of winter, like the deepened crimson of the robin's breast, and the pale purple of the crocus-like colchicum starring the meadows by the Sweet Waters. For those who chose, it would be summer. And all the vices of the Old World and the New came out to bask in the warmth and the beauty. And the roar of traffic and the confusion of tongues in the offal-ridden, stinking thoroughfares and on the filthy quays, above the broad belt of discarded straw slippers, rusty tin kettles, and wooden basins, and decomposing cats and dogs, that rose and fell upon the margin of the crystal-blue Bosphorus—deafened the ears and dazed the brain.

The roadsteads of Beshiktash were packed with French and English battleships and transports. The vessels of the Turkish Fleet, with the great golden lions sprawling on their prows, were anchored lower down. Innumerable gilded caïques, richly draped and cushioned, propelled by rowers in gay liveries and crowded—not only by Turkish ladies veiled in the yashmak, and swathed in the feridjeh, but by English and French women of Society—dressed in the latest Parisian fashions, and accompanied by uniformed officers and civilian friends in correct afternoon attire—shot to and fro over the surface of the harbor; seeming to avoid, yet encircling and following a large galley, gorgeous as a dying dolphin in colors of crimson and silver and green, and closely attended by one or two vessels of magnificence only inferior to the first, which had been waiting all the morning at the Dolma Bâghchi Palace Stairs.

His Sublime Majesty, the Padishah, a sallow, black-bearded, impassive personage—suggestive, in his tightly-buttoned frock coat and plain fez, of a dark blue glass medicine-bottle with a red seal—attended by one or two privileged Ministers, corpulent and spectacled dignitaries with gray beards, was pleased to take the air of the harbor instead of seeking the refreshment of the Sweet Waters; and it was etiquette to follow, at a respectful distance, the galley containing the Luminary of the World. Thus, the gilded caïques containing the veiled inmates of the harems of Stamboul and Pera and

Therapia, or the well-dressed ladies of the Legations and Consulates with their male companions, followed the turns and windings of the monster dolphin, like a flock of variegated Pacific parrot-fish, while the fervid sunshine poured down upon the glory and the loveliness, the filth and the degradation of the ancient seat of the Byzantine and Ottoman Empires, and all the vices of the East and of the West mingled in the olla-podrida of nations and of tongues.

Veiled and muffled Turkish ladies, elevated above the mud upon wooden clogs, went by, with chattering Nubian women in attendance on them. Old men in green turbans hawked *coco* and sweetmeats; gypsy-girls, brazen of glance and bold of tongue, trafficked in fortunes and did business in smiles. Turkish soldiers of the Reserve, garrisoning the capital—the fine flower of the Ottoman Army being with Omar Pasha at Eupatoria—shambled by, smoking cigarettes, or munching lumps of coarse ration-bread. And Jews, Armenians, Germans of the Legion, Styrians, Levantines, Africans, Bulgarians, Wallachs, Czechs, rubbed shoulders with men of every rank and branch of the Sister Services of Britain and her Ally of France.

And amongst the English officers who thronged the European Clubs, and crowded the hotels, and strolled upon the public places, were well-groomed, dandified, curled and whiskered Adonises who had been the spoiled and petted beauty-men of their regiments at Home, and were going out to Balaklava under the impression that they were heroes. But when they encountered the men who had come down invalided from the Front, the luster fled from their Macassared whiskers, and the assurance of their manners underwent alteration. For these were the Real Thing—the genuine article—and only for the genuine article were the ladies, English and French, Greek or Italian—possessed of ears and eyes.

Upon the deck of a large, luxurious steam-yacht, anchored with other private vessels in the roadstead below Beshiktash, and flying the Ensign of St. George, with the white, red-crossed, gold-crowned burgee of the Royal Yacht Squadron, were gathered so many men and women representative of Society in Paris or London, that the background might have been Cowes, or Ryde, or Henley at the height of the season, instead of the European shore of the Bosphorus in November drear. And though many brilliant uniforms were present, with handsome men inside some of them, the loveliest ladies, icily ignoring these, vied with each other in attentions to certain hairy, ragged, bandaged, and limping tatterdemalions, who sported their rags with insufferable arrogance, or the profound reposeful pride of old Egyptian kings. For they were officers of Infantry and Artillery who had been wounded at the Alma, or they were Cavalrymen whose stained red jackets, striped overalls, and battered brass helmets, proclaimed them to be of Redlett's Heavy Brigade.... And he who lolled under the green-and-white after-deck awning in a big Indian cane chair, with a little court of admiring beauties gathered round him, and the wife of the English Ambassador sitting upon his right hand—the man whose astrakhan-trimmed Hussar jacket, stiff with tarnished gold lace, was slashed to ribbons; whose busby had been shorn by a sword-cut of its red plume and gilded cord—whose crimson overalls were stained like the tights of a street tumbler—who had lost his sabretasche and half a spur, and whose boots—once the pride of a Pall Mall maker's heart—were slit in places and had burst in others, was the most cosseted, complimented, caressed and waited-on of all those who basked in the light of admiring glances and the warmth of approving smiles.

As Houris in rustling silks, marvelous lace mantles, and bonnets of the latest Parisian mode hovered about him, ministering with champagne-cup, Russian tea, caviar-sandwiches, little Turkish pastries, and large Turkish cigarettes to his imperial needs, you saw him as a man of forty-nine or thereabouts, tall and lean in figure, sinewy of muscle, long of bone. His features were boldly aquiline and not unhandsome; his eyes were of keen, sparkling yellowish hazel, his reddish curling hair and bushy, untrimmed whiskers of the same shade were just sprinkled with gray. The outline of his jaw had the sharp salient line that distinguished the bows of the brand-new pivot-gun screw-steamer that lay anchored with the French and British line-of-battleships in the roads at Beshiktash; his smile revealed a magnificent unbroken row of shining white teeth, and his left arm was bandaged and slung. Also, he had a Russian saber-cut on his sharp cheekbone, and a Russian bullet in the muscles of his ribs made him catch his breath and grimace occasionally. For this egregious dandy, the owner of the luxurious steam-yacht and many things more desirable; who said "aw" for "are" and "wheiah" for "where," and "Bay Jove!" with the drawl one has heard Bancroft use in Robertson comedies, was Lord Cardillon, the Brigadier who had led the famous Light Cavalry Charge at Balaklava, on the white-legged, big brown horse—who was even then being pampered with cakes and sugar in his loose-box in the 'tween decks—and whose tail the hero-worshiping crowd were to pluck bare when he got back to London.

Now, as the gold-and-crimson twenty-six-oared State caïque with the gilded whorl and the preening peacock at the prow, shot up-stream towards Therapia, Cardillon laughed, and said to the middle-aged handsome woman who sat near, the diamonds on her white hands flashing in the sunlight as she stitched at a masculine garment of coarse white calico....

"You haven't asked how my audience went off, Lady Stratclyffe?"

"I had forgotten," she answered, "but I presume nothing new or original was said or done, and that you were dismissed with the customary compliments?"

His laugh, rather sharp and hard, rang out again clearly. People were listening, and his white teeth gleamed in rather a self-conscious smile.

After the usual stage-wait—filled up with coffee and *chibuks*—we found his Sublimity at the top of a long crystal staircase, illuminated with red glass lusters. The Shadow of Omnipotence took exception to the condition of my toggery. He said to Prince Galamaki, who presented me: "*Mâshallah!* but the infidel's clothes are torn and filthy! Does the Queen of England pay her Pashas so badly that they cannot afford to buy new uniforms?"

There was a burst of laughter, masculine and feminine. He went on, in the dandified drawl, pulling at his bushy whiskers with the free unbandaged hand:

"Galamaki—who had the honor of meeting you at Petersburg, Lady Stratclyffe—and who had attended to make his bow prior to leaving for the Embassy at Vienna, looked civilly agonized, not having mentioned to the Padishah that I understand Turkish pretty well. So I said, in that language, that in England we considered that the uniform of a soldier who had seen Service was his robe of honor. And that I had dressed to wait upon the Sultan as I should dress to wait upon the Queen!"

There were "bravos" and the clapping of hands. Faces of both sexes turned towards the speaker; and though he hid his pride and exultation at the homage under an affectation of cynical indifference, it expanded his sharply-cut nostril and burned in his light hazel eyes. He went on:

"Though the look of some of these fellows we're waiting for might scare her...."

"Oh no!" said Lady Stratclyffe, looking up from her work. "How could you possibly imagine that?"

"English ladies are all so brave, nowadays!" he returned, with an inflection of sarcasm.

Said a velvet voice behind him, with a sweet foreign accent that added honey to the implied compliment:

"Milord, the English ladies but follow the example of the English gentlemen!"

"Capital, Madame de Roux!" called out a handsome gray-haired man, rather formally and stiffly dressed for a yacht-party, who had been conversing with a French officer in Zouave uniform. "You scatter your sugar-plums broadcast!—even a diplomatist may hope to pick up one in the scramble.... Now, if you had said 'The English Army,'—Lord Cardillon would have taken the compliment to himself!"

Cardillon returned, ignoring the prick of sarcasm:

"Madame de Roux, who is upon her way to the Crimea, to confer supreme happiness upon a gallant countryman, can afford to give English ladies due credit for bravery. When do you sail, Madame?"

She thought in two days' time.... He said, with gallant regret:

"I wish I might have had the pleasure of carrying you there in the *Foam Star*. But I am compelled to return to England, worse luck!"

She said, with her lovely smile, as Lord Stratclyffe was buttonholed by a gray-whiskered bluff-faced Rear-Admiral:

"There are many who will rejoice at what you so much regret. For me, I have been granted a passage upon one of my country's war-steamers—thanks to the influence of one who is soon to become far nearer than a friend...."

He said, with a certain sharp subtlety, understanding that she referred to her approaching marriage with one of the Generals of France's Eastern Army:

"He should be grateful for whom you risk so much! But at Kamiesch you will not suffer the inconveniences of Balaklava. Your countrymen have already built a harbor and macadamized the principal roads. They have a railway to their Front—public conveyances—field and general hospitals—ambulances, and a corps of trained attendants, supplemented by Sisters of Charity. In fact, everything that we have not—and that we ought to have!"

"And whose is the fault," she asked, "that you have not what you ought to have?"

His debonair face suddenly changed into a mask of stiff Officialism. His eyes hardened. His lips lost their jocund curve as they dropped out the formula:

"I am really not aware!"

He shrugged his shoulders, and turned the conversation to the beauty of the sables in which she was wrapped, leaning close as he spoke of them with the air of a connoisseur, and looking at the wearer. Some other women present there were younger and more brilliant. Not one, he thought, exhaled the charm that breathed from Madame de Roux. He noted the fine lines about her eyes and mouth, and on her forehead, and the thread or two of white that showed amidst the silken black hair. Its superb coils were crowned with a wide-brimmed hat of cavalier fashion, black with drooping plumes of mauve. The tone of half-mourning characterized the exquisite array of one who had been widowed a year previously; conveying the impression of sorrow that had mellowed into resignation, bereavement not unwilling to be consoled.... Bands of mauve velvet, fastened with clasps of cameos set in brilliants, closed her full lace sleeves at the wrists and encircled the lovely throat that rose above the chemisette. Ample skirts of black *gros de Naples*, stamped with mauve velvet flowers, billowed about her; exquisite feet adorning little kid boots peeped from the expansive folds. With his eyes upon the perfect arch of the revealed instep, Cardillon sighed, envying this exquisite creature's future husband, that noted fire-eater Leguerrier.

We remember Grandguerrier, formerly Governor-General of Algeria, whom the retirement of Boisrobert was soon to place in the chief command of France's Expeditionary Forces. Thick-set, short, hot-tempered—burnt brown by African suns, with a close cap of gray hair coming down low on the sagacious forehead—with bloodshot brown eyes, snub nose, deep-cut mouth pouting under the bristling black mustache, the middle-aged commander of Zouaves and Spahis appeared what he was, a gallant soldier.... How loyally he stood by England when the imperious hand at the Tuileries checked maddeningly at the electric bridle, we never should forget!

"*On the 7th of June the Mamelon Vert, the Ouvrages Blancs and the Quarries must be taken. Lord Dalgan and I have decided it. Ours is the responsibility.*" And so broke up the Council of War. But when the stout little man on the white Arab rode through the English camps on the day after the successful attack, what roaring cheers went up from British throats at the sight of him.... And that he was tender-hearted as well as brave we know.

Cardillon had sighed, and his sighs were not generally wasted. Henriette turned upon him the eyes that had always reminded Dunoisse of moss-agates gleaming under running brook-water, and said with the subtle, half-mischievous smile that crinkled the corners of her eyelids, and hardly curved her mouth:

"*You* should have nothing left to sigh for at this hour!"

He said:

"But I have! I sigh for one of those violets you are wearing."

She glanced down at the knot of pale purple blossoms pinned at the bosom of her lawn chemisette, revealed by the unfastened mantle of sables. Emboldened by her smile, he stretched a hand to them. But she leaned back, avoiding the contact of the sinewy, sunburned, covetous fingers. She had grown pale, her eyes and lips had shadows round them—she looked older, more worn. Then, as he hesitated whether to pursue his intent or withdraw his hand, she rose in a frou-frou of silken draperies, and was gone upon the arm of Lord Stratclyffe, leaving only a perfume and a desire behind her.... And Lady Stratclyffe, looking across her sewing, said quietly:

"Answer *me*, since even our exquisite ally must not be trusted with official secrets!... With whom does the blame rest? Need our Army of Invasion have suffered all these hardships and privations and miseries? How comes it that we are so lamentably deficient in Commissariat and Transport arrangement? Why—I quote your own words—have we 'nothing that we ought to have'?"

He glanced about him before replying. But, seeing him engaged in talk with the Ambassadress, his guests had moved away, leaving an island of gleaming white planks about them. He said:

"Dear Lady Stratclyffe, the system of our Army Administrations has been, from first to last, a system of Contracts. One must own it has not been a success. Contractors are not, as a rule, trustworthy or conscientious.... Ours have not proved themselves exceptions to the rule!"

His shrug spoke volumes. She said, with hesitation:

"Surely the resources of the country——"

He answered harshly:

"The resources of the country, reported to be vast, were in our case non-existent. We could get nothing! We were upon the soil of a nation for whose liberty we were about to fight, and they treated us from the first as enemies. There's no question about it! The native Bulgarians refused to sell us grain, forage, fuel and provisions, nor would they supply us with wagons, and beasts of burden and draught, or serve us as drivers, guides or interpreters! They let us encamp where cholera and fever were rife—and so we invaded the Crimea with a weakly, invalidy, crippled army, two-thirds of 'em too weak to carry their packs and the rest horizontal—disabled or moribund! And Burgoyle rode up to the head of Varna Harbor when his Division was being put on board the transports. He shook his fist and howled—he was quite beside himself. 'Sick men to fight the Russian Imperial Guards with! Better give me dead ones!' But that we have achieved what we have, ma'am, we owe to the pith and pluck and endurance of these sick men."

"They're glorious!" she said. "They're glorious...."! And the Brigadier went on:

"They were exhausted from exposure, dropping from want of sleep, half-starved from shortage of rations when they carried the Great Redoubt, and smashed two-thirds of Menschikoff's army into gray lumps on the Alma. On the day of the Balaklava Attack neither men nor beasts had had bite or sup since the middle of the day before.... How the Light Brigade charged I hardly know; their horses' legs were tottering under 'em! And they lay down after the battle, round their smoky fires of green wood, with their baggage and camp equipment knocking about on board the transports, and nothing but a sopping wet blanket between half of 'em and the sky! And then they couldn't sleep for the neighing of the horses, and the row made by the camels and mules and bullocks. For you can't teach animals to starve in silence!—they've no pride like two-legged brutes! There's a verse I'd liked at Eton, about the lions roaring and asking their meat from God. Well, the row made me think of that and wonder whether He heard them?... And—— But I suppose they're quiet enough now!"

XCI

They were—but there a silence that is clamorous in the hearing of the Eternal. Do you see those pinched ghosts of gallant Cavalry horses tethered in the driving blizzards behind the low stone walls? A few rags of tents shivered in the piercing wind that blew from Sevastopol.... Here and there shanties of mud and earth sheltered officers, but the rank-and-file of Britannia's Army had gone down into the ground where the dead were, that they might keep the life in them. And for Blueberry and his kind there was nothing but to stand and wait for death.

Blueberry's beautiful blue-black eyes were glazed with fever, and gaunt with famine. Dreams of the full rack and the brimming manger tortured the suffering beast. And Joshua Horrotian leaned his cheek upon the broad front of his dying charger, and begged him to keep up!—and tried to comfort him. He had no fodder to give the horse—nothing but promises and kind words. He promised him Old England and plenty of sound oats again—a grassy paddock to kick his heels in—everything else a good horse might desire, if only he would keep on living.... He scraped wood-shavings fine as paper and offered them to him—and when Blueberry snuffed at them feebly, and turned his sorrowful eyes away, the tears rolled down his master's weather-beaten cheeks for the creature he had bred. He took the dying head in his ragged arms and fairly moaned over him:

"Oh Lord! Oh Lord!—my poor old Blueberry! why ever did us go a sogering?"

Blueberry had done with that hungry profession for good and all.... And Joshua Horrotian kissed him again, and staggered away to borrow a mattock to dig his grave with.... When he returned with this, narrowly escaping destruction at the hoofs of a frenzied Brocken-hunt of ownerless, starving Cavalry horses, he found that great pieces had been torn from Blueberry's yet quivering sides by these perishing comrades: and that his mane and tail had been gnawed away....

Perhaps Somewhere Else it was all made up to these blameless four-legged martyrs?... Perhaps Blueberry woke up in radiant meadows beside crystal-clear pools?... Stern theologian, do not shake your head.... You can be sure no more than I can. And there is room enough in Eternity for every soul, be it human or brute.

XCII

Still speaking of the horses, Cardillon ended:

"It sounds brutal to say it, perhaps, but they're better dead. Even if forage could have been got up to the camps in time to save them, they haven't a chance—with the Russian winter coming upon them, and no shelter of any kind. Take my word for it, we shall fight no more Cavalry actions on the soil of Crim Tartary—as sure as I'm a Brigadier on my way home to be heckled by a Government Commission of Inquiry for obeying a written order of Her Majesty's Commander-in-Chief!"

He tugged at his sandy bush of whisker and frowned. Lady Stratclyffe returned mellifluously:

"Granted that the order was an error, scrawled in a moment of perplexity or confusion—the loyal obedience and high discipline of the commanding officers and the men, have turned a blunder into a blaze of glory."

He took her hand and touched it lightly with his lips:

"Never believe, though, that my fellows cheered as they rode down the Valley under the plunging fire of all those Ruski batteries. They cursed and swore. Jove! how they did just swear!" He chuckled like a schoolboy.

"But they rode on, nevertheless," said Lady Stratclyffe; "and knowing what they are, I burn with indignation to think how they have been wronged! For it is a grievous wrong, to have cast them out upon an unfriendly foreign shore and denied them their rights of food and fuel and shelter. Without which, I quote your own words in reference to the horses, 'with the Russian winter coming upon them, they haven't a chance!'"

He begged her not to pelt him with his own rash words to his undoing. Winter clothing—stores of all kinds, huts for the troops, were even then on their way up the Bosphorus *en route* for the Black Sea.

"And," he went on, dexterously changing the topic of conversation, "you spoke of 'flurry and confusion' just now, in connection with the Commander-in-Chief. He was cool enough to perpetrate a clever epigram at the very moment when he must have realized that the order was disastrous. After all was over, it appears—a French *chef d'escadron* attached to his Staff got down from horseback, and—not to put too nice a point upon it! was violently sick. When he had somewhat recovered, he said to Lord Dalgan: 'Monseigneur, I entreat your pardon for my weakness. I have been in action many times, but this is the first massacre I ever saw!' And *he* raised his eyebrows and said in his charming French: 'Really, Major? I had imagined that you, with your regiment, played rather a prominent part in clearing the streets of Paris at the time of the *coup d'État*.' Not bad for a 'flurried' man, was it? And he was cool enough two hours later, when he rode up to me, and said, almost in the words he had used to the Chief of the Division: *'Do you know what you have done, Lord Cardillon? You have thrown away the Light Brigade!'*

"If Lord Dalgan be sometimes guilty of an injustice," she said, looking full at him with her clear gray eyes, "he has never shirked his share of privation and hardship."

The hit told. For the Brigadier had clung to the comforts of his yacht in Varna Bay and Balaklava Harbor. He had never tasted the discomforts, and knew nothing of the hardships, of the campaign.

"You are in pain?" she asked, for he had winced and thrown up his hand with the gesture of a hit fencer, and the hot color had mounted to his reddish hair.

"No, no!" He stooped to pick up her forgotten work, without concealing the twinge that the bullet gave him, for Fate had bestowed the title of the bravest upon one of the vainest of men. He added, as he laid the mass of coarse white calico back upon her knee; "Do say what this is you have been sewing at? It looks like—dare I say?—a nightshirt?"

"It looks as it ought," she answered, placidly threading a gold-eyed needle. "And Ada will applaud me. Your recognition of the garment should lend it value in her eyes."

"It is for the Hospital?" He added as she signified assent:

"How is Miss Merling, by the way? She got in yesterday morning, I understand, with her staff of nursing ladies—of all denominations, according to the newspapers.... One hopes they exaggerate?"

She answered:

"Of the thirty-eight trained nurses who have arrived with Ada, fourteen are Church of England Sisters, three or four are Congregationalists, there are a certain number of Presbyterians; and ten are Catholic Sisters of Charity from the London East End."

He screwed his mouth into the shape of a whistle, and elevated his eyebrows dubiously:

"By George! I fancy I hear the whoops of the ultra Low Church Party against Popish proselytizers and priestesses of the Romish Mysteries. The gale will break, though there is calm at present. And then—there will be a heckling of the Minister at War!"

She said, displeased:

"The Sisters are strictly bound not to speak of religious matters to any patient who is not of their Church.... I am sure that they can be depended upon. So far as I can judge, their demeanor is perfect. It struck me that they accorded a more prompt obedience to Ada's orders than the other nurses displayed. And when one remembers that they only arrived yesterday morning, the changes that have already been wrought are astonishing. I could not have believed it had I not seen!"

He asked:

"And the Lady-in-Chief. One hopes she is serenely confident in the success of her great undertaking?"

Something in his tone stung. Lady Stratclyffe answered, with her eyes upon her work:

"The undertaking is great, undoubtedly. As you must know, her letter volunteering to assume its burden crossed that which Robert Bertham had written entreating her to accept it. The Barrack Hospital here and the General Hospital will be under her sole direction. She has also the supervision of all other British Military Hospitals in the East. But I can detect no 'confidence' in her bearing.... It would be more appropriate to describe it as calm."

"The Mediterranean is calm," Cardillon said, smiling and shrugging. "Yet I've been three times wrecked in it, and once in the Ionian Sea!"

"There is no storm behind Ada's calm," said Lady Stratclyffe, "though when she found that the head and foot-pieces of two thousand iron bedsteads sent out from England in our transport *The Realm* for use in the Barrack Hospital here, had been buried under mountains of shot and empty shell, destined for the batteries of Balaklava, she was certainly not complimentary to the contractor who supplied, and the agent who undertook to pack and ship them! For the shot and shell must be unloaded at Balaklava before Ada can receive the missing parts of the beds. And that may mean a matter of weeks: From the windows of the Embassy I saw the transport pass this morning—a magnificent vessel!"

He asked:

"You are speaking of *The Realm*?" Adding, as she signified assent: "It was to her I referred just now when I said that all stores and clothing needed by the Army were even now on their way up the Bosphorus to the Black Sea. Your bungling agent is a well-known middleman between Government and its purveyors. Has a son, by the way, for whom he got a commission in the Guards, and who has good blood in him—however he may have come by it! Was mentioned in Dispatches from Headquarters after the Alma. Not bad for a callow Ensign, it appears to me!"

"Do tell me what he has done!" she begged. "I have missed so much that has been reported!"

"I'll do better than tell you. You shall hear the story from his company Captain, Caddisbroke!"

The hirsute and bandaged wearer of a superlatively shabby red coat which had formed the center of a group gathered near the saloon-cabin companion came limping on a crutch across the deck, followed by the silken swish of feminine skirts and the creak of masculine boots.

"You called me, Lord Cardillon?"

"To tell Lady Stratclyffe what young Jowell said at Alma to the dandy False Retreat in the Hussar jacket and red forage-cap."

A pretty woman with an infantile lisp wanted firtht to know what wath a Faith Retreat? The crutched newcomer answered, exchanging a glance with the Brigadier:

"We're beginning to get used to 'em, Madame de Bessarine, in moments of crisis. In fact, they're a feature of this campaign. They're mounted officers with airs of authority, and Staff epaulets and brassards as correct as their English accent. Buglers with 'em too, up in all our calls—particularly numbers Four and Seven.... And when the Light Division were beginning to reckon with the six Vladimir battalions, the 'Retire' was sounded, and down they came pell-mell, officers and men, smack into the middle of the White Tufts, who were coming on towards the river in first-class form.... They disordered their center, and jumbled the Bearskins Plain, who were advancing a little to the right of 'em. And in the confusion the Ruskis broke in on their center and left—and tried to take the Colors, and there was trouble. So Sir Bayard Baynes rode back to us—and you may guess we were well in the background, having Royalty to keep in a bandbox!—and suggested an onward movement. And the Duke of Bambridge gave in. And we came up at the double, hurraying like mad to have got the chance of a crack at 'em!—and formed on the left of the White Tufts; and had no sooner begun to pound the two great columns of gray coats into smithereens—the White Tufts file-firing while we poured volleys in—than up comes a dandy False Retreat riding with an order. *'The Duke requests the Cut Red Feathers to retire without delay!'* And the bugler-blackguard blew—and our bugles sounded down the line—and the men called out 'No, no!' And this young Jowell—acting as Lieutenant for his half-company in place of Ardenmore killed—calls out—and I heard him from the ditch I'd tumbled into when they shot me: 'The Duke never gave that order—and I'm dam' if I'll obey it!—I'm blest if I do, so there!' And when His Royal Highness heard it, he was uncommonly tickled—and said they should hear it at home!"

XCIII

The laugh went round. Men said there was thoroughly fine stuff in that fellow. Women wanted to know what he was like? Lady Stratclyffe hoped he had a mother to be proud of him. Cardillon was tugging at his auburn whiskers and, thinking of the missing head and tail-pieces of the bedsteads destined for the Hospital, wondered how many of them lay at the bottom of the holds under the munitions? Two or three hundred, he guessed, knowing the Jowellian methods. Damn the man! You came across him everywhere. He really went a bit too far!

The Ambassador's wife went on to tell him of the four miles of mattresses already laid upon the pavement in default of bedsteads, and ranged in double rows down the sides of the Barrack Hospital corridors. She was afraid the stones would strike cold, and that the long passages would be draughty in the winter.

"The men won't complain," Cardillon told her. "But are all the wards so full?"

"Four large wards," she answered him, "and half-a-dozen small rooms were found available. But there are sixteen hundred sick and wounded—including cholera patients—already within the walls. And nearly six hundred in the General Hospital, of which Ada also has superintendence.... And if the patients there, lie in filth and misery such as I saw yesterday...."

Her brows contracted and her fine lips quivered. He asked:

"You went through the wards yesterday?"

"Yesterday morning, with Ada and the Sisters of Charity. And the horrors of them were like nothing of which I ever heard or read. To start with, the condition of the floors was indescribable. Luckily we thought of Turkish clogs. And mounted on them we followed Ada through the Inferno——"

He gloomed. Oblivious of his displeasure, she went on: "There were no vessels for water, or utensils of any kind. They had no soap, or towels, or Hospital clothing. The sick were lying in their uniforms, stiff with filth, upon the dreadful pallets. Unwashed—untended—covered with vermin—"

She could not go on. He said between his teeth:

"I have said from the first that women have no business in War-Hospitals. They're the necessary complement of the camp and the battlefield, and they'll be horrible and ghastly as long as the world lasts. The things that are seen in them are too grim to be talked about! But why need we talk? We can't better things by talking!"

"I agree with you perfectly," she said, with a fine smile of sarcasm. "But the condition of things I have described is, since yesterday, astonishingly improved.... To begin with, those Augean floors have been thoroughly scrubbed!"

"Surely not by—ladies?"

"By the Sisters of Charity, aided by the Hospital orderlies who had told them—'*It cannot be done!*' They said: '*It must!*'—and set the example forthwith!"

He commented:

"That's the pace that kills. They'll never be able to hold on at it!"

"Wait and prove! I credit Ada and her nuns with immense reserves of energy. They waste no words. But, oh! Lord Cardillon, when I think that all this abomination and misery lay close at our doors—here in Constantinople—and that I and others never knew of it—never dreamed of it!—I burn with shame and sicken with disgust. No! I do not exaggerate!"

Her sewing had fallen to the deck. Her white hands wrung themselves in her lap. Her matronly calm face was contracted and quivering. She continued:

"I sent from our kitchen at the Embassy quantities of broth and jelly and other articles of invalid diet. Wine from the cellars and so on. But neither I nor Stratclyffe ever went there—to our shame never thought of going there! And but for those articles in the English papers we never should have known——"

He ground his spurred heel into the deck, and something very like an oath escaped from him.

"Confound the London newspapers! As for the men who came out here to cater for news—paid Paul Prys and chiels in butcher-boots and traveling-caps, taking notes—they go too far. It is unbearable espionage—presumption!—insolence! I'd hang up every one of them, if I had the authority and the privileges the Provost-Marshal enjoys! Why, one of those rags of papers actually published information as to where we'd stored our powder! What business have Fleet Street journalists nosing about at the Seat of War?"

She said with spirit:

"They make mistakes occasionally, like the rest of us. But nearly all of them are gentlemen of education, good sense, and good feeling. Could anything but honest, fearless indignation have penned those articles in the *Times*? And—if there is maladministration—lack of organization—are they not right in pointing where the fault lies? The British Public, who give their fathers, husbands, sons and brothers to the service of the country—surely have a right to know how they fare!... Lord Cardillon!—could not much of this horrible suffering and waste of life have been prevented by a little forethought?"

He frowned, but answered:

"Since you will have it—yes!" He added, as she thanked him with a look for the truth, seeing that it had galled in the utterance:

"Please, no more now on that subject. Here's Miss Delavayle!" And their conversation ended with the rustling arrival of a tall, elegant woman, who hurried up and sank down into a chair between them, saying with an affectation of breathlessness:

"I'm dead, hearing people sing your praises, and telling them that you don't deserve any!"

She was a blonde of rather hard and brilliant coloring, dressed as brilliantly as a tropical bird. Her cheeks and eyes were burning with suppressed, none the less evident, excitement; her nerves seemed tense and strung. As she looked at the man, her glance was feverishly bright and hungrily possessive. He moved uneasily as though he felt it so.

"Rest; why don't you rest?" he said to her. "But you never rest. I wonder when you will?"

Lady Stratclyffe had risen and joined the Ambassador's circle. The answer was given:

"When your wife dies, and we're married; then I shall rest—not before!"

He moved restlessly and bit his lip. She went on:

"Do you think I didn't see you playing the gallant with Madame de Roux? Don't protest! I've eyes in the middle of my back," she said, quivering, "for every petticoat that comes near you. Don't I know your charming ways with women, poor idiots that we are!"

"Laura!" he muttered, as her ringed hand clenched upon his chair-arm, and her fever-bright eyes shot challenges at him. "For Heaven's sake don't make me a scene of jealousy!"

"All right! Tell me what you thought when the Brigade got fairly in movement. Was it anything about me?"

"By Gad! no!" he said, wounding her unintentionally. "What I thought to myself was: 'Here goes the last of the Paradynes!'"

"Trot! Canter! Gallop! Charge!" She imitated the staccato tones of the officer commanding. "Why wasn't I born a man, so that I might have followed you—and fought for you—and died for you when I got my chance! There! Lady Granbyson is beckoning to me.... I'm compromising myself hopelessly, sitting here with you like Darby and Joan...."

She flashed a disdainful eye-dart at Lady Granbyson, a portly dowager in voluminous cinnamon satin, fluttering in distress afar off, like a large maternal hen. Then she rose, and stooped over him, clasping the wrist of the unwounded arm that he had thrown across the chair-back, and whispered, with her blazing eyes looking into his, as her burning breath beat upon his cheek, and a long, snaky ringlet of her hot-colored golden hair trailed across the tarnished Brandenbourgs of his Hussar jacket:

"Do you know what I would have done if the last of the Paradynes *had* gone that way? Drowned myself in the Bosphorus when the news came from the Front!"...

He flushed crimson to the temples and caught his breath.

"Laura!"

But she was gone—and the attendant ladies, who had melted into the background when she drew near, were bearing down on him. He cursed women, in his heart, for the mulls they dragged one into. Compunction, pity, strove in him with anger and resentment. Poor Laura! Yet how the clasp of her hand had burned, and how green her eyes had gleamed with jealousy! He foresaw hideous complications with her family—more terrible with his wife's people. Confound it! And just now when one's Sovereign—always down like bricks upon conjugal offenders—notoriously strict in matters of morals—might be expected to smile on a popular Brigadier....

"No, Lady Hathermore, no iced lemonade, thank you. You're too kind, Madame de Mirecourt, but I've three cushions and a footstool now!"

So forbidding was his frown, that they rustled away in search of more accessible divinities. Then—lovely eyes—greenish hazel with golden lights and dusky shadows playing in them—looked down into his and a lovely mouth smiled bewilderingly. A small white hand with clusters of rubies and diamonds like drops of blood mingled with tears sparkling on its slender, pink-tipped fingers, held under his nose a little bunch of violets....

Henriette had charmed—she must charm again—she had been asked for a single flower—she must give the whole bunch in her lavishness. You remember that she could never say No! to a man?...

"I was unkind just now.... You asked—and I denied you. See—I will make amends! Smell them—are they not sweet?"

"Divinely sweet!—both the gift and the giver!" He forgot his new-born prejudice against her sex, as she sank with a whispering rustle of silken draperies into the vacant chair at his side. Suave enchantress! Exquisite witch! How these ivory-white, supple, small-boned creatures vulgarized high-colored, big-boned women! Laura, who would presently have to lead her own forlorn hope down into the Valley of Death under the plunging fire of the eyes of Society, was high-colored and big of bone.

"You were angry with me, and for good cause.... I offended, and I have been punished...."

She said, delighting him with her voice, with her smile, with the play of her mobile features:

"The fault lay not in your words, Milord, or in your actions, but in your eyes. Men with such blue eyes are inimical to me. I believe 'unlucky' is your English word? Ah, no! Do not suppose I do not like the color.... Unhappily, I liked it but too well!"

Her glance was enchantment. Her voice was a song. She allured and drew and provoked him. Laura, under cover of her chaperon's parasol, glared at him tigerishly from the other side of the deck. But he had forgotten Laura. He wondered, noting the delicate spider-lines about Henriette's lovely eyes, and on her ivory temples, where the blue veins melted in the bluish shadows of her jetty, silken hair, how old she was? Thirty-four or five. Worth a dozen of younger women. He thought this as he asked whether she was not staying at the Embassy?

"No, not at the French Legation.... I am engaged to visit there when I return from the Crimea. For the present I share, with Madame de Bessarine, some rooms at the Hotel of Missiri." She added, as he asked if he might not call? "Alas! I leave for the Crimea so soon—it will not be possible to receive visitors!"

But Cardillon pressed for an appointment and she yielded.

"You are an angel of kindness!" he declared.

She returned, with lovely gravity:

"You are of those who have faith in Angels and Heaven? You believe in the existence of another world beyond this earth of ours?"

"Certainly. But you could make this earth so sweet for a man that he wouldn't barter it for Mahomet's Paradise."

She said, ignoring the compliment:

"When you were near to death—not long ago, did you feel more sure of the existence of that other world than your tone now indicates?"

He answered with reluctance:

"I cannot say. To be sure, one would have to die, and come back to life again."

She rose up with her supple exquisite grace, and moved to the yacht's side, and stood with one jeweled hand upon the taffrail looking over at the opposite shore of Asia, as from the thousand minarets of Stamboul came clear musical voices calling the Faithful to the prayer of afternoon.

"I am sure, because I once died, and returned to life again. And I came back out of that dim, strange country that lies beyond this world, with a secret to tell, and a gift to bestow. And he to whom I would tell my secret, and give my gift, had departed—where I know not! It may be we shall never meet on earth any more! And well for him if it were so! For I have come to believe that if he is ever to know peace or happiness, his path and mine must never cross again!"

What strange impulse of confidence moved her? One cannot answer. She went on, not looking at the Brigadier:

"This seems strange to you—will seem stranger when I tell you that I go to the East to marry another.... But Love and Marriage—are they not different things, Milord? Does not your experience teach you so?"

He was silent. Her voice sighed on:

"The gift I spoke of but now, is Love—perhaps you have guessed it? I tell you that a woman may yield to passion—may be much beloved, without ever having learned that!... It was revealed to me when I lay as one dead, and one whom I had despised and ill-used stood by what he and another believed to be a dead body. And in the face of scandal, dishonor—the mockery and contempt of the world!—he said—I shall never forget the tone in which he said it: *'Because that other man has left you, I stay beside you here!'*"

Cardillon said, possessed by a sudden, savage jealousy:

"Was that the man with the blue eyes?"

She shook her head. The pearly line of her white profile, as she turned her face from him, seemed the subtlest thing he had ever looked on. Her plume of herons' feathers gleamed black-blue against the night of her coiled and knotted hair. The little delicate shell-like ear had a ruby hanging from it, like a blood-drop. She said, in that voice of exquisite, sighing cadences, looking at a shabby caïque containing a single passenger, that was being paddled from the steamer-quay of Tophaneh across to the landing-place of Scutari,—and half-consciously noting the struggles of the little craft as it battled against the stiff rush of the current that sweeps past the promontory where transformed Io landed....

"No, Milord. This man had black eyes. When they looked at you.... Ayme!... Madre de Dios, misericordia! C'est lui!—c'est lui!"

The final words were unheard; they had exhaled in a sigh from lips suddenly bleached pale as poplar-leaves. As her head fell forwards on her breast, and the tall, rounded, supple figure swayed as though about to fall, Cardillon threw his strong unwounded arm about her; knowing by the dead weight that the swoon was unfeigned—wondering what had brought it about?

Nothing had happened to alarm her. Only the toiling rower had pulled up-stream diagonally, as though making for the point above the landing-place of Scutari, and had then let the head of the frail craft swing round. And the pasenger, a white-haired, black-eyed man, in worn gray traveling dress, had thus been brought plainly into view of those on the steam-yacht's after-deck.

The man had never glanced at the two people who leaned upon the rail, talking. His eyes were for the green slope and the great quadrangle of yellow stone masonry reared by Sultan Suleiman....

Madame de Roux recovered almost instantly. The caïque had shot out of sight past the bend of the promontory. The traveler had landed and passed on about his business—an accidental likeness had deceived her, that was all. She lifted her head, smiled with lips still white, and declared herself well again. And the Brigadier, whose keen light eyes had the instant before seen a European lady—seated in a caïque with others—start back and hide her face in horror, as something grim and shapeless rose up at the boat's side, said:

"Do not explain! I can guess what happened. You were looking at the water.... One of those dead men!..."

She said, with a shadowy, troubled glance at the deep, rushing tide that swept downwards round the promontory of Scutari:

"I do not fear the dead. The living can be more terrible sometimes!"

"Still," he said, with an effort of unselfishness, "if certain sights affect you so painfully, it would be well not to wait to see the arrival of the Hospital-ships."

"Are we not all assembled," she asked, "to honor the brave unfortunate? And, if I could not support tragic, or grim, or squalid spectacles, should I be now upon my journey to the scene of war?"

"Must you go there? Is Grandguerrier so exigent? Have you really set your hearts upon being married amidst the tragic spectacles to which you refer?"

She told him, with her shadowy smile:

"I go, not because I desire to, but because I am destined to.... All my life long I have done what I wished not to do, at the bidding of an inexorable Fate...."

He did not know how true it was. But the sensual fever she had kindled in his veins abated. He looked at her with more sympathy and less desire. She went on:

"Besides, I must tell you that I have campaigned with my first husband's regiment in Algeria, and helped to nurse the wounded. Recently at Toulon and Marseilles I visited the transports that had brought in our invalided soldiers from the War-Hospitals of the Levant. Now I would cry, *'Bravo, mes amis!'* and wave my handkerchief to your wounded heroes of Alma and Balaklava and Inkerman.... Listen, Milord! Surely that was a salute of guns!"

XCIV

She did not err. The south-westerly breeze had shifted. Sky and water darkened, a cold north wind blew, scattering some sleety drops of rain. And as the squall broke, and the awnings tugged at their reevings, came the splitting crack of the old brass Turkish cannon from the batteries of Deli Talian, and the deeper, more sonorous boom of ships' guns answering back again.

Eighteen guns. They were coming! they were coming! The quays of Pera and the landing-places of Tophaneh and Scutari were crowded with eager, many-colored sightseers. On the balconies and roofs of houses, on the gardenwalls bordering the Bosphorus, on the decks and in the rigging of the warships anchored in the roadsteads, human figures thronged and clustered. A *susurration* of excitement—a hum of expectation, quickened into a clamor—broadened into a roar. For they were coming—they were coming! the men of Alma and Balaklava and Inkerman, whom their country and the nation they had fought for could never praise and honor enough.

They had passed Therapia, for from the nearer fortresses of Europe and Asia the salute crashed deafeningly. Columns of white smoke rose beyond the promontory, slanted and came down upon the wind. As nervous ladies stopped their ears, expectant of an answering salute, the gorgeous king-dolphin, followed by the flying cloud of variegated parrot-fish, darted round the promontory that as yet hid the first of the approaching ships from view, and fled downstream towards Seraglio Point.

What could have scattered the glittering flotilla? They had gone out, led by the Golden Peacock and the Sublime Umbrella to do honor to the brave. They had fled in panic before something unexpected and appalling; for the retreat was most palpably a flight.

Even as the spectators wondered and questioned, a dark blue mist came down like a lowered curtain upon the scene that had been instinct a moment before with light and movement, and color. The wooded hills, the palaces, and mosques, and shops, and kiosks, the thronged terraces and quays, the vessels, with their manned yards and decks crowded with gayly dressed sightseers, were seen dimly as through a thick gauze veil. And the cold breeze brought with it an appalling stench—a cold and deadly exhalation as of the battle-field, the charnel-house, and the plague-pit—as the first of the three great transports came gliding into view.

They came! and from the flagships of the English, French, and Turkish Admirals anchored at Beshiktash the guns boomed out their welcome—the Three Ensigns dipped as in a royal salute. But the cheers and acclamations died in the throats of the thousands whose eyes were nailed upon those mighty argosies, deep-laden, deck-piled, with Death's blackening harvest.... The shouts went up, quavered, and broke, and died....

The transports followed each other at an interval of a cable's length. They moved slowly, laboriously, painfully, like living creatures enfeebled by famine and sick to death. Such canvas as they spread hung crookedly; their tangled cordage, hanging in neglected loops, gave to them a strange air of neglect and dishevelment. Their sails had proved useless; their auxiliary steam-power alone had proved available. For the wounded and the pestilence-smitten, the dead and the living, were herded and packed and crowded on those dreadful decks, as wantonly as though some giant child had been playing at soldiers with real men and real ships—and had wearied of the game half through, jumbled the men in anyhow—and given each ship a spiteful shake, and gone sulkily away.

Filth flowed from their scuppers and streaked their flanks as the three transports moved slowly towards their anchorage. Bevies of the pretty little Adriatic gull accompanied them, screaming and mewing as in derision; dropping upon the water that had become oily, dark, and malodorous, to feed eagerly; rising, wheeling, and dropping again. And flocks of the tiny blue-breasted gray shear-water that haunts the Bosphorus and the Dardanelles fluttered above them, twittering and piping: "See here! See here!"

Faces crowded at their ports, and beyond these you could see more and more faces.... The bulwarks were hedged with faces; the decks were heaped with them.... The bodies belonging to them were clad in discolored rags of uniforms, or thin, and torn, and tattered shreds of linen underwear, and shivered in the bitter wind unceasingly; with a chattering of the teeth that sounded like the rattle of hail upon wood or canvas—with a vibration that communicated itself to the timbers of the ship.

But you could think of nothing but those faces, haggard and worn with privation and suffering, gaunt and terrible with famine, disfigured with wounds, or hideous from the ravages of pestilence. There were faces lividly blue or greenish-yellow with the discoloration of cholera or dysentery, darkly spotted with typhus, fiercely flushed with rheumatic fever or pneumonia, black with the decomposition of gangrene. And, swathed in clotted rags of bandages; or nakedly exposed to the shuddering sight of men, were faces mutilated by loss of noses or lips; and blind faces, showing red, empty eye-sockets; or mere fragments of faces, shattered, and split, and mutilated by grape, and shrapnel, and shell-splinters; or cloven with great sword-strokes from the forehead to the chin. And among these were faces snow-white, or yellow as wax—upheld by the pressure of the living crowd about them—that showed in the glassy stare and the dropped jaw where Death had taken toll. For the Red Reaper was busy gathering in his harvest. Many of these men would not live to be carried up the hilly road that was to serve as England's Calvary. They died even as you looked, inwardly crying.... What wanton wreck and waste of splendid life, what reckless spill of strength, and hope, and courage! Was it for this, O God! that Britain has sent forth her pride and flower?—her manly, gallant officers, her stark and sturdy men?

It is a sacred duty to fight for one's country, a glorious fate to die for her, if need be. But to perish, gaunt with famine and rotten with gangrene, through the neglect and indifference of that same country; to become, living, the prey of flies and the food of maggots that little middlemen may grow fat and flourish—and great Contractors become multi-millionaires—and Nobs and Bigwigs build unto themselves palaces, and the secret animosities working in crowned heads be gratified and glutted—that is to be a martyr, not a hero! Surely the gulls and the little gray shearwaters were crying: "Betrayed! Betrayed! Betrayed!"

One day a great writer will rise up, who will tell this story as it should be told. You will burn and thrill, you will weep and laugh as you read.... Meanwhile, be patient with the feebler pen that stumbles and falters, lost amidst a wilderness of nameless, forgotten graves.

Not that they suffered and died for nought, these men who upheld the honor of England at Alma, and Balaklava, and Inkerman. With the odor of their filthy garments, the stench of their gangrened wounds, the exhalations of fever and pestilence, they brought with them the perfume of sublime obedience and the fragrance of great acts of heroism, forever buried in the silence of official reports.

And the sight of them, grotesque, and strange, and awful as the pipe-dream of an opium or hashish-smoker, fascinated and held those thousands that beheld. In silence, with suspended breath, the men and women of many nations looked, and could not cease from looking; while the gulls shrieked and wheeled, and the tiny gray shearwaters piped and twittered—and a stranger sound than either of these grew upon the ear and filled it, and presently drowned out every other sound:

"*A-a-a-a-a-a!*"

It was feeble, and faint, and broken, and unutterably pitiful.... It reminded you of the bleating of sheep buried in a snowdrift—or the complaint of young calves being bled by the butcher's knife—or the whimpering of dogs, bound and tortured by the vivisector's cruel, skillful hand.... Most of all it suggested the wailing of innumerable pauper babies, pining in the grim nursery-wards of the many workhouses of great grimy London....

"*A-a-a-a-a!*"

It was a sound that plucked at the heart-strings, and brought a choke into the throat, you knew not why or wherefore. Women broke into tears and sobs as they heard it, and a salt stinging mist came before the harder eyes of the men. Not until the warships of the Three Nations anchored at Beshiktash had dipped their Ensigns to the leading transport—not until, in her slow course, she came abreast of the luxurious steam-yacht that displayed the Light Cavalry pennant under her burgee of the Royal Yacht Squadron—were even those who wept to understand.

Then the wail of the dying pauper babies, the bleating of the perishing sheep upon the mountain, came louder than ever.

"*A-a-a-a!*"

And blackened hands waved rags of caps, and even gory bandages; and the woman he had called Laura rushed to Lord Cardillon, as the Brigadier stood—center of the deep half-circle of well-known men and women assembled on the steam yacht's after-deck—and a gallantly conspicuous figure by reason of his height and bearing, and the brilliant tatters of his Hussar uniform—and clutched him wildly by the arm, and shrieked:

"Oh, Arthur! stop them!—stop them! Oh, for God's sake, don't let them moan like that! Oh! will no one have pity and stop them?"

And he thrust her from him, crying:

"You idiot! Can't you understand they're cheering? They've seen us!... They've recognized their officers!... Mildare! Leighbury! Southgrave!" he shouted to the other wearers of soiled and tattered uniforms: "What the devil has come over you that you don't know your own Guards and the fellows of the 555th and 442nd? Briddwater! Gauntless! there are your plungers of the Heavies! And the rest are my own!—my men of the Light Brigade!"

And he ran forwards, forgetful of his wound, and leaped upon the bulwarks; and so stood; holding to the ratlines with the hand that was uninjured—and gave back the cheer in his clear, hard, ringing tones:

"Hurrah, my men! hurrah!"

And as though a spell had been broken, a mighty shout of acclamation went up from every British throat in all that vast assemblage, drowning out the *vivas* of the French, and the *Hochs* of the German Legion, massed upon the crowded slopes of Scutari:

"Hurrah! Hurrah! Hurrah!"

XCV

"*Whom the gods would destroy, they first make mad*" is a hackneyed adage, undeniably true in the case hereunder quoted. For when young Mortimer's not very shining repartee to the False Retreat in the dandy red forage-cap was mentioned in Dispatches, by request of the Duke of Bambridge, and reproduced, with additions and embellishment, in all the daily papers, headed "Amusing Incident During The Action Of Alma," or "Good For The Guards," or "Smart Retort Of A Young Ensign," the joy of Thompson Jowell almost turned his brain.

The man exulted like a triumphant ogre. He had said to the boy "Win distinction!—it's in your blood!" and by Gosh! the youngster had gone and done it! He wearied Cowell, Sowell, Dowell, and the rest to the verge of tears with endless boasts—with windy prophecies of Morty's future greatness. At home, or at his office or Club, or in the sacred ante-rooms of stately Government Departments, he would sit heaving and swelling and fermenting like a large moist, crimson heap of beetroot being distilled into the old Jamaica rum supplied by Mowell to Her Majesty's Forces—until he broke and burst in bubbles of pride. On an average he must have repeated the "I'm dam' if I retreat! I'm blest if I do, so there!" utterance upwards of a hundred times a day.

The fact of his son having ceased to write to him since his unrelenting reply to the letter we know of, did not shake the monstrous egotism of the father's certainty that all would be well between them by-and-by. Meanwhile he laid domineering, greedy hands on all letters that the son wrote to his mother—opening them first, and permitting that much-bullied woman, as a favor, to read them when he had done. He had only to get richer, and Mortimer would come to heel, like a blundering young pointer, none the worse in his owner's estimation, for having shown spirit in threatening to break away.

And every day that dawned *did* see the man rise up with a thicker coating of golden mud upon him, to be scraped off and invested in safe things. He had boasted to his heir that he stood to make millions by the War, and his boast was verified. There had been moments when his success had almost frightened him.

But now, between paternal pride and gratified vanity, his greed of gain was quickened, and his few remaining scruples sailed down the wind like thistle-blow. His conscience slept behind his gorgeous waistcoat, seldom calling for Cockle's pills or any other helpful remedy. He left off jolting up in bed o' nights with the gray sweat of terror standing on him, when the north-west wind roared among the elms of his country place near Market Drowsing, or bellowed among the sooty chimney-pots of Hanover Square. He could think placidly under these circumstances of *The Realm* thrashing on her way to the Bay of Balaklava, looking for the Black Sea gale she was not meant to weather through. He could await with calmness the arrival of the cablegram which should cram the coffers of Cowell, Towell, Powell, Sowell, Bowell, Crowell, Dowell, and Co. with solid golden drops wrung from the veins of victimized firms of underwriters—and materially hasten the hour that should transform himself into a glittering joss of solid bullion, before whom the world—and chief of all the world—his son—should burn incense and bow down.

And all the time his Fate was drawing nearer, sword uplifted.... And a day dawned when the blade flashed and fell. And it bit deep through the little slanting forehead, behind which all the creatures of the Noah's Ark—the Goose and the Donkey uppermost lately—were jumbled and packed away.

It had been a wild wet summer in the British Isles that year, and a wild wet autumn had followed. November had set in with gales and thunderstorms. The floods were out when Jowell went down to his little place in Sloughshire. Suppose him humming "Marble Halls" and building castles in the air of Government hay-trusses at twenty pounds a ton, as the train carried him through the submerged country, where men in punts were lassoing the floating stacks and cornricks, and fishing with grapnels for drowned pigs, sheep, and cows.

Where the land was not under water, laborers were breaking up the green fallows for the Spring sowing. They were veterans or striplings for the most part. Middle-aged men and young men were almost as rare as strawberries in winter—so many had been taken by the War.... And the cry was for more men, and more, unceasingly. At every barracks and police-station, at every town-hall or railway booking-office, gayly-pictured placards were posted offering bounties, baited lines were dangled, to catch the Recruit.... Brakes carrying brass-bands, and with beribboned warriors on the box, drove through the country towns on market days, to the strains of "Rule, Britannia" and "See the Conquering Hero"; the alluring stories of the dashing sergeant, battled with newspaper-reports of a country where there was wonderful little in the way of eating, and scarce a drop o' beer.

But the bounties scored in the long run. Gearge and Tummus, Market-Day over, would go back to their field-work and plod behind the teams, whistling stray bars of "See the Conquering" and "Rule, Britannia!" Then, as the bright steel share clogged with the fat brown clay, Gearge would throw down the plow-stilts, swearing bitterly:

"Ten shillin' to-wick and nowt but bread for dinner! I'll stand it no more—be danged if I do now! Wut say, lad? Ool't jine th' Army?"

"Ay! wi' all my heart!" Lad would say. And they would leave the farmer's team in mid-furrow in charge of the whimpering plowboy—tramp the six, ten or fifteen miles to the nearest recruiting station—take the Queen's shilling, and be sent up to Regimental Headquarters with the very next draft.

A month of drill, a week at home to say "Good-by!" and then the rookies would be shipped to the distant land where very often there was not even the tough crust to gnaw for dinner; and you plowed your way, not amidst cleanly clods, but through deep and stinking mud, where dead bodies of men and beasts that had perished lay bloated and corrupting, until swine or dogs or ravens had picked their bones.

Arrived at his "little place," the large pretentious country mansion standing in its brand-new shrubberies and experimental gardens on the outskirts of a rustic hamlet within a mile of Market Drowsing, the Contractor sent for his agent—who in a petty way was another Thompson Jowell, and went—thoroughly as was his wont—into his rents and dues.

His gross shadow loomed large upon the village, the greater part of which belonged to him, in virtue of his benevolent habit of advancing money upon mortgage to small freeholders who were in difficulties, and subsequently gulping down their land. His trail was upon the ancient Church—where the brazen pulpit-lamps by which the Parson read his sermon on winter evenings—the font in which infant pagans were made Christians—the harmonium that chased the flying choir to the last line of the hymn, the copper shovels upon which the Church wardens collected halfpennies and buttons—bore brazen plates, testifying that they had been presented by Thompson Jowell, Esq. And in the churchyard an imposing vault, containing the remains of his deceased mother, transferred from a remote burying-ground in the neighborhood of Shadwell—where the honest soul had kept a little tobacco-shop—awaited the hour when her son should condescend to die.

Death did not hover in the mind of Jowell at this particular juncture. He was happy as he issued mandates for Distraint upon the goods of non-paying cottage tenants, and indicated those mortgagors who were to have a little rope, and those others who were to be shown no quarter. Chief of these unfortunates was Sarah Horrotian, to whom her kinsman had, some seven years previously, lent cash upon her freehold of the Upper Clays.

"She's letting the place go to rack and ruin," said the agent. "For her own good, sir, you ought to foreclose!"

His master pondered, routing in the stiff upright hair that had perceptibly whitened lately. Then he roused himself with a snort, and said that as it was a fine morning after yesterday's rain, and the Clays not two miles distant, he would walk over there, by Gosh, he would! and see the widow himself.

When he set out, a tussle was going on between the business side of him and the part that was paternal. The woman owed him money, but her son had saved his son.... One may suppose, that at first he had some vague idea of appearing before his debtor in the character of a grateful father. But as exercise quickened Jowell's brain, he perceived that this would be wrong. People who had the impudence to borrow money without the means to pay it back, were presumptuous no less than improvident. *Ergo*, to waive his claim to arrears of interest, was to encourage Sarah Horrotian in presumption and improvidence. Moreover, other people in the same boat as the widow would hear, and expect Thompson Jowell to extend to them a similar benevolence. Further, it was the bounden duty of the trooper to have saved young Mortimer Jowell from the sea. In common Christianity he couldn't have done otherwise. He ought to think himself lucky that he had got the chance.

And to delay foreclosing would be to wrong this same son Mortimer, who had won distinction as he had promised his old Governor, and through whom the name of Jowell was to strike deep root in the County and spread wide and tower high. Whether the boy wanted it or not, he should have The Clays for a stud-farm and hunting-box. Tip-top nobs needed these things. And, by Gosh! Jowell's son was going to be a tip-top nob.

Baron Jowell of Drowsing, K.C.B., Lord-Lieutenant of Sloughshire. He said the words to himself over and over, chewing them, ruminating over them, extracting their juice. And set his face—by dint of their constant repetition—into so coarse a cast of greed and mercilessness, that when his squat shadow fell over the half-door of the farm-kitchen, Sarah Horrotian looked up from the tub of clothes she was washing, and the feeble spark of hope that had kindled in her gaunt black eyes at the sight of her great kinsman died out there and then.

Things had gone ill at The Clays since the Second Exodus of Joshua Horrotian. Betsey Twitch, the half-widow, having been taken on as dairymaid in place of Nelly, had, in company with the pigman, Digweed, been detected in scarlet doings, and, with her fellow sinner, incontinently cast forth. And without even such clumsy supervision as the departed Jason's, Sarah's laborers had ceased laboring and her weeders took their rest.

Stock had to be sold ere long, to pay up interest due on Jowell's mortgage. The stately hayricks vanished one by one. After the Declaration of War, read by the Mayor from the balcony of the Town Hall in Market Drowsing, Sarah ceased to sell her eggs, chickens and butter on Thursdays in the shadow of the civic edifice. She even left off attending the local Bethesda, where the Mayor was regarded as a shining light.

For the Almighty would judge the man, she prophesied, for bringing on the War between England and Russia. If he had set his foot down firmly, the Lord Mayor of London and Queen Victoria might have been led to see the error of their ways.

She preached this belief of hers unceasingly, in tones that clanged like beaten fire-irons. It was no use to argue.—Sarah knew best.... Ere long, when Tudd Dowsall and Joe Chinney took the Queen's shilling and trudged away in the wake of the recruiting sergeant, flying ribbons of patriotic colors, Sarah made no attempt to fill their vacant places. The last beast had been sold to pay the poor-rates. Her purse was as empty as the heart behind her wedge-shaped apron-bib, when Thompson Jowell threw open the half-door, and rolled into the kitchen, keeping his curly-brimmed, low-topped hat upon his pear-shaped head, and flourishing his gold-mounted cane.

"What's this I hear?" he said blusteringly. "Now what does this mean, Mrs. Horrotian? Here have I come marching up your muddy lane to know! You're a religious woman and you don't pay your debts! Do you call that a-keeping up of your profession? Four hundred pounds of my money has gone to bolster up this here farming-business of yours, and two years' interest will be due in a week. You may tell me that Juffkins has taken stock and what-not from time to time, on account of my Twenty-five per cent. Ay! and he may have—but Cash Payments should be made in cash. Those cows and pigs and that hay of yours fetched nothing—I'm a loser by the sum I allowed you for 'em. I am, and by Gosh! ma'am, what have you got to say?"

"It is the will of the Lord," returned Sarah Horrotian, returning Jowell's stare unflinchingly, though her thin face was as white as chalk between her graying hair-loops, and her heart beat in sickening thumps. "Though, if my son were here he would find a word to say for the mother that suckled him, and the farm be his, take it how you like it. He have been of age these ten years, and ought to ha' been considered. There would be lawyers should say as I ought never to ha' borrowed money on th' property wi'out his written name!"

She had put her bony finger on the weak place in Thompson Jowell's mortgage. If he had for a moment intended to spare her, the flicker of pity died out in him as he stood rolling his moist eyes and blowing at her in his walrus-style. His mind was made up. He would foreclose at once, in case the bumptious ne'er-do-well of a son should live to come home, and—taking dishonest advantage of the flaw—rob his son Mortimer of his hunting-box. There should be no delay.

Meaning to turn the widow out, without fail, upon the morrow, he spoke of time to pay, even hinted at a further loan. Then Sarah broke down and wept with loud hard sobs. This brought the ready tears into the eyes of Thompson Jowell. He called her his dear Cousin Sarah, quoted the adage about blood being thicker than water, even made an uncertain dab with his pursed-up mouth at the knobby forehead between the black-gray hair-loops, as though to plant a cousinly kiss there—thought better of it, took leave, and went upon his way.

Fate, the grim executioner, walked behind Thompson Jowell as he waddled across the Upper Clays farmyard, sloppy as of yore, but populous no longer with squattering ducks, musing pigs reclining on moist litter, and hairy faces of cows and plow-horses contemplating their world across the half-doors of stables and sheds.

The white gate clashed behind Fate as well as the Contractor; and, when he struck into the narrow hedgerow-bordered lane dividing the westerly slope of the clay-lands, whose deep, sticky mire had made havoc of his brown cloth spatterdashes on the way up, Fate followed at his heels.

He was portentously cheerful at dinner that evening. Fate stood behind his chair as he gobbled, and cracked his bottle of Port. When he pulled his tasseled nightcap down to his great mottled ears and flounced into bed after his aggressive fashion, Fate snuffed the candle and drew the brocaded bed-curtains close. And when the meek, dowdy woman, lying sleepless beside him, wondered why he groaned and snorted?—he was having his Fate-sent dream.

You are to know that it seemed to Thompson Jowell that he arose from bed, and without even waiting to throw on his Oriental dressing-gown over the brief and airy garment of slumber, straightway flew to the Seat of War.

And presently, with a sound in his ears as though two prehistoric beasts of inconceivable size were roaring at each other, he found himself hanging over the Advanced Line of Siege Works, scanning three finger-shaped plateaus, powdered with snow, and divided from each other by deep ravines.

Beyond a strip of plain, tufted with scrub, and humped with the crumbling ruins of Greek churches—that had been reared above the tombs and temples of ancient Scythian Kings—lay the proud fortress-city of Tsar Nicholas, in the crook of an arm of glittering blue-black sea. And from the marvelous array of Defense-works that had sprung up since the Army of the South had rolled away towards Simferopol, puffs of white smoke accompanied the ringing crash of brazen 64-pounders, and the dull boom of the mortar-firing answered similar puffs, booms, and crashes, hailing from the French and British batteries.

Even as Jowell gazed—hanging suspended under a leaden sky-arch in which pale, luminous meteors crossed and recrossed, whistling like curlews, and sometimes bursting in mid-air, a tremendous explosion not far beneath his naked feet, accompanied by a sound as though an express train, loaded with scrap-iron, had passed upon its journey to Sevastopol, warned him that the Lancaster batteries were upon the cliffs immediately behind him, and that his position had its risks.

"This is all very well," said the Contractor, "and uncommon like what I have a-read of in the newspapers, proving that the blackguards who write for 'em tell the truth once in a way. But what I have come here for is to see my son, Ensign Mortimer Jowell, Second Battalion Cut Red Feathers. And I'll give anybody a sovereign who'll take me to their Lines."

With the words, Jowell began to sink; and—firmly convinced that he was being taken in the wrong direction—presently found himself standing in a slushy alley-way.

Upon his right was a ten-foot parapet of yellow clay, strengthened with sandbags and earth-filled gabions. Upon his left was a low cliff, in which caves that were magazines for ammunition, and magnified rabbit-holes that made bomb-proof shelters for human beings, had been delved and burrowed out. There were embrasures in the right-hand parapet, and a row of thirty-two pounders was mounted on the platforms facing the embrasures; and haggard, hairy-faced sentries in tattered great-coats, wearing leg-bandages of sacking and canvas, were placed at intervals on mounds of clay, so that their eyes were raised above the level of the parapet.

The men who worked the guns were Royal Artillery, but the sentries, and two of a group of haggard men who sat with their backs against the parapet were Guards, wearing the forage-cap badge of the Garter Star, peculiarly distinctive of the Cut Red Feathers. Save for those shabby tarnished badges, and the stained and ragged silk sashes the two men wore over clumsy coats of rabbit-skin, there was nothing to distinguish them as officers, except an authoritative manner. Not even the fact that he knew himself to be in his nightshirt would have kept Jowell from breaking in upon their conversation. But even as he opened his mouth, there was a cry of "Shot!" followed by a crash; and earth and stones flew in showers, mingled with clouds of yellow dust.

A solid projectile from one of the Barbarians' big brass sixty-two pounders had struck the parapet, knocking a good-sized piece away. One of the look-out men had toppled off his earth-mound, and lay sprawling in the shin-deep icy slush that was all stained with red about him. Men with gabions and shovels hastened to make good the damage to the epaulement. One of the seated officers got up, strode over, stooped down and examined the fallen private. Even to Thompson Jowell's unskilled eyes there was no repairing *him*.

But something in the gait of the tall, broad-shouldered, weather-beaten young officer quickened the beating of the Contractor's heart, and brought the tears into his eyes. It was his son, bronzed and whiskered, hard-bitten and lean, who said, "Gaw! Poor beggar!" as he rose up and turned away from the headless private. Regardless of his naked legs, and the freezing blasts that sported with his single garment, Thompson Jowell ran forwards, with hands outstretched, crying, in a gush of tenderness:

"Morty! My own boy!"

The face of the young officer had not previously been turned towards the visitor in the nightshirt. But now it met his fully, and the heart of Jowell stopped beating with a jolt. For that cold, ignoring look disowned him and unfathered him. It told him that he had been warned, and had ignored the warning; and that henceforth, of his own act, he must be a stranger to his only son.

In the horror of this revelation he screamed out, and awakened. He leaped out of bed and floundered to the window, pulled aside the blind, and looked upon a calm, bright dawn. Not a breath of wind creaked his elms, but far away in the Bay of Balaklava, Fate was brewing that Black Sea gale *The Realm* had waited for so long.

XCVI

She had got into harbor on the previous evening. Some of the troops on board—a draft of the 146th—had already been landed. The others came ashore after the ship broke up.

Fate sent young Mortimer Jowell down from the Front that morning, in charge of a fatigue-party, detailed to draw rations of hard biscuit, salt-pork, and the green coffee-berries supplied by a maternal Government to men who had no fires to roast or mills to grind them with.

The tramp of eight miles through knee-deep, sometimes waist-deep slough would have been no joke to men full-fed and in hard condition. They were muddy to the hair, weary and sore-footed, when they passed the camps of the Four British Divisions—lying under the Argus-eyes and iron mouths of the French Artillery, whose breastworks crowned the line of cliffs along their rear and flank. For the Red Snake lay coiled about the grim fortress-city of Tsar Nicholas, and the Blue Snakes had lapped themselves between the Red Snake and retreat.

To the eye of Hector Dunoisse that disposition of the Allied Forces would have spoken volumes. To the uninstructed glance of young Mortimer Jowell it merely suggested a barely-possible contingency. He said to himself:

"My eye! Suppose the Emperor of the French and that pasty chap, the Sultan, were to turn those whacking big guns on us one of these fine mornin's! Gaw! I wonder where we should all be then?"

It was the most brilliant thing the Ensign had ever said in the whole of his life, but he was not conscious that he was being clever. He was only glad that he had got his draggled party of muddy scarecrows safely into Balaklava. He was inhaling almost with relief the smells of that ramshackle, rag-and-bone town.

They went down into her by the Kadikoi Road that skirts the top of the retort-shaped, jug-mouthed harbor, presided over by the Star Fort and the Mortar Batteries. Stacks of sleepers and rusty lengths of rail marked the site of the proposed railway between the Front and Balaklava. A living-wagon, reversed upon the summit of a mountain of mud, bore upon its canvas tilt the pithy inscription:

> "NO PAI FOR 6 MUNTHS AND HARDLY ENNY VITTALS.

PRESHUS SIK OF THE HOLE JOBB."

A forest of masts fringed the harbor. You saw vessels of every imaginable class, from the stately Indiaman to the paddle-wheeled gunboat, tied up in tiers like the mackerel-boats of a Cornish fishing-village. Upon the oily pewter-colored waters bobbed and wallowed innumerable carcasses—canine, porcine, equine, and bovine.

"Hair-trunks" the sailors called these unpleasantly-inflated objects; and as every ship was supposed to tow those in her immediate vicinity, she naturally left her neighbors to carry the business out.

One bottle-nosed Commander of a screw line-of-battle-ship, putting by the desire for promotion, earned the gratitude of his fellow-men, and a deathless name in History, by an appreciation of the peculiar sanitary demands of the situation, that was at least sixty years in advance of the age.

Said he, in effect: "These carcasses, ignored by the Executive Heads of the Army, the Harbor-Master and the Port Captains, are as perilous to the life of man as effective shelling.... Let others serve their country after their own fashion. I tow dead cows henceforth."

So his boats were sent regularly to collect the bobbing hair-trunks packed with fetid odors, and tow them out of the roadstead crowded with shipping of three nations, away to the open sea.... And the Fleet and the Army gave their benefactor the Chinese-sounding appellation of "Commander Tow Cow." And the nickname adhered to him to his dying day.

Suppose that you see the Ensign, with his sergeant and section, tramping down the miry main street of the South-Crimean coast-town, between villas that had been clean and dapper and habitable when the Allied Armies rolled down from the North.

An endless procession of men on foot, men on horseback, men driving beasts or charioteering vehicles of various descriptions, passed up and down that swarming thoroughfare, all day and nearly all night. Lean dogs and ownerless swine routed in piles of offal and garbage. And—for Death constantly dropped in in the shape of shell or round-shot—and dysentery and cholera were always with the Army—human refuse lay sprawled or huddled in strange fashion, waiting for the burial which did not always come....

Shrieking stenches saluted young Jowell's nose, the din of voices mingled with the distant bellow of the Lancasters, and the fainter answer of the great brass sixty-two pounders from the batteries of Sevastopol.... Faces he knew nodded cheerily to him from windows of improvised Clubs and temporary restaurants. Hands waved, voices shouted hospitable invitations. He shook his head and passed on.

Dreadful women beckoned with ringed chalked hands and leered at him with painted faces, from the upper balconies of abominable houses where the business of vice went on ceaselessly by day as by night. Roulette-balls clicked—occasionally revolvers cracked, and knives were used—under the canvas of gambling-booths where French and German, Greek and Italian and British gamesters crowded about the green-covered trestle-board.

Cracked pianos vamped accompaniments to villainous songs, screeched by red-tighted sirens in *soi-disant* music-halls. Barrel-organs ground out popular waltzes for the revelers in crazy dancing-saloons, where shadows of revolving couples passed and re-passed, thrown on the crimson blinds by flaring naphtha-lamps. Next door to a house of this type was another that was an hospital; a single-storied, mud-walled, windowless and doorless building that stood close upon the thoroughfare. A lean hog shambled over the threshold as Mortimer Jowell passed. He looked in, and saw green men, blue men, yellow men and black men lying upon the bare earth floor in rows, side by side....

Many had been dead for days. The silence of the others rivaled that of Death itself, for the most part. But sometimes a thready voice cried on God or Our Lady, or faintly cursed, or asked in vain for drink. And Mortimer Jowell halted his men; and went in and drove out the hog, and barricaded the threshold with a broken shutter. As he left the dreadful place a man came in.

He was a priest, tall, broad-shouldered and sufficiently clean-shaven to be remarkable, where nineteen men out of twenty were hairy-faced. He wore a rusty biretta and a thin, torn cassock, and had no other protection against the piercing cold. He had a canvas wallet slung about him, and moved with his hands crossed upon his breast as though something were hidden there.... He glanced at Mortimer Jowell as he stepped aside to make room for him in passing—and his hard blue eyes and jutting underlip and long, powerful chin were features distinctive of a man we have met before.

His name was known to no one in Balaklava. He came over three or four times a week from the French base at Kamiesch—where he wrought with many others among the wounded in the hospitals—to minister to the dying Catholic soldiers in this and similar places of misery and woe. Their dull and glassy eyes flickered a little at the sight of him. He made the sign of the Cross, drew out the purple stole—passed it round his neck—and knelt down by one of the prostrate bodies, murmuring a Latin benediction. And, too ignorant of his high, awful function to be conscious of intrusiveness, the Ensign watched and listened to him as he drew a silver pyx from the bosom of his cassock and fed the starving with the Bread of Life.

The ex-State official, diplomat and *viveur* who had become a priest, and the bullet-headed young English subaltern were never to exchange one word, never again to meet—and yet there was a link between them.... Both were—one quite unconsciously—seeking the Peace that is only gained by the Way of Expiation. And one of them was to find it before the sun went down.

Ignorant of this, the Ensign tramped on, and, having dropped his party at the Commissariat Stores—a row of sheet-iron roofed sheds that had sprung up, with many other buildings of the same kind, on the offal-strewn beach, above high-water mark—was free to wander where he would.

So he strolled along the muddy foreshore among the huge stacks of planking for stables and huts, and the great mountains of food and forage that lay piled up and rotting—rendered useless by lack of transport and plenitude of Red Tape—doomed never to supply the needs of perishing beasts and starving men.

A store-ship sent out many months previously had just unloaded a cargo of Showell's Army boots by the simple process of digging them out from the hold with shovels, filling boats with them, and emptying the boats on the beach close to low-water mark. And a half-company of Fusiliers, barefooted, and several degrees more ragged than those of Morty's fatigue-party, had been marched down and directed to take what they needed from the pile.

The boots were all too small. You saw men eagerly turning over the heaps, sorting and comparing, pitching away and swearing, sitting down and trying in vain to force the ridiculously inadequate coverings on their swollen, bleeding feet. A minority succeeded in getting shod—after a fashion. But upon the hairy faces of the muddy, ragged, hunger-bitten majority, anger and disgust and disappointment were vividly painted; and presently found vent in words.

Their N.C.O's—in like case with them—vainly endeavored to cast oil upon the troubled waters. Then the officer in command of the party emerged from a low-browed beach *café*, built of mud, mules' bones and Army Mess-tins, where a red-fezzed Greek sold coffee, vodka, rum, and

Crimean wine. He said—shouldering a net of potatoes, tucking the head of a dead fowl under his sword-belt, and Sucking his mustache, gemmed with ruby drops of generous liquor:

"Whass this, Rathkeales? Sergeant-Major Lonergan, bring these mutinous divvies up before me! Can't get the boots on, is that whass the matter wit' you? And whoever thought you could?—and your feet swelled to the size of pontoons with chilblains and frostbite! Whass that you're saying, Private Biles? 'Women's and children's sizes'? Get to the divvle with your women and children! Do you suppose the Government's a fool?"

But the production of a bundle of elastic-sided foot-coverings of unmistakably feminine proportions reduced even the Captain to silence; and a pair of little clump-soled shoes brandished in a gaunt and grimy hand, put a clincher on the case.

"Who says they're not child's sizes now?" shouted the owner of the grimy hand hoarsely. "Are these men's boots? Maybe you'll look and say!" He added: "And may the feet o' them that has palmed 'em off on us march naked over Hell's red-hot floor, come the Day o' Judgment! If there's a God in Heaven, He'll grant that prayer!"

He threw down the little hobnailed shoes, and went over, muttering, and scowling, and staggering in his gait, to where the stark body of a long-booted navvy lay in the shadow of a pyramid of Commissariat crates.

His comrades and officers and Mortimer Jowell watched in silence, as he sat himself down opposite the dead man, and measured the soles of his feet against the rigid feet. They were of a size. He nodded at the livid blue face of their late owner, and said grimly:

"You and me, matey, seem about the same size in corn-boxes. Maybe you'll not grudge to part with your boots to a covey who'll be in your shoes next week or to-night!"

Mortimer Jowell sickened as the ghastly process of removal was completed, but the ugly fascination of the scene held him as it did other men. Nobody had noticed the blue haze creeping in from the sea, pushed by a wind that had veered suddenly. As the soldier stood up in the dead navvy's boots, the gale yelled, and broke....

XCVII

It came from the southwest with hail and blizzards of snow in it. Tents scattered at its breath like autumn leaves—iron roofs of Army store-sheds took wing like flights of frightened rooks. Thunder cracked and rolled incessantly—fierce blue lightnings cleft the mirk with jagged yataghans of electric fire. Huge waves beat upon the narrow beaches, and leaped upon the towering cliffs, dragging mouthfuls of acres down. Ships and steamers, large and small, crowding the Harbor, were jumbled in wild confusion. The smashing of bowsprits and cutwaters, bulwarks, paddle-boxes and stern-boats may be better imagined than described. Outside in the Bay, Hemp, Iron, and Steam waged war with the unleashed elements of Wind and Water. And through all, the siege-batteries of the Allies went on bellowing; and from the wonderful array of Defense Works that had sprung up as by magic since the Army of the South rolled away on the road to Simferopol—Sevastopol answered, with canister, and round-shot, and shell.

As store-ships and troop-ships beached, and pivot-gun war-steamers foundered—and great line-of-battle ships staggered out to sea—*The Realm* set herself to ride out the gale with full steam up and both anchors out. But as red sparks and black smoke weltered out of her funnels, and the great iron cables rolled off her capstan-drums—one after the other those port and starboard anchors went to the bottom with a roar. And the gale took the brand-new two-thousand-six-hundred-ton Government transport, twisted her round, lifted her up and broke her, as a child breaks a sugar ship that has come off the top of a birthday-cake.

A petty officer of artificers—his rating is unknown, but he ranks as Second-Class Scoundrel—had been bribed with the sum of fifty pounds not to clinch the cable-ends. When the great stern-wave lifted the doomed ship, this man, with another, was on the poop. He shrieked to his mate to dive, but the heart of the poor wretch failed him. And the Second-Class Scoundrel dived—and, looking down into an awful gulf of sliding black-green water, his mate saw him swimming like a frog, far down below the surface, straight for the open sea.... And then *The Realm* bumped thrice—and broke into barrel-staves and flinders. And her cargo of good goods and bad goods—bogus goods and no goods—and nearly every living soul aboard her—went to the bottom of the Euxine. And young Mortimer Jowell, who had skirted the Harbor on its windward side, and climbed the towering wall of rock that gates it from the Bay, shut up the Dollond telescope through which he had witnessed the tragedy—and sat down upon the hailstone carpeted ground behind a big boulder of pudding-stone to recover and think over things....

"O God, save those poor beggars!" he had groaned out over and over, as the little red and black specks that were men bobbed about in the boiling surf. It was quite clear to him that they were shrieking, though the howl of the sleety gale had drowned their cries.

"Damn the old man! He's done it, as he said he would!" he muttered, hugging his knees and blinking as the stinging tears came crowding, and a sob stuck in his throat. "And I used to chaff him for being such a thundering old Dodger! Gaw!" He shuddered and dropped his haggard young face into his grimy, chilblained hands.

He knew he could never again face his brother-officers. He knew he could never, never again go home. He roused himself out of a giddy stupor presently at the sound of voices. Two officers of the Fleet had taken refuge from the blizzard in a buttress-angle of the Fort wall, not far distant. They were talking about the wreck of *The Realm*, and, sheltered as they were from the wind, their voices reached the ear of Jowell's son.

"It's a gey guid thing for the Contractors," said one man. "They've saved their bacon by letting the Army salt-pork and junk go to Davy Jones's locker, ye ken!"

And his companion answered significantly:

"Supposing it ever was aboard!"

"Ay!—now I come to think of it," said the first man, who had a North of the Tweed accent, "that was varra odd the way the port and starboard cables went ripping oot o' her. Will we be getting any explanation of that circumstance, do ye suppose, later on?"

"Undoubtedly, if we wait until the Day of Judgment," said the second speaker, who seemed a bit of a cynic. "And meanwhile—I'll bet you a sovereign that more stuff will be proved to have gone down in her than ever could have been got into her holds. She'll be the scapegoat of the Commissariat—and by Gad! they want one!"

Said the other man:

"Ay! do they—gey and badly! Come, let's be ganging doon. I'm sorely wanting a nip!"

And their figures crossed the threshold of the broken doorway, and Mortimer Jowell heard the pebbles rolling under their sliding feet as they negotiated the downward path.

"If I were the kind of man I'd like to be, I wouldn't even take the twenty-five thousand pounds *he* settled on me when I got my Commission," he muttered. "No, sir! I'd send it back—and send in my papers—and get a berth in the Sultan's pay. Turn Bashi, perhaps, though I hate Turks, filthy beggars! Still.... Gaw!... that ain't half a bad idea!"

Momentarily he forgot his keen unhappiness in contemplation of a glowing portrait of Mortimer—not Jowell Pasha—riding to war upon an Arab charger of dazzling beauty, presented by his royal master in conjunction with a gold and jeweled scimitar—in recognition of His Excellency's distinguished services as Commander of an Imperial Order.

He saw the Pasha, followed by a lengthy train of aide-de-camps, orderlies, and pipe-bearers, returning to his luxurious tent at nightfall, to be welcomed by his mother—an English lady of pleasant but dowdy appearance—and His Excellency's young and lovely bride. And he put his hand into his breast and pulled out a note-case—and took from this the oddest little scrawly letter—that had been brought to him at the camp of the First Division before he went to the Front.

"Honored Sir,

"I am told it is thus one begins a letter to a gentleman of Ingiland. Pardon me if I am wrong! When my nurse binds the pencil to my wrist with a ribbon I can write as the Ingliz ladies at the school at Pera taught me, though it is not so well as I speak.

"I have much heard of your deeds at the Alma Battle, and of your noble answer to the false messenger of the English Emir, and I am proud to the bottom of my heart! For so brave a man has told me that he loves me. Honored Sir, you have given me what I thought to have never! I pray Our Lord Isa and the Lady Maryam to bless and guard you! Do we, I wonder, meet again?

"Honored Sir,

"I am yours respectfully,

"Zora,
"Of the House of Jones."

The Ensign folded up the funny little letter and kissed it—and put it back in his note-case, and stowed the note-case away. And then he remembered the sergeant and section, waiting at what was left of the Commissariat-Sheds, and hoisted himself by that rope of Duty, up upon his stiff and aching legs.

He looked at his watch. It was twelve o'clock. The storm that had brewed and burst with the diabolical suddenness peculiar to Black Sea hurricanes had begun to pass over. Tears in the pall of sooty vapor rushing north-east showed patches of chill blue sky and blinks of frosty-pale sunshine. The batteries had never for an instant ceased bellowing and growling. Now men who had left off work, or play—to stare from the cliffs at the sight of war-steamers buckling up, and transports smashing like matchwood—went back to play or work again.

But, where the cliff lowered to a saddleback below the Fortress, a rescue-party of men of both Services—with lifebuoys and lines and a rocket-apparatus—were energetically busy—and the Ensign joined them and asked the reason why? When they pointed to the brink of the cliff, he crawled on his hands and knees, and, craning his neck over—saw that shipwrecked mortals no bigger than swarming bees were clinging to a fragment of wreckage—jammed amidst jagged rocks and boiling surges, a sheer three hundred feet below.

The question argued was, who should be lowered down and make fast a line, by which these perishing wretches might be hauled into safety? They would have settled the thing by drawing of lots. But Fate stepped in in the person of the bullet-headed young subaltern of the Cut Red Feathers, who shouted as he unbuckled his sword-belt, untied his sash, and threw off his mud-stained fur-coat.

"I'm the owner's son, and this is my affair, I'm blest if it ain't! I'm dam' if anybody goes down that cliff but me!"

He had not the least desire to die, but it had suddenly been revealed to him as by a mental lightning-flash, that there was but one way to cleanse the tarnished name of Jowell. Not by discarding it—but by good deeds purifying it, and sweetening it in the nostrils of honest men.

As they made fast the line about him, he fumbled in his breast and pulled out a little note-case, calling out:

"I want some fellow to take charge of this!"

No one volunteering, he scanned the faces of the throng about him— and lighted on one that, despite a shag of crimson beard—he knew. He said, moving over to the owner, a tall, broad-shouldered, ragged soldier, in the tatters of a Lancer uniform, and holding out his hand to him:

"You're the man who saved me in the wreck of *The British Queen*, and wouldn't tip me your fist afterwards. Have you any objection to doing it now?" He added, as Joshua Horrotian complied shamefacedly: "And as you're a kind of cousin, you might look after this 'ere note-case. There are some flimsies in it, and two letters that are to be posted, supposing I don't come up from down there! You can keep the tin in the event I've mentioned, and spend it as you choose! Do you twig? And have my sword and sash sent to my mother! Now, ain't you beggars about ready to lower away?"

And they lowered away—swimmingly for a hundred-and-fifty feet or so, and then the gale—that had been crouching and holding its breath—roared and leaped. And the hope of the house of Jowell was beaten into a red rag against the face of those stupendous precipices of pudding-stone, in less time than it takes to write these lines.

He sobbed out "Mummy!" as the life went out of him, and something plucked at the vitals of a dowdy woman, separated from him by thousands of miles of dry land and bitter water, and she cried out: "My boy!..." And then there was nothing left for those on the cliff-top, but to haul the limp and broken body up again.

XCVIII

Upon the morning that saw the wreck of *The Realm* in Balaklava Bay, Thompson Jowell traveled up to London, big with the determination that what he had planned should not be carried out. It would be difficult to arrest the hand of his hired Fate, but with tact and promptitude it could be managed. He eased his mind by saying that it could, as the London Express carried him to Paddington at the Providence-defying speed of thirty miles an hour.

Even as he composed his cautiously-worded cablegram a wire from the Admiralty was lying on his office-desk. But he felt happier than he had done for months, and correspondingly virtuous as he chartered a hackney cab and drove to the City—and got out at the paved entrance to the narrow alley of squalid houses in the shade of the Banking House of Lubbock and Son.

It was a moist, foggy November forenoon, and the yellow gas-jets made islands of light in the prevailing murkiness.... Broadsheets papered the gutters, advertising the Latest Intelligence from the Crimea. Fate had arranged that Jowell's newspaper should not be delivered at his country seat that morning, and that—absorbed in the composition of his message—he should have omitted to buy one at the railway station. It occurred to him that he would buy one now.

He thrust his big hand in his trousers-pocket and wagged his umbrella at a scudding newsboy. The boy darted on, and Jowell condemned him for a young fool. Then a coatless, shivering misery, with wild eyes staring through a tangle of matted hair—padded up on blue and naked feet and thrust a paper under the nose of the Contractor, saying:

"Buy it, sir! It's the last I have!"

"Give it here!" snorted Jowell, grabbing it and fumbling for a penny. As he dropped the copper in the dirty hand, he knew that he and the sea-green Standish had met again. The ex-clerk laughed huskily as he recognized his old tyrant, and said, in a voice that shook and wobbled with some strange emotion:

"Keep your damned money! I'll make you a present of the paper! I've prayed for a chance like this ever since my wife died!"

With a shrill, crazy laugh he shoved the penny back into the stout hairy hand with the big showy rings upon it, and was swallowed up in the moving crowd and blotted out. And Jowell damned him for an impudent hound, and pitched the coin angrily after him. And a guttersnipe pounced on it, turned a Catherine-wheel with a flourish of dirty heels, and vanished. And Jowell, standing under the gas-lamp at the head of the alley, tucked his umbrella under his arm, and opened the newspaper. These headlines caught his eye:

"GREAT GALE IN BALAKLAVA BAY.

DAMAGE TO ALLIED FLEETS' WAR-SHIPS.

FOUNDERING OF 'THE REALM' TRANSPORT
WITH ALL HANDS.

Heroic Conduct of Young British Officer

Meets Death in Effort to Save Shipwrecked Men."

By Gosh! the thing had happened, and would have to be made the best of. The boy would come round, by-and-by. Thompson Jowell folded the newspaper, and walked down the alley to his office, and rolled in amongst the pale-faced clerks, who did not dare to lift their heads from their ledgers, knowing what they knew already, and went in silence to his private room.

And Chobley, the Manager, peeping out of his own little glass-case, said to himself that it would be better to leave his employer to himself for a little. Hence we may gather that Chobley had peeped into the Admiralty telegram that lay waiting on the blotting-pad.

Jowell opened it, sitting at his table. It briefly conveyed the news, and condoled with him on the irreparable loss of his gallant son. He did not collapse as on a previous occasion. He sat very still after he had read the message, with his ghastly face hidden in his thick, shaking hands.

His son, for whom he had saved, and planned, and plotted, and swindled, who was to become a Titled Nob and found a race of Nobs that should carry down into remote posterity the glories of the paternal name, had repudiated the name, and cast off his father, and gone down to death, defying and disowning him.

He lifted his livid face and rolled his bloodshot eyes about the office, and the sentences of the letter he had burned seemed written on the dingy wall-paper and woven into the dirty carpet on the floor. An organ in the street was grinding out a popular air, and they fitted themselves to it, were jarred out over and over in maddening repetition. He knew that he must soon go mad if this sort of thing went on.

There was courage in the man. He took pen and paper and wrote a letter to the firm of underwriters who had insured *The Realm*, making it clear that he would accord no grace in the matter of the great sum they would have to pay. His name was Peter Prompt in such matters, he added, and had always been. And then he penned an additional sentence or so that made the Senior Partner open his eyes.

His letter directed, sealed and stamped, he pulled himself out of his chair, took his umbrella from its usual corner, and went about his City business in the usual way. Save that his eyes were bloodshot, and that he wore no hat, there was nothing out of the common in his appearance. Yet, wherever he went, by something that, unknown to him, kept cropping up in his conversation—he left the impression that grief had turned his brain.

He became conscious ere long that he was bareheaded, and supplied himself with the needed article—with the latest thing in mourning bands upon it—at his hatter's in Cornhill. Leaving the shop, he blundered into the capacious waistcoat of Sowell, who was walking arm-in-arm with Powell and Cowell. And they wrung his hands and tenderly condoled with him, lengthening their faces that were expanded in irrepressible smiles of happiness, and squeezing tears into eyes that were twinkling with relief and joy.

For the wreck of *The Realm* had saved the credit of the Army Contractors. The quills of Tussell of *The Thunderbolt* and those other War Correspondents who told barbed truths were robbed of their venom. They were to be feared no more. Henceforth everything that was lacking to the health and comfort of the British Eastern Expedition would be proved to have been contained in that capacious scapegoat. There would be no end to the possibilities of the transport—safe at the bottom of Balaklava Bay.

And the sacrifice of young Mortimer had wreathed the crime of Jowell with a halo of impeccability. Sowell, Cowell, Powell and Co. could hardly refrain from chuckling, and digging him in the ribs. And they bore him off to lunch with them in a private room at a well-known City tavern, where Bowell, Dowell, Crowell, Shoell, and others of the fraternity were to meet them by appointment. And they plied the bereaved parent with meats and wines, and flattered and cockered him. After the cloth was drawn, their exultation bubbled over. There were toasts and speeches, full of allusions of the sly and subtle kind. And the health of their idol being drunk with acclamations, he got up heavily out of his chair to make a speech.

"Gentlemen..." he began.

There were protestations. Cowell would rather have heard the words *"My friends"* from the lips of a man so endeared to those present by long years of business association and successful enterprise, as his honored friend, Thompson Jowell. There were cries of "Hear, hear!" at this.

"By Gosh! You shall have your way!" said Jowell thickly, beating his big knuckles heavily on the shiny mahogany. Then he cleared his throat and began:

"My friends, if you do this thing that you have planned to do I will never come home again or call myself by your name, or take another sixpence of your money. Don't do it, Governor! Don't do it, for God's sake! He might forgive you! I never should, I know!"

He smiled upon the sickened faces round the table, waiting for the applause that should have greeted the shoddy sentiment he had intended to dish up for them.... He did not know that he had repeated the words of his dead son's last letter; or that he had wound up his communication to the underwriters by quoting them.

He must have left the confederates staring, for he found himself in the street, walking Westwards at a great rate.... It was now dark, and very wet—and the people who passed him were for the most part sheltered by umbrellas, and omitted to notice the stout man in the mourning hatband and flaring waistcoat, who walked with his coat unbuttoned heedless of the pouring rain.... But it seemed to Jowell that eyes followed him, and fingers pointed at him—and that the sentences of Mortimer's last letter flared at him from every hoarding, and were written in fiery characters upon the pavement under his feet.

He let himself into the great house in Hanover Square, shut up and blinded and looked after, in his absence from town—by a housekeeper and an under-butler. He was expected, and preparations had been made to receive him. But, explaining to the curtseying housekeeper that he would want no dinner, he passed into his sumptuous library and locked the door. Nobody ventured to disturb him, and when he came out it was nearly midnight. To the under-butler, who was waiting up to valet him, he spoke quite gently, bidding him fasten up the house and go to rest.

And then he took his candlestick from the hall-table and passed up the wide, shallow-stepped, softly-carpeted staircase and went into the splendid suite of rooms he had furnished for his boy....

Evidences of the young man's sporting tastes were not lacking in the driving-whips and fishing-rods, single-sticks, fencing-foils and boxing-gloves that—in conjunction with divers brilliantly-colored pictorial representations of Stars of the Ballet, and Beauties of the Harem, yachts winning cups, favorite racers winning the Derby, and Pets of the Prize-Ring winning Championships—decorated the walls.

The costly inlaid banjo, upon which the hope of the House of Jowell had been wont to thrum out the accompaniment to "Villikins and His Dinah," lay upon a cedar cigar-cabinet, beside an Oriental divan stood the gilded *huqua* that had never failed to make its owner deadly sick. A Turkish dressing-gown lay over a chair—an embroidered smoking-cap hung upon the corner of a gilded reading-stand.... Upon a table stood the Ensign's library, consisting of an English Dictionary, a Bible presented by his mother on his tenth birthday; some Manuals of Infantry Drill and Musketry; sundry lives of celebrated pugilists, Ruff's *Guide to the Turf*, the *Stud Book*, *Stonehenge on the Horse*, *Hoyle on Whist*, and the *Sporting Almanac*.

It had been the father's whim that Mortimer's rooms should be kept exactly as Mortimer had left them, and that nothing the Ensign had forgotten should be moved, or put away. There was a pair of doeskin military gloves he had worn, lying upon the toilet-table in the bedroom. And a strap that had formed part of a sword-belt lay forgotten upon the Brussels carpet near the foot of the bed.

Thompson Jowell picked up the strap, and as he set down his candlestick, he ran it between his fingers, remembering that it had belonged to his son, who, rather than be defiled by the golden mud that every roll in the gutter crusted more thickly upon him, had cast him off and chosen to die.

"I'm piling it up for you, Morty, my boy," he heard himself saying, as he laid himself down heavily into the armchair by the huge carved four-poster, and sat there staring, and drumming heavily with his fists upon his knees.

He had throughout his life been a man destitute of imagination. Now, at this final hour, the gift was born in him. He heard thousands of voices cursing him. He saw thousands of blackened hands pointing at him. He knew himself a murderer. He realized that the millions he had gained by fraud and trickery had bought him estate in Hell.

"My name's Done Brown—that's what it is," he muttered, thickly.

He lifted a shaking hand to wipe the cold sweat from his forehead, and started as the strap of the sword-belt dangled before his eyes. He lowered his hand and looked intently at the narrow band of tough, doubled buff-leather; pipeclayed, and having a solid gilt-brass ring stitched and riveted in the loop at either end. As he turned it musingly about in his fingers, he found that, doubled, and pushed through one of the gilt rings, it made a slip-noose. Then Imagination suggested the thing that he might do. No thought of the dowdy woman weeping for her son in the lonely house at Market Drowsing came to stay him. She had never been anything to Thompson Jowell but the mother of his son....

The thought of Mortimer spurred him to the act of desperation. He got up and went to the door that led from the bedroom into the luxuriously-furnished apartment adjoining, where the Stars of the Ballet and the Beauties of the Harem simpered from the walls. He measured its height with his eye—rolled an ottoman, worked in Berlin wools by Mortimer's mother, to the right position—got heavily upon it—threw an end of the buff strap over the top of the door—shut the door, and put the noose about his short, thick neck. Then, supporting himself by the wooden molding of the upper framework—he drove the ottoman from him with a clumsy kick and flourish of his stumpy legs....

Lights danced before his eyes that might have been the fires of a distant camp. There were explosions in his ears that might have been the thirty-four pounders speaking from the batteries. There was a hissing as of steam from flooded engine-furnaces—and a crying and shouting as of men packed and crowded together upon the bursting decks of a great transport that was going down....

And then there was nothing but the dead body of a gross stout man in shiny broadcloth—hanging behind the door of the bedroom—waiting to scare the life out of the housekeeper when she looked in at seven upon a bright November morning to pull up the window-blinds.

The decision of the Coroner's jury was that grief for the death of his son had temporarily unhinged the mind of the great Contractor, and there were many expressions of sympathy for the widow, and there was a pompous Funeral.

Cowell, Sowell, and the rest of the fraternity attended the solemnity. They shook their heads regretfully, and the water stood in their eyes. They said that he had been the very devil, sir! and that there never had been a man like him, and that there might never be another; and added that they were surprised he had left as little as three millions behind him—

considering his opportunities!—and that they shouldn't wonder if the gross amount turned out to be a great deal more!

It did; much to the benefit of the various charities among which the great fortune was divided by his widow, carrying out the expressed wishes of the son who would never have been his heir.

But even from the grave, his gross and greedy hand bore heavily upon the Army; nor has his spirit been altogether exorcised up to the present day. A Jowell was mixed up in the Forage and Remount scandals—which occupied the attention of a Commission of Inquiry—subsequently to the close of the most recent South African War.

It was a Neapolitan descendant of his—one Thompsono Jowelli—who washed the oats destined for the Artillery horses of the Italian Army in Tripoli, who filled up the Commissariat cattle with dry hay and coarse salt—drove them to the weighing-machines past those water-tanks in the Via Angioina—kept back part of the shipments of coffee and sugar intended for the troops—carried it back to its original starting-point, and re-sold it to the Government. And of these, as in the case of their distinguished forerunner, the inevitable lesson must be learned in the long-run.

No man can plunder and defraud the community without injuring and despoiling himself.

XCIX

When Sarah Horrotian heard of the strange and terrible ending of Thompson Jowell, she found it hard to believe that she was never to see his coarse red face again, never to be uprooted and ruined by him.... Even when weeks passed without foreclosure, she was still expectant of his turning up suddenly, big and gross and greedy as ever.... When at length she realized that he was dead, she forbade herself to hope.

For the man had a son, and the son would be no more pitiful than the father, thought Sarah Horrotian. When the legal representatives of Jowell's widow wrote, saying that the interest and principal of her debt would be remitted—when the deed of mortgage was returned to her with "Canceled" written across it—the widow faintly wondered, having gone too numb to be joyfully surprised.

Nothing now was needed to set the farm upon its legs again but a little money and a certain amount of energy.... The money she might have found, but the springs of vitality had dried up. Though there were hours, when, sitting in the gaunt, bare farm-kitchen towards nightfall, staring at the handful of coals that burned in the capacious fire-grate, she knew that the desert of her heart might grow green things again, if only Josh and his wife came home.

And, though she told herself they never would, something in her secret heart gave the lie to her. She would have died rather than admit it to herself—but for fear lest they should come, after all, and miss her, and go away to return no more—she ceased to leave the house. Presently the news spread that Widder Horrotian had come down in the world, and gone crazy-like, and never even crept outdoors to look for eggs in the tenantless sheds and empty pigsties—and that you could range over the whole place wi'out coming athirt the woman at all.

Gangs of marauding boys ventured first, after ungathered apples and unharvested turnips; and then their seniors began to take a fearful joy in nocturnal visits from which they returned, bending under mysterious loads.

The fowls disappeared—the wood-stack melted—the farm and garden tools took to themselves wings, and the vegetable shed was broken into one night, and gutted. Discovering this, the widow realized that when the flour in the garret, and the potatoes in the cellar; the sides of bacon hanging in the kitchen, and the cheese under the press in the dairy should be eaten, Want would come knock at the door of Upper Clays Farm.

Yet when the threshold was approached by ragged tramps with mendacious stories of misfortune, or lean and hairy men with scurvy-marked faces, who said simply that they were invalided soldiers who had been sent home from the Front—Sarah gave of what she had, without reproach or girding. To these last, especially when they came limping on crutches, or showed bandaged wounds, or sleeves empty of arms, she was almost gentle. None of them could tell her anything of Joshua Horrotian, except that two squadrons of the Hundredth Lancers had ridden in the Charge of the Light Brigade.

Hope was all but dead in the woman, when upon a sultry summer evening, the white gate clashed behind a tall, thin, ragged, red-haired and bearded man—and a shabby woman carrying a baby—wrapped in the folds of a faded plaid shawl. As they stood faltering, doubtful of their reception, the heart of Sarah leapt within her faded wincey bodice, and the ice of her frozen nature broke up.

Always of formal gait and scanty gesture, there was now something eloquent, free, and almost noble in the woman's action. She had no words—she was bankrupt of a single text to fit the occasion. But she set back the half-doors, and knelt down upon the worn stone threshold. Bowing her head, she crossed her thin arms upon her aching bosom, then spread them open wide, and waited so.

"Oh! my dear son, whom I have ill-used; and cast out and denied the right of heritage. Come, take your own, and forgive me, my son!—my son! Oh! my dear daughter, whom I have wronged so cruelly—try—try to pardon me! Teach your child to think of me forgivingly. For I have sinned, and the Lord has punished me with rods and scourges. Yet He must have relented towards me—for He has sent you home!"

In words like these the silent action and the mute gesture spoke to the returned wanderers. So they lifted Sarah up, and kissed her; and she wept and kissed them and their child, and was comforted. And they went into the house together. And with them Happiness, and in the end Prosperity, came back to dwell at Upper Clays Farm.

C

The three hospital-ships slowly rounded the promontory. Their anchors fell with a sudden plunge. The bugles sounded, the gangways opened, the ladders fell—the barges of the Turkish hospital-hulk below the Point of the Seraglio, hurried, with a host of other craft, to receive their load of wretchedness. No surf beat on the rotten planks and shifting stones of the landing-place, and yet the process of disembarkation was lengthy and slow.

Day waned, the sickly haze fell dead, and the atmosphere grew denser. A round, red sun, hanging over Constantinople, stared through the dark blue fog malevolently, like some ogre's solitary eye. Presently by the light of flaming torches the endless procession of litters—carried by English and French sailors, Turkish gendarmerie, porters of the markets, and soldiers of the militia regiments of Artillery that had been recalled from Tripoli to man the batteries and garrison the forts of the Bosphorus—moved over the crazy planks of the landing-quay, and climbed the steep paved road that led to the great yellow stone Barrack Hospital, between the crowds of sightseers of all nations that walled them in on either side.

For men and women could not tear themselves away from the awful fascination of the spectacle, as scourged and thorn-crowned England staggered, bleeding, up her Hill of Calvary—even as it had been prophesied to Prince Gortschakoff by the Tsar, his master—who was so soon to lie a-dying on his sack of leather stuffed with hay.

There was one woman among the many who held to blackened hands that hung over the sides of litters, or staggered upwards, aiding some tottering cripple's steps with the little strength they had.... You saw her as a lean, tanned, big-boned creature, with ropes of coarse black hair tumbling down over the tatters of a cavalryman's cloak. Passionately she resisted some sailors who shouted at her—gesticulating and crying herrings on them.... All the litters were in use, they said. Her man was no worse off than hundreds! Let him bide by the roadside with the others, dead and living, who lay there waiting for bearers! What call had a common soger to be treated any better than the rest?

What call? But that the blaggyardly rapscallions would not stop and listen to her, Moggy Geogehagan would have let them hear a thing or two.... As it was, with her Jems drawing every breath like a bucketful of stones, there was no time to waste in arguing with the likes of them....

So she bowed herself, and hoisted the yellow parchment-covered skeleton that had been her man upon the shoulders that had carried many a brimming creel of herrings, and, leaning on a knotted staff she had, began to make the ascent.

A few steps, and the woman tottered. But that a black-eyed, white-haired and bearded man, in worn gray traveling clothes, broke through the hedge of spectators, and lent his wasted strength to eke out hers, she would have fallen with her precious load.

So together they carried Jems Geogehagan up the stone-paved road that led to England's Calvary. As long as Moggy lived—and she did not die for many years—she remembered that stranger's face.

The man was Hector Dunoisse. Nor did he ever forget how—as they reached the summit of the toilsome ascent, and the great archway of the Barrack Hospital gaped before them—he saw at last the woman he had come so far to find.

She stood upon a rising knoll of ground, upon the right of the entrance to the Hospital. As in his dream of her, she wore a plain black dress, and a black silk kerchief was tied over the frilled white cap. She was very pale; her eyes burned gray-blue fire beneath her leveled brows, and her lips were colorless and closely set.

Officials of various grades, in mufti and in uniform, were grouped behind her. Nurses in gray, or brown holland dresses and white caps gathered about her: the black habits and white guimpes of the Sisters of Mercy were actively conspicuous among the rest. And as her keen, observant eyes glanced hither and thither—and swift orders dropped from her lips—one nun after another would dart from her side and vanish; to return and speed forth again—diligent as little black-and-white humble-bees obeying the orders of their Queen.

It is upon record that all through the day, all through the night of fog-bleared moonlight and far into the morning that followed, Ada Merling stood while the sick and wounded were being carried into the Hospital.

Strong men grew weary, and went away in search of rest and refreshment. Nurses collapsed, and were succeeded by other nurses. Relays of bearers were replaced by fresh relays. But the Lady-in-Chief remained at her post unflinchingly, and the white-haired man toiled on, and never stopped. For the strength and endurance that breathed from the still composure of Ada Merling seemed, despite his weakness, to communicate itself to Dunoisse. He was giddy, and faint, and breathless—his shoulders were galled, his hands were raw—his boots were in rags upon his blistered feet, when a rose-red dawn suffused the sky behind the wooded slopes of Bûlgurlû, and the last burden of wretchedness was carried in.

Then, and not until then, Ada Merling quitted her post, and followed. He who watched saw the tall, slight figure pass under the deep archway, saw the sentries present arms, saw the heavy gates shut. The last sightseers straggled away, and Dunoisse went down the hill-path, weary, and faint, and limping, yet happier and more at peace than he had been for many years. A tumbledown wooden eating-house, kept by a Greek named Demetrios, stood in those days near the landing-quay of Scutari. Dunoisse obtained a miserable room with a poor bed in it, slept for an hour or two, ate what they put before him, and returned to the Hospital.

CI

Changes were taking place in that vast, uncleanly caravanserai. Soldiers' wives were washing linen, surgeons and nurses were passing to and fro. Working-parties of orderlies with barrows, brooms, and shovels, were gathering up waste-paper and vegetable refuse; removing from the great quadrangle derelict tin cans, piles of cast-off rags, and decomposing carcasses of cats and dogs. Others were bringing buckets of broth, milk, tea, and coffee, and trays of bread from the huge untidy kitchens, soon to be transformed into models of good management and economical excellence. Others—for the Red Reaper made his harvest daily—so that there was always room for more—no matter how many were received into the Hospital—were carrying the dead to the long trenches full of quicklime that scarred the hillside under the nightingale-haunted cypresses of the vast Cemetery of Scutari.

Fortune favored Dunoisse in his search for Ada Merling. He found her standing near a storehouse, barred, and fastened with its heavy Turkish lock, and guarded by a stolid Irish infantryman. Two nuns were with her—a minor official of the Hospital argued and gesticulated—the situation was evidently one of strain. As Dunoisse drew near, he heard her say to this personage:

"But, my good sir, this store contains most of the bales and cases that I brought with me from England. And I am in authority here!"

The man stammered something about an order from the Deputy Inspector-General.

She returned:

"It has been applied for, and has not been received; and patients are hourly dying for want of the nourishment and comforts that are contained in this store. Under the circumstances———"

"Under the circumstances there is nothing for it but to wait! Excuse me, madam!"

The official spread his hands, shrugged his shoulders, bowed and evaporated. She looked from his retreating back to the nuns' faces, saw loyalty framed in bands of starched linen, and issued a mandate in unfaltering tones.

"Find me a hatchet, Mother Aquinas. Look for an iron bar, or a beam light enough for us to handle, Sister Jerome! For we are going to break open that door!"

The sentry muttered, bringing the butt of his musket sharply to the flagstones.

"Ma'am, av ye do, 'tis myself will smarrut for ut!... Flogged, an' broke will I be, an' divil a lie!"

His starting eyes and scarlet face confirmed his sincerity. She said to him:

"You shall not be flogged! I would strip my own shoulders to the lash rather than that you should suffer! Stand aside!" She caught up a stone and struck upon the wooden lock.

One of the nuns had found, and now brandished, an ancient, rusty chopper. The other had a bent poker, disinterred from a heap of scrap. As they advanced upon the door, the sentry whimpered, gave in, and put down his musket, crying:

"Stand away, ma'am! Hould harrud, Sisthers! I'll do ut, be the hokey! The knife to my buttons—the lash to my back—divil a one av me cares wan way or the odher! Give me a hoult av the chopper!" He amended, for Dunoisse, with a brief word to the nun, had already possessed himself of the weapon. "The poker, thin—since the gintleman has a taste for the other article!—and we'll be in among the blankuts and broth-bottles before yez can say 'knife!'"

The door yielded to their united attack upon it. As the Sisters darted joyfully in, as the sentry resumed his musket, Dunoisse knew that he was recognized. For Ada Merling's eyes were fixed on him, and a faint tinge of color suffused her paleness. He threw down the chopper on the scrap-heap and approached her, saying hurriedly:

"Miss Merling, I trust I have not alarmed you by an appearance you were not prepared for? When you have time to listen to me, I will explain why I am here.... Meanwhile, let me serve as best I may in this house of sickness and anguish, under an assumed name, for it will be best that my own should be forgotten! You will not deny me that comfort, I hope?"

"Not if it is a comfort," she said, with her great eyes fixed upon him, and her delicate lip quivering. "But—are there not grave reasons for your desire to remain unknown? I cannot but suspect it and fear it. You look so worn, and changed from what you were!..."

"I am changed, as you say," returned Dunoisse, "but the change is not altogether due to long sickness and close imprisonment———"

"Can it be possible?... You have really been a prisoner?" she asked, looking at him strangely; and he replied:

"I have been confined in a military fortress of Northern France for the last six months."

"I dreamed it!"

The words had broken from her despite her will to stay them. To Dunoisse the utterance brought revival of life and hope. He drew nearer, and said, with deep, vibrating earnestness:

"Miss Merling, I was imprisoned without trial, for no crime, but for a desperate effort to retrieve a great wrong that I had done—at the instance of my superiors, unknowingly.... Should you hear ill of me, do not judge me!—do not condemn me!—try to believe that I have told you the very truth!"

"I do believe you!"

The words, softly spoken, conveyed unfaltering sincerity. He looked his gratitude, and said, in broken tones:

"You have no time to listen to the story now, but when you are free, you will hear me tell it?" He added, as she bent her head in assent: "And until then I will do what service I may in the Hospital. Years back, had I listened to you, I should have plucked myself from the morass of vanity and sensuality in which I was slowly, surely sinking. But I had gone too far to draw back. So I took, and spent, that money I had vowed never to touch, and leagued with rogues to put myself upon the throne of Widinitz, and was repaid, and richly, in disgrace and failure. You see, I hide nothing from you! Even in my days of blindness, you were for me the ideal of a woman, noble and pure, disinterested and true!"

She said, putting out her hand entreatingly:

"Your praise is undeserved. I have often reproached myself since, for the lack of tact and discrimination which I showed that night in our conversation at the Embassy. Upon the first occasion of our meeting, you may remember that you bestowed your confidence upon me very freely, very generously.... Possibly that is why I spoke to you candidly, as an old friend or an elder sister, forgetting that I had no right...."

"The right was yours!" said Dunoisse, gripping his thin hands together and speaking low and eagerly. "It is yours to-day! it will always belong to you! In exchange, you have given me a noble woman to believe in, an earthly angel to be my guardian and guide. How can I speak to you, who are so much above me, of what is in my heart towards you? How dare I dream——"

He broke off, for she had silenced him with an entreating look.

"I must go!" she said, and pencilled a hasty line in a memorandum-book taken from her apron pocket, and tore out the scribbled leaf, and put it in his hand. "Give this to the Head of our Medical Department, Surgeon-Major Cray, if you are in earnest in your wish to help us? When I have leisure, we shall meet again, and I will hear your story. And in the meantime, have courage! You are among friends here!"

"If I have one in you," said Dunoisse, deeply moved, "I need no other, for God has given me the best of all!... Yet one question I must entreat you to answer, before you leave me. You said just now that you had dreamed I was a prisoner.... To me, as I walked upon the ramparts under guard one day last March, came a message, in answer to a cry of waking anguish. For I called upon a woman's name in my loneliness and desolation, and the woman answered—

"'*I hear you! Oh! where are you?*...'"

It was the unforgettable voice, the very words that were graven upon his memory. Her bosom heaved, her eyes were starry, the rosy flush had risen to her very hair. He said, with a shock of joy in the revelation:

"I am sure, but I need words to confirm the belief that is mine already. Answer me, I entreat you! Was not the voice that answered yours?"

She bent her head and hurried swiftly from Dunoisse, leaving him standing in the great Hospital quadrangle, under the hot, blue, November sky.

The blood in his veins sang a song of hope. New life had come to him. He pressed the scribbled memorandum to his lips, and hurried in search of the Head of the Medical Department. Helpers were sorely needed; the services of the new volunteer were eagerly accepted. And for weeks Dunoisse wrought among the wounded in the Hospital of Scutari. No one cared to ask his name; to those he nursed he was a hand that raised and fed—a voice that spoke consolation—nothing more tangible. Nor during the weeks of toil and exertion that followed did he exchange a word with the woman who had become the one star of his lonely night. But he saw her, and that was enough. Wherever help and sympathy, skill and courage, were most needed, she was to be found unfailingly. Slight creature that she was, her strength seemed superhuman; the fire of zeal that burned in her was quenchless. She breathed her spirit into those who worked with her: they seemed to need no rest.

The most revolting cases, the most arduous duties, were hers invariably, by right, and claim, and choice. Anæsthetics were not supplied by Britannia for use in her military hospitals; surgical science was as yet in its infancy—but the presence, the voice, the touch, of Ada Merling nerved men to endure, unflinchingly, the atrocious agonies of amputation; if she stood by, there was no outcry when the sharp saw cut into the flesh, or bit through the bone.

And at the end of the long day, when Night had fallen upon the ancient city of the Byzantine Emperors, and porters, hawkers, and beggars slept, wrapped in their ragged mantles, on the grass slopes where Io rested—and only a few silent nuns on night-duty moved through the corridors of the Hospital of Scutari—a twinkling light would grow into vision at the end of those dark halls of anguish—echoing with shrieks of delirious laughter—death-rattles, and groans....

Like a Will-o'-the-Wisp of charity and mercy, a little brass lamp, carried in a woman's hand, would move forwards—deviate to right or left, stop for a moment—then flit on again.... It is upon record how the blackened lips of the dying soldier kissed the shadow of the pure, clear profile of her who bore it, as it glided over his pillow. He buried his haggard cheek where it had been, and slept, when she had passed.

CII

When fever touched Ada Merling with his scorching wing, there was consternation among the staff, and grief among the patients of the Hospital. The attack was severe, but short; she was removed, during its continuance, to a small garden-villa adjoining the great Cemetery of Scutari.

And there, as she walked on the short, sweet grass, under the vast and ancient cypresses, Dunoisse—having been sent for—came to her; and had no words, seeing her pale and wan and wasted. She held out to him her thin, white hand, and said, with her smile of infinite sweetness:

"Now that I have leisure, I keep my promise. I do not think you need an introduction to Sister Jerome, who has nursed me so kindly and so well."

Dunoisse exchanged a handshake and a smile with the Sister, who was a round-faced, bright-eyed little creature, with a voice sweet as a piping bullfinch's, and the activity of a kitten or a child. To see Sister Jerome kiss a baby was to think of a blackbird pecking at a cherry.... When she dressed her patients' cruel wounds, she joked and laughed with those who were able to enjoy chatter. But tears dropped from her bright eyes on the dressings whenever they could drop unseen.

Sister Jerome flitted up and down like a little black-and-white humble-bee between the alleys of turban-capped or flower-decked tombstones, while Dunoisse told his story to the accompaniment of the doves' hoarse cooing in the branches overhead. And as he spoke, he sometimes looked for belief and sometimes for comprehension; and never failed to find them in Ada Merling's eyes.

"I did not need to be told," she said, when he had ended, "that you have suffered most cruelly. It is written on your face.... Possibly another might tell you you blame yourself needlessly—you were a tool in the hand of a master who was responsible—but I shall not do so!"

She sank down upon the prone trunk of a great cypress that old age had leveled, and in the characteristic way clasped her hands about her knee. She had on a plain gray dress of some soft material; a white silk shawl was wrapped about her. Not being on duty, she wore no cap, and the pure Greek outlines of the lovely head, with its classic coils and braids of golden-brown hair, were revealed in all their beauty—and the pale sea-shell pink of returning health was upon the oval cheek.

"I knew it!" she said, as though communing with herself, and forgetful of the man who stood beside her. "That the secret feeling of this man towards England and her people was fanged and venomous hatred, something has told me whenever I looked him in the face.... For the very generosity that harbored him, as for the indifference that merely tolerated while it despised him, he was bound to repay in his own coin. And that coin has been minted in Hell! And it has not only scorched and blistered the fingers that took it, but it has carried with it a pestilence that scourges and devastates.... And now that mourning, and sorrow, and ruin and desolation, sit in ashes by Britain's hearth—*he* comes knocking at the door with soft words of sympathy. For those who are the victims of his vengeance will never realize it! he has learned in those years of poverty, obscurity and humiliation, to hide his hate so well!"

She might have been a Fate as she linked her long white fingers and looked out beneath her leveled brows over the olive-groves and gardens fringing the Cemetery, and beyond the sapphire-blue water, populous with boats and shipping, towards the European shore. A moment she waited, gathering her forces, and then she drew a deep breath, and rose, and said to Dunoisse, holding out her hand:

"You tell me that it is your purpose to leave here and go to the Crimea, obtain an audience of Lord Dalgan, and unfold the plot to him. It will be a difficult task to convince him—almost an impossible task. Still—since to you as to me the voice of conscience is the Voice of God—go—and Heaven be with you and bring you safely back again!"

The thrill in her sweet voice, the magic of the hand that gently touched his, thawed the old ice about Dunoisse's heart. He fell down upon his knees before her, and caught a fold of her dress and kissed it, crying passionately:

"Oh! my good angel, from whom once I turned away! oh! dearest and noblest of women, I bless you for those words that hold out hope to me! I swear to you that I will atone!"

He sought her hands, and she yielded them to his clasp, and he kissed them lingeringly. He folded them in his own, and laid them upon his heart, and cried:

"How can one speak to one so spotless of an earthly passion? And yet I will earn the right, one day. Tell me—when I have erased all those black entries from the book of the Recording Angel—when I have washed my soul clean of the guilt of all this blood—tell me that I may come to you and claim my priceless joy—my great reward of you! Give me some sign, even though you do not speak!"

Their eyes met. For answer she leaned over him, and kissed him once, upon the lips, divinely.... Her mouth was a chalice of strengthening. The clasp of her hands gave new life.... He said, exultantly, as they rose up, still looking in each other's faces:

"Oh, my beloved! I will deserve so much of God, that one day He will give me even you!"

"Hush—hush!" she said, and touched his lips with her cool hand to bid them silence. He kissed the hand, glanced downwards and stooping, disentangled from the soft material of her dress a trailing branch of delicate, vividly-green creeper, hardly larger in leaf than the climbing rose, and set with long sharp thorns.

"What is that? How beautiful and how unusual!" she commented. Then—as he twisted the dewy green leaves and the sharp prickles into a rough circlet and offered it to her, she took it from him silently—saying to herself: *"It is always the hand we love that gives us the crown of thorns!"*

And then she called the nun, and bade him good-night, and went back to the little painted wooden villa standing in its nightingale-haunted garden on the main road to Ismid.

And Dunoisse knew a mad impulse to follow the tall, lightly moving figure, clutch at the softly flowing garments—stay her with desperate prayers not to leave him without one more kiss or at least a word of tenderness. But he fought it down, and went by the northern avenue back to his narrow, stuffy quarters at the Hospital, said farewell to his fellow-workers, and left next morning for the seat of war.

CIII

"French Headquarters, "Before Sevastopol, "*December, 1854.*

To His Excellency, the Commander-in-Chief of the British Forces. Staff Headquarters, near Balaklava.

"My Lord,

"I have to inform your Lordship that a person, passing under the alias of M. Cain, and who is known to have left Scutari *en route* for the Crimea, is an ex-Brigadier General of His Imperial Majesty's private staff, named von Widinitz-Dunoisse, who was employed upon Survey in Bulgaria a few years previously, and upon his return to Paris, in May last, committed a gross outrage upon the person of the Emperor, and was consequently deprived of his rank in the French Army, and imprisoned in the Fortress of Ham. Of exceptional ability—this officer—who was released by the clemency of his Imperial Master—rendered excellent service to his Majesty, who has attributed his fantastic conduct and the strange suspicions that apparently possess him, to an intermittent fever contracted in the Dobrudja, the effects of which have permanently unhinged his mind.

"Madness is in the family of this unhappy gentleman, who, as a pupil at the Technical School of Military Instruction, attacked and dangerously wounded a fellow-student with a broken fencing-foil. His mother, the late Princesse Marie-Bathilde von Widinitz-Dunoisse, was for many years in confinement, and died as the inmate of a lunatic asylum a few months ago.

"Should your lordship find yourself annoyed by the assiduities of this person, you are respectfully requested to send him under guard to our Headquarters, where he will be placed under the human surveillance that his malady requires.

"I beg to assure your Lordship of my distinguished considerations,

"A. Boisrobert,

"Commander-in-Chief."

Lord Dalgan, Commander-in-Chief of the British Forces in the Crimea, stood leaning an elbow upon the narrow mantelshelf of the clay-brick fireplace that had been built in the corner of the bare, comfortless room of the farmhouse that served him as Headquarters, as he perused this letter—which was penned upon a square sheet of blue official paper, emblazoned with the eagle of Sire my Friend.

The handsome, high-bred, resolute face of Moggy Geogehagan's bould ould gintleman bore the stamp of weariness and exhaustion. The gallant martial figure in the blue frock-coat that looked so absurdly plain beside the profusely gold-laced and bestarred uniforms of the French Generals, had gained a stoop; the dark gray trousers hung loosely on the wasted limbs.

It was dusk; by the light of the low-burning fire, and by the flicker of the stable-lantern that was held by an orderly who waited just inside the door as though for instructions—you saw the significant disorder of the place.

Papers were piled upon the central stove, papers were heaped upon the trestle-table, upon the three chairs and my lord's narrow camp-bedstead. Papers filled the wine-hampers that served as waste-paper baskets, papers littered the floor of beaten earth, yet every moment fresh telegrams and dispatches were being brought in by breathless messengers.... One of my lord's Staff aides-de-camp, a handsome, fair-haired, long-legged young Lieutenant of Lancers, came in, bringing a great handful, as my lord thoughtfully folded the letter that he had been reading and scratched his strong old chin with it in rather a characteristic way he had, and said to the orderly in quiet, level tones:

"Sergeant-Major Ransome, if the person who has again applied for an interview be still waiting in the courtyard, perhaps you had better bring him here!..." He added, taking three telegrams and a couple of bulky envelopes from the aide-de-camp: "And you will wait in the ante-room, Foltlebarre, and see that they have the horses in readiness. I purpose to visit the Cavalry Camp and the Camp of the Second Division before I go to bed."

"But you had no sleep last night, my lord, or the night before that!"

The boy, scarlet to the ears, met the kindly, almost quizzical look that responded. My lord said, and condescension and hauteur mingled in his tone:

"I am obliged to you, my dear Foltlebarre, but rest will come for me in the due course of things. At present there is duty to be done."

He opened a telegraphic message from the War Office. It read:

"*Communicate whether Captain Cronan Hundredth Fusiliers has been bitten by a snake or a centipede? Family urgently desirous to know.*"

A second telegram repeated this message with the addition of the words: "*Highly urgent.*" Amidst the innumerable interrogations, advices, demands, orders and counter-orders that had reached my lord that day, the casualty of Captain Cronan—who was son-in-law to a personage high in power at the Horse Guards, had figured prominently. My lord, with a stifled sigh of weariness, crossed the room and added the telegram to a file of others, as the orderly sergeant-major ushered in the person who had so urgently sought an interview, and saluted and retired, on the heels of the aide-de-camp.

We know who the stranger was. The interview was brief, and as Ada Merling had prophesied, fruitless. Dunoisse had no sooner made the purport of his visit plain, than my lord said, gently but authoritatively, checking him with a gesture of the hand:

"No more, sir! You have sought me, it may be, in all sincerity, but the obligations of my post forbid me to hear you to the end. You have suffered imprisonment—possibly ill-usage—and your views have become distorted. My sympathy for your evident suffering induces me to be lenient. Otherwise, I should not hesitate to hand you over to the representatives of your country, who would deal with you, harshly, it might be...."

He added: "Do you not suppose that reports and accusations of treachery have not already reached me, as they probably have the French Commander-in-Chief! You must have little experience if you doubt this!... Yet I tell you, that were these accusations true, I should not alter, by one single hair's-breadth, my method of procedure. For it would be better that the British Army of the East should perish to a man in the trenches before Sevastopol than that England should stoop to show suspicion of her Ally. Our interview is over.... Sir, good-night to you!"

And my lord struck upon a bell that stood upon his portable writing-table, and consigned the dismissed visitor to the guidance of the orderly. So, with a burning brain, and dazed eyes and unsteady feet, Dunoisse passed out into a frosty night, bitten in with cold, white, twinkling stars—and went down, stumbling over the deep ruts of the snow-covered road, towards the lights of the Khutor Farm.

It was all over, all over! No atonement was possible!... Weary and weak, and sick at heart, he reached the farmstead, turned in under a shed where some sacks had been thrown upon the ground, flung himself face downwards upon these, and either slept or swooned.

When he awakened or revived it was daybreak. A couple of Zouaves passed him, making their way northwards towards the French headquarters after a night of drink and gambling. One of them was singing in a nasal tenor voice. As though in mockery the words came:

"*Thy Fate in the balance, thy foot in the stirrup, before thee the path of Honor. Ride on! Who knows what lies at the end of the long journey? Ride on!*"

"O God!" cried Dunoisse, as the men passed, "be merciful and send me Death! For I cannot keep my vow to Thee and to the woman who has my earthly worship. It is not in my power to atone!"

A flush of rosy color filled his haggard eyes. He lifted them and saw—beyond the heights that were dotted with the Turkish defense-works, beyond the deep glen through which the darkling flood of the Tchernaya rolled downwards to the sea—topping the rugged line of hills to the eastward, where the fires of the Cossack camps sent up thin lines of smoke, blue-white and slanting northwards, the rising of the sun. And the disk of the luminary was pale, dazzling as burnished silver. And a broad, vertical bar of crimson rose above and below it—and a transverse bar of the same glowing, ruddy splendor made the semblance of a Crimson Cross with a central glory. And in that moment knowledge and power and strength came to the son of Marie-Bathilde. He knew what his atonement was to be.

He had money that had been returned to him upon his release from the Fortress. He bought a donkey and a canvas saddle with panniers that day in Balaklava, and with a store of simple comforts, bought at a great price from the masters of the store-ships in the Harbor, he began to go about amongst the camps of the Divisions, and to frequent the pest-houses called hospitals, and to visit the soldiers dying of hunger, and bronchitis, and pneumonia in the slushy, freezing trenches, and to do what good he might.

He wore a sheepskin cap and coat, and leggings of pig-leather. He made himself a dwelling in the crypt of a ruined Greek church. Under the inlaid picture of Our Lady on the wall he made his bed of withered leaves and Army sacking. He lived on the coarsest, plainest food—taking no more than was needed to sustain the life in him. It is not for nothing that one has Carmel in the blood.

And toiling thus, he forgot his griefs, for labor is a powerful anodyne. And still the war went on, and still the eyes of England turned towards the Upland, and still her sons died in thousands, and were buried in its marly soil.

The great Tsar died. Marshal Boisrobert retired, and was succeeded by Grandguerrier, the hot, fierce, stout little warrior of whom we know. When Dalgan breathed his last—when the gallant gray head sank under its overwhelming burden of overwork, exertion, grief, and anxiety—that is an unforgettable picture of the French Marshal standing by the deathbed in the bare room of the wooden farmhouse, his broad shoulders heaving—his swarthy, convulsed face hidden in the thick stout hands—weeping and sobbing unrestrainedly as a child for the friend who was no more.

He had a tender heart, that little, fiery man who had become Commander-in-Chief of France's Imperial Army. Henriette might have been happy, had she married him.... And how exquisitely she would have played her part as Madame la Maréchale one may imagine, had not Fate stepped in, in the person of a little drummer of the Line.

For she visited the military hospitals of Kamiesch a few days subsequently to her arrival. As she was leaving the last ward, one of the Sisters of Mercy in charge pointed out to her this youth of eighteen, who had been blinded in both eyes by the explosion of a shell. And Henriette, glancing pitifully at the swollen, bandaged face upon the pillow, said with a shudder:

"Poor young man! How sad that he should suffer so cruelly! Ah! if his mother could only see him now!"

Some tone of the speaker's seemed to reach the consciousness of the fevered sufferer upon the narrow pallet. He stretched out yellow, bony arms, groping towards the unseen sweetness. He turned his bandaged head towards it, and said, in a voice between a rattle and a gasp:

"Mother, mother, mother! They have brought you to me at last! Come and hold me, mother, my mother! Come and kiss me, and I shall get quite well!"

The nun in charge would have dissuaded Henriette, saying that the patient was not only wounded, but was suspected to be suffering from a malignant kind of fever, the true character of which had not yet declared itself. But Henriette was obstinate. She felt so strangely happy that day—it seemed to her that she must do something for somebody. And she ran to the squalid pallet and knelt beside it, saying, as though the little drummer had been a child indeed:

"Yes, yes!—I am your mother!... Come, now, be good! You disturb the other little ones. Be patient!—be quiet!—by-and-by you shall get well!"

She had never been so tender to one of the little pig-tailed girls who had been brought up by the market-gardener's wife at Bagnères—but you will remember that Henriette could never say No! to a man. So, as the drummer still moaned to be held and kissed and cosseted, Henriette yielded, and touched with her own lips the poison-breathing lips of the pestilence-stricken—and laid the bandaged head upon her beautiful bosom—and hushed and soothed it there. She coaxed the drummer into taking food and medicine. She sang a cradle-rhyme and she rocked the dying lad to rest. Not the naughty little witch-song about the Archbishop's cupboard, but a vague, tender lullaby, dealing with Our Lady, lilies, roses, angels and stars.

And the delirious parrot-cry was stilled in sleep, but a few days later Henriette was smitten with smallpox, of which the wounded drummer was already dead.

Symptom followed symptom in ugly, familiar procession. When the fever abated, there was no beauty left in the once witching face. The voice of honey, the sweet, enthralling smile, and the seductive shape were left, but beyond these, nothing. By-and-by she asked for a mirror.... The nun who nursed her brought her one, after repeated refusals. She looked in it, and said, almost with a smile to Grandguerrier, who had insisted upon being admitted to her bedside:

"I am even uglier than that poor boy, am I not? Well,—the best thing I can do now is to go back to my little girls."

Grandguerrier raved and stormed, they say, but Henriette said No! this time, and said it firmly. And so she went away—she who upon that night you know of had made choice of Christ before all earthly lovers—she whom I, like so many others, have loved against my will.

True to her character of enchantress, she bewitched all those about her. For the nuns held her a saint—and to his dying day Grandguerrier believed her to be the noblest of women. And would you be surprised to learn that she played the *rôle* of perfect mother to the three little pig-tailed girls?

Man is merciless to the Henriettes, yet once there lived One Man who understood them; Who was merciful and chivalrous to the erring, perishable thing of clay His Hands had made. He drank pure water from the vessel of the Woman of Samaria—who was an elder sister of this Henriette of my story. As also was Mary of Magdala, who loved much, sinned greatly, and was forgiven. And, like the first, my sad, sweet prodigal, her store rifled, her treasure spent, held drink to the parched lips that thirsted; and even as the second, broke the box of spikenard—wiped the Sacred Feet with the silken veil of her tresses—embraced with passion the Holy Cross.

CIV

A day came when the Malakoff only replied with one shot to three that were fired from the batteries of the Allies, and the Second Bastion answered not at all. Between the yellow, smoke-wreathed hills and the glittering blue, wind-swept bay the fortress-citadel lay dying—she who had for so long owed life to the invigorating genius of Todleben.... Presently along her whole line of bastions no living creature moved. Ruin, Destruction, and Death, held sole possession. Amidst the red glare of conflagration—the shock of repeated explosions—the clouds of pale dust, and sooty smoke shot with ruddy flames that veiled the face of day—the clashing of bayonets and the roll of iron wheels—the garrison and the population streamed over the swaying bridge of boats that led to the northern shore; and when night came, and earth and sea and sky were wrapped in fire, it is on record that but three representatives of the invading Army of England witnessed the destruction of Sevastopol from the summit of Cathcart's Hill.

"Oh, hang the place! Let it burn!" said the others. "We're going to have a night in bed!"

And they had it. There were banquets subsequently, expeditions to the evacuated citadel, meetings and fusions of friends who had been foes; regimental balls and bonfires; Royal and Imperial congratulations. And then the camps of Balaklava and Kamiesch were deserted; and, to the strains of *Partant Pour La Syrie* and "Cheer, Boys, Cheer!" the diminished Army of Sire my Friend, and the crippled remnant of England's Eastern Expedition, were recalled from the Crimea.

My Aunt Julietta will never forget that day, when the shabby, battered-looking transport steamed in slowly to the Dockyard quayside, and the bugle blew, and the gangways opened, and the ragged, hairy men—not a vestige of uniform remaining on the backs of nineteen out of twenty of them—began to march, or limp, or halt, or hobble ashore by companies, as the band that had come to meet them struck up "Home, Sweet Home." And Captain Goliath McCreedy was not seen amongst them—and in her bitter distress and disappointment my Aunt ran up crying to a thin, ragged maypole of an officer with a long red beard—he would have called it a "bird"—reaching down to his middle. She meant to ask him where her husband was?—but her sobs prevented the words from coming. And the lean, red-haired giant shouted, "Juley! don't ye know me?" and caught her in a huge embrace....

There was a Triumph in Paris and there were rejoicings in London, including a Service of Thanksgiving at St. Paul's. All the Bigwigs and Nobs attended in state, and Cowell, Powell, Dowell, Bowell, Crowell, Towell, Rowell, and the rest of the fraternity, were present; and gave thanks behind their shining hats with ostentatious devoutness. It would have been a peculiarly appropriate season for a National Fast, and a Litany, with special clauses having reference to Cabbaging, but nobody seems to have thought of that.

Though that lamentable public spirit of distrust of the Army Contractor—instilled into the national bosom by the malignant demon Tussell, was never to be exorcised—has not been laid unto this hour.... And a day was to dawn when the crowned Imperial charlatan who had made France his mistress and his slave, was to see Great Britain—awake at last, if only in part, to the truth that she herself had been his dupe and victim—stand by with white arms folded over those old ineffaceable bosom-scars of 1854-56; while he whom she had befriended, believed in, championed—for whom her sons had been offered up in hecatombs of slaughter, wallowed in the dust, a fallen Power.

Not a single taunt, O my England! not the shadow of a smile of contemptuous pity; only the stern silence, the grave, immovable regard, and the arms folded over the bosom marred by those old, old cruel scars of THE CRIMEA. But, if his hidden hate of her long years before had amounted to obsession, judge to what a pitch of secret frenzy it was wrought when she afforded him, an exile, refuge from the well-earned vengeance of those whom he had ruled and ruined—a roof to shelter his disgraced and humbled head.

CV

In April, 1910, a radiant celestial traveler, with flaming silvery hair, came rushing back out of the inconceivable, immeasurable spaces that lie beyond the orbit of the planet Neptune, drawn by that strange mysterious need that impels it—at the close of each successive period of eighty to eighty-five years—to revisit the dim glimpses of this speck of Earth, where once the Supreme Architect of the Universe dwelt, a poor man amongst men—and make its transit of the cooling sun, before it passes into the Southern Hemisphere, beyond the reach of the astronomer's lens, pursuing the path appointed it to follow towards the unknown end....

In the opal dawn of mornings in late April it gleamed, a pale and sinister radiance under the white knee of the waning moon. In May it made a luminous streak of whiteness in the north-west after sunset, where an unknown comet had hung in the February of the year.

That strange new comet of February, and now this.... Old Hector Dunoisse was vaguely uneasy as he gazed at the dazzling-pale wonder. Did it presage some great approaching misfortune? Some visitations of War, or pestilence, or famine? Some cataclysmic disaster, such as the earthquake of Messina? Some great irreparable loss to the world in the sweeping away, by one swift stroke of the Death Angel's sword, of some lofty, notable, familiar figure of man or woman, raised in virtue of high gifts, or lofty deeds, or elevated ranks above the heads of the rest?....

To each bird's breast its own nest is the nearest. Old Hector trembled, remembering the great age of the woman who was the one joy and comfort of his life. But early in May, when the faces of men and women of British race were drawn and livid with suspense, as the electrical waves throbbed out from London, telling the hushed and waiting world how a great King's last sands of life were dancing out of the glass, he breathed more freely, despite the sorrow that he felt.

"He was a pretty boy when first I saw him," he said to one who brought him the latest, saddest news. "He was a splendid sportsman and an accomplished *viveur*, besides one of the greatest diplomats that have ever lived. He never spoke a discourteous word, or revenged a private grudge. He never pardoned an impertinence, or asserted his high rank, or forgot it! He fought for the political freedom of creeds he did not hold—he honored Art—and practiced hospitality. The world is better for his nine years' reign! Take off my cap, my Sister," he bade the nun, "and make for me the Sign of the Cross. May the soul of Edward the Peacemaker and the souls of all the faithful departed, by the Mercy of God, rest in peace!"

Thenceafter he was mentally less troubled, but yet in body he was failing. Those about him shook their heads. It was what they had long anticipated—what else, indeed, should be looked for but that one so laden with years should let their burden slip from the bowed shoulders? They did not know of his determination not to lay down life while yet his loved one lived.

The summer was gray, and wet, and cold. He suffered as all Nature did, for lack of wholesome vivifying sunshine. Rheumatic pains racked his paralyzed limbs; his great black eyes were less brilliant under their bushy arched eyebrows, his memory was less vivid, his speech less clear and concise. Sleep rarely visited him, to whom sleep was nourishment and tonic. When it came it brought terrible dreams. Dreams in which endless pageants of tortured faces and mutilated bodies, in bullet-pierced and shot-torn uniforms, defiled before him, and clashing martial music drowned the cries of dying men. And other dreams in which he, Dunoisse, died and passed into a gray void of Nothingness, in which no ray of the Divine Love might reach his groping soul—and wandered in a formless, boundless wilderness, peopled with dim intangible shapes that flitted by him—and when pursued turned on him faces of despair and horror unspeakable, crying: "Away! Trouble us not! We once were Christian men and lived on earth, were guided by priests and clergymen, and believed in the fair promises of Religion. Where now is God of Whom the preachers talked? Where are the spirits of those who have gone before with the Sign of Faith, in the blessed hope of Salvation? We cannot find One or the others—yet this is the World beyond the Grave!"

He would wake from such a dream in an agony. What consolation, then, to see, shadowed against the purple-black sky of midnight or the gray-white sky of dawn, the sculptured outline of the thoughtful bending head and the pure gentle face of his dear lady. He would look from it to the walnut Crucifix with the Emblems of the Passion, and reflect:

"God made her good, therefore He must be Goodness. And though a whole lifetime has gone by since my eyes saw, and my hands touched her—yet she lives, and is, and has her being beyond those snowy mountains of Switzerland and the broad fertile fields of France—and across the restless Channel, in the big black city of London I should find her—had I but strength to follow my will—had I but courage to disobey her command."

For that had been the guerdon of his great and tireless labors, to be sent away empty-handed, beggared of all but a little hope. He had gone on patiently toiling among the sick and wounded soldiers in the camps at the

Crimea, shunning no service that could be rendered, bearing the heaviest and most irksome burdens; always repeating to himself, over and over, the words he had said at parting to his beloved:

"When I have erased all those black entries from the Book of the Recording Angel!—when I have washed my soul clean of the guilt of all this blood, I will come and claim my priceless joy—my great reward of you! I will deserve so much of God that He will give me even you!"

Even when he knew her there, engaged in her great work of reforming and reorganizing the war-hospitals at Balaklava, he had made no attempt to see or speak with her; he had waited to be worthier still.... Sometimes a distant glimpse of the tall, slight figure was vouchsafed him, as she went from hospital to hospital with her nurses and Sisters of Charity; or her mule-drawn basket-wagon would rattle by, upon the uneven tracks that led to the various camps. But the man in the sheepskin coat and cap, who led the little donkey with panniers, was not recognizable among hundreds of other men, clad similarly. Or at least Dunoisse thought so.

But the yearning to touch her hand and hear her voice again was torture. One night, looking from afar at the light in the windows of the hut she occupied, it seemed to him that he could bear it no more. Trembling, he ventured to the door and knocked. A Sister, with a fair, kind, placid face, opened.... From her he learned that some days previously the Lady-in-Chief had been stricken down with a second attack of fever and conveyed to the Sanatorium; that the illness had yielded to treatment; but that the doctors would not hear of her remaining in the Crimea. And that she had, that very morning, been carried down to the harbor upon a stretcher, borne by soldiers, and accompanied by nurses and Sisters of Charity, and embarked, upon the yacht of a friend, for Scutari.

It was Summer, and the myriad wild-flowers of the Tauric Chersonese had sprung up upon the brown plains, and between the stones and boulders; and as in the beech-forest near the Inn of the Three Herons long ago, Dunoisse flung himself face downwards amidst the flaunting blooms and wept. Then he rose up and went back to his labors among the sick and suffering. But he wrote to her; and presently received a letter in the beloved handwriting, telling him that she had returned to England in feeble health.

The Allied Armies were withdrawn from the seat of war—the hospitals were closed, yet Dunoisse hesitated to follow her. He had not earned the right, it seemed to him. He volunteered as a surgeon's assistant on one of the French hospital-ships and returned to Marseilles. Here he rendered service to his wounded countrymen, and—simultaneously with the outbreak of the Indian Mutiny—was called back to Paris, to be present at the death-bed of Marshal Dunoisse.

The stately mansion in the Rue Chaussée d'Antin had fallen into decay. A dusty board upon the weather-stained portico advertised it as Unfurnished and To Let. In the little ground-floor back room of the porter's lodge, inhabited by Auguste and his plump-faced wife, the late master of the big house lay dying, his fur-lined cloak spread above the patchwork coverlet and drawn up to his long-unshaven chin. The curly-brimmed beaver hat was perched upon the top of the wardrobe—the gold-mounted teeth were in their morocco case on the deal toilet-table—the ambrosial wig hung upon the looking-glass—the big Malacca cane, its chased golden top replaced by a knob of tarnished pewter, lay beside the Marshal on the frowsy bed.... Monseigneur would have it, Auguste's stout wife explained, to shake at devils that worried him. When he got too weak to do this she had set a plaster Crucifix on the chest of drawers that stood at the foot of the bed.

The Marshal's race was nearly run, that was evident. But he was conscious, with lapses into semi-delirium. He recognized his son.

"When I said that Flemish Buonaparte should never pick my bones, I forgot you!" he told Hector. "So, when that woman of yours came to me for money for her dear imprisoned one—I gave, though I knew myself a fool! Then de Fleury sent to me, saying that—though your sentence was for life and the Emperor's resentment was implacable—he could insure your freedom for—I forget how much, but I know it was a thumping sum of money!—and what in the name of a thousand thunders was a man with bowels to do? You were a poor creature, but Marie's son, after all!—and so I let them plunder me.... Ah-h! What are you up to now, you rascals, you?"

He saw devils, and roared and brandished his big cane at them. Only in imagination, because his voice had sunk to a crackling whisper, and his hand was powerless. A little child—the year-old son of the ex-coachman's daughter—sat on the bed, holding one of the shrunken fingers—undismayed by the fierce glare of the bloodshot eyes.... Monseigneur had been kind to Toto, Auguste's wife whispered.... Dunoisse, seeing the end approach, signed to her to take the boy away.

A change of mood came upon the old man presently.

"Let me rise up!" he said to the coachman's wife, a trifle wildly. "I tell you that I am in the presence of the great!..."

He added, with the rattle in his throat:

"Guilty, M. the President, upon all these counts and charges. But I never showed my back to an enemy, or gave the cold shoulder to a friend in trouble.... I am a soldier of Napoleon, I! And when I see him—even if he be chained down in Purgatory with imps swarming over him, I will draw my sword and cry: *'Be off, you singed rapscallions!—I come, my Emperor!'* For I fear God,—but He knows me better than to suppose I shall turn tail before a rabble of fiends...." He made an ineffectual grasp at the cane—rose in imaginary stirrups, and thundered, in that crackling whisper: "Form column of squadrons! Behind the enemy is our rallying-point! Charge!"

Then he fell back into the hollowed bed limply as an empty saddle-bag, and Dunoisse, with an indescribable pang at the heart, knew that his father, who had loved him after all, was dead, and that he had died without a word of love or gratitude from the son for whom he had gone down beggared to the grave.

The poor remnant of a once handsome fortune was left to that son without conditions. The funeral over, Dunoisse sold what remained of the lease of the house—the furniture, plate, and pictures having mysteriously vanished—and left Paris for the East. Wherever the red star of battle burned, thenceforwards the son of Marie-Bathilde was to be found aiding the torn and mutilated victims of that grim Moloch we adorn with gold and scarlet; bow down before; give honorable titles to; hang with Orders and Crosses, as though in mockery of the Son of Peace, who died for Love upon the bitter tree.

When the Austrians crossed the Ticino and the French troops entered Piedmont, he quitted the hospitals of Lucknow and hurried to Italy. At Solferino he met with a kindred spirit, and erelong became enrolled a member of a band of high-souled men and women of many nations, who presently were gathered together under the banner bearing the symbol of the Crimson Cross. The funds that were needed to establish the Society upon a sound working basis were supplied from an unexpected source: for when Luitpold, Regent of Widinitz, quitted this life, having been predeceased by his wife, his son, and both his daughters, it was found, by some strange freak of will, that he had bequeathed his vast private estates to the son of Marie-Bathilde. Thus, the dowry of three hundred thousand silver thalers having been repaid to the Prioress of the Carmelite Convent at Widinitz, Dunoisse spent the huge sum that remained in the realization of his dream; and when Love and Pity, Charity and Mercy, were leagued all the world over, in a vast, comprehensive Society—when Kings and Emperors praised and thanked the man whose genius for organization and consummate mastery of detail had perfected this vast machine for the alleviation of suffering—whose riches had been poured out unstintingly to further the cause—it seemed to him that he might now seek out the woman of his worship. And he wrote to Ada Merling asking, "May I come to you?" and she answered: "Come!"

It was after the fall of the French Empire. MacMahon had succeeded Thiers as President. Upon the journey Dunoisse, whose exertions had been unceasing during the Franco-Prussian War, scarcely ate or slept. He answered at random those who spoke to him. When he reached the door of the house in Park Lane he trembled, so that he had to lean for support against the railings. He had changed and aged much in the last fifteen years.

He was admitted to the beautiful, quiet drawing-room. An elderly servant knocked at a door communicating with this, and went away. The door opened, and the wraith of Ada Merling stood upon the threshold. So white, so wan, so frail, that but for the indomitable fire burning in the blue-gray eyes, and the resolute, energetic setting of the lips, he who loved her, would hardly have known her.... He cried out, stricken to the soul with anguish.... She said to him, with no sign of emotion beyond a tremble in her voice:

"You too are changed—you too have suffered! That you should suffer no longer I have decided to tell you all. There can be no question of any closer tie between us—but while I live you have my faithful friendship. And it may be that I shall live for years—though I shall never leave my room again!"

She added, as Dunoisse sank down in a chair, and covered his face with his hands:

"Do not grieve. Try to be glad that the path I am to tread has been pointed out so clearly...."

"Oh! my beloved!" said Dunoisse brokenly. "If you have never loved me I am glad of it for your sake!... But, remembering that evening in the Cemetery at Scutari—can you tell me truly that it is so?"

"I will answer you in a letter," she said, "when I have gathered strength sufficiently. How soon you will receive the letter, I cannot say!" She added, when they had sat together for a little space in silence: "Now bid me good-by and leave me. Never seek me!—do not follow me! If you can, find earthly happiness elsewhere. For we are set apart while we both live, by the Will of God. Nevertheless, in His good time, and in the place He has appointed, I believe that you and I shall meet again!"

And so he had left her, and never since seen her. Yearly a letter from her had reached him, but it had never been *the* letter. Now you know why Dunoisse would not consent to die. He was waiting for the letter that told him of her love.

He had already waited fifty-six years. Well! he would go on waiting.... The letter was sure to come.

CVI

She died in August, and the letter would never come now....

September paved the chestnut-woods with golden leaves, the ripened blackberries vanished before the onslaughts of children and the attack of birds. The snow-peaks turned into pyramids of ice, blizzards swept screaming down the gorges, there were frost-frogs in the valleys and icicles upon the edges of the rocks over which the waterfalls hung in blocks of frozen foam. The Promenade of Zeiden grew empty—people had migrated to Davos or Grindelwald. The familiar figure of the old white-haired man in the Bath-chair had not been seen for many a day. For he lay in his large bedroom at the Home, dying at ninety-three years of age, of a complaint the existence of which is, by the physicians, denied....

He was tended with the kindest care. Nor, when the land and submarine telegraphs tapped out the news East, West, North, and South, and the Wireless sent it to the ears of the helmeted operators in the Marconi Installation Room on the upper decks of the great passenger steamers, hurrying with their human cargo to distant countries, did expressions of sympathy fail.

People were very sorry. Extremely sorry. Though hardly anybody had ever in their lives before heard the name of the dying man. Of the Society of the Crimson Cross, they knew quite certainly. An excellent institution. Had done heaps of good. But they had rather imagined it to have been founded by the Prince Consort in 1859, if they were English; and if they happened to be Germans, they boldly said that the-never-to-be-sufficiently-esteemed and-now-with-his-mourned-ancestors-and-beloved-wife-reposing Imperial Chancellor, Prince Bismarck, had laid the egg of the idea that another less eminent had hatched.... Italians draped with fine art their own innate convictions that Garibaldi or the Pope was responsible. French people shrugged, superior, for even an Austro-Helvetian, born and bred in Paris, becomes by the most subtle of transitions, a Frenchman of France.

Several Crowned Heads and Scientific Associations cabled sympathetic messages, the Council of the Society of the Crimson Cross pressed for the latest bulletin, the State Council of Widinitz despatched a delegate; the Mayor of Zeiden, with two of his town councillors, made a visit of ceremony to the dying man's bedside.... Two Little Sisters of the Poor were with him—mild-eyed religious who had taken it in turns for years with others of their Community, to visit him daily. Lights were burning between vases of flowers before a Crucifix set upon a little white-draped table. They were ending the recitation of the Sorrowful Mysteries of the Rosary as the officials were ushered in.

The man they sought lay, snow-white and barely conscious, a fitful breathing stirring the white hairs of his upper lip. A bleak pinched look was on the brave old face, the great black eyes were closed and sunken. But sometimes their lids would flutter and lift, and they would wander until they fell upon an object that might have been a woman's bust upon a pedestal draped in a heavy veil of crape that hid its lineaments. And then— the look in them was not good to see.

"M. Dunoisse is barely conscious," said the elder of the two Sisters. "The doctors hold that the end is close at hand. That he is quite prepared is happily certain,—Monsieur has ever been a devout Catholic. His confessor is to bring him the Viaticum at noon." The pale face of the speaker flushed as a carriage was heard to stop before the hall-entrance. "It is here!" she said, and hurried to the double doors and flung them wide apart.

CVII

There were muffled footsteps upon the druggetted landing. The Sisters were already kneeling, two black-robed, white-wimpled, motionless images of Prayer. The Mayor of Zeiden, a devout Catholic, hastily crossed himself and knelt down. The delegate from the State Council of Widinitz followed his example—the municipal councillors backing, in exquisite discomfort and embarrassment, against the white-papered wall.

The manager of the Home and his chief assistant entered. Each carried a lighted candle in a tall silver candlestick. Their faces were common, ordinary faces, dignified by an expression of absorbed careful attention rather than devoutness. The tall, bulky, bald, aged man who followed them was not the priest who usually confessed the patient, but an ecclesiastic in the violet cassock that is distinctive of a Cardinal of the Church of Rome. His nervous, energetic-looking hands were folded against his breast; a great amethyst upon the forefinger of the right gleamed purple and rose between the wavering yellow flame of the tapers and the keen dazzle of the autumn sunshine that bathed the lovely landscape seen beyond the lofty windows. His face—pale, heavily-jowled and with the jutting underlip of an orator and a statesman—was absorbed, and rapt, and set. And, keeping his hands always folded over Something hidden in his bosom, he moved forwards slowly, continuously, as St. Christopher might have waded the drift of the icy black river, bearing the world's Redeemer. The kneeling Catholics received the episcopal benediction, the cold blue rapier-points of the Cardinal's keen eyes flashing, as he raised the fingers that bestowed it, at the two standing figures by the wall. A single finger waved, and there was a change. The silver candlesticks, with their burning tapers, now added to the illumination upon the temporary altar, the room was emptied of all human presence save the stately, imposing figure of the ecclesiastic and scarcely-breathing form upon the bed.

You saw the tall, bulky figure bend over the prone form. The sunk, sealed eyelids twitched and lifted. Recognition flashed in the great black eyes. The Cardinal said low and distinctly:

"My son, the priest who was to administer the Last Sacraments has been seized with sudden illness. Knowing me to be staying at Mölkenzell—where I have been taking the whey-cure—he telegraphed, entreating me to supply his place." He added: "And I hesitated not to come—for it may be that Our Lord requires of you this act of final obedience. Will you consent to receive His Body from the hands of one who has been your enemy, but who has already humbly entreated your forgiveness—who renews his penitence at this final hour?"

With a great effort the dying man faltered:

"Yes!"

Then tears dimmed the eyes that had lost their brilliance, the hollow cheeks palpitated—the chin quivered—Old Hector wept.... And the visitor soothed him, bending over the pillow, and the Confession was completed; the thready, breathless whispers of the penitent replying to the resonant undertones of the priest.

He received Absolution then, and the Final Blessing. The noiseless nuns stole back at the sound of the strong, resonant voice rolling out the glorious Latin sentences—the Mayor and the delegate returned.... You are to see the dying body asperged with the holy water, the dying mouth fed with the Blessed Sacrament for the nourishment and support of the soul upon its awful journey over the great Unknown Desert, that I who write, and you who read must travel before very long.

Extreme Unction followed the Communion of the Dying. And as the sacred rite went on, an awful sternness settled over the grave old aquiline face. All the long life of Hector Dunoisse lay unrolled as a map before his mental vision. He hung poised on albatross-wings above his past. He knew as he lay speechless, sightless, scarcely sentient under the deft ministering hands, listening as the deep, melodious voice of Holy Church spoke for the penitent in accents of contrition, judged, rebuked, condemned, pardoned for God,—he knew how great a burden were his trespasses, how small a pack his justifications. He appraised, he valued, he weighed.... And, weighing, he was made aware how Self, in the opposing scale of the just balance, weighed down the seeming stately pile of noble sacrifices made and good deeds done for Heaven. Ah! little wonder that the grand old face grew sterner and sterner as the Sacrament reached its close, and he who ministered by the deathbed, passed to the Recommendation of the Departing Soul.

Do you know it, that tremendous valediction following the brief Litany, that calls upon One Who vanquished Death and trod down the powers of Hell under His Feet, to deliver and save? To pardon sin, remit the pains of present and future punishment, open the gates of Paradise—welcome the wanderer home?...

"Go forth, O Christian soul! from this world. In the Name of God the Father Almighty, Who created thee; in the Name of Jesus Christ, the Son of the Living God, Who suffered for thee; in the Name of the Holy Ghost,

Who was poured out upon thee; in the Name of the Angels and Archangels; in the Names of the Cherubim and Seraphim; in the Names of the Patriarchs and Prophets; in the Names of the Holy Martyrs and Confessors; in the Names of the Holy Monks and Hermits; in the Names of the Holy Virgins and all the Saints of God, may thy place be this day in peace!... Per Christum Dominum! Amen."

It was quiet, very quiet, the passing of this soul. The grand old face grew sterner, sterner. The jaw dropped—the great dim black eyes turned slightly upwards under the thin, withered lids. The sweat of death rolled shining down the dark-veined hollows of the temples: bathed the icy body.... He was gone.... The Cardinal said the final prayers, sprinkled the body with holy water, placed a small crucifix upon the pulseless breast, stooped above the pillow, and kissed the cold forehead, ere he withdrew, followed by the two visitors, leaving the Little Sisters of the Poor to complete their pious task.

CVIII

He was very weary, the great Churchman who had traveled from Mölkenzell—but when he reached his private rooms at the hotel he could not rest. Something urged him with a soundless voice, plucked at him with invisible hands, constrained him to return to the death-chamber.... He dined, and snatched brief sleep beset with dreams upon a preposterous, green-plush sofa. Then he obeyed the entreaty, or the mandate, and took his *biretta*, and threw a heavy cloak about him, for it was night and cold; and stepped out upon the Promenade.

It was a dazzling night of stars; great blazing jewels spilt with a lavish hand upon the purple lap of the Night. From south-west to north-east the Milky Way made an arch across the sky-dome. Bootes made the outline of a kite, its fiery tail Arcturus. Vega in Lyra made a wondrous show. Cardinal de Moulny looked up at them, and murmured a prayer for the soul he had helped to depart. The Home was but a few minutes' walk from the Promenade; he reached it in a few moments. The hall-door stood open; some silent-footed men in black came out as His Eminence mounted the steps.

The vestibule was fragrant with laurel-leaves, with leaves of fern and scattered petals of pure white blossoms, dropped in the hasty unpacking of memorial wreaths and crosses from the florists' boxes that had already begun to arrive. Men and women and children of many nations and ranks and classes had also brought flowers. Many of these people were standing on the pavement near the door, and a crowd had gathered in the street, and were pointing out, with sorrowful faces, the half-open, blinded windows on the floor above the *entresol*.

"He is lying there," a peasant woman said to her little daughter, as the Cardinal passed. And the keen, austere blue eyes of the Churchman turned upon the speaker, and he said to her in a kindly tone of rebuke:

"'*Was*' lying there, my daughter. He is now with God. He died a blessed death. May yours and mine be as holy!"

He traversed the vestibule and passed upstairs. The diligent hands of the Little Sisters had already completed the last arrangements. Into the middle of the lofty room, with its consecrated burning candles and massed votive wreaths and crosses, the narrow, white-draped bed had been drawn. At the foot of it stood the altar, with its Crucifix, and its vases of flowers, and burning tapers. The pure frosty night breeze, scented with larch and pine needles, flowed in through the open windows; in the bay of the one that looked south-east stood the black-draped bust, with a great Cross of violets and bay-leaves leaning against its pedestal, and a crown of white lilies on its crape-veiled head.

One of the Little Sisters of the Poor knelt on a *prie-Dieu* near the bed-foot. There would be a public Lying-in-State upon the morrow, when members of Religious Sodalities would take part in the solemn function; when a guard of honor, drawn from the Army of the Swiss Republic, would be posted to watch the illustrious dead. Meanwhile, the Little Sister, with her fellow-nun to relieve her at intervals, would thus keep watch through the night-hours. His Eminence must know it would be not only a duty but a pleasure to render these sacred duties to the remains of one so good as Monsieur.

Then, as de Moulny turned towards the bed to sprinkle it and its occupant from the little stoup of holy water that stood upon a small stand close by, an oblong patch of whiteness showing relief against its purple cover drew his attention. The meek, good eyes of the Sister had followed the Cardinal's. They now encountered them.

"It was I who placed it there," the Sister explained, with a little innocent confusion. "It arrived by the afternoon post. It is a letter from England—M. Dunoisse received one in that handwriting regularly once a year at Noël ... its arrival was Monsieur's great festival!" She added, as the Cardinal took the letter in his hand: "The good God permitted Monsieur to suffer a terrible bereavement in the death of the dear friend who thus remembered him!" She glanced at the crape-veiled bust in the window-bay, and added: "In August he received the news. At the close of September comes this letter—a message from the dead to the dead."

The Cardinal's expression of composed stem gravity did not change as the Sister made her explanation.

"Leave me, my child," he said to the nun, "and rest until I again summon you. I desire to remain alone awhile by this bed of holy death."

The Sister withdrew, leaving the Cardinal standing with the letter in his hand by the old white head that rested upon the flower-strewn pillow. A snow-pure veil of unutterable peace had been drawn by the hand of gentle Death over the splendid, powerful brow, the sealed eyes, and the high, clear-cut, aquiline features. The face was wonderfully noble, marvelously grand.

A great prelate, a subtle theologian, a profound scholar, no priest was more deeply read than Cardinal de Moulny in the pages of the Book of Life and Death. Long years of experience among the living, stores of knowledge accumulated beside innumerable deathbeds, had taught him that the deeper you read between the pages of that Book, the less you know that you know.

An idea struck him as he looked from the dead face to the envelope, obviously yellowed, addressed in a delicate old-fashioned handwriting—handwriting faded as though by the passage of many years—to an address in Paris that had belonged to Dunoisse many years previously—now re-addressed in blacker ink in a modern upright hand. And as he looked, yielding to a sudden impulse, he tore open the envelope and mastered the contents. He read by the light of the death-tapers that flickered on the altar at the bed-foot, set on either side of the Crucifix, carved in dark walnut with the Emblems of the Passion, that had hung above the head of the bed. The letter bore the date of thirty-nine years back. It ran thus:

"It has been made clear to me that what it is my determination to reveal to you in this letter cannot be known by you while the hand that penned it is yet warm and living. So, once written, it shall lie in the shabby desk most people laugh at until my summons comes from that High Power Whose call we must all obey. There was a time, though you have never suspected it, when for the sake of the sweetness of the earthly love you had not then offered me, I would have taken my hand from the plow.

"Nor when the gift was made, was I without my hour of doubt and hesitation, for, had I linked my life with yours, I must have broken a vow. Well!—I was spared the choice by the verdict of the London physicians—the relentless progress of the disease that bound me prisoner to this room within whose four walls I have now for so many years lived and labored.... Dear friend!—dearest of all earthly friends!—there is no marriage in that world where blessed spirits dwell, but there is Oneness. It is the gift of God to souls that have purely loved upon earth. Oh my beloved! whom I loved from the first—whom I shall love to the last—and this world is not the last, thanks be to God for it!—I do most humbly trust in Him that we who have been so long divided here on earth shall meet and be one in Heaven."

CIX

Cardinal de Moulny was not ordinarily prone to yield to emotion—not commonly open to the appeals of sentiment—yet the tears rolled down his heavy cheeks as he read. It seemed to him so exquisitely piteous that the reward of his dead friend's unswerving devotion and lifelong fidelity should have come too late to yield him joy.

Was it fancy? Was it some shadow cast athwart the dead face by a wind-blown taper-flame that made the stern old beautiful mouth under the white mustache that charitable hands had trimmed and waxed for Dunoisse, seem to be smiling? The glassy, fixed eyes were a little open. Had they not been shut a little while before? The steady nerves of the questioner knew a strange thrill of awe.... He stepped to the bedside, gazed earnestly in the still, white face. No doubt, death was there! He touched the icy wrist,—bent his ear close to the cold, shrouded heart—Death, beyond all doubt! Yet, remembering that he had solemnly sworn, many years before, to be the friend of Dunoisse to the edge of Death, and, if possible, beyond—he would do as some unseen Mentor now prompted.... There was no sin in the thing.... It was an act of charity....

So, as he would have shouted in the ears of an expiring penitent, following the retiring consciousness to the remotest bounds of vitality with the sacred words, the gracious consolations of Holy Church, now with all the power of his splendid lungs de Moulny shouted the letter of the dead woman in the ears of her dead lover. There was not a spark of life in the glassy eyes glimmering between the rigid, livid eyelids. The deadly chill of death bit him like a frost as he slipped the letter within the folds of the shroud where the leather case that held its comrades was hidden on the breast of Hector Dunoisse. He was a little contemptuous of his own weakness as he dipped his fingers in the china shell of holy water—sprinkled the head and feet of the corpse, and murmured a Latin prayer commending the departed soul to the Divine Mercy. Then he lifted his fur-lined mantle from the floor where he had dropped it—and went out of the room with long, light, noiseless steps, shutting the door.

The man who lay upon the flower-decked, white-draped bed, with dimly burning tapers at his head and feet, and his dead love's letters lying upon his dead breast under the stiff white hands that held a Rosary, saw the tall, corpulent figure in the purple cassock pass out of the room. He heard the closing of the door.

He had heard the letter, every word of it. And the revelation of her long-hidden secret had brought him unutterable joy—joy of which he knew he must infallibly have died, had he not been already dead.

For he knew quite well that he was dead; but that his spirit had not yet passed beyond the gates of its earthly tenement. He waited in a great, cold, quiet void. The little busy world spun on, forever divorced from him. He was one with the Immensity of Eternity. He hung, an isolated point in Illimitable Space, upon the borders of the Otherwhere. He knew no shrinking. Terrors are for nerves of flesh, fears for the finite, mortal, perishable.... He lay like a drop of water that is yet a boundless ocean, enclosed in the hollow of the Almighty Hand.

It has been said and written by learned men, dead ages ago—that the soul remains a prisoner for hours, perhaps days, when the spark of Life is extinguished, and the heart is forever stilled. Perhaps it was the third hour after death, perhaps the third day—who knows?—when Dunoisse became aware that four walls no longer bounded his horizon—that the peaks and ranges of the ancient snow-crowned mountains now rose up about him.... He stood beside a new-made grave, covered and surrounded with crosses and wreaths of fading flowers, in the cemetery that lies on the hillside below Zeiden. The flush of dawn was upon all Nature, the frosted grasses at his feet bowed to the earth in slumber; the lake far below, lying in the lap of the wintry woods and meadows, seemed to slumber and dream ... and in the East, to which his face was turned—the mysterious East that has been, since the childhood of this old world, the threshold across which Revelation has stepped with shining feet—the moon was rising more gloriously than he had ever known the great silvery-golden planet rise—or was it the sun?...

Or was it a Lamp of inconceivable radiance upheld in the hands of a Woman who stood upon the mountains, robed in the glory of sun and moon and stars, adorned with all the beauty of earth and sea and sky, lovely with the loveliness which human words are powerless to convey. A Wind, going whither it listed, soughed past; it brought with it the sound of rustling leaves and falling waters, with the cooing of doves; it whispered in his ear a Name, the second his first childish lispings had been taught to utter in prayer—reverenced and beloved above all on earth or in Heaven, save One.

It was no Lamp she held, it was a Child of Wonder. A Child above Whose Brow crossing and intertwisting and interweaving rays of light formed the semblance of a Crown of Thorns. And from the Eyes of the

Child, as from its thorny diadem, all the Light emanated, all the glory flowed.

The vision faded, but the Light of those Eyes remained. He whom their ineffable mild gaze had turned on, standing by his own new grave in Zeiden Cemetery, understood at last. He comprehended now the breadth and depth and height of the Divine Love. He saw how Supreme Beneficence had worked for good and ultimate happiness through all the disappointments, labors, agonies, sorrows, and sufferings of his own ended life on earth. He saw it dispersing through a million million channels, to irradiate, cleanse, and transform the souls of men and make them fit for Heaven. He saw it flowing outwards through the gentle hands of the woman, his soul's beloved, appointed to carry out the great work by which his own had been prompted and inspired. He reaped his harvest bountifully. And what had been a trembling Hope in Life became now after Death a glorious certainty of work not done in vain by any laborer, however humble or unskilled, whose aim and end are the honor and glory of God.

And he realized the huge dynamic force of Prayer, wielded by Christian men and Christian women, and saw in Faith the fulcrum of the lever that is daily moving the world. And by the Body of Christ, veritably present in the Blessed Sacrament—in the Blood of Christ shed again for us—in the Sacrifice that shall daily be renewed by Catholic priests at Catholic altars until the End of Time—he knew that all the nations of the earth shall be saved and pardoned and justified. He saw them with the brightness that is the shadow of the ineffable Light upon their faces, destroying their hideous engines of destruction, laying down their weapons of war. He heard them crying: "Since we are the Sons of God, let us be brothers in deed and verity!" And he saw purified holy souls that have passed through Purgatory; blessed spirits that are now in Paradise; all the Hierarchy of Angels, all the Thrones and Powers and Dominations, all the crowned saints, martyrs, virgins, hail with joy that day....

The solemn mountains were no longer round him. His temples were no longer kissed by a breeze that was chill with the frosts of earthly night. A balmy warmth, an exquisite fragrance, an enveloping, embracing sense of light and peace and rest, were his now. He stood amidst vast, illimitable fields of lilies,—tall blossomed stems that bowed and swayed and whispered as though a wind were passing over them. Yet the atmosphere was still—so still, so clear, so pure, that his unspoken thought stirred it, sending waves of vibrations eddying through its celestial ether, as uttered words of earthly speech set in motion the mundane air:

"These are the Fields of Paradise," was his thought. And—oh! with what bliss unutterable he heard the Beloved answer in that wordless, thrilling language that is common speech with the Blest:

"These are the Fields of Paradise—and I am here with you!"

He cried out: "Blessed be God!" seeing her coming.

She answered: "Blessed be God!" even as she came.

He had had earthly dreams of meeting her after Death in some roseate land beyond the sunset, dressed in the well-loved, sober black silk gown, white cap and little cape, walking upon the virgin shores of some tideless, opal ocean.

This was the Divine reality—that she should move to him through a whispering sea of lilies; robed in the spotless glory of her unstained virginity, with the shining halo of her long martyrdom hovering over her pure brow, reflected in her radiant eyes.

"O my Love!" she said, in that thought-speech of Paradise that is sweeter than all the singing of all the nightingales of earth, "there is no marriage in Heaven, but there is Oneness. It is God's gift to souls that have faithfully loved on earth!"

"O my Love!" he said, "I never dreamed you half so beautiful."

"And ah! my Love," she answered back, "I never knew before how glorious you were!"

They were speechless for a moment, gazing on each other, while the little years of our earth flitted by, and its men and women were born, and grew up and grew old. She held out both hands to him then, and he would have fallen at her feet, but, "No!" she said, and opened her dear arms, and took him to her breast instead.

And heart to heart they stood; lips hushed on lips in the kiss of Paradise that outweighs all the joys we covet. And the lilies kept whispering as though they knew a secret. "*Who* is coming?" they rustled to each other. "We know!—we know!"

There was a Footstep in that holy place. The lilies ceased whispering—it was still, so still! Who came, moving through His Garden of Paradise as of old time He moved through His earthly Eden, calling the man and the woman? The lilies knew, but they did not say.

The woman and the man heard His Voice. They turned, hand clasped in hand, to see the Face of Love smiling under the Crown of Thorns; and, oblivious even of each other in the bliss of the Beatific Vision, they fell in adoration at those nail-pierced Feet that trod the Dolorous Way under the weight of the Cross; toiling under the burden of their sins and yours and mine—that, repentant—we might find pardon and salvation.

THE END